Origins and Method

Towards a New Understanding
of Judaism and Christianity

Essays in Honour of John C. Hurd

edited by
Bradley H. McLean

Journal for the Study of the New Testament
Supplement Series 86

Published by JSOT Press
JSOT Press is an imprint of
Sheffield Academic Press Ltd
343 Fulwood Road
Sheffield S10 3BP
England

Typeset by Sheffield Academic Press
and
Printed on acid-free paper in Great Britain
by Biddles Limited
Guildford

British Library Cataloguing in Publication Data

Origins and Method: Towards a New
Understanding of Judaism and Christianity
—Essays in Honour of John C. Hurd.—
I. McLean, Bradley H. II. Series
291.1

ISBN 1-85075-441-1

CONTENTS

Foreword   9
Editor's Preface   15
Abbreviations   17
List of Contributors   23

Part I
NEW UNDERSTANDINGS OF PAUL

GERD LÜDEMANN
Paul, Christ and the Problem of Death   26

HEINZ O. GUENTHER
Gnosticism in Corinth?   44

JOHN REUMANN
Church Office in Paul, Especially in Philippians   82

WENDY COTTER, CSJ
Our *Politeuma* is in Heaven: The Meaning of Philippians 3.17-21   92

EDGAR M. KRENTZ
Military Language and Metaphors in Philippians   105

KARL P. DONFRIED
2 Thessalonians and the Church of Thessalonica   128

JOHN L. WHITE
Apostolic Mission and Apostolic Message: Congruence in Paul's
Epistolary Rhetoric, Structure and Imagery   145

6   *Origins and Method*

ALAN F. SEGAL
Conversion and Universalism: Opposites that Attract   162

TERENCE L. DONALDSON
Thomas Kuhn, Convictional Worlds, and Paul   190

KENNETH J. NEUMANN
Major Variations in Pauline and Other Epistles in Light of
Genre and the Pauline Letter Form   199

Part II
NEW UNDERSTANDINGS OF THE NEW TESTAMENT

JOHN S. KLOPPENBORG
Edwin Hatch, Churches and *Collegia*   212

BRADLEY H. MCLEAN
The Agrippinilla Inscription: Religious Associations and
Early Church Formation   239

LLOYD GASTON
The Uniqueness of Jesus as a Methodological Problem   271

WALTER E. AUFRECHT
The Son of Man Problem as an Illustration of the *techne* of
NT Studies   282

ROBERT M. GRANT
Ancient and Modern Questions about Authenticity   295

WILLARD MCCARTY
Discontinuity, Metamorphosis and Coherence:
Methodologies for Computer-assisted Textual Analysis,
with Reference to the *Metamorphoses* of Ovid   302

Part III
NEW UNDERSTANDINGS OF THE RELATIONSHIP BETWEEN JUDAISM AND CHRISTIANITY

G. PETER RICHARDSON
Philo and Eusebius on Monasteries and Monasticism:
The Therapeutae and Kellia   334

WAYNE O. MCCREADY
Sectarian Separation and Exclusion—The Temple Scroll:
A Case for Wholistic Religious Claims   360

ERNEST G. CLARKE
The Bible and Translation: The Targums   380

John Coolidge Hurd, Jr: *Cursus Vitae*   394
Bibliography of John C. Hurd   396
Index of Biblical References   399
Index of Authors   405

John Hurd at Trinity

When Francis Wright Beare was facing retirement as Professor of New Testament at Trinity College, he told the Provost and Divinity staff, 'You must get John Hurd'. In those days there was little or no formal consultation and no search procedure. So after one short visit John was appointed full Professor of Divinity with tenure. Already his book *The Origin of 1 Corinthians* had established his stature as one qualified to succeed his distinguished predecessor in Canada's major centre for graduate studies in Divinity and one of the largest Anglican theological schools in North America. Even so, the story goes, John was only finally persuaded to migrate from the Episcopal Theological Seminary of the Southwest, in Austin, Texas, when his family convinced him that Toronto is a great place for Scottish dancing. The fact that he and his wife Helen came originally from Massachusetts, and spend their summers 'on Golden Pond' (Squam Lake) in New Hampshire, no doubt made the move north more congenial. With their daughters, Elisabeth and Louisa, and son Lyman, they moved to Toronto in the summer of 1967.

In those days, the required programme for Divinity was relatively rigid, allowing few electives. Students were often considered the objects of education, and staff people were those who knew and would teach what others learn. Recalling those days, Howard Buchner remarks that 'we prayed "Bless those who teach and those who learn" believing that these are not necessarily the same people!' But change was in the air. The student movement led to demands for student representation on governing councils. The student government was elected by fellow students, no longer appointed by the Provost. Faculty and students began to have representation on the Executive Committee of Corporation (Trinity's board of directors, hitherto dominated by Arts *alumni/ae*). Over the years, John has had his full share of such responsibilities, serving in the year before retirement as Dean.

In 1966–67 the American Association of Theological Schools—now ATS (the North American accrediting organization)—completed a review involving teaching staff, students and other constituencies, which led to major course changes and greater co-operation among the six denominational schools on the campus of the University of Toronto. Trinity is one of the original 'federating colleges' of the university, retaining its independent university charter with the right to grant degrees in Divinity, while amalgamating its Faculty of Arts with that of the secular university. For a while, John taught both undergraduates in Religious Studies and ordinands in Divinity. He remains cross-appointed to the Graduate Centre for the Study of Religion in the University of Toronto.

In earlier times Canadian ordinands aspiring to do graduate work were advised to go to Europe or the United States. But Charles Fielding, former Dean at Trinity, and his colleagues at Emmanuel, Wycliffe and Knox, founded the Toronto Graduate School of Theological Studies and pushed for greater attention to graduate research as part of the collective responsibility. At first only a master's degree (MTh) was awarded. At St.Michael's College (the Catholic federating college) an independent MA—PhD sequence was maintained. Over the next two years St. Michael's and Regis (the Jesuit college) joined the TGSTS. With the advice of Dr. Charles L. Taylor (John's Dean when at seminary and former director of ATS) the Committee on Theological Education in Toronto (COCTET) came into being, and the full schedule of basic and advanced degree programmes of what is now the Toronto School of Theology began to evolve. John joined Eugene Fairweather and Howard Buchner as the Trinity members of COCTET, which brought the Toronto School of Theology (TST) into being.

In Canon Buchner's words, 'John joined us in the middle of this rather exciting mess' giving special attention to the advanced degree program. For over twenty years he was Trinity's Director of Advanced Degree Studies and representative on the Advanced Degree Council of TST. There he used his familiarity with comparable programs at Harvard and Yale to good effect. At various times he has served as Chair of the Advanced Degree Council, Chair of the Biblical Department and a key member of the Executive Committee of the

Board of Trustees of TST. Over the same period he was active on the Library Committee of both Trinity and TST, helping the consortium to pool resources to the point where research in all departments has become increasingly easier. By now there were seven member colleges of TST (St. Augustine's, the Catholic diocesan foundation for training ordinands joining for basic degree studies only). Of all the components at TST, the Advanced Degree Council has been the most effective, overseeing the ThM and ThD degrees, awarded by each college conjointly with the University of Toronto, as well as the MA and PhD degrees awarded through St. Michael's College.

Such a large consortium as TST is able to allow its combined staff of over a hundred faculty to specialize early in their teaching. Within the basic degree program, John and his New Testament colleagues have been the only ones to combine forces in offering a common ·introductory course for all colleges, known not always affectionately by the students as 'baby Bible'. Their ambivalence is due to the steady diet of solid meat, as a result of which parochial pieties are challenged and the historical critical method is instilled in liberals and conservatives alike. John conducts the Trinity tutorials for this course, as well as giving his share of the combined lectures and taking his turn as course administrator. He has followed this up with a required course on Paul which has been a staple in the Trinity basic degree program (John's lecture on eating meat offered to idols is renowned).

John's undergraduate training in natural science and precise, systematic cast of mind have been most demonstrated in his classroom teaching of New Testament Greek. One of the first to grasp the potential of computer-aided language training, he has painstakingly developed what is now known internationally as 'the Greek Tutor'. In his own words, this is 'a general information retrieval system for investigating the inflectional characteristics of the Greek language'. It can be used to assist teaching *Koine* Greek at every level, allowing the addition of Attic and other texts as needed. The ten-megabyte dictionary and full text of the New Testament enables the student to see for each word the English equivalent of the dictionary form, its morphemic expansion, its inflectional identification and the complete set of paradigms governing its uses. A set of lessons teach the student how to use the computer terminal, learn the alphabet, acquire vocabulary, type in Greek and learn to punctuate and add diacritical marks. The student can leave questions for an instructor, have right and wrong answers recorded for each lesson and register in or out of any stage of the course of instruction. Over the years John has collaborated with others developing professional expertise at the University of Toronto for computing in the Humanities and has received a number of research grants and teaching awards in this area. In 1987 he downloaded the Greek Tutor from the university's IBM mainframe computer to an IBM PC-XT, redesigning the screen display and creating new fonts for various printers. The system has now been shared with St. Paul's University in Ottawa (which houses one of the best theological libraries in North America); the universities of Edinburgh, Glasgow, Oxford, Durham and Manchester in the UK; the University of Pennsylvania and other sites in the USA; and the Yarra Theological Union in Australia. As more and more students become computer-literate, appreciation for the meticulous, scholarly work invested in this project continues to grow, as does the number who can make full use of it.

In addition to directing a number of doctoral theses himself, John has served over the years on numerous thesis committees and examining boards. In Toronto he has carried on the approach to New Testament studies exemplified by the late John Knox. He is a past President of the Canadian Society for Biblical Studies, a former Editor of the *Anglican Theological Review* and a consultant to both the ATS and the University of Toronto in his special fields. He was one of three senior Fellows recently asked by Trinity College to develop proper grievance policies and procedures and has been a faithful member of the committee to advise the Bishop of Toronto on candidates for ordination. For over twenty years, John and Helen have been parishioners at St. Clement's, Eglinton, where he has served as an honourary assistant to successive rectors and she has been an active member of the Anglican Church Women.

In 1992 John stepped into the breach to serve the Faculty as Dean ('pro tem') at a critical juncture in the College's history. He enlisted his colleagues to work as a team as never before, guiding the Faculty to redefine its goals and objectives in meeting demands for financial stringency and bringing stability to the administration of student concerns. In previous years, John and Helen introduced successive generations of students, staff, and friends of Trinity to the intricacies of Scottish reels, showing a tolerance of others' lack of precision while encouraging even the most inept of beginners to experience the joy of taking graceful steps in the right directions. In many such large and small ways they have demonstrated the qualities which have won them friends from coast to coast and made their partnership one of the current strengths of Trinity Divinity.

Howard W. Buchner
C. Peter Slater

EDITOR'S PREFACE

The present volume of essays is a tribute to John C. Hurd. A unifying theme in all of Professor Hurd's writings is the importance of sound method, especially as he applied it to the study of Pauline biography and theology. In the light of his writings, it is painfully clear how Pauline scholarship has often been characterized by an indiscriminate use of ancient sources, unargued assumptions, and an ignorance of the methodological issues involved. Hurd's own advances in New Testament research testify to the startling impact which attention to method can have on our understanding of the origins of Christianity.

Much of the pleasure which the contributors and editor have gained from the making of this *Festschrift* has come from the knowledge that John Hurd's insights into the New Testament continue to bear new fruit in their own research. As one of his previous students, I have witnessed the tremendous impact which John Hurd's insights and learning have had upon his students and colleagues alike.

Essays in Part I of this volume directly address subjects, issues and themes in Professor Hurd's research such as Pauline chronology (Lüdemann), Paul's letters to Corinth (Guenther), Philippi (Reumann, Cotter, Krentz), Thessalonica (Donfried), Paul's epistolary structure (White), theology (Segal, Donaldson) and finally papers dealing with computer-aided biblical research (Neumann, McCarty). Part II includes essays which pursue New Testament topics more central to their author's minds—topics such as Christian origins (Kloppenborg, McLean), Christology (Gaston, Aufrect), and authenticity (Grant). Essays in Part III address the relationship between Judaism and early Christianity focusing on such topics as the Therapeutae and Kellia (Richardson), the Temple Scroll (McCready) and the targums (Clarke). All share an indebtedness to one man whose plea for clear thinking on methodological issues has formed the foundation of their own understanding of Christianity or Judaism. His critical method has fruit yet to bear, as we pursue it in the Jewish and Christian Scriptures and the literature that clusters around them, in directions unknown or unventured in the past.

The editor has many thanks to express to those who have assisted in bringing this project to fruition. First of all, I wish to thank all of the contributors, without whom there would be no book at all. Secondly, John Kloppenborg whose initial encouragement got the project started and who was always ready to assist me in addressing the numerous difficulties which inevitably arise in a project such as this. Nor should I omit to mention here the support for this project received from the Anglican Diocese of Toronto, the University of Trinity College (Toronto), and St Clement's Church (Toronto). Finally, I wish to thank the editorial staff of the Sheffield Academic Press who have supported the project.

Bradley H. McLean

ABBREVIATIONS

a. *Ancient Authors and Works*

A.	Aeschylus, *Pers.—Persae*
A.D.	Apollonius Dyscolus, *Synt.—Syntax*
Aen. Tact.	Aeneas Tacticus
Ar.	Aristophanes, *Lys.—Lysistrata*
Arn.	Arnobius Afer
Ath.	Athenaeus
Aug.	Augustine, *Civ. Dei.—De Civitate Dei*; *De Doctr. Christ.—De Doctrina Christiana*
Cal.	Callimachus, *Cer.—Hymnus in Cererem*
C. Herm.	*Corpus Hermeticum*
Cic.	Cicero, *Tusc.—Tusculae Disputationes*; *De Nat. Deor.—De Natura Deorum*
Clem. A.	Clement of Alexandria, *Strom.—Stromateis*
D.	Demosthenes
D.H.	Dionysius of Halicarnassus, *Amm.—Epistula ad Ammaeum*; *Ant. Rom.—Antiquitates Romanae*
DS	Diodorus Siculus
E.	Euripides, *HF—Hercules Furens*
Epict.	Epictetus
Eus.	Eusebius, *EH—Ecclesiastical History*
Hdt.	Herodotus
Herm.	Hermes Trismegistus
Hierocl.	Hierocles
Hippol.	Hippolytus, *Comm. Dan.—Commentary on Daniel*
Hom.	Homer, *Il.—Iliad*
Iren.	Irenaeus, *Her.—Adversus omnes Haereses*
Isoc.	Isocrates, *Or.—Oration*
Just.	Justin, *Apol.—Apologia*; *Dial.—Dialogues*
MH	Middle Hebrew
Onas.	Onasander, *Strat.—Strategicus*
Onos.	Onosander
Or.	Origen, *Prin.—De Principiis*
Ov.	Ovid, *Met.—Metamorphoses*
Ph.	Philo, *Contemp.—De Vita Contemplativa*; *Confus.—De Confusione Linguarum*; *Flacc—In Flaccum*; *Legat—*

	Legatione ad Gaium; *Migr.*—*De Migratione Abrahami*
Pl.	Plato, *Alc.*—*Alcibiades*; *Ap.*—*Apologia*
Plin.	Pliny the Younger (C. Plinius Caecilius), *Ep. Pan.*—*Epistulae Panegyricus*; *HN*—*Historia Naturalis*
Plot.	Plotinus, *Enn.*—*Enneads*
Plu.	Plutarch, *Fab.*—*Fabius Maximus*; *Vitae Par.*—*Vitae Parallelae*
Ps-Clem. Hom.	*Pseudo-Clementine Homilies*
Quint.	Quintilian, *Inst.*—*Institutione Oratotriae*
Sen.	L. Annaeus Seneca, *Ep. Mor.*—*Epistulae Morales*; *Dial.*—*Dialogui*
Stob.	Joannes Stobaeus
Str.	Strabo, *Geo.*—*Rerum Geographicarum*
Tac.	Tacitus, *Germ.*—*Germania*
Tert.	Q. Septiums Florens Tertullian, *Ad. Herm.*—*Adversus Hermogenem*; *Ad. Marc.*—*Adversus Marcionem*; *Apol.*—*Apologeticum*
Th.	Thucydides
Theophil.	Theophilus, *Auto.*—*To Autolycus*
Tyrt.	Tyrtaeus
Var.	Varro, *R.R.*—*Res Rusticae*
X.	Xenophon, *An.*—*Anabasis*; *Cyc.*—*Institutio Cyri* (*Cyropaedia*); *HG*—*Historica Graeca* (*Hellenica*); *Mem.*—*Memorabilia*

b. *Periodicals, Reference Works and Serials*

ABD	D.N. Freedman (ed.), *Anchor Bible Dictionary*
AEPHE	*Annuaire Ecole Pratique des Hautes Etudes*
AHR	*American Historical Review*
AJA	*American Journal of Archaeology*
AJP	*American Journal of Philology*
AJS	*American Journal of Sociology*
AnBib	Analecta biblica
ATR	*Anglican Theological Review*
BA	*Biblical Archaelogist*
BAGD	W. Bauer, W.F. Arndt, F.W. Gingrich and F.W. Danker, *Greek–English Lexicon of the New Testament*
BARev	*Biblical Archaeology Review*
BCH	*Bulletin de correspondance hellénique*
BCSBS	*Bulletin of the Canadian Society of Biblical Studies*
BETL	Bibliotheca ephemeridum theologicarum lovaniensium
BJRL	*Bulletin of the John Rylands University Library of Manchester*

BMI	C.T. Newton (ed.), *The Collection of Greek Inscriptions in the British Museum* (4 vols.; Oxford: Clarendon Press, 1874–1916)
BTB	*Biblical Theology Bulletin*
BZ	*Biblische Zeitschrift*
BZAW	Beihefte zur *ZAW*
CBQ	*Catholic Biblical Quarterly*
CHum	*Computers and the Humanities*
CIG	*Corpus inscriptionum graecarum*
CIL	*Corpus inscriptionum latinarum*
CJT	*Canadian Journal of Theology*
ConBNT	Coniectanea biblica, New Testament
ConNT	*Coniectanea neotestamentica*
CP	*Classical Philology*
CQR	*Church Quarterly Review*
CR	*Classical Review*
EIL	G. Wilmanns, *Exempla inscriptionum latinarum in usum praecipue academicum* (2 vols.; Berlin: Weidmann, 1873)
EKKNT	Evangelisch-Katholischer Kommentar zum Neuen Testament
EPRO	Etudes préliminaires aux religions orientales dans l'empire romain
ETR	*Etudes théologiques et religieuses*
EvQ	*Evangelical Quarterly*
EvT	*Evangelische Theologie*
ExpTim	*Expository Times*
.FO	*Folia Orientalia*
FRLANT	Forschungen zur Religion und Literatur des Alten und Neuen Testaments
GRBS	*Greek, Roman and Byzantine Studies*
HNT	Handbuch zum Neuen Testament
HNTC	Harper's NT Commentaries
HR	*History of Religions*
HSCP	Harvard Studies in Classical Philology
HTR	*Harvard Theological Review*
HUCA	*Hebrew Union College Annual*
HZ	*Historische Zeitschrift*
I.Eph.	R. Merkelbach, *et al.* (eds.), *Die Inschriften von Ephesos* (8 vols.; Bonn, 1979–81)
IG	F.F. Hiller von Gaertringen (ed.), *Inscriptiones graecae* (Berlin: de Gruyter, 1913–1940; repr.; Chicago: Ares, 1974)
IGLAM	P.Le Bas and W.H. Waddington, *Inscriptions grecques et latines recueillies en Asie Mineure. I. Textes en majuscules. II. Textes en minuscules et explications, Voyage archéologique en Grèce et en Asie Mineure. III. Cinquième Partie: Asie Mineure* (2 vols.; Paris: Firmin-Didot & Cie., 1870)

IGLS	W.H. Waddington, *Inscriptions grecques et latines de la Syrie: Recueillies et expliquees*. I. *Texts en Majuscules*. II. *Textes en minuscules et explications* (2 vols.; Paris: Firmin-Didot & Cie., 1870)
IGR	R. Cagnat and G. Lafaye (eds.), *Inscriptiones graecae ad res romanas pertinentes* (Paris, 1911–27)
ILS	H. Dessau, *Inscriptiones latinae selectae* (5 vols.; Berlin, 1892–1916)
I.Mag.	O. Kern (ed.), *Die Inschriften von Magnesia am Maeander* (Berlin, 1900)
Int	*Interpretation*
I.Perg.	M. Fraenkel, *Die Inschriften von Pergamon* (2 vols.; Berlin, 1890–95)
JAAR	*Journal of the American Academy of Religion*
JAC	*Jahrbuch für Antike und Christentum*
JBL	*Journal of Biblical Literature*
JCHE	*Journal of Computing in Higher Education*
JETS	*Journal of the Evangelical Theological Society*
JJS	*Journal of Jewish Studies*
JL	*Journal of Linguistics*
JP	*Journal of Politics*
JQR	*Jewish Quarterly Review*
JSJ	*Journal for the Study of Judaism in the Persian, Hellenistic and Roman Period*
JSNT	*Journal for the Study of the New Testament*
JSNTSup	*Journal for the Study of the New Testament*, Supplement Series
JSOT	*Journal for the Study of the Old Testament*
JSS	*Journal of Semitic Studies*
JTS	*Journal of Theological Studies*
KEK	W. Meyer (ed.), *Kritisch-exegetischer Kommentar über das Neue Testament*
KJV	King James Version
LCL	Loeb Classical Library
LSAM	F. Sokolowski, *Lois sacrées de l'Asie Mineure* (Ecole française d'Athènes, Travaux et mémoires, fasc. 9; Paris: E. de Boccard, 1955)
LSCG	F. Sokolowski, *Lois sacrées des cités grecques* (Ecole française d'Athènes; Travaux et mémoires, fasc. 18; Paris: E. de Boccard, 1969)
LSCGSup	F. Sokolowski, *Lois sacrées des Cités grecques: Supplément* (Ecole française d'Athènes, Travaux et mémoires, fasc. 11; Paris: E. de Boccard, 1962)
LSJ	Liddell–Scott–Jones, *Greek–English Lexicon*
LTP	*Laval théologique et philosophique*

MB	*Le Monde de la Bible*
MDAI(A)	*Mitteilungen des Deutschen Archäologischen Instituts (Athens)*
MTZ	*Münchener theologische Zeitschrift*
NedTTs	*Nederlands theologisch tijdschrift*
Neot	*Neotestamentica*
NICNT	New International Commentary on the NT
NIGTC	The New International Greek Testament Commentary
NovT	*Novum Testamentum*
NovTSup	*Novum Testamentum*, Supplements
NRSV	New Revised Standard Version
NTS	*New Testament Studies*
OGIS	W. Dittenberger, *Orientic Graeci Inscriptiones Selectae* (Leipzig, 1903–1905).
OLD	*Old Latin Dictionary*
PAPS	*Proceedings of the American Philosophical Society*
PG	J. Migne (ed.), *Patrologia graeca*
PhS	*Philosophical Studies*
PW	Pauly–Wissowa, *Real-Encyclopädie der classischen Altertumswissenschaft*
Quandt	W. Quandt, *De Baccho ab Alexandri Aetate in Asia Minore Culto* (Diss.; Halis Saxonum: Ehrhardt Karras, 1912)
RA	*Revue archéologique*
RAC	*Reallexikon für Antike und Christentum*
REG	*Revue des Etudes grecques*
RevQ	*Revue de Qumran*
RhM	*Rheinisches Museum*
RQ	*Römische Quartalschrift für christliche Altertumskunde und Kirchengeschichte*
RSR	*Recherches de science religieuse*
RSV	Revised Standard Version
SAG	L.C. Reilly, *Slaves in Ancient Greece: Slaves from Manumission Inscriptions* (Chicago: Ares, 1978)
SBL	Society of Biblical Literature
SBLASP	SBL Abstracts and Seminar Papers
SBLDS	SBL Dissertation Series
SBLSBS	SBL Sources for Biblical Study
SBS	Stuttgarter Bibelstudien
SBT	Studies in Biblical Theology
SIG²	W. Dittenberger, *et al.*, *Sylloge Inscriptionum Graecarum* (Lipsiae: S. Hirzel, 2nd edn, 1898–1901)
SIG³	H. von Gaertringen, *et al.*, *Sylloge Inscriptionum Graecarum* (4 vols.; Lipsiae: S. Hirzel, 3rd edn, 1915–1924)
SJT	*Scottish Journal of Theology*
SNTS	Studiorium Novi Testamenti Societas
SNTSMS	SNTS Monograph Series

SR	*Studies in Religion*
TDNT	G. Kittel and G. Friedrich (eds.), *Theological Dictionary of the New Testament*
TJT	*Toronto Journal of Theology*
TLZ	*Theologische Literaturzeitung*
TRu	*Theologische Rundschau*
TU	Texte und Untersuchungen
USQR	*Union Seminary Quarterly Review*
VT	*Vetus Testamentum*
VTSup	*Vetus Testamentum*, Supplements
WBC	Word Biblical Commentary
WUNT	Wissenschaftliche Untersuchungen zum Neuen Testament
ZNW	*Zeitschrift für die neutestamentliche Wissenschaft*
ZTK	*Zeitschrift für Theologie und Kirche*
ZWT	*Zeitschrift für wissenschaftliche Theologie*

LIST OF CONTRIBUTORS

Walter E. Aufrecht
The University of Lethbridge, Lethbridge, Alberta, Canada

Howard W. Buchner
Dean of Divinity 1961–1983, University of Trinity College, Toronto, Ontario, Canada

Ernest G. Clarke
Victoria University, Toronto, Ontario, Canada

Wendy Cotter, CSJ
Loyola University, Chicago, Illinois, USA

Terence L. Donaldson
College of Emmanuel and St Chad, Saskatoon, Saskatchewan, Canada

Karl P. Donfried
Department of Religion and Biblical Literature, Smith College, Northampton, Massachusetts, USA

Lloyd Gaston
Vancouver School of Theology, Vancouver, British Columbia, Canada

Robert M. Grant
University of Chicago, Chicago, Illinois, USA

Heinz O. Guenther
Emmanuel College, University of Toronto, Toronto, Ontario, Canada

John S. Kloppenborg
University of St Michael's College, Toronto, Ontario, Canada

Edgar M. Krentz
Lutheran School of Theology at Chicago, Chicago, Illinois, USA

Gerd Lüdemann
University of Göttingen, Göttingen, Germany

Willard McCarty
University of Toronto, Toronto, Ontario, Canada

Wayne O. McCready
Department of Religous Studies, The University of Calgary, Calgary, Alberta, Canada

Bradley H. McLean
St John's College, University of Manitoba, Winnipeg, Manitoba, Canada

Kenneth J. Neumann
Fairy Glen Lutheran Parish, Fairy Glen, Saskatchewan, Canada

John Reumann
Lutheran Theological Seminary, Philadelphia, Pennsylvania, USA

G. Peter Richardson
University College, University of Toronto, Toronto, Ontario, Canada

Alan F. Segal
Columbia University, New York, NewYork, USA

C. Peter Slater
Dean of Divinity 1985–1990, University of Trinity College, Toronto, Ontario, Canada

John Lee White
Loyola University, Chicago, Illinois, USA

Part I

NEW UNDERSTANDINGS OF PAUL

PAUL, CHRIST AND THE PROBLEM OF DEATH*

Gerd Lüdemann

Introduction

It seems to be a platitude to call attention to the fact that large portions of the NT are written by people about whom nothing or almost nothing is known. To attempt a biography of each of the four Gospel writers would be more or less guess work and since the names Matthew, Mark, Luke and John are second-century ascriptions, many scholars have doubts as to whether or not their true names are known. The scholarly opinions about the origin of the different Gospels vary considerably since it is not only the authors of the four Gospels who remain anonymous, but also the hero they tell stories about. Even though scholars may agree on a basic outline of his teachings and about his death, to give a sketch of Jesus' life on the basis of the Gospels is impossible. One major difficulty is that Jesus, like Socrates, does not seem to have written anything himself. The earliest records of Jesus stem from the second generation of Christians and the portraits of Jesus from the four evangelists differ considerably and even contradict each other. Finally, we have to remember that the synoptics give mainly a report of one year in Jesus' life. In terms of the time prior to his last year, the evangelists have only a blank sheet to offer apart from stories about his youth.

But whereas the reconstructions of Jesus' life even today stand in

* This essay goes back to a lecture that I gave at various occasions and places in Canada and in the United States (1977–82). Although some of my opinions concerning the way we should approach Paul have changed since then, I leave it unchanged and would like to dedicate it to my old friend, John Hurd, whose book on 1 Corinthians (*The Origin of 1 Corinthians* [London: SPCK, 1965; rev. edn; Macon, GA: Mercer University Press, 1983]) has played a decisive role in the way I read Acts and Paul. I would also like to thank Kang Na, an exchange student for helping me work on the English manuscript.

improper proportion to the difficulties mentioned above, it seems appropriate to remember that there is one person in the NT who is not anonymous and concerning whom enough evidence is left for reconstructing his life and thought: namely Paul. There exists some of his letters in which he expresses his feelings, argues with opponents, and talks about his past, present and future. In short, through his letters we become acquainted with Paul as a human being.

But curiously enough, if we compare the number of scholarly books on Paul with that of books on Jesus we can make an interesting observation: despite the difficulties involved in writing a book on Jesus and the possibility of writing one on Paul, far more books on Jesus are published than on Paul. The reason for this is quite clear. The life and teachings of Jesus seem to be more important for more Christians than Paul's.

Turning to the significant number of books on Paul or to parts of books that deal with Paul as well as to commentaries that have been written in the last two decades, we get the impression that Paul's thought is related in many cases to doctrinal issues disputed in contemporary systematic theology. An example is the question of justification: for some exegetes it seems to be particularly important to determine whether the genitive θεοῦ after δικαιοσύνη is subjective or objective. In either case, Paul becomes *the* theologian of justification by faith and all the other aspects of Pauline thought are organized under this theme. However, in view of the absence of theme of justification from 50 percent of the extant letters, this attempt becomes very questionable and must be regarded as a premature systematization.

Even more questionable is the systematic presentation of Paul's theology in the traditional dogmatic order, according to which we start with his thoughts on creation, then deal with his view on the Fall, and end up with the final judgment, and the question of whether or not Paul thought that all people would be saved. Such an approach (for example, D.E.H. Whiteley's *Theology of St Paul*, 1964) overlooks the fact that Paul's thought was shaped by particular situations and circumstances.

There are some modern scholars whose approach is basically correct in the way they pay attention to the fact that Paul's letters are a part of his career and vice versa. An example is Günther Bornkamm's *Paul* which may be the most widely read book on Paul in North America. His book is divided into two parts: 'I. Life and Work' and

'II. Gospel and Theology.' At the beginning of Bornkamm's book he asserts correctly that

> Paul's letters are the primary and normative source not only for his message and theology, but also for the first subject to be discussed in this book, his life. All that we are told of Paul elsewhere will need to be measured against them.[1]

In the course of reading Bornkamm's book, it is interesting to note that he usually avoids the term 'missionary journey', a notion which is based on Acts, according to which Paul undertook three missionary journeys. Although most scholars use this term quite casually, Bornkamm correctly avoids it on methodological grounds.

But even before him the American scholar, John Knox, already criticized the pattern of three missionary journeys:

> If you had stopped Paul on the streets of Ephesus and said to him, 'Paul, which of your missionary journeys are you on now?', he would have looked at you blankly without the remotest idea of what was in your mind.[2]

However, Bornkamm makes an additional statement which governs his whole work: in his estimation, Paul's letters 'were all written within a short space of time in the last phase of his life, when his work was at its peak but was also drawing to its end.'[3]

Where does Bornkamm get this information? Is it evidenced in the primary and normative source for Paul's, that is, the letters? This does not seem to be the case: it is not according to the letters themselves but rather the Acts that Paul founded communities such as Philippi, Thessalonica and Corinth towards the end of his career. In asserting that all of Paul's extant letters belong to the last phase of Paul's career, Bornkamm abandons the principle that Paul's letters have to be normative for reconstructing the life of the apostle to the Gentiles. Bornkamm fails to base his chronological judgment on the sole basis of the letters.

Another point of criticism against Bornkamm's book is closely related to the first. In Part II ('Gospel and Theology') Bornkamm expounds Paul's theology which as the introductory chapter of Part II

---

1.   G. Bornkamm, *Paul* (New York: Harper & Row, 1971), p. xiv.
2.   J. Knox, *Chapters in a Life of Paul* (Nashville: Abingdon Press, 1950), pp. 41-42; revised in 1987 (Macon, GA: Mercer University Press), p. 26.
3.   Bornkamm, *Paul*, p. xiv.

('Paul and the Gospel of the Primitive Church') reveals, can be properly understood only when taken in close connection with the doctrine of justification by faith. In this way Bornkamm arrives at a rather uniform picture of Paul's theology. How was Bornkamm able to do so? He laid the foundation for such an approach in Part I with his conclusion that all extant letters of Paul were written within a short period of time at the end of his career. Hence, the interpreter would seem to be justified in relating all the elements of Paul's letters in one uniform system. Luther's rule that scripture has to be interpreted through scripture would stand on very solid chronological ground in the case of the Pauline letters.

But what if the groundwork as presupposed and further developed in Part I of Bornkamm's book turns out to be insufficiently prepared? And if so, would Bornkamm's approach not collapse for methodological reasons? This is one obstacle which Bornkamm and his many followers must overcome and which concerns everyone who deals with Paul's theological thought: before anything we must consider the chronology of Paul's life.

The other obstacle is the question of whether or not it is appropriate or justifiable to present Paul's thought, which we know from occasional letters, as a system, that is to say, a fixed pattern of beliefs implying that it was revealed as such to Paul at the very time of his conversion?

In calling this view into question, several objections may be raised. First of all, it would be only natural to think that Paul, a human being, changed his mind on at least one or two theological points. Or to put it more abstractly, history means endless change and this is also true for Christian heroes, no matter how hard their devout followers try to preserve the holy within reality. Furthermore, it would also be natural to assume that persons involved in the Christian movement at its very beginning expressed different beliefs at various stages. As can be seen in the different strata of the earliest tradition, Christianity began as a reaction to the appearance of the risen Jesus. Aside from the belief in his resurrection from the dead (or his exaltation), everything or almost everything was open, specially in the first generation to which Paul belongs. Hence, a change in Paul's theological viewpoint becomes probable when we consider the very character of early Christianity.

If it is acknowledged that these points against a systematic approach to Paul's theological thought are valid or at least sufficient enough to call for a different methodology, we may now proceed to examine Paul's thoughts concerning one specific topic to see whether or not his opinions did in fact change over time. If we succeed in demonstrating this, we should be able to understand Paul better and could gain some insight for our own theological thought.

But before proceeding, a good foundation should be laid by directing attention to the chronology of Paul's life. We should bear in mind that a specific chronology of Paul facilitated a systematization of his thought in the case of Bornkamm. Is Bornkamm's chronology accurate and is my attempt to demonstrate a development in Paul's thinking therefore doomed to failure? Or can I indeed challenge his chronology?

1. *The Relative Chronology of Paul's Letters* [4]

I mentioned above that Bornkamm fails to apply his methodological principle of the priority of Paul's letters to Acts when determining a chronology.[5] Instead, Bornkamm presupposes that the placement of Paul's world mission in Acts after the apostolic council is correct (Acts 15). But is this order of events not doubtful for redaction–critical reasons? There is a theological reason why Acts would place the council before Paul's independent mission which constitutes the second part of Acts: before Paul sets out on his mission every dispute must be settled, such as the mission to the Gentiles, the food laws that the Gentiles are required to keep, and the circumcision issue. It is Luke's theological concern that Paul, the hero of Luke's own church, is rooted in the Jerusalem church and is sanctioned by the apostolic council in Acts 15. The church of Luke's time is exclusively the Pauline church which lives in the tradition of the apostles. Thus, in Acts the apostles legitimize Paul's mission and then disappear afterwards.

---

4.   For a detailed study of Pauline chronology see Lüdemann, *Paul: Apostle to the Gentiles* (Philadelphia: Fortress Press, 1984).

5.   On the priority of Paul's letters over *Acts* see Hurd, *Origin*, pp. 22-44; J.C. Hurd, 'Pauline Chronology and Pauline Theology', in W.R. Farmer *et al.* (eds.), *Christian History and Interpretation: Studies Presented to John Knox* (Cambridge: Cambridge University Press, 1967), pp. 225-48, esp. 225-34.

It is obvious that once Luke's redactional method of relating Paul's mission to the apostolic council and the Jerusalem church is detected, the chronological order of Acts can no longer be used to establish a sound chronology of Paul. If in fact Paul had started his great mission before the apostolic council, it would be absolutely certain that Acts would have inverted the order of events for the reasons mentioned above.

One must nevertheless admit that observations about the Lukan way of arranging texts do not help us greatly in establishing a chronology of Paul. The question we have to ask is whether it is possible to develop a safe method for reconstructing a sequence of events on the sole basis of the Pauline letters. Fortunately, the answer is yes. One of the greatest milestones of American biblical scholarship was when John Knox and his followers such as John Hurd[6] pointed a way out of the chronological impasse. I shall try to build on and improve Knox's attempt below.

In Galatians 1–2 Paul recounts that about seventeen years have elapsed between his conversion and the apostolic council. Since the council was a crucial issue in Galatia, Paul gives a full account of it. He had promised to make a collection among his gentile churches for the poor in Jerusalem and stresses that he had set off immediately after the council to fulfill this promise. Most of the extant Pauline letters bear witness to this claim and show Paul organizing this collection: in 1 Cor. 16.2 he gives instructions on *how* to collect the money; in 2 Corinthians 8–9 he admonishes the churches of Achaia (and indirectly Macedonia) not to delay the collection of the money; and in Rom. 15.25 Paul can look back on the completion of the collection and indicates that together with delegates of the churches, he is about to deliver the money to Jerusalem.

The beginning of this collection, its progress and its completion can be monitored in Paul's letters. Moreover, the collection itself can be used to establish a sequence for these letters: 1 Corinthians 16 was written before 2 Corinthians 8–9 and Romans was written after Corinthian correspondences.

If we combine this sequence with the chronological and geographical information of Paul's whereabouts which are preserved in .his letters, we get a more or less exact sequence of events, dates and

6.   J.C. Hurd, 'The Sequence of Paul's Letters', *CJT* 14 (1968), pp. 189-200; Hurd, 'Pauline Chronology', pp. 225-48.

places. That is to say, we can reconstruct a relative chronology of the three or four years between the council of Jerusalem and Paul's last stay in Corinth where he was about to start on his last trip to Jerusalem in order to deliver this collection.

After reconstructing this order of events between the apostolic council and Paul's last trip to Jerusalem we have to ask: is it possible to place Paul's mission *before* the council?

This does seem to be possible. First of all, we know that the time span between Paul's conversion and his council visit was about seventeen years. Secondly, the case for Paul's presence in Greece before the council can be made with a high degree of probability, even though most scholars reject this probability on the basis of Acts and Galatians 1 where Paul does not mention a visit to Greece to have taken place before his council visit.

To conclude, however, from Paul's silence in Galatians that he was not in Greece at that time is an argument which cannot replace the evidence. The evidence requires a mission in Greece to have taken place for the following reasons. First, the references in the Corinthian correspondence to a foundation visit presuppose a long period of time between this event and the writing of 1 Corinthians: in the meantime many have died (1 Cor. 11.30); Apollos has been in Corinth and has already returned to Ephesus (3.5; 16.12); Paul has written the previous letter (5.9) and has already received a response with further questions; and factions have arisen in Corinth. Bornkamm and his followers are ready to admit these occurrences presuppose more than one or at least two years. If we allow a longer time span, we have to place Paul's foundation visit before the council.

Secondly, Paul states in Phil. 4.15:

> As you know yourselves, Philippians, in the early days of my mission, when I set out from Macedonia, you alone of all our congregations were my partners in payments and receipts.[7]

What does the apostle explicitly say here? He clearly regards the mission in Greece as belonging to the early days of his Gospel. If, as most scholars think, the mission in Greece occurred twenty years after Paul's conversion it is very difficult, if not impossible, to explain how

---

7.   This is taken from the New English Bible. All other biblical quotations in this essay are taken from the NRSV.

Paul could consider this mission as belonging to the early days of his preaching.

Thirdly, 1 Thessalonians does not refer to the collection. If we strictly apply our method, this would indicate that this letter was not written within the period of two to three years during which Paul organized the collection. This conclusion would be questionable only if we assume that the community of Thessalonica was not involved in the collection. But 2 Corinthians 8–9 shows that it was indeed. Another possible objection to our conclusion may be that 1 Thessalonians was written after the period of the organization of the collection. But this is excluded because 1 Thessalonians refers to the foundation visit which implies a time prior to the collection. Therefore, 1 Thessalonians was probably written around 40 CE, and is the only extant letter from the period between Paul's first Jerusalem visit and his second visit during which the council took place. (Although Philippians also does not mention the collection it cannot be dated with that period because it presupposes a long time span between the first visit and the time of its writing.)

What is the upshot of the foregoing arguments? We have seen that the reconstruction of a chronology of Paul based solely on his extant letters is not impossible. Bornkamm's chronology was partially confirmed in that all extant letters except one were indeed written within a period of two to three years. However 1 Thessalonians is an exception which argues against Bornkamm's claim since it stems from the first decade of Paul's missionary activity and is also ten years older than the next letter, 1 Corinthians. Hence Bornkamm's implicit appeal to chronology as a justification for systematizing Paul's thought has to be rejected and our own attempt to apply a new method to the interpretation of Paul's theological thought is well grounded.

We can now finally turn to our major task and ask: does Paul have a different view in 1 Thessalonians than in the later letters? Let us examine a specific topic and ask: how does he deal with the problem of dead Christians in 1 Thessalonians in comparison with other letters where this issue is dealt with? When making this comparison we have to ask one further question: what constant theological view point, if any, becomes visible in each of the different cases?

2. *A Case for a Development in Paul's Theology* [8]

It has been well said that the early Christians did not think of themselves as early Christians. On the contrary, they thought of themselves as the very last Christians. The letters of Paul bear witness to this observation, especially 1 Thessalonians, his oldest extant letter.

From a short summary at the beginning of this letter (1.9-10) we learn what Paul has preached to the Thessalonians about the future. He has taught them 'to serve a living and true God, and to wait for his son from heaven, whom he raised from the dead—Jesus, who rescues us from the wrath that is coming'. In this summary three things are closely connected: Jesus' resurrection, Jesus' coming from heaven, and Jesus' future deliverance of the Christians from the judgment.

But what is so peculiar about this belief? After all, it appears that most Christians today believe this as did the early Christians. The peculiar thing is, as mentioned above, that the first Christians and Paul, who transmitted such a belief did not think of themselves as first Christians but as the very last: unlike later Christian generations they expected all this to happen within their own lifetime. At the time of 1 Thessalonians the resurrection of Jesus was for Paul the first sign of his coming from heaven. The time between these two events and the mission around the world were not an issue and the concept of salvation focused mainly on a future event, the expected coming of Jesus from heaven, who would provide salvation for the Christians.

A close parallel to this kind of belief can be found in the missionary instruction given in Mt. 10.23: 'for truly I tell you, you will not have gone through all the towns of Israel before the Son of Man comes.' Since this passage in Matthew excludes a gentile mission there is an important difference between it and Paul's preaching to the Thessalonians. Nevertheless, there can be no doubt that both Mt. 10.23 and 1 Thess. 1.9-10 expect the coming of Jesus within the lifetime of the first generation of Christians (cf. Mk 13; Jn 21).

But time marched on and eventually some Christians in Thessalonica died. In trying to cope with this problem the Thessalonians turned to Paul for help, whose answer is preserved in 1 Thess. 4.13-18. The formula 'we do not want you to be uniformed',

8.   Some of the ideas in this section can also be found in my article, 'The Hope of the Early Paul', *Perspectives in Religious Studies* 7 (1980), pp. 195-201.

in v. 13 indicates that up to this point Paul had not dealt with the problem of dead Christians with the Thessalonians.

Paul gives a twofold answer. He first assures the believers that as Christ died and rose, God will bring the dead Christians together with the Lord (v. 14). Death will not prevent them from being together with Jesus at his coming. The second part of the answer is given in vv. 15-18 where Paul describes how he thought the end drama would happen. He quotes a word of the exalted Lord which he supplies with some additions: the Lord will come from heaven and the dead Christians will rise first; then they will be lifted up to meet the Lord in the air together with those who had not died.

When Paul writes, 'we who are alive, who are left until the coming of the Lord', he clearly implies that he will be alive at the time of Jesus' coming. We must go even further: he surely thought that the majority of Christians would be alive at this time. This fact can be deduced from Paul's argumentation in 1 Thess. 4.13-18 itself.

We have said that the first part of Paul's answer in v. 14 consisted in the assurance that the dead Christians would be together with Christ at his coming. In the second part of the answer we saw how Paul related this to the fate of the living Christians: the dead Christians are resurrected so that they may be caught up together with the living Christians to meet the Lord. We get the impression that the disadvantage of having died is cancelled through the resurrection: after rising, those who have died enjoy the same fate as those who have never died.

Hence, there are two different concepts in our passage: (1) resurrection and (2) translation. But which concept prevails? Surely the latter since the resurrection is merely related to it: Paul makes use of the concept of resurrection only to be able to employ the concept of translation. The idea of resurrection is an auxiliary thought enabling Paul to maintain his old concept of translation.

If this had not been the case, Paul would have argued differently and claimed that since God raised Jesus from the dead after he had fallen asleep, so he will raise those Christians who have fallen asleep. However, the awkward structure of 1 Thess. 4.14 indicates that Paul's hope centers around the encounter of the living generation with the coming Jesus. And in such a context the resurrection of the Christians can only be of minor importance, since their death was simply not anticipated.

The result of our analysis of 1 Thess. 4.13-18 fits in well with what we asserted about the summary of Paul's missionary preaching in 1 Thess. 1.9-10. For Paul the resurrection of Jesus is a sign of his immediate coming from heaven and the time between these two events is extremely short. That no one would die in the meantime was surely assumed and Paul did not take pains to think about the intermediate state of the few Christians who died. Furthermore, the future aspect of salvation is stressed in 1 Thess. 4.13-18 as well as in 1 Thess. 1.9-10 where salvation consists of Jesus' deliverance of the Christians from the coming wrath. In 4.13-18 salvation takes place when Christians are united with Christ at his parousia by means of translation.

There is another similarity between 1.9-10 and 4.13-18. In both texts Paul considers Jesus' (death and) resurrection as the reason for Jesus' union with believers at the parousia. Just as Jesus rose, the believers, whether dead or alive, will be safe at the parousia. This causal connection between Jesus' resurrection and the believer's future seems to be an important theological pattern in 1 Thessalonians and thus of the early Paul who did not anticipate more deaths to occur prior to Jesus' coming.

However, as time went on and more Christians died during the ten years between the writing of 1 Thessalonians and 1 Corinthians, the next extant letter, was Paul able to take this into account and adjust his beliefs accordingly? And if so, how? In order to secure a good chance for answering these questions, two conditions have to be fulfilled: (1) we must have a text which can be regarded as a reworking of 1 Thess. 4.13-18 and (2) the audience of Paul's previous teaching must be the same as that of the altered thought (otherwise the contingent situations and issues in another community may be responsible for a different answer).

Fortunately both conditions can be fulfilled. To begin with the question of the audience we should recall that 1 Thessalonians was written from Corinth. Therefore, the teaching about the coming of Jesus which appears in 4.13-18 must have been a part of Paul's first preaching in Corinth. That is to say, Paul also must have told the Christians in Corinth that they would soon be taken up into the air to meet the Lord along with the small number of those who would be raised from the dead to take part in this event.

We now can turn to the question of whether there is a text which can be understood as a deliberate reworking of 1 Thess. 4.13-18 and which is sent to Corinth. In 1 Cor. 15.51-52 Paul writes:

> Listen, I will tell you a mystery! We will not all die, but we will all be changed, in a moment, in the twinkling of an eye, at the last trumpet. For the trumpet will sound, and the dead will be raised imperishable, and we will be changed.

How can we assert that 1 Cor. 15.15-16 is a reworking of 1 Thess. 4.13-18? First of all, the expression 'mystery' in v. 51 corresponds to the 'word of the Lord' in 1 Thess. 4.15. Both contain apocalyptic information about something that was previously unknown. Secondly, the same vocabulary occurs in both contexts: 'die' in v. 51 and 1 Thess. 4.13, 14, 15; 'the dead' in v. 52 and 1 Thess. 4.15; and 'trumpet' in v. 52 and 1 Thess. 4.16. Thirdly, the structure of both passages is similar: after referring to the 'mystery' or the 'word of the Lord', Paul does not quote it but offers a summary in the first person plural ('we will not all die, but we will all be changed' and 'we who are alive, who are left until the coming of the Lord, will by no means precede those who have died' in 1 Thess. 4.15). It is not until he has summarized the mystery that he quotes it. The last reason why we may claim 1 Cor. 15.51-52 to be a reworking of 1 Thess. 4.15-18 is that these two passages are the only ones in which Paul makes a statement about the number of Christians to survive until the parousia occurs.

After recognizing this historical link between these two texts we proceed to ask: is there any common element in them? What are the differences? Is there evidence for a change in Paul's theological thought?

In answering the question of whether or not there are common features in the two passages, I must emphasize that both texts are concerned with the fate of Christians at the parousia. This implies that Paul does not deal with the intermediate state. Neither 1 Thessalonians 4 nor 1 Corinthians 15 is concerned with the question of what happens to the dead Christians in the time between their death and the parousia.

As to the differences between the two passages, I must point out that in 1 Thessalonians 4 the dead Christians are treated as an exception whereas in 1 Corinthians 15 the survivors are the exception. This can be concluded from the larger context of 1 Corinthians. For example, in 11.30 Paul says that many (ἱκανοί) have died. Furthermore, Paul

writes in 15.15: 'we will not all die [that is, most of us will die], but
we will all be changed'. Although 'we' includes those who have
already died and those still alive, it is difficult to determine whether
Paul expected to be among the survivors. (I would be inclined to
assume it from the end of v. 52.)

Another difference between the two texts can be seen in the notion
of the resurrection. We have already seen that the resurrection of the
dead Christians in 1 Thessalonians meant being restored to the body
prior to death, that is to say, to be made like the survivors. In
1 Corinthians 15, however, a shift has taken place: being resurrected
means being transformed or becoming imperishable. From the
immediate context of 1 Cor. 15.51-52 we learn that Paul ascribes to
the resurrected Christians a *pneumatic* body as opposed to the *psychic*
body which belongs to this world and has to perish.

Hence, we must conclude there are considerable differences between
1 Thessalonians 4 and 1 Corinthians 15. But how are they to be
explained? In what way did a change in Paul's theological thought take
place? In order to answer these questions correctly, we must be
reminded that an eschatological teaching like the one in
1 Thessalonians 4 was a part of Paul's first preaching in Corinth. The
implication, if not an explicit part of such a teaching, was that there
would be no deaths before the parousia. After Paul left, however,
some Christians died. This fact raised doubts concerning the former
model of translation since it was mainly concerned with the surviving
Christians. Paul had to modify his beliefs and find new concepts that
were adequate both for expressing the Christian hope and for coping
with history which could no longer be overlooked because of its most
characteristic feature, death. It is not until this later point in time that
Paul tries to come to terms with death and to deal with it from a
theological perspective.

Despite such differences in his concept of the resurrection of
Christians and of the imminence of Christ's parousia, we detect an
astonishing consistency in Paul's thought between 1 Corinthians 15
and 1 Thessalonians 4. In 1 Corinthians 15 he relates the transform-
ation/resurrection of both alive and dead Christians. They will receive
a *pneumatic* body at the parousia of the second man from heaven,
whose likeness the Christians will wear: 'as is the man of heaven, so
are those who are of heaven' (1 Cor. 15.48). As in 1 Thessalonians 4
it is from his Christology that Paul again derives a new theological

concept for expressing his hope. Death is unable to destroy the Christian hope because the Christians will be like Christ, the second man, whose likeness they will wear. 'As with Christ, so also with the Christians'—this is the logical pattern which underlies Paul's exciting theological struggle in 1 Corinthians 15. This model is used elsewhere in 1 Corinthians. For example, in 1 Cor. 6.14: 'God raised the Lord and will also raise us by his power.'

This theological model, in spite of its similarity with the one in 1 Thessalonians 4, seems to be a significant step beyond the latter. The model underlying 1 Thessalonians 4 was a causal connection between Jesus' resurrection and the believers' union with him at the parousia. Paul did not say 'as Christ was raised, the Christians will also be raised.' Not so long after Paul had developed this model of thought he had to undertake a fresh attempt to come to terms with the phenomenon of death in Corinth, even though the christological centre remained one and the same.

However, once the explication of this christological point of departure had been modified, other changes followed. In particular the dualistic aspects of Paul's thought in 1 Corinthians 15 must be directly related to his struggle with the problem of death. In 1 Corinthians 15 the *psychic* body has to perish for flesh and blood cannot inherit the kingdom of God (15.50). The *psychic* body, as flesh and blood, belongs to the realm of sin and death which will ultimately be destroyed with the parousia. Paul deliberately concludes his discussion of the resurrection with these words:

> When this perishable body puts on imperishability, and this mortal body puts on immortality, then the saying that is written will be fulfilled: 'Death has been swallowed up in victory.' 'Where, O death, is your victory? Where, O death, is your sting?' The sting of death of sin, and the power of sin is the law. But thanks be to God, who gives us the victory through our Lord Jesus Christ. (1 Cor. 15.54-57)

In contrast we will find no hints of a dualism—the pair spirit/flesh is lacking—and no reflection on the problem of death in 1 Thessalonians. This omission should not be regarded as accidental. At the time of the writing of 1 Thessalonians death was no concern for Paul because of the expectation of an imminent parousia!

Furthermore, we must recognize that 1 Corinthians 15 was not Paul's last word on this subject. Although Paul had dealt with the theological problem of death, one issue was still open: the state of the deceased Christians between death and parousia. The issue was negligible as long as the parousia was expected to happen shortly. But what if the coming of Christ was further delayed and not even a minority of Christians of the first generation, including Paul, could hope to be alive at the parousia? With this question in mind I turn to 2 Cor. 5.1-4:

> For we know that if the earthly tent we live in is destroyed, we have a building from God, a house not made with hands, eternal in the heavens. For in this tent we groan, longing to be clothed with our heavenly dwelling—if indeed, when we have taken it off we will not be found naked. For while we are still in this tent, we groan under our burden, because we wish not to be unclothed but to be further clothed, so that what is mortal may be swallowed up by life.

I begin with the question of whether or not there are any common elements in Paul's thought in 2 Corinthians 5 in relation to 1 Corinthians 15. What is called an 'earthly tent we live in' in v. 1 is described afterwards in terms of a garment: 'longing to be clothed with our heavenly dwelling' (v. 2). But whether Paul speaks of a building or a garment, the important fact is that there will be a new immortal body to replace the mortal body which is thus absorbed into immortal life (v. 4). The new body which Paul looks forward to cannot be distinguished from the *pneumatic* body that he expected to receive at the parousia (in 1 Corinthians 15). Hence, the notion of a bodily existence remains constant in both texts.

Another feature which underlies both 1 Corinthians 15 and 2 Corinthians 5 is the christological vantage point: 'as with Christ, so also with the Christians'. In the case of 2 Corinthians 5, the immediate context serves as a basis for the excursus in chapter 5. In 4.14 Paul writes: 'because we know that the one who raised the Lord Jesus will raise us also with Jesus'. The theological pattern 'as with Christ, so also with the Christians' cannot be better expressed.

As for the differences between 1 Corinthians 15 and 2 Corinthians 5, we have to emphasize that the destruction of the earthly tent in 2 Cor. 5.1 refers to the moment of death and to what will happen immediately afterwards. Therefore, we may say that at the time of the writing of 2 Corinthians, Paul no longer thinks of the parousia as the moment when the Christians receive a new body. He now expects the Christians to receive a heavenly body immediately after their death. This is an exciting innovation which Paul incorporated into his theology around the time of 2 Corinthians 5.

Can we somehow specify the historical and theological motives for this development? As far as the historical motives are concerned, we should turn to 2 Cor. 1.8-9 where Paul informs the Corinthians of something that had happened recently:

> We do not want you to be unaware, brothers and sisters, of the affliction we experienced in Asia; for we were so utterly, unbearably crushed that we despaired of life itself. Indeed, we felt that we would have received the sentence of death so that we would rely not on ourselves but on God who raises the dead.

This incident had taught Paul that he no longer could expect to be among the survivors.

As for the theological reasons for the shift in 2 Corinthians 5, we have to recognize the growing impact of the person of Christ on Paul which reaches its peak in 2 Corinthians 5. This growing importance of Christology is but a consequent development from his early days. At that time his concept of salvation was dependent on the traditional scheme of the coming world which was to happen with the parousia of Jesus who would save the Christians from the wrath to come. At a second stage this scheme was still in use, although under the impact of history and the ongoing delay of the parousia, Paul introduced a concept of resurrection different from that in 1 Thessalonians. But he was able to do so only because his Christology had provided him with the theological pattern 'as with Christ, so also with the Christians'.

When the delay of the parousia became too obvious to be ignored and Paul himself had been close to death, he abandoned the traditional scheme. At the same time, the impact and the importance of the person of Christ broke through: Christ has both the present and the future in his hands. Present Christian existence means to be in Christ and future Christian existence to be with Christ. Nothing is able to keep Paul from a union with Christ either in this life or at the moment of death. No apocalyptic time scheme is able to make the Christians wait for union with Christ between their death and the parousia. This union, previously expected to take place at the parousia, will happen at the moment of death. Moving from a concept of salvation in the future more and more to an emphasis of the fullness of time in the very present, Paul found a new understanding of time. This fullness of time, however, is not confined to the present but encompasses the future with Christ as well. To belong forever to Christ is Paul's hope—either 'in Christ' on this earth or 'with Christ' at the moment of his death—and he will not tolerate conceptions which may jeopardize the certainty and the full reality of this personal life with Christ.

That is the final, mature result of Paul's theological thought concerning the impact of Christ's death and resurrection on the future of the Christians which an exegesis of Philippians 1 and Romans 8 would only serve to confirm. We may add here that the basic theological principle 'as with Christ, so also with the Christians', which had provided Paul with the original response to the problem of death, was also applied to other issues such as the question of whether a Christian should suffer. It is easy to see how the example of Christ became for Paul a weapon against any theology of glory. We may add further that once Paul had developed this fundamental principle, he also managed to interpret baptism as dying and rising with Christ. In any case, these brief remarks show that our findings in one specific area of Pauline thought could be significant for other areas of Pauline theology.

Concluding Remarks

My preliminary remarks about the emergence of one aspect of Pauline theology have come to a close. As we look back now on this exegetical exercise we encounter a great man and a great theologian during the first three decades of the Christian movement as he was interpreting the meaning of Christ's resurrection for the future of Christians. We observe him making different statements which cannot be harmonized with each other. But we also see him starting again and again from the same theological conviction: namely, that Christ died and was raised. Perhaps we may realize now that an immature systematization of Paul's thought concerning the future of Christians could overlook the problems Paul had to face and would deprive us also of a chance to get to know Paul's theological method.

If these concluding remarks are not too far from the truth about the real Paul, then the apostle to the Gentiles becomes important once again to contemporary Christians, be they professional theologians or lay persons. Paul's theology could be seen as a model for responsible theology which pays sufficient attention to both the creed and the world. When we see Paul himself working out his theology, we can observe how and why theology is an endless task of interpretation, an interpretation with which we are entrusted even today. The theological method for this task can still be learned from Paul. Thus, we hope that theologians today become like Paul and that his principle may also be true for us: as with Paul, so also with every theologian.

GNOSTICISM IN CORINTH?

Heinz O. Guenther

John C. Hurd's reconstruction of the origin of Paul's first letter to the Corinthians[1] is a masterpiece in Pauline methodology. His detailed analyses demonstrate to the reader that solutions in Pauline studies must be based on Paul's own writings. Hurd's concern at each stage of his investigation is to allow the internal evidence of the letter to determine its context and content. He warns that reconstructions which draw too quickly on extra-biblical evidence not only misdirect the energy of responsible scholarship but also invite speculations to haunt the work of the exegete. Any solution to the Corinthian controversy based chiefly on external evidence is by necessity burdened with far too many suppositions. Hurd's patient insistence on exploring every piece of inside information before going to outside sources has produced significant results. The contours of Paul's strained relationship with his Corinthian counterparts appear with much greater clarity than any one at this distance of time could reasonably expect.

In tune with the literary methodology underlying all parts of his study, Hurd begins his investigation into the Corinthian situation with a fresh examination of the letter itself. In a cautious but imaginative step-by-step approach he works back from the letter to earlier written exchanges between the Corinthian community and Paul, the founder of that Greek church. In the course of his study it becomes clear that 1 Corinthians is not an isolated writing of canonical prominence but rather the climax of a series of unhappy communications between two parties drifting more and more apart. The letter is Paul's reaction to tensions which unexpectedly began to overshadow the originally intimate relationship between him and the community of his founding. More specifically, 1 Corinthians is for Hurd Paul's response to the

---

1. J.C. Hurd, Jr, *The Origin of 1 Corinthians* (Macon, GA: Mercer University Press, 1983).

Corinthians' adamant rejection of directives given by the apostle in his so-called *Previous Letter*, of which a displaced fragment is still available in 2 Cor. 6.14-7.1, apart from some brief reference to it in 1 Cor. 5.9-12a. Although Paul responds in 1 Corinthians to the Corinthians' position, the philosophy of the letter reinforces in more organized form the instructions expressed already by the apostle in his *Previous Letter*. No change in Paul's perspective is in evidence in the relatively short interval from the *Previous Letter* to the writing of 1 Corinthians. Neither is it possible to note any major change in the Corinthians' own critical attitude to Paul during that same period of time. The apostle had to write 1 Corinthians because leaders and members of that church continued to react frostily to his various attempts to clarify his position.

Throughout his study Hurd points out that the origin of the Corinthians' displeasure with Paul's position cannot lie in their fascination with gnostic teachings. No indication is implied in the letter of any sudden intrusion of gnostic Christian outsiders into this Pauline church. The Corinthians' glaring discontent with the Paul of the *Previous Letter* led Hurd to suspect that at the founding visit the two parties must have been in agreement over most of the issues now seriously in dispute. For Hurd the cause of the conflict has not been the Corinthians but Paul's change of attitude. The apostle surprised his Corinthian counterparts with what they regarded as newfangled provisions of unknown origins. Hurd suggests that it was most probably the *Apostolic Decree*, issued after his founding visit, which occasioned a change in Paul's missionary strategy. It is important to note that Hurd does not view the *Apostolic Decree* as a Lukan composition. In a bold interpretive move he assumes, with K. Lake, an origin and purpose of the *Decree* different from that accorded to it by the writer of Acts 15. The directives laid down in the *Previous Letter* regarding idolatry, improper diet and sexual morality are in this perspective Paul's attempt to reciprocate Jerusalem's recognition of his Gentile apostolate. It is these same directives which apparently set Paul apart from the Corinthians. To do justice to the *Decree*, Paul had to revise his earlier preaching, a move the Corinthians watched with increasing suspicion.

The purpose of this essay is to demonstrate that Hurd's rejection of gnosticism as the origin of the Corinthian controversy cannot be taken as a denial of all gnostic influences upon the Corinthian Church. One must not lose sight of the fact that the purpose of Hurd's study is to probe into the *immediate* source of the Corinthians' falling-out with the founder of their church. The wider cultural horizon of Paul's frustrating debate with his counterparts is not the focus of his study. It is not even a passing interest. The examination of key passages such as the painful divisions within the community (1 Cor. 1), the Corinthian attitude to idol meat (1 Cor. 8), the issue of sexual relations within marriage (1 Cor. 7), and the doctrinal tenet of physical resurrection (1 Cor. 15) leads Hurd to the conclusion that the disagreement between Paul and the Corinthians resulted not from any external interference but from shifts in Paul's strategy. Formerly unknown gnostic leanings on the part of some or all Corinthians cannot possibly have been the cause of their uneasiness with Paul. The search for a gnostic background to specific issues discussed in the letter is motivated, Hurd charges, not by the textual evidence of 1 Corinthians itself but by preconceptions carried to the letter. Nowhere in 1 Corinthians is there any evidence that Paul dealt with gnostic inclinations peculiar to his Corinthian opponents. Neither are there gnostic intruders in sight, alienating the church from its founder. 'It is exceedingly improbable', says Hurd, 'that the indirect influence of any outside teacher could have affected the entire Corinthian Church'.[2]

A brief review of Hurd's thought in the four areas of Paul's disagreement with the church of his founding (factions in the church, idol meat, sexual attitudes, resurrection) will bear out these observations. In the course of our discussion it will become clear that in addition to clashes between Paul and his counterparts, the Corinthian imbroglio has an important but widely ignored cultural side. The controversy is not merely the result of changes in Paul's missionary strategy. The Corinthian cultural mind and milieu determined the intensity of the dispute and added to it a dimension of which even Paul may not have been fully aware.

1. *The Alleged Gnostic Christ Party*

Mindful of the major role that 1 Cor.1.12-13 has played in most scholarly reconstructions of the Corinthian situation, Hurd made the passage into a steppingstone in order to investigate the general background of the Corinthian correspondence. Needless to say, quite a few

---

2.   Hurd, *Origin*, p. 215.

leading critical scholars have sought the origin of the Corinthian debate in the spread of a certain brand of gnostic anthropology. Gnostic interest in the Christ figure gave rise, for these scholars, to the so-called 'Christ party'. 'Some of you,' writes Paul, 'side with Apollo, others rally round Cephas or even flock to me, while again others ally themselves with Christ.' On the face of it, Paul seems to deal here with the slogans of four opposing parties: 'I belong to Paul', 'I belong to Apollo', 'I belong to Cephas', 'I belong to Christ' (1 Cor. 1.12). Are these slogans to be taken as the identifying marks of four distinct parties within the Corinthian church or are they merely hermeneutical vehicles of Paul's own making? Scholars disinclined to read them as rhetorical devices demonstrating the absurdity of all Christian disunity have taken these slogans at face value. They regard them as self-identifications, as watchwords used by members of these four parties to pledge allegiance to their respective spiritual leaders. In this essay the ambitions of the first three parties can be left aside. What is important here is that scholars of various persuasions have tended to characterize the 'Christ-party' as the representation of an interesting blend of gnostic Christian mythology.

Walter Schmithals, for instance, regards the slogan 'I belong to Christ' (ἐγὼ δὲ Χριστοῦ) as the aggregate of a gnostic myth, as the watchword of those who conceived of their 'self' in terms of entrap- ment. The self was here the 'alien' within the body, the spark separated from its pneumatic source, but wistfully yearning for reunion with it. The advocates of this gnostic teaching, Schmithals holds, found the worth of the individual exclusively 'in a super-terrestrial pneumatic substance' lying helplessly encased in the body, waiting to be rescued from the bodily prison.[3] 1 Corinthians is evidence, Schmithals claims, that together with Apollo and Cephas, Paul defended the apostolic tradition in the face of attacks on it by this type of gnostic belief.[4] In both canonical letters (1 Cor. 1.12 and 2 Cor. 10.7), the apostle had

---

3. W. Schmithals, *Gnosticism in Corinth: An Investigation of the Letters to the Corinthians* (trans. J.E. Steely; Nashville: Abingdon Press, 1971), p. 155; cf. p. 199.

4. Writes Schmithals: 'In Corinth apostolic tradition stands against free pneumatic status! The appeal to the Christ without against the appeal to the Christ within!' (Schmithals, *Gnosticism*, p. 202). A 'unified anti-Gnostic front,' represented by Paul, Peter and Apollo struggled with this type of gnostic 'Christ-party' (Schmithals, *Gnosticism*, p. 202 n. 124).

to square up to one single party of opponents, to intruders representing 'a pneumatic-libertine Gnosticism'[5] whose origins may well reach
back into pre-Christian times. To believe in Christ was for the
Corinthian gnostics tantamount to being a part of Christ.[6] Schmithals
holds this intruding gnostic party and their Corinthian supporters
'responsible for all the disorder' in the church.[7] The 'Christ people'
and particularly their gnostic anthropological myth are in Schmithals's
reconstruction the sole target of Paul's reprimand in 1 *and* 2
Corinthians.

Schmithals's study of the Corinthian brand of gnosticism is a large
scale elaboration of Rudolf Bultmann's exegetical investigation into
the religious background of Paul's opponents in 2 Corinthians.[8] Like
Schmithals, Bultmann holds that the apostle's adversaries in
1 Corinthians are identical with those combatted more intensely by
Paul in the second letter. Bultmann points to the topic of resurrection
as the major issue at stake in both letters. What transpires in
1 Corinthians 15 and 2 Corinthians 5, he argues, is that the mind of
the Corinthian intruders was steeped in gnostic mythology. Gnostic
ideas, he says, dominate 2 Corinthians 5 in the same measure as they
control 1 Corinthians 15.[9] In both letters, insists Bultmann, Paul
struggled with Hellenistic pneumatics of gnostic persuasion.[10]

Bultmann's attempt to accord primacy to the tenet of resurrection at

---

5.   Schmithals, *Gnosticism*, p. 117; cf. pp. 114-15, 124, 203-205.

6.   Behind the 'I belong to Christ' (ἐγὼ δὲ Χριστοῦ) lies for Schmithals 'the
typically Gnostic EGO EIMI formula…which conforms to the myth that man is only
a part of the Christ' (Schmithals, *Gnosticism*, p. 199).

7.   'I belong to Christ' is 'the watchword of those against whom in all his letters
Paul takes a position as against a *single* front…' (Schmithals, *Gnosticism*, p. 202;
emphasis added; cf. pp. 201, 203 n. 126).

8.   R. Bultmann, *Exegetische Probleme des Zweiten Korintherbriefes: Zu 2 Kor
5:1-5; 5:11-6, 10; 10-13; 12:21* (SBibUps, 9; Uppsala: Whetmans Boktryckeri
A.-B., 1947).

9.   'Es sind gnostische Vorstellungen [in 2 Corinthians 5], und es handelt sich
im Grunde um das gleiche Thema wie 1. Kor. 15' (Bultmann, *Exegetische
Probleme,* p. 4).

10.   'Das Pneumatikertum, gegen das Paulus kämpft, kann nur das hellenistische
Pneumatikertum sein, das wir als charakteristisch für die gnostiche Bewegung
kennen' (Bultmann, *Exegetische Probleme,* p. 25). For Bultmann, the gnostic
pneumatics are *intruders* (Bultmann, *Exegetische Probleme,* pp. 21, 26-27 etc.).
1 Corinthians itself does not warrant this conclusion.

the expense of other major items of 1 Corinthians cannot convince. Ernst Käsemann pointed this out with great clarity.[11] Käsemann notes that Paul's strivings in the two letters are by no means on a par.[12] He also refrains from placing Paul's opponents squarely in the gnostic camp.[13] He notes that 'weakness' (ἀσθένεια) in personal appearance and in speech mirrors for Paul the way of the cross (2 Cor. 11.30; 12.5, 9-10; 13.4). Thus, the hallmark of Paul's apostolate is 'weakness' in carrying out his own vocation. Apostles cannot be prepossessing in appearance. Arrogant spiritual demeanor is the cachet of false prophets. Paul's stern insistence on his own 'gnosis' in 2 Corinthians (10.5; 11.5-6) is for Käsemann not a sign of the apostle's boasting. It is evidence that Paul's Corinthian opponents must have impugned his pneumatic gifts. Paul openly acknowledges his 'weakness' in order to deal with accusations that he lacked spiritual power.

For Paul's opponents, observes Käsemann, the bench mark of apostolic dignity was their ability to free speech (either in tongues or otherwise), along with the power to perform miracles and experience ecstatic journeys into the upper world through visions or auditions. All these marks of pneumatic responsibility were, in their judgment, absent from Paul's life. They regarded him as a spiritual simpleton, unable to meet their own high standards. He displays spiritual power only from a distance, in written communications, they said disparagingly, while his oral performance is painfully disappointing (2 Cor. 10.10; 11.6). Käsemann concludes from his examination of pertinent passages in 2 Corinthians that Paul's Corinthian adversaries must have been intruders into his church, Hellenistic pneumatics who knew no moderation when boasting of their spiritual power.[14] They claim to furnish what Richard Reitzenstein called Hellenism's 'proof of the possession of πνεῦμα: the ability of free and improvised dialogue'.[15]

Contrary to Bultmann and Schmithals, Käsemann hesitates to designate these pneumatic intruders as gnostics, pure and simple. For him

11. E. Käsemann, 'Die Legitimität des Apostels: Eine Untersuchung zu II Korinther 10–13', *ZNW* 41 (1942), pp. 33-71.

12. Käsemann, 'Die Legitimität', p. 41.

13. Käsemann, 'Die Legitimität', pp. 36, 39-40.

14. Käsemann, 'Die Legitimität', pp. 36, 39-40, 70, etc.

15. R. Reitzenstein, *Hellenistic Mystery-Religions: Their Basic Ideas and Significance* (trans. J.E. Steely; Pittsburgh: The Pickwick Press, 1978), p. 461.

they are not the forerunners of the later infiltrators of the second century church. It is anything but certain, he maintains, 'that the [Corinthian] pneumatics were gnostics.'[16] The absence of any clearly outlined gnostic soteriology in Paul's own summary of their activity dissuades him from following Bultmann and Schmithals' lead in this regard. Paul's image of them as men 'measuring themselves by clearly defined rules' (τὸ μέτρον τοῦ κανόνος), using these rules as a yardstick to determine their own rank (συγκρίνοντες ἑαυτούς, 2 Cor. 10.12-14), suggests to Käsemann that in addition to their spiritual credentials as Hellenistic pneumatics, they must have been envoys from the Jerusalem Church, carrying 'letters of recommendation' (2 Cor. 3.1) to prove their official status. As pneumatics of Hellenistic persuasion they were, for Käsemann, apostolic emissaries dispatched and empowered by Jerusalem, 'the head office of the early church' (K. Holl).[17]

The three attempts to unveil the origins of Paul's opponents show that no consensus exists in contemporary critical scholarship a) on their mental (gnostic or otherwise) persuasion and b) on the topical interrelation between the issues addressed in 1 and 2 Corinthians. While Bultmann and Schmithals describe Paul's adversaries as 'gnostics', Käsemann designates them as 'Hellenistic pneumatics' of Jewish-Christian descent. For Bultmann and Schmithals, Paul was faced with the same type of opponents in both letters. Käsemann disagrees. He points out that the issues addressed in 1 Corinthians are different from those touched upon in 2 Corinthians. In the first letter, says Käsemann, a variety of issues figure prominently, such as the unity of the church, the Lord's supper, moral laxity and appeal to pagan judges. 2 Corinthians is conspicuously silent about these issues. Without fully understanding all the ramifications, Paul refutes what must have been 'gnostic' ideas about resurrection in 1 Corinthians. In 2 Corinthians, however, no opposition is raised to the gnostic

---

16. 'Daß sie Pneumatiker etwa im Sinn der hellenistischen Gnosis waren... ist alles andere als gewiß' (Käsemann, 'Legitimität', p. 40).

17. The Church, 'die in Jerusalem ihren eigentlichen Sitz hat' (K. Holl, 'Der Kirchenbegriff des Paulus in seinem Verhältnis zu dem der Urgemeinde', in *Gesammelte Aufsätze zur Kirchengeschichte*. II. *Der Osten* [Darmstadt: Wissenschaftliche Buchgesellschaft, 1964], p. 56).

interpretation of resurrection.[18] Contrary to the first letter, 2 Corinthians focuses its attention on the legitimacy of apostleship,[19] an issue of no prominence in 1 Corinthians.

We have delineated the views of Schmithals, Bultmann and Käsemann to show that the gnostic solution to the Corinthian controversy is only attractive at first sight. Upon closer scrutiny into the evidence, this solution breaks down at various points. To uphold it, corroborative evidence first had to be created by each of the three scholars. Moreover, each of the three offers a slightly different reading of the key texts cited in support of the gnostic solution, often based on a rather whimsical exegesis. To seek the *immediate* reasons for Paul's strained relationship with the Corinthian church in some form of gnosticism, embryonic or full-fledged, is a decision based more on preconceptions than on Paul's own writings. Personal affinities begin to determine the mesh of the scholars' sieve. The gnostic solution is sustainable only if one is ready to take supposition for evidence. The research of Käsemann into Paul's opponents particularly bears out the fact that the thought of Paul's Corinthian adversaries was shaped more by hellenism than gnosticism. It is the speculative nature of this research which inspired Hurd to take a fresh look at 1 Corinthians itself and to provide a textually more sustainable solution. Hurd offers several observations which speak against Schmithals's assumption that 'the gnostically inclined Christ people were the one opposing party in Corinth'.[20] To these I must now turn.

It cannot go unnoticed that 1 Corinthians, taken in its entirety, does not affirm the existence of factional divisions along the lines suggested by 1 Cor. 1.12-13. There is no corroborative evidence in the letter that four opposing factions were active in Corinth. 'The perplexing fact is,' said Hurd, 'that the remainder of 1 Corinthians does not seem to give any information about the issues which separate these four

18. 'An die gnostische Auferstehungslehre wird [in 2 Cor] mit keinem Wort gerührt' (Käsemann, *'Legitimität'*, p. 40).

19. '...dominierend steht...das 'Amt' des Paulus im Vordergrund' (Käsemann, 'Legitimität', p. 40).

20. 'Since...Paul does not indicate with a single word that he connects one of the false teachings which he is opposing with Peter or Apollo, it naturally follows that only the [gnostic] Christ people came into consideration as the opposing party' (Schmithals, *Gnosticism*, p. 205).

parties'. [21] Just as there cannot have existed an anti-Pauline Cephas or
Apollo party, so no antagonistic 'Christ-party', gnostic or not, can be
assumed to have aspired after the leadership of that church. The letter
supports the view that Paul was not opposed by different groups
within the Corinthian church; instead he was rejected by the *entire*
church. In Hurd's terms, '1 Corinthians apparently was addressed by
Paul to a single, more or less unified, opposing point of view'.[22]

Had there been four major conflicting viewpoints within the
Corinthian community, Paul would undoubtedly have commented on
them in one form or another. Moreover, the arguments advanced in
his effort to secure the unity of the church fit the alleged 'Christ-
party' like a glove. Both he and the Christ people, had any such group
ever existed, would have agreed that Christ is not divided and
that Christians are not baptized in anyone other than Christ himself
(1 Cor. 13). Paul's silence in 1 Corinthians about the teachings of the
four parties strongly suggests that none of them existed. 1 Cor. 1.12-
13 is a rhetorical device demonstrating the absurdity of Christian
disunity. Nothing more.

A second observation strengthens the conclusions of the first. Paul's
insistence that Christ is *not* divided (1 Cor. 1.13), coupled with his
claim that *all* Christians belong to Christ (1 Cor. 3.21b-23), is apparently an assumption he would have shared with the alleged Christ
party. More has to be said. Paul's statement that Christ cannot be
divided would have made him into the spokesman of any such party.
The claim 'I belong to Christ' represents the best of Paul's thought.[23]

21. Hurd, *Origin*, p. 96.
22. Hurd, *Origin*, p. 96; cf. pp. 126, 147, 207, 269. He is here in agreement
with Schmithals who also holds that 'only one decisive conflict pervades the epistle'
(Schmithals, *Gnosticism*, pp. 114; cf. 115, 117, 124, 202 n. 124, 203, 205). But
Hurd disagrees with Schmithals's conclusion that the conflict was the result of gnostic intrusion.
23. The affinity of Paul's own Christology to that of the alleged 'Christ party'
presents Schmithals with no small difficulty. He is forced to explain away the agreement between the two with a slight of his exegetical hand. The 'I am Christ', says
Schmithals, is 'the watchword of those against whom in all his letters Paul takes a
position as against a single front' (*Gnosticism*, p. 202). Why then do two opposing
parties share a common Christology? Paul's antithesis to a group representing his
own position ('I am of Christ') implies, Schmithals opines, that at first the apostle
'has not recognized the 'Christ people' as Gnostics or understood them as such in
their concern' (*Gnosticism*, p. 205; cf. p. 201 n. 123). Relatively late in the game

In addition, while Apollo and Cephas reappear in the letter at least once or twice (1 Cor. 3.4, 22; 4.6; 9.5; 15.5), the 'Christ-party' disappears entirely from sight in the rest of the letter. It stands out, says Hurd, 'as an anomaly'.[24] Paul does not lose a single word about it anywhere. 2 Cor. 10.7 cannot be linked to 1 Cor. 1.13. Here Paul claims the Χριστοῦ εἶναι for himself: 'If anyone is confident that he is Christ's, I am too!' No mention is made in 2 Cor. 10. 7 of a 'Christ-party'.

Thirdly, some tinkering with the extant text is required if the responsibility for the Corinthian disorder is placed on the shoulders of a gnostically inclined 'Christ group'. Hypotheses necessarily begin to dictate conclusions. It is not surprising that Schmithals is forced to assume first, that for strategic reasons the 'Christ party' had to modulate its favourite 'I AM' watchword ('I *am* Christ') into the Christianized slogan of 1 Cor. 1.12: 'I *belong* to Christ'.[25] Secondly, Schmithals can sustain the gnostic hypothesis only by reckoning with the possibility of Paul's initial misunderstanding of the gnostic ΕΓΩ ΕΙΜΙ. This is a formula, says Schmithals, whose background was unknown to the apostle.[26] In order to read the slogans in 1 Cor. 1.12, moreover, as actual watchwords of four existing parties he posits the existence of small Jewish house churches in Corinth, originally founded by Peter but later probably placed under the supervision of

the apostle recognized, for Schmithals, their gnostic intention as a distinct group. Käsemann faces a similar difficulty. For this scholar too the Christ party is an existing group antagonistic to Paul. But why does Paul in 1 Cor. 1.13 not mark off his own Christology from a party otherwise hostile to him? Why does he merely affirm that Christ is not divided, a belief he shared with this alleged Christ party? Käsemann gets around the difficulty by claiming that the 'Christ group' must have appeared at a relatively late stage in the conflict: Χριστοῦ εἶναι (1 Cor. 1.12) 'taucht...nur an der Peripherie der Debatte auf und markiert allenfalls eine letzte Konsequenz des gegnerischen Angriffs' ('Legitimität', p. 36). This is speculation at its best.

24. Hurd, *Origin*, p. 104.

25. The watchword of the Christ party, argues Schmithals, was modelled on the 'typically Gnostic EGO EIMI formula', even though the slogan of 1 Cor. 1.12 reads 'I belong to Christ' (*Gnosticism*, p. 199). The gnostic 'Christ party' in Corinth, suggests Schmithals, 'had to refrain from the extreme self-expression of every Gnostic...' (*Gnosticism*, p. 200 n.121).

26. Schmithals, *Gnosticism*, p. 206. 'I consider it unlikely that [at an early stage of the conflict] Paul had comprehended the position of his opponents...' (*Gnosticism*, p. 201 n.123). At first, Paul 'has not recognized the "Christ people" as Gnostics or understood them as such in their concerns' (*Gnosticism*, p. 205).

Apollo.[27] It cannot be said that any of these three claims enjoys the immediate support of 1 Corinthians. Understandably Hurd is not prepared to endorse them.

Lastly, Paul's rebuttal in 1 Cor. 1.12-13 does not constitute any serious challenge to the alleged 'Christ party'. That Christ is not divided would have been a foregone conclusion for any of the four parties, had they ever existed. Neither Paul nor the alleged Christ party would have taken issue with such statement. 1 Cor. 1.12-13 thus does not suggest the existence in Corinth of a gnostically inclined 'Christ party'. Its existence is indeed, as Hurd points out, 'extremely doubtful.'[28] Moreover, the fact that the Christology of such a party is not fleshed out in the remainder of the letter weighs against its existence.

1 Corinthians informs the reader of a number of topics which have been the immediate source of the Corinthian controversy. Large parts of the letter deal with the question of idol meat, the appropriateness of sexual asceticism within marriage and with the doctrinal issue of resurrection. Hurd's reconstruction of the Corinthian situation rests on the examination of these three items.

2. Friction over Idol Meat

Paul's double reference to *gnosis* (γνῶσις οἴδαμεν) in 1 Cor. 8.1a ('We *know* that all of us have *gnosis-knowledge*') has become one of the key texts marshaled by commentators in support of the assumption that the Corinthian controversy resulted from some gnostic intrusion in Paul's church. Admittedly, most scholars, including J.C. Hurd, affirm that the slogan 'We all possess knowledge' (8.1a) is not a statement of Paul's own making. The apostle cites here a catchword borrowed from his Corinthian opponents. The literary observation, however, that 8.1a is a Corinthian catchword is no justification for assigning it immediately to gnostic intruders or their sympathizers

---

27. The slogans with the familiar names (Peter, Paul, Apollo) hail for Schmithals from some unified anti-gnostic front. 'The majority of the communities can be traced back to Apollos' (Schmithals, *Gnosticism*, p. 202 n. 124). How did the small Petrine group come into existence? Schmithals conjectures that it may have been the 'result of the missionary work of Peter' (*Gnosticism*, p. 204 n. 124).

28. Hurd, *Origin*, p. 105. 'The so-called Christ party probably did not exist' (Hurd, *Origin*, p. 269).

within the Corinthian church. It must be kept in mind that the citation 'All of us possess *gnosis*' is only one of three quotes used by Paul in ch. 8. It stands side by side with two other statements which equally stem from the Corinthians.[29] Together with 'gnosis-knowledge' (8.1a), Paul's Corinthian counterparts also insisted that 'Idols have no real existence' (8.4a) and that 'there is no God but one' (8.4b), two statements with no particularly gnostic overtones. As ch. 8 discloses, the three slogans, taken together, all relate in one form or another to one single topic. The chapter focuses not on *gnosis*, but on the issue of *idol meat*, a topic which found Paul and the Corinthians on opposite ends of the spectrum.[30] Paul's warning in one of his earlier communications against eating such meat in public upset the Corinthians. In fact, one purpose of writing 1 Corinthians was Paul's intention to set the Corinthians' mind at ease or, at least, to counter their objections to his earlier communications about immortality (ch. 5), idolatry (ch. 8) and sexual abstinence (ch. 7).[31] The issue at stake in 1 Corinthians 8 is not gnosis. Idol meat dominates the agenda.

Gnosis-knowledge was not a bone of contention between Paul and the Corinthians. Both took it for granted that 'all Christians possess knowledge'. What is in dispute in ch. 8 is the advisability of eating 'idol meat' in public. It is here that the Corinthians suspected Paul to be poles away from their own position. Is it appropriate to eat such meat in the presence of Christians questioning the propriety of such diet? Or, should Christians better refrain from touching it, in deference to 'weaker' members of the community (8.10-13), whoever they may have been? Once it is clear that the real issue in Corinth is idol meat, and the Christian attitude to it, the reference to *gnosis* loses its centrality within the ongoing debate. The catchword 'We all possess knowledge' can now no longer be isolated from the larger

29. The three statements are 'all most probably slogans quoted by Paul from a source' (Hurd, *Origin*, p. 121).

30. *Idol Meat* is meat that at one point had been dedicated to idols. Later it was sold in public meat markets across the city. Paul is not concerned with the eating of such meat in the privacy of Christian homes. The question is whether it should be consumed in full public view, at fellowship meetings open to all members of the church.

31. In ch. 8 Paul modifies the three Corinthian affirmations 'in a way which indicates that he [could] not accept them without severe reservations' (Hurd, *Origin*, p. 122).

context of the Corinthian conflict. It can no longer be taken by itself or made into the motto of only one single group within the Corinthian community. The dispute about diet concerned not one party but the *whole* Corinthian church. It was not a marginal issue. The whole community was engaged in it.

To put the catchword 'gnosis' (1 Cor. 8.1a) into the mouth of gnostic intruders (or their supporters) is ill-founded for yet another reason. Nowhere in 1 Corinthians 8 are gnostic teachings at stake. The Corinthian catchword that 'there is no God but one' cannot have been the result of gnostic leanings either. All early or later gnostics assumed that multitudes of higher and lower divine beings dwell in the *pleroma*, the place of perfection and peace beyond all evil and suffering.[32] Stress on only one divine being has never been a strong gnostic suit. Gnostics tended to speak of the 'Unknown God', the 'Alien God' or the 'Highest God' rather than of the 'One God'.

Paul's plea for monotheism would not have been an effective refutation of gnostic leanings, had they dominated the Corinthian church. The Corinthians coined the catchword ('there is no God but one') in defense of their practice of eating idol meat. Idols have reality only for those who lack faith in 'the one God'. By contrast, Paul cited the same catchword to challenge the Corinthians' naive monotheism. In defining God's inner unity, the apostle's Christology called for a greater degree of sophistication. Paul takes issue with the Corinthians because their affirmation of the one God jarred somewhat with his image of Christ's divine role at creation and redemption. Christians affirm, says Paul, that 'there is one God... *and* one Lord, Jesus Christ, through whom are all things and through whom we exist' (8.6:

---

32. The *pleroma*, says K.L. King in her introduction to Valentinian gnosticism, is 'the dwelling place of the highest God... the place where the spirits of light, rescued from their human bodily prison, will rest forever' (K.L. King, 'What is Gnosticism?', *The Fourth R* 4/3 (1991), pp. 1-6, esp. 3). All sorts of heavenly beings dwell in the light-world of the pleroma. *Pleroma* includes 'the Alien Father and the Alien Mother along with other figures belonging to the rich divine light-world' (*Pleroma* signifies 'die reiche Figurenwelt zu der der unbekannte Vater und die unbekannte Mutter gehören' (W. Bousset, 'Gnosis, Gnostiker', *Religionsgeschichtliche Studien: Aufsätze zur Religionsgeschichte des Hellenistischen Zeitalters* [ed. A.F. Verheule; NovTSup, 50; Leiden: Brill, 1979], p. 58). 'The Valentinian divine world, or Pleroma, is composed of a core of thirty aeons which are arranged in [male-female] pairs' (M.R. Desjardins, *Sin in Valentinianism* [SBLDS, 108; Atlanta, GA: Scholars Press, 1990], p. 13).

emphasis added). While both affirmed that 'there is no God but one', the affirmation functions differently in their respective systems of thought.

Is it possible to recover from the use of these three slogans the reasons for the Corinthians' disagreement with Paul? Why did they challenge Paul's position on idol meat with these three catchwords? And why was the Paul of ch. 8 so cautious in his use of the slogans? He continues to warn against any unrestricted consumption of idol meat while at the same time reaffirming that 'idols have no real existence'. Appeal to gnostic opposition in Corinth does not contribute much to solving these questions. Paul is under attack here. He is anxious to let the three slogans stand while dithering helplessly about their exact meaning.

Paul's modification in 1 Corinthians 8 of the three Corinthian catchwords[33] suggests that he read and understood them as a serious challenge to his own position on idol meat. Otherwise he would not have dealt with them in such detail. The way in which he responds to the Corinthians' challenge bespeaks a dilemma on Paul's part. He affirms without any reservations the Corinthian claim that 'idols have no real existence' (8.4a). But for reasons undisclosed in the chapter, he jeopardizes his own affirmation by making some allowances for the perceptions of 'weak Christians'. Idols thus indeed have existence for some, he implies, even if only in their minds. Paul befuddles his claim that 'idols do not really exist' by insisting that those who attribute reality to them ought to determine church policy! To paraphrase Paul's caution: 'Take care lest your insistence on the unreality of idols alienate those for whom idols still exist' (8.9).

In like manner, he agrees with the Corinthians that 'all Christians possess knowledge' (8.1a). But he jeopardizes the inner logic of his point by adding that despite the commonality of this knowledge, some have not yet acquired it: 'Not all possess this knowledge' (1 Cor. 8.7). His affirmation of the unrestricted freedom to eat idol meat (10.25: 'Eat whatever is sold in the meat market without raising any question on the ground of conscience') unites him with his Corinthian challengers while, at the same time, separating him from them. Freedom to consume idol meat is misused if the faithful walk over the

33. 1 Cor. 8.1a: 'We know that all of us possess knowledge'; 1 Cor. 8.4a: 'We know that an idol has no real existence'; 1 Cor. 8.4b: 'We know there is no God but one'.

minds of those who are unprepared for the exercise of this freedom
(8.9: 'Take care lest this liberty of yours becomes a stumbling block
to the weak').

What is the reason that Paul espouses such an equivocal position on
these matters? The apostle seems to be playing both ends. Since the
freedom to eat idol meat is nowhere disputed by him, his call to
refrain from it reads like a *petitio principii,* that is, a logical fallacy
which takes for granted what in itself is not clear at all. On the one
hand, he gives a restrained but unmistakable nod in the direction of
eating idol meat. On the other hand, he disapproves of implementing
this freedom in the presence of those unprepared to exercise it. No
power of persuasion, he holds, ought to be applied to the weaker
members. No attempts must be made to lead them into the freedom
shared by all Christians. The tension between approval and
disapproval points to an earlier stage of Paul's relationship with the
Corinthians, a time when both parties were in agreement on matters
now sharply disputed. Paul is cautious not to reject any of the
principles underlying the three slogans because they seem to be the
Corinthians' summary of his own preaching at the founding visit.
Unable to understand Paul's sudden restraint on their freedom, the
Corinthians presented him with what they considered the gist of his
own earlier preaching: all possess knowledge; idols are unreal; God
alone is real.

Hurd solves the problem of Paul's oscillation between approval to
eat idol meat in public and disapproval of doing so in the presence of
those who object to it by drawing the reader's attention to the content
of the apostle's *Previous Letter* (1 Cor. 5.9; 2 Cor. 6.14-7.1). It
cannot be accidental, he notes, that among other things this fragment
of Paul's earlier communication with the Corinthians refers to
idolatry. What transpires here is that shortly after his founding visit,
Paul must have stunned the Corinthians with his instruction to avoid
anything unclean: 'What agreement has the temple of God with
idols... Touch nothing unclean' (2 Cor. 6.16, 17). As could not be
expected otherwise, the Corinthians read this as a warning sign against
an unrestricted diet. In fact, the controversy between the apostle and
his counterparts seems to have erupted from what the Corinthians
regarded as novel injunctions. It is not difficult to reconstruct the
Corinthians' response to the *Previous Letter*: 'How can we avoid
contact with immoral people in everyday life?' (1 Cor. 5.9), 'We

never eat idol meat in pagan temples, we eat it in Christian fellowship meetings' (1 Cor. 8.10). 'Most of the time we do not even know whether or not the meat bought or served to us had at one point been dedicated to idols' (1 Cor. 8.10).

Unable to understand the origin, reason or purpose of Paul's call to avoid things unclean, the Corinthians submitted to Paul a summary of what they had heard him say at the founding visit. In their request for clarification they accused the apostle of inconsistency in argumentation. 'You yourself taught us,' they may have said, 'that Christian recognition of only one God implies the nonexistence of idols! Why must we now abstain from eating idol meat if idols do not exist?' The memory of the 'younger, more vigorous Paul' of the founding visit (who had probably eaten idol meat himself) exacerbated their dissatisfaction with the Paul of the *Previous Letter*.[34] What caused Paul to change his mind shortly after the Apostolic Council? Why did he call upon the Corinthians in the *Previous Letter* (written after the Apostolic Council) to abstain from anything unclean, even though he himself had possibly been unconcerned about these things at the founding visit?

For Hurd the answer to this question lies hidden in the language of the *Apostolic Decree*, a series of dietary laws imposed by Jewish circles upon Paul's brand of Gentile Christianity. According to the book of Acts this *Decree* calls upon Gentile Christians to 'abstain from the pollution of idols, from unchastity and from meat of animals killed by strangulation' (Acts 15.20, 29; 21.25). Hurd suggests that the *Decree* might first 'have given rise to the *Previous Letter*'.[35] Should this be correct, everything falls into place. In return for being acknowledged by the Jerusalem Church as a fully fledged apostle (Gal. 2.7-9; Rom. 15.31),[36] Paul agreed in a spiritual *quid pro quo* to enforce the rules of the *Decree* among his Gentile churches. Since the Corinthians had not been party to the new agreement, Paul decided to

---

34. At the time of the founding visit, says Hurd, the Corinthians met 'a younger, more vigorous Paul, fired with enthusiasm in his new faith, less cautious in his theological statements than he later became, little conscious of the weakness of human nature' (*Origin*, p. 287).

35. Hurd, *Origin*, p. 246.

36. 'What Paul wanted and needed...was the recognition by the Jerusalem Church of his missionary work and the confirmation of his authority in the Churches he had founded' (Hurd, *Origin*, p. 263).

withhold from them full information about it. Such information, says
Hurd, 'would only have angered them without serving any useful
purpose' in the apostle's missionary endeavours in Asia Minor and
Greece.[37] It is the silence about matters he should perhaps have
disclosed to his partners which seems to have given rise to the
growing unrest in Corinth, leading to the Corinthians' determined
opposition to what for them were Paul's newfangled diet regulations.

To trace the Corinthians' opposition back to gnosticism grossly
ignores the fact that ch. 8 is devoted to the topic of idol meat.[38]
Hurd's reconstruction is persuasive: nowhere does Paul reject 'any of
the principles of the Corinthians as being...the result of gnostic
influence.'[39] Rather, the entire church is engaged in a dispute over
strictures Paul himself had tried to impose on them. A brief look into
Paul's discussion about sexual abstinence within marriage will further
discredit the gnostic hypothesis. Gnostic intruders cannot be held
responsible for the Corinthian conflict.

3. *Marriage versus Celibacy*

Paul wrote 1 Corinthians 7 in response to a Corinthian letter[40] which
must have strongly favoured total sexual abstinence among Christian
spouses. The statement, 'it is well for a man not to touch a woman!'
(7.1b)[41] is another typically Corinthian slogan. But it is more than
that. Paul's obvious agreement with its intent suggests that at an early
point of their association, he must have countenanced some sort of
sexual asceticism himself. The apostle's subdued reaction to the
Corinthian slogan, together with the gist of ch. 7,[42] implies that

37. Hurd, *Origin*, p. 265.

38. Had the Corinthians been motivated by gnostic concerns, they would not
have been startled by Paul's attitude to such meat. The gnostic solution is further
weakened by the fact that some gnostic circles (Satornil, Marcion etc.) strictly
prohibited meat diet (Bousset, 'Gnosis, Gnostiker', p. 69).

39. Hurd, *Origin*, p. 147.

40. 'Concerning the matters about which *you wrote*' (7.1a; emphasis added).

41. 'To touch a woman' (γυναικὸς [μὴ] ἅπτεσθαι) is in LXX jargon the precise
idiom for sexual relations (Gen. 20.6; Ruth 2.9; Prov. 6.29b). Observes Hurd,
'clearly the slogan of 7.1b could apply to marriage in general as well as to marital
intercourse' (*Origin*, p. 166).

42. 'He who refrains from marriage will do better' (1 Cor. 7.38); 'Whoever is
firmly established in his heart...to keep her as his betrothed [not to have intimate

earlier on both parties must have been at one in their basic recognition that intimacies between spouses would run counter to the stirrings of the spirit. Both may have held it as axiomatic that sexual relations serve the flesh, not the spirit. Spouses engaging in marital intercourse enjoy what is of no lasting value. Had no such principal agreement between them ever existed, Paul might have been expected to have reacted more severely to the Corinthians' radical proposition 'not to touch a woman'. Moreover, 1 Corinthians still reflects Paul's tacit concurrence with the principle underlying the Corinthian slogan. Why else would he have hailed celibacy as the most appropriate Christian life style: 'It is well to remain single' (7.8)?[43]

The restraint shown by Paul in discussing the wisdom of entering into lasting marriage relationships indicates that he himself had a stake in the matter. At an early point of their mutual history, he and the Corinthian's must have agreed that in view of the imminence of the Lord's return (7.26-27) sexual relations had not only to be kept in check, but had to be resolutely renounced. In 1 Corinthians 7 sex is put under taboo: 'It is well for Christians to abstain from any such intimacies' (7.1b). Early in their history both must have contended that life-long relationships would by necessity sap the strength of the spouses' faith in the Lord's coming. When it appeared to the Corinthians that Paul had withdrawn from his earlier commitment to ascetic intramarital lifestyles, relations between them, personal and communal, began to turn sour.

Paul's sudden advocacy, in a letter preceding 1 Corinthians, of traditional marriage relationships between Christian spouses must have stunned the Corinthians. They did not hesitate to accuse him of a serious volte-face in his position. The tone of 1 Corinthians indicates that the protracted controversy about the pros and cons of celibacy within marriage had roiled relations between the two parties. The letter which, in Hurd's reconstruction of the Corinthian situation, must have caused the Corinthians to object to Paul's new stance (7.1a) is again likely to have been the *Previous Letter*. Just as Paul had warned the Corinthians against any unqualified exercise of their

relations with her] he will do well' (7.38; cf. 7.7.8; 7.26-27, 34).

43. Celibacy is highly regarded by Paul: 'I think that in view of the impending disaster it is well for a person to remain as he is... Are you free from a wife? Do not seek marriage' (7.26-27); 'Unmarried people are anxious about the affairs of the Lord...' (paraphrase of 7.34); cf. 7.37-38.

freedom to eat idol meat (ch. 8),[44] so he cautioned them against any form of sexual *hybris*—within marriage (7.5) and/or without (7.2, 9, 36): 'Because of the temptation to immorality, each man should have his own wife, and each woman her own husband' (7.2).

It cannot escape notice that, in both cases, Paul continues to uphold this principle controlling the Corinthians' own radical approach to the problem in question. His advice to abstain from eating idol meat aside (8.10-13), the principle that 'idols have no real existence' (8.4) remains untouched. Similarly, despite his practical advice to enter into normal marriage relations (7.2.5),[45] the principle that 'it is better to refrain from intimate relations in marriage' (7.37-38) still continues to stand. The fact that the Corinthians turned a deaf ear to the apostle's reaffirmation of these principles speaks for itself. Virtually disregarding his preference for celibacy, the Corinthians continued to take issue with Paul's casuistic distinctions,[46] a clear indication that in their view the apostle had abandoned the position of unconditional celibacy. The apostle's reaffirmation of the principles underlying their position must have appeared to them as mere lip service.

The slump in relationships between Paul and the Corinthians started for Hurd with the apostle's *Previous Letter*. In it Paul speaks of 'defilement of body and spirit' in general (2 Cor. 7.1), as well as against matching believers with unbelievers (2 Cor. 6.14); he is probably referring here to courtship with the intent of marriage. What is missing is a clear statement against marriage between Christians as such, and against intramarital relations. Paul's acceptance of normal sexual relations between spouses must have displeased the Corinthians. They noted that no support had been given in the fragment of the *Previous Letter* (2 Cor. 6.14-7.1) to sexual asceticism within marriage. Significantly, 1 Corinthians 7 still echoes faintly an earlier agreement on the strict injunction not to engage in marital intercourse. Paul urges them: 'Do not refuse one another *except perhaps by agreement*, and for only a brief period of time' (7.5; emphasis added). A former rule inculcating total abstinence has

---

44. 'Take care lest this liberty of yours somehow becomes a stumbling block to the weak' (8.9).

45. 'It is better to marry than to be aflame with passions' (7.9).

46. 'If the unmarried cannot exercise self-control, they should marry...' (7.9); 'if any brother has a wife who is an unbeliever, and she consents to live with him, he should not divorce her...' (7.12), etc.

apparently been modulated here into a concession to abstain *temporarily* from sexual relations. It is well possible, says Hurd, that in their response to the apostle (7.1a), the Corinthians protested 'against what they believed to be Paul's exaggeration in the *Previous Letter* of the dangers from πορνεία and from ἄπιστοι.'[47]

Hurd affirms that 1 Cor. 7.1b[48] is one of the slogans coined by the Corinthians in their reply either to Paul's *Previous Letter* or to some other earlier Pauline communication.[49] The slogan even purports to be a catchword effectively shared by both parties at the founding visit.[50] But Hurd contests the view that the slogan derived from gnostically inclined groups within the Corinthian community. There is evidence in the Corinthian correspondence indicating the increasingly strained relationship between Paul and the whole Corinthian church about issues such as idol meat and sexual relationships. 'The Corinthians' question on the subject of marriage', says Hurd, 'came solely from an ascetic point of view'.[51] But no evidence exists for the assumption that gnostic intruders (or their sympathizers) had goaded the Corinthian community into opposition to Paul.

In short, opposition to Paul was not fanned by some obscure party of gnostic persuasion but rather resulted from what the apostle himself had written to the Corinthian church. His own written directives *after* the founding visit are the immediate source of the controversy. The Corinthians' insistence on continuing with their practice of eating idol meat goes hand in hand with their plea for sexual asceticism within marriage and without. The two Corinthian claims stem from one single point of view.[52] 'Confident of their [spiritual] strength,' notes Hurd, 'they boasted that they were able to expose themselves safely to the temptation of idolatry [1 Corinthians 8] and the lure of

47. Hurd, *Origin*, p. 224. It is quite possible that in the *Previous Letter* Paul 'had advocated marriage as a bulwark against immorality' (p. 223).

48. 'It is well for a man not to touch a woman' (7.1b).

49. Cf. Hurd, *Origin*, pp. 164-67.

50. At the founding visit, Paul had 'apparently...taught that in general, it is best for a man not to touch a woman. Paul's own unmarried status confirms this supposition' (Hurd, *Origin*, p. 275).

51. Hurd, *Origin*, p. 164.

52. The two concerns (idol meat and intramarital relations), argues Hurd, most probably 'emanated from a single point of view' (*Origin*, p. 164; cf. 207).

sexual immorality [1 Cor. 7.1-7].'[53] Their continuing practice of eating idol meat and their advice on refraining from normal intramarital relations opposed the Corinthians to Paul, and created an episode in their relationship that later both would have preferred to forget. Whatever the impact of the gnostic religion on Corinth might have been, the written evidence of 1 Corinthians 7 definitely rules out gnosticism as the *immediate* source of disagreement between Paul and his counterparts. The inconsistency between Paul's earlier (founding visit) and later written articulations (*Previous Letter*, etc.) engendered the tensions underlying 1 Corinthians 7.

4. *Resurrection: Flaws in Logic*

Does 1 Corinthians 15 support the assumption that gnostic intruders (or their supporters) had turned away from traditional Christian teachings about the resurrection? J.C. Hurd does not think that sufficient textual evidence can be marshaled in support of this assumption. Indisputably, 1 Corinthians 15 shows that the Corinthian controversy was not limited to ethical matters alone. Their challenge to Paul went beyond practical matters such as idol meat (1 Corinthians 8) and intramarital relations (1 Corinthians 7). Even the core of the Christian proclamation itself, the resurrection, was at issue. The key phrase epitomizing the seriousness of the rankling is 1 Cor. 15.12: 'There is no resurrection of the dead!' Who used this notorious statement? Was this a slogan used by Paul's opponents to castigate his brand of Christianity? Or was the veiled accusation that '*some of you say* there is no resurrection' merely a rhetorical device used by the apostle to throw his point into relief—a Pauline warning perhaps against the dire consequences of belittling faith in *bodily* resurrection?

It is virtually inconceivable that Paul's Corinthian counterparts ever intended to dismiss life after death outright. They cannot have been the trailblazers of modern atheism or agnosticism. Had they denied the resurrection *in toto,* their mythico-magical practice of vicariously baptizing believers on behalf of the deceased (1 Cor. 15.29) would have made no sense at all. Why should someone be anxious to be baptized for a departed relative or friend if resurrection had been

---

53. Hurd, *Origin*, p. 167. For Hurd's reconstruction of the Corinthians' letter to Paul cf. Hurd, *Origin*, pp. 207-208.

discarded altogether?[54] The statement that 'there is no resurrection of the dead' thus cannot possibly have been part of the Corinthian vocabulary. It cannot have been one of their catchwords along the lines of 'All of us possess knowledge', 'Idols have no real existence' or 'It is well for a man not to touch a woman'. It must have been a Pauline formulation, pre-emptive in its intention, directed against the adversaries of *physical* resurrection. 'There is resurrection', Paul's counterparts must have said, 'but not of the flesh.' The physical body was for them part of the natural state of life, unfit to share eternal glory.

Our suggestion that Paul himself was responsible for the misleading slogan (15.12) raises a further issue. Is it possible that, in accusing his adversaries of denying all resurrection of the dead, Paul grossly over-stated what they had intended to say? Did Paul perhaps coin the slogan because he seriously misunderstood at first the Corinthian position on the matter? Some scholars have advocated this view. Following Bultmann's lead, they read 1 Corinthians 15 against the background of Paul's more subtle arguments in 2 Corinthians 5. These scholars claim that in the heat of the battle, the Paul of 1 Corinthians 15 wrongly believed that the Corinthians had denied resurrection in any form. Disturbed by their boastful posture, he had understood them to mean that 'there is no resurrection at all'. Hence his warning in 1 Cor. 15.13-14: 'If there is no resurrection then our faith and our preaching are in vain!' It did not take long though before he became aware of his unfortunate misjudgment. Dawn broke when he realized that the Corinthians had only denied resurrection of the *physical* body. Mindful of his misinterpretation, he wrote 2 Corinthians 5, a chapter dealing with the Corinthians' real concerns, with their insistence on spiritual resurrection, resurrection *from* the body.

For scholars claiming that 1 Cor. 15.12 rests on Paul's miscompre-hension, 2 Corinthians 5 shows that any outright denial of resurrec-tion was not at all on the minds of the Corinthians. Rather, some gnostically inclined circles in Corinth had been unhappy with the

54. Far from rejecting life beyond death, some gnostic sects viewed baptism as a means to free believers from the demonic rule of the stars. Baptism is necessary, these gnostics claim, lest the self (soul) on its ascent to heaven fall prey to demonic powers lying in wait all over the cosmos. Vicarious baptisms are hardly of Christian origin. They are part of pre-Christian religiosity (cf. Bousset, 'Gnosis, Gnostiker', p. 67).

physical implications of Christian resurrection thought, as well as with its images. In true gnostic style, they claimed that the heavenly self is released at death from the inexorable laws dominating the mortal body. Resurrection thus was for them the release of the divine self held captive within the body, not by its own fault, but by some inner divine disturbances in the heavenly *pleroma* long before the creation of the world.[55] For these scholars Paul countered the claims of the Corinthians by insisting that even the heavenly self will not remain without a 'body'; it will 'not be found naked' (2 Cor. 5.3), but have 'a *house,* though one not made with hands' (οἰκία ἀχειροποίητος). Gnostically inclined Christians are purported to have said that death marks the point at which the mortal body is swallowed by the spiritual body (καταποθήσεται τὸ θνητὸν ὑπὸ τῆς ζωῆς). 2 Corinthians 5

---

55. The Corinthian gnostics, Bultmann argues, reinterpreted the resurrection *of* the body in terms of resurrection *from* the body (*Exegetische Probleme*, p. 4). Similarly to ideas laid down in hermetic literature, resurrection was for them the liberation of the self (soul) from its incarceration in the prison of the physical body. (C. Herm. 1, 24-26; 7, 2; Plot. Enn. III, 6, 6.69; cf. Bultmann, *Exegetische Probleme,* p. 5). Bultmann follows here W. Bousset who claims that 'gnosticism adamantly rejected the idea of bodily resurrection' ('Gnosis, Gnostiker', p. 69). Although Paul had in 2 Corinthians 5 a clearer picture of his opponents' position than in 1 Corinthians 15 (where he had grossly misunderstood their aspirations), he himself, observes Bultmann, did not change his mind much on the subject of resurrection in the course of the debate. Admittedly, in his earlier ministry the apostle had expected the majority of the believers to experience the parousia during their own lifetime (1 Thess. 4.17). But even then he expected the physical body to be changed into a heavenly one (1 Cor. 15.51-52). History forced him in his later ministry to rethink his earlier expectations. Even if death should take away some before the coming of Christ, their self (soul) would not remain in a naked state. Not unlike seeds of grain, a *new* body will emerge. The physical body (σῶμα ψυχικόν) will be changed into a heavenly one (1 Cor. 15.44: σῶμα πνευματικόν; 2 Cor. 5.1: οἰκία ἀχειροποίητος) (Bultmann, *Exegetische Probleme,* p. 9). The common denominator is in both cases Paul's emphasis on the transformation of the physical body into some form of heavenly 'body', either at the parousia or at death. Bultmann reckons with the possibility that Paul borrowed the idea of the body's disintegration (2 Cor. 5.1: ἡ ἐπίγειος ἡμῶν οἰκία καταλύσεται) from his gnostic counterparts. But even if this should have been the case, the apostle was still not in agreement, notes Bultmann, with their outlook on resurrection. While for them the destruction of the body was to take place at the moment of death, Paul gave a new positive twist by denying the 'nakedness of the self (soul)' at any point of its transformation. At the parousia, the self (soul) does not appear by itself, it appears rather enclothed in its new 'body'.

thus casts a new light on Paul's whole treatment of resurrection in 1 Corinthians 15. The ignoble statement that 'there is no resurrection of the dead' is a caricature in the perspective of 2 Corinthians 5, a misunderstanding or exaggeration which Paul himself corrected when he understood what constituted the Corinthians' real concern.

The attempt to read 1 Corinthians 15 with Bultmann and others in light of 2 Corinthians 5 raises immensely difficult new questions. The major problem is that this reading fails to do justice to the intimacy of Paul's relationship with the Corinthians. The accuracy of the apostle's knowledge of the Corinthian situation in other parts of 1 Corinthians does not suggest that Paul ever misunderstood their views of the resurrection so completely. To begin with, Bultmann's gnostic solution to the Corinthian controversy, together with his assumption that 1 Cor. 15.12 misrepresents the Corinthians' own view of resurrection, is in conflict with what we know from the letter itself about the exchange of news between the two parties. As founder of the church, Paul knew his Corinthian counterparts personally. At no point was the flow of information between them ever interrupted (1.11; 5.1, 11; 7.1, etc.). Any misunderstanding, if it had occurred at all, would immediately have been cleared up with the next batch of information. It is inconceivable that any misunderstanding could ever have developed into misconceptions on the scale assumed by the advocates of this theory.

The outright denial of the resurrection within the Corinthian church would furthermore have been such a break with traditional Christianity that Paul can be expected to have sought independent confirmation before putting such a radical view into the mouth of his counterparts. To assume that Paul at first mistook their arguments on the return of the heavenly self in a naked state to God as an outright denial of all resurrection would make the apostle into a maverick whose theological judgments are random, incalculable and unreliable. In his reconstruction of the Corinthian controversy, Hurd notes, rightly, that at all stages of their association, Paul 'knew [exactly] what he was talking about'.[56] He also knew what the Corinthians had on their minds. The idea of an inchoate Paul who heard the Corinthians say what they did not mean to say does not coincide with what is known from the letter about the intimate relationship between the two parties.

56. Hurd, *Origin*, p. 197.

Thirdly, we have seen earlier that the assumption of a gnostic Christ party anxious to transform the Pauline heritage into a more spiritualized version of Christianity is not rooted in the letter itself. 1 Cor. 1.12 is rhetorical in nature, not a description of the actual state of Corinthian affairs. The same must now be said about the discussion of the resurrection in 1 Corinthians 15. Paul responds here to news received from the Corinthian church.[57] He resists Corinthian attempts to bowdlerize the crudely physical tenets of traditional Christian resurrectionist language. It is likely that Paul himself had supported the idea of bodily resurrection in one form or another in his communications, perhaps even in the *Previous Letter*. Increasing cases of death within the community probably made the Corinthians wonder about the adequacy of these teachings.[58] In view of this, the assumption that a specifically gnostic group within the Corinthian church had defied Paul's ideas about the resurrection, while other circles continued to remain loyal to him, cannot be ascertained from the letter itself. The assumption is also in conflict with what we know of gnosticism's own affirmations of the salvific efficacy of Jesus' flesh.[59]

---

57. Admittedly, the typical περὶ δέ, as the indicator of Paul's response to a Corinthian communication, is conspicuously absent from 1 Corinthians 15. But the apostle still reminds the church of his earlier preaching (15.1), he urged the Corinthians to adhere to what he had told them about the issue (15.2), and he authenticates his teaching authority by citing a generally accepted formulation (15.3b-4). His references to a selection of christophanies (15.5-7), all regarded as constitutive of the Christian faith, serve the same purpose. All this shows that in 1 Corinthians 15 too Paul defended his teaching against challenges from the Corinthians.

58. Statements concerning the resurrection may have emerged 'as a result of the passage of time and death of some believers' (Hurd, *Origin*, p. 241).

59. The *Gospel of Philip* is a relatively late gnostic writing. It represents a typically gnostic view of the resurrection. 'Those who say that the Lord died first and then rose up are in error, for he rose up first and then died' (W.W. Isenberg, 'The Gospel of Philip [2,3]', in J.M. Robinson [ed.], *The Nag Hammadi Library in English* [San Francisco: Harper and Row, 1981], p. 134 [56, 15-20]; cf. M.L. Peel, 'The Treatise on Resurrection [I, 4]', *Nag Hammadi Library in English*, p. 51 [45, 40: 'spiritual resurrection'; 49, 10-15: 'flee from the divisions and fetters, and already you have the resurrection']). Following Paul's lead, the Gospel of Philip notes that 'flesh and blood shall not be able to inherit the kingdom' (*Nag Hammadi Library*, p. 134 [56, 30]). However, it still speaks highly of the flesh of Christ. 'His flesh is the word, and his blood is the Holy Spirit' (*Nag Hammadi Library*, p. 134 [57, 6-7]). Rising takes place in *this* flesh (*Nag Hammadi Library*, p. 135 [57, 15-

Whatever Paul's reading of the Corinthians' concept about resurrection may have been, statements critical of the resurrection, as can be found in 1 Cor. 15.12, cannot be expected to have been issued by any early gnostic group.

Lastly, there is no reason why the Pauline rendering of the Corinthian position[60] should be taken at face value. It must rather be read against the background of Paul's own literary conventions and in light of his overall style of argumentation. Throughout 1 Corinthians Paul exhibits the tendency to exaggerate his arguments. For instance, he concludes the discussion about idol meat declaring that 'if food is a cause of my brother's falling, *I will never eat meat,* lest I cause my brother to fall' (8.13; emphasis added). This is clearly an overstatement. It can hardly mean that in the interest of accommodating objections to meat, Paul turned vegetarian. By the same token, his advice to 'shun immorality' (6.18) cannot be taken as a call to withdraw from public life. Similarly, Paul's charge that 'some among you say that there is no resurrection of the dead' (15.12) cannot be made to mean that those accused had denied *all* resurrection. Hurd's suggestion stands to reason: 'Paul has taken an objection to belief in bodily resurrection and declared it to be tantamount to a rejection of all belief in life after death.'[61]

The gnostic solution to 1 Corinthians 15 does not stand the test of a closer reading of the chapter. Paul addressed the subject matter of resurrection because in one of their many communications with him the Corinthians had denied *bodily* resurrection. 1 Corinthians 15 is Paul's response to this challenge. Not that the Corinthians had sought the apostle's advice. As in the case of idol meat and abstinence from intramarital relations, they had stated their position rather boldly and without reserve.[62] Their objection to Paul though did not occur in a

---

19]). Says Klaus Koschorke to the point, 'the natural flesh cannot inherit the kingdom. The flesh of Christ, however, sacramentally received, has the potential of rising' ('Paulus in den Nag Hammadi Texten: Ein Beitrag zur Geschichte der Paulusrezeption im frühen Christentum', *ZTK* 78 [1981], pp. 177-205, 192). Even though the *Gospel of Philip* is late, statements such as 1 Cor. 15.12 are incompatible with its message; cf. 'The Treatise on Resurrection', *Nag Hammadi Library*, p. 52 [48, 10]: '... do not think the resurrection is an illusion').

60. 1 Cor. 15.12: 'There is no resurrection of the dead.'

61. Hurd, *Origin*, p. 197.

62. What may be called a Corinthian question 'is actually more an objection than a question. The Corinthians have not asked for Paul's opinion; they have stated their

spiritual vacuum. It was part of the changing relationship between the two parties. Mindful of Paul's preaching at the founding visit, the Corinthians seemed to have resented his turn to positions out of line with their own thought on the matter. They challenged Paul's plea for bodily resurrection not only 'because they considered it an unspiritual, grossly corporeal idea,' as Hurd contends,[63] but also because his stress on bodily resurrection seemed to them to have lost the lustre and force of his early preaching.

5. *Gnosticism Revisited*

Up to this point we have sketched in broad outline J.C. Hurd's graphic reconstruction of Paul's struggle with the Corinthian church in order to show that gnostic leanings within the community cannot have been the *immediate* cause of the controversy. Shifts in Paul's own thought were responsible for both the extent and the intricacy of the conflict. Events in the interval between his founding visit and the Apostolic Council in Jerusalem caused Paul to re-examine some of his earlier positions, forcing him to adapt them to the newly emerging situation in the church at large. The modulation of his earlier pronouncements on ethical and doctrinal issues into the new reality of a rapidly expanding church must have goaded the Corinthians into action. Their uneasiness with the 'new' Paul began to drive a wedge between them and the apostle, threatening to pull the two parties irredeemably apart. Paul wrote 1 Corinthians to establish the integrity of his teachings and to restore his erstwhile credibility as founder of the church. With fastidious care Hurd traces the sequence of the events leading up to the Corinthians' alienation from Paul. The countermeasures the apostle took to contain the conflict are analyzed in this reconstruction with unusual sensitivity.

Why did Hurd's convincing reconstruction not make a more pro-found impact upon contemporary studies of 1 Corinthians? Why did he not succeed in laying to rest the gnostic solution to the Corinthian controversy once and for all? One of the major reasons must be the limited scope of his reconstruction, his reluctance to situate the Corinthian dispute in the larger context of Hellenistic culture. Given the fact that Paul himself was the *immediate* cause of the Corinthian

position and made an attempt to defend it' (Hurd, *Origin*, p. 200.)
    63. Hurd, *Origin*, p. 199.

imbroglio, can all outside influence upon it be so categorically dismissed, as Hurd's study seems to suggest? Can it be ignored that the Corinthian debate took place in the wider arena of Hellenistic culture? All culture, Hellenistic or otherwise, reflects a broad array of socio-political constituencies and religious mentalities. Hurd himself speaks of the need to elucidate 'the general understanding of the religiosity of the period,'[64] He stresses that 'the general religious and cultural influences (for example, the influence of Hellenistic teaching and gnosticism)...must have been present.'[65] But instead of penetrating these larger influences, he merely cautions that they are 'difficult to assess.'[66] Weighing in on them is hardly more difficult than assessing the forces behind the Corinthian controversy, an exercise so masterly carried out in Hurd's study.

Whatever the beginnings of gnosticism may have been, chronologically, geographically or religiously, the mentality which eventually gave rise to it must have been in the air in Paul's day. The claim that the wider cultural climate of Hellenism, and included in it 'gnostic' thought and mentality, must in some form have influenced the Corinthian controversy does not rest on the assumption that, as a religion, gnosticism had definitely consolidated itself in pre-Christian times. W. Bousset in particular vaulted the view of gnosticism's pre-Christian origin to prominence. Since the gnostic beginnings are wrapped in darkness, it is indeed difficult to assess them. But Bousset does not surrender in despair. All gnosticism, he holds, grew out of what he cautiously calls *Gnosis*. Gnosis, says Bousset, is an ingenious blend of Persian, Babylonian, Jewish and Greek ideas. 'In its narrower sense, Gnosis is a significant, probably the most significant factor in the development of the larger movements of gnosticism.' [67] The pioneers of early gnostic speculations separated these ideas from their own religious home and built them into a new powerful religion, one bent on the redemption of the soul. 'Gnostics were possessed with a passion to enter heaven'; they were busy in 'recovering their roots in the Great Mother of all life'.[68] The assumption here is that, due to

64. Hurd, *Origin*, p. 96.
65. Hurd, *Origin*, p. 213.
66. Hurd, *Origin*, p. 213.
67. Bousset, 'Gnosis, Gnostiker', p. 93. All translations from Bousset are mine.
68. 'Sehnsucht der G[nosis] ist, in die himmlischen Regionen zu kommen' (Bousset, 'Gnosis, Gnostiker', p. 83). 'Was die Gläubigen ersehnen, ist die

disturbances in the *pleroma* long before the creation of the world, divine sparks had come to be imprisoned in the dark realms of matter. For Bousset, the starkly dualistic nature of the gnostic thought system[69] cannot be attributed to Christian influences. Rather, he infers from gnosticism's insistence on the incurable human situation that the roots of Gnosis must lie in pre-Christian times.[70]

Bousset acknowledges that all gnostic literature bears the stamp of the movement's epoch-making encounter with Christianity. In fact, the merger of Gnosis circles with Christianity first gave rise to the type of gnosticism known to us today. Gnosis thus heralded for Bousset the arrival of gnosticism. The transformation of the one into the other has been so radical that it is next to impossible, admits Bousset, to

Heimkehr zur Mutter' (Bousset, 'Gnosis, Gnostiker', p. 85). The idea of the 'Mother' (Isis) suggests that this type of Gnosis originated in Egypt (Bousset, 'Gnosis, Gnostiker', p. 87).

69. Bousset, 'Gnosis, Gnostiker', pp. 49-53, 63-64, 76.

70. Cf. Bousset, 'Gnosis, Gnostiker', pp. 44, 78. Relying mostly on the accounts of Christian heresiologists (Justin Martyr, Ireneaus, Hippolytus, Epiphanius, etc.), Bousset describes *Gnosis* as a multitudinous congeries of salvational theories and practices relating mostly piecemeal to a diversity of Hellenistic and Near Eastern ideas. The dualistic Zervan speculation of Persia (Bousset, 'Gnosis, Gnostiker', pp. 55-56), coupled with features borrowed from Babylonian astral fatalism, based partly on the inexorable laws of the seven hostile planets (Bousset, 'Gnosis, Gnostiker', pp. 51, 54-55, 56-57, 60), are linked in Gnosis with concepts describing the rescue of the fallen Sophia by the Anthropos-Urmensch (Bousset, 'Gnosis, Gnostiker', pp. 49, 51, 58-62) and further enriched with elements of the OT Genesis myth (Bousset, 'Gnosis, Gnostiker', pp. 53, 63-65, 70). Some elements deriving from the Mithras cult (Bousset, 'Gnosis, Gnostiker', pp. 67-68) even left their mark in one form or another on Mandaeism and Manichaeism (Bousset, 'Gnosis, Gnostiker', pp. 51, 70). All these tenets and many others converged in pre-Christian Gnosis to form a dualistic religion highlighting the soul's (or self's) dramatic return to its divine origin. It is significant that early Gnosis, although strongly influenced by Jewish ideas (Bousset, 'Gnosis, Gnostiker', pp. 70, 74, 87), was not at all favourably disposed towards the religion of Judaism. Bousset distinguishes sharply between the contribution of OT ideas to the rise of Gnosis and the movement's disdain for Jewish literature as sacred writ. For Bousset, it is clear that 'the contact of Gnosis with Judaism was largely hostile in nature' (cf. Bousset, 'Gnosis, Gnostiker', pp. 70; also pp. 54, 75). Only after its encounter with the Christian community, and with Christian ideas, did the gnostic schools change their attitude to the OT. The change though was largely cosmetic. Even in later gnosticism, OT texts were not appreciated for what they said; they were merely read allegorically (Bousset, 'Gnosis, Gnostiker', p. 75).

delineate the teachings of pre-Christian Gnosis with any measure of certainty. What makes it so difficult is that no unalloyed product of pre-Christian gnostic literature has survived the *rencontre* of Gnosis with Christianity, its powerful former rival. Bousset does not paint a favourable picture of the history and teachings of pre-Christian Gnosis. He suggests that originally most Gnosis sympathizers probably limited themselves 'to forming small sectarian fellowship groups, not unlike the seclusive circles of the mysteries. These groups showed no interest in shaping wider culture in any appreciable measure'.[71]

Gnosis teachings first gained momentum after being infused with Christian content. The amalgamation of the two, says Bousset, was a process which left its marks indelibly on all available gnostic writings. Profound though the impact of Christian thought upon gnosis proved to be, the Christian overlay on all gnostic literature is nonetheless still nothing more than a thin veneer of ideas which remain throughout intrinsically alien to Christianity. It is therefore not difficult to crystallize the non-Christian bedrock out of its superimposed Christian décor. None of the gnostic systems, for instance, succeeded in weaving the earthly figure of Jesus of Nazareth seamlessly into the gnostic teachings of redemption. It is clearly discernible that the early Gnosis did not know anything of an earthly redeemer. Even later gnosticism proved unable to integrate the earthly Jesus fully into its own myth.[72] In all gnostic systems the figure of the divine redeemer continues to jar with the life and work of Jesus, the earthly redeemer. It is here that even at this distance of time, despite endless efforts to reconcile the two, the remnants of pre-Christian gnosis shine through.[73]

71. Cf. Bousset, 'Gnosis, Gnostiker', p. 73.

72. Bousset, 'Gnosis, Gnostiker', pp. 70-72.

73. For Bousset, the pre-Christian Gnosis lies buried under the rubble of often weird later gnostic images. He attributes the teachings about the seven archons (demonized planetary deities) to pre-Christian Gnosis (cf. 'Gnosis, Gnostiker', pp. 84, 87, 91), together with the paeans to the Great Mother (Bousset, 'Gnosis, Gnostiker', p. 84). Gnosticism's dualism and all speculations about the androgynous *Urmensch* (Bousset, 'Gnosis, Gnostiker', p. 88) (hymns to the celestial redeemer figure) are part of early Gnosis as well (Bousset, 'Gnosis, Gnostiker', p. 90). The references to *Jaldabaoth*, however, go back to Jewish influences upon Gnosis (Bousset, 'Gnosis, Gnostiker', pp. 87, 91). Bousset finds these pre-Christian elements preserved in the fragments of Simonianism, in Bardesanian gnosticism, Hermetic literature (Poimandres) and the Acts of Thomas (Hymn of the Pearl) (Bousset, 'Gnosis, Gnostiker', pp. 93-94).

What prompted the strange alliance between two basically and originally independent religions. What attracted the only loosely organized
Gnosis fellowship groups in pre-Christian times to the early Christian
movement? Why were assumed gnosis circles allegedly anxious to
enter into close contact with Christianity? Bousset holds that it did not
take the advocates of the intrinsically syncretistic pre-Christian gnostic
movement long to become aware of the affinity of certain of their
own key teachings and practices with those of Christianity. Inspired
by Christianity's meteoric rise, they decided to make common cause
with it. In doing so the pre-Christian Gnosis movement integrated the
powerful Christian concept of redemption into its own religious
thought system, an attempt from which the former benefited more
than the Christian community itself.[74] The alliance between the two
strengthened the Christian religion only in some limited way. It made
the young Christian movement aware (1) of its superiority to Judaism;
it encouraged Christians (2) to rank the NT higher than the OT; it
contributed (3) to the spiritualization of Jewish eschatology, prompted
the development (4) of sacramental piety, and prepared the way
(5) for linking celestial redeemer figures such as Manda d'Hayye with
the earthly Jesus.[75]

74. Bousset's overall judgement upon gnosticism is negative. Gnosticism, he
says, is another version of fanciful wisdom teachings known from the mysteries.
Everything in it rests on visions, ecstasies and arcane traditions (Bousset, 'Gnosis,
Gnostiker', p. 78). Small wonder, 'Christianity could not thrive within the oppres-
sive and stuffy climate which had given birth to Gnosis' (cf. Bousset, 'Gnosis,
Gnostiker', p. 76). Its influence upon Christianity ought not to be overestimated,
Bousset cautions. It was primarily a negative influence, and an indirect one for that
matter. Not the gnostics, only the apologists were the first real theologians (Bousset,
'Gnosis, Gnostiker', p. 77). For Bousset, Gnosticism did not reshape the teachings
of Christianity. It merely tried to coax the early Christian thinkers into allying their
teachings with spiritualized oriental mythologies and their coarse-grained dualism
(Bousset, 'Gnosis, Gnostiker', p. 78). Christianity did not yield to this temptation.
Even the later founders of gnostic schools (Valentinus, Heracleon Gnosticus, etc.)
are for Bousset men who lingered between the lines, without contributing any
innovative ideas of their own to the basics of the Christian religion. 'They were not
men of the future; they did not run ahead of their time' (Bousset, 'Gnosis,
Gnostiker', p. 78).
75. Originally, the gnostic myth, which underwent various changes in its long
history, spoke of a divine redeemer seeking to rescue his lost but equally divine
female companion. The celebration of a ἱερὸς γάμος marked the reunion of the two
(cf. Bousset, 'Gnosis, Gnostiker', pp. 90-91). This type of gnostic myth provided

It must be noted that for Bousset the initiative for the merger of the two originally independent religions did not lie with Christianity. The early gnostics initiated the alliance. Gnosticism is a religious movement, he says, which approached Christianity with the intention of forging some union with it.[76] Gnosticism thus is for Bousset more than a manifestation of Christian religiosity. 'Viewed as a whole Gnosis did not grow on Christian soil proper but is older than Christianity.'[77] As to Bousset, gnosis sympathizers decided at one point to hitch their star to that of Christianity. What exactly motivated them in this decision Bousset does not say. He merely suggests that the aloofness of the gnostic vision towards life on earth probably forced them to rethink their position.

To substantiate his assumption of gnosticism's pre-Christian history, Bousset points out that all gnostic systems have proved impervious to Christian thought. In their reconstruction of the gnostic systems, Christian apologists and church fathers therefore refused to look upon gnosticism merely as a heretical aberration from Christian teachings. Rather, they regarded it as a religion of its own.[78] Bousset distinguishes between gnosticism's prime time (Basilides, Carpocratus-Marcellina, Valentinus, Cerdon, Marcion etc.) and its early history as

no room for an earthly redeemer figure. On the contrary, Christianity borrowed the idea of 'Christos', the heavenly redeemer, from Gnosis. 'The origin of the "Christos" redeemer figure does not lie in the Christian religion, despite the fact that in all the gnostic systems known to us "Christos" has come to be identified with Jesus of the Christian church' (Bousset, 'Gnosis, Gnostiker', p. 90).

76. Cf. Bousset, 'Gnosis, Gnostiker', p. 44. Only occasionally does Bousset attribute some initiative to Christianity as well. 'Gnosticism and Christianity are two distinctly different religious systems which attracted *each other* magnetically through their affinity in certain areas of teaching' (Bousset, 'Gnosis, Gnostiker', p. 72; emphasis added). 'Gnosis and Christianity, soon after the birth of the latter, attracted each other with magnetic power. The attraction resulted from one definite point of interest, i.e., the Christian concept of redemption and the figure of the Christian redeemer' (Bousset, 'Gnosis, Gnostiker', p. 70).

77. Bousset, 'Gnosis, Gnostiker', p. 49. Similarly, 'the syncretistic religion of gnosticism emerged at a time when the religions of antiquity were at the point of disintegration. It is possible to look upon it as an independent phenomenon without casting a side-glance at Christianity' (p. 70). Gnosticism is 'a self-contained religion of its own [fertige Erscheinung]' (p. 49).

78. The *logos* speculations of the apologists, says Bousset, run parallel to those of Gnostics. However, none of them is entirely dependent upon the other (cf. Bousset, 'Gnosis, Gnostiker', pp. 77-78, 94).

a gnosis religion rooted mainly in Babylonian, Samarian and Syrian soil. The youthful pre-Christian gnostic movement had neither a renowned leader, nor did it have any single founder venerated by all its groups. Simon, Helena and Dositheus are virtually the only names that have survived from the time of early Gnosis. Yet despite its heavy Christian overlay[79] the resplendent image of pre-Christian Gnosis still continues to outshine all its later mutations. Although pre-Christian gnostic literature is lost to us, it is quite possible, Bousset conjectures, that some of the apologists still had access to gnosis writings. [80]

A movement of this magnitude, Bousset holds, cannot be ignored in Christian studies. At the time of the Corinthian controversy, gnosticism itself may still have been *in statu nascendi*. Gnosis circles, however, must have been active within the same area and within the same groups from which the Christian church recruited its followers. The reconstruction of 1 Corinthians must take into account the shaping influence of those forces which in Paul's time increasingly turned their attention to the Christian movement.

Conclusion

Hurd's study into the origin of Paul's Corinthian controversy has lifted the veil which for decades covered the beginnings of the church in Corinth. The major players behind the events leading up to the Corinthians' confrontation with the founder of their church were not gnostic infiltrators roaming the western realms of Paul's missionary hinterland. Gnosticism is, in 1 Corinthians, not the issue of the evidence. The integrity of Paul's own 'gospel' is the chief focus of attention. The apostle did not wish to lose credibility on his early preaching. 1 Corinthians is the climax of a lengthy debate between the apostle and the Corinthians, a dispute which, with the exception of the letter itself, has left us nothing but a few unmistakable fragments. They are enough to give the reader a good idea of the vitality of a once spirited exchange between Paul and his Corinthian counterparts.

79. Cf. Bousset, 'Gnosis, Gnostiker', p. 45.

80. Justin Martyr, he suggests, may have had access to the now lost *Syntagma*. Hippolytus was perhaps familiar with it as well, in addition to other pre-Christian documents (cf. Bousset, 'Gnosis, Gnostiker', pp. 47-48). Traces of early gnostic writings may also be preserved in Apocalypse of Jaldabaoth, the literature of Sethian gnosticism etc. (Bousset, 'Gnosis, Gnostiker', pp. 94-95).

The main source for reconstructing the conflict remains 1 Corinthians itself. The chief topics at issue in this letter are the proper administration of Christian knowledge, the expediency of eating idol meat in public, the appropriateness of practising intramarital asceticism and the meaning of Christ's resurrection, literal or symbolic, physical or spiritual. Nowhere in 1 Corinthians does Paul discredit the Corinthians' position on any of these issues. What surprises is that despite his general agreement with them, the two parties are nonetheless throughout the letter strangely at cross-purposes with each other. Paul's defensive mode of expression suggests that the apostle himself was most probably the source of the controversy, and he himself knew it. He wrote 1 Corinthians to disavow, or at least disallow, the Corinthians' interpretation of some of his own earlier statements. It seems that the Corinthian church had turned more Pauline than Paul himself was prepared to allow.

Hurd's analysis of 1 Corinthians demonstrates clearly that Paul's opponents came from inside the Corinthian church. No evidence is found in the letter of gnostic intruders trying to trench on his authority or to upset the hermeneutics of his Christian interpretation. There is no trace in 1 Corinthians that the tension between the two parties was prompted by (anti-Pauline) circles of Corinthian Christians bent on forming an alliance with gnostic missionaries. Rather, policy decisions at Jerusalem and Antioch are likely to have forced Paul to nuance his former teachings in ways unacceptable to the Corinthians. The terminology and conceptual framework of his written communications subsequent to the founding visit suggested to them a major change in Paul's outlook on both christology and eschatology. Negotiations at the *Apostolic Council* as well as consultations with those responsible for the formulation of the *Apostolic Decree* may indeed have convinced Paul that a price had to be paid for maintaining the unity of the church at large, a multi-racial community threatened in Paul's day by disintegration. When Paul, in keeping with the agreements reached in Jerusalem and Antioch, tried to win over the Corinthians to directives of the larger church, he found himself faced with stiff opposition from them. The church's resistance might have dissipated, had it not been for Paul's failure to disclose to them the background of and the rationale underlying these major policy decisions. His embarrassing silence about the political and strategic concerns of the larger church was bound to exacerbate the uneasiness of the Corinthians with what seemed to them Paul's newfangled approach to major ethical and doctrinal issues. The apostle himself thus installed the suspicions which led to an increasingly strained relationship with his church. A type of distrust developed which was bound to haunt him for the rest of his life. No future study into the background of 1 Corinthians can ignore Hurd's careful examination of events which threatened to disrupt crucially relations between the apostle and the church of his founding. The reader is informed here of the wider church context within which this part of early church history must be placed.

Bousset's introduction to *Gnosis* shows that the problems surrounding the origin and history of churches in Asia Minor and Greece cannot be satisfactorily resolved within the perspective of their Christian history alone. As Hurd demonstrates admirably, the *Apostolic Council* and, probably, the *Apostolic Decree* effected significant changes in Paul's outlook on Christian mission and unity. However, the rather complex cultural milieu deserves attention as well. The Corinthians' Hellenistic mentality intensified the debate to no small degree. 'Gnostic' mentality and thought patterns were not unfamiliar in Paul's day. The Corinthians' cultural proclivity towards Hellenism made them by inner compulsion suspicious of Paul's compromising new style. Admittedly, W. Bousset's study of *Gnosis* and *Gnosticism* abounds with speculation. His claim that gnosticism ensued from an incipient gnosis movement remains as unproven as his assumption that pre-Christian gnosis circles, dissatisfied with their own introverted depth vision, sought to revitalize their religious sentiments by devising a mechanism of compromise, approaching the Christian movement with the intention of forging some sort of unity between the two formerly distinct religious movements. Bousset's observation that the pre-Christian gnostic redeemer myth, together with its emphasis on celestial saviour figures, is only poorly glued on to the Christian idea of Jesus, the earthly redeemer, leaves as much to be desired as his overall negative evaluation of pre-Christian gnosis. Bousset himself can hardly be blamed for his inadequate approach to these hefty issues. He had no access yet to the Nag Hammadi codices. His image of *Gnosis-Gnosticism* rests almost entirely on a very limited assortment of gnostic literature. Most of his source material derives from citations found in the writings of the heresiologists.

Enormous strides have been made in recent years in the study of gnosticism, due to the discovery and analysis of Nag Hammadi mate-rial.[81] The movement's origin and early history, however, are still wrapped in darkness. To which extent gnosticism had consolidated itself in NT times continues to remain another open question. All these uncertainties notwithstanding, scholars such as W. Bousset and others have never allowed the absence of conclusive evidence to discourage them from offering intuitive insights into the rise and growth of a movement whose influence upon the early church can hardly be over-estimated. Its origins must in one form or another reach far back into pre-Christian times. Whether or not Bousset's claim that gnosticism's roots lie in sequestered gnosis circles searching for deeper knowledge bears scrutiny, his assumption that the birth of the movement must have preceded its impressive role and literary output in first and second century Christian history continues to stand up. Bousset was not satisfied with acknowledging gnosticism's influence upon the NT writings in some general sense. He took it upon himself to reconstruct from very limited source materials the background out of which the gnostic movement must have emerged. His claim that the same mental climate which gave rise to the gnostic religion can be postulated to have also engendered the Christian religion cannot readily be disputed.

The passion to explore the deeper meaning of religious language and its thought is a distinctive feature of *Gnosis-Gnosticism*. The beginnings of the drive to seek the truth *behind* verbal articulation reach back into pre-Christian eras of antiquity. All near Eastern sapiential writings, the Bible included, seek to penetrate into the secrets of life. As J.M. Robinson has shown, the search for deeper meaning, particularly in parables and aphorisms, constitutes a hermeneutical trajectory of its own, one which is as old as wisdom teachings themselves. This hermeneutical trajectory provides data which cannot be muted even by the historical uncertainties as to the exact origin of the movement. The inner assurance that only the wise understand, together with the hermeneutical vocabulary ensuing from it, says Robinson, 'is hardly an *ad hoc* creation with the process of

---

81. Cf. J.M. Robinson, 'Gnosticism and the New Testament', in B. Aland, *et al.* (eds.), *Gnosis: Festschrift für Hans Jonas* (Göttingen: Vandenhoeck & Ruprecht, 1978), pp. 125-43. Robinson places the changing meaning of παραβολή from illustration to conundrum on a hermeneutical trajectory. Its origins run parallel to the development of wisdom literature.

interpreting Jesus' parables [or any other NT literary devices]. Rather it is indicative of the context in which that process took place—the broader hermeneutical undertaking of Late Antiquity.'[82]

The fact that the Corinthians challenged the casuistic strictures Paul intended to impose upon them bespeaks their independent Christian mind. Their propensity to find truth behind the surface meaning of words disinclined them to Paul's later written instructions. The freedom to eat idol meat ensued for them from their type of Christian 'gnosis-knowledge', just as their practice of sexual asceticism signaled their possession of this same type of knowledge. Claims to physical resurrection did not meet the standards set by their hermeneutics of Christian wisdom. Paul's advice to abstain from idol meat on behalf of a hypothetical group of 'weak Christians' signified to them a change in religious definitions, a shifting of the frontiers he himself had set in and through his early preaching. There was respect in Corinth for Paul, the founder of the church. This respect did not translate into support for his attempt to turn the clock of Christian understanding back. No sympathy was found in Corinth for Paul's dietary and behavioural directions. The return to traditional marital conventions was as unacceptable to them as Paul's appeal to belief in physical resurrection. The apostle's change of mind was for them not only in violation of his own early preaching at the founding visit; it was also in conflict with their own Hellenistic notions of culture and religion.

Paul's instructions in the *Previous Letter* may indeed have triggered the crisis in Corinth. The decisions of the larger church attendant upon the Apostolic Council, and the deliberations leading to the *Apostolic Decree*, may have more to do with Paul's change of mind than is generally supposed. However, the Corinthian milieu, rife with Hellenistic sentiment and tradition, cannot be relegated to the background. It is more than a pendant to the inner-church controversy. The Corinthians' Hellenistic 'gnosis' mentality, their drive to search for deeper meaning in religion, made them object to Paul's instructions in the *Previous Letter*. Teachings of this type alienated even those among them who otherwise might have been congenial to Paul's leadership in the Corinthian church.

The immediate cause of the Corinthian imbroglio, admirably identified in J.C. Hurd's study, is part of the wider *cultural horizons* of the

82. Robinson, 'Gnosticism and the NT', pp. 138-39.

Mediterranean mind. It is in this wider sense that the Corinthian brand of 'gnosis' continues to claim scholarly attention, either as a mental climate gradually growing into consciousness or as a more consolidated movement knitting vast soteriological blankets from the skeins of ancient Greek and Near Eastern religiosity. The results provided by Hurd in his reconstruction of the *immediate* causes of the Corinthian problem still have to be applied with full force to a second, as yet outstanding, inquiry into the cultural milieu of the controversy.[83]

83. The significant role played by cultural conditioning has been beautifully illustrated in a collection of essays published under the title *Scriptures and Cultural Conversations*, J.S. Kloppenborg and L.E. Vaage (eds.), *TJT* 8/1 (1992), pp. 7-173.

CHURCH OFFICE IN PAUL, ESPECIALLY IN PHILIPPIANS

John Reumann

'Church office' (Ger. *Amt*, 'ministry'),[1] though not prominent in
1 Corinthians—on the origins of which as a letter John Hurd has contributed greatly to our knowledge[2]—has become increasingly
important in Pauline studies since 1965 and in ecumenism. The Faith
and Order statement, *Baptism, Eucharist and Ministry* (1982), reflects
widespread agreement when it states that threefold ministry is not
found in the NT but became established in the second or third
centuries.[3] This working consensus reflects hard-won gains through
historical-critical studies such as Edwin Hatch articulated over a
century ago, that, for example, 'the traditional doctrine of the
episcopate is wholly discontinuous from anything contained in the
New Testament'.[4] There exists today greater freedom than ever from

1. Traditionally 'ministry' meant the ordained, but recent studies in the NT and
ecumenically have placed such persons within the ministry of the entire community.
The German term *Amt* can be used, but one must remember there were all sorts of
'offices' in antiquity. Edward Schillebeeckx usefully speaks of 'leadership in the
community of Jesus Christ' as the subtitle of his *Ministry* (New York: Crossroad,
1981; Dutch, *Kerkelijk ambi: Voorgangers...*) I have usually opted for the term
'church office', reflecting in part E. Schweizer's still basic *Church Order in the New
Testament* (trans. F. Clarke; SBT, 32; London: SCM Press, 1961). See now
Schweizer's 'Ministry in the Early Church', *ABD* 4.835-42.
2. J.C. Hurd, *The Origin of 1 Corinthians* (London: SPCK, 1965; 2nd edn
reprinted, 1983) and *A Bibliography of New Testament Bibliographies* (New York:
Seabury, 1966) reflect the situation when there was less interest in ministry, but
cf. *Origin*, pp. 14-15, 192 and 240-70 on topics touched on below.
3. *Baptism, Eucharist and Ministry* (Faith and Order Paper, 111; Geneva: World
Council of Churches, 1982), Ministry nos. 19-20.
4. The summary is K.E. Kirk's in *The Apostolic Ministry* (London: Hodder &
Stoughton, 1957 [1946]), p. xxi with reference to Hatch's Bampton Lectures of
1880, *The Organization of the Early Christian Churches* (London: Rivingtons, 3rd
edn, 1888), see lectures 2 and 4.

denominational postulates, whether for threefold, presbyteral or congregational polity, as *iure divino* and biblically sanctioned.

Nonetheless, questions of methodology remain, in part involving new sources like the Dead Sea scrolls, application of historical criticism to patristic materials with rigor equal to NT use, and new methodologies. Here 'social world' approaches are particularly promising. At points influences from Jewish communal structures on Christian church offices are possible, but Jewish data too are in course of reassessment, as the sibling synagogue and church structures emerged. In addition, there are now new interest groups, women, for example, along with 'hierarchy' and 'laity'.

In the spirit of this volume for John Hurd the aim of the present essay is to set forth some cautions and clarifications for methodol-ogical research on church office, where principles have often gone unarticulated. The focus will be on Paul, especially his letter(s) to Philippi. Here the evidence on church office may be fullest among the acknowledged letters, though 'apostleship' or lists in 1 Cor. 12.28-30 and Rom. 12.6-8 are more commonly made the starting point. Only in Philippians do *episkopoi* and *diakonoi* occur together (1.1), in a phrase that one should first try to explain in its setting rather than declare it a gloss on the basis of later notions about 'bishops and deacons';[5] Epaphroditus provides a clear example of a congregational *apostolos* at work (Phil. 2.25, NRSV 'messenger'); women of importance are named (Phil. 4.2, Euodia and Syntyche; if Acts is included, Lydia too, Acts 16.14-15, 40); and house churches (Acts 16.15, 34, 40). Of course, there is Paul the apostle (title unused in Philippians) and his missionary team (Timothy, Phil. 1.1; 2.19; cf 'we' in Acts; Silas, Acts 16.19, 25). Much can only be sketched here, with fuller treatments to be found elsewhere.[6]

1. In seeking origins of church offices one should exercise care *not to read in evidence from later sources or theories*. Of course, we look for lines of development ('trajectories'), but these are historically more complex—with ups and downs, bifurcations and dead ends— than later theory usually assumed. This caution applies especially to

---

5. So, among others, W. Schenk, *Die Philipperbriefe des Paulus: Kommentar* (Stuttgart: Kohlhammer, 1984), pp. 78-82.

6. See the literature in the notes below and in my Anchor Bible *Philippians* (in preparation), 'Excursus B: *Episkopoi* and *Diakonoi* in the Emerging Pauline Church at Philippi.'

attempts to read threefold ministry of bishops, presbyters and deacons back into the NT, or to assume it was there but unstated. The motto has often been 'When in doubt, follow the tradition' (though the traditions, when examined, prove more varied than supposed). Alan Richardson's treatment of ministry is an example: 'it is right to interpret the NT documents in light of what we know of the development of the Church's ministry in NT times'; 'the NT writings must be understood...in relation to a development...in...Clement of Rome or St. Ignatius'.[7] Hence Richardson can find monepiscopacy in Jerusalem and emphasize the 'fact' of succession by laying on of hands.

The actual discontinuities in history involved here can be illustrated with the concept of 'apostle'. Traditionally the notion was of twelve apostles, appointed by Jesus, who in turn appointed bishops (so Irenaeus). Historical scholarship has come to see a much larger group of *apostoloi*, including Paul, by no means synonymous with 'the twelve'. The NT does not record them appointing bishops. The *šālîaḥ* theory has had its influence in NT and ecumenical studies but gone (rightly) into decline, though with some recent attempts to revive it.[8] Clearly Paul had an understanding of himself as having been commissioned an apostle by the risen Christ, and his letters breathe such authority.[9] But there existed also 'congregational *apostoloi*' like Epaphroditus and the 'apostles of the churches' mentioned in 2 Cor. 8.23, who were sent by Paul to Corinth to spur on the collection there. They were Macedonians, at least one of them elected by the churches in democratic Greek fashion[10] (2 Cor. 8.19, Thessalonica? Philippi?). Is the 'congregational apostle' a local derivative from acquaintance with Paul the apostle, indigenously reworked?

A second example involves the *episkopoi kai diakonoi* at Phil. 1.1. This is the first time the word later translated 'bishop' appears in a

7. A. Richardson, *An Introduction to the Theology of the New Testament* (London: SCM Press, 1958), pp. 329 and 332 (quoted), cf. pp. 291, 312-13, 325-36.

8. K.H. Rengstorf, 'ἀπόστολος', *TDNT* 1.398-447 (German 1933); J.A. Kirk, 'Apostleship since Rengstorf: Towards a Synthesis', *NTS* 21 (1974–75), pp. 249-64; F.H. Agnew, 'The Origin of the Apostle-Concept', *JBL* 105 (1986), pp. 75-96.

9. K. Berger, 'Apostelbrief und apostolische Rede/Zum Formular frühchristlicher Briefe', *ZNW* 65 (1974), pp. 190-231.

10. H.D. Betz, *2 Corinthians 8 and 9* (Hermeneia; Philadelphia: Fortress Press, 1985), pp. 74-75 on *cheirotonētheis*.

Christian document about church leaders. But it is plural here, and so not monepiscopacy. And though coupled with *diakonoi*, the reference is not threefold, for presbyters do not appear in Philippians or anywhere else in Paul's acknowledged letters. All this suggests to modern interpreters some other rendering than KJV's 'bishops and deacons'. Thus even Richardson (p. 333), 'bishops and other ministers' and NAB (Revised NT) 'overseers and ministers'. We have in Philippi something different and not directly continuous with later patterns of ministerial leadership.

2. Traditional approaches of various sorts have sought not only to link NT references, often all too easily, with later outcomes; they have also sought to connect passages in Paul and later writers, all too smoothly, with Jesus, the OT or at least 'Palestinian Christianity,' preferably with the twelve (apostles) in Jerusalem. In seeking origins, however, one should exercise caution *not to read in earlier backgrounds without good evidence or contrary to likely historical probabilities.*

Often this misuse of scriptural references has involved an overemphasis on the historical Jesus. The very canonical sequence of books encourages a pattern that runs, 'Old Testament forerunners in Israel, Jesus's institution of a ministry, early church reception of it.' But two hundred years of *Leben-Jesu* studies have made it clear that he did not, pre-Easter, 'found' a church in any usual sense of the word, let alone structure an ongoing ministry. This is clear if only because of the imminent apocalyptic expectancy involved. The Jesus movement had little organization (except for a treasurer!) and the charismatic, prophetic impulses it generated scarcely looked to church order as a high priority. Attempts to root ministry in sacraments which Jesus instituted have fared little better because of the admitted origin of baptism in a *post*-Easter mandate (Mt. 28.16-20) and the lack of reference to officiants in any version of the *verba* for the Lord's Supper. We have no idea who was 'celebrant' in Paul's Corinthian churches.[11]

While the desire to link church ministries of the fifties CE with Palestinian, Aramaic-speaking communal origins or with the synagogue may, in our time of interreligious rapprochement, reflect philo-Semitism, the more likely factors have included a desire to find

---

11. Cf. R.E. Brown, *Priest and Bishop: Biblical Reflections* (New York: Paulist Press, 1970), pp. 40-42.

earlier, pre-Pauline origins and an assumption that 'Jewish/Semitic is better than Graeco-Roman thought.'[12] The emergence of a particular church office is, however, no worse (or no better) because its closest analogue is Hellenistic-Roman, rather than ancient Near Eastern. Indeed, given the Graeco-Roman setting of churches Paul planted, probability favors a style of governance and leadership with which converts were familiar, in the absence of evidence for one imposed by Jersualem, Antioch or Paul (see 5.a, below).

This search for backgrounds will be illustrated below in point 4 with regard to *episkopoi* and *diakonoi*.

3. With these cautions in mind about later developments and putative backgrounds, we are freer to look at pertinent *texts in their own right, in their historical, social setting*, before proposing theories of development. The mention of *episkopoi* (and *diakonoi*) at Phil. 1.1 has often been taken up only in relation to, or even after, discussion of later documents, like the reference in Acts 20.28, the Pastorals or Ignatius, without asking first about the Philippians phrase in its own setting. So Richardson;[13] then the alternative readily becomes 'gloss'.

In the social-ecclesial setting of all such first and second century references, the 'house church' must be taken as the norm.[14] This is not to overlook *collegia* and even philosophical and rhetorical schools but to take seriously Wayne Meeks's considered judgment that 'the household remains the basic context' for Pauline groups.[15] Pauline references to 'the church in so-and-so's house' include 1 Cor. 16.19, Phlm. 2, Rom. 16.5, cf. Col. 4.15, with its shift in later MSS and KJV from 'her' to 'his house', and 1 Cor. 16.15. For Philippi there are examples in Acts 16 of the household of Lydia (Acts 16.15, cf. 40) and the Roman jailer's family (Acts 16.34-35). Such cells made up the 'base communities', a group of *Hausgemeinden* that comprise an

12. A reflection of the widespread view articulated by T. Boman, *Hebrew Thought Compared with Greek* (Philadelphia: Westminster Press, 1960).

13. Richardson, *Introduction*, p. 333, after 325-33

14. See, e.g., F.V. Filson, 'The Significance of the Early House Churches', *JBL* 58 (1939), pp. 105-12; H.-J. Klauck, *Hausgemeinde und Hauskirche im frühen Christentum* (SBS, 103; Stuttgart: Katholisches Bibelwerk, 1981); V. Branick, *The House Church in the Writings of Paul* (Zacchaeus Studies, NT; Wilmington, DE: Glazier, 1989).

15. W. Meeks, *The First Urban Christians: The Social World of the Apostle Paul* (New Haven: Yale University Press, 1983), p. 84.

Ortsgemeinde. Yet Paul refers to the several likely house groups in Philippi as an *ekklesia* (Phil. 4.15).

Without being able to explore here the growing archaeological data for house churches until after Constantine and the importance of the *oikos* in Graeco-Roman life, economy, politics and philosophy, including understandings of friendship, as presented in recent social-world research, we may simply note the legal role played by the head of a household as patron to clients and as protector (*prostatis*). Such persons provided for a house church not only a meeting place but also validity with the authorities, a core group of family and slaves, hospitality for visitors and skills in leadership. The number of women in such roles in Paul's day stands out (Lydia; Phoebe, Rom. 16.2; perhaps Euodia and Syntyche, Phil. 4.2-3; and others).[16] It was likely in the house church that *episkopoi* arose (see 5.b, below).

A point to be made in passing is how older authoritative texts were sometimes pressed into service to justify what had emerged in social-ecclesial structures (e.g., Deut. 25.4 at 1 Cor. 9.9 and 1 Tim. 5.18). At 1 Clement 42.5 a Greek mistranslation of Isaiah 60.17 is cited about *episkopoi* and *diakonoi* (likely two groups, not a hendiadys) to refer to *presbyteroi*-leaders and ministers. This may reflect what obtains in Clement's Rome or the situation addressed in Corinth.[17] In any case, the verse seems *ad hoc* application to ministries that exist on other grounds, rather than the blueprint that created them. In Philippians, significantly, Paul does not evoke any such warrants in his references to church offices. He simply accepts them.

4. In employing *word studies* in connection with the origins of church offices, one needs to be aware of the *complexity* of issues, as well as *methodological problems* long discussed.[18] We illustrate with the two terms at Phil. 1.1.

For *episkopos* a certain smokescreen has been laid down in modern ecumenical discussion by appeal to *episkopē* as an umbrella term. Rare

16. E. Schüssler Fiorenza, *In Memory of Her* (New York: Crossroad, 1984), pp. 176-84.

17. H.W. Beyer, '*diakoneō*, etc.', *TDNT* 2.92-93; Schweizer, *Church Order*, §16, pp. 146-49; H.O. Maier, *The Social Setting of the Ministry as Reflected in the Writings of Hermas, Clement and Ignatius* (Dissertations SR, 1; Waterloo, Canada: Wilfrid Laurier Press, 1991), pp. 87-146.

18. Recall the debate touched off by J.M Barr, *The Semantics of Biblical Language* (New York: Oxford University Press, 1961).

in non-biblical Greek, this word means primarily 'visitation.' It could involve oversight of goods and possessions. At Acts 1.20 (= Ps. 109 [LXX 108].8b) the 'position' (of Judas), originally financial, is that of *apostolos* as witness to Jesus and the resurrection (1.21-22) in the Lucan view of the twelve; 'overseership' is less apparent. At 1 Tim. 3.1 *episkopē* likely 'is newly coined on the basis of the title *episkopos*, which had meanwhile established itself…'[19] Beyond that, 'overseership' is a social, communal phenomenon capable of being filled in various ways. It is unlikely any ancient ever said, 'We have *episkopē*, let's call the officials *episkopoi*'. How did the title arise?

The *episkopoi* of Philippi have often been explained by appeal, on the one hand, in the OT/Jewish world, to the LXX and the synagogue (though there is little evidence that helps), and more recently to the *mᵉbaqqēr* occasionally mentioned in the Damascus Document, 1QS 6.12-20 and a few other Qumran references.[20] The result was much speculation, but little to convince one that such a title had migrated into Christianity first at Philippi. On the other hand the data assembled by Hans Lietzmann in 1914 and subsequently expanded by others make a far better case for *episkopos* as a supervisory office in the state, in various societies, and other groups in the Graeco-Roman world, often with financial responsibilities. More specifically Dieter Georgi lifted up as background the Cynic-Stoic itinerant preachers who scout out (as *kataskopoi*) and 'oversee' (*episkopein*) human beings for the gods. All in all, adaptation of this title by the Philippians from their Hellenistic environment seems more likely than some Jewish background.[21]

19. H.W. Beyer, '…*episkopos*, etc.', *TDNT* 2.608.
20. H. Braun, *Qumran und das Neue Testament* (Tübingen: Mohr [Paul Siebeck], 1966), II, pp. 329-32; J. Fitzmyer, 'Jewish Christianity in Acts in the Light of the Qumran Scrolls', in L.E. Keck and J.L Martyn (eds.), *Studies in Luke–Acts* (Nashville: Abingdon Press, 1966), pp. 247-84, reprinted in Fitzmyer's *Essays on the Semitic Background of the New Testament* (SBLSBS, 5; Missoula, MT: Scholars Press, 1974), pp. 293-94.
21. H. Lietzmann, 'Zur urchristlichen Verfassungsgeschichte', *ZWT* 55 (1914), pp. 97-153, reprinted in K. Kertelge (ed.), *Das kirchliche Amt im Neuen Testament* (Wege der Forschung, 189; Darmstadt: Wissenschaftliche Buchgesellschaft, 1977), pp. 93-143; M. Dibelius, '"Bischöfe" und "Diakonen" in Philippi,' in *An die Philipper* (HNT, 11; Tübingen: Mohr [Paul Siebeck], 3rd edn, 1937), pp. 60-62, reprinted in Kertelge, *Amt*, pp. 413-17. D. Georgi, *The Opponents of Paul in Second Corinthians* (Philadelphia: Fortress Press, 1986 [1964]); J. Hainz, 'Die

With *diakonoi* the matter is more complex because of (1) the larger number of examples of *diakonein* words, (2) the question of when *diakonos* becomes a technical term and (3) John N. Collins's challenge to most existing wordbook articles when he claims the classical usages do not bear out what he terms a modern shift from 'minister' to 'service'.[22] Again appeal has been made on the Semitic side to, among other places, the LXX, Levites, rabbinic committees of seven *parnāsîm*, and the synagogue *ḥazzān*. More satisfying, in my judgment, is the evidence for *diakonoi* in Greek guilds and again among the itinerant Cynic philosophers in the *diakonia* of God.[23] Among Collins's clusters of meaning for *diakonos* are 'go between' messengers, agents and attendants. Greek examplars of the term seem to have been readily at hand in Philippi for church use.

Word studies will take us only so far. A final step is to move beyond individual terms to the full phrase, 'the saints in Philippi together with *episkopoi* and *diakonoi*' and its context historically and socially.

5. The reconstruction of emerging offices must *fit* a picture of *development likely for the document in its context.*

    a.   Paul brought no overall, uniform plan of organized leadership for his churches on his own or from authorities in Antioch or Jerusalem. Even the 'Council' of Jerusalem in Acts 15 and the Apostolic Decree, on which John Hurd laid such emphasis in shaping Paul's work, in no way dealt with congregational offices. The surest proof is the very variety in Paul's congregations, which can scarcely be homogenized into a pattern. There are leaders at Thessalonica who labor, give care and admonish (5.12, *proïstamenoi*; cf. Rom. 12.8),

Anfänge des Bischofs- und Diakonenamtes', in J. Hainz (ed.), *Kirche im Werden: Studien zum Thema Amt und Gemeinde im Neuen Testament* (Munich: Schöningh, 1976), pp. 91-107. J. Rohde, *Urchristliche und frühkatholische Ämter* (Theologische Arbeiten, 33; Berlin: Evangelische Verlagsanstalt, 1976), pp. 54-56. E. Lohse, 'Die Entstehung des Bischofsamtes in der frühen Christenheit', *ZNW* 71 (1980), pp. 57-83.

    22. J.N. Collins, *Diakonia: Re-interpreting the Ancient Sources* (New York: Oxford University Press, 1990). See also Dibelius, 'Bischöfe', Hainz 'Die Anfänge des Bishofs' (pp. 94-102), and Rohde, *Urchristliche und frühkatholische Ämter*.

    23. Georgi, *Opponents*, pp. 27-32. But see the contrary opinion in J. N. Collins, 'Georgi's "Envoys" in 2 Cor. 11.23', *JBL* 93 (1974), pp. 88-96.

at Corinth, 'apostles, prophets, teachers,' and then all sorts of charismatic functions (1 Cor. 12.28). The Letter to the Galatians sheds little light (but cf. the teacher at Gal. 6.6). Philemon depicts a house church. Philippians alone names *episkopoi* and *diakonoi*. Each congregation seems to develop *ad hoc* and on its own, with what Collins calls in Philippi 'local idiosyncracy'.[24]

b.   The Philippians chose their terms for leaders from a world they know, of government, guilds, societies and the *oikos*. Possibly they elected representatives, like the delegate to Corinth (2 Cor. 8.19). But the *oikos* structure in Greek society must not be forgotten for the house churches. The *oikodespotēs* would, as patron and *pater familias*, exercise great influence and so there is good chance that *episkopoi* first appeared as house-church supervisors (hence the plural at Phil. 1.1).[25] In Paul's day women were likely to be included among them. *Diakonoi* or agents helped with various tasks. For Philippi the necessary tasks included fund-gathering and distribution to Paul, and for Jerusalem, missionary advance, oversight over congregational *apostoloi* and maintaining unity and discipline in and among house churches.[26]

c.   Elsewhere in early Christianity there existed communities led by presbyters, as in the synagogues (see Acts, 1 Peter, James, the Pastorals, 2 and 3 John). Space does not permit even out-

---

24. Collins, *Diakonia*, p. 236, quoting H. von Campenhausen, *Ecclesiastical Authority and Spiritual Power in the Church of the First Three Centuries* (Palo Alto, CA: Stanford University Press, 1969), p. 69 with regard to 'overseers' at Phil. 1.1.

25. E. Dassmann, 'Hausgemeinde und Bischofsamt', in *Vivarium: FS Theodor Klausner zum 90. Geburtstag* (JAC Ergänzungsband, 11; Münster: Aschendorff, 1984), pp. 82-97; G. Schöllgen, 'Hausgemeinden, *oikos*-Ekklesiologie, und monarchischer Episkopat', *JAC* 31 (1988), pp. 74-90; E. Dassmann and G. Schöllgen, 'Haus II (Hausgemeinschaft)', *RAC* 13 (1986), pp. 801-905, esp 886-901, cf. also Schöllgen's, 'Was wissen wir über die Sozialstruktur der paulinischen Gemeinde?', *NTS* 34 (1988), pp. 71-82.

26. For a fuller list, see E. von Dobschütz, in *Die Thessalonischer-Briefe* (KEK, 10; Göttingen: Vandenhoeck & Ruprecht, 7th edn, 1909), pp. 216-27, cited by B. Holmberg, *Paul and Power: The Structure of Authority in the Primitive Church as Reflected in the Pauline Epistles* (ConBNT, 11; Lund: Gleerup, 1978), p. 102, and by Maier, *Social Setting*, pp. 36-37.

lining other variations and how in the Pastoral Epistles *presbyteroi-episkopoi* and *diakonoi* provided two types of leaders[27] and how Ignatius, 'man of the Spirit' and/or 'entrepreneur', forged monepiscopacy as a new step in Antioch.[28] The Pastorals also took the fateful step of excluding women from being *episkopoi*, though they might still function as *diakonoi*.[29] Sociological studies can help explain the dynamics—good, bad or inevitable—of increasing institutionalization.[30]

6. Only at this point should one begin to talk of a *norm*, by selecting a particular stage in the process, a date or document(s) to serve as standard or a theme, doctrine or goal (like *koinōnia*, justification, mission) to help judge all developments. Subsequent church history is full of discussions declaring what is the *esse, bene esse*, happy result or just plain happenstance. Careful study of the NT provides a framework for options by depicting how and why church offices arose and were so varied.[31]

27. So, for example, among many commentators, M. Dibelius and H. Conzelmann, *The Pastoral Epistles* (Hermeneia; Philadelphia: Fortress Press, 1972), p. 55-57.

28. For Ignatius as 'man of the Spirit', see Campenhausen, *Ecclesiastical Authority*, p. 104; as 'entrepreneur', see C.J. Friedrich, 'Political Leadership and the Problem of Charismatic Power', *JP* 23 (1961), pp. 3-24; for recent discussion, see Maier, *Social Setting*, pp. 147-97.

29. Schüssler Fiorenza sees this compromise, women as deacons, perhaps for a time as presbyters (*In Memory of Her*, pp. 288-91).

30. For example M.Y. Macdonald, *The Pauline Churches: A Socio-historical Study of Institutionalization in the Pauline and Deutero-Pauline Writings* (SNTSMS, 60; New York: Cambridge University Press, 1988).

31. The role of the local church, organizationally and in other ways, is stressed in my paper for the 1992 SNTS meeting, 'Contributions of the Philippian Community to Paul and to Earliest Christianity', forthcoming in *NTS*.

OUR *POLITEUMA* IS IN HEAVEN: THE MEANING OF PHILIPPIANS 3.17-21

Wendy Cotter, CSJ

The meaning of Phil. 3.17-21 has produced considerable scholarly theses, but none of them has been sufficiently compelling to win consensus.[1] One of the central problems is the identity of the 'enemies of the cross of Christ' (Phil. 3.18). Does Paul refer back to those who 'mutilate the flesh' (Phil. 3.2), that is, those who endorse Torah observance, or to some other threatening group? The answer to this question sets the interpretive context for Paul's responding reminder, 'But our πολίτευμα is in heaven'.

Scholars like Helmut Koester and Walter Schmittals who identify 'the mutilators' as 'the enemies of the cross' must face the problem of reconciling a group enmeshed in religious perfectionism (Phil. 3.2-11) with Paul's insult in Phil. 3.19b, 'their god is the belly' (Phil. 3.19b). Drawing largely on Phil. 3.2-11 Koester proposes that these opponents are:[2]

> Christian missionaries of Jewish origin and background...preaching a doctrine of perfection based on the Law and the continuation of Jewish practices (circumcision).

Koester argues that Phil. 3.19 is consistent with this portrait if κοιλία ('belly') is only understood correctly. Admitting that κοιλία often refers to carnal appetite in Graeco-Roman literature, he nonetheless holds that this meaning cannot be assumed for Phil. 3.19 because no

---

1.   For a review of the major scholarly positions see R. Jewett's 'Conflicting Movements in the Early Church as Reflected in Philippians', *NovT* 12 (1970), pp. 362-90.

2.   H. Koester, 'The Purpose of the Polemic of a Pauline Fragment', *NTS* 8 (1961–1962), pp. 317-32; W. Schmittals, 'Die Irrlehrer des Philipperbriefes', *ZTK* 54 (1957), pp. 297-341.

NT text uses κοιλία in that way. Therefore, Koester maintains that the context of Phil. 3.19 must dictate the significance of κοιλία. Since Paul has just been addressing the question of Torah observance, it seems clear to Koester that Phil. 3.19 must refer to the fanatical observance of dietary laws.[3]

But Koester's interpretation must minimize the context afforded by the second insult of Phil. 3.19, 'and they glory in their shame'. Again he argues that since no NT text uses αἰσχύνη ('shame') in reference to carnal excesses, the context provided by Phil. 3.2-11 should determine its meaning. In this case the notion of shameful behaviour must refer to the preoccupation with Torah observance. Koester concludes 'it is very doubtful that Paul even hints at the sexual connotations of the Greek word αἰσχύνη.'[4]

First, Koester's jettisoning of ordinary Graeco-Roman meanings on the basis that they are not upheld by NT usage fails to recognize that Paul's letters predate most NT material. Secondly, his separate treatment of κοιλία and αἰσχύνη minimizes the contextualization which these words provide for each other. It is unlikely that Paul, who was so aware that he was writing to a Gentile community, would have used two insults so loaded with sexual connotations if he meant to refer to religious fanaticism over the observance of dietary laws. Finally, Koester himself admits that Paul *does* use κοιλία in a sense closer to ordinary Graeco-Roman usage in Rom. 6.18, where he says of those who cause strife in the community, 'For such persons do not serve our Lord Christ, but their own appetites (κοιλία).' Koester's efforts to reconcile Phil. 3.18 with Phil. 3.2-11 fail to convince because they are dependent on special pleading.

Walter Schmittals maintains that Phil. 3.2-11 and Phil. 3.17-21 refer to a group of libertinistic gnostics. These 'enemies of the cross' teach that salvation depends only on spiritual perfection, not on external conformity to Torah, nor any other behavioral norm. Schmittals claims that 'their god is the belly' (v. 19) is a denunciation of the gnostics' practice of eating idol meat in order to flaunt their 'freedom'.[5]

His reconstruction of a heretical movement from only these few verses draws its support from the Corinthian and Galatian

3.   Koester, 'Purpose of the Polemic', p. 331.
4.   Koester, 'Purpose of the Polemic', p. 326.
5.   Schmittals, 'Die Irrlehrer des Philipperbriefes', pp. 332-34.

correspondence.[6] The 'wise ones' of Corinth and the 'bewitchers' of Galatia are also denounced by Paul as opponents of Christ's cross (1 Cor. 1.18-19; Gal. 6.12-14). Schmittals concludes that the gnostic movement has also penetrated the Philippian community. But his argument cannot hold, as Koester has astutely observed. Schmittals' gnostics eschew the observance of Torah, and it is plain from Paul's argument in Phil. 3.3-11 that the opponents against whom he fights are enjoining Torah observance on the Philippian community.[7] Thus, neither Koester nor Schmittals can successfully reconcile the Torah observant opponents of Phil. 3.2-11 with those whose god is the 'belly'.

Of the scholars who recognize Phil. 3.17-21 as referring to a group distinct from the Torah observers, S. Schulz, D. Georgi and J. Gnilka argue persuasively that Paul's opponents are 'divine-man' missionaries who teach that the time of glory and ecstasy has been realized.[8] Relegating the cross to the past they preach that humiliation and suffering have no place now. These persons continually seek charismatic experiences of power, miracles, ecstasies and other spiritual manifestations. This theory fits Paul's accusation in Phil. 3.19 where he accuses them of keeping their mind on earthly things. But one cannot help asking how a group that is given over to expectations of spiritual power on earth deserves the insult, 'their god is the belly'.

Like the gnostic theory of Schmittals, the proposal that the group is composed of 'divine-man' missionaries requires an appeal to the Corinthian and Galatian texts, and many of the same ones, to supply the details that Phil. 3.18-21 cannot. Thus, two separate heretical groups, the libertinist gnostics and the 'divine-man' missionaries are completely reconstructed from the little material provided in Phil. 3.18-21, while each of them relies on almost the same texts found in other letters.

───

6. W. Schmittals, 'Die Haretiker in Galatien', *ZNW* 47 (1956), pp. 25-67. See also 'Zur Abfassung und ältesten Sammlung der paulinischen Hauptbriefe', *ZNW* 51 (1960), pp. 225-45.

7. Koester, 'Purpose of the Polemic', p. 319.

8. S. Schulz, 'Die Decke des Moses. Untersuchungen zu einer vorpaulinischen Überlieferung in 2 Kor 3, 7-18', *ZNW* 49 (1958), pp. 1-30; D. Georgi, *Die Gegner des Paulus im 2 Korintherbrief, Studien zur religiösen Propaganda in der Spätantike* (Neukirchen–Vluyn: Neukirchener Verlag, 1964); J. Gnilka, 'Die antipaulinischen Mission in Philippi', *BZ* NS 9 (1965), pp. 258-76.

The method used above to identify the 'enemies of the cross' in Phil. 3.17-21 is tenuous at best. One of the most important tenets of John C. Hurd's rigorous method is that the interpretation of any text from Paul's letters must rely mostly on the evidence provided by the letter in which it actually occurs. Since Paul writes to each particular community with attention to its special concerns, its membership and cultural orientation, his statements to one community, no matter how similar to the vocabulary and imagery in another letter to another community, cannot be used as proof of similar situations and similar enemies. Common vocabulary and imagery may be explained more simply by the fact that it is the same missionary who is writing the letters.[9]

In this case it is still questionable whether the Corinthian 'wise ones' and the Galatian 'bewitchers' are either gnostics or 'divine-man' missionaries or even that the opponents in the two communities are the same. In any case the application of either heresy to Phil. 3.18-21 requires greater substantiation from the Philippian letter as a whole. One fact of the letter which speaks against the opponents being heretics is that Paul does not treat the persons mentioned in Phil. 3.18-19 as he does the 'Judaizers' of Phil. 3.3-11. With the group that urges the adoption of Torah, Paul launches an argument in which his own conversion is cited as the proof against the idea that righteousness will be found in the observance of the Law. On the other hand in Phil 3.18-21 Paul simply dismisses this group with negative labelling (vv. 18-19) and by a reiteration of basic Christian eschatological hopes (vv. 20-21). Paul does not combat any real teaching, as he would certainly have done if libertinist gnostics or 'divine-man' missionaries were contesting his teachings to the community.

Secondly, Paul's *tertium comparationis* between himself and these persons is περιπατεῖν, their lifestyle. Paul enjoins the Philippians to copy his way of living (περιπατεῖν). The opponents come to mind as the example of those who should never be imitated. Paul thinks of these opponents in terms of their way of life, not in terms of a heretical teaching they are spreading.

Thirdly, not only have these scholars neglected to contextualize Paul's remarks with attention to the letter as a whole, but they have

9. While this method may be observed in all J.C. Hurd's scholarly work, it is most assiduously demonstrated in his book, *The Origin of First Corinthians* (London: SPCK, 1965).

also neglected to set the remarks against the backdrop of ordinary
Graeco-Roman city life. Only if Paul's remarks can be shown to stand
apart from usual situations found on the first-century street can they
be presumed to apply to a more esoteric group, like gnostics or other
heretical sects.

This is what must be addressed here. Examining Paul's statements
about these enemies we cannot begin with the presupposition that they
are or once were Christians on the grounds that Paul says he weeps
when he thinks of them or because he describes them as 'enemies of
the cross'. The appeal to tears is far too common in rhetorical
speeches to act as proof of the enemies' identity.[10] Culturally Paul's
tears are appropriate since Paul wants to be seen as a man of
humanitas. It is not necessary that *Paul* know these persons who will
be destroyed (Phil. 3.18), but that he knows the *Philippians* do! Since
the destruction to come will surely then include persons known by the
members of the Philippian community, friends or neighbours, it is
only seemly that Paul demonstrate some sign of regret for their fate.
In fact Paul's tears allow him to raise the subject of these oft-
mentioned opponents once again. Thus the tears are able to stress the
irrevocability of the doom awaiting these persons, while
demonstrating respect for the Philippians' possible distress about it.

Similarly, Paul's description of these opponents as 'enemies of the
cross of Christ' need only relate to the Philippians, not the opponents.
That is, Paul's label makes it clear that any member who imitates these
persons places himself or herself at variance with the cross.

But to what does Paul refer when he calls these opponents enemies
of the cross of Christ? Here it is interesting to note a pattern that
emerges in an examination of Paul's letters to the Corinthians and the
Galatians. Whatever the platform of Paul's opponents he will describe
the cross so that it stands in direct contrast to them. His own conversion or life story will be then told in such a way as to place Paul in

---

10. '[The accomplished orator] establishes his sway over the emotions of his
audience, forces his way into their very hearts...' (Quint., *Inst.* 2.5.8). Also
Augustine, 'Just as the listener is to be delighted if he is to be retained as a listener,
so also is he to be persuaded if he is to be moved to act. And just as he is delighted if
you speak sweetly, so is he persuaded if he loves what you promise, fears what you
threaten, hates what you condemn, embraces what you commend, sorrows at what
you maintain to be sorrowful...flees those whom you, moving with fear, warn are
to be avoided', (Aug., *De Doctr. Christ.* 4.13).

unity with his particular description of the cross. In Corinthians Paul combats the 'wise' by presenting the cross, and his own call as well, as devoid of 'wisdom' and 'empty of power' (1 Cor. 1.17-18). In Galatians Paul fights those who insist on circumcision by claiming that persons want to evade the sufferings of the cross and win glory for themselves (Gal. 6.12-14). His own call is shown to be in complete harmony with that cross,

> It is those who want to make a good showing in the flesh that would compel you to be circumcised, and only in order that they may not be persecuted for the cross of Christ... But far be it from me to glory except in the cross of our Lord Jesus Christ, by which the world has been crucified to me and I to the world.

It is more complicated to examine how Paul has presented the cross in Philippians because Phil. 2.5-10 is regarded by notable scholars as part of a separate letter (Phil. 1.1-2.30).[11] If that be the case, the use of Paul's presentations of Jesus' cross to interpret Phil. 3.18 is less sure. But what is notable here is that Paul's presentation of his own call in Phil. 3.2-11 brings out the same elements that he emphasizes in his treatment of the cross in Phil. 2.5-10. The coherence between the aspects Paul stresses in his presentation of Christ's sacrifice serve to highlight weaknesses that require this teaching and example.

In Phil. 2.5-10, Paul emphasizes Christ's surrender of his exalted place to take on the abject human condition. The cross becomes a sign of greatest humiliation. Then God raises up Jesus and restores him to his power, where he receives the world's adulation.

Correspondingly in Phil. 3.3-11, Paul shows that he too left the life of prestige and honour as a scrupulous observer of the Law. He too counted all his gains as loss in his glad discovery of new life in God.[12]

> But whatever gain I had, I counted as loss for the sake of Christ. Indeed I count everything as loss because of the surpassing worth of knowing Christ Jesus my Lord. For his sake, I have suffered the loss of all things and count them as refuse, in order that I may gain Christ... (Phil. 3.7-8).

---

11. See F. Beare, *The Epistle to the Philippians* (London: A. &. C. Black, 1959). For structural reasons against accepting Phil. 1.1–2.30 as a separate letter, see J.L. White, *The Body of the Greek Letter* (SBLDS, 2; Missoula, MT: Scholars Press, 1972), p. 84. For a review of the scholarly argument over the integrity of Philippians see Koester, 'Purpose of the Polemic', p. 317 nn. 1, 2, 3.

12. I am indebted to my colleague J.L. White for this insight.

Significantly, both Christ's example of humility (Phil. 2.5-10) and Paul's own example (Phil. 3.4-11) occur in exhortative passages where Paul is calling on the community to regulate their community life so that it will be unified, joyful and loving (Phil. 1.27-2.4; 2.12-16; 3.12-16). While it is true that the warmth of Phil. 4.1 shows that the Philippians have not veered dramatically from their loyalty to Paul's teachings, his exhortations and warnings about the importance of community unity and love suggest that the community did have some internal division. Paul's description of Jesus' cross and his own conversion show the Philippians that they too must surrender their love for prestige, and a prominent name in society, and taking authority over others. In fact Paul's introduction to his presentation of Jesus' cross addresses these issues directly,

> Do nothing from selfishness or conceit, but in humility count others better than yourselves. Let each of you look not only to his own interests, but also to the interests of others. Have this mind in you which was in Christ Jesus... (Phil. 2.3-5).

After Paul describes his own conversion and daily struggle to remain faithful he enjoins the community,

> Brothers, join in imitating me, and mark those who so live as you have an example in us. For many, of whom I have often told you and now tell you with tears, live as enemies of the cross of Christ (Phil. 3.17-18).

In the Philippian context to be an enemy of Christ's cross would mean a person opposed to any sort of humiliation. In contrast to Christ and to Paul too, such persons would be working for the increase of their own public name and vying for positions of importance without regard for others, a clear violation of the Christian mandate.

The search for the identity of such persons must include any evidence that can be drawn from Paul's negative labelling of them in Phil. 3.18-19. It is interesting that his denunciation finds a resonance in Philo's record of Augustus' indictment of the voluntary associations,[13]

> He [Augustus] ordered that the Jews alone should be permitted by them [the governors of Asia] to assemble in synagogues. These gatherings, he said, were not based on drunkenness and carousing (μέθης καὶ παροινίας) to promote conspiracy and so to do grave injury to the cause

---

13. Ph., *Legat.* 10.311-12.

of peace, but were schools of temperance and justice (σωφροσύνης καὶ δικαιοσύνης) where men while practising virtue subscribed the annual first fruits to pay for the sacrifices which they offer and commissioned sacred envoys to take them to the temple in Jerusalem.

Philo also reports that Flaccus, Tiberias's governor of Egypt, banned the voluntary associations for their drunken and outrageous behaviour because it led to seditious conduct,[14]

> The sodalities and clubs which were constantly holding feasts under the pretext of sacrifice in which drunkenness vented itself in political intrigue, he dissolved and dealt sternly and vigorously with the refractory.

Much earlier Varro had also denounced such groups,[15]

> [There are] organizations in the city in whose fellowship you could find no sound elements but only liquor, tippling, drunkenness and the outrageous conduct they lead to, associations and 'couches' as they are called locally [in Alexandria]. In all or most of these religious associations Isidore reigned supreme, under the nickname Party Leader, Couch Captain, or Master of the Rebels.

The reputation of the associations cannot be said to be completely undeserved. Clubs without benefactions were obliged to use the local taverns for their meetings. In fact, Claudius closed down the taverns in Rome and Ostia as part of his suppression of clubs.[16] But associations that did have benefactors and a special meeting place other than a tavern also practiced heavy drinking. For example, in examining the content of the twenty-three by-laws of the religious society,[17] 'the Worshippers of Diana and Antinoüs' (c. 136 CE), thirteen of them deal with: (a) the provision of wine (the entrance fee, for example, is one hundred sesterces and 'an amphora of good wine'); (b) the responsibility for providing the society with its banquets and (c) the fines for misbehaving during the dinner. Only eight concern the obligation to bury deceased members of the group.

14. Ph., *Flacc.* 4.
15. Var., *R.R.*, 3.2.16. See R. Macmullen, *Roman Social Relations* (New Haven: Yale University Press, 1974), p. 78.
16. Cassius Dio, *History* 60.6-7.
17. Although associations might gather on the basis of a common trade, a common location or a common devotion, all associations were 'religious' as J.P. Waltzing observes, 'A l'époque lointaine dont nous parlons, une corporation sans culte ne se conçoit pas' (J.P. Waltzing, *Etude historique sur les corporations professionelles* [4 vols.; Louvain: Forni Editore Bologna, 1895–1900], I, p. 75.)

Of the remaining two by-laws, one stipulates the clothing to be worn by the head officer at the liturgy and the other reminds him that he .must provide free oil to the members when they go to the baths just prior to the banquets.[18]

If such associations had been few, geographically limited or insignificant in their influence, the citation of this evidence would be irrelevant with respect to the Macedonian city of Philippi. But the associations were plentiful and very popular throughout the Mediterranean, as the inscriptional evidence proves.[19] Furthermore, Frank Beare has already established that,[20]

> A highly significant feature of the religion of the period is the multipli-
> cation of private brotherhoods, cult-associations (*sodalitates, thiasoi*)
> devoted to the worship of a chosen god; *and there were many such groups
> at Philippi.*

The influence of such clubs was significant enough to warrant their periodic suppression by the emperors and governors. The inscriptions show that it was not so much the drinking and outrageous conduct as it was the opportunity for political protest that concerned rulers most.

The strongest sign of the popularity of these clubs is that despite the movements to suppress them they always sprung up again, almost immediately.[21] There are two main reasons for the popularity of these clubs. First, they provided a group with common interests an opportunity for frequent socializing. Clubs helped to fill the void created by the rather unsettled and lonely circumstances of city life for a poor person. Secondly, clubs created an order in which the members could

18. For the full text see N. Lewis and M. Reinhold (eds.), *Roman Civilization* (2 vols.; New York: Harper & Row, 1955), II, pp. 274-75.

19. For evidence of the associations throughout the Mediterranean world see the inscriptional evidence in F. Poland, *Geschichte des Griechischen Vereinswesens*; J.P. Waltzing, *Etude Historique sur les Corporations Professionelles;* F.M. de Robertis, *Storia delle Corporazioni e del Regime Associativo nel Mundo Romano* (2 vols.; Bari: Adriatica Editrice, 1934); G. Clemente, 'Il Patronato nei Collegia dell'Impero Romano', *Studici classici orientali* 21 (1972), pp. 142-229. For a treatment of the popularity of the various voluntary associations, especially the trade associations see MacMullen, *Roman Social Relations*, pp. 71-87.

20. Beare, *Philippians*, p. 9 (emphasis mine).

21. This evidence is discussed in an unpublished paper, W. Cotter, 'The Collegia and Roman Law: The State Restrictions on Private Associations: 64 BCE–200 CE' for the 1989 meeting of the Canadian Society of Biblical Studies at Laval University, Quebec City, Canada.

achieve honours, prestige and exercise authority which would not have otherwise been possible for them.[22] It must be presumed that the Philippians had the same needs as the other members of their time and culture, and that they too were attracted by these two prominent features of the clubs.

When Paul's denunciation of the opponents, 'Their god is the belly and they glory in their shame, with minds set on earthly things' is set against the backdrop of the city and its many voluntary societies and religious clubs, it is in no significant way different than the repudiations launched against associations by Varro, Augustus, Flaccus and Claudius. Furthermore, if we allow that Paul is referring to the members of the most prominent and popular clubs in Philippi, it would explain his acknowledgement that he has spoken about these opponents many times before (Phil. 3.18). It is less easy to explain how heretical groups like the gnostics would gain strength so early. The proposal also explains why Paul would be inclined to raise the warning about these persons once again. The steady presence of these associations would constitute a continual threat. There is no 'teaching' of theirs that needs to be contested but it is their περιπατεῖν that Paul denounces. This way of life must never be copied. The reiteration of Christian expectations and beliefs explains the appropriateness of the separation which must be maintained between the Philippian Christians and these persons whose behaviour is at enmity with the cross of Christ.

It remains to discuss whether Paul's main distinction, '*Our* πολίτευμα is in heaven' fits naturally with our proposal that Paul is referring to members of the prominent, popular clubs in the city. The meticulous philological treatment of πολίτευμα by P.C. Böttger proves that the most reliable translation should address the civic character of the word in a rather general way, the best Latin equivalents being *res publica* or *civitas*, and the best German rendering, 'Stadt'.[23] Böttger notes that Paul's placement of the pronoun ἡμῶν in the initial position of the statement ἡμῶν γὰρ τὸ πολίτευμα ἐν οὐρανοῖς ὑπάρχει suggests that he is using the opponents' terminology.[24] The proposal

22. See Macmullen, *Roman Social Relations*, p. 76.

23. P.C. Böttger, 'Die eschatologische Existenz der Christen. Erwägungen zu Philipper 3.20', *ZNW* 60 (1969), pp. 244-63, esp. 245 and 247.

24. Böttger, 'Die eschatologische Existenz der Christen', pp. 244-63, esp. 245 and 247.

that πολίτευμα belongs to outsiders seems plausible since Paul
appears to use this technique in Phil. 3.2-12 against the advocates of
circumcision[25] and because πολίτευμα is found nowhere else in
Paul's letters. But certain evidence suggests that Paul may be using
language that reflects the particular interest of the Philippians
themselves. First, a verbal form of πολίτευμα occurs in Phil. 1.27
(πολιτεύεσθαι) where he addresses the community about their own
self organization. While the RSV translates πολιτεύεσθαι 'manner of
life' we suggest that the civic character of the verb is better
represented by the term 'self-governance'. The verb is another *hapax*
in Paul's letters.[26] It appears to have been chosen with the specific
character of the Philippian community order in mind.

Secondly, it is curious that Paul's letter to the Philippians is the only
letter where he greets ἐπίσοκοποι and διάκονοι (Phil. 1.1) and there
is no textual evidence to show scribal interference here. The office of
the ἐπίσοκοπος was already well known in the towns and cities of the
Mediterranean. The ἐπίσοκοπος was required to oversee projects
such as the construction of public buildings, or to supervise the local
market like the ἀγορανόμος.[27] The office was often copied by the
voluntary associations where it required the same responsibilities but
operated within the parameters of a club.[28]

The word διάκονος is so broad in usage that it must be translated
according to context. In Paul's letters διάκονος is usually used to
describe someone's relationship with Christ or with God: (a) Paul's
relationship to Christ (1 Cor. 3.5; 2 Cor. 3.6; 11.23); (b) Timothy's
relationship to God (1 Thess. 3.2); (c) Jesus' relationship to God
(Rom. 15.8) and (d) the earthly ruler's relationship to God (Rom.
13.4). But in Rom. 16.1 Paul's endorsement of Phoebe as a deacon
from Cenchreae shows that διάκονος is also an office there. It is this
sense that obtains in Phil. 1.1, because the mention of the διάκονοι
follows the salutation to the ἐπίσκοποι which is indisputably an office.

The sign of internal organization with attention to civic order leads
to the natural conclusion that Paul's use of πολίτευμα reflects the

25. F.J. Klijn, 'Paul's Opponents in Philippians iii', *NovT* 7 (1964),
pp. 280-82.

26. In the NT, it occurs elsewhere only in Acts 23.1.

27. See G. McLean Harper, Jr, 'Village Administration in the Roman Province of
Syria', *Yale Classical Studies* 1 (1928), pp. 132-34.

28. See Poland, *Geschichte*, pp. 377, 381, 448.

interest of the Philippians who take pleasure in considering their community as something of a civic entity.

The modelling of a club or association along civic lines was the rule rather than the exception in Graeco-Roman antiquity.[29] Even the slaves of a household imitated the city's organization, as Pliny the Younger remarks, 'for the house provides the slave with a country (*res publica*) and a sort of citizenship (*civitas*)'.[30] Here it is instructive to note that Pliny uses the two Latin terms that Böttger claims are the best translations of πολίτευμα. Pliny too defines the attraction and function of the association as one that gives its members a sure citizenship of their own.

But what exactly is the point Paul makes with his statement, 'Our πολίτευμα is in heaven'? Frank Beare proposes that Paul is contrasting heaven with Rome because Philippi was only a colony, '[Philippi was] an outpost governed by the laws of the homeland and attached to it by the deepest sentiments of loyalty'.[31] He therefore concludes that the πολίτευμα of the Philippians is Rome.

But Beare misunderstands the expectations that Romans had for their colonies. Colonists were to settle in and establish a city of their own, as Philo states,[32]

> For surely, when men found a colony, the land which receives them becomes their native land instead of the mother city, but to the traveller abroad the land which sent him forth is still the mother to whom he also yearns to return.

This is certainly true for Philippi which had been settled by Roman veterans[33] and was proud of the fact that it was governed by the *ius*

---

29. See Poland, *Geschichte* pp. 337-423; Waltzing, *Les Corporations*, I, pp. 357-446.

30. 'nam servis res publica quaedam etquasi civitas domus est', Plin., *Ep. Pan.* 2.8.16. See the unpublished paper, 'Collegia' by J.S. Kloppenborg, presented at the meeting of the CSBS in 1989 at Laval University, Quebec, esp. p. 14.

31. Beare, *Philippians* (London: A. & C. Black, 1973), p. 136.

32. Ph., *Confus.* 4.78.

33. Philippi was first colonized by Italian settlers in 45 BCE following Marc Anthony's victory over Cassius and Brutus. It was called *Colonia Victrix Philippensium* (Strabo 7, frag. 41; Dio Cassius 51.4.6; Plin., *HN* 4.42). Augustus renamed the colony *Colonia Iulia Augusta Philippensium,* dispossessed Anthony's veterans and gave the land to his own. See J.A.O. Larsen, 'Roman Greece', in T. Frank (ed.), *An Economic Survey of Ancient Rome* (6 vols.; Baltimore: The

Italicum, the highest privilege obtainable by a provincial municipality.[34] Therefore, when Paul creates a contrast between the πολίτευμα
of the Christians and that of the opponents, he is not contrasting
heaven with Rome, because the home city of the Philippians is Philippi
itself. Or it might be that the 'home city' model is in reference to the
associations and clubs which flourished all around and provided so
many disparate people with their own special citizenship. In either
case, Paul's distinction lays bare the fact that Philippians are no longer
citizens of any earthly city, real or community created. When he says,
'*our* home city is in heaven', the ἡμῶν broadens out the addressees of
this maxim to include Paul himself and indeed, all Christians. All
Christians have become 'foreigners' since their true home city is in
heaven.

In a similar vein, Philo describes the wise men who realize that they
will never find their citizenship (πολιτεύονται) on earth but only in
heaven,[35]

> Their souls are never colonists leaving heaven for a new home... to them
> the heavenly region, where their citizenship lies (πολιτεύονται) is their
> native land; the earthly region in which they became sojourners is a
> foreign country.

It must have been difficult for the Philippians to find a community
model that would allow them to adopt certain offices of civic order
without the attending ambitious and worldly behaviour typical of
political and civic organizations. Paul's statement, 'But our home city
is in heaven' serves in two important ways. First, it dispels any idea
that a midground exists for the appropriation of popular associations'
practices. Secondly, it acknowledges the separateness that the community is suffering and reminds them of the greater honours awaiting
them, for they have their citizenship in heaven, God's own *politeuma*
where the *cursum honorum* includes only the names of the faithful.[36]

Johns Hopkins University Press, 1936), IV, pp. 443-53.

34. '[The privilege of the] *ius Italicum* [means that] the land is free from *tributum
soli* (land tax) and can be possessed in full ownership *ex iure Quiritium* (not subject
to the laws of Roman patrician privilege); the inhabitants are not liable to *tributum
capitis* (poll tax)... Under the Empire, this was the highest privilege obtainable by a
provincial municipality. Augustus gave it only to genuine citizen colonies, mostly his
eastern foundations. See A.N. Sherwin-White, '*Ius Italicum*', *OCD*, p. 559.

35. Ph., *Confus.* 4.77-78.

36. My sincere thanks to J.L. White for his helpful critique of the paper.

MILITARY LANGUAGE AND METAPHORS IN PHILIPPIANS*

Edgar M. Krentz

John Hurd has been a conversation partner in Pauline studies for over twenty years. He has been a pioneer in the use of computer technology in Biblical studies, a creative teacher of the Greek language, a sensitive colleague who argues gracefully with those who hold opinions different from his own. It is an honour to contribute to this Festschrift an examination of one paragraph in Philippians, part of a larger study of military language in the Pauline corpus. It uses data from a generally disregarded body of literature to supplement linguistic data gathered by computer database searching. In that sense it breaks some new ground.

New Testament scholarship pays little attention to ancient writers of military tactics—to their loss. In this paper I propose to show that Paul used military metaphors extensively in Philippians, as did contemporary Graeco-Roman writers. By the end of the first century the imperial system had radically changed the old Roman concepts of *virtus* and *gloria*. Under the principate one no longer earned individual glory. Donald Earl puts it well:

> *Gloria*...was to be tempered by obedience, *obsequium,* above all a military virtue. Public men must act as soldiers, winning by their deeds in the service of the state such glory as was consistent with their position, but obedient always to their commander, the emperor.[1]

* Many of the passages from Greek literature cited in this paper came from searching the *Thesaurus Linguae Graecae* Pilot CD ROM #C disk, prepared under T.F. Brunner's leadership (Irvine: University of California, Irvine, 1987). I used the search program *Pandora* 2.3 (Santa Barbara: Intellemation Library for the Macintosh, 1990), developed by the Classics Department of Harvard College, project editor E. Mylonas, on a Macintosh IIsi computer. I use the abbreviations of *OCD* and LSJ for the authors and titles of Latin and Greek writers in the footnotes.

1 D. Earl, *The Moral and Political Tradition of Rome: Aspects of Greek and*

In his biography of his father-in-law Cn. Iulius Agricola, governor of Britain, Tacitus contrasts the now somewhat servile relation of the optimates to the emperor with the non-Roman tribes who still show the traditional Roman virtues:

> When they [the *Germani*] join battle it is shameful for the chief (*princeps*) to be surpassed in *virtus* and shameful for his retinue not to equal the *virtus* of the chief. Indeed, the man who leaves the battle alive when his chief has been killed suffers lifelong infamy and opprobrium. The essence of their oath is to defend him, protect him and to attribute to his *gloria* their own brave deeds. The chiefs fight for victory, their companions for their chief.[2]

Military language also appears in many other contexts. It was a familiar τόπος in philosophic argumentation.[3] Though used infrequently in texts of the fifth to fourth centuries BCE, Socrates compared his teaching style to remaining firmly in place in a military line:

> Strange, indeed, would be my conduct, O men of Athens, if I who, when I was ordered by the generals whom you chose to command me at Potidaea and Amphipolis and Delium, remained where they placed me, like any other man facing death—if now, when, as I conceive and imagine, God orders me to fulfil the philosopher's mission of searching into myself and other men, I were to desert my post through fear of death, or any other fear.[4]

Roman era Stoics frequently use this military metaphor to urge a life dedicated to ethical actions. Epictetus uses the soldier's oath of

Roman Life (Ithaca, NY: Cornell University Press, 1964), p. 90.

2.   Tac. *Germ.* 14.1, as translated by Earl, *Tradition of Rome*, p. 90; J.G.C. Anderson, 'Germania and Agricola', in H. Furneaux (ed.), *Cornelii Taciti Opera Minora* (Scriptorum Classicorum Bibliotheca Oxoniensis. Oxford: Clarendon Press, 1949), gives a trustworthy Latin text.

3.   The basic work is H. Emonds, 'Geistlicher Kriegsdienst. Der Topos der militia spiritualis in der antiken Philosophie', in O. Casel (ed.), *Heilige Überlieferung* (Münster: Aschendorff, 1938), pp. 21-50.

4.   Pl. *Ap.* 28d.5-29a.1, cited according to J. Burnett (ed.), *Platonis Opera* (Scriptorum Classicorum Bibliotheca Oxoniensis; 5 vols.; Oxford: Clarendon Press, 1900), vol. 1 (trans. B. Jowett, *The Dialogues of Plato*; New York: Oxford University Press, 1892), II, p. 122. In his annotated edition of *Plato's Euthyphro, Apology of Socrates and Crito* (Oxford: Clarendon Press, 1924), p. 119, Burnett comments that 'Socrates regards himself as a soldier of God, whose orders he must not disobey. This had nothing to do with the "divine sign" which gave only prudential and negative intimations.'

allegiance to the emperor (*sacramentum*) as a model for the philosophic life dedicated to the god within:

> ...when you close your doors and make darkness within, remember
> never to say that you are alone, for you are not alone; nay, God is within,
> and your own genius is within. And what need have they of light in order
> to see what you are doing? Yes, and to this God you also ought to swear
> allegiance, as the soldiers do to Caesar. They are but hirelings, yet they
> swear that they will put the safety of Caesar above everything; and shall
> you, indeed, who have been counted worthy of blessings so numerous
> and so great be unwilling to swear, or, when you have sworn, to abide by
> your oath? And what shall you swear? Never to disobey under any
> circumstances, never to prefer charges, never to find fault with anything
> that God has given, never to let your will rebel when you have either to do
> or to suffer something that is inevitable. Can the oath of the soldiers in
> any way be compared with this of ours? Out there men swear never to
> prefer another in honour above Caesar; but here we swear to prefer
> ourselves in honour above everything else.[5]

Hierocles, a second century CE Stoic, wrote an epitome of Stoic
philosophy, preserved in fragments cited by John Stobaeus. In the
section περὶ ἀδελφίας Hierocles describes life as follows:

> On the whole, we must conclude that our lives appear to be a *long sort of
> war* which lasts many years, partly because of the nature of things them-
> selves which possess a certain resistant quality, and partly because of the
> *sudden and unexpected incursions* of fortune, but especially because of
> vice itself, which does not abstain from any *violence* or from guile and
> *evil stratagems*.[6]

Seneca also uses military language in several places to describe the
philosophic life: 'And so, Lucilius, to live is to serve as a soldier.
Therefore those who are tossed about and who go up and down

---

5. Epict. 1.14.13-17, trans. W.A. Oldfather in *Epictetus* (2 vols.; LCL;
London: William Heinemann; Cambridge, MA: Harvard University Press, 1925), I,
p. 105. Cited according to H. Schenkl, *Epicteti Dissertationes ab Arriani digestae*
(Bibliotheca Teubneriana, ed. maior; Stuttgart: B. G. Teubner, 1965 [1916]).

6. Stob. *Flori* 4.27.20. Italics indicate military language. Translated by
A. Malherbe, *Moral Exhortation, A Greco-Roman Sourcebook* (Philadelphia:
Westminster Press, 1986), p. 95. Malherbe translates from the standard five-volume
edition of Stobaeus by C. Wachsmuth and O. Hense. I cite the Greek from the earlier
edition ΙΘΑΝΝΟΥ ΣΤΟΒΑΙΟΥ ΑΝΘΟΛΟΓΙΟΝ IOANNIS STOBAEI
FLORILEDIUM (ed. A. Meineke; Bibliotheca Teubneriana; 4 vols.; Leipzig:
Teubner, 1856), III, p. 129.

through toilsome and harsh circumstances and go to meet most perilous military operations are brave men and the most illustrious of those in the fortresses...'[7] Seneca cites approvingly a certain Sextius, a philosopher who promoted Roman virtues in Greek words:

> An image put forward by him moved me: an army in a fourfold line, ready for battle, goes to a place where an enemy is suspected on every hand. 'The wise man,' he said, 'ought to do the same. He spreads out his virtues in every direction, in order that wherever something hostile arises, there the defenses are ready and react without tumult at the nod of the commander.' That in those armies, which great commanders put in order, we see it happen that all the forces sense the command of the leader at the same time, and thus disposed, that a command (*signum*) given by one runs through the foot and the horse at the same time: this, he said, is considerably more necessary for us. For they often fear an enemy without cause, have a most safe road which was highly suspect: stupidity has no peace. Fear hangs over it as much as it is [actually] below it: its flank is anxious in every direction. Dangers follow it and meet it; it quakes in fear at everything, is unprepared and terrified by its own auxiliary troops. The wise man, however, is prepared for every attack, its mind set fast; not if poverty, not if mourning, not if ignominy, not if grief should make an attack, does it retreat: it goes its way, undisturbed, against them and among them. [8]

7.   Sen. *Ep.Mor.* 96.5 (my translation): *Atqui vivere, Lucili est militare. Itaque, hi, qui iactantur et per operosa atque ardua sursum ac deorsum eunt et expeditiones periculosissimas obeunt, fortes viri sunt primoresque castrorum...* Cited from A. Beltrami (ed.), *L. Annaei Senecae ad Lvcilivm Epistulae Morales* (Scriptores Graeci et Latini consilio Academiae Lynceorum editi; 2 vols.; Rome: Typis Pubicae Officinae Polygraphicae, 1949).

8.   Sen. *Ep.Mor.* 59.7-8. (my translation): *Movit me imago ab illo posita: ire quadrato agmine exercitum, ubi hostis ab omni parte suspectus est, pugnae paratum. Idem, inquit sapiens facere debet: omnes virtutes suas undique expandat, ut ubicumque infesti aliquid orietur, illic parata praesidia sint et ad nutum regentis sine tumultu respondeant. Quod in exercitibus is, quos imperatores magni ordinant, fieri videmus, ut imperium ducis simul omnes copiae sentiant, sic dispositae, ut signum ab uno datum peditem simul equitemque percurrat: hoc aliquanto magis necessarium esse nobis ait. Illi enim saepe hostem timuere sine causa, tutissimumque illis iter quod suspectissimum fuit; nihil stultitia pacatum habet. Tam superne illi metus est quan infra: utremque trepidat latus. Secuntur pericula et occurrent: ad omnia pavet, imparata est et ipsis terretur auxiliis. Sapiens autem ad omnem incursum munitus, intentus, non si paupertas, non si luctus, non si ignominia, non si dolor impetum faciat, pedem referent: interritus et contra illa ibit et inter illa.*

In short ethical teachers used military language constantly. E.V. Arnold says that Roman Stoics put ethical ideals before young men by referring to the training of the athlete, the gladiator and the soldier, but most of all the soldier.[9]

One should not, then, be surprised if a similar use of language appears in Paul.[10] And it does. Paul refers to armour and weapons in 1 Thess. 5.8 (all defensive). 1 Cor. 14.8 refers to using the trumpet to give orders in the army,[11] while 1 Cor. 16.13 uses military commands in parenesis. But, to my knowledge, there is no systematic survey of any Pauline letter based on a comprehensive knowledge of Greek military terminology.

Paul uses such military language extensively in Philippians. He calls Epaphroditus and Archippus fellow-soldiers.[12] Bauer,[13] citing

9. E.V. Arnold, *Roman Stoicism* (New York: The Humanities Press, 1958 [1911]), pp. 363-64: '...the soldier's oath serves as an example, when he pledges himself to serve Caesar faithfully all his life: let the young philosopher pledge himself to serve his God as faithfully, to submit to the changes and chances of human life, and to obey willingly the command to act or to suffer'. Arnold cites Sen. *Dial.* 7.15.7 (*ad Gallionem de vita beata*): *Quicquid ex universi constitutione patiendum est, magno suscipiatur animo. ad hoc sacramentum adacti sumus, ferre mortalia nec perturbari iis, quae vitare non est nostrae potestatis. In regno nati sumus. deo parere libertas est.* Cited according to F. Haase (ed.), *L. Annaei Senecae Opera quae supersunt* (Bibliotheca Teubneriana; 3 vols.; Leipzig: Teubner, 1894–1895).

10. The topos also appears in early Christian literature. Ig., *Pol.* 6 uses an extended military metaphor (note the sequence of *συν- compounds [συγκοπιᾶτε, συναθρεῖτε, συντρέχετε, συμπάσχετε, συγκοιμᾶσθε, συνεγείεσθε] which describe the experience of soldiers in battle and the description of Polycarp's armor). In *Smyr.* 1, Ignatius speaks of Jesus' resurrection as erecting a standard (σύσσημον). Ignatius is only the first of many to use military language with reference to the Christian faith. See also 1 Clem. 21 and 28. A. Harnack, *Militia Christi: The Christian Religion and the Military in the First Three Centuries* (Philadelphia: Fortress Press, 1981), p. 41, cites *Pol.* 6.2, but overlooks the significance of 6.1. There is a graphic description of this unified effort by soldiers in V.D. Hanson, *The Western Way of War: Infantry Battle in Classical Greece* (New York: Alfred A. Knopf, 1989), pp. 152-84. Though he writes of hoplite warfare, much of what he says applies to any battle of foot soldiers in pre-gunpowder days.

11. P. Krentz, 'The *Salpinx* in Greek Warfare', in V.D. Hanson (ed.), *Hoplites: The Classical Greek Battle Experience* (London and New York: Routledge & Kegan Paul, 1991), pp. 110-20.

12. συστρατιώτης, Phil. 2.25, Phlm. 1. Paul never uses the simple term στρατιώτης; the term does appear in 2 Tim. 2.3.

13. BAGD, *s.v.*, 'συστρατιώτης'.

Polyaenus 8.23.22,[14] calls it a 'term of honor (which in Polyaenus 8.23.22 makes the soldier equal to the commander-in-chief, and in Synes.[ius], Kingship 13 p. 12c makes a warrior equal to the king).' Paul links the 'fellow soldier' with the terms ἀδελφός and συνεργός, both terms of respect. Paul mentions the praetorium, the camp of the emperor's guard, in Phil. 1.13.

Recent literature on the social setting of early Christianity pays almost no attention to the Roman army as a social factor—though Roman historians recognize its great significance.[15] The lower officers of the Roman army, when mustered out of the military, often became the upper class in provincial towns dependent on the military.[16] When mustered out these veterans emerge as holders of every type of civic office. 'Veterans were prominent, influential and sought after as magistrates, senators, patrons and sons-in-law...'[17] Neither Abraham Malherbe[18] nor Wayne Meeks[19] list the army or military matters in their indexes—and their indexes reflect their content. Meeks cites the judgment of the Roman historian A.H.M. Jones that 'Soldiers might rise to the equestrian order or even the senate.'[20] Meeks himself

14. (Καῖσαρ τοὺς στρατιώτας ἐκάλει συστρατιώτας, τῷ ἰσοτίμῳ τοῦ ὀνόματος προθυμοτέρους ποιῶν ἐς τὰς μάχας). Polyainus wrote his Στρατηγικά under Marcus Aurelius. He dedicated the book to him and Lucius Verus in 162 CE when the Parthian War broke out. See A. Neumann, 'Polyainos 2', in *Der kleine Pauly*, IV, pp. 981-82. The standard edition of Polyainus is E. Woelfflin and J. Melber (eds.), *Polyaeni Strategematon* (Bibliotheca Teubneriana; Leipzig: Teubner, 2nd edn, 1967 [1887]). There is no modern English translation; R. Shepherd's translation, *Polyaenus's Stratagems of War* (Chicago: Ares, 1974) reprints a 1793 translation.

15. See G.R. Watson's chapter 'The Soldier in Society', in *The Roman Soldier: Aspects of Greek and Roman Life* (Ithaca, NY: Cornell University Press, 1969), pp. 143-54. R. MacMullen evaluates the role of the army in *Soldier and Civilian in the Roman Army* (Harvard Historical Monographs, 52; Cambridge, MA: Harvard University Press, 1963).

16. MacMullen, *Soldier and Civilian*, pp. 99-103, uses the inscriptions from Aquincum (modern Budapest) to examine the activity of army veterans in one provincial town.

17. MacMullen, *Soldier and Civilian*, p. 103.

18. A. Malherbe, *Social Aspects of Early Christianity* (Philadelphia: Fortress Press, 2nd edn, 1983).

19. W. Meeks, *The First Urban Christians: The Social World of the Apostle Paul* (New Haven: Yale University Press, 1983).

20. Meeks, *Urban Christians*, p. 20.

mentions the army as a 'means of social advancement', but goes on to say:

> ... so far as our sources permit us to judge, this kind of career has little or no relevance for the first generations of Christians, although later on Christians in the army would constitute a problem for the empire and the church's leaders. More germane, as we shall see in the next chapter, are questions about the status and opportunities of artisans and trades people, of slaves and freedpersons, and of women.[21]

Meeks is basically correct though the references to the centurion of Capernaum in the Gospels and Cornelius in Acts 10 might urge some caution. One is surprised that Meeks raises no questions about the presumed absence of the Roman army from NT texts and does not ask whether there are any texts in which one might expect them to be mentioned—as they are in Acts.

1. *Philippi as Roman Military Colony*

The history of Philippi suggests that military language was peculiarly appropriate for the Christians there. Philippi passed under Roman control after the Battle of Pydna (168 BCE). Its history is obscure until its destiny changed in the last half of the first century BCE. After Mark Antony and Octavian defeated the tyrannicides Brutus and Cassius on the plain of Philippi in 42 BCE, Antony settled army veterans at Philippi, gave it the status of colony (memorialized in its name, *Colonia Victrix Philippensis*) and the *ius Romanum*, local government by Roman law.[22] As a colony it was a 'military settlement with exceptional civic privileges.'[23] After defeating Antony in the battle in the Bay of Aktion, Octavian (soon to be called Augustus)

21. Meeks, *Urban Christians*, p. 20
22. The name is inferred from the coin legend AICVP. See P. Collart, *Philippes Ville de Macédoine depuis ses origines jusqu'à la fin de l'époque romaine* (Travaux et Mémoires publiés par les professeurs de l'Institut supérieur d'Etudes françaises et les membres étrangers de l'Ecole français d'Athènes, 5; Paris: E. de Boccard, 1937), p. 227. Strabo describes the town very briefly: after locating it in Thrace he says that 'Philippi was earlier called Crenides, a very small settlement; but it increased in size after the defeat of Brutus and Cassius' (οἱ δὲ Φίλιπποι Κρηνίδες ἐκαλοῦντο πρότερον, κατοικία μικρά· ηὐξήθη δὲ μετὰ τὴν παρὶ Βροῦτον καὶ Κάσσιον ἧτταν [Str. 7.41]).
23. The phrase comes from F.W. Beare, *A Commentary on the Epistle to the Philippians* (HNTC; New York: Harper & Brothers, 1959), p. 6.

settled a second contingent of Roman soldiers at Philippi and named it
Colonia Augusta Julia Philippensis. It bore that name until at least the
first half of the third century, as its coinage and inscriptions testify.[24]

Philippi in the first century bore a distinctly Roman face in its civic
life. As a Roman colony Philippi was probably a *colonia civium
Romanorum*[25] whose citizens had full citizenship in Rome; the colony
was a portion of Rome in a foreign place. Roman citizenship gave
highly prized privileges: the right to hold political office, to participate in Roman deliberative assemblies, to inherit and own property
(*ius commercii*, the right to buy, hold and sell) and to contract a valid
marriage under Roman law. At the same time the citizen owed allegiance to Rome.[26]

The inscriptions[27] from the site testify to the supremacy of Latin
over Greek, at least in official notices. Greek continued in use, but did
not become the predominant language in Philippi again until after
Constantine.

2. *The Rhetorical Importance of Philippians 1.27-30*

Duane F. Watson claims that Phil. 1.27-30 functions as the *narratio*,
the proposition which Paul argues in Philippians.[28] The *exordium*
describes Paul's situation, while Phil. 1.27-30 introduces Paul's goal

24. Collart, *Philippes Ville*, pp. 237-38, pl. XXXI, 1-9. Pl. XXXII, 1 shows
the name on an architrave block from the forum.

25. D. Medicus, 'Coloniae', in *Der kleine Pauly*, I, pp. 1248-50. It is possible
that Philippi was a *colonia Latina,* that is, a colony whose citizens had status equal to
the Latin, non-Roman inhabitants of Italy.

26. See the description in F. Lyall, *Slaves, Citizens, Sons: Legal Metaphors in
the Epistles* (Academie Books; Grand Rapids: Zondervan, 1984), pp. 61-62. Lyall
refers readers to W.W. Buckland, *A Textbook of Roman Law* (Cambridge:
Cambridge University Press, 4th edn, 1970), pp. 96ff., and H. Jolowicz, *Historical
Introduction to the Study of Roman Law* (Cambridge: Cambridge University Press,
3rd edn, 1972), pp. 58-71.

27. Citing B.M. Levick (*Roman Colonies in Southern Asia Minor* [Oxford:
Oxford University Press, 1967], p. 161), P. O'Brien (*The Epistle to the Philippians*
[NICNT; Grand Rapids: Eerdmans, 1991], p. 4 n. 4), points out that '421
inscriptions in Latin and only sixty in Greek, dating from 42 BC to AD 330 had been
found in Philippi'.

28. D.F. Watson, 'A Rhetorical Analysis of Philippians and its Implications for
the Unity Questions', *NovT* 30 (1988), pp. 57-88. Watson's basic rhetorical analysis
is Phil. 1.3-26: *exordium*; 1.27-30: *narratio*; 2.1-3.21: *probatio*; 4.1-20: *peroratio.*

in writing the letter: an exhortation to stand firm in the faith under pressure. Hawthorne[29] points out that in Phil. 1.27-30:

> battle terms, or terms from the athletic games, are present: 'stand firm', 'struggle' [twice], 'suffer' (στήκειν, συναθλοῦν, ἀγών, πάσχειν) characterize this section. One is tempted to compare Paul with a commanding officer or a coach who is determined to inspire his troops, or to encourage his contestants, as he sends them into the fray, with the hope of getting back a good report about how they conducted themselves.

Hawthorne does not go on to provide supporting evidence for what he is tempted to affirm.

In this article I propose to show that Phil. 1.27-30 makes consistent and clear use of military, not athletic, language, to demonstrate the use of that language in historical, tactical and other writers and then to ask how this historical context influences our understanding of other passages in the letter and contributes to Paul's theological insights. While it is not an argument about the structure of the letter, it will support the view of Duane F. Watson that this paragraph contains 'the chief proposition' of the letter (the *narratio*). Moreover, Phil. 1.27-30 forms an *inclusio* with Phil. 3.17-4.1, as the repetition of both language and motifs show. The paragraph deserves special attention.

3. *A Question of Method*

What texts or authors does one read to discover the semantic domain of Paul's letters? Contemporary scholars rarely address that question.[30] One should answer the question posed above by reading (1) the surviving texts from the city (city territory) for which a document is written (inscriptions above all), (2) the (earlier) literature read in the standard education of the time and (3) texts that are earlier or contemporary with the text studied. In addition one should consider the subject matter discussed, the possibility that some later writers reflect the usage of earlier periods, etc.

In examining the military cast to the language of Philippians I will base my conclusions on historians (Herodotus, Thucydides,

---

29. G.F. Hawthorne, *Philippians* (WBC, 43; Waco, TX: Word Books, 1983), p. 54.

30. See F.G. Downing, 'A Bas les Aristos: The Relevance of Higher Literature for the Understanding of the Earliest Christian Writings', *NovT* 30 (1988), pp. 212-30.

Xenophon, Polybius, Dionysius of Halicarnassus, Diodorus Siculus, Appian, Arrian), orators (Lysias, Aeschines, Demosthenes) biographers (Plutarch), writers of military tactical manuals (Aeneas Tacticus, Asclepiodotus, Onosander, Polyaenus) and inscriptions. Unfortunately the tacticians are not yet in the *Thesaurus Linguae Graecae* data base, and word indexes or concordances are practically non-existent. I have read Aeneas Tacticus, Asclepiadotus, Onosander, and Polyaenus, the most important of all, rapidly[31]—though I am not certain I discovered all relevant references.

4. *Philippians 1.27-30*

Onosander[32] refers to two kinds of speeches made by generals to troops. After battle a general should encourage the survivors (παραμυθησάμενος τοὺς ἀνασωθέντας), if defeated; if victorious he should guard against suffering harm through negligence (36.2). He also suggests that a general should encourage his army when losing by shouting out good news, even if it is false! (23). In giving the qualifications one should look for in a general he includes 'a ready speaker' (ἱκανὸς λέγειν, 1.1). In 4.3-6 he describes the kind of speech a general gives before war and the reasons for doing so.

Paul, in the language of Phil. 1.27-4.2, does for the Philippians what Onasander encourages the general to do for the army. The language of obedience in 2.12 correlates with this view. Onasander does not describe the speeches made by generals before battle, though there are significant examples in the historians (for example Cyrus in Xenophon).

Paul uses political and military language to urge the Philippians to

31. The Illinois Greek Club translated *Aeneas Tacticus, Asclepodotus, Onasander* in the Loeb Classical Library (Cambridge: Harvard; London: William Heinemann, 1986 [1928]).

32. Onasander wrote his treatise *Strategicus* [*The General*] in the first century, under Claudius, i.e. he is an exact contemporary of St Paul. A late Platonist, he also wrote a commentary on Plato's *Res Publica.* He dedicated the work to Q. Veranius, consul in 49 CE, who died in Britain in 59 CE. See A. Neumann, 'Onasandros', in *Der kleine Pauly*, IV, p. 300; F.A. Wright, *A History of Later Greek Literature* (New York: Macmillan, 1932), p. 260. The best edition is that of W.A. Oldfather in *Aeneas Tacticus, Asclepiodotus Onasander* (ed. The Illinois Classical Club; LCL; Cambridge: Harvard; London: William Heinemann, 1928). I will also cite Aeneas Tacticus and Asclepiodotus from this edition.

remain firm in their faith. His words resemble, in part, a speech given during battle, though there are significant differences. πολιτεύεσθαι (Phil. 1.27), a *hapax legomenon* in Paul's authentic letters,[33] is a striking term.[34] It occurs primarily in the middle, as in this passage. Its fundamental sense is 'to be a citizen' or 'freeman, to live in a free state'.[35] It can also mean to engage in public life. So, for example, Epictetus claims that Epicureans avoid the life of the citizen: διὰ τοῦτο φησὶν ['Επίκουρος] οὐδὲ πολιτεύεσθαι τὸν νοῦν ἔχοντα (1.22.6; cf 3.9.9). In his long discourse on the Cynic philosopher, Epictetus asks whether the Cynic will participate in public life (εἰ πολιτεύσεται, 3.22.83) and answers that he will engage in a greater public life rather than debating about imports and exports by discussing the blessed life and the unfortunate life, good fortune and misfortune, slavery and freedom. 'When a man is engaged in such exalted politics, do *you* ask me if he is to engage in politics?' (τηλικαύτην πολιτείαν πολιτευομένου ἀνθρώπου σύ μου πυνθάνῃ εἰ πολιτεύσεται; 3.22.85). In that way the Cynic contributes to the preservation of life in community (διασώσει τὴν κοινωνίαν, 3.22.77).

In his 1954 article Brewer calls attention to the political status of Philippi as a colony governed by *ius Italicum*, whose citizens included *Augustales* devoted to the worship of the divine Augustus, and where the ruler cult continued throughout the first century.[36] Brewer

33. In Acts 23.1 Paul uses the term to describe his life-style.

34. The two major studies in English are R.R. Brewer, 'The meaning of πολιτεύεσθε in Phil 1:27', *JBL* 73 (1954), pp. 76-83, and E.C. Miller, 'πολιτεύεσθε in Phil. 1.27: 'Some Philological and Thematic Observations', *JSNT* 15 (1982), pp. 86-96. See also L. Portefaix, *Sisters Rejoice: Paul's Letter to the Philippians and Luke–Acts as Received by First-Century Philippian Women* (ConBNT; Stockholm: Almqvist & Wiksell, 1988), pp. 138-43.

35. LSJ, *s.v.*; see Th. 2.46: X. *An.* 3.2.26, etc.

36. Brewer, 'The meaning of πολιτεύεσθε', p. 80. He cites a Neapolis inscription which refers 'to an unnamed Roman magistrate (*duumvir*) at Philippi' as *'pontifex, flamen, divi Claudi Philippi'*, cited from J. Lightfoot's commentary (*Saint Paul's Epistle to the Philippians: A Revised Text with Introduction, Notes, and Dissertations*, [London: Macmillan, 7th edn, 1883], p. 51 n. 4). Surprisingly Brewer nowhere cites Collart's magisterial work, which cites seven inscriptions relevant to ruler cult at Philippi from before the time of Vespasian. Collart cites the fuller text of the Neapolis inscription: *P. Cornelius Asper Atiarius Montanus / equo publico honoratus, item ornamentis decu / rionatus et IIviralicis, pontifex, flamen*

suggests that Paul formulated Phil. 1.27-30, 2.9-11, and 3.20 in conscious opposition to the ruler cult of the emperor Nero. He summarizes his interpretation as follows:

> Read in the light of the three passages referred to they [the terms πολιτεύεσθε in 1:27 and πολίτευμα in 3:20] seem to be chosen deliberately and for a good reason. Paul seems to have employed these words to say, 'Continue to discharge your obligations as citizens and residents of Philippi faithfully and as a Christian should; but do not yield to the patriotic pressure to give to Nero that which belongs to Christ alone. Remember that while you are members of a Roman colony you are also a colony of heaven from which you are awaiting the return of your divine Lord and Savior. So stand firm. Never waver in the conflict. You may have to suffer for Christ, but remember that he is your deliverer too.'[37]

Brewer cites numerous passages from early Judaism (Philocrates to Aristeas, Philo, Josephus) and the Apostolic Fathers to support his case, but only one text from earlier Greek authors: Xenophon, *Cyropaedia* 1.1.1: 'The thought once occurred to us how many republics have been overthrown by people preferred to live under any form of government other than a republican...' (῎Εννοιά ποθ' ἡμῖν ἐγένετο ὅσαι δημοκρατίαι κατελύθησαν ὑπὸ τῶν ἄλλως πῶς βουλομένων πολιτεύεσθαι μᾶλλον ἢ ἐν δημοκρατία...)[38] His insistence on interpreting Philippians in the light of public life in a Roman colony, however, is entirely persuasive to me and is one of the stimulants for this paper.

Brewer's singular use of emperor cult to explain the language is possible, but not compelling. Excavators have found evidence that the colonists paid special attention to military events both local and elsewhere in the empire. The goddess Victoria appears in an *ex voto*, winged, holding the palm of victory in her left hand and a wreath in her outstretched right.[39] She appears in similar iconographic pose on a series of coins of Philippi, with the legend VIC(toria) AVG(usta). The reverse shows three military standards ringed by a beaded 'milling',

divi Claudi Philippis, / ann. XXIII, h. s. e. (*CIL* III.650). Note the reference to public honors, equivalent to the ἔντιμος of Phil. 2.29.

37. Brewer, 'The meaning of πολιτεύεσθε', p. 83.

38. Cited from W. Miller, *Xenophon V; Cyropaedia* (2 vols.; LCL; Cambridge, MA: Harvard University Press; London: William Heinemann, 1914), I, pp. 2-3.

39. Collart, *Philippes Ville*, p. 410; pl. LXVII, 2.

with the legend COHOR(s) to the left and PRAE(toria) to the right, and below the standards PHIL.[40] Collart points out that 'Ces pièces apportent la preuve que Philippies fut colonisée aussi par une cohorte de prétoriens.' The cult of Victoria Augusta was therefore early on present at Philippi.

The phrase ἀξίως τοῦ εὐαγγελίου (Phil. 1.27) modifies πολιτεύεσθε, thus describing the fitting mode of living as a citizen. Herodotus 6.102-108 describes the preliminaries to the battle of Marathon. The Plataeans alone came to support the Athenians (108). Herodotus recounts the battle itself in 6.109-117. Though the Greeks were fewer in number, they charged the Persians, so that the Persians thought they were mad. 'The Athenians, however, when they engaged in close ranks with the barbarians, fought in a manner worthy of record,'[41] (6.112), that is, their exploits deserved reporting. Greeks before them had feared the very name Mede—and the Persians wore Medic dress.[42] That made the Athenian united front victory worthy of the historian's report.

The criterion of worthiness is the gospel (εὐαγγέλιον), a term which also has a long history in the imperial cult. The parade case is the well known calendar inscription from Priene:

'WHEREAS Providence that orders all our lives has in her display of concern and generosity in our behalf adorned our lives with the highest good: **Augustus**, whom she has filled with *arete* for the benefit of humanity, and has in her beneficence granted us and those who will come after us [a Savior] who has made war to cease and who shall put everything [in peaceful] order; and whereas Caesar, [when he was manifest], transcended the expectations of [all who had anticipated the good news], not only by leaving no expectation of surpassing him to those who would

40. Collart, *Philippes Ville*, p. 232, pl. XXX, 8-11.
41. Hdt. 6.112. Ἀθηναῖοι δὲ ἐπείτε ἀθρόοι προσέμειξαν τοῖσι βαρβάροισι. ἐμάχοντο ἀξίως λόγου. The translation is from *Herodotus* (trans. H. Cary; London: George Bell and Sons, 1904), the Greek text according to C. Hude (ed.), *Herodoti Historiae* (2 vols.; Scriptorum Classicorum Bibliotheca Oxoniensis; Oxford: Clarendon Press, 3rd edn, 1927).
42. See W.W. How and J. Wells, *A Commentary on Herodotus* (2 vols.; Oxford: Clarendon Press, 1928), II, pp. 112-13. Cyrus's speech to his commanders before the Great Battle in X. *Cyr.* VI, 4.20 urges each to show himself 'worthy of command by showing himself fearless in his bearing, in his countenance and in his speeches' (ἐπιδεικνύτω τις τοῖς ἀρχομένοις ἑαυτὸν ἄξιον ἀρχῆς, ἄφοβον δεικνὺς καὶ σχῆμα καὶ πρόσωπον καὶ λόγους).

come after him, with the result that the birthday of our God signalled the beginning of Good News for the world because of him...[43]

The term 'gospel' is at home in ruler cult, though Stuhlmacher argues from the plural in the calendar inscription that the NT use of the term is not drawn from this usage.[44] The term may have political and, possibly, military implications.[45]

Generals fought alongside their troops in ancient warfare. Generals were not far-off officers in a command post; they genuinely wanted to fight beside and share the dangers of their soldiers. Archilochus described the ideal commander as follows: 'Give me a man short and squarely set upon his legs, a man full of heart, not to be shaken from the place he plants his feet.'[46] Later theorists were less certain that commanders should undergo such danger.[47]

---

43. *OGIS* II, 458.32-41. The translation is from F.W. Danker, *Benefactor: Epigraphic Study of a Graeco-Roman and New Testament Semantic Field* (St Louis: Clayton Publishing House, 1982), p. 217. The Greek text is reprinted in P. Wendland, *Die hellenistisch-römische Kultur in ihren Beziehungen zu Judentum und Christentum: Die urchristlichen Literaturformen* (HNT, 2; Tübingen: Mohr, 2nd and 3rd edns, 1912), pp. 409-10, Beilage 8. W.H. Buckler, 'An Epigraphic Contribution to Letters', *CR* 41 (1927), pp. 119-21, issued a revised text. I reproduce his text as printed by P. Stuhlmacher, *Das paulinische Evangelium. I. Vorgeschichte* (FRLANT, 95; Göttingen: Vandenhoeck & Ruprecht, 1968), p. 186 n. 3.

44. Stuhlmacher, *Das paulinische Evangelium*, I, pp. 199-220. Julius Schniewind proposed a major examination of the term in fifteen sections. The two Lieferungen he published carried it only through section 7—and he intended to treat Hellenistic sacral use and Emperor cult in sections 9 and 10. See *Euangelion: Ursprung und erste Gestalt des Begriffs Evangelium. Untersuchungen* (Darmstadt: Wissenschaft-liche Buchgesellschaft, 1970 [1929–31]).

45 See G. Friedrich, 'εὐαγγελίζομαι, εὐαγγέλιον, πρευαγγελίζομαι, εὐαγγελιστής', *TDNT*, III, pp. 721-25.

46. Fr. 93 [= Fr. 60, Diehl, Fr. 58 Bergk]: ἀλλά μοι σιμικρός τις εἴη καὶ περὶ κνήμησ' ἰδεῖν / ῥοικός, ἀσφαλέως βεβηκὼς πόσσι, καρδίης πλέος. F. Lassere (ed.), *Archiloque Fragments* (trans. and commentary by A. Bonnard; Collection des Universités de France; Paris: Société d'édition 'Les Belles Lettres', 1958), p. 30. Translation from V.D. Hanson, *The Western Way of War: Infantry Battle in Classical Greece* (New York: Alfred A. Knopf, 1989), p. 110. The first two lines of Archilochos read 'I don't like the towering captain with the spraddly length of leg, one who swaggers in his lovelocks and clean shaves beneath his chin'.

47. See X. *Mem.* 3.1; Onos. 33.1: 'The general should fight cautiously rather than boldly, or should keep away altogether from a hand-to-hand fight with the enemy.'

One result is that '...a Greek commander's absence on occasion
could set off panic among the men at his side who watched him go
down.'[48] Xenophon advised his officers (στρατηγοί, ταξίαρχοι καὶ
λοχαγοί) that they should be more brave than their troops, exercise
forethought for their good, and set an example of enduring hard-
ship.[49] The commander was in many ways another soldier, fighting
alongside his troops.

Paul's captivity in Rome meant his absence from Philippi. But
Paul's exhortation is not dependent on his physical presence. He
stresses that he is concerned about their conduct whether he is present
in Philippi or not: ἵνα εἴτε ἐλθὼν καὶ ἰδὼν ὑμᾶς εἴτε ἀπὼν ἀκούω
τὰ περὶ ὑμῶν (Phil. 1.27). One purpose Paul has in writing the
Philippians is to assure them that he is still working with and for
them. He sends Epaphroditus (his ἀδελφὸς καὶ συνεργὸς καὶ
συστρατιώτης, Phil. 2.25) back to them so that his presence would
bring joy (Phil. 2.28), and he urges the Philippians to receive him and
regard all such as worthy of civic honour (καὶ τοὺς τοιούτους
ἐντίμους ἔχετε, Phil. 2.29). The term ἔντιμος comes from civic life.
Thus Xenophon, *Cyr.* 3.1.8, describes Armenians of high rank as
ἔντιμος, the antonym to ἄδοξοι ('without reputation or honor').

'No one alive today has ever experienced anything really like a
hoplite battle.'[50] That truism has a wider application. No one has
experienced anything like the Macedonian phalanx or the Roman
legion in battle either. Ancient warfare in Homeric times seems to be
primarily multiple individual combats.[51] The hoplite λόχος which
succeeded it was in turn replaced by the Macedonian φάλανξ. The
Roman *legio* later replaced the Macedonian phalanx. In all three
however it was massed mankind, not individual prowess that won

48. See Hanson, *Way of War*, p. 109.

49. X. *An.* 3.1.37. On the relation of leader to soldier in classical Greece see
E.L. Wheeler, 'The General as Hoplite', in V.D. Hanson (ed.), *Hoplites: The
Classical Greek Battle Experience* (London: Routledge & Kegan Paul, 1991),
pp 121-70. Wheeler gives extensive documentation from both classical and later
Hellenistic historians such as Polybius and Plutarch and from the tactician
Polyaenus. This volume also has a short glossary of Greek military terms discussed
in the book. A dictionary of Greek military terms is a desideratum.

50. J. Lazenby, 'The Killing Zone', in Hanson (ed.), *Hoplites*, p. 87.

51. Wheeler, 'General as Hoplite', pp. 122-24.

battles. Individual skills were not important.[52] It was rather the force of the massed unit that won battles and wars.

στήκετε ἐν ἑνὶ πνεύματι, μιᾷ ψυχῇ συναθλοῦντες (Phil. 1.27) describes the attitude of the soldiers drawn up in line, τασσόμενοι. Onosander 27 points out that soldiers should stay in formation, not leaving their ranks, whether pursuing a fleeing enemy or themselves retreating. 'In short, let him see that nothing is better for them than to remain in order, nothing more dangerous than to break ranks.'[53] Nothing leads to more certain defeat than having one or another soldier break the line and allow the enemy to pour through. Thus Cyrus, when ordering (τάττειν) his army for a march, 'always kept drawn up in order one body of troops who were to pursue and another who were to stay with him; but he never suffered his main line to be broken' (πᾶσαν δὲ τὴν τάξιν λυθῆναι οὐδέποτε εἴα).[54]

The verb most used to describe staying in line in classical Greek is μένειν. Euripides says the test of a man's courage is 'to stand (μένειν) and look and outface the spear's swift stroke, keeping the line firm.'[55] Remaining in line is the key to victory.[56] According to Xenophon the Theban general Epaminondus held the opinion that it was very difficult to discover those who want to stay in line when they see some of their own men in flight.[57] Even one who rushed ahead of the line and did glorious deeds was a danger, as the case of the Spartan Aristodemos suggests:

> However, when it was debated which of them had been the bravest, the Spartans who were present decided that Aristodemos, evidently wishing to die on account of the disgrace attached to him, and acting like a madman,

52. Lazenby, 'The Killing Zone', p. 103. P. Connolly, *Greece and Rome at War* (Englewood Cliffs, NJ: Prentice–Hall, 1981) gives a good overview of the changing formations and tactics.

53. ὅλως δὲ μηδέν σφισιν ἄμεινον εἶναι λεγέτω τοῦ μένειν ἐν τάξει μηδ' ἐπισφαλέστερον τοῦ λύειν.

54. X. *Cyr.* 5.3.58. In *Cyr.* 6.1.43 Cyrus suggests that if an army changes their order on the spur of the moment, they will be thrown into confusion.

55. ἀνδρὸς δ' ἔλεγχος οὐχὶ τόξ' εὐψυχίας, ἀλλ' ὃς μέων βλέπει τε κάτιδερκεται δορὸς ταχεῖαν ἄλοκα τάξιν ἐμβεβώς. E. *HF* 162-165, English translation from Lazenby, 'The Killing Zone', p. 91.

56. See D. 3.17.

57. μάλα γὰρ χαλεπὸν εὑρεῖν τοὺς ἐθελήσαντες μέδνειν, ἐπειδάν τινες φεύγοντας τῶν ἑαυτῶν ὁρῶσι. X. *HG* 7.5.24.

and leaving the ranks, had performed great deeds; but that Posidonius, not wishing to die, had shown himself a brave man; and therefore that he was the better.'[58]

The value placed on not breaking ranks is clear. The case is no different in the Roman army. Vegetius (4–5 CE) describes training for battle formation (single line, double line, square, wedge and circle) as follows:

There is nothing which has proved to be of greater service in action than for the men to learn by constant practice to keep their allotted positions in the line, and nowhere to close or to open their ranks disadvantageously. Men packed closely together have no room for fighting and merely get in one another's way. Similarly, if they are scattered and there is too much daylight between them they give the enemy an opportunity of breaking through. Inevitably, if the line is cut through and the enemy attacks the fighting troops from behind, there is immediate panic and universal disorder... If the young soldiers perfect these movements by constant practice they will more easily keep their ranks in real fighting.[59]

Thus soldiers needed to preserve unity of stance and purpose in an ancient battle. If the line broke at any point, there was danger of a rout and the battle (and war) was lost. Most ancient wars were one battle affairs. The Theban general (στρατηγός) Epaminondas made a strong incursion (ἔμβολον ἰσχυρόν) with his cavalry and drew up in line all his foot soldiers too, thinking that, if the horse should cut through (διακόψειεν), the entire opposing force would be conquered. 'For it is extremely difficult to find those who want to stand fast, when they see people of their own army in flight.'[60]

Paul uses the verb 'stand' (στήκετε), a late formation from the perfect ἔστηκα of ἵστημι, as the antonym to flee (φεύγειν).[61] The verb ἵστημι is not frequent in a military sense. Xenophon describes a

58. Hdt. 9.71.3. Most of the references above came from the article by Lazenby ('The Killing Zone').

59. Vegetius 1.26, as translated in Watson, *Roman Soldier*, pp. 70-71. For the Latin text see Flavius Vegetius Renatus, *Epitoma Rei Militaris*, edit. with an English translation by L.F. Stelten (New York: Peter Lang, 1990), pp. 49-51. After Paul, Ignatius praised the Magnesians for their orderliness (πολυεύτακτον, 1.1), using a military metaphor.

60. X. *HG* 7.5.24. μάλα γὰρ χαλεπὸν εὑρεῖν τοὺς ἐθελήσαντες μένειν, ἐπειδάν τινας φεύγοντας τῶς ἑαυτῶν ὁρῶσι.

61. LSJ, *s.v.*, gives references only to the LXX, NT, papyri and Ath. 10.412e.

debate in the Spartan league in *HG* 5.2.23. Choosing a man as leader, the Acanthians argued, and a force from Lacedaimon as quickly as possible would lead the undecided city states (πόλεις) to stand firm (στῆναι), while those compelled by force would fight together less. Hierocles includes a joke about a horse in his *Facetiae*: When a learned simpleton was asked whether the horse he was selling was cowardly, he responded 'No, by my father's well-being; for he stood fast all alone in his stall.'[62] This reply by a naïve young man shows that 'standing fast' is a mark of bravery—though in this case it is nonsense that provides the humor.

The phrases ἐν ἑνὶ πνεύματι, μιᾷ ψυχῇ describe the mind-set needed to function militarily. 'Unit skills were...important.'[63] Battles were won or lost on the basis of unity of mind, purpose, and action. Lazenby[64] calls attention to the elegiac poet Tyrtaeus, who exhorts the Spartans to fight standing by one another because then fewer of them will die.[65] Morale was also a key component in an army's success. Aeneas Tacticus urges the defender of a city to make it a major goal to 'win over the mass of the citizens to a spirit of loyalty' (ὁμόνοια).[66] Similarly, a wise commander does not send defensive troops out in 'small and scattered groups,' since that leads to self-service and defeat. Rather they must be close together on the march.[67]

The compound verb συναθλοῦντες stresses the need for joint

62. οὐ μὰ τὴν τοῦ πατρός μου σωτηρίαν· ἐν τῷ στραύλῳ γὰρ μόνος ἕστηκεν. Hierocl. 10. Cited from A. Thierfelder (ed. and trans.), *Philogelos der Lachfreund von Hierokles und Philagrios* (Tusculum-Bücherei; Munich: Heimeran Verlag, 1968), pp. 32-33.

63. Lazenby, 'The Killing Zone', p. 103.

64. Tyrt. fr. 6-7 [regarded by Diehl as one poem, cited by Lazenby as Nr. 10], p. 15. Ὦ νέοι, ἀλλὰ μάχεσθε παρ' ἀλλήλοισι μένοντες, μὴ δὲ φυγῆς αἰσχρῆς ἄρχετε μηδὲ φόβου. Cited from E. Diehl (ed.), *Anthologia Lyrica Graeca*. I. *Poetae Elegiaci* (Bibliotheca Teubneriana; Leipzig: B.G. Teubner, 1954). The 'classical' edition of T. Bergk, *Poetae Lyrici Graeci* (Leipzig: Reichenbach, 1853), p. 319, gives the older numbering followed by Lazenby ('The Killing Zone').

65. Lazenby refers to Tyrt. fr. 8.11-13 [= 11.11-13 Bergk]: οἵ μὲν γὰρ τολμῶσι παρ' ἀλλήλοισι μένοντες ἔς τ' αὐτοσχεδίην καὶ προμάχους ἰέναι, παυρότεροι θνήισκουσι, σοῦσι δὲ λαὸν ὀπίσω·

66. 14.1: τὸ δὲ πλῆθος τῶν πολιτῶν εἰς ὁμόναιαν τέως μάλιστα χρὴ προάγειν. In 17 Aeneas describes the dangers to a city in which harmony (ἁρμονία) is missing.

67. Aen. Tact. 15.2: σποραδὴν καὶ κατ' ὀλίγους.

action in war. The verb, which recurs in Phil. 4.3, occurs in athletic, gladiatorial and military contexts. O'Brien comments that the occurrence of the term ἀγών in Phil. 1.30 leads most English commentators, following Lightfoot, to stress the [Panhellenic] games metaphor, while German commentators stress gladiatorial combat.[68] He misinterprets Lightfoot. ἀγών is also a military term. Herodotus describes the battle at Thermopylae in book seven. The Persian Xerxes could not believe that his immortals could not conquer so few Greeks. But the Lacedamonians fought with intelligence and discipline.

> ... and whenever they turned their backs, they retreated in close order; but the barbarians seeing them retreat, followed with a shout and clamour; then they, being overtaken, wheeled around so as to front the barbarians, and having faced about, overthrew an inconceivable number of the Persians... Thus they strove at that time. On the following day the barbarians fought with no better success (τότε μὲν οὕτως ἠγωνίσαντο, τῇ δ' ὑστεραίῃ οἱ βάρβαροι οὐδὲν ἄμεινον ἀέθλεον).[69]

One might compare the use of the term συναγωνίζεσθαι in relation to warfare. Pericles said Athenians should not fear that the Lacedaimonians might appropriate money and hire away the mercenary sailors from Athens, since 'how many of our foreign sailors would, for the sake of a few days' extra pay, fight on the other side (συναγωνίζεσθαι) at the risk not only of being defeated, but also of being outlawed from their own cities.'[70] According to Plato, Socrates said that a trierarch should be so superior to his crew that 'they, regarded as inferior by him, will fight together with him against the enemies' (καταφρονηθέντας συναγωνίζεσθαί σοι πρὸς τοὺς πολεμίους).[71]

68. O'Brien, *Philippians*, pp. 150-51. O'Brien misinterprets Lightfoot, in my opinion, who makes no comment about the metaphor in συναθλέω and says of ἀγών quite simply '"a gladiatorial or athletic contest," as in 1 Tim. 6.12, 2 Tim. 4. 7; compare , ver. 27'(see Lightfoot, *Philippians*, p. 106).

69. Hdt. 7.211.3-212. In 1.67.1 he uses ἀθλέω in similar fashion.

70. Th. 1.143.2, translation from *Thucydides History of the Peloponnesian War* (trans. R. Warner, with introduction and notes by M.I. Finley; New York: Penguin Books, 1972). LSJ, *s.v*, also cites X. *Cyr.* 4.5.49. Pericles uses the term in a speech in 2.63.1 when encouraging the Athenians after two incursions by the enemy into Attica; cf. 5.109.1. These last two references from T.C. Geoffrion, 'Philippians: Paul's Letter of Exhortation Calling Citizens of Heaven to Remain Steadfast' (Dissertation, Lutheran School of Theology at Chicago, 1992).

71. Pl. *Alc.* 119c.1-2. See also Hdt. 7.21

Paul urges the Philippians to fight together τῇ πίστει τοῦ εὐαγγελίου, 'for the *pistis* of the Gospel' (1.27). The phrase clarifies what Paul meant by 'in a manner worthy of the Gospel' earlier in the verse. But just what does πίστις mean in this context? In the Greek political arena πίστις means a pledge of good faith, the assurance given to seal a treaty.[72] 'For the Samians immediately gave a pledge of their faith and oaths about confederation with the Greeks.'[73] Later, after the defeat of the Persians, the Athenians 'took into the alliance (ἐς τὸ συμμαχικὸν ἐποιήσαντο) the Samians, Chians, Lesbians and other islanders, who were then serving with the Greeks (οἳ ἔτυχον συστρατευόμενοι τοῖσι ῞Ελληνες), binding them by pledges and oaths that they would remain firm and not revolt' (πίστι τε καταλαβόντες καὶ ὁρκίοισι ἐμμενέειν τε καὶ μὴ ἀποστήσεσθαι).'[74] The coincidence of language with Phil. 1.27-38 is striking.

Fear (φόβος) is the great enemy of unity of purpose in war. Where fear stalks the troops, there is danger of sudden turning tail and running. Commanders therefore deal with fear whenever they detect it—and rapidly. When Cyrus detected fear arising from the army's perception of the apparent numerical superiority of the Persian army, he dealt with it immediately in speeches that reminded his soldiers of their earlier victories, their increased strength, and their superior equipment (Xenophon, *Cyr.* 6.2.13-20).

Therefore Paul urges the Philippians not to fear in the phrase μὴ πτυρόμενοι ἐν μηδενί (Phil. 1.28). The verb πτύρομαι is an unusual term, used infrequently. Plutarch recounts an incident from the Second Punic War. When Hannibal invaded Italy and threatened Rome itself, Q. Fabius Maximus counseled not engaging him in direct combat. Flaminius determined not to wait to fight in Rome, but to engage Hannibal in battle. When he mounted his horse, for no reason it trembled, against all reason grew frightened and threw Flaminius. He did not recognize the omen, marched out, and was destroyed with

72. See the numerous references in LSJ, *s.v.* II.1.

73. Hdt. 9.92.1: αὐτίκα γὰρ Σάμιοι πίστιν τε καὶ ὅρκια ἐποιεῦντο συμμαχίης πέρι πρὸς τοὺς ῞Ελληνας. LSJ translates 'make a treaty by an exchange of assurances and oaths'. The same two words are used together in Ar. *Lys.* 1185, and numerous other passages.

74. Hdt. 9.106.4, trans. by Cary, called to my attention by Geoffrion, *Philippians: Paul's Letter of Exhortation*, pp. 66-67.

his army at the Trasimene Lake.[75] When the praetor Pomponius heard the news, he called a popular assembly to consult about safety and security (περὶ σωτηρίας αὐτῶν καὶ ἀσφαλείας, 3.5). Diodorus Siculus uses the term of frightened horses in similar fashion.[76]

ὑπὸ τῶν ἀντικειμένων describes the opposing army. I have not found a good example of ἀντικείμαι in military contexts. The usual term there is οἱ πολέμιοι. But LSJ (*s.v.*) calls attention to Exod. 23.22 and Isa. 66.6 in the Septuagint and Luke 13.17 in the NT. These make opposition clear, but not opposition in war. In Exodus Yahweh promises that if Israel keeps the covenant stipulations, they will be his people, a royal priesthood and holy nation. 'I will be an enemy to your enemies and I will set myself against those drawn up against you' (ἐχθρεύσω τοῖς ἐχθροῖς σου καὶ ἀντικείσομαι τοῖς ἀντικειμένοις σοι). Isa. 66.6 uses the term similarly: 'a shouting voice from the city, a voice from the temple, a voice of the Lord giving vengeance to those drawn against you' (φωνὴ κραυγῆς ἐκ πόλεως, φωνὴ ἐκ ναοῦ, φωνὴ κυρίου ἀνταποδιδόντος ἀνταπόδοσιν τοῖς ἀντικειμένοις). Luke 13.17 uses the term of Jesus' opponents in a Sabbath controversy.

The antithesis 'for them a demostration of destruction, but of your victory' (αὐτοῖς ἔνδειξις ἀπωλείας, ὑμῶν δὲ σωτηρίας, 1.28) also finds a good home in military contexts. The messenger in Aeschylus' *Persae* reports the outcome of the Battle of Salamis to Atossa, the Persian Queen. He contrasts the good fortune of those who died quickly with the misfortune of those who lived after the battle (ὅσοι δὲ λοιποὶ κἄτυχον σωτηρίας).[77] The noun here means survival. In Thucydides 2.60 Pericles 'called an assembly to put fresh courage' into the Athenians after the second incursion of the Spartans into Attica has disheartened them. He tells them they are 'losing [their]

---

75. Plu. *Fab.* 3.1 αὐτὸς δ' ἐπὶ τὸν ἵππον ἀλάμενος ἐξ οὐδενὸς αἰτίου προδήλου παραλόγως ἐτρόμου τοῦ ἵππου γενεομένου καὶ πτυρέντος, ἐξέπεσε... Cited according to C. Lindskog and K. Ziegler (eds.), *Plutarchi Vitae Parallelae* (Bibliotheca Teubneriana; Leipzig: B.G. Teubner, 2nd edn, 1959), I, 2, p. 50.

76. DS 2.19; 17.34.6.

77. A. *Pers.* 508, cited from G. Murray (ed.), *Aeschli Septem quae Supersunt Tragoediae* (Scriptorum Classicorum Bibliotheca Oxoniensis; Oxford: Clarendon Press, 1938).

grip on the common safety' (τοῦ κοινοῦ τῆς σωτηρίας ἀφίεσθε, 2.60.4; cf. διασώσωμεν, 2.62.3).[78]

τὸ ὑπὲρ Χριστοῦ, τὸ ὑπὲρ πάσχειν (Phil. 1.29) is a striking phrase. The verb πάσχειν is regularly used of suffering harm from a military opponent.[79] The preposition ὑπέρ is used of the one on whose behalf one fights. Onosander advises placing brothers, close friends and lovers next to each other in the ranks (τάττειν), because one fights more recklessly on behalf of the beloved who is near by.[80] Paul uses the phrase ὑπὲρ Χριστοῦ twice, though only in the second instance is the verb πάσχειν added. Compare, for example, the phrases in 1 Cor. 15.29, 2 Cor. 5.20, 2 Cor. 12.10; in these passages Christ suffers on behalf of others. The idea that Christians suffer 'on behalf of Christ' is unique in Paul.

The term ἀγών (Phil. 1.30) is frequently used of a military engagement. Dionysius Halicarnassus *(Ant. Rom.* 3.16.2), speaks of 'the struggle on behalf of all' (τὸν ὑπὲρ ἁπάντων ἀγῶνα).[81] In his Introduction, Aeneas Tacticus uses the term ἀγών in conjunction with κίνδυνος to describe dangers encountered by an army invading foreign territory and to describe the desperate struggle to defend one's own city when attacked. The citation of Onosander above uses the verb ἀγωνίζεσθαι.[82] Dibelius comments on Phil. 1.30 that 'ἀγών is here, when preceded by ἀντικείμεναι, translated as "battle"'.[83]

Phil. 1.27-30 contains the first extended description of the Philippians in the letter. The convergence of such a large amount of military language in this paragraph is not accidental. Phil. 1.27-30 uses a consistent linguistic field to describe Christians as those engaged in a battle against people who fight against the gospel. Such a battle demands unity of mind and action. Paul summons the Philippians to

78. Cf. G.F. Hawthorne, 'The Interpretation and Translation of Philippians 1.28b', *ExpTim* 95 (1983), pp. 80-81

79. Onos. 36.2 (τοῦ μὴ παθεῖν).

80. Onos. 24: ὅταν γὰρ ᾖ τὸ κινδυνεῦον τὸ πλησίον προσφιλέστερον, ἀνάγκη τὸν ἀναπῶντα φιλοκινδυνότερον ὑπὲρ τοῦ πέλας ἀγωνίζεσθαι.

81. See also 3.18.19. Cited according to C. Jacoby (ed.), *Dionysi Halicarnasensis Antiquitatum Romanarum quae supersunt* (Bibliotheca Teubneriana; 4 vols.; Leipzig: B.G. Teubner, 1885).

82. Onos. 24: ἀνάγκη τὸν ἀγαπῶντα φιλοκινδυνότερον ὑπὲρ τοῦ πέλας ἀγωνίζεσθαι...

83. M. Dibelius, *An die Thessalonicher I II An die Philipper* (HNT, 11; Tübingen: Mohr [Paul Siebeck], 3rd. edn, 1937), p. 71.

'act as citizens of a city ought to act' (πολιτεύεσθε, 1.27). The paragraph opens up a section that corresponds to a general's military harangue before battle, encouraging his soldiers to fight bravely with a common purpose on behalf of family, city and fame. Paul uses language that the Philippians, citzens of a Roman military colony, would understand well. He appropriates the language to encourage the Philippians to stand fast in his absence.

2 THESSALONIANS AND THE CHURCH OF THESSALONICA

Karl P. Donfried

It is with gratitude that I contribute this essay in honor of John Hurd. In over twenty years of friendship our common work on 1 and 2 Thessalonians has demonstrated both remarkable affinity[1] and substantial divergence.[2] Always, however, I have learned and been stimulated by John's creativity and originality and it has been a high privilege, over a long period of years and in a wide variety of Pauline seminars within the Society of Biblical Literature, to observe his careful analysis of texts and to engage his probing mind in dialogue. In what follows I will attempt to continue the conversation about a key concern to both of us and one for which no scholarly agreement has yet emerged.

In my article 'The Cults of Thessalonica and the Thessalonian Correspondence'[3] I argued that both the civic and religious cults of the city are a decisive factor in understanding the milieu in which the Thessalonian Christian congregation existed and that much of Paul's argument in 1 Thessalonians could be interpreted with greater accuracy when these components were studied with care. In the comments that follow it will be urged that this same cultic background also serves as a critical factor for the comprehension of the intention of 2 Thessalonians. Since this has not been the usual interpretation of

1. J.C. Hurd, 'Paul Ahead of his Time: 1 Thess. 2.13-16', in P. Richardson (ed.), *Anti-Judaism in Early Christianity: Paul and the Gospels* (Studies in Christianity and Judaism, 2; Waterloo: Wilfrid Laurier Press, 1986), I, pp. 21-36, and 'Concerning the Structure of 1 Thessalonians' (unpublished; presented at the Paul Seminar, Society of Biblical Literature Annual Meeting, Los Angeles, 1972).

2. J.C. Hurd, 'Concerning the Authenticity of 2 Thessalonians' (unpublished; presented at the Paul Seminar, Society of Biblical Literature Annual Meeting, Dallas, 1983).

3. K.P. Donfried, 'The Cults of Thessalonica and the Thessalonian Correspondence', *NTS* 31 (1985), pp. 336-56.

the setting of 2 Thessalonians it will be necessary at the outset to comment briefly on the setting of 2 Thessalonians in terms of its rhetorical intention, its authorship and its concrete background.

There is an emerging consensus that 2 Thessalonians belongs to the deliberative genre of rhetoric. This genre includes honor and advantage as the standard topics and in 2 Thessalonians these topics are used to advise the audience concerning their actions in the present and their outcome in the future. Recognizing that 2 Thessalonians is an example of deliberative rhetoric permits the interpreter to be sensitive to the argumentation of the letter. An examination of the various components of the rhetorical structure allows one to be perceptive to the neuralgic issues at stake in the dialogue that this author is having with his audience. Thus, the *partitio* (2.1-2; statement of the proposition) immediately indicates that a major point of contention between the writer and his adversaries is related to the claim 'that the day of the Lord has already come' (2.2) and the *probatio* (2.3-15; proof) makes evident that the source of this false teaching is related to the Spirit (2.15). Another example of the importance of examining carefully the various rhetorical units can be seen in the exhortation in 2 Thess. 3.1-15. Hughes has demonstrated that even though 'exhortation is not a standard *pars orationis*, we are justified in identifying certain sections of certain letters in the Pauline corpus as exhortation sections, because of a variety of parallels to both "literary" and "nonliterary" letters, and because of the strong connection of deliberative rhetoric to exhortation'.[4] This last point is supported by the long section on exhortation, especially given the brevity of 2 Thessalonians, and the rather detailed mandate to work (3.6-15) presented in four different ways. Even these cursory glimpses at the rhetorical structure of 2 Thessalonians have provided us with some important indications concerning the goal that the author of this document is pursuing.

Contemporary scholarship is not of one mind concerning the authorship of 2 Thessalonians and the range of opinion is broad: some hold that the Apostle is indeed the author; other scholars suggest that this is a pseudepigraphical letter written in the late first century to a situation quite different than the one addressed in 1 Thessalonians, even, many would insist, to a church other than Thessalonica itself.

4. F.W. Hughes, *Early Christian Rhetoric and 2 Thessalonians* (JSNTSup, 30; Sheffield: JSOT Press, 1989), p. 64.

Factors most frequently mentioned in connection with the authenticity
of 2 Thessalonians include: (1) the apparent literary dependence of
2 Thessalonians on 1 Thessalonians; (2) the tensions, if not contradictions, that are said to exist between 2 Thess. 2.3-12 and 1 Thess. 4.13–
5.11; (3) the paucity of personal references and the formal, solemn
tone of 2 Thessalonians; and (4) the references to forgery in 2 Thess.
2.2 and 3.17.[5]

For our present purposes it must suffice to examine briefly the first
two items on this list, the first certainly being the most neuralgic topic
in the current scholarly debate.

1. Perhaps the single most important aspect of the current discussion concerning the authenticity of 2 Thessalonians is the claim that it
reveals an unusual dependence on and imitation of 1 Thessalonians,
not only in terms of ideas but also terminology and phrases. The best
known advocate of this position is William Wrede who in his 1903
study compared 1 and 2 Thessalonians in parallel columns.[6] He determined that much of the first letter is repeated in the second, a fact not
evidenced similarly in the remainder of the Pauline corpus. Even
more striking is that many of these parallels occur in the same order.
Such dependence, for example, can be seen in the relationship between
1 Thess. 1.4 and 2 Thess. 1.7-8; 1 Thess. 2.13, 14 and 2 Thess. 2.12,
13; 1 Thess. 2.16 and 2 Thess. 3.11; 1 Thess. 3.1 and 2 Thess. 4.1;
1 Thess. 3.6, 7 and 2 Thess. 4.1-2; 1 Thess. 3.10-12 and 2 Thess.
4.10-12; 1 Thess. 3.16 and 2 Thess. 5.23. Unless one assumes
coincidence or that Paul slavishly imitated his earlier letter, the only
logical conclusion for Wrede is that of forgery. Wolfgang Trilling's
two subsequent monographs, one a full-scale commentary on
2 Thessalonians, have served both to augment and to keep the insights
and arguments of Wrede in the forefront of the current discussion.[7]

5. See further G. Hollmann, 'Die Unechtheit des zweiten Thessalonicher-
briefs', *ZNW* 5 (1904), pp. 28-38; and J. Bailey, 'Who Wrote II Thessalonians?'
NTS 25 (1979), pp. 131-45. See the discussion in R. Jewett, *The Thessalonian
Correspondence: Pauline Rhetoric and Millenarian Piety* (Philadelphia: Fortress
Press, 1986), pp. 3-18.

6. W. Wrede, *Die Echtheit des zweiten Thessalonicherbriefs untersucht* (TU NS,
9/2; Leipzig: Hinrichs, 1903).

7. W. Trilling, *Untersuchungen zum zweiten Thessalonicherbrief* (Erfurter
theologische Studien 27; Leipzig: St Benno, 1972) and *Der zweite Brief an die
Thessalonicher* (EKKNT, 14; Zürich: Benzinger Verlag, 1980). For a summary of

Based on a stylistic, form-critical and theological analysis of this second letter, Trilling concludes that although the vocabulary is in general Pauline, all other factors, particularly the style and rhetoric of this letter, suggest non-Pauline authorship.

To date there has been no comprehensively compelling refutation of Wrede's analysis. His investigation, reinforced and augmented by Trilling's studies, introduces a most persuasive series of arguments against the direct Pauline authorship of 2 Thessalonians. Yet in finding Wrede's literary study demonstrating the dependence of 2 Thessalonians on 1 Thessalonians forceful, we do not believe that this research either furnishes[8] or, by itself, provides the basis for any specific forgery hypothesis or discernible historical/social setting in which 2 Thessalonians was composed. Further, little compelling evidence has been provided in the literature to help understand how a letter purportedly addressed to Thessalonica by Paul would be pertinent and compelling to a non-Thessalonian church some thirty years after the Apostle has died.

2. Despite this artificial similarity between the two letters, 2 Thessalonians exhibits a remarkably different eschatological emphasis and agenda. Thus it is argued that the eschatological assertions made in 2 Thess. 2.1-12 are incompatible with those found in 1 Thess. 4.13–5.11. It is observed that the eschatology of the second letter is more thoroughgoing apocalyptic than the first and dependent on apocalyptic devices about time-calculations that are not only uncharacteristic of the first but, in fact, rejected there. Further, a dependence on the apocalyptic thought of Revelation is urged; so, for example, the idea of punishments and rewards as coming from God (2 Thess. 1.5, 6) is found in Rev. 6.10; 7.14; 11.18; 13.6; the phrase 'mighty angels' (1.7) is paralleled in Rev. 19.14 as are the phrases 'flaming fire' (1.8) in Rev. 19.12 and 'eternal destruction' (1.9) in Rev. 20.10.

Although I find the most cogent argument for non-Pauline authorship to be that of literary dependence, I am not persuaded that these critics have correctly or compellingly described the circumstances that prompted the writing of this letter, particularly those scholars who

Trilling's major observations, see C.A. Wanamaker, *Commentary on 1 & 2 Thessalonians* (NIGTC; Grand Rapids: Eerdmans, 1990), pp. 21-28.

8. I thus reject Wrede's own attempt (*Die Echtheit*, esp. pp. 95-96) to place 2 Thessalonians as a forgery in the period 100–110 AD.

place it in the late first or early second century in a location other than Thessalonica. It is difficult to imagine a setting where a letter purportedly addressed to Thessalonica by Paul would be relevant and convincing to a non-Thessalonian church some thirty or more years after the Apostle's death. Compelling evidence simply has not been provided for these conjectures.

I am neither convinced that Paul wrote 2 Thessalonians nor that this letter was written late in the first century and unrelated to a concrete situation in Thessalonica. While agreeing that 2 Thessalonians is non-Pauline in the technical sense I do hold that it is related to a specific situation in Thessalonica. In all likelihood the circumstances that provided the primary motivation for the writing of 1 Thessalonians continued and escalated. 2 Thessalonians alludes to this intensification not only by use of the term τοῖς διωγμοῖς (persecutions; 1.4) and the harsh response to the afflictors (1.5-12), but also by the bellicose description of the lawless one in 2 Thess. 2.3-12. In terms of authorship, perhaps one of his two co-workers, Timothy or Silvanus, who are listed as joint authors with Paul in both 1 and 2 Thessalonians, wrote the letter. It is not improbable to think that one of them may have been in the city when the newest phase of the problem erupted. Since the first letter was co-authored by Paul, Silvanus and Timothy, would Silvanus or Timothy have difficulty in co-authoring this second letter and modelling it after the first? But who is the more likely candidate—Silvanus (Silas) or Timothy? The answer is not uncomplicated by the fact that we do not have much information concerning either. Silvanus's Jerusalem background and his identification as a 'prophet' in Acts 15.32 might point to him as the author of 2 Thessalonians; but speaking against this is the absolute silence about Silas as an associate of Paul after their stay in Corinth (Acts 18.5). Pointing in the direction of Timothy, in addition to his key role as Paul's representative to the Thessalonian Christians, are two facts: (1) we know from Acts and I Corinthians that Timothy made at least two further trips to Macedonia (1 Cor. 4.17, cf. 1 Cor. 16.10-11; Acts 19.22, cf. 20.4)[9]; and (2) the close association of Paul

---

9.   In citing the references to 1 Corinthians, I assume that Timothy traveled from Ephesus to Corinth via Macedonia. This visit would have been earlier than the one mentioned in Acts 19.22 which is probably to be correlated with Phil. 2.22-24. Timothy could have authored 2 Thessalonians at either time, although we would opt for the earlier reference in 1 Cor. 4.17.

and Timothy in the authorship of at least four letters: 2 Corinthians, Philippians, 1 Thessalonians and Philemon.

Regardless which option one selects with regard to authorship, 2 Thess. 3.17 ('I, Paul, write this greeting with my own hand. This is the mark in every letter of mine; it is the way I write') presents difficulties for each view. Those who select Pauline authorship have to resolve the problem that, if 1 and 2 Thessalonians are Paul's first letters, there is no evidence of a Pauline letter prior to 2 Thessalonians that contains a greeting in the hand of the Apostle. Those who understand 2 Thessalonians as a pseudepigraphical letter must assume that the writer purposely inserted 2 Thess. 3.17 to mislead the readers into thinking that Paul was the actual author of the letter.

Before attempting to answer the question just raised, it is important to realize that 3.17 bears a close relationship to both 2 Thess. 2.2 ('not to be quickly shaken in mind or alarmed, either by spirit or by word or by letter, as though from us, to the effect that the day of the Lord is already here') and 2.15 ('So then, brothers and sisters, stand firm and hold fast to the traditions that you were taught by us, either by word of mouth or by our letter').[10] Several comments are in order.

First, there is an allusion to a problem related to an unspecified letter. Theses abound in attempting to explain this reference. In our view the letter that is being referred to in both cases is 1 Thessalonians. In 2.2 it appears that some persons misrepresented its meaning. In 2.15 the reference is again to 1 Thessalonians, specifying in this case that it contains authentic traditions taught by Paul, Silvanus and Timothy which the Thessalonian Christians would do well to uphold and maintain.

Secondly, both in 2 Thess. 2.2 and 2.15 it is made clear that this un-specified letter, which in our view is 1 Thessalonians, was written by 'us', namely, Paul, Silvanus and Timothy. We have here, as we just observed, a case of joint authorship,[11] a situation that coheres nicely

10. Hughes, *Rhetoric*, pp. 75-79.

11. This is not to deny that Paul is the primary author of 1 Thessalonians, even though the 'we' style is found throughout. The two exceptions to this 'we' style in 1 Thessalonians, namely, 2.18 and 3.5, serve to underscore both his deep concern for the Thessalonian Christians and to eradicate the notion that his absence is either the result of a low regard for them or the result of a neglect of the difficult situation that this church finds itself in. See further, K.P. Donfried, 'War Timotheus in Athen? Exegetische Überlegungen zu 1 Thess. 3,1-3' in J.J. Degenhardt (ed.), *Die*

Origins and Method

with the evidence in 1 Thess. 1.1 and elsewhere in that letter. Paul, Silvanus and Timothy are intimately involved not only in the joint authorship of 1 Thessalonians but also in a shared ministry that Paul describes as apostolic in 1 Thess. 2.7 where he refers to all three as 'apostles.' If one of them, probably Timothy, is writing in 2 Thessalonians on behalf of the apostolic group it would only be natural that Pauline tradition and authority receive an emphasis here that was not the case in the first letter.

Now if one of Paul's co-workers, probably Timothy, is the author of 2 Thessalonians, how would that affect our understanding of the Pauline autograph in 3.17? If one were to consider seriously a concept like that of the 'corporate personality' in ancient Israel or what Conzelmann and others have described as the 'Pauline school,'[12] it may well be that this 'I' might be viewed more broadly. If, indeed, 2 Thessalonians is attempting to partially augment and correct a misunderstanding of 1 Thessalonians, and if Paul and Timothy were co-authors of that letter, could not Timothy refer to Paul in the way he does? Although Paul and his other two co-workers share in this same 'geistigen Eigentum' [intellectual property], it is Paul, who because of his high profile in Thessalonica, becomes the target of misunderstanding. If Paul is being attacked as a result of the gospel that he and Timothy jointly share, and, further, since Timothy knows well what was intended in the original letter (1 Thessalonians), is it not possible that the final rhetorical clincher of 2 Thessalonians is to draw explicitly upon the Pauline apostolic authority, in which Timothy shares, as the final rebuttal to the misunderstandings rampant in Thessalonica? Certainly a letter from Timothy alone would not carry the same weight or be as effective in refuting distortions directed primarily at Paul.

Given our understanding that 2 Thessalonians is addressed to the same Christian community as 1 Thessalonians, and written not long after that first letter, the descriptions of the historical settings of Thessalonian Christianity described elsewhere need not be repeated and the reader is referred to them.[13] Thus our present task will be to understand the distinctive factors in Thessalonica that necessitated the

Freude an Gott—unsere Kraft: Festschrift für Otto Bernhard Knoch zum 65. Geburtstag (Stuttgart: Katholisches Bibelwerk, 1991), pp. 189-96.

    12. H. Conzelmann, 'Paulus und die Weisheit', *NTS* 12 (1965-66), pp. 231-34.

    13. Donfried, 'The Cults of Thessalonica and the Thessalonian Correspondence'.

composition of 2 Thessalonians. The letter reveals a continuance and intensification of the persecution attested to in 1 Thessalonians. Evidently the Thessalonian Christians' proclamation of the Kingdom of God (2 Thess. 1.5) generates hostility among non-Christians (2 Thess. 1.8; 2.12). 2 Thess. 1.4 refers not only to τοῖς θλίψεσιν (afflictions), as in 1 Thessalonians, but also to τοῖς διωγμοῖς (persecutions). Whereas θλῖψις (affliction) needs to be specified according to its context, διωγμός always refers to persecution. But there is also a noteworthy reference to this later theme in 2 Thess. 2.15: 'So then, brethren, stand firm (στήκτετε) and hold fast to the traditions that you were taught by us, either by word of mouth or by our letter.' This motif, 'stand firm,' is part of a well-formed tradition of teaching in the context of persecution.[14]

Given this environment of protracted and escalated persecution, there are some in the congregation who are proclaiming that 'the day of the Lord is already here.' What was meant by this slogan is not altogether clear.[15] It might refer either to a spiritualized, almost gnostic-like, understanding, namely, that there will not be any future, physical coming of the Lord, much like the problem described in 1 Cor. 15.12-28;[16] or it might suggest that the day of the Lord was at hand, that it would occur before long. Critical for the interpreter of 2 Thessalonians is to understand how this originally Jewish concept, the day of the Lord, would be interpreted in a congregation composed predominantly of Gentiles in a milieu permeated by Graeco-Roman cults. For the author of this letter, contrary to some in the Thessalonian congregation, this event, this day of the Lord, will be real, dramatic, observable and future.

In all likelihood we are dealing with a misinterpretation of Paul's alleged 'realized eschatology' in 1 Thessalonians. The author of the second letter is not only concerned about this misreading but also with

14. E.G. Selwyn, *The First Epistle of St Peter* (London: Macmillan, 1961), pp. 454-58.

15. The Greek verb translated as 'already here' is ἐνεστῆκεν. Further references to its meaning can be found in Trilling, *Untersuchungen*, pp. 124-125; *idem, Der zweite Brief*, pp. 78; H-M. Schenke and K.M. Fischer, *Einleitung in die Schriften des Neuen Testaments* (Berlin: Evangelische Verlagsanstalt, 1978), I, p. 192; Jewett, *Thessalonian Correspondence*, pp. 97-98.

16. See further, K.P. Donfried, *The Dynamic Word* (San Francisco: Harper & Row, 1981), pp. 22-28.

its consequences. For if the day of the Lord is already present, and not
a future event yet to be consummated, then, of course, the foundation
of the Thessalonians' faith becomes very fragile. Our author responds
to this dilemma by presenting an apocalyptic time-table that distances
the present situation from the yet future day of the Lord. This shift in
eschatological emphasis from the first letter does not mean, however,
a contradiction between the two. Different situations call for distinct
nuances and emphases.

There are two factors, both of which will be described more fully
as we proceed, that suggest that the day of the Lord is being
misunderstood in a pseudo-spiritual, gnostic way: (1) The problem of
the spirit in 2 Thess. 2.2 and 2.15; and, (2) The identification of τὸ
κατέχον / ὁ κατέχων in 2 Thess. 2.6 and 7 as a seizing or possessing
power, some 'pseudocharismatic spirit or agent' that is 'a false
imitation of spiritual illumination and inspiration' and that has seized
power.[17]

Not only must our author correct a false understanding of the day
of the Lord, but he must also urge his readers to stand firm in their
afflictions and not to be unsettled or troubled when some proclaim
that the day of the Lord has already arrived. In order to accomplish
this goal, 2 Thess. 1.5-13, which contains a major expansion of
1 Thessalonians, makes clear that the Lord's vengeance will come
against those who are involved in this persecution against the
Thessalonian Christians and that they will suffer 'the punishment of
eternal destruction' when the Lord appears (2 Thess. 1.9). 2 Thess.
2.3-12, using strikingly apocalyptic categories and language and
marking a major insertion into the framework of 1 Thessalonians,
intends to combat the assertion made by some that 'the day of the
Lord is already here' (v. 2). It is argued, on the contrary, that the day
of the Lord is not yet here, or even close at hand, because certain
future events about to be described must first take place. Glenn
Holland has shown that we are dealing in this passage with a three-fold
apocalyptic schema in which a present phenomenon is portrayed and
then personified at a future moment of crisis. What 'has been and
continues to be active in the present, will in the future be unveiled as a
personal force, part of the battle between the personalized forces of

17. C.H. Giblin, 'The Heartening Apocalyptic of Second Thessalonians', *The
Bible Today* 26 (1988), p. 353.

good and evil (cf. Dan. 10.18-11.1; Rev. 12.7-9).'[18]

This triple repetition of the impending crisis as already partially operative in the present is presented as follows in 2 Thessalonians 2:

Present	*Future*
1a. ἡ ἀποστασία [the rebellion]	1b. ὁ ἄνθρωπος τῆς ἀνομίας [the lawless one] (2.3)
2a. τὸ κατέχον [the seizing power]	2b. ὁ κατέχων [the seizer] (2.6-7)
3a. τὸ μυστήριον τῆς ἀνομίας [the mystery of lawlessness]	3b. ὁ ἄνομος [the lawless one] (2.7-8)

In each case it is apparent that what occurs in the future is a personification of those evil forces already operative in the present. Therefore the use of neuter and masculine participles of the verb κατέχω is determined not by that to which these two participles refer but to the apocalyptic pattern itself.[19] In contemporary scholarship the most widespread translation for τὸ κατέχον / ὁ κατέχων is 'what is restraining/the one who restrains.' Giblin has urged an alternative translation: 'the seizing power/the seizer.'[20] This translation is defended on the following grounds:

    a.   κατέχειν is an intensive form of ἔχειν. Its usual meaning when followed by positive clauses and/or 'in contexts where death, curses or demonic power are mentioned'[21] is 'to hold on to, to seize, to grasp, to possess and to spellbind.' Thus for Paul, Giblin points out, κατέχειν normally means 'to possess.' That is not to say that κατέχειν cannot mean 'to restrain' in the sense of 'to detain/ hold on to,' but when it does it is usually followed by a negative clause as in Luke 4.42.

18. G.S. Holland, *The Tradition that you Received from us: 2 Thessalonians in the Pauline Tradition* (Hermeneutische Untersuchen zur Theologie, 24; Tübingen: Mohr, 1988), p. 112.

19. Holland, *Tradition*, p. 112.

20. C.H. Giblin, *The Threat to Faith: An Exegetical and Theological Re-examination of 2 Thessalonians 2* (AnBib, 31; Rome: Pontifical Biblical Institute, 1967), p. 201. See now also Giblin's article, '2 Thessalonians 2 Re-read as Pseud-epigraphical: A Revised Reaffirmation of *The Threat to Faith*' in R.F. Collins (ed.) *The Thessalonian Correspondence* (BETL, 87; Leuven: Leuven University Press, 1990), p. 459-69.

21. Giblin, 'Pseudepigraphical', p. 465.

b.   Many exegetes understand κατέχον/ων as a benign
     restraining force such as the Spirit or the preaching of the
     Gospel which keeps the Lawless one at a distance. However,
     in the NT the Gospel is described as unimpeded and '...not as
     itself impeding anything, much less, even indirectly, the
     Lord's coming.'[22] The relevant texts in the NT warn about
     the day of the Lord but never describe any force, benign or
     otherwise, as involved in devising a delay in its appearance.

In his 1967 study of 2 Thessalonians, Giblin drew some interesting
links between the use of τὸ κατέχον / ὁ κατέχων in 2 Thessalonians
and the cults of Serapis and Dionysus in Thessalonica and concludes
that a 'generic allusion to pagan religious practice, especially to
pseudo-prophetic seizure, would seem to account for Paul's choice of
this particular term.'[23] This is a thesis that has been generally
overlooked or rejected in the literature.[24] Yet Giblin's suggestion
needs to be taken more seriously not only in light of my previous
description of Thessalonica (see n. 3 above) but also in view of Ernst
Koeberlin's work in which he shows that 'the mysteries instituted by
Caligula and linked with emperor worship partook of Isiacism, the
colossal statue intended for the Temple of Jerusalem being a blend of
Neos Gaius and Zeus *Epiphanes*.'[25] Based on Koeberlin's study Rex
Witt is tempted to suggest that Paul in the ἄνομος passage is 'hitting
out possibly at a Thessalonian cult in which emperor worship was
combined with the cult of Isis and Serapis.'[26]

This perspective is strengthened by a closer examination of the
negative (2 Thess. 2.6a, 7b, 11a) and positive (2 Thess. 2.8, 13)
references to the Spirit. Not unimportant is that 2 Thess. 2.13

22. Giblin, 'Pseudepigraphical', p. 466.
23. Giblin, *Threat*, p. 201.
24. It is heartening to note in Holland, *Tradition*, p. 114, that the work of τὸ
μυστήριον finds its conclusion in the appearance of ὁ ἄνομος and is parallel to and
contemporary with ἡ ἀποστασία and that he 'would suggest that the author is using
the metaphor of a pagan mystery cult for the apocalyptic antagonism to Christ, a cult
that is already "in operation" in the present'.
25. E. Koeberlein, *Caligula und die ägyptischen Kulte* (Beiträge zur klassischen
Philologie, 3; Meisenheim am Glan: Verlag Anton Hain, 1962), pp. 21, 61 as cited
in R. Witt, 'The Egyptian Cults in Ancient Macedonia' in *Ancient Macedonia* II
(Thessaloniki: Institute for Balkan Studies, 1977), p. 331.
26. Witt, 'The Egyptian Cults', p. 331.

concludes any further reference to the Spirit, either as a pseudo-spiritual activity or as Spirit-lead sanctification. Further, in 1 Thess. 5.21, a letter our author/s had clearly in mind, κατέχω—is used precisely with regard to spiritual discernment and prophecy. Already in 1 Thessalonians 5, especially in vv. 5-7 and 19-22, the Apostle does not wish the gift of the Spirit to be confused with the excesses of the Dionysiac mysteries; for Paul the Spirit does not lead to 'Bacchic frenzies.' In short, then, this lawless one, this seizer, whose rebellion and seizing power is exercised in the present, will continue to mislead and confuse all people until the God of justice, through the manifestation of the Lord Jesus, will ultimately dethrone him. Therefore the eschatological day of the Lord has not yet arrived; much wickedness and lawlessness must yet be played out on the world's corrupt stage before God's ultimate show of victory.

Rhetorical criticism has made clear that the intentions of 1 and 2 Thessalonians are quite different. The rhetorical genre of the first letter is epideictic and has as its purpose to encourage and console, that is, it is primarily a paracletic letter. The genre of the second letter is deliberative and has as its purpose exhortation, that is, it is primarily a paraenetic letter.[27] These observations are confirmed by the use (or non-use) of three key verbs in the letters: παρακαλέω, παραγγέλω and παραμυθέω.

Although the verb παρακαλέω has a wide-range of meanings, in the two Thessalonian letters the translations 'to comfort, to encourage, to urge' are appropriate. The word is used eight times in the first letter (2.12; 3.2,7; 4.1, 10, 18; 5.11, 14), but only twice in 2 Thessalonians (2.17; 3.12). The opposite pattern can be observed when we examine the usage of the verb παραγγέλω—which, in general, has the meaning 'to give orders, command or instruct.'[28] This word is used four times in the second letter (3.4, 6, 10, 12) but only once in the first (4.11) and this single reference in 1 Thess. 4.11 has a quite different context from that of 2 Thessalonians. In the former, παραγγέλω is twice preceded with the verb παρακαλέω (4.1,10)

27. This is not in any way to suggest a rigid demarcation between a 'paracletic' and a 'paraenetic' letter. Each may contain and combine both elements, although their overall emphasis and focus is different.

28. W. Bauer, *A Greek–English Lexicon of the New Testament and Other Early Christian Literature* (W.F. Arndt, F.W. Gingrich and F.W. Danker [eds.]; Chicago: The University of Chicago, 1979), p. 613.

which strengthens the view that this paraenesis 'was intended to reinforce them in their current forms of behavior rather than direct them to a different pattern of behavior';[29] in the latter the primary section of ethical exhortation uses only the verb παραγγέλω, which lends to support to the perspective that 2 Thessalonians is attempting to change the future behavior of the Christians in Thessalonica. To further substantiate our thesis that paraenesis is found in the context of paraclesis in 1 Thessalonians and paraclesis in the context of paraenesis in 2 Thessalonians is the fact that the verb παραμυθέω, meaning 'to encourage, to cheer up, to console someone concerning someone' is found twice in 1 Thessalonians (2.12; 5.14) and not at all in the second letter.

2 Thessalonians, belonging to the genre of deliberative rhetoric, is urging the Thessalonian Christians both to believe and to conduct themselves in a different manner. The former intention is primarily located in the first proof, 2.1(3)-12, and the latter in the command to work, 3.6-15. It is now to 2 Thess. 3.6-15 that we turn. In v. 6 both the source of Paul's authority is stated, 'in the name of our Lord Jesus Christ,' as well as the command to work, expressed negatively, 'to keep away from every brother who is living in idleness (ἀτάκτως; used also in 3.11) and not according to the tradition παράδοσις that they received from us.' Central to our understanding of what is at stake in the argument is the meaning of ἀτάκτως (also ἀτακτέω in 3.7) and παράδοσις.

With regard to ἀτακτέω, Louw and Nida write: 'Traditional translations have often interpreted ἀτακτέω—in an etymological sense of "not being ordered" and hence with a meaning of "to behave in a disorderly manner", but this is quite contrary to the context.'[30] The adjective ἄτακτος 'means primarily "out of order", "out of place" and...is readily employed as a military term to denote a soldier who does not keep the ranks, or an army advancing in disarray'.[31] The verb ἀτακτέω has much the same meaning and 'is extended to

29. Wanamaker, *1 and 2 Thessalonians*, p. 48.

30. J.P. Louw and E.A. Nida, *Greek-English Lexicon of the New Testament based on Semantic Domains* (New York: United Bible Societies, 1988) I.768-769 [88.246-247].

31. G. Milligan, *St Paul's Epistles to the Thessalonians* (New York: Macmillan, n.d.), p. 152.

every one who does not perform his proper duty...?[32] Is this original meaning really so contrary to the context as Louw and Nida would have us believe?

Since the interpretation of 2 Thess. 3.6-15 is heavily dependent on the translation of the Greek, it will be useful at this point to offer our own translation of vv. 6-12:

> [6]Now we command you, brothers, in the name of our Lord Jesus Christ, to keep away from brothers who are not living a well-ordered life and are not in accord with the tradition that you received from us. [7]For you yourselves know how you ought to imitate us; we did not depend on others for our support when we were with you [8]and we did not eat anyone's bread without paying for it; but with toil and labor we worked night and day, so that we might not burden any of you. [9]This was not because we do not have that right, but we waived our right in order to give you an example to imitate. [10]For even when were with you, we gave you this command: Anyone unwilling to work should not eat. [11]For we hear that some of your number are leading ill-ordered lives, and, instead of attending to their own business, are busy with what does not concern them. [12]Now such persons we command and exhort to attend quietly to their own work and to earn their own living.

This translation varies from several common translations in translating ἀτάκτως / ἀτακτέω as 'ill-ordered' or 'not well-ordered' rather than 'in idleness' and in translating περιεργάζομαι as 'not attending to their own business' rather than as 'busybody'.[33] This rendering of 2 Thess. 3.6-12 gives support to the thesis of Bengt Holmberg that the author of this letter is critical of a 'charismatic authority' being exercised by some in the congregation who are claiming that because of this self-claimed authority they are to be supported by others in the congregation.[34] This view of the situation also allows us to see the relationship between the problem of the 'spirit' and the 'seizing power' that is already at work in the present. In this connection it is noteworthy that of only two references to οἴδατε[35] [you know] in this second letter, one of them appears in the first proof at 2.6a: 'And now

32. Milligan, *Thessalonians*, p. 153.

33. I have been greatly assisted in these renderings by the translation of Milligan, *Thessalonians*, p. 112.

34. B. Holmberg, *Paul and Power* (Philadelphia: Fortress Press, 1980), p. 159. Not unimportant is the use of the word εὐτάκτως [good order] in 1 Clem. 42.2, a section dealing with church leadership.

35. 2 Thess. 2.6; 3.7.

you know by experience the Seizing power...' Perhaps the use of the phrase 'you know' implies that this problem may have already been present in an embryonic fashion as Paul wrote the first letter (1 Thess. 1.9; 4.12-13, 14, 19-22).

This circumstance of an economic elitism by a few, based on the claim to charismatic authority, is refuted by 2 Thessalonians on the basis of tradition [παράδοσις], a term that is used in 2 Thess. 2.15 in the plural ('So then, brethren, stand firm and hold fast to the traditions that you were taught by us, either by word of mouth, or by our letter') and in 3.6 in the singular ('Now we command you, brothers, in the name of our Lord Jesus Christ, to keep away from brothers who are not living a well-ordered life and not in accord with the tradition that you received from us'). With Trilling I agree that the plural refers to a body of tradition and the singular to a specific item of that larger tradition.[36] The first reference is to the third argument of the second proof, namely, that by holding to the traditions already taught by Paul through word and letter they will make evident their orthodoxy. The second reference is found in the fifth section of 2 Thessalonians pertaining to exhortation. Again in this context the appeal is made to Pauline tradition: living an ill-ordered life does not accord with this tradition.

Although the term παράδοσις ('tradition') does not appear in 1 Thessalonians, Caroline Vander Stichele[37] has examined the use of the verb παραλαμβάνω ('to receive' or 'accept') in 1 and 2 Thessalonians, discovering a significant connection between the two. The verb is used in 1 Thess. 2.13; 4.1 and in 2 Thess. 2.15 and 3.6. Further, Vander Stichele finds a 'striking similarity in place and formulation' between the use of the verb παραλαμβάνω in 1 Thess. 2.13 and 2 Thess. 2.15 and between 1 Thess. 4.1 and 2 Thess. 3.6.[38] With regard to the first linkage she points out that in addition to the formal agreements between the two, in both cases the author refers to himself as 'the source of tradition.'[39] Even though 2 Thess. 2.15 is a more explicit statement than 1 Thess. 2.13 and the fact that the latter one emphasizes more the reality that the Thessalonians accepted the

36. Trilling, *Untersuchungen*, p. 116.

37. C. Vander Stichele, 'The Concept of Tradition and 1 and 2 Thessalonians' in Collins (ed.), *The Thessalonian Correspondence*, pp. 499-504.

38. Vander Stichele, 'Tradition', p. 501.

39. Vander Stichele, 'Tradition', p. 502.

word of God, nevertheless both focus on a general rather than a particular tradition. In comparing 1 Thess. 4.1 and 2 Thess. 3.6 it is indicated that in both cases we find παραλαμβάνω together with παρ' ἡμῶν ('from us') as well as the connection with the verb παραπατέω ('to live', 'conduct oneself'). Also, in these latter two verses a specific ethical issue receives attention.

The use of the term παράδοσις in 2 Thessalonians may have implications with regard to the issue of authorship. The absence of this term from 1 Thessalonians, it is argued, supports the non-Pauline authorship of 2 Thessalonians. Yet it could be argued that in view of the fact that παράδοσις is used elsewhere in the Pauline letters (1 Cor. 11.2 and Gal. 1.14), 2 Thessalonians is Pauline. More likely, however, is the conclusion that Vander Stichele reaches at the conclusion of her study: 'The structural agreement and the terminological affinity between 1 and 2 Thessalonians can hardly be accidental. It looks as if 2 Thessalonians used 1 Thessalonians as a model.'[40] The use of the term παράδοσις alone does not contribute significantly to solving the issue of authorship; rather, the critical issue is why the first letter serves as a model for the second.[41]

Not unrelated to this theme of παράδοσις in 2 Thessalonians is its relationship to sanctification. In 1 Thessalonians there is a strong emphasis on sanctification which is closely linked to the theme of the parousia. In 2 Thessalonians the terms ἀγιάζω (1 Thess. 5.23) and ἀγιωσύνη (1 Thess. 3.13) do not appear at all and the term ἀγιασμός (1 Thess. 4.3, 4, 7) is used only once in 2 Thess. 2.13. Obviously our author values the concept of sanctification, but because of the different pressures to which he is reacting, 'to be worthy' (1.5, 11) of God's kingdom and call is now presumed to be an adhering to the traditions that Paul and his associates have passed on to them. These include, on the one hand, adherence to Paul's teaching about the day of the Lord and the rejection of the idea inspired by some of the cults of Thessalonica that it is already here, and, on the other hand, fidelity to Paul's instruction about leading an orderly life in a culture that prizes behavior quite the contrary.

It has become apparent, then, that the Thessalonian church is faced with a variety of dilemmas in the midst of an overall situation of increased persecution. Even though one of Paul's co-workers rather

40. Vander Stichele, 'Tradition', p. 504.
41. See the more detailed discussion on pp. 130-31.

than the Apostle himself is the author of the letter, it makes perfectly
good sense to read it as addressed to the Thessalonian church
sometime after the writing of 1 Thessalonians. The presence of the
κατέχον/ων references, the refutation of the belief that 'the day of the
Lord is already here' and the tendency toward a charismatic authority
by a few in this letter do suggest the possible influence of the pagan
cults in this crisis. The intention of the author of 2 Thessalonians
becomes evident as one observes the manner in which he addresses
and refutes these unsettling circumstances current in the Thessalonian
church.

APOSTOLIC MISSION AND APOSTOLIC MESSAGE: CONGRUENCE IN
PAUL'S EPISTOLARY RHETORIC, STRUCTURE AND IMAGERY

John L. White

Introductory Comments

I argue in this essay that Paul's way of writing letters reflects his particular sense of mission. This does not mean that his letters all belong to the same type nor that, in any simple sense, he created a new hybrid type. In fact, Nils Dahl argues in an unpublished paper that all of Paul's letters are to a greater or lesser degree mixed types.[1] Nonetheless, because of his ability to combine epistolary types to fit situational needs, he is one of the outstanding letter writers of antiquity. Therefore, comprehension of Paul as a letter writer requires subtlety and flexibility of analysis.

John Hurd shares Dahl's conception of Paul as a creative letter writer. Unfortunately, according to Hurd, scholars concern themselves too much with harmonizing the theological content of *what* Paul says and too little with the situational occasion of *why* he says something and with *how* he expresses it.[2] Hurd, Dahl and I share a common interest in epistolary structure and rhetoric as indices of theology. Though I focus on Paul's letters collectively, whereas Hurd

---

1. See N.A. Dahl, 'Paul's Letter to the Galatians: Epistolary Genre, Content, Structure' (paper presented at the 1973 annual SBL meeting), pp. 10-11.

2. These criticisms are expressed by Hurd in an unpublished paper: 'Concerning the Structure of 1 Thessalonians' (1972 annual SBL meeting), p. 3. Hurd extends his emphasis on individuality by arguing that Paul's letters need to be ordered chronologically. See 'Paul Ahead of his Time: 1 Thess. 2:13-16', in P. Richardson with D. Granskou (eds.), *Anti-Judaism in Early Christianity*. I. *Paul and the Gospels* (Waterloo: Wilfrid Laurier University Press, 1986), pp. 31-33. See also '"The Jesus Whom Paul Preaches" (Acts 19.13)', in P. Richardson and J.C. Hurd (eds.) *From Jesus to Paul. Studies in Honor of Francis Wright Beare* (Waterloo: Wilfrid Laurier University Press, 1984), pp. 73-89, esp. p. 89; J.C. Hurd, 'The Sequence of Paul's letters', *CJT* 14, 3 (July 1968), pp. 189-200, esp. p. 200.

and Dahl emphasize the distinctiveness of each letter, our emphases
are not finally antithetical. The purpose of this essay is to identify the
features that characterize Paul as a letter writer.

In the first section below I describe epistolary patterns in the
opening and closing. Then, in a second section I identify chiastic
patterns and rhetorical argumentation in the letter body. Finally, in a
conclusion, I assess what the preceding analyses show about how Paul
wrote letters and, in turn, what they indicate about Paul's conception
of his apostolic mission.

1. *Opening and Closing Conventions in Paul's Letters*

1.1 *The Importance of Family Imagery and Orality for Defining Paul's Letters*

I acknowledged above that Paul's letters do not belong to a common
type. Nonetheless, it is possible to describe social and literary factors
that contributed to the way Paul wrote letters. In particular, all of the
letters except Philemon are longer than ordinary letters. This length
derives from their function as letters of instruction and Paul's
metaphors show he had a recurring conception of community in mind
in all his correspondence.

It will become clear in the following analysis that kinship is Paul's
fundamental metaphor for his Gentile churches. However, since none
of the existing institutional models—synagogue, philosophical schools,
voluntary associations and family household—are able fully to explain
Paul's idea of the church as a household, I need to say a few things
about his use of kinship imagery.[3] It is obvious when Paul represents

---

3.   These are the structures Wayne Meeks identifies as operative in Paul's urban
centers. See *The First Urban Christians* (New Haven: Yale University Press),
pp. 75-84. Because Christian communities were an offshoot of Judaism, Meeks
says the synagogue is the most natural model by which to understand communities
(pp. 80-81). Though synagogue and church are comparable in many respects, we
must resort to a redefinition of Jewish life to describe Paul's churches as
synagogues. Paul *never* uses the word synagogue for churches and neither
1 Thessalonians, Philippians, nor Philemon cite Jewish Scripture as a source of
authority. Paul only seems to cite Scripture for polemical purposes. Nor did he
require circumcision of gentile converts, the observance of dietary laws, and adherence to Moses' Law. In fact, he insists that community norms must be based on
something other than popular markers of Jewish identity. To be sure, Paul was still
interested in ethical norms of conduct and the necessity, as God's chosen people, of

his converts as a family, he does not have literal kinship in mind. The
social institution that best fits is the symbolic family provided by the
voluntary associations. Both Paul's groups and the associations were
founded on intimacy of relationship. Members met in households,
sharing table fellowship and other fraternal activities. Membership
was by free decision rather than by birth and often grew out of
participation in a common trade. Despite these similarities, Wayne
Meeks says Christian groups were more exclusivistic in supplanting
other loyalties than the voluntary associations were.[4] The association
with family households served as a fortuitous means whereby Paul
could convey his spiritual experience of God as father.

There is ample evidence that Paul conceived of God's life giving
paternity not only as father of the family but as father of a new
spiritual race and even, more broadly, as father of a new creation.[5]
Something of this broader intention is expressed by Paul's description

being holy and distinct. Yet he did not link such necessities in a racially defined way
to Judaism. In this connection Wayne McCready observes that there is minimal NT
evidence which shows Christianity imitated synagogue organization. See his
unpublished paper, *'Ecclesia'* (prepared for the 1989 annual meeting of the CSBS)
(pp. 3-4). Regarding the philosophical schools as a model, Stanley Stowers notes
that Paul's instruction differs in two respects from the philosophical schools: his
focus is on building up communities, not individual character; moreover, he
attributes the development of communal life to God, not to any activity of community
members themselves. See S. Stowers, *Letter Writing in Greco-Roman Antiquity*
(Philadelphia: Westminister Press, 1986), p. 42.

4.   Meeks, *The First Urban Christians*, pp. 77-80. See also McCready,
'Ecclesia', pp. 2-3.

5.   See the explicit references to God as father in 2 Cor. 1.2-3; Gal. 1.1, 3-4;
1 Thess. 1.1-2. When Paul refers to converts as 'beloved by God' (or as Paul's
beloved children) the affection is that of the father of the family (see 1 Thess. 1.4;
Phil. 2.11; 1 Cor. 4.14-15). When Paul addresses God as 'Abba' ('daddy') in Rom.
8.15 and Gal. 4.6, the intimacy is especially marked. Despite explicit reference to
God as father, Paul also attributes nourishing functions to God characteristic of the
mother. God's identity as father of a people/race is implied when converts are
described as Abraham's seed in Rom. 4.1, 11-13, 17-25 and Gal. 3.7, 16. The
description of converts as the spiritual/true circumcision also is racial (see Rom.
2.28-29; Phil. 3.3). God's life-giving nature as universal father is indicated in Rom.
8.21: 'creation itself will be set free from its bondage to decay and obtain the glorious
liberty of the children of God.' In 2 Cor. 5.14-27 Paul says anyone who is in Christ
is a new creation and that the old has passed away. In Gal. 6.15, he says it does not
matter whether one is circumcised, but it does matter that one is a new creation.

of his communities as the ἐκκλησία (the 'assembly'/'church'), a word which often translates the Hebrew term *qahal* in the Septuagint. The same Hebrew word is also rendered by συναγωγή ('gathering place'). Though both words may represent the collective assembly of Israel as God's holy people, ἐκκλησία was the term earlier used of the assembly of citizens in the Greek city states. Paul selected ἐκκλησία deliberately to differentiate his communities from traditional Judaism and to indicate the political level of status which he claims, in a Graeco-Roman sense, for the organization.[6] At the same time the word retains the Jewish idea of the assembly as God's people.

We want to identify one other factor that influences the conventions and rhetoric of Paul's letters, their oral character. The citation of liturgical materials show Paul imagined his letters as a surrogate expression of the speech he would have spoken had he been present. He compensated for his absence by having the letters read aloud in the house churches.[7] Since Paul imagined his letters as an approximation of spoken presence and since most community members 'heard' Paul's letters, and did not actually read them, we should attend to his use of concrete images as a means of embodying orality. Paul's kinship imagery is a good example.

1.2 *Conventions in the Letter's Opening and Closing*
My earlier analyses of Paul's letters were overly formalistic and the choice of comparative materials too narrow. I tried to understand the entirety of Paul's letters in terms of conventions found in nonliterary papyrus letters.[8] It is still feasible to delineate the beginning and end

6. This explanation is offered by McCready in his paper, '*Ecclesia*', p. 4.
7. See 1 Thess. 5.27 where Paul exhorts recipients to read his letter to the brethren. Paul's threat in 1 Cor. 4.18-21 shows he regarded actual presence more highly than written presence. R. Funk identifies three forms of Paul's apostolic presence with his recipients: the letter, his messenger, and Paul's own presence through a visit. The prospect of a visit appears in final position as the most potent form of Paul's visit. See 'The Apostolic Parousia', in W.R. Farmer, C.F.D. Moule and R.R. Niebuhr (eds.), *Christian History and Interpretation: Studies Presented to John Knox* (Cambridge, MA: Cambridge University Press), pp. 258-61.
8. As much as I like the study of letter structure by Ann Jervis, the work is inadequate at the same point my earlier work was deficient. She understands Paul too much in terms of the way he begins and concludes his letters. See L.A. Jervis, *The Purpose of Romans: A Comparative Letter Structure Investigation* (JSNTSup, 55; Sheffield: JSOT Press, 1991).

of Paul's letters by such means but, for the large intermediate part of the letter's body, we need to look to the literary letter tradition for our model. Therefore, in the present section we examine the opening and closing of Paul's letters, along with the introduction and conclusion to the letter's body. In the essay's second section, we study the stylistic devices and argumentative rhetoric in the letter's body with an ear to the rhetoric of literary letters. The following outline illustrates stock features in the opening and closing of Paul's authentic letters.[9]

OPENING

Address: Paul, an apostle of Jesus Christ, to the church of God at
_____, sanctified (beloved, called, etc.) in Christ.

Grace greeting/salutation: Grace to you and peace from God our Father and the Lord Jesus Christ.

Thanksgiving prayer: I thank God (always) for (all of) you, because of... and I pray that the Lord may make you increase (mature) in such activity so that you may be pure and blameless when Christ returns.

CLOSING

Greetings: from (to) third parties

The Holy Kiss greeting:

Grace benediction: The grace of our (the) Lord Jesus Christ be with you.

Opening and closing conventions originated in spoken salutations, greetings and well-wishing. The extensive kind of greetings we find in Paul were used between friends and family members. By contrast, chancery and business letters had brief opening conventions and minimal or no closings.

Though Paul wrote as his churches' leader, the familial tone of his opening and closing sections makes it clear that he regards community members as fellow siblings of free-born status in a spiritual household. The most common word of address, both in the openings/closings and in the body is the egalitarian 'brothers' (ἀδελφοί), which Paul uses collectively for men and women.[10] In addition to identifying

9. The seven letters about which there is consensus are: Romans, 1 and 2 Corinthians, Galatians, Philippians, 1 Thessalonians, and Philemon.

10. The designation occurs in 1 Corinthians as follows: 1.10-11, 26; 2.1; 3.1; 4.6; 7.24, 29; 10.1; 11.2, 33; 12.1; 14.6, 20, 26, 39; 15.1, 50, 58; 16.15. The use of 'brethren' in the vocative of address occurs with comparable frequency in Paul's remaining six letters. Paul also refers to the spiritual family/people status of his recipients in his letter openings by means of such words as 'saints', 'called' (elect), 'sanctified' and 'beloved'.

himself as a fellow sibling, Paul refers to himself as father because he is the communities' founder.[11] In the letter body he describes his anguish in trying to give spiritual birth to the Galatians as a mother in labor pains (Gal. 4.19). In trying to nourish converts to maturation Paul refers to himself as a nurse (see 1 Thess. 2.7-8; 1 Cor. 3.1-2) and manager of the household (1 Cor. 4.1-4). Consequently, though Paul and his brethren have egalitarian ties because of common spiritual generation, Paul shows he is responsible for his converts' maturation.

Paul uses the typical form of opening address, that in which the sender's name is written first. However, he modifies the word of salutation, 'greetings' (χαίρειν), by using the same root to express a fuller religious greeting: 'Grace (χάρις) to you and peace from God our Father and the Lord Jesus Christ.' Though Paul never expresses the health wish common in family letters, his grace greeting is the religious equivalent.

Following the opening grace greeting, Paul thanks God for some virtuous activity of his converts which exhibits their spiritual welfare.[12] This convention is seldom expressed in nonliterary letters and, then, the writer usually thanks a deity for his own deliverance from harm.[13] Like the opening grace greeting, Paul adapts the thanksgiving to ecclesiastical ends. Following the initial thanks Paul

11. 'Apostle' is the term in the letter's opening that conveys this founding authority. However, Paul's words of affectionate address in the opening greeting and thanksgivings of Philippians, 1 Thessalonians and Philemon imply Paul's status as father (see Phil. 1.7-8; 1 Thess. 1.4, 6; Phlm. 1). Paul states explicitly in the letter-body he is his correpondents' father.

12. The thanksgiving prayer occurs in five of the seven authentic letters. The two letters which do not have a thanksgiving prayer are situations in which relations with correspondents are strained. Thus, Paul replaces thanksgiving with a blessing formula in 2 Cor. 1.3 and with an expression of extreme dissatisfaction (θαυμάζω) in Gal. 1.6. Though there is a difference in mood in the two letters, they convey the same function as the thanksgiving prayers. Both express Paul's attitude toward his recipients and, by means of the subject of satisfaction/dissatisfaction, they anticipate the main theme of the letter.

13. For example, J.G. Winter cites letters from young military recruits who have travelled to Rome from Egypt by sea in which, among other things, they express thanks to a deity for preserving them from harm at sea. Thus, by expressing this thanksgiving to a god in the letter's opening, the writer informs family members of his welfare and, accordingly, the thanksgiving functions as an extension of the health wish. See 'In the Service of Rome: Letters from the Michigan Collection of Papyri', *CP* 22 (1927), pp. 237-56.

continues by entreating God to bring the virtuous activity for which he gives thanks to full maturation by Christ's return.[14] Thus, both in the grace greeting and the thanksgiving, Paul's concern is not with ordinary well-being but with spiritual welfare.

Family letters often conclude with greetings, health wish and/or a word of farewell. Paul also closes his letters with greetings, but he departs from the common pattern in his exhortation, 'Greet one another with a holy kiss' (1 Cor. 16.20b; 2 Cor. 13.12; 1 Thess. 5.26; Rom. 16.20). He replaces the farewell with a grace blessing nearly identical to his opening convention. Therefore, the grace blessing forms a ring that opens and closes the letter. It expresses Paul's most essential desire, the church's spiritual welfare.[15]

1.3 *Conventions that Introduce and Conclude the Body*

Though we are not able to compare most of the Pauline letter-body with nonliterary letters, we can compare formulas which introduce and conclude the body.

> BODY
>
> *Introductory formula:*
> either: I want you to know, brethren, that... (I/we do not
>   want you to be ignorant, brethren, that/of)...
> or: I appeal to (request) you, brethren, that...
>
> *Concluding convention*: Paul's Apostolic Presence
> 1. Autobiographical reference to the letter and Paul's expression
>   of confidence in his recipients' willingness to comply with
>   instruction.

14. See P. Schubert, *Form and Function of the Pauline Thanksgivings* (Berlin: Töpelmann, 1939), pp. 3-4.

15. Some scholars include the doxology as a letter closing item but, since it occurs only in Phil. 4.20 and Rom. 16.25-27 and since the Romans passage is disputed on textual grounds, it seems better to exclude it as a convention. Scholars also include Paul's reference to his autograph as a letter-closing convention. For example, Paul states explicitly that he is closing the letter in his own hand in 1 Cor. 16.21 and in Gal. 6.11. By this means he shows he has been using a secretary up to the point he takes the pen in hand. The accompanying warning in 1 Cor. 16.22, 'If anyone has no love for the Lord, let him be accursed', indicates Paul's signature conveyed his authority as well as his friendship. The same double nuance is found in Gal. 6.11-17 and perhaps, also, in 1 Thess. 5.26-27. We suggest below, however, that Paul's assertion of personal authority belongs more naturally to the close of the body than to the letter-closing.

    2. Identification/recommendation of Paul's apostolic messenger.
    3. Announcement of Paul's anticipated (hoped for) visit.
    4. Parenetic section: Reminder of Paul's instruction, appeal to Paul's and the congregation's former conduct, appeal to the example of Christ.
    5. Prayer/wish for eschatological peace.

Paul introduces the letter-body with two epistolary phrases: a disclosure formula in five cases (Romans, 2 Corinthians, Galatians, Philippians and 1 Thessalonians) and a request formula in the other two letters (1 Corinthians and Philemon). Besides Paul's use of the vocative of address, ἀδελφοί, and the religious subjects addressed, these formulas do not differ from disclosure and request phrases in ordinary correspondence.

We find a spectrum of phrases that close the body of letters. Writers plead, cajole and threaten recipients to attend to some duty specified in the letter. In this case the body closing functions as a means of finalizing and underscoring the reason for writing. In the attempt to 'nail down' how the recipient should respond, the letter writer also tends to convey his/her disposition toward the recipient as a means of securing compliance.[16]

Paul uses comparable phrases to conclude the body of his letters. In fact his stereotyped pattern is more elaborate than anything we find in ordinary letters. Robert Funk shows that the analogous use of the multi-element convention from letter to letter conveys an important apostolic function for Paul.[17] Paul uses the first three elements of the convention to persuade recipients to attend to his instructions. On the other hand, the fourth and fifth elements indicate that the community's welfare is contingent on its complete congruence with the norms established in Christ as its ruler. Thus, Paul is less concerned with compliance to his situational instruction than with his recipients' general maturation. The community must be spiritually blameless by

16. See the description of these conventions and how they function in J. White, *Light from Ancient Letters* (Philadelphia: Fortress Press, 1986), pp. 204-207.

17. R.W. Funk, 'The Apostolic Parousia', pp. 249-268. See the comments on note 7. Funk identifies the first three elements of the apostolic presence convention in the body's closing and I identify the fourth and fifth items. For a fuller explanation of this convention, see J.L. White, 'Saint Paul and the Apostolic Letter Convention', *CBQ* 45 (July 1983), pp. 440-442.

Christ's return. By way of summary to this point, the beginning and end of Paul's letters form a ring composition. The outer most circle is formed by Paul's grace blessing and expresses Paul's desire for his recipients' spiritual welfare. The next inner ring is formed by the thanksgiving and the body closing convention. This ring specifies the means of achieving spiritual welfare and the temporal limits that attend actualization. Conformity to Christ's spirit is identified as the church's means of achieving maturation. Christ's return marks the temporal limit allowed for growing up into Christ.

2. *Rhetoric in the Letter-Body*

Just as salutations, greetings and well-wishing originated in oral convention, so too rhetoric in the letter-body arose in oral speech. Whereas the greetings and health wish formulas were spoken in ordinary life, oral patterns in the body reverberate with the training of the academy. In ancient Greek culture rhetoric referred above all to public speaking and oratory. The earliest handbooks on rhetoric, such as Aristotle's *Art of Rhetoric*, arranged its principles into a scientific 'art' to show how, why and what kind of rhetoric was effective in specific situations. Even after it became common to write down speeches and to study them as written texts, orators composed speeches with an ear to oral performance.[18]

For some time scholars have been noting rhetorical patterns in the body of Paul's letters. The features we discuss below are representative. We examine the rhetoric under two headings. First, we look at chiastic patterns and then we compare Paul's rhetoric with classical argumentation.

2.1 *Chiastic Patterns in the Letter-Body*
Joachim Jeremias argues that Paul arranges words, phrases and whole sentences according to the chiastic schema *a b/b a*. Indeed, Paul organizes the whole of Galatians according to the *a b/b a* pattern.[19] On the

---

18. Ancient literature retained aspects of its oral roots more than modern literature since the invention of the printing press. See W.J. Ong, *Orality and Literacy. The Technologizing of the Word* (London: Routledge, 1988), pp. 9-10.

19. See 'Chiasmus in den Paulusbriefen', *ZNW* 49 (1958), pp. 145-56. Regarding the chiastic structure of Galatians, Jeremias notes that in 1.10-12 Paul identifies two criticisms of his apostleship: his gospel is κατὰ ἄνθρωπον (1.10-11)

other hand, John Hurd notes that Jeremias thinks of *chiasmus* too much in terms of the reversal of only a pair of items and usually limits this pattern to short passages.[20] Thus, Jeremias is critical of Nils Lund who identifies multiple member reversals.[21]

Hurd's study of *chiasmus* is closer to Lund than to Jeremias since he finds several multiple member inversions in 1 Thessalonians.[22] Though Paul may have had the main chiastic lineaments in mind as he dictated the letter, it is likely he refined the patterns further before he sent off his clean copy.

Unfortunately, traditional ideas about structure present Paul's logic narrowly in terms of linear sequence and fail to take account of *chiasmus* as an organizing factor. For example, 1 Thess. 2.13-16 is interepreted as an interpolation, because of its similarity to 1.2-10. However, I argue that Paul's frequent use of *chiasmus* shows repetition is typical of his style.[23]

In particular, John Hurd defends the authenticity of 1 Thess. 2.13-16 by means of an *a b a* form of *chiasmus*. In this structure, Paul discusses one point, digresses to a second and then recapitulates the first point. Hurd argues that this pattern occurs in full form two times in 1 Thessalonians and organizes the whole of the letter.[24] The first *a b a* pattern occurs in 1.2-2.16. I illustrate the parallelism of the two framing members below.

and it stems παρὰ ἀνθρώπου (1.12). He defends himself in chiastic order: παρὰ ἀνθ. (1.13-2.21), κατὰ ἀνθ. (3.1-6.1).

20. See Hurd's unpublished paper, 'Concerning the Structure of 1 Thessalonians', pp. 21-22.

21. Lund, *Chiasmus in the New Testament: A Study in Formgeschichte* (Chapel Hill: University of North Carolina Press, 1942). Jeremias's criticism is in 'Chiasmus in den Paulusbriefen', p. 145.

22. E.g. see Hurd's analysis of the multiple member chiastic chains in 1 Thess. 2.19-20; 4.3-8; 4.15-17 and 5.2-8 ('Concerning the Structure of 1 Thessalonians', pp. 21-25).

23. See Hurd, 'Paul Ahead of his Time', pp. 28-30. See also his unpublished paper on 1 Thessalonians, 'Concerning the Structure of 1 Thessalonians', pp. 25-27.

24. See the subsequent discussion for illustration of this thesis. Hurd says there are a number of examples of this *a b a* pattern in Paul's letters. For example, in 1 Corinthians 8 Paul discusses the eating of meat offered to idols, then in ch. 9 he discusses his rights as an apostle before returning in 10.1-11 to the subject of meat offered to idols. Similarly, in 1 Corinthians 12 he introduces a certain subject, ch. 13 is a digression and ch. 14 marks the return to the subject of ch. 12. See Hurd, 'Paul Ahead of his Time', p. 28.

	1.2-10		*2.13-16*
a	we give thanks to God	a'	We also give thanks to God
b	always for you all, constantly	b'	constantly
c	knowing...your election;	c'	that when you received
d	for our gospel came to you	d'	the word of God which you heard from us
e	not only in word,	e'	you accepted it not as the word of men
f	but also in power	f'	but as what it really is, the word of God,
g	and in the Holy Spirit	g'	which is at work in you believers.
h	And you became imitators of us and of the Lord...	h'	For you, brethren, became imitators of the churches...
i	For you received the word in much affliction	i'	for you suffered...
j	(The success of the missionaries)	j'	(The suffering of the missionaries)
k	You turned to God from idols,	k'	hindering us from speaking to the Gentiles...
l	to serve a living & true God & to wait for his Son...	l'	that they may be saved...
m	who delivers us from the wrath to come	m'	But God's wrath has come upon them at last.

Paul runs through the same sequence of thought in 2.13-16 that he uses in 1.2-10, but he varies the phraseology and attributes a different effect to the Gospel's reception. Whereas the Gospel brings joy and success to the missionaries in 1.7-8, it brings suffering in 2.14b-15. Thus 2.13-16 is not a slavish imitation of 1.2-10. The middle member between the two series is found in 2.1-12. All three members close with an eschatological climax: 'wrath' (1.10), 'kingdom and glory' (2.12), 'wrath' (2.16).[25]

The same *a b a* parallelism exhibited in 1.2-2.16 is found in 2.17-3.13, with 2.17-20 and 3.9-13 framing 3.1-8. The section is similar in the way formulas introduce the framing members in 2.17 and 3.9 and both sections close on an eschatological climax, 'the coming of our Lord Jesus'.[26]

25. See Hurd, 'Paul Ahead of his Time', pp. 29-30.

26. The introductory and concluding phrases of the middle panel (1 Thess. 3.1-8) are not marked so well. On the other hand, the eschatological climax in 2.19-20 make it clear that 3.1 introduces the new middle member. Though, the end of the middle panel in 3.8 is only mildly eschatological ('For now we live, if you stand fast in the Lord'), the preceding verse signals the end of the section: 'Therefore we have been

The *a b a chiasmus* of 1.2–2.16 and 2.17–3.13 appears to be largely missing from the letter's third main section in 4.1–5.22. To be sure, there are other chiastic structures (for example 4.3-8; 4.15-18; 5.2-8), and we may speak loosely of 4.13–5.11 being a middle panel in 4.1–5.22, but the organizing principle differs somewhat from that in the first three chapters.

1 Thess. 4.1–5.11 is a series of four essays that address ethical issues.[27] The next section, in 5.12-22, repeats concerns voiced in the four essays before turning to general paranetic emphases that appear in Paul's other letters (see 1 Cor. 16.13-18; 2 Cor. 13.5-11; Gal. 5.16–6.10; Phil. 4.2-6). The topics in 1 Thess. 4.1–5.11 were written in reply to questions the Thessalonians sent in a letter. Thus, the questions themselves organize 4.1–5.11.[28]

Though Paul's response to the Thessalonians' questions in 4.1–5.11 interrupts the double *a b a* pattern of the first three chapters, we have noted that 4.13–5.11 appears to function like the middle panel in the two previous cases. Moreover, the subject matter of the three middle members appears to form an overarching pattern for 1.2–5.22. The theological virtue of love is the subject of 2.1-12, faith is the subject of 3.1-8, and hope is the focus of 4.13–5.11. It is hardly coincidental that Paul thanks God for the concrete expression of the Thessalonians' faith, hope and love in the opening thanksgiving prayer: '…remembering before our God and Father your work of faith and labor of love and steadfastness of hope in our Lord Jesus Christ' (1 Thess. 1.3). Correspondingly, near the close of the letter, Paul

comforted, brethren, about you' (3.7). Paul concludes two other sections in the same way (see the discussion of 4.18 and 5.11 below).

27. The issues are: sexual morality (1 Thess. 4.1-8); love of the brethren (4.9-12); resurrection of deceased Christians (4.13-18); and signs of the *parousia* (5.1-11).

28. Hurd proposes that Paul wrote 1 Cor. 7-16, like 1 Thess. 4-5, mostly to answer questions which his recipients had sent to him. Thus, 1 Corinthians and 1 Thessalonians may be described as 'Response Letters', because they are written in large part to address specific questions. After expressing epistolary conventions more or less comparable to his other letters, in these two letters Paul turns by means of a transitional passage to topics in his correspondents' letter. Though we do not know the sequence of topics in the correspondents' letter, it is significant that in both cases Paul discusses sexual morality first (see 1 Corinthians 7 and 1 Thess. 4.1-8) and eschatological matters more or less at the end (see 1 Corinthians 15 and 1 Thess. 4.13-5.11). See Hurd, 'Concerning the Structure of 1 Thessalonians', pp. 32-38.

expresses the same triadic list of virtues: 'Put on the breastplate of faith and love, and for a helmet the hope of salvation' (1 Thess. 5.8). Consequently, Paul's interior expression of faith, hope, and love cuts across the entirety of the letter. The first two intermediate members of the *a b a* structure contain the virtues of love and faith respectively and organize the body up to Paul's response to the Thessalonians' letter. The third virtue, hope, provides an appropriate eschatological note on which to end the letter as a whole. Hurd argues that since Paul dictated the letter, he probably organized material mentally. The triad of virtues is just the sort of organizing device that a speaker like Paul would have carried into his epistolary pulpit.[29]

Chiasmus is an important stylistic aspect of Paul's correspondence generally. For example, we noted at the beginning of this subsection that, according to Jeremias, all of Galatians is organized on the basis of an overarching chiastic structure. Shorter inversions also abound within the letter. We may point to the correspondence between Gal. 1.1-5 and 6.16-18 and the parallelism of 1.6-10 and 6.11-15, which illustrate the ring composition I identified earlier in the essay. By way of summary for this section, I cite John Hurd's assessment of Paul's chiastic ability: 'Paul does seem capable, often in surprising detail, to work his way to the center of an idea and then to unwind the sequence so as to end where he began'.[30]

2.2 *Rhetorical Forms of Argumentation*

According to Aristotle, there were three types of argumentative rhetoric: deliberative, forensic and epideictic. Deliberative oratory directed itself to the Greek city state's assembly and urged the most expedient political course, for example, should we go to war or stay at peace? Forensic rhetoric was spoken at the law court and attacked or defended a citizen's past conduct. Epideictic rhetoric was used at customary celebrations (military victories, funerals, etc.) in order, through praise or blame, to clarify what was honorable or shameful. Traditional kinds of argumentation were expanded, adapted, and combined in the Graeco-Roman period and philosophical schools began to use rhetoric in letters of instruction. Since letter-writing had its own roots, the shape of rhetoric in letters was not fully delineated in antiquity. Nonetheless, the dominant form of epistolary rhetoric in

29. Hurd, 'Concerning the Structure of 1 Thessalonians', pp. 38-42.
30. Hurd, 'Concerning the Structure of 1 Thessalonians', p. 22.

the early period of the empire was the loosely defined epideictic branch.[31]

What is the difference in saying Paul's emphasis in any particular letter is forensic, deliberative or epideictic? If forensic, Paul's intention would be apologetic or accusatory. He would defend his own conduct as trustworthy and/or he would argue against the reliability of alternative views. This type of judicial rhetoric could arise in situations like Galatians and 2 Corinthians where people with an alternative view had confused recipients about Paul's trustworthiness. If the emphasis were deliberative Paul would offer advice appropriate to the issues that occasioned the letter and the advice would be designed to procure specific actions. Finally, if the emphasis were epideictic Paul would use praise or censure to gain adherence to values he and recipients shared. We survey alternative views of two letters to focus what is at stake in Paul's use of rhetoric.

Hans Dieter Betz argues that Paul defends himself against false charges in Galatians and that, formally speaking, it is an apologetic (forensic) letter. This viewpoint is supported by Paul's uncharacteristic description of apostleship in the opening address: 'not from men nor through man, but through Jesus Christ and God the father' (1.1). The gravity of the situation is supported by Paul's failure in 1.2 to identify the Galatians with any designation other than 'the churches of Galatia'. Even more striking Paul replaces his usual thanksgiving with censure in 1.6-11 (the *exordium*).

In Gal. 1.12-2.14 Paul establishes the legitimacy of his past conduct by rehearsing how he received his commission by divine intervention (the *narratio*). The supernatural origin of Paul's commission is verified by the radical change from persecutor to advocate of Christianity. Paul also shows his contact with Jerusalem apostles was

---

31. According to Stanley Stowers, accusing and apologetic letters fell under forensic rhetoric. The letter of advice should be classified as deliberative rhetoric. Most other kinds of letters could be regarded as belonging to epideictic rhetoric. To be sure the strict distinction between epideictic (praise and blame) and deliberative (giving advice) rhetoric breaks down in the hortatory and paranetic tradition (see *Letter Writing in Greco-Roman Antiquity*, p. 52). For the most part Paul's letters are complex paranetic/hortatory letters. In general, hortatory letters dominate in first and second century Christian letter writing. Judicial and deliberative rhetoric only come to the fore in fourth and fifth century letters from Christian bishops (*Letter Writing*, pp. 42-43).

too limited and so long after conversion to be the source of his authority. Moreover, Paul demonstrates that the Jerusalem leaders publically acknowledged his status as apostle to the Gentiles. Finally, by means of the issue of table fellowship at Antioch, Paul shows by his defense of the equality of Gentile converts that he was true to the gospel. In Gal. 2.15-21 (the *propositio*) Paul adduces the following 'proposition' from the dispute at Antioch: both Paul and his fellow Jewish converts agreed that right relation with God was no longer based on traditional observances. In Gal. 3.1-4.31 (the *probatio*) Paul 'proves' that right relation with God is effected by faith in Christ, not observance of the law. He does this by appealing to the Galatians' own experience of the salvation effected in their former response to Paul. Without going further, we may assume that we understand the main lineaments of a forensic reading of Galatians.

Contrary to Betz's view, Robert Hall argues that self-defense is less an issue in Galatians than an error in judgment which needs correcting.[32] In this reading, Galatians fits the deliberative species of rhetoric better than the forensic. Thus Hall asks: 'Is the letter to the Galatians primarily concerned with defending some past action of Paul?' It is difficult to reconcile this hypothesis with the second half of the letter (Gal. 3.1–6.18), where Paul's past actions are hardly considered. Paul's goal is to persuade the Galatians to cleave to Paul and to reject opponents.[33]

Unfortunately, advocates both of the forensic and of the deliberative reading of Galatians assume too narrowly that historical circumstance determines Paul's argument. To comprehend Paul's primary intent we must look to the social reality which Paul conceives as a possibililty in Christ. In this sense epideictic rhetoric best describes Paul's intent, because it sought to fix or alter the disposition of people toward certain values. To be sure, Paul concerns himself with the future conduct of the Galatians, as Hall suggests. However, the central issue is the past and how it impinges upon the future as a basis of commitment. Namely, Paul concerns himself with the authenticity of the

---

32. R.G. Hall, 'The Rhetorical Outline for Galatians: A Reconsideration', *JBL* 106 (June 1987), pp. 277-87. See also G.A. Kennedy, *New Testament Interpretation through Rhetorical Criticism* (Chapel Hill: University of North Carolina Press, 1984), pp. 144-52. See further Dahl, 'Paul's Letter to the Galatians', pp. 50-52.

33. Hall, 'The Rhetorical Outline for Galatians', pp. 278-79.

Galatians' former relationship with God. In this respect Betz is right in emphasizing the significance of Paul's narration of the past because it establishes what is certain. Paul composed Galatians in such a way as to evoke the effective power of the spirit, a reality which the Galatians had already experienced. Thus, the letter functions as a reminder of the experience of the divine spirit encountered in the crucified one.

At the level of formal argumentation I agree with Nils Dahl that Paul's letters are all mixed types. On the other hand, there is an essential sense in which, at the level of primary intentionality, epideictic rhetoric provides the explanatory principle that best accounts for the adherence to community concord which Paul regularly requires. This viewpoint may be illustrated further. For example, Stanley Stowers concludes that the genre which is most determinative of 1 Corinthians is deliberative rhetoric, even though he identifies parts of the letter as epideictic.[34] Wilhelm Wuellner argues against Stowers by contending that Paul was not concerned with what story there *was* of divisions at Corinth but by what story of unity there *is* in Christ, which the Corinthians have already experienced as a reality. Thus, Paul refuses to attribute the Corinthians' discord to the authentic basis of community which God has created in Christ. Division and destructiveness at Corinth comes not from Christ's spirit but from human perversion of God's intention. Thus, Paul's goal is to reinforce God's life giving concord as the true basis of human community.[35]

Conclusion

There is fundamental congruence in Paul's use of rhetoric in the theological argument of his letters, both in the formal features that characterize the beginning and end of his letters, and in his conception of his churches as a spiritual family. Paul's concern with his converts' spiritual welfare is evident in his use of a grace blessing to introduce and conclude his letters. Blamelessness in Christ is the condition of spiritual well being and this idea is regularly exhibited in Paul's opening thanksgiving prayers and in the body-closing convention. Moreover, both the body-closing conventions and the thanksgiving prayers agree that a temporal limit is fixed for the community's

34. Stowers, *Letter Writing in Greco-Roman Antiquity*, p. 52.
35. See W. Wuellner, 'Epistolography and Rhetoric in 1 Corinthians' (unpublished paper delivered to the SNTS , 1988), pp. 8-10.

maturation. They must be prepared by the time of Christ's return. In his emphasis on the community's purity and blamelessness, Paul maintains the traditional Jewish idea that God's people must be a kingdom of priests.

This conception of Paul's converts as God's people leads, in turn, to his use of family imagery to characterize the converts' relation to one another and to God. They are a spiritual family. The imagery is of a piece with Paul's epistolary features and his rhetorical argumentation. The root idea is Paul's conception of God's life giving character. God's ability to father and mother (nourish) is exhibited not only in the generation of sonship out of the sterility of Christ's ignominious death, but also in the creation of a spiritual family and race. The life giving character effected in Christ and in the community show that the creator is at work effecting the new birth of the world. Just as God is life giving and nourishing in his effect, so too his offspring must create unity not division; they must be productive and not sterile; they must build up and not tear down.[36] By this root idea of growth and life we see that Paul's rhetorical purpose is epideictic. As the apostle to the Gentiles Paul must produce adherence to a system of convictions that places unerring trust in God's ability to effect life out of death.[37] The maturation process whereby Gentiles converts conform to the model of Christ must be completed by his return.

36. Paul expresses the analogous ideas of productivity (versus sterility), building up (versus tearing down), and maturation (versus 'childishness') in 1 Cor. 3.1-4.21

37. This viewpoint is also advocated by W. Wuellner in 'Greek Rhetoric and Pauline Argumentation', in *Early Christian Literature and the Classical Tradition* (Festschrift R.M. Grant; Paris: Beauchesne, 1979), pp. 177-88. See also Wuellner, 'Paul's Rhetoric of Argumentation in Romans: An Alternative to the Donfried-Karris Debate over Romans', in K.P. Donfried (ed.), *The Romans Debate* (Minneapolis: Augsburg, 1977), pp. 152-74. Though Daniel Patte does not discuss Paul's religious viewpoint in terms of epideictic rhetoric, he supports the same perspective. See *Paul's Faith and the Power of the Gospel* (Philadelphia: Fortress Press, 1983).

CONVERSION AND UNIVERSALISM: OPPOSITES THAT ATTRACT

Alan F. Segal

It is a pleasure to contribute this work to a Festschrift in honour of John Hurd, my colleague at the University of Toronto in the late 1970s, and my teacher in computing and New Testament.

There is much to be gained by interleafing the reading of Jewish literature and Christian documents. I can illustrate the benefits by asking some simple questions: what was the Jewish view in the first century of the place of the Gentiles in God's scheme? Is there a relationship between the notion of conversion and the concept of a universal mission in Judaism and Christianity?

As with all deceptively simple questions, there is no single answer. For instance, *Judaism* did not have a single policy on the status of the Gentiles; there was no single Judaism of the day. *Jews* did have opinions about Gentiles but that is not the same as a policy. Various Jewish sects had policies or theologies that involved Gentiles in some way. And most Jews and Jewish sects had ambivalent opinions. This paper will attempt to address the ambivalence and show how various communities dealt with it. Within the various choices available to them, the Christian and the rabbinic communities found new answers to the questions, answers which were appropriate to their social outlook and purposes. We shall discover that the Christian community designed its understanding of universal mission in the first century, as it dealt with the issue of the conversion of the Gentiles. Conversely, rabbinic Judaism designed its specific understanding of universalism in the second and third centuries, as it dealt with the issue of remaining Jewish in a hostile world, without having a Jewish national homeland, a world that looked askance at any Jewish mission to convert.

A major point of this essay will be that the NT evinces the same ambivalence on the issue of the inclusion of Gentiles as do the other Jewish sects. Indeed, the history of early Christianity is a history resolving that ambiguity after a great deal of conflict. So the easy contrasts made between the early Christian community and the variety of Jewish sects do not work. It is not just a question of Jewish parochialism being replaced by Christian universalism. Each community discussed universalism and answered the question in a different but similar way, resolving that quandary in a similar but unique way. In both communities the solution favors universalism. In both communities the path to universalism is an aspect of the intellectual climate of late Hellenism mediated by the special and differing historical circumstances of the nascent rabbinic Jewish and Christian communities.

I want to trace the relationship between various Jewish definitions of conversion and the Christian one. Social scientists tell us that each community defines uniquely what it means by conversion. We do not know everything we need to know about the origins of the rabbinic version of conversion. But we can tell a great deal about the Dead Sea Scroll community. In different ways both communities outlined a period of learning, followed by a change of identity based on oath and ritual. The Christian definition of conversion, however, is quite different. It is concerned with a reorientation of the mind, a psychological decision. How did it come about? To find out we will have to ask basic questions of the entire relationship between Judaism and Christianity in the first century.

1. *Jewish Mysticism, Apocalypticism and Conversion*

All Jewish mysticism, indeed even the doctrine of resurrection itself, depends on a very peculiar passage in Daniel 12, the only apocalyptic work accepted into the Hebrew Bible:

> At that time shall arise Michael, the great prince who has charge of your people, and there shall be a time of trouble, such as never has been since there was a nation til that time, but at that time your people shall be delivered, every one whose name shall be found written in the book. And many of those who sleep in the dust of the earth shall awake, some to everlasting life, and some to shame and ever-lasting contempt. And those who are wise shall shine like the brightness of the firmament; and those who turn many to righteousness, like the stars for ever and ever. (Dan. 12.1-3)

And we often gloss over the rather peculiar aspects of this prophecy. It says that two kinds of people will be resurrected—the very good and the very bad (not the usual understanding of the later communities). More interesting to me is the idea that the *maskilim*, those who are wise, will shine as the stars in heaven, יזהרו כזהר הרקיע—this is literally where Zohar, the principal book of Jewish mysticism, gets its name. Essentially this document tells us that those who make themselves wise will become stars, but it actually means that the good people on earth will become stars. Angels in heaven and stars are equated. The history of Jewish mysticism is deeply concerned with the experience of becoming a star. But that is precisely what Paul tells us. We must wait to see how.

I want to underline two aspects of this mystical tradition and show how it is fundamental to Paul's experience. The first aspect of the Jewish mystical experience is the vision of a principal angelic mediator who like 'the son of man' or the angel of the Lord in Exodus carries the name of God or participates in God's divinity somehow. All the passages describing a principal angelic mediator, sometimes more technically called the Glory of the Lord, especially Dan. 7.3 and Ezek. 1.26—the human figure on the throne in Ezekiel's vision—are pulled into this angelic figure, making a consistent figure of a principal angelic mediator. This mediator figure can be called a variety of different names—Yahoel, Melchizedek, and even the son of man—and as I have tried to show in *Paul the Convert*, it was this figure that Paul saw and with whom he identified the crucified Christ. So for Paul the figure was the traditional one except, as he says in 2 Corinthians, it has the face of Jesus.

The second aspect of this tradition which is important to the study of Paul is *transformation*. In the Jewish mystical tradition adepts or heroes or patriarchs can be transformed or subsumed into the mediator figure. This is more or less the equivalent of becoming an angel or becoming a star, which is the exact point of Daniel 12. The most obvious example of this phenomenon, though by no means the only one, is Enoch, who is transformed into the Son of Man in *1 Enoch* 71. I would submit that what is narrated there is the very experience of being made a star, the same experience which is narrated in Daniel 12. From an historical point of view, the problem with this tradition is that ch. 71 of *1 Enoch* cannot be proven to be pre-Christian. Most scholars believe it to be pre-Christian but that is not the same thing as a proof.

Since *1 Enoch* cannot be proven pre-Christian, Paul's testimony becomes the most important. Furthermore, Paul gives us first person, confessional experience about what these experiences are. He tells us about the man who went to heaven and he tells us what it is like to be in Christ.

2. *Paul's Use of Mystical Vocabulary*

Paul himself rarely uses the concept of conversion, but his writing is full of that kind of radical religious experience which we in the West have called conversion. When Paul says that he preaches that Jesus is Lord and that God 'has let this light shine out of darkness into our hearts to give the light of knowledge of the glory of God in the face of Christ' (2 Cor. 4.6), he seems to be describing his own conversion and ministry, just as he described it in Galatians 1, and just as he is explaining the experience to new converts for the purpose of furthering conversion. His apostolate, which he expresses as a prophetic calling, is to proclaim that the face of *Christ* is the glory of God.

Concomitant with Paul's worship of the divine Christ is *transformation* and it is this experience which dominates Paul's religious life. Paul says in Phil. 3.10 'that I may know him and the power of his resurrection and may share his sufferings, becoming like him (συμμορφιζόμενος) in his death'. Later, in Phil. 3.20-21, he says: 'But our commonwealth is in heaven, and from it we await a Savior, the Lord Jesus Christ, who will change (μετασχηματίσει) our lowly body to be like (σύμμορφον) his glorious body, by the power which enables him even to subject all things to himself'. The body of the believer eventually is to be transformed into the body of Christ.

Paul's depiction of salvation is based on his understanding of Christ's glorification, partaking of early Jewish apocalyptic mysticism for its expression.[1] In Rom. 12.2 Paul's listeners are exhorted to 'be

---

1. Scholars like S. Kim (*The Origin's of Paul's Gospel* [WUNT, 2/4; Tübingen: Mohr, 2nd edn, 1984]), who want to ground all of Paul's thought in a single ecstatic conversion experience, which they identify with Luke's accounts of Paul's conversion, are reticent to accept this passage as a fragment from Christian liturgy because to do so would destroy its value as Paul's personal revelatory experience. But there is no need to decide whether the passage is originally Paul's (hence received directly through the 'Damascus revelation', since ecstatic language normally is derived from traditions current within the religious group. Christian mystics use

transformed' (μεταμορφοῦσθε) by the renewing of your minds'. In
Gal. 4.19 Paul expresses another transformation: 'My little children,
with whom I am again in travail until Christ be formed (μορφωθῇ) in
you!' This transformation is to be effected by becoming like him in
his death (συμμορφιζόμενος τῷ θανάτῳ αὐτοῦ, Phil. 3.10).

Paul's central proclamation is: Jesus is Lord and all who have faith
have already undergone a death like his, so will share in his resurrection. As we have seen, this proclamation reflects a baptismal liturgy,
implying that baptism provides the moment whereby the believer
comes to be 'in Christ'. Christianity may have been a unique Jewish
sect in making baptism a central rather than a preparatory ritual, but
some of the mystical imagery comes from its Jewish past.

Alternatively, Paul can say, as he does in Gal. 1.16 that 'God was
pleased to reveal His Son in me (ἐν ἐμοί)'. This is not a simple dative
but refers to his having received in him the Spirit, in his case through
his conversion. Being in *Christ* in fact appears to mean being united
with his heavenly image. The same, however, is available to all
Christians through baptism.

The meaning of Romans 8.29 can be likewise clarified by Jewish
esoteric tradition. There, Paul speaks of God as having 'foreordained
his elect to be conformed to the image of his Son' (προώρισεν
συμμόρφους τῆς εἰκόνος τοῦ υἱοῦ αὐτοῦ). Paul uses the genitive
here rather than the dative as in Philippians 3.21, softening the
identification between believer and savior. But when Paul states that
believers conform to the image of his Son, he is not speaking of an
agreement of mind or ideas between Jesus and the believers. The word
σύμμορφον itself suggests a spiritual reformation of the believer's
body into the form of the divine image. Paul's language for
conversion develops out of mystical Judaism.

Christian language, Muslim mystics use the languages developed for mysticism in
Islam and no mystic is ever confused by another religion's mysticism unless it is the
conscious and explicit intent of the mystic's vision to do so. See R.C. Zaehner
Hinduism and Muslim Mysticism (New York: Schocken Books, 1969); S. Katz,
'Language, Epistemology, and Mysticism', in S. Katz (ed.) *Mysticism and
Philosophical Analysis* (New York: Oxford University Press, 1983). In this case the
language is not even primarily Christian. The basic language is from Jewish
mysticism, though the subsequent exegesis about the the identification of the Christ
with the figure on the throne is Christian; the vision of God enthroned is the goal of
Jewish mystical speculation.

Paul speaks of the transformation being partly experienced by believers already in their pre-parousia existence. His use of present tense in Rom. 12.2 and 2 Cor. 3.18 underscores that transformation is an ongoing event. However in 1 Cor. 15.49 and Romans 8 it culminates at Christ's return, the parousia. This suggests that for Paul transformation is both a single, definitive event yet also a process that continues until the second coming. The redemptive and transformative process appears to correspond exactly with the turning of the ages. This age is passing away, though it certainly remains a present evil reality (1 Cor. 3.19; 5.9, 2 Cor. 4.4, Gal. 1.4, Rom. 12.2). The Gospel, which is the power of God for salvation (Rom. 1.16), is progressing through the world (Phil. 1.12, also Rom. 9–11).

Paul describes the 'Glory of the Lord' (2 Cor. 3.16-4.6) in the very places where he describes his own conversion, which he also uses as a pattern for experience by which other believers come to be in Christ. As an heir of Christ the believer shares the glory of Christ (Rom. 8.17), which eclipses any suffering which may have been experienced in the believer's life (Rom. 8.18, 2 Cor. 4.15-17). This exchange of suffering for glory will occur at Christ's coming, according to Col. 3.4, which may have been Paul's opinion but can as easily be the considered judgment of a close disciple after Paul's death. Paul himself appears less sure of the exact relationship between the various processes. He talks both of a progressive process and a final consummation of the faithful being changed or transformed into the 'image of Christ' (Rom. 8.29, 1 Cor. 15.49), which again resembles Ezekiel's language of 'the appearance of the likeness of the Glory of the Lord' (Ezek. 1.28 cf. LXX). Central to Paul's Christian experience is the transformation of believers at the apocalypse. More importantly, Paul anticipates the technical terminology of the transformation of believers into angels in Jewish mysticism.

Of course, the mystical experience of conversion is not only with the *risen* Christ but with the *crucified* Christ. The most obvious relationship between the believer and Christ is suffering and death (Rom. 7.24; 8.10,13). By being transformed by Christ one is not simply made immortal, given the power to remain deathless. Rather one still experiences death as the Christ did, and like him survives death for heavenly enthronement. This is a consequence of the Christian's divided state. Although part of the last Adam, the Christian also, living through Spirit, is still part of the world of the flesh. As

James Dunn has noted: 'Suffering was something *all* believers experienced—an unavoidable part of the believer's lot—an aspect of experience as Christians which his converts shared with Paul.[2]

Thus, the persecution and suffering of the believers is a sign that the transformation process has begun; it is the way to come to be *in* Christ. Paul is convinced that being united with Christ's crucifixion means not immediate *glorification* but *suffering* for the believers in this interim period. The glorification follows upon the final consummation. The connection between suffering and resurrection has been clear in Jewish martyrology; indeed the connection between death and rebirth was even a prominent part of the mystery religions as well. But the particular way in which Paul makes these connections is explicitly Christian.

3. *Paul and Luke Compared*

There are many important differences between Paul and Luke, mostly stemming from their different purposes. Paul wants to vindicate his position as apostle, while Luke wants to portray the progress of the church from the Jewish community to the Gentile one. The sequence basic to Luke's history of the church is unemphasized in Paul's own writing. Paul tries to express the content of his revelation while Luke uses Paul's ecstatic experience as a model for Gentile conversions. Lastly and most importantly, although Paul certainly calls his conversion a revelation, Luke substitutes a revelatory audition unknown in Paul's writing.

Luke was writing with more historical perspective than Paul and, of course, less personal knowledge of the experience, but he understands the importance of Paul's conversion in ways which Paul himself perhaps did not fully realize. The most significant aspect of Luke's description is the radical distinction between resurrection appearances of Christ and experiences of the spirit.[3] Neither Paul himself nor John

---

2.   Rom. 5.3 ('we'); 8.17-18 ('we'), 2 Cor. 1.16 ('you endure the same sufferings that we suffer'); 8.2; Phil. 1.29-30 ('the same conflict which you saw and now hear to be mine'); 1 Thess. 1.6 ('imitators of us and of the Lord'); 2.14 ('imitators of the churches of God in Judea: for you suffered the same things'); 3.3-4 ('our lot') 2 Thess. 1.4ff. (cf. J.D.G. Dunn, *Jesus and the Spirit*, [Philadelphia: Westminster Press, 1975], p. 327).

3.   Dunn, *Spirit*.

distinguishes so clearly between 'spiritual' and 'resurrection' appearances. In 1 Cor. 15.45, for instance, Paul shows no sensitivity to Luke's interpretive categories when he conflates the appearance of the risen Jesus as 'a life-giving spirit.'

Luke, on the other hand, distinguishes Paul's experience from that of the original twelve apostles. For Luke the authentic resurrection appearances of Jesus in the Gospel and Acts are far more mundane and 'realistic.' Jesus walks and talks with wayfarers, blesses them, eats and is sometimes unrecognized at first. For Luke these are not visionary appearances but meant to be descriptions of ordinary consciousness. Luke understands the first sightings of Jesus as actual physical manifestations. The resurrection appearances are brought to an end by the ascension (Acts 1.9-11).[4] Conversely, for Luke, Paul's conversion is a visionary audition, with no specific image described. Even though Paul's experience may have been visionary in some way, it falls into a second category of sightings, an expression of the spirit after Jesus' ascension.[5] Luke identifies the original twelve disciples as apostles, limiting apostolic status to those who had accompanied Jesus during the length of his ministry (Acts 1.21-6); by implication then, Paul falls into a secondary category, that of converts to Christ by means of the holy spirit.

Paul may accept the status of the twelve as special disciples, but he argues for his apostolate. For him, the appearance of Christ to him vindicates his equal status as apostle, even though it occurred in a revelation and vision. Indeed, he includes himself in the list of those to whom Jesus' resurrection was made manifest (Galatians 1, 1 Cor. 9.1, 15.8-9). Paul may recognize that he is 'last of all' and 'untimely born' but he will not give up his claim to be an apostle, because Christ appeared to him. He uses the same simple word, 'see', to describe his and the other apostles' experience of the Christ. Paul therefore does not distinguish between the kind of appearance made known to him and those of his forebears.

For Luke, ecstatic experience is already the established role model for the conversion of Gentiles, because of Paul. But it is not the model for resurrection appearances, which are treated literally and give a

4. Indeed, there are two different ascensions in his history. The Gospel implies an ascension with the resurrection, which is fulfilled at the beginning of Acts.

5. Ananias, Peter and others receive 'visions' (ὀπτασία) e.g. Acts 2.17; 9.10; 10.3, 17; 11.5. Paul's experience is also a 'trance' (ἐκστάσις [Acts 22.17]).

special status to the first apostles. For Paul, in contrast, the revelatory vision of the Christ functions as a bid for power, since he was a peripheral figure in Christianity, as his battle for apostolic acceptance shows.[6] The motif of realistic appearances in Luke is similar to a Graeco-Roman apologetic designed to impress critics and friends with the power of Jesus' resurrection, whereas the ecstatic visions of Paul are more in line with the original Jewish apocalypticism out of which Christianity.

Luke's and Paul's description of the risen Christ is significant in social ways as well. The contrast between them points to an incipient crisis in the church—between those, mostly Jewish Christians, who based their new faith on an experience of Jesus in the flesh and those, mostly Gentile Christians championed by the ex-Pharisee Paul, who based their faith on a spiritual interpretation of the Christ, seen primarily in his resurrection or spiritual body. The theology, in other words, parallels the social distinction in early Christianity between those who knew Christ in a fleshly way and those who knew him in his spiritual body. This vision and the subsequent success of the Gentile mission convinces Paul that the new age is not only imminent but that it has already begun. It also convinces him that his Jewish opponents see the Christ in a fleshly rather than a spiritual way.

Paul's own experience stands squarely within Jewish mysticism. Luke's description is cognizant of that connection, but Luke is more taken with the issue of spirit possession in the later Church. Luke's model for Paul's conversion reflects a more evolved definition of conversion within the Church, a model for many converts to follow. For Luke, Paul's ecstatic conversion on the road to Damascus is the first of a large number of ecstatic conversions.

Another interesting exposition of the new developing definition of Christian conversion comes toward the end of Luke's narration of Paul's life. When Paul is interrogated by King Agrippa and the Roman Procurator Festus in Acts 26, the following dialogue takes place:

6.   Of course, one can take the distinction too far, for in 2 Corinthians 12, in the same passage that Paul describes a revelation and ascent to the heavens, he argues against other Christians who claim yet more authority for ecstatic experiences. So Paul represents a compromise position between pure periphery and pure centrality in early Christianity. If he were more characteristic of a peripheral prophet he would not oppose the charismatics so vigorously. On the other hand he feels that all have a proper place (1 Cor. 12.4-13).

And as he thus made his defense, Festus said with a loud voice, 'Paul, you are mad; your great learning is turning you mad'. But Paul said, 'I am not mad, most excellent Festus, but I am speaking the sober truth. For the king knows about these things, and to him I speak freely; for I am persuaded that none of these things has escaped his notice, for this was not done in a corner. King Agrippa, do you believe the prophets? I know that you believe'. And Agrippa said to Paul, 'In a short time you think to make me a Christian!' And Paul said, 'Whether short or long, I would to God that not only you but also all who hear me this day might become such as I am—except for these chains.' (Acts 26.24-29)

Luke has fashioned this encounter into a conventional confrontation between the wise man and the ruler. But it is not thereby devoid of historical meaning. As Abraham Malherbe has pointed out, The wit, irony and sarcasm in this passage depends very much on understanding differing communities' definitions of conversion.[7] Philosophical (and I might add most Jewish) definitions of conversion were characterized by long training; they depended on this trait for their credibility. Therefore, Paul is being criticized for thinking to make converts too quickly. Luke's Paul answers that he does not care whether it be a quick or slow conversion, provided that the king is converted. Luke thereby certifies that his contemporary Christian missionaries could hope for quick conversions, as well as slow, more conventionally Jewish or philosophical ones. By the time of Justin, who keeps to a more philosophical definition of Christianity, such a conversion would have been viewed with suspicion among some Christians as well. But in Luke's time the quickness of the conversion apparently emphasizes the miraculous power of the spirit. So Luke also portrays Paul's conversion as a sudden Damascus Road experience. Luke uses Paul's example doubly, both as an paradigm of a convert and as model for Christian missionaries.

Paul himself certainly portrays his conversion as thorough and radical. But he does not necessarily think of his conversion as quick. On the other hand, he clearly has made conversion to Christianity easier and perhaps shorter than the normal conversion to Judaism, as his opponents will charge.

Unlike Luke, Paul himself could scarcely have suggested that his spiritual experience was typical of all believers. When we look at his

7. '"Not in a Corner": Early Christian Apologetic in Acts 26.26', *The Second Century* 5.4 (1986), pp. 193-210, see pp 208-210.

ecstatic experiences, such as those narrated in 2 Corinthians 12, we shall see that it provides Paul with special credentials as an apostle. It is not meant to be a universal experience, though it reveals to Paul a universal and hidden meaning to history. However, Paul's narrative is by no means coterminous with the events, either of his conversion or his subsequent revelations.

A long period of time had passed between Paul's actual conversion experience and his account of himself. According to his autobiographical statements in Galatians 1, a minimum of fourteen and perhaps more than seventeen years must have passed, by our counting.[8] So Paul's own description is affected by his Christian calling.

This use of Paul himself as a role model for the convert is even clearer in the pastoral epistles. 1 Timothy 1.12-17 purports to be Paul's own description of his conversion but has much more in common with Luke's ideas about Paul:[9]

> I thank him who has given me strength for this, Christ Jesus our Lord because he judged me faithful by appointing me to his service, though I formerly blasphemed and persecuted and insulted him; but I received mercy because I had acted ignorantly in unbelief, and the grace of our Lord overflowed for me with the faith and love that are in Christ Jesus. The saying is sure and worthy of full acceptance, that Christ Jesus came into the world to save sinners. And I am the foremost of sinners; but I received mercy for this reason, that in me, as the foremost, Jesus Christ might display his perfect patience for an example to those who were to believe in him for eternal life. To the King of Ages, immortal, invisible, the only God, be honor and glory for ever and ever. Amen.

8.   Hellenistic conventions for counting years give a different total than we might expect. Scholars have estimated on the basis of Hellenistic reckonings that from twelve to seventeen years could actually have passed. Since the counting could include the present year, even if it were a bare fraction of a year, as well as what we would consider the first year and the same inclusionary policy was possible at the end of the time period, a wider time span is possible than we would normally allow. See H. Koester, *Introduction to the New Testament* (Berlin: de Gruyter), I, pp. 101-106. Koester demurs from the use of the term 'conversion' on the basis of Paul's self-understanding as a prophet. But once both the change and the mission are brought out, any differences in terminology are likely to be semantic.

9.   See S.G. Wilson, *Luke and the Pastoral Epistles* (London: SPCK, 1979) for the notion that the pastorals were written by Luke. His discussion of 1 Timothy 1.12-17 appears on p. 109.

This passage stresses the contrast between the two periods of Paul's life, his life before conversion and after it. But before conversion Paul is portrayed as the foremost of sinners (1.16) in this pastoral letter, while the Paul of the authentic letters asserts that he is blameless according to the law (Phil. 3.6). Although Paul emphasizes his conversion, and may even regret his former life as a persecutor of Christianity, he never considers himself to be the foremost sinner. This passage in 1 Timothy then has a distinctly post-Pauline character. This conversion is depicted as a model (ὑποτύπωσιν, 1 Tim. 1.16) for the conversion of all non-believers. The theme of repentant sinners is appropriate to the Gentile mission, where repentance from a sinful life was a prominent theme. While the message is mostly Pauline—the narrative reflection upon it comes from the historical distance—it is closer to Luke's than to Paul's authentic voice. And it points out how, by means of Luke's narrative, Paul's life came to be a model for Christian conversion. Thus, we have at least three distinct stages of development in the early Church's understanding of ecstatic conversion: (1) Paul's own ecstatic, emotional experience, which is intensely personal, special, and visionary and which he uses to establish his apostolate, as well as to exemplify the power of the spirit; (2) Luke's contention that Paul's experience is typical of Gentile conversions (but not equivalent to the experience of the disciples); and (3) the deliberate attempt to make Paul into a paradigm for Gentile conversion experiences. Stages two and three are typical of Luke but stage three continues into the pastoral epistles.

4. *The Salvation of the Gentiles: Luke, Paul and the Rabbis*

The problem of the Gentile is played out against the community's growing sense of the uniqueness of its own experience, the sense that there is something new into which to convert. Let's take the Christian community first, because its history on this issue is actually clearer than that of the rabbinic community. According to Acts 15 the issue arises at Antioch before the Jerusalem council, because emissaries from Jerusalem maintain that one cannot be saved unless one is circumcised according to the custom of Moses (ἐὰν μὴ περιτμηθῆτε τῷ Μωϋσέως, οὐ δύνασθε σωθῆναι, Acts 15.1). Sometimes the rejection of this principle is taken by a Christian readership to show the beginning of the process by which Christianity rid itself of painfully parochial ideas in Judaism. Yet, leaving aside the issue of dating in rabbinic Judaism, one puzzling aspect of this report is at odds with normative rabbinic thought of later centuries, which feels that the *righteous* of *all* nations have a place in the world to come. The ambiguity appears due to the time and distance that has elapsed between the actual issue and Luke's narrative, as I will try to show.

Of course, one does not take issue with an ancient historical source without some sense of also taking on the burden of proof. Almost all New Testament critics distrust Luke's chronology of the events of Paul's life for several reasons, not least of all that he is writing at least a generation after the fact. When it comes to issues of historical interpretation the situation is more subtle and less satisfying. As I will show, Luke appears correct in saying that there were Jews who refused to allow that some Gentiles could be saved as Gentiles, who even would not accept *any* Gentiles into the Israelite faith, or who imposed certain ritual requirements on them. So it is entirely possible that the conservative members of the Church do not go along with the Jerusalem church's decision. (A new directive from Jerusalem is not likely to have changed their opinion either, since these positions are variously founded in Jewish law, which the conservative members of the church continued to observe.) The restrictive understanding of salvation is characteristic of some kinds of apocalyptic Judaism. But we shall see that it is certainly not at all uniformly accepted within the Jewish community. Paul will partly help us resolve this dilemma of unravelling the ancient Jewish positions and datings for this issue because Paul is the only Pharisee who ever gave us his personal writings.

In this thicket a few things are exceedingly clear and that is perhaps where we should start: Paul's opinion is that Gentiles do not need to be circumcised to be saved, as he says so clearly. I shall not resolve whether Paul makes this statement before or after the Jerusalem conference. It is not important for the purposes of this paper. Instead I will try to show that Paul's statement is not uniquely characteristic of Pauline Christianity and is not likely to be Paul's innovation. It is characteristic of some pharisaic and later rabbinic Judaism but emphatically not true of apocalypticism. A stronger statement attributable to Paul—namely, that *no one* needs to be circumcised to be saved (which I believe he says, *pace* Gaston)—also appears to have some precedent within the Jewish community, but it is a very minority position, limited to that class of Jews represented by the 'radical allegorizers' mentioned by Philo (*Migr.* 89-94), who apparently identify as Jews but do not perform the rituals.[10] Thus, Luke and Paul taken together are witness to some of the rough spectrum of Jewish opinions as well as the early Christian opinions on that issue. What differs in the Jewish community is the relative weight to be given to the various positions, but the alternatives are roughly the same as those outlined in the writings of the early church.

Luke equates the idea that there is no *salvation* without circumcision with the position of the party of the Pharisees who say 'It is necessary to circumcise them, and to charge them to keep the law of Moses' (Acts 15.5). For Luke, writing from a slight but perceptible historical distance, the questions appear to be part of the same single issue of the inclusion of Gentiles into the community of the saved. But for rabbinic Judaism the two questions which Luke mentions in this passage are hardly identical. In the first instance (Acts 15.1), we are talking about justification and salvation; in the second (Acts 15.5), we need only be talking about proper conversion. Rabbinic Judaism (as evidenced by the Mishnah, which is redacted at the beginning of the third century) distinguishes radically between conversion and salvation. It does say all Israel will be saved. But it allows that some Gentiles can be saved *qua* Gentiles without conversion: conversion to Judaism is hence not necessary for salvation, though it is certainly admirable. The rabbis do not define as exclusive a club for salvation as does Christianity and the reasons for it are not hard to find in the historical context, as will shortly become clear. On the other hand, rabbinic Judaism requires that *all converts to Judaism be strictly charged to keep the law of Moses*: No doubt this is something like what Paul had in mind when he says: 'Now I, Paul, say to you that if you receive circumcision, Christ will be of no advantage to you. I testify again to every man who receives circumcision that he is bound to keep the whole law' (Gal. 5.2-3). Viewed in this way, Paul can tell us that the rabbinic notion that Gentiles can be saved without conversion is already in existence (on which see the brief discussion below of Romans 2).[11]

---

10. L. Gaston has made the case repeatedly that Paul was proclaiming an antinomian way for gentiles only. Gaston believes that Jews can continue to be saved through the law (see, *Paul and the Torah*, Vancouver: University of British Columbia Press, 1987).

11. *m. Sanh.* 10, *t. Sanh.* 13.2, *b. Sanh.* 105a, *Sifra* 86b, *b. B. Qam.* 38a.

Rabbinic writings debate the issue of the salvation of the Gentiles, as they debate almost every issue.

> Rabbi Eliezer said: 'All the nations will have no share in the world to come, even as it is said, "the wicked shall go into Sheol, and all the nations that forget God" (Ps. 9.17). The wicked shall go into Sheol— these are the wicked among Israel.' Rabbi Joshua said to him: 'If the verse had said, "The wicked shall go into Sheol with all the nations," and had stopped there, I should have agreed with you, but as it goes on to say "who forget God," it means there are righteous persons among the nations who have a share in the world to come.' (*t. Sanh.* 13.2)

According to the rabbinic writings, Luke is half right. Some Pharisees (let us for argument's sake identify Pharisees and Tannaim, even though the two are not exactly coterminous), represented by Rabbi Eliezer, said that only Israel will be saved. Others, represented by Rabbi Joshua, said that the righteous Gentiles would be saved as well. Would that we could trust that these were the actual positions of the rabbis. We cannot any more, given our natural skepticism about the value of oral reports. But we should not assume that the texts are deliberately misinforming us either. Like Luke, the midrash is not necessarily totally at error; it has probably foreshortened and conflated in a way that seems justified from its own perspective.

We do note that the Mishnah and Midrash are at least consistent on this issue, which one can hardly claim about a number of other issues: the positions attributed to Rabbis Eliezer b. Hyrcanus and Joshua b. Hananiah, two Pharisees of the late first century, are typical of other remarks that rabbinic literature has attributed to them. Rabbi Eliezer is a severe critic of Gentiles. Rabbi Joshua b. Hananiah is more liberal. He removes all distinctions between Jew and Gentile in attaining salvation through the doing of good deeds. He says that everyone who walks in blamelessness before his Creator in this world will escape the judgment of hell in the world to come. He even disagrees with Rabbi Gamaliel by maintaining that the blameless children of wicked heathen will also have a share in the world to come. Though Rabbi Joshua probably does not allow conversion without circumcision, he at least looks at the positive side of the issue by stating that baptism without circumcision makes one a *ger*, (that is a proselyte, a convert)—that is, all the ritual has to be done, but if the circumcision is to be performed, the status of convert can be regarded as beginning with baptism from some points of view (see *b. Yeb.* 46a).

If the argument between Eliezer and Joshua were historical, then they would be directly coterminous with the first generations of Christians; and they are to be found in early rabbinic sources—the Tosefta is as important as the Mishnah in terms of authority and dating. But if the early third century is our *ad quem*, the attribution to the first century is the very thing which we must question, unless we have evidence to establish it. Furthermore, the rabbinic discussions are certainly not *ipsissima verba* of the rabbis, just as Luke's statements are not the exact words of the conservative party of Jews within the Christian movement. But the midrash does leave us with the impression that the same issues which were debated in the Church were also being debated by the rabbis. It is possible that all the Christian Pharisees were of the most conservative persuasion, and some more liberal ones show up in rabbinic Judaism, but that seems statistically unlikely. Note too that this issue is crucial for understanding Paul's program for Christianity, to which I shall return at the end of this essay.

It is possible that the rabbis debate this issue because it is raised by the Christian community and that they take their cues from them. This has always been an unpopular hypothesis in the study of rabbinic texts but it should not be automatically excluded, as Jews have perennially learned significantly from their friends and neighbors, creating throughout their history similar as well as contrasting formulations of issues which they absorbed from outside sources. But the questions in Luke and the rabbis are suffcently different in formulation and logic in my eyes to preclude direct borrowing. We seem to have two different but originally loosely related (and, as we shall see, probably contemporaneous) formulations of the issue of God's universal concern for humanity. The most satisfactory understanding of the problem appears to be that it was an issue of late Hellenistic Judaism, exacerbated and interpreted by each community in terms of their increasingly separate historical predicaments.

Before we come to Paul directly we have to look at the wider context of these ideas in more detail. And the wider context includes some sociological observations about the nascent Christian and Jewish communities.

5. *The Jewish Environment*

The ambiguity of these traditions is promoted by the fact that there are two different models for Gentile inclusion in Jewish tradition. The status of the Gentiles is discussed in later rabbinic Judaism both through the rubric of the *resident sojourner* and the doctrine of the *Noahide Commandments*. They conflict, in the first place by making different assumptions about the purpose and motivation of Gentile interest in Judaism.The conflicts had to be systematically worked out, both in Christianity and rabbinic Judaism, as it turns out. The ambiguity in both cases is worked out in the direction of universalism.

The issue of the resident sojourner derived from the biblical rules incumbent upon 'the stranger in your gates'.[12] Resident sojourners were obliged to abstain from offering sacrifices to strange gods (Lev. 17.7-9), from eating blood in any form (Lev. 17.10-12), from incest (Lev. 18.6-26), from work on the Sabbath (Exod. 20.10-11), and from eating leavened bread during the Passover (Exod. 12.18-19).[13]

The second model is the rabbinic doctrine of the 'Noahide Commandments'. This rabbinic doctrine is derived from a sophisticated and theological formulation that some legal enactments were given before Sinai, during the primeval history, to all human beings. Furthermore, the sign of the Noahide covenant, the rainbow, is available to all humanity to symbolize God's promise of safety. And it is completely outside of the special covenant with Abraham and his descendants. The covenant with Noah is expanded to the entire primeval period, encompassing all the revealed commandments preceding Sinai. The Noahide Commandments (for example *t. 'Abod Zar.* 8.4

---

12. Here the work of D. Novak, *The Image of the Non-Jew in Judaism: An Historical and Constructive Study of the Noahide Laws* (Toronto: Edwin Millen Press, 1983) is right on the mark. But Christian scholarship has preceded him. See J.C. Hurd, *The Origin of 1 Corinthians* (Macon, GA: Mercer University Press, 2nd edn, 1983 [1965]), pp. 250-53 for the basic bibliography; also see P. Richardson, *Israel in the Apostolic Church* (Cambridge: Cambridge University Press, 1969) and N.A. Dahl, *Das Volk Gottes*: Eine Untersuchung zum *Kirchenbewusstsein des Urchristentums* (repr.; Darmstadt: Wissenschaftliche Buchgesellschaft, 1963 [1941]).

13. See S.G. Wilson, *The Gentiles and the Gentile Mission* (Cambridge: Cambridge University Press, 1974). My interpretation softens Wilson's arguments a bit but agrees with it in principle.

SEGAL *Conversion and Universalism* 179

and more fully in *b. Sanh.* 56b) function somewhat like a concept of 'natural law,' which any just person can be expected to follow by observation and reason. In more Christian theological language, it is available by God's grace to all humanity. Here is the earliest rabbinic version, as stated in the Tosefta to Avodah Zarah:

> Seven commandments were the sons of Noah commanded: (1) concerning adjudication (*dinim*), (2) and concerning idolatry (*avodah zarah*), (3) and concerning blasphemy (*qilelat ha-shem*), (4) and concerning sexual immorality (*giluy arayot*), (5) and concerning bloodshed (*shefikhut damim*), (6) and concerning robbery (*ha-gezel*), (7) and concerning a limb torn from a living animal (*ever min ha-hayy*).[14]

In the basic version, nothing is mentioned which crosses into the purview of the special ordinances encumbent upon Jews in Jewish law. The rabbis immediately bring up more questionable ordinances, presumably asking whether a particular rule is specifically Jewish or should apply to all humanity. For instance, the rabbis mention crossbreeding (*kilayim*), castration (*sirus*), eating blood from a living animal (*dam min ha-hayy*) and witchcraft (*kishuf*). To these, in later discussions, is sometimes added the recognition that YHWH, the God of Israel, is the one true God. Other Tannaim limit the Noahide Commandments to the prohibition of idolatry, or those concerning with idolatry, blasphemy and adjudication (see *y. Kil.* 2.7). As David Novak says in his discussion of the Noahide Commandments: 'What emerges from all of this discussion is that in the Tannaitic period, there was a debate over the number and content of the Noahide laws. We have no record, however, that any authority in that period rejected the doctrine per se'.[15]

Of course, the minute we mention a rabbinic doctrine from a third century text we risk anachronism in assuming that it comes from the first century. To find out what was practiced in first century Judaism, we have to consult other varieties of Judaism, including Christianity. But for a minute, in order to avoid circular logic, let us look at a pre-Christian document. Once it can be ascertained that the ideas are prevalent in pre-Christian Judaism, we can safely use Christianity as another variation on a pre-existent theme.

14. The technical terminology of these sections is so commonly transliterated into English that I forego the more scientific notation for clarity's sake.
15. Novak, *The Image of the Non-Jew in Judaism.*

Another close parallel to the Noahide Commandments can found in
Jub. 7.20-21, which is pre-Christian:[16]

> And in the twenty-eighth jubilee Noah began to command his grandsons
> with ordinances and commandments and all of the judgments which he
> knew. And he bore witness to his sons so that they might do justice and
> cover the shame of their flesh and bless the one who created them and
> honor our father and mother, and each one love his neighbor and preserve
> themselves from fornication and pollution and from all injustice.

The particular ordinances thought to be universally humane by
Jubilees are establishing justice, eschewing incest, honouring parents,
loving neighbors and prohibiting adultery, promiscuity and *pollution*
from injustice.[17] In *Jubilees*, this short law code forms the basis of the
judgment against the giants, which brings on the flood and sets the
scene for the myths contained in the Book of Enoch.

It would be unwise, however, to assume that *Jubilees* is
promulgating such ideas in order to find a basis for humane
universalism—which is more or less what the rabbis and Christians do
with it. Quite the contrary, *Jubilees* has a strictly dualistic view of the
world, both on the divine and human level, in consonance with the
ideas of Qumran sectarians, in whose library it figured prominently.
Israel is identified as a good kingdom. God selected it as special and
above all other peoples (*Jub.* 2.21) to be marked by circumcision (*Jub.*
15.11). It alone can participate in the Sabbath and the other God
ordained festivals. The other nations are condemned and God has
placed spirits in authority over them to lead them astray. *Jub.* 22.16
warns Jews not to eat with a Gentile. *Jubilees* forcefully says that there
is no salvation without circumcision on the eighth day (*Jub.* 15.26-27).
That virtually means that conversion of the Gentiles is impossible.
Even a charitable reading supposes that only the children of converts
can enter the community:

16. See Novak, *The Image of the Non-Jew in Judaism,* pp. 3-35. Novak dates
the laws to Maccabean times, albeit with no textual support, because it seems to him
to be appropriate to the time of forced conversions. Then he discounts the witness of
Jubilees. Neither hypothesis convinces me. But Novak's main emphasis is on the
later discussion of these rules in talmudic and post-talmudic times, which is more
convincing.

17. Notice that as in Paul's writing and parallel with the others Judaisms of the
day, *Jubilees* here uses pollution as a metaphor for unrighteousness.

And anyone who is born whose own flesh is not circumcised on the eighth day is not from the sons of the covenant which the Lord made for Abraham, since (he is) from the children of destruction. And there is therefore no sign upon him so that he might belong to the Lord because (he is destined) to be destroyed and annihilated from the earth and to be uprooted from the earth because he has broken the covenant of the Lord our God. Because the nature of all of the angels of the presence and all of the angels of sanctification he sanctified Israel so that they might be with him and with his holy angels.[18]

The obvious reason for the inclusion of the Noahide Commandments at this place is to provide *Jubilees* with a legal warrant for condemning the Gentiles. God would not consign most of humanity to destruction without reason; the Gentiles know His law and have spurned it. This is entirely appropriate to a sectarian position, where all the Gentiles and but a saving remnant of Israel are scheduled for destruction. We know from this evidence that there were sects within Judaism which did not subscribe to any liberal ideas about the capabilities of Gentiles.[19]

6. *The Apostolic Decree*

Luke tells us something about the status of the discussion about the Noahide Commandments in first century Judaism. Acts 15.20, 15.29, and 21.25 describe an Apostolic Decree defining a minimum of practice for the new Gentile Christians:

Therefore my judgment is that we should not trouble those of the Gentiles who turn to God, but should write to them to abstain from the pollutions of idols and from unchastity and from what is strangled and from blood. For from early generations Moses has had in every city those who preach him, for he is read every sabbath in the synagogues. (15.19-21)

That you abstain from what has been sacrificed to idols and from blood and from what is strangled, and from unchastity. (15.29)

18. So translates O.S. Wintermute in J.H. Charlesworth (ed.) *The Old Testament Pseudepigrapha* (Garden City: Doubleday and Co., Inc., 1985), II, p. 87.

19. The rabbis also clarified that when a child is not circumcised, his future reward is not automatically imperiled. Such a lack is, in the opinion of the later rabbis at least, a sin of his father (*Shulhan Arukh*, 'Yoreh Dea' 260.1). Sabbath laws took precedence over circumcision laws for children born by caesarean section. So for later rabbinic tradition, it was not even necessary to be circumcised on the eighth day to be Jewish, part of Israel, or deserving of the world to come.

Thus all will know that there is nothing in what they have been told about
you but that you yourself live in observance of the law. But as for the
Gentiles who have believed, we have sent a letter with our judgment that
they should abstain from what has been sacrificed to idols and from blood
and from what is strangled and from unchastity. (21.24-5)

In other words, the Christian discussion of Gentiles is evidence that
the issue of the legal and ceremonial responsibilities of Gentiles was
being debated in Judaism too, even if the argument had special
characteristics within the Christian community. The Apostolic Decree,
as Luke transcribes it, is neither exactly the laws of the resident
sojourner nor the Noahide Commandments; it is a peculiar,
ambiguous *mélange*, perhaps even a combination of both. The new
Christian 'God-fearers' (σεβόμενοι, φοβούμενοι), as such Gentiles
are sometimes called, had to abstain from idol sacrifices
(εἰδωλόθυτον), from blood (αἷμα) (whatever that may mean:
perhaps from eating blood entirely, or perhaps from blood sacrifices,
as the Sibylline Oracles says, or perhaps from bloodshed). They must
also stay away from πνικτός, evidently a ritual requirement of some
sort, perhaps avoidance of animals which had been throttled and killed
as prey—hence a translation of the Hebrew term *terefa*, or perhaps, as
the later church sometimes interpreted it, from animals killed and
prepared by stewing or boiling—what the French and especially the
Cajuns would call *la viande étoufée*—perhaps a remembrance of the
rule against meat and milk or perhaps another reference to improper
slaughter. If I had to guess, I would say that πνικτός refers to *terefa*,
since πνικτός is a reasonable Greek translation of the Hebrew word
denoting the carcass of an animal caught as prey and because not
eating *tref* foods is one of the most basic requirements of Jewish food
laws. Similarly, the resident sojourners should observe the basic
moral code of the Jews, staying away from forbidden marriages,
incest and unchastity (πορνεία).[20]

The question is: what kind of a code is the Apostolic Decree? Is it
moral or cultic? What does it forbid? Which model does it evince?
Even terms like 'moral' and 'cultic' are not easy to use because they
contain some ambiguities as well. The Apostolic Decree can hardly be
a complete moral code, because such obvious sins as theft are entirely
missing, although they are present in the rabbinic formulation of the
Noahide Commandments. Thus, the Apostolic Decree is not exactly

---

20. See Wilson, *The Law in Acts*, pp. 87-100, for more detail on these issues.

what the Noahide Commandments are supposed to be. Obviously, Christians are expected not to steal, though that is not covered above. Probably the Ten Commandments and other virtue lists were in effect for all the community. εἰδωλόθυτα is often taken to be cultic, while εἰδωλολατρία would be moral. But the rabbis might see the issue differently. No doubt they would see both as morally wrong, but the term εἰδωλολατρία is too general; thus it is less helpful than εἰδωλόθυτα, which has the advantage of specifying which types of behavior are forbidden. The question here is only the rules specifically appropriate for those Gentiles who do not convert to Judaism. Thus, these laws are not exactly the Noahide Commandments, because they assume a social situation where the Christians are subject to other moral standards as well. But they are not exactly the received rules for resident sojourners either since there are fewer rules and the situation is somewhat different. Obviously the Apostolic Decree, as it stands, is another formula of the same type as both of them but adapted to a unique purpose: just rules for Jewish Christians and Gentile Christians living together. In other words, in the Apostolic Decree, some issues were taken for granted because they were obviously eschewed by all Christians. The decree concerned only those things which Jewish Christians might impose on Gentile Christians to allow them to live in their midst.[21]

Stephen Wilson suggests that *Luke* understands the Apostolic Decree as a universal moral code, a kind of Noahide Commandments, because he appears to interpret αἷμα as bloodshed and because he already knows that the food laws and ceremonial laws of Judaism are now suspended, from the stories that he relates about Peter. Thus, the only purpose of the code for Luke is as a universal moral code for Gentiles. Furthermore, there is a significant textual variant in the Western text, which adds a negative version of the golden rule at this point and eliminates the πνικτός clause. Thus, the textual tradition, which is most easily understood as a theologically sophisticated early gloss, underlines that the church has followed Luke in taking a 'moral' rather than a 'ceremonial' interpretation of these early Christian laws.

In this regard, the interpretation of the Greek words αἷμα and

---

21. See the helpful articles of K. Lake, 'The Apostolic Council of Jerusalem', and 'Paul's Controversies', in *The Beginnings of Christianity: The Acts of the Apostles*. V. *Additional Notes* (Grand Rapids: Baker, 1966), pp. 195-211 and pp. 212-23.

πνικτός is crucial for understanding the original intent of the Apostolic Decree. πνικτός probably means *terefa*, but whatever it means, it seems clearly ceremonial or ritual, ensuring that the approach of the first church council was at least partly 'ceremonial' as well as 'moral'. The ambiguity in the rules hides a change in church perspective over time and it possibly also hides a deliberate attempt to express both sides of the conflict, perhaps even a strategy not to alienate needlessly one Christian community. Here we lay bare one of Luke's basic methods. He cannot drop out the original edicts of the conference but he places them in a context which changes their import somewhat, in line with his more universal perspective. As it is, αἷμα and εἰδωλόθυτα can be interpreted ceremonially or ethically. In its original Jewish context there would not be much need to distinguish; but the import of the rules was probably to make the earliest Gentile Christians pure enough to interact with their Jewish co-religionists.

It is for this reason that Wilson suggests that moral universalism was not necessarily the original intent of the decree and I agree wholeheartedly. There is little point in detailing 'ritual' requirements after they are suspended. The ritual requirements must be more original, reflecting a time in the church when the Gentiles were viewed by the framers of the decree more like resident sojourners who must conform their practice to the minimum practice within the community. It must have come from a time when Luke's summary historical theology had not yet penetrated, a time which Luke has no interest in detailing accurately and perhaps did not understand either. Thus, the history of the Apostolic Decree is incomplete as it stands now.

There are comparable problems in reading the Christian evidence as there are in reading the Jewish evidence. Just as there are problems reading the history of the Noahide Commandments, so too there are insoluble problems in tracing the history of the Apostolic Decree which is, indeed, known to us in far more detail than rabbinic history. But it will turn out that these two documents should be seen as strategies to resolve the same problems, two chapters in the same history; and when they are, the same tendency towards universalization will become evident in both communities.

All of these formulations are attempting to deal with a similar issue from a variety of social situations. Once the social significance of the different formulations is outlined, the reasons for the ambiguity will become clearer: the difference between the Noahide Commandments and the rules for the sojourner is clear from a social point of view. The resident sojourner must, because of the close association with Israelites, observe some of the laws of Judaism, while the Noahide Commandments refer to the ultimate disposition of Gentiles and thus entirely to Gentiles who are not observant. The resident sojourners may be ethical or not; the issue is irrelevant. The law of the sojourner is formulated for the benefit of the Israelites who need not tolerate certain impieties within their own political or social territory.

The social issue in the Noahide Commandments is quite different. With the Noahide Commandments first a different theological issue enters: can God entirely spurn the Gentiles? Both Christians and rabbinic Jews answer 'No!' but they formulate the process of inclusion in different ways. In the rabbinic consensus the Gentiles need not observe any Jewish law at all; the sole question is whether they can be righteous, hence worthy to inherit the world to come. The issue has to do with the place of Israel within the wider category of humanity.

The original historical context suggests the social function of the two models. They correspond to the two different but related social situations of Jews in the hellenistic world. The first, the resident sojourner, refers to a situation where Jews are in the majority and have political power. In that situation they can maintain that Gentiles ought to do a certain amount of Jewish ritual—even including circumcision—if they want to eat the passover sacrifice. This formulation of a *ger*, a resident sojourner, later becomes the major legal basis for discussions of conversion in Judaism. Rabbinic discussion can use the same word to cover both conceptions, stimulating the distinction between an ordinary *ger* and a *ger tsedek*, a full convert.

Thus, the issue of how to accommodate Gentiles depends on the social landscape. It is not directly caused by the existence or destruction of the temple or the old land of Israel/diaspora split. But one can see that both history and geography have an effect on which model will be adopted in specific situations. In the land of Israel under Israelite law, the resident sojourner is the easiest model to apply. But wherever Jews are not the majority of the population or have very limited political power to affect or control their neighbors, the second model can become more relevant. In such a situation, there is even a danger of Gentile backlash in being too open to converting Gentiles.

We have ample evidence of the concern of the pagan community that the Jews and Christians are stealing their children from them.[22] In these situations the concept of a righteous Gentile, who eschewed sin but did not explicitly take up the special rules of Judaism, would have a positive value. So before the third century when the mature doctrine is voiced in rabbinic Judaism, certain ambiguities would naturally obtain. In areas around Palestine with a Jewish majority and certain rights of self-rule, one set of procedures would be more relevant. In other areas, the other might. During the hostilities with Rome when circumcision was forbidden, the only alternative for an interested Gentile would have been becoming a god-fearer. So too in mature Christianity and Judaism, both of whom work with a Gentile majority as the given, the concept of righteous Gentile is much more important. In the first and early second century, before the situation clarified, the situation was more fluid, as the Christian evidence shows us. The ambiguity of the Christian formulation of the Apostolic Decree merely underlines the imprecision of the earliest discussions of the issues.[23]

Of course, there would never have been any necessity or purpose for adopting this vocabulary within the Christian Church had the moral and ethical universalism so evident to Luke been evident to the earliest Christians. The vocabulary was probably adopted because some Christian Jews viewed the first Gentile Christians through the rubric of the law of the sojourners. They might convert to Judaism if they wished. But if they did not seek such a privilege, evidently by circumcision, they should at least make some cultic or ceremonial accommodations to Jewish observances so that the whole group could interact. Conversion to Judaism is thus not the only cultic approach to the inclusion of Gentiles within the community. It is merely the most

22. See A.F. Segal, *Paul the Convert: The Apostolate and Apostasy of Saul the Pharisee* (New Haven: Yale University Press, 1990), pp. 84-96.

23. Whether 'αἵματος' refers to a moral action or a ritual one is not entirely clear in church tradition, which has taken it in both ways. Traces of the decree appear in Rev. 2.14, 20, 24; Did. 6.3; Just. *Dial.* 34-35; Tert., *Apol.*; Eus. *EH* 5.1.26 (in a letter dated 177 CE, from Lyons); Minucius Felix *Octavius* 30; *Sib.Or.*, 2.93; *Ps.-Clem. Hom.* 7.8.1. The early Christians more closely approximate the ordinances of *Jubilees* than did the third-century rabbis. Thus the ambiguity in the Christian evidence as to whether the term αἵμα refers to a Jewish rule of slaughter or bloodshed shows that this ambiguity was rather early. See J.C. Hurd, *Origin*, pp. 250-53 for the basic bibliography.

conservative one. Possibly this is why James and Peter agreed that circumcision was not necessary. They may have understood that there was another option: the Gentiles did not have to become Jews but they may have had to make other ceremonial accommodations. This is logical because the earliest church was largely a Jewish majority with a small Gentile minority. While many Jewish Christians seemed positive to the idea of being one community with Gentiles, many thought that some kind of accommodation to the ritual purity of the Jewish community should and could be reached. Only a few took Paul's position that no ritual accommodations were necessary. Furthermore, Paul himself was forced to compromise in place after place, by saying that although Christian *freedom* permitted the abandonment of Jewish ceremonial observance, no ἔργα τοῦ νόμου, Christian *unity* demanded that the strong always accommodate to the feelings of the weak for the sake of peace in the community.

This ambiguity about the true referent of the apostolic enactments has a positive social function for the Christian community even after Paul, as the maximalist Gentile position grows inexorably stronger. Take the issue of αἷμα—whether *blood* be idolatrous, ethical or ritual. Paul told Gentiles that they were free of all the special laws, but they should consider other Christians' feelings. For them, Luke's αἷμα is ethical—bloodshed. Other Christians insisted that Gentiles observe at least some of the laws. Or they may have assumed, as Paul did when he was a Pharisee, that *converts* must keep all the laws, but that resident sojourners need not. Obviously, Paul is fighting against there becoming two classes of Christians. After Paul, the ambiguity served to allow both opinions to be precedented in the text. So a variety of perspectives is protected by a certain ambiguity in Luke's rendering of the Apostolic Decree. We can see that there is no need to make accommodations unless the opposing group is the vast majority. But it is possible that Paul himself may have sought this compromise as a way to gain legitimacy for his Gentile congregations.[24]

24. Of all the possible reconstructions of Paul's career, and especially his policy about the Jewish law, that proposed by John Hurd in *Origin* seems the most logical. With allowances for the fact that the course of events does not necessarily follow the most logical path, let me outline Hurd's solution. According to Hurd's reconstruction of the events, the regulations contained in the Apostolic Decree were not part of Paul's original preaching at Corinth because they had not yet been formulated. Paul adopted them after the council, in which he participated, and sent a letter to the

The result of this policy of conciliation could easily have produced confusion for Paul's hearers and readers. He begins by assuming that the Gentiles need observe none of the Jewish laws, in effect assuming the model of the Noahide Commandments. The dominant model of some of the other church fathers is apparently close to that of the rules of the sojourner, not the Noahide Commandments. This means, in effect, that they understand that there are a few Gentiles mixed into a larger Jewish sect. Paul, on the other hand, reflects the position of a majority of Gentiles in which a few Jewish Christians have to live.

Paul does not openly in any place discuss the Apostolic Decree. Either he did not know it (meaning that it had not actually yet been formulated by the church in the way that Luke expresses it), or he chooses to ignore it. In that case, it is plausible to argue that to have acknowledged the modified sojournor model which underlies the Apostolic Decree would have jeopardized Paul's radical position on Christian freedom. Instead Paul begs moderation and continues his basic attack that the Gentiles are to be added to the community of the faithful through the model of the Noahide Commandments, with no specific rules of Judaism in place, especially not circumcision. Either of the two alternatives is understandable within the Christian formulation of the discussion. But one must realize that even if the church had not formally ratified anything like the Apostolic Decree, it is quite likely that early Jewish Christian church communities were

Corinthians later, informing them of his intentions to live by the compromise adopted at the Jerusalem council. None of this is possible if one assumes that Paul exploded the system of works-centered righteousness of Judaism. But it is possible if the position of Paul was against the aspects of Jewish law that separated his gentile congregations from the Jewish Christian ones. This was a religious issue driven by a sociological fact. Because the events are still unresolved in our minds, and the majority of New Testament scholars in fact favor the alternative ordering, I shall not assume either reconstruction but, instead, try to stick to the specific issues. Evidently, when the Corinthians receive Paul's letter informing them of their responsibilities, they immediately respond by challenging his lack of consistency. Paul then replies again (1 Cor. 7-14) in an attempt to preserve the principles of his earliest teaching, without transgressing his agreement with the other church fathers. The result is what we know as his policy of freedom tempered by a diplomatic policy of conciliation, which begs the Corinthians to observe the rules of the council, at least to the extent that they can understand them (Hurd, *Origin*, pp. 259-70). This policy is only possible if one understands Paul to be operating as a rabbi would, on a case by case basis, without an overwhelming critique of works righteousness.

automatically applying their Jewish understanding of what was necessary for Gentiles to join their midst. The issue would have had to be present, as Paul's letters so amply testify, even if the specific solution had not yet formally evolved.

But Paul's message goes considerably beyond the issue of Gentiles. Instead, Paul is primarily concerned with the process of transformation by faith that brings justification, a process which he sees to be universal, required for both Jewish and Gentile converts to Christianity. Still, he has agreed that the feelings of Jewish Christians are to be considered in practical community. So even though Gentile Christians have the freedom to eat anything and not to observe any of the festivals of Judaism; yet they should forbear where others may be offended by their behavior. Thus, Paul's arguments do not burst through Jewish parochialism; rather they absolutely depend on knowing that he is relying on what the rabbis will call the 'Noahide Commandments.' He is fighting against both the conversion to Judaism model and the model of the resident sojourner, which apparently have been active in the early Christian community, because they have been already active in Judaism. Instead he promulgates a new conception of conversion, which involves a spiritual metamorphosis.[25] But he is willing to accept some of the rules of the sojourner if that will achieve peace and unity within his community of Christians. Indeed, his usage merely gives us one more piece of evidence that Judaism contained such ideas, even before the redaction of the Mishnah.

It seems fair to conclude that a significant part of the Christian Church continued to analyze the issue of the role of the Gentiles in God's scheme in the traditional Jewish way. On the other hand, a new definition of the center of the community's definition—one that started in Paul's mystical visions and ended in a new definition of conversion—entailed a new approach to the problem of universalism as well. Following on Paul's argument that inclusion in the community was by means of faith, everyone in the community, regardless of their Jewish or Gentile identity, should be united by their faith. This eventually obviated the differences between Gentile and Jew completely within the community and made moot the issue of righteous Gentiles which remained central for Jews.

---

25. See Segal, *Paul the Convert*, pp. 117-49 for more detail.

THOMAS KUHN, CONVICTIONAL WORLDS, AND PAUL[*]

Terence L. Donaldson

The problem of making sense of Paul's letters, already observed by the author of 2 Peter (2 Pet. 3.16) has been vividly described by Albert Schweitzer:

> In the effort to understand Paul some started out from his anthropology, others from his psychology, others from his manner of thought in his pre-Christian period (as though we knew anything about that!), others from his personal idiosyncrasy, others from his attitude to the Law, and others from the experience on the way to Damascus. In thus taking hold of any thread which came to hand they tangled the skein to start with, and condemned themselves to accept an inexplicable chaos of thought as Pauline teaching.[1]

Attempts to untangle the skein have generally fallen into several broad categories. One line of approach has been to look for a centre or core around which the remaining elements can be suitably arranged. Schweitzer himself took this approach, as he relegated another putative centre—justification by faith—to the status of a subsidiary crater existing within the main crater, Paul's mystical doctrine of 'being in Christ'.[2] Another approach has been to search in Hellenism or Judaism for the religious background to his thought, finding here either a coherent framework presupposed in the foreground[3] or the

[*] In his seminars on the Synoptics and Pauline chronology, I have learned much from John Hurd, especially with respect to matters of methodological awareness and logical precision. Since we both have backgrounds in the natural sciences, I chose this topic as an appropriate way to express my appreciation.

1. A. Schweitzer, *The Mysticism of Paul the Apostle* (New York: Seabury, 1968 [1931]), p. 40.

2. Schweitzer, *Mysticism*, pp. 205-26.

3. Schweitzer's own explanation of Paul's mysticism in terms of Jewish eschatology is a good case in point. See also W.D. Davies, *Paul and Rabbinic Judaism* (London: SPCK, 1948).

poles of an unresolved tension or duality in his thought.[4] As already noted in the quotation from Schweitzer, others have argued that Paul's conversion (or call) often taken together with his pre-conversion opposition to the Christian movement, provides the necessary inter-pretative starting point.[5] Still others have posited theories of develop-ment, seeking a dynamic rather than static pattern of coherence.[6] And a few have denied that Paul was a systematic thinker at all, arguing that the attempt to reconstruct a system of 'Paulinism' is mis-conceived, either since it is in his religious life and pastoral concern that his true significance is to be found,[7] or (blaming Paul himself for the tangle) since his argumentation is so riddled with contradiction and inner inconsistency as to render it inherently incoherent.[8]

In a number of recent studies, however, a new and promising approach to the problem seems to be emerging. Informed to a certain extent by insights from the social sciences, and stimulated by the posi-tive advances in understanding that it has already opened up, this approach is characterized by a different way of conceiving the problem. Rather than seeing Paul's letters as presenting us with a skein—a linear file of concepts and terms, existing on the same level, and linked together in some (presumably) ascertainable way from beginning to end—it seeks to understand what has customarily been described as Paul's thought in terms of a structured framework functioning on several levels. While this structure is conceived of in different ways, in general terms the new approach is characterized by a development outwards from traditional constructions of Paul's theology in two directions: one looks behind the text to the rhetorical context, emphasizing the dynamic interaction between gospel and cir-cumstance, as Paul articulates the gospel afresh in terms appropriate

4. See the discussion in A. Schweitzer, *Paul and his Interpreters* (London: A. & C. Black, 1950), pp. 28-32.

5. As early as F.C. Baur, *The Church History of the First Three Centuries* (London: Williams & Norgate, 1878) I, p. 46.

6. See, e.g., C.H. Dodd, 'The Mind of Paul' *BJRL* 17 (1933), pp. 91-105; 18 (1934) pp. 69-110; L. Cerfaux, *The Christian in the Theology of St Paul*, (trans. L. Soiron; New York: Herder & Herder, 1967); H. Hübner, *Law in Paul's Thought* (trans. J.C.G. Greig; Edinburgh: T. & T. Clark, 1984).

7. A. Deissmann, *St Paul: A Study in Social and Religious History* (trans. L.R.M. Strachan; London: Hodder & Stoughton, 1912); J.S. Stewart, *A Man in Christ* (London: Hodder & Stoughton, 1935).

8. So H. Räisänen, *Paul and the Law* (Tübingen: Mohr [Paul Siebeck], 1983).

to each new situation; the other looks beneath the text, differentiating between the shifting rhetorical surface of the text and a more fundamental set of basic convictions operating at a deeper level.

Among the studies I have in mind here are the significant seminal treatments of Paul by J. Christiaan Beker, Daniel Patte and E.P. Sanders,[9] as well as the ongoing work of the Pauline Theology Group of the Society of Biblical Literature.[10] The authors here represented can by no means be cast into the same mold. Beker's differentiation between coherent core and contingent interpretation is broadly analogous to Patte's categories of convictions and ideas; but Beker places much more emphasis on situational contingency. Sanders, too, differentiates between a core set of convictions, and the arguments by which Paul attempts to defend and develop those convictions in response to specific questions; but he allows a larger interpretative role for tensions within Paul's convictional core (especially between those derived from Paul's native Jewish upbringing and those stemming from his conversion) than do either of the other two. And the material from the SBL group presents us with a proliferation of structural levels and functional metaphors.[11] Despite the differences in emphasis and detail, though, there is a family resemblance to be discerned.

Drawing on these insights I have adopted for my own work on Paul a three-level framework for understanding his theological discourse and argumentation. The bottom level consists of a system of basic convictions, undergirding his semantic universe, derived both from his native Jewish upbringing and from his conversion experience. The surface level is constituted by the rhetorical situation of the letters themselves, as Paul represents and responds to particular sets of circumstances in his ministry with local congregations. In between, mediating the two and driven in different but interconnected ways by

9.   J.C. Beker, *Paul the Apostle* (Philadelphia: Fortress Press, 1980); E.P. Sanders, *Paul and Palestinian Judaism* (Philadelphia: Fortress Press, 1977), and *Paul, the Law, and the Jewish People* (Philadelphia: Fortress Press, 1983); D. Patte, *Paul's Faith and the Power of the Gospel* (Philadelphia: Fortress Press, 1983).

10.   The first collection of papers from this group is now available in J.M. Bassler (ed.), *Pauline Theology. Volume 1* (Minneapolis: Fortress Press, 1991). Other material can be found in the *SBL Seminar Papers*.

11.   In J. Bassler's 1989 paper, for example, she proposes a five-level model for understanding Paul's theology, involving analogies of lenses and prisms; see 'Paul's Theology: Whence and Whither?' in D.J. Lull (ed.), *SBL Seminar Papers 1989* (Atlanta: Scholars Press, 1989) pp. 412-23.

each, is a process of theological reflection and development. What we are accustomed to call Paul's theology, then, is to be seen as a dynamic hermeneutical process taking place in the space between his structured set of convictions on the one hand, and his contextual ministry on the other.[12]

It is not my purpose here to develop this model in dialogue with the authors referred to above, nor to defend it over against any of them. Rather, I would like to raise some more theoretical considerations, and in particular to contribute to the ongoing discussion by suggesting a conceptual ally.

With the exception of Patte, the three scholars mentioned above proceed in an apparently instinctive exegetical fashion; explicit theoretical reflection on their interpretative procedure is rare.[13] Patte's structuralist approach is more self-consciously theoretical. And indeed, his concept of a structured set of convictions as providing a 'semantic universe' within which people order their lives and make them meaningful is very useful. This concept could be elaborated in connection with work being done in the social sciences, especially the sociology of knowledge,[14] linguistics[15] and cultural anthropology.[16] Sociology of knowledge, in particular, offers a way of seeing Paul's letters in their full social dimension (and not simply as collections of 'ideas') while retaining a place for what has more traditionally been investigated under the category of Paul's 'thought': Paul's letters can be seen as attempts to present, defend and preserve a particular 'social world' (or construction of reality) with inner symbolic structures and outer social forms.[17]

12. On Paul's theology as an *activity*, see Bassler, 'Paul's Theology', pp. 418-19.

13. Though Beker does observe in passing that his approach could be described in structuralist categories; (*Paul the Apostle*, p. 16).

14. The seminal work in this area is P.L. Berger, *The Sacred Canopy* (Garden City, NY: Doubleday, 1967).

15. See R.B. Hays' use of Chomsky in 'Crucified with Christ: A Synthesis of the Theology of 1 and 2 Thessalonians, Philemon, Philippians and Galatians', in Bassler (ed.), *Pauline Theology. Volume 1*, pp. 227-46.

16. For an application of Mary Douglas' theory to Paul, see J.H. Neyrey, *Paul, in Other Words* (Louisville, KY: Westminster/John Knox, 1990).

17. The basic category of 'social world' as Berger defines it is congruent in essential respects to Patte's 'faith.' For a stimulating introduction to the whole NT

But as an alternative I would like to suggest that the conceptual framework developed by Thomas Kuhn in his book *The Structure of Scientific Revolutions*[18] provides a model that can be adapted very fruitfully to the study of Paul's letters. Kuhn's analysis of cognitive structures is strikingly congruent with sociology of knowledge approaches[19] and thus provides just as useful a theoretical framework for the three-level approach to Paul described above. But it has two added advantages. Because of its origin with reference to the world of science and scientific innovation, where individual perception plays an important role,[20] it is more adaptable to the case of a semantic universe as perceived by an individual. And more important, since his central concern has to do with shifts of convictional framework (in his case, those accompanying scientific revolutions), the conceptual tools he develops are fundamentally suited to a characteristic feature of Paul's convictional world—namely that his semantic universe has been decisively shaped by a conversion experience.[21]

In his book, Kuhn stakes out a position over against an empiricist view of science and scientific progress—that is, a view stressing the primacy of detached observation over scientific theory and seeing scientific progress simply as an ever-growing accumulation of observation-based knowledge. Instead he argues that normal science takes place within 'a strong network of commitments—conceptual, theoretical, instrumental and methodological—that tell the [scientist] what both the world and his science are like.'[22] Only within such a

from a sociology of knowledge perspective, see L.T. Johnson, *The Writings of the New Testament* (Philadelphia: Fortress Press, 1986).

18. T. Kuhn, *The Structure of Scientific Revolutions* (Chicago: University of Chicago Press, 2nd edn, 1970).

19. The social basis of scientific paradigms is stressed even more strongly in the postscript to the second edition (pp. 174-210).

20. I recognize and fully endorse Kuhn's emphasis on the social basis of scientific knowledge, indeed, of all knowledge. Nevertheless, individual perceptions, discoveries, and theoretical proposals have had a decisive role in scientific revolutions, as Kuhn himself makes clear.

21. For the appropriateness of describing Paul's Damascus experience as a conversion, see my article, 'Zealot and Convert: The Origin of Paul's Christ–Torah Antithesis', *CBQ* 51 (1989) esp. pp. 680-82, with the literature cited there; to which can now be added A.F. Segal, *Paul the Convert* (New Haven: Yale University Press, 1990). This article concludes with some brief observations on Kuhn and conversion.

22. Kuhn, *Scientific Revolutions*, p. 42.

sense-giving framework can observations have any meaning. Consequently, as his title suggests, he argues in addition that scientific progress takes place through revolutions, in which one theoretical network of world-ordering commitments comes to be seen as inadequate and is abandoned in favour of another.

Kuhn's best known and most characteristic category is that of the 'paradigm' and this is as good a place as any to begin a more detailed description of his analysis. Actually he uses the term in two distinct (though organically connected) ways. In its most basic sense a paradigm is a specific scientific achievement—including 'law, theory, application and instrumentation together'[23]—successful enough in resolving a set of hitherto intractable problems that it sets a pattern and a framework for scientific work to follow. Copernicus' theory of a rotating earth revolving with other planets around a stationary sun is a good example. Providing a simpler and more satisfying account of astronomical observations than the earth-centred system of Ptolemy, it set the framework for astronomical investigation from that time onward. Kuhn also uses 'paradigm' in an extended sense to refer more broadly to the set of basic assumptions and convictions described in the previous paragraph. But it is clear from his discussion that the two are closely linked. Not only does the paradigm in the narrow sense provide the foundation out of which the set of guiding convictions develops, but since the convictions are implicit in the paradigm, the paradigm itself, rather than an explicitly formulated set of assumptions, rules and procedures, often provides the more immediate point of reference for scientific work.[24]

Paradigms do not solve all of the problems in a given scientific field, of course; they represent the beginning, not the end, of what Kuhn calls 'normal science'. Normal science involves extending the accomplishment of the paradigm to the whole field of knowledge— 'paradigm articulation' as he describes it—attempting to replicate the achievement of the paradigm in the case of other recognized problems, and exploring new problems suggested by the paradigm itself. The paradigm thus sets the framework for normal science, providing the criteria for appropriate problems, the rules for tackling

23. Kuhn, *Scientific Revolutions*, p. 10.

24. To use Polanyi's terminology, the '*paradigm*' in the extended sense of the term is just an articulation of what was *tacitly* apprehended in the basic paradigm; see M. Polanyi, *Personal Knowledge* (New York: Harper & Row, 1964).

the problems, and the standards for admissible solutions.

Kuhn's main concern has to do with the process by which one convictional framework—and the normal science to which it gives rise—is replaced by another, a process he describes as a 'paradigm shift'. An important element in the process is the recognition of an anomaly—a counter-instance unforeseen by, or not consistent with, the predictions of the theory. By themselves anomalies do not cause the rejection of a paradigm; at most they create a sense of crisis, a feeling that the tools a paradigm supplies are no longer capable of solving the problems that emerge. A paradigm is never simply abandoned; it is always exchanged for another more suitable:

> The decision to reject one paradigm is always simultaneously the decision
> to accept another, and the judgment leading to that decision involves the
> comparison of both paradigms with nature and with each other.[25]

In this discussion of paradigm shifts it becomes apparent that Kuhn's concept of paradigm, especially in its extended sense, and Patte's categories of 'conviction' (a truth taken as self-evident by the knower) and 'faith' (the structured aggregate of convictions)[26] are essentially congruent. Once a paradigm has been accepted, Kuhn asserts, it takes on an axiomatic quality. What within the former paradigm were seen as anomalies—irritants to be explained away—now 'seem very much like tautologies, statements of situations that could not conceivably have been otherwise'.[27] A paradigm in its extended sense, then, corresponds closely to Patte's definition of 'faith' as a system of convictions that relate various elements of human experience together in an orderly way, providing a framework of meaning for human action and existence. Indeed, Kuhn can describe a paradigm as a 'set of received beliefs'.[28] Further, because a paradigm shift represents a shift of allegiance from one system of convictions to another, he describes the process as a 'conversion'.[29] A paradigm cannot simply be accepted as the result of a logical proof, since it is the paradigm itself that provides the rules governing the standards for such proofs. A paradigm shift is not a step by step process of logical reasoning, but a

---

25. Kuhn, *Scientific Revolutions*, p. 77.
26. Patte, *Paul's Faith*, pp. 10-14.
27. Kuhn, *Scientific Revolutions*, p. 78.
28. Kuhn, *Scientific Revolutions*, p. 5.
29. Kuhn, *Scientific Revolutions*, p. 150.

transfer of allegiance from one set of convictions to another.

I suggest, then, that Kuhn's analysis presents us with a fruitful model for discerning the structure of Paul's thought. In his terms, Paul can be seen as one who experienced a paradigm shift, a transfer of allegiance from one set of world-structuring convictions to another. Paul began with a semantic universe defined by the Torah and the 'traditions of [his] fathers' (Gal. 1.14). His commitment to this way of ordering the world was anything but casual: he describes himself as a 'zealot' who 'advanced in Judaism beyond many of [his] contemporaries' (Gal. 1.14). Because of this commitment, when he encountered the early Christian movement he perceived—perhaps more clearly than the Jewish Christians themselves—the incompatibility of the message of a crucified and risen Messiah with his Torah-centred way of looking at the world. This is not the place to attempt any precise determination of the nature of the conflict between Christ and Torah as Paul perceived it.[30] Nevertheless, it is clear from Gal. 1.13-14 and especially Phil. 3.6 that he attempted to suppress the Christian message precisely because he perceived it as posing in some way a threat to the Torah.

The message of a crucified and risen Messiah presented itself to Paul, then, as an anomaly, or at least as something that would have been an anomaly if he believed it were true. In this connection, it is worth noting Kuhn's observation that commitment to an established paradigm is a prerequisite for recognizing the presence of an anomaly: 'novelty ordinarily emerges only for the man who, knowing with precision what he should expect, is able to recognize that something has gone wrong.'[31] With his experience outside Damascus the anomaly ceased being merely hypothetical, and Paul came to believe that something had indeed 'gone wrong' with his inherited world of meaning. Contrary to his expectation, God had raised Jesus from the dead. Though it threatened to shatter his semantic universe, Paul became convinced that the crucified Jesus was after all God's anointed Messiah.

How Paul was able to make sense of this new conviction and to resolve the conflicts it presented for his old system of convictions are questions that cannot be entertained here. For our present purposes all we need to note is that he apparently did so, and that, in Kuhn's

30. See my paper 'Zealot and Convert'.
31. Kuhn, *Scientific Revolutions*, p. 65.

categories, this initial resolution of the conflict between Christ and Torah can be seen as a basic paradigm, in the more restricted sense of the term, setting the pattern for what was to follow. This basic paradigm provided the framework for a more general reconsideration of the convictions that made up Paul's former semantic universe or system of convictions. The result of this reconsideration was a new constellation of convictions, a new way of ordering the world in a meaningful way—a new paradigm, in the more extended sense of the term.

This new paradigm was anything but abstract and general; indeed, central to it was Paul's highly personal conviction that he had been called as Christ's apostle to the Gentiles. In carrying out this calling, he found himself confronted by a variety of contextual situations needing to be brought within the organizing framework of his paradigmatic gospel. At the same time the press of circumstances, and especially of opposition, forced him to wrestle with the implications of his convictions and to attempt to deal with residual tensions among them. Kuhn's model provides us with analogues, then, to the other two levels of the interpretive structure: in the process of theological explication we see, I suggest, the apostolic equivalent of what Kuhn calls normal science, the ongoing work of paradigm explication; and in the epistolary responses to contingent circumstances, the analogue (though Kuhn does not much dwell on it) of applied science.

My proposal, then, is that we can best make sense of the tangled rhetorical surface of Paul's letters by conceiving of three structural levels, lying behind or beneath the surface, that constrain the discourse and govern its meaning: (1) *contextual* or *circumstantial*—arising from the situation of the readers being addressed, Paul's intentions with respect to that situation, and the nature of the relationship between Paul and his readers; (2) *convictional*—the basic set of convictions, or the semantic universe, that structures Paul's apostolic ministry and undergirds his thought; and (3) *theological*—the developing pattern of explicatory thought that emerges through the dynamic interaction of the other two. Kuhn's analysis provides us with both a helpful analogue to this three-level structural approach, and workable categories that will enable us to include within our analytical structure the fundamental and formative element of Paul's conversion experience.

MAJOR VARIATIONS IN PAULINE AND OTHER EPISTLES IN LIGHT OF
GENRE AND THE PAULINE LETTER FORM

Kenneth J. Neumann

The untapped capabilities for the computer to assist in biblical and
other literary research have been a recurring theme in pioneering
courses and seminars conducted by John C. Hurd since the early stages
of computer technology. As a result, under his direction a statistical
investigation of the style of epistolary literature from the early
Christian period was undertaken to shed light particularly on the
letters of the Pauline corpus disputed by critical scholars (Ephesians,
Colossians and 2 Thessalonians). It was found by the statistical
approach of discriminant analysis that, if one assumes that the
author(s) of the disputed letters must be one of four authors (Paul,
Ignatius, Clement or the author of Hebrews), all three letters were
assigned to the Pauline group with a clear 100 percent likelihood.
However, another statistical measure gives more precision to the
results. On the basis of the distance from the Pauline 'centroid' (an
imaginary statistical point where the Pauline style is centered) the
statistical probability that they were written by Paul ranged from less
than 20 chances per 100 for the third Ephesian sample to less than 5
per 100 for all other samples except for Colossians (less than 10 per
100). This means from a statistical viewpoint one would expect, at
best, less than 20 Pauline samples out of 100 would be as different
from the typical Pauline style as those of the disputed letters.

  These results may seem to question seriously the authenticity of
these letters until one notes two more points. First, the disputed letters
are generally much further from the non-Pauline centroids than the
Pauline centroid; Ephesians has less than 5 chances in 1,000 that it is
by one of the other three writers. 2 Thessalonians is the closest to any
non-Pauline group with a less than 2.5 chance in 100 that it is created
by the author of Hebrews. Secondly, sample writings from some

recognized Pauline epistles, especially the Galatian sample, are as distant from the Pauline centroid as the disputed letters. On the basis of the most effective style indicators the text sample from Galatians, although assigned statistically to the Pauline group, has a probability of less than 10 chances in 100 that it belongs to the Pauline group and less than 5 chances in 100 it fits with Ignatian writings. This is the most extreme result for an undisputed Pauline letter found in this study.[1]

What do these figures mean? On the one hand, Pauline authorship of the disputed letters is not ruled out, but, on the other hand, the statistics as they stand give cause for doubts about this classification. Is the answer to these puzzling results that there are other factors bringing about more variation than might normally be found if the primary sources of variation were only differences of authorship? It should be noted that in the original study an attempt was made to reduce or eliminate the impact of some factors besides authorship causing variation. The salutations of letters were deleted since they could not be compared with the philosophical and theological argumentation of other writers lacking salutations.[2] Besides, since salutations are full of concise formulae and standardized phrases[3] and are more consciously and carefully crafted than other parts of a letter, they are not very typical of an author's style. Furthermore, quotations of the Old Testament, early Christian tradition, and other quoted sources were deleted prior to taking samples. Introductory phrases to quotations were eliminated as well. However, quotations were not deleted if they were grammatically part of the author's sentences.[4]

An attempt was made to select samples reasonably close in genre although the degree of similarity in genre required was not seen in advance. The first stage of the investigation employed non-Christian authors (Josephus, Epictetus and Philo) writing treatises or philosophy similar in some ways to the Pauline letters. However, the research

---

1.   K.J. Neumann, *The Authenticity of the Pauline Epistles in the Light of Stylostatistical Analysis* (SBLDS; Atlanta, GA: Scholars Press, 1990), pp. 158, 194-99.

2.   Neumann, *Authenticity*, pp. 127-28, 132.

3.   B. Rigaux, *Letters of St Paul: Modern Studies* (trans. S. Yonick; Chicago: Franciscan Herald Press, 1968), pp. 133-34.

4.   Neumann, *Authenticity*, pp. 131-32.

showed there was a very sharp difference between those writings and the four Christian writers employed. One of the factors separating them is probably genre.

Epictetus' style, however, being oral presentations written down, resembled the Pauline style slightly more than Ignatius. Epictetus still was closer in style to Josephus and Philo.[5] These results especially show the need to be careful about comparing writings of similar 'genre'.

Another unexpected result from the investigation showing the importance of only comparing writings of similar genre was the classification of 1 Timothy and 2 Timothy with different authors (1 Timothy with Hebrews, 2 Timothy with Ignatius). One could have anticipated this perhaps since non-statistical studies have recognized a difference in form—1 Timothy is described by Werner Kümmel as a book of 'church order', while 2 Timothy tries to sound autobiographical and has the form of a 'literary testament'.[6] A closer examination of the letters shows they contain a number of examples of 'seriation', that is, syntactically parallel lists of items, such as virtues or vices (1 Tim. 1.9-10). Since these may not be examples of an author's normal writing style, on a second trial the sections with seriation were deleted, and new samples taken. Only then are the two works classified together in the Ignatius group and nearer one another, although 1 Timothy is still far from either the Hebrews or Ignatian centroids.[7] These results suggest attention needs to be paid to genre and special material within sections.

In some non-biblical studies by Barron Brainerd genre analysis has been helpful. The use of definite articles and pronouns, especially personal pronouns, varies according to the genre in which they are located.[8] These results should make one more careful in using such stylistic indices and in comparing works from the same genre. Anthony Kenny's statistical study of the entire Pauline corpus employs these and several other indices likely consistent within the same genre

. 5. Neumann, *Authenticity*, pp. 183-84.

6. W. Kümmel, *Introduction to the New Testament* (trans. H.C. Kee; Nashville: Abingdon Press, 1975), p. 384.

7. Neumann, *Authenticity*, pp. 95-96, 200-202; see graphs, pp. 198-99.

8. B. Brainerd, 'An Exploratory Study of Pronouns and Articles as Indices of Genre in English', *Language and Style* 5 (1972), pp. 239-59; B. Brainerd, 'Pronouns and Genre in Shakespeare's Drama', *CHum* 13 (1979), pp. 3-16.

but varying from other genres, and therefore his results, finding little significant difference among the thirteen letters attributed to Paul except for Titus, are to be expected for features consistent in letters.[9]

This brief study proposes to begin investigating some other possible reasons for the variation within Paul. *One hypothesis to be given a partial test is that part of the variation discovered is due to significant differences in the proportions from the major sections of Paul's letters.* In other words, if the original samples and the samples tested have too great a difference in the proportion of, for example, the parenetic sections of the letters, this may explain the unexpected results. It has been observed that in many ways Paul varies his style in the various major sections of his letters; the salutation, thanksgiving and closing follow certain customary patterns and set formulas which the apostle alters 'according to the situation presupposed by the letter'.[10] In the letter body Paul deals with the main issues 'at length' and is 'least bound by epistolary structures'. The exhortations and commands in the parenetic sections 'are by and large traditional materials'[11] and appear to be brief and direct. Are these variations so great as to assign test letter samples into the wrong authorship group?

In this study the various samples employed in the statistical analysis of Paul's letters will be examined to discover what proportion of the various sections are included. A prior necessary step is to determine the exact boundaries of those sections, if possible. Obviously, there will be great dependence on previous studies of the form of the Pauline letters. In some cases, there will not be agreement on the nature and extent of particular sections, in which case both possible analyses will be given from which one may choose.

For the *three original Pauline samples* (from 1 Corinthians and Philippians) used to describe statistically Paul's style in relation to other writing styles, an important question is under what section(s) to place 1 Cor. 5.1–16.18, where Paul replies to various oral and written information he has received.[12] John L. White and William G. Doty

---

9. A.J. Kenny, *A Stylometric Study of the New Testament* (Oxford: Clarendon Press, 1986), pp. 80-100.

10. Kümmel, *Introduction*, pp. 248-49.

11. W.G. Doty, *Letters in Primitive Christianity* (Philadelphia: Fortress Press, 1973), pp. 34, 37-38.

12. J.C. Hurd, Jr, *The Origin of 1 Corinthians* (London: SPCK, 1965), pp. 47-94.

both agree that the main body embraces 1 Cor. 1.10–4.21, with the latter saying a parenetic section is lacking in the letter.[13] However, for 1 Thessalonians Doty includes under the category of parenesis Paul's responses to comments or questions, likely in letter form (1 Thess. 4.9–5.11).[14] The closing section for 1 Corinthians, he says, does not begin until 16.19, and since 5.1–16.18 is analogous in form to responses by Paul in 1 Thessalonians, the section can best be categorized as parenetic.

As for Philippians, the thanksgiving and body sections in the first part of the letter are clear (1.3-11 and 1.12–2.30).[15] For the sample used in the statistical analysis, the questionable section is ch. 3. Again, Doty does not find a parenetic section in Philippians. However, he does not classify ch. 3.[16] The nature of the verses, a warning against those who teach the need for Jewish customs such as circumcision, is paralleled by Gal. 5.1-12, which can be part of the body[17] or the parenetic unit. Paul appears to start off with a parenetic general interest, which is repeated again in the parenetic section of 5.13–6.10, but he decides instead to return once more to his warnings in earlier chapters against those urging submission to Jewish customs (5.2-12). Similarly, in Philippians Paul begins with general parenesis but decides to devote many verses to warnings against his opponents and their teachings (3.3-21). To this writer Gal. 5.1-12 and these verses in Philippians should be considered part of the letter body primarily, although statistics for these sections as parenetic will also be presented.

For the two Pauline samples used to test if the statistical formula is effective, the one requiring discussion is 1 Thessalonians. The body consists of 1 Thess. 2.1–3.13, and definite parenetic sections are 1 Thess. 4.1-12 and 5.1-22.[18] The debatable passage is the one concerning the dead in Christ (4.13-18). Both 4.9 and 5.1 are

13. J.L. White, *The Form and Function of the Body of the Greek Letter: A Study of the Letter-Body in the Non-Literary Papyri and in Paul the Apostle* (SBLDS; Missoula, MT: Society of Biblical Literature, 1972), pp. 73, 122-23, 131-35, 146, 149-50; Doty, *Letters*, p. 43.

14. Doty, *Letters*, p. 43; Hurd, *Origin*, p. 64, cites several scholars supporting the view that 1 Thessalonians is a response to a letter.

15. White, *Form and Function*, pp. 71-73; Doty, *Letters*, p. 43.

16. Doty, *Letters*, p. 43.

17. Doty, *Letters*, p. 43.

18. Doty, *Letters*, p. 43.

introduced by περὶ δέ clauses associated with the verb γράφω implying a response to a written letter, and 4.13-18 is linked with 5.1-22 in form and content (περί; 5.10, 14).[19] This paragraph will be classed then with the parenetic section.

Since the boundaries for the major sections of the various Pauline letters employed in the first stage of research have now been discussed, word counts from those sections are given below for the original samples used to define the typical Pauline style and for the test samples used to evaluate whether the statistical definition can classify samples correctly:

Number of Words from Major Sections of Pauline Letters

Name of Sample	Thanks-giving	Body	Parenetic	Closing
PLA (1 Cor. 4.7–6.19)	0	216	534	0
PLC (1 Cor. 11.33–12.23; 15.56–16.24)	0	0	688	62
PLF (Phil. 1.3-26; 2.27–3.30)	142	608	0	0
or PLF*	142	296*	312*	0
PLR (Rom. 2.20–3.25; 6.22–7.19)	0	750	0	0
PLT (1 Thess. 2.13–5.4)	0	393	357	0

Means of Sections and Percent of Samples

Original samples	Thanksgiving	Body	%	Parenetic	%	Closing
with PLF	47.3	274.7	(36.6)	407.3	(54.3)	20.7
with PLF*	47.3	170.7*	(22.8)	511.3*	(68.2)	20.7
Test samples (PLR & PLT)	0.0	571.5	(76.2)	178.5	(23.8)	0.0

(* Phil. 3.1-21 is classed as parenesis, not body)

The difference in the sources for the samples is clearly seen. The 1 Corinthian samples (PLA, PLC) come from mostly *parenetic sections*, while those from Romans and 1 Thessalonians (and possibly Philippians) draw from the *main body* of the letter. Little use is made of thanksgiving and closing sections. There is a striking difference between the original samples and the test samples in their means from the respective parts, the former coming mainly from parenetic sections (and possibly not as representative of much of the Pauline

19. Hurd, *Origin*, p. 64.

style?). In the test runs of the various stylistic criteria, when the test samples were not classified with the correct authors, perhaps this was due to the difference in the proportion from body or parenetic sections. Even correct classifications could have been misleading.

The next step is to analyze the samples used in the second stage of research, those from the disputed letters and more samples from undisputed Pauline letters used to further verify the validity of the statistical methodology. Doty does not analyze the disputed letters; however, he observes, 'The Deutero-Pauline letters...rather closely copy the Pauline letter form.'[20] If one uses the Pauline models for the undisputed letters, Ephesians, Colossians and 2 Thessalonians can be divided into the usual Pauline sections without much debate over boundaries, as follows:

Section	Eph.	Col.	2 Thess.
Salutation	1.1-2	1.1-2	1.1-2
Thanksgiving	1.3–2.10	1.3-29	1.3-12
Body	2.11–3.21	2.1–3.4	2.1–3.5
Parenesis	4.1–6.20	3.5–4.6	3.6-15
Closing items	6.21-24	4.7-18	3.16-18

The recommendations of the letter bearers are seen by Doty as part of the conclusion to the letter body,[21] but they will be treated here as part of the personal greetings and information usually found in the closing. Doty sees two possible lengths to the body of Galatians (1.6–5.16 [6.17?]), but since he assigns 5.13–6.10 to the parenetic section,[22] we will view Gal. 1.6–5.12 as the body. The closing items are 6.11-18. 2 Corinthians is more difficult to treat. Doty's analysis viewing the body (or bodies) occurring in various places is accepted.[23]

Employing the above-mentioned sections in the letters, the following results are obtained for a similar analysis of various Pauline letters and the disputed Pauline letters:

20. Doty, *Letters*, pp. 65-66.
21. Doty, *Letters*, pp. 36-37, 43, 45-46.
22. Doty, *Letters*, p. 43.
23. Doty, *Letters*, p. 43. The body for 2 Corinthians is 1.8–2.13, 7.5-6, 2.14–7.4, 10.1–13.14; there is no parenesis section listed, and he says the closing consists of the blessing in 12.14 (does Doty mean 13.14 [RSV]?) and 13.12-13. For this research 2 Cor. 13.10 will be regarded as the body's final verse, and 2 Cor. 13.11-13 the closing items.

Origins and Method

Number of Words and Percent of Samples

Name of Sample	Thanks-giving	Body	%	Paren-etic	%	Closing
GAL (3.10–4.9; 5.10–6.17)	0	401	(53.5)	254	(33.9)	95
COR2 (2 Cor. 1.12–2.8; 12.14–13.13)	0	701	(93.5)	0	(0)	49
COR1 (1 Cor. 6.19–7.22; 9.13–10.11)	0	0	(0)	750	(100)	0
EPH1 (1.3–3.5)	485	265	(35.3)	0	(0)	0
EPH2 (3.5–5.3)	0	257	(34.3)	493	(65.7)	0
EPH3 (5.3–6.24)	0	0	(0)	684	(91.2)	66
COL (2.8–3.8; 3.17–4.17)	0	324	(43.2)	240	(32.0)	185
TH2 (2 Thess. 1.3–3.16)	207	381	(50.8)	153	(20.4)	9

When this table is compared with the results from the original investigation, there appears to be a correlation between the kinds of sections in the samples and the degree of similarity to the Pauline style. In general, the closer the sample resembles the original samples with respect to the proportions from the various sections, the closer the sample is to the Pauline centroid. The 1 Corinthians sample, being totally from the parenetic section, is very near, while the samples from 2 Corinthians, 2 Thessalonians, and Galatians, containing more body material than parenesis, are relatively distant. Of the Ephesian samples, the one most similar to 'Paul' is the one consisting of mostly parenesis (EPH3, 5.3–6.24). The one exception to this pattern, EPH2, which is very similar to the original samples in having more parenesis than words from the letter body, is slightly more distant from the Pauline centroid than EPH1 consisting of only thanksgiving and body.[24] However, the pattern with other samples is clear enough that it may be concluded that one of the factors of variation between samples is the kind of sections from which they come, whether from the body or parenetic section or other parts. For samples assumed to be Pauline the variation is not major enough to classify the samples into the wrong groups, but the table here may help to explain why there are samples appearing to be on the fringes of the Pauline group (Galatians, the three disputed letters) when they may have been well within normal Pauline ranges if the samples chosen would have taken

24. Neumann, *Authenticity*, pp. 195, 198-99.

into account the sections of Pauline letters. It would be better to compare body sections with body sections, parenetic sections with parenetic, etc., to obtain more accurate results.

To complete the picture one should compare the Pauline samples with the writings of *the other authors* in the original study and see from what sort of sections their samples are derived, for if the samples are from markedly different sections of the letters, then the original research, in part, was separating not just authors but major forms of writing. The other authors do not generally follow the Pauline pattern of letters closely even though apparently they were all strongly influenced by Paul's letters.[25] Ignatius's letters are similar to the Pauline letter pattern in their salutations and closings, but the central sections of the letters do not have clearly defined thanksgiving and parenetic sections. They appear to be most similar to the body sections of Paul's letters. Clement's letter also contains well-defined opening and closing sections although far longer than Ignatius'. No samples were taken from those parts but only from the body of the letter, again a mixture of instruction most comparable to the Pauline letter body. Hebrews, according to Doty, goes beyond the letter form to become a 'letter-essay' alternating sermon and parenesis during most of the work but concludes in chapter 13 with parenesis (13.1-19) and closing benediction, greetings and 'a wooden travelogue' (13.20-25).[26] In conclusion, the samples from the three writers appear to be mainly similar to Paul's letter body section (although this should be tested), and thus one may wonder how much of the clear differences between author groups found in the research is due to differences in proportions from major sections.

Now that the non-Pauline letters have been briefly analyzed by form, an examination of the Pastoral letters is appropriate. Doty finds 'characteristic' for them that the parenetic section is 'now lost to view formally', but the letters are 'thoroughly permeated with the sort of advice and instruction which Paul usually treated in the fourth part of his letters'.[27] 1 Timothy has not one basic body of regulations but 'a collection of various materials'. Even 2 Timothy with its personal references 'belongs to the genre of parenesis'.[28] There are the usual

25. A.E. Barnett, according to Doty, *Letters*, p. 66.
26. Doty, *Letters*, pp. 68-69.
27. Doty, *Letters*, pp. 69-70.
28. M. Dibelius and H. Conzelmann, *The Pastoral Epistles: A Commentary on*

opening and closing sections (1 Tim. 1.1-2; 6.21b; 2 Tim. 1.1-2; 6.9-22) and even a section resembling the Pauline thanksgiving (2 Tim. 1.3-7). Thus, the samples from 1 and 2 Timothy could be considered primarily parenetic except for 65 words of thanksgiving in 2 Timothy. One would expect if they were written by Paul, they would be close in style to the original Pauline samples, which are more parenetic in nature; however, there is a very significant difference from them, and they are clearly in the non-Pauline stylistic groups. 2 Timothy, the closest, only has a probability of being Pauline of less than one chance in 100, while the 1 Timothy sample remote from any author group has less than a one in 1,000 chance.[29] From a stylistic point of view it is next to impossible to put these letters in the Pauline group. Since the section of the letters from which the samples were taken were about the same as the Pauline samples, the significantly different style is due to another cause, probably a difference in authorship.

The results showing the effect of Pauline sub-divisions of letters are likely due, in part, to the different forms within such units, that is, forms such as doxologies. Even closer scrutiny should be given to sentences based on traditional formulations and structure, particularly in parenetic sections.

A closing statistical comment is good to keep in mind. From a mathematical viewpoint, since the discriminant analytical tool is based on certain samples and tries to find the very best indices to maximize the spread between authors and minimize the spread between just a few samples from the same author, any other samples compared with them will almost invariably be further away from the centroid. Some variation therefore is accounted for by this factor.

In conclusion, the results call for a whole new study comparing only the same sections of letters and deleting forms within the sections heavily influenced by traditional structure and content (for example, doxologies). The thanksgiving sections and closing sections are too short to provide samples by themselves and should be omitted from any new study. Since Paul is least bound by structure in his letter body sections, research should probably concentrate on them. All these considerations will result in a reduced amount of potential text for

the Pastoral Epistles, (trans. P. Buttolph and A. Yarbro; Hermeneia; Philadelphia: Fortress Press, 1972), pp. 5-8.

29. Neumann, *Authenticity*, pp. 198-201.

samples, but the results will be more reliable. The sample size (750 words) may need to be reduced, but other effective studies have employed much smaller size samples.[30] Since Clement and Ignatius do not have clearly defined thanksgiving or parenetic sections, and it is difficult in advance to label the central section of their letters, it would be best to perform an analysis similar to genre analysis, that is, discriminant analysis on the known body and parenetic sections in undisputed Pauline letters to see what stylistic indices particularly separate the two forms and then apply the best combination to Clement and Ignatius to determine whether they are more typically like the Pauline letter body or parenetic section. Similar testing should be done with Hebrews. Sections clearly parenetic and those clearly like the Pauline letter body may be separated. However, the researcher may conclude that Hebrews is too different in genre to include in Pauline comparative studies. Finally, with samples that are similar in form and genre, the variations discovered will be more likely due to a difference in authorship rather than some other factor. This procedure should clarify the place of the disputed letters within the entire Pauline corpus.

30. Neumann, *Authenticity*, pp. 135-36.

Part II

NEW UNDERSTANDINGS OF THE NEW TESTAMENT

EDWIN HATCH, CHURCHES AND *COLLEGIA*

John S. Kloppenborg

The convergence and conflict between Acts and Paul regarding the chronology of Paul's activities and the interpretation of his mission and theology are well known, though, as John Hurd has observed repeatedly, not always taken as seriously as they might. Converge and conflict are likewise observed in the description of the Pauline churches given by Acts and that which can be derived from Paul's own letters. Luke and Paul agree in calling these groups ἐκκλησίαι. Luke's treatment, however, implicitly characterizes churches as extensions of the synagogue. Although he depicts Paul as finding converts outside the structure of the synagogue, the Lukan Paul is in constant contact with the synagogue, and draws members from the so-called 'god-fearers'. Moreover, when describing the indigeneous leadership of churches, Luke adopts the term πρεσβύτερος, a term which is entirely non-Pauline but which, in view of its use in Luke's Gospel, allows for the conclusion that Pauline churches are in a continuum with synagogues. The apologetic value of this for Luke is clear. Whether it should be allowed to inform our reconstruction of the social organization of Pauline churches is another matter.

In this tribute to John Hurd I deliberately disconnect the evidence of Paul's churches from the Lukan representation, and propose to look at Pauline churches through the lens of Greek and Roman voluntary associations or *collegia*. I begin with the sometimes maligned but mostly neglected work of Edwin Hatch.

1. *Edwin Hatch*

More than a century ago Hatch, whose name is perhaps best remembered for his monumental *Concordance to the Septuagint and the*

Other Greek Versions of the Old Testament,[1] delivered the 1880 Bampton Lectures at Oxford University under the title, *The Organization of the Early Christian Churches*.[2] He was riding the crest of a wave of epigraphical publications during the 1860s and 1870s, including collections of Greek and Latin inscriptions from Greece, Asia Minor and Syria[3] and the important work of Paul Foucart on religious associations.[4]

Epigraphy made plain the fact that professional, athletic, literary, dining and cultic associations flourished in every city of the Empire, despite the best efforts of several emperors to eradicate them. They shared, at least nominally, a 'religious' character and most, even those of a professional nature, had a tutelary deity. They offered people, according to Hatch, a religion 'which they believed' alongside the rather sterile state religion 'which they professed'.[5]

From this it was a very short step to the observation that as Christianity spread, it did not have to invent the notion of a religious society distinct both from the family and the *polis* or state. Forming associations was already a 'fixed habit'. Indeed, in most respects,

1. E. Hatch, and H.A. Redpath, *A Concordance to the Septuagint and the Other Greek Versions of the Old Testament* (2 vols.; repr.; Graz: Akademische Druck-u. Verlagsanstalt, 1954 [1897–1906]).

2. E. Hatch, *The Organization of the Early Christian Churches: Eight Lectures* (Bampton lectures for 1880; London: Rivingtons, 1881).

3. G. Wilmanns, *Exempla inscriptionum Latinarum in usum praecipue academicum* (2 vols.; Berlin: Weidmann, 1873); P. Le Bas and W.H. Waddington, *Inscriptions grecques et latines recueillies en Asie Mineure. I. Textes en majuscules. II. Textes en minuscules et explications* (Paris: Firmin-Didot & Cie., 1870); W.H. Waddington, *Inscriptions grecques et latines de la Syrie: Recueillies et expliquées. I. Textes en majuscules. II. Textes en minuscules et explications* (Paris: Firmin-Didot & Cie., 1870); J. Turtle Wood, *Discoveries at Ephesus: Including the Site and Remains of the Great Temple of Diana* (repr.; Hildesheim: Georg Olms, 1975 [1877]).

4. P. Foucart, *Des associations religieuses chez les Grecs—thiases, éranes, orgéons, avec le texte des inscriptions rélatives à ces associations* (Paris: Klincksieck, 1873). Also G. Battista De Rossi, 'I collegii funeraticii famigliari e loro denominazioni', in *Commentationes philologae in honorem Theodori Mommseni scripserunt amici* (Berlin: Weidmann, 1877), pp. 705-11; O. Lüders, *Die dionysischen Künstler* (Berlin, 1873); and the earlier work of T. Mommsen, *De collegiis et sodaliciis Romanorum. Accedit inscriptio lanuvina* (Kiliae: Libraria Schwersiana, 1843).

5. Hatch, *Organization*, p. 28.

Christian churches would simply have been regarded as another form of association. In many associations and in Christian groups, contributions were made to a common fund, and in both cases, Foucart's evidence had shown, membership was extended to women, noncitizens, and even slaves, rather than being restricted to citizens, as tended to be the case with civic cults.[6]

Hatch's chief interest lay in accounting for the formal organization of Christian churches, in particular, for the offices of bishop and deacon. At the heart of Christian associations was support of the poor[7] and practically speaking, this meant that financial administration became an important structural element in Christian groups. Thus, Hatch argued, ἐπίσκοπος commended itself as an administrative title for Christian churches precisely because, along with ἐπιμελητής,[8] it was the key title for a financial administrator in associations and in the *polis*.[9] The terms 'elders' (πρεσβύτεροι) and 'bishops' (ἐπίσκοποι) referred to the same persons, but to different roles: as members of the council they would be called πρεσβύτεροι but as administrators they were ἐπίσκοποι.

Hatch's claims about the nature of the episcopacy attracted much criticism, but he was not alone in seeing analogies with voluntary

6. See Foucart, *Des associations religieuses*, pp. 5-12. '[Civic associations] n'admettaient que les membres d'une même famille ou d'une même tribu, les citoyens d'une même ville ou d'un même dème. Il en était tout autrement pour les thiases et les éranes. Non-seulement ils étaient ouverts aux femmes, mais encore les étrangers, les personnes de condition ou d'origine servile y avaient accès' (p. 5).

7. Hatch, *Organization*, p. 36: 'Other associations were charitable: but whereas in them charity was an accident, in the Christian associations it was of the essence.' He quotes J. Chrysostom, *Homilae in Epistulam ad Hebraeos* 12, Hom. 32 (*PG* 63.224) οὐδὲν οὕτω χαρακτηριστικὸν Χριστιανοῦ ὡς ἐλεημοσύνη.

8. Ἐπιμελητής is the principal term used for financial administrator. See *LSCG*, p. 338, *s.v.* ἐπιμελητής. The title is also found for municipal officers: see, e.g., F. Oertel, *Die Liturgie: Studien zur ptolemäischen und kaiserlichen Verwaltung Ägyptens* (repr.; Aalen: Scientia Verlag, 1976 [1917]), pp. 214-21, 302-308.

9. See C. Wescher, 'Note sur une inscription de l'île de Théra publiée par M. Ross relative à un société religieuse', *RA* NS 13 (1866), p. 246: δέδοχθαι· ἀ[ποδε]ξαμένος τὰν ἐπαγγελίαν τὸ μ[ὲν ἀρ]γύριον ἐγδανεῖσαι τὸς ἐπισκό[πος] Δίωνα καὶ Μελέϊππον... 'It is resolved that the ἐπίσκοποι Dion and Meleippus shall accept what has been promised and invest the money...' The term also appears in inscriptions in the Hauran (Auranitis): *IGLS*, nos. 1989, 1990, 2298. For usage outside of voluntary associations, see *IG*, I² 10, ll. 12-13; *IG*, V, 2; *IG*, XII, 1 49, ll. 42-44.

associations or *collegia*. In 1866 Ernest Rénan's book on the apostles had devoted a chapter to voluntary associations and the restrictions placed upon them by various emperors.[10] Rénan had not argued that the structure of Christian communities derived from that of voluntary associations, only that Christian communities provided their members with many of the same benefits and, like voluntary associations, would have been regarded with the same (or more) suspicion by anxious prefects and governors. Just four years before Hatch's Bampton lectures, Georg Heinrici had renounced the *opinio communis* established by Campegius Vitringa, that Pauline churches were organized as synagogues,[11] and compared the church at Corinth with Graeco-Roman cultic associations.[12] Like Hatch, Heinrici was impressed by an array of convergences between Graeco-Roman associations and Pauline churches: associations sometimes bore the name ἐκκλησία,[13]

10. E. Rénan, *Les apôtres* (Histoire des origines du christianisme, 2; Paris: Michel Levy, 1866), pp. 262-74.

11. C. Vitringa, *De synagoga vetere libri tres: quibus tum de nominibus structura origine praefectis ministris et sacris synagogarum agitur, tum praecipue formam regiminis et ministerii earum in ecclesiam Christianam translatam esse demonstratur: cum prolegomenis*, Editio altera emendatior (Leucopetrae: apud Io. Frid. Wehrmannum, 1726).

12. G. Heinrici, 'Die Christengemeinden Korinths und die religiösen Genossenschaften der Griechen', *ZWT* 19 (1876), pp. 465-526; G. Heinrici, 'Zur Geschichte der Anfänge paulinischer Gemeinden', *ZWT* 20 (1877), pp. 89-130; G. Heinrici, 'Zum genossenschaftlichen Charakter der paulinischen Christengemeinden', *TSK* 54 (1881), pp. 505-24; G. Heinrici, *Der erste Brief an die Korinther* (Kritisch-exegetischer Kommentar über das Neue Testament, 5; Göttingen: Vandenhoeck & Ruprecht, 8th edn, 1896). Heinrici also observed that the Corinthians brought disputes to a civic forum rather than judging them in an internal forum (1 Cor. 6), concluding that this indicates that they were not part of a synagogue structure (see on this, Jos., *Ant.* 14.10.17). A similar argument was mounted by Hermann Weingarten, 'Die Umwandlung der ursprünglichen christlichen Gemeindeorganisation zur katholischen Kirche', *HZ* 9 (1881), pp. 441-67. There is, however, no indication that Hatch knew either Heinrici's or Weingarten's work.

13. *IGLAM*, no. 1381 (Aspendus [Pamphylia]): Ζήνων [Θεοδώρου ἀρχιτ]έκτων τοῦ θεάτρου ἀνέθηκεν· ἀ[πέδωκεν εἰς ἀγῶνα] γυμνικὸν γενέθλιον τοῦ θεάτρου πρισχείλια, [καὶ εἰ]ς εὔφημον ἐκκλησίαν ἐχαρίσατο κήπους πρὸς τῷ ἱπποδ[ρόμῳ...] The editors comment: 'Εὔφημος ἐκκληία signifie peut-être une assemblée non politique, une réunion de plaisir' (2.336). No. 1382 (Aspendus): ἡ βουλὴ καὶ ὁ δῆμος ἐτείμησεν Ζήνων[α] Θεοδώρου ἀρκιτέκτονα τοῦ θεάτρου [καὶ] τῶν τῆς πόλεως ἔργων, ἐπιδεδωκότα [εἰς] ἀγῶνα γυμνικὸν γενέθλιον τοῦ θεά[τρου] δηνάρια τρισχείλια καὶ εἰς

they were often religious in character, and Christian groups, conversely, were sometimes described with terms drawn from associations.[14] While civic organizations tended to restrict membership to citizens, associations extended their membership to others. Moreover, associations provided both financial support and festal occasions which 'were the highlight in the lives of many poor, despised or lonely persons'.[15] Heinrici saw further similarities in the fact that both Pauline churches and Roman associations used the metaphor of a 'body' to describe themselves,[16] and in the common use of familial terms in respect to members.[17]

εὔφημον ἐκκλησ[ίαν ἐχαρίσα]μενον κήπους π[ρὸς τῷ] ἱπποδρόμῳ... See further, W. Liebenam, *Zur Geschichte und Organisation des römischen Vereinswesens: 3 Untersuchungen* (Leipzig: B.G. Teubner, 1890), pp. 272-79.

14. Lucian (*Peregr.* 11) calls Christianity a 'new mystery' (καινὴ τελετή) and refers to the leaders with the terms προφήτης, θιασάρχης, ξυναγωνεύς, νομοθέτης and προστάτης. Tertullian (*Apol.* 39) refers to *christiana factio* and states: *corpus de conscientia religionis et disciplinae unitate et spei foedere; coimus in coetum et conjugationem.* Celsus (*apud* Or. *Cels.* 3.23) calls the disciples θιασῶται Ἰησοῦ. Cf. Eusebius (*EH* 1.3.12) who refers to Christians as θιασῶται.

15. Heinrici, 'Die Christengemeinden Korinths', p. 487.

16. Heinrici refers to *EIL*, p. 631 (index, *s.v.* 'corpus'); see now J.P. Waltzing, *Etude historique sur les corporations professionnelles chez les Romains depuis les origines jusqu'à la chute de l'Empire d'Occident* (Mémoire couronne par l'Academie royale des Sciences, des Lettres et des Beaux-Arts de Belgique; 4 vols.; repr.; Hildesheim: Georg Olms, 1970 [1895–1900]), IV, pp. 546-52. Waltzing (*Etude*, I, pp. 340-41) comments: 'Il y a un mot qui se distinguie de tous ceux qui précèdent: c'est *corpus* (σύστημα). Quand on veut indiquer de plus que le collège est autorisé, reconnu comme un organisme public et, par conséquent, doté des droits qui constituent la personnification civile, on l'appelle *corpus*. Tel est le sens juridique de ce mot; mais dans l'usage ordinaire, il est employé concurremment avec *conlegium*, quand il s'agit d'un collège authorisé: *collegium pistorum* ou *corpus pistorum*.'

17. Heinrici, 'Die Anfänge paulinischer Gemeinden,' pp. 98-99; Liebenam (*Geschichte und Organisation*, p. 185) refers to *CIL* VI 406: *fratres carissimos et collegas hon(oratos)* [cult of Juppiter Dolichenus]; VI 9148 [*domestic collegium*]; VI 10681; VI 21812; VI 377 [cult of Mithras]: *fratres et sorores*; V 7487 [professional association]: *fabri fratres.* Other terms connoting friendship (*CIL* VI 6220: *amici*; X 6699; V 4395; 4483) are attested. F. Poland (*Geschichte des griechischen Vereinswesens* [repr.; Leipzig: Zentral-Antiquariat der DDR, 1967 (1909)], p. 55), however, notes that ἀδελφοί is not as common in Greek associations as it was in Roman: 'Gerade in dem Fehlen dieser gemütlichen Bezeichnung besteht eine der merkwürdigsten Verschiedenheiten vom römischen Brauch, der, wie er von Vater und Mutter spricht, so vor allem Brüder in den Kollegen sieht.' See further,

The reaction to Rénan, Heinrici and Hatch was both swift and mixed. On the one hand, Hatch's book achieved the distinction of being among the few to make a southward voyage across the English Channel in other than its original language, being translated into German in 1883 by the young Adolf Harnack.[18] Harnack embraced Hatch's suggestion that the ἐπίσκοπος was associated with financial administration, although he argued that the bishop's role also included 'Cultus, Correspondenz, kurzum Ökonomie im weitesten Sinn des Wortes'.[19] But with the discovery of the Didache in that same year, Harnack's interests modulated into a discussion of two forms of ministry, one institutional and the other charismatic—his famous distinction between the διακονία τῶν τραπεζῶν and the διακονία τοῦ λόγου.[20] Attention shifted from the general thesis propounded by Rénan, Heinrici and Hatch to two more limited issues: whether πρεσβύτεροι and ἐπίσκοποι were alternate designations for the same persons, a position also advocated by Lightfoot[21] and whether the episcopal office was originally one of financial administration.

On the other hand, the negative reaction to Hatch[22] and Heinrici[23]

F. Bömer, *Untersuchungen über die Religion der Sklaven in Griechenland und Rom* (Mainz: Akademie der Wissenschaften und der Literatur, 1958–63), I, pp. 172-79.

18. E. Hatch, *Die Gesellschaftsverfassung der christlichen Kirchen im Alterthum: Acht Vorlesungen gehalten an der Universität Oxford im Jahre 1880* (Giessen: J. Ricker'sche Buchhandlung, 1883).

19. A. von Harnack, *Die Lehre der zwölf Apostel nebst Untersuchungen zur ältesten Geschichte der Kirchenverfassung und des Kirchenrechts* (Texte und Untersuchungen 2/1-2; Leipzig: Hinrichs, 1884), pp. 88-151, esp. p. 144.

20. In 'On the Origin of the Christian Ministry' (*The Expositor* 3.5 [1887], pp. 321-43) Harnack insists that ἐπίσκοπος emerged not from the LXX but 'from a purely Gentile Christian ground' (p. 338). The ἐπίσκοπος, however, belonged to the διακονία τῶν τραπεζῶν to be distinguished from the διακονία τοῦ λόγου, which fell to the charismatic figures, the apostles, prophets and teachers.

21. J.B. Lightfoot, *Saint Paul's Epistle to the Philippians: A Revised Text with Introduction, Notes and Dissertations* (repr.; London: Macmillan & Co., 4th edn, 1881), pp. 95-99. Like Hatch, Lightfoot also recognized that ἐπίσκοπος in Greek commonly referred to supervisors or inspectors.

22. *The Expositor* devoted many of the essays in the 1887 issue to an evaluation of the proposals of Lightfoot, Harnack and Hatch, although, curiously, Hatch himself did not (or was not asked to) contribute. See *The Expositor* 3.5 (1887): W. Sanday, 'The Origin of the Christian Ministry. I. Recent Theories', pp. 1-22; W. Sanday, 'The Origin of the Christian Ministry. II. Criticism of Recent Theories', pp. 97-114; J. Rendel Harris, 'Dr. Sanday on the Christian Ministry', pp. 225-35;

was immediate. Most of the criticism had to do with Hatch's apparent views on the origins of the episcopacy. William Sanday, who was otherwise favourably disposed to Hatch's thesis, remained unconvinced that the texts cited by Hatch indicated that the role of ἐπίσκοπος was one of financial administration[24] and unconvinced of a Greek origin for the term ἐπίσκοπος.[25] The LXX was a more obvious

A. von Harnack, 'On the Origin of the Christian Ministry', pp. 321-43; C. Gore, 'The Origin of the Christian Ministry', pp. 411-25.

23. Heinrici ('Zum genossenschaftliche Charakter', p. 507) reports (and responds rather apologetically to) a review by C. Holsten (*Das Evangelium des Paulus, Teil 1. Die äussere Entwicklungsgeschichte des paulinischen Evangeliums. Abt. 1. Der Brief an die gemeinden Galatiens und der erste Brief an die Gemeinde in Korinth* [Berlin: Georg Reimer, 1880], pp. 237, 243) who dismissed Heinrici's thesis because it implied that Christian churches 'die Lebensformen einer Kultusgenossenschaft der Dämonen (1 Kor. 10.20) benutzte'.

24. Sanday, 'The Origin of the Christian Ministry. II. Criticism of Recent Theories', *The Expositor* 3.5 (1887), pp. 98-99. Sanday rightly observed that the inscription from Thera (above n. 9) does not indicate whether financial administration was the sole concern of the ἐπίσκοπος and that the inscriptions from Auranitis do not provide any concrete indications of the responsibilities of the ἐπίσκοποι. Waddington's inscriptions from Syria provide ten occurrences of the noun ἐπίσκοπος (*IGLS*, nos. 1989, 1990, 2298) and the verb ἐπισκοπεῖν (nos. 1911; 2070, 2308, 2309, 2310, 2412e 2412^f) but none specifies the role of the ἐπίσκοπος. In no. 1990, however, five persons are called ἐπίσκοποι ἐκ τῶν τοῦ θεοῦ. Waddington (*IGLS*, 474 [on no. 1990]) comments: 'Les magistrats appelés ἐπίσκοποι sont souvent mentionnées dans les inscriptions du Haourân (nos. 1989, 2298, etc.). Leurs function sont ainsi définies par le jurisconsulte Charisius, qui écrivait sous Constantin: episcopi, qui praesunt pani et caeteris venalibus rebus, quae civitatum populis ad quotidianum victum usui sunt (Digest 50.4.18); elles étaient donc analogues à celles des agoranomes, et il est possible que les magistrats appelés agoranomes en Grèce et géneralement dans les pays helléniques aient porté dans l'interieur de la Syrie le titre d'épiscopes; dans tous les cas, j'ai n'y ai trouvé recontré plusiers épiscopes dans les textes du Haourân, et je n'y ai trouvé qu'un seul exemple d'un agoranome, à Kanatha (no. 2330). Notre inscription semblerait prouver que les épiscopes exerçaient aussi quelque surveillance sur les revenus sacrés; mais l'expression τὰ τοῦ θεοῦ est assez vague, et peut s'appliquer à des amendes infligées par les épiscopes, et dont le produit était consacré aux réparations des temples.'

25. Sanday, 'The Origin of the Christian Ministry. II', p. 102: 'I have indeed no objection in principle to the use of analogies from the Greek and Roman civil or religious organizations, but where the option is given of going either to these or to the LXX for the groundwork of a theory, the latter seems to me distinctly preferable.' For a similar position, see C. Gore, *The Church and the Ministry: A Review of the*

source. The same criticism was echoed by Loening[26] and Lietzmann.[27] Charles Gore was prepared to concede that churches would have *appeared* as *collegia* to many and that the existence of *collegia* would have facilitated the spread of the church. But he was quite unprepared to concede that *collegia* exerted any substantial influence on the organization of churches, particularly in the realm of official terminology. The terminology of Christian ministry came from Jewish rather than Gentile usage.[28]

Johannes Weiss, Heinrici's successor as the commentator on 1 Corinthians in the Meyer (KEK) series, was also reluctant to accept Heinrici's views:

> It is perhaps not open to any doubt that in general the Christian community on Corinthian soil had to accept various features from the associations and in many respects had to operate like a new θίασος of an oriental religion. However, the difficulty begins when we ask: 1) did Paul or his helpers in the community consciously take over forms or institutions from Greek associations? and 2) which *individual* forms of this type can be detected?[29]

Weiss conceded immediately that the first question could not be answered but surmised that at least some Christians in Corinth may have been (former) members of other associations. What told against the analogy of *collegia* and the Corinthian church had to do with particular details. First, there was no evidence at Corinth of a common chest. Paul's instructions regarding the collection (1 Cor. 16.1-4) implies that the church did not regularly administer monies, and there is no hint that the common meal was paid for from a common fund. Secondly, the Corinthian church did not elect its officers and there is no evidence of a common rule regulating behaviour of members.

Rev. E. Hatch's Bampton Lectures (London: Longmans, Green, 4th rev. edn., 1900 [1882]), pp. 16-17.

26. E. Loening, *Die Gemeindeverfassung des Urchristentums: Eine kirchenrechtliche Untersuchung* (repr.; Aalen: Scientia Verlag, 1966 [1888]), pp. 21-22.

27. H. Lietzmann, 'Zur altchristlichen Verfassungsgeschichte', *ZWT* 15 (1914), pp. 97-153, esp. pp. 101-106.

28. C. Gore, *The Ministry of the Christian Church* (London: Rivingtons, 1888), pp. 31-36.

29. J. Weiss, *Der erste Korintherbrief* (Kritisch-exegetischer Kommentar über das Neue Testament, 5; Göttingen: Vandenhoeck & Ruprecht, 9th edn, 1910), pp. xxiii-xxiv.

Finally, while noting that the practices of baptism and exclusion admittedly had parallels within voluntary associations, Weiss argued that the fact that baptism originated in Palestine with John and that 1 Corinthians 5 closely resembled a synagogue ban made it more advisable to compare the Corinthian church with a diaspora synagogue.[30]

2. *Recent Assessments of Hatch*

For most of the first part of this century, the Hatch-Heinrici thesis did not find many advocates and could, it would seem, be safely ignored.[31] It has been only in the last two decades that Hatch's thesis was revived. Asking how Christianity would have appeared to others in the Roman world, Robert Wilken suggested that it would have been seen as a burial society (*collegium funeraticium* or *collegium tenuiorum*) or as a philosophical club. Wilken argued that these two types of organizations in fact overlapped in several important ways, sharing some of the same terminology (*secta*, σύνοδος, θίασος), often having a cultic dimension, and usually meeting for common meals.[32] His

30. Weiss, *Der erste Korintherbrief*, pp. xxiv-xxv. Similarly Loening, *Die Gemeindeverfassung des Urchristentums*, 9: 'der Versuch, aus den heidnischen Cultvereinen die Verfassung der christlichen Gemeinden herzuleiten, ist bis jetzt nicht geglückt.' Liebenam, *Geschichte und Organisation*, p. 271: 'Ich kann diesen Ausführungen Heinricis nicht überall zustimmen, da es sich zum Theil um Formen handelt, wie sie eben bei jedem Gemeinwesen, jeder Assoziation wiederkehren, andrerseits um Beziehungen, die keineswegs den Genossenschaften eigentümlich sind... (φιλοτιμεῖσθαι, ζῆλος, ζηλοῦν, κυροῦν, δοκιμάζειν, προθυμία, κατ' ἐπιταγήν, καλῶς καὶ εὐσχημόνως, u.a.) und nur einer vorgefaßten Ansicht zu Liebe als spezifisch technische Begriffe der Vereine gedeutet werden können.' F. Poland's assessment, based on a much broader survey of associations, was strikingly different: 'In den Festmahlen, in den Versammlungen der Genossen, in den patriarchalischen Verhältnissen der Hausgemeinden, in der Glossalalie (?) und mancher andern Erscheinung steht das Christentum unter der Einwirkung des griech. Vereinswesen: man darf nur diese Verwandtschaft nicht zu sehr auf Einzelheiten wie die Bezeichnung der Ämter u.a. ausdehnen wollen. Denn gerade hier zeigt sich die Eigenart des Christentums. Was in Griechland Zufälligkeit der Erscheinung ist, tritt hier bald als festes, bewußtes Gesetz auf' (*Geschichte*, p. 534).

31. For example it is not discussed, but only briefly alluded to in a footnote by E. Schweizer, *Church Order in the New Testament* (SBT, 1/32; London: SCM Press, 1963), p. 201 n. 761, without, however, naming Hatch or Heinrici.

32. R.L. Wilken, 'Collegia, Philosophical Schools and Theology', in S. Benko

point was not to treat philosophical groups and *collegia* as the same, nor was it to claim that Christian groups *were collegia*; instead, he tried to show both the social character of philosophical groups, and the religious and ethical character of *collegia* and thus to indicate the significant overlap, an overlap shared with Christian organizations.[33]

Perhaps the most suggestive, if brief, commentary was offered by Abraham Malherbe. Taking his cue from Heinrici, Malherbe suggests

and J.J. O'Rourke (eds.), *Early Church History: The Roman Empire as the Setting of Primitive Christianity* (London: Oliphants, 1972), pp. 268-91, esp. p. 279. In his later book (*The Christians as the Romans Saw them* [New Haven: Yale University Press, 1984], p. 44) Wilken writes of Christians of a slightly later stage: 'To the casual observer, the Christian communities in the cities of the Roman Empire appeared remarkably similar to religious societies such as the one described above [i.e., the Iobacchi, *IG* II² I, 2, no. 1368] or to a burial society such as the one at Lanuvium [*CIL* XIV 2112]. Like these other associations, the Christian society met regularly for a common meal; it had its own ritual of initiation, rules, and standards for members; when the group came together, the members heard speeches and celebrated a religious rite involving offerings of wine, prayers and hymns; and certain members of the group were elected to serve as officers and administrators of the association's affairs. It also had a common chest drawn from the contributions of members, looked out for the needs of its members, provided for a decent burial, and in some cities had its own burial grounds. Like the followers of Heracles who were called Heraclists, the devotees of Asclepius called Asclepiasts, or the followers of Isis called Isiacs, the Christians were called *Christiani*.'

33. See also J. Gagé, *Les classes sociales dans l'Empire romain* (Bibliothèque historique; Paris: Payot, 2nd edn, 1971), p. 308: Christian groups 'offere, à première vue, une resemblance étonnante avec une espèce d'assocation confraternelle qui avait fleuri depuis le IIe siècle, dans le cadre du paganisme et avec une très ouverte tolérance des pouvoirs, des municipaux comme de l'impérial: les *collegia funeraticia*, ou "collèges" funéraires.' More recently, H.-J. Klauck ('Die Hausgemeinde als Lebensform im Urchristentum', *MTZ* 32 [1981], p. 11) drew attention to the fact that private cultic associations, like Pauline groups, often used private homes as meeting places. This is developed in much greater detail by H.O. Maier, *The Social Setting of the Ministry as Reflected in the Writings of Hermas, Clement and Ignatius* (Dissertations SR, 1; Waterloo: Wilfrid Laurier University Press, 1991), pp. 22-23, 29-39. A century ago, Liebenam, *Geschichte und Organisation,* p. 272 n. 4 drew attention to the parallel between Pauline house churches (κατ' οἶκον ἐκκλησίαι) and domestic collegia for the dependents of households. E.g. *CIL* VI 9148: 'collegium quod est in domu Sergiae Paullinae' (also *CIL* VI 9149, 10260-10264); *CIL* VI 404: collegium quod consistit in praedis Larci Macedonis'. Pliny (*Ep.* 8.16) states: 'nam servis respublica quaedam et quasi civitas domus est'.

that a significant sector of the Corinthian Christian groups would have been handworkers,[34] and hence familiar with the structure and dynamics of professional *collegia*. This type of *collegia* functioned not like a modern labour union, to protect labour markets, but for social reasons, providing a quasi-civic structure in which members could receive and bestow honours on their fellows.[35] The consciousness of social stratification and the interest in promoting (fictive) status elevation that was typical in professional *collegia* may be factors in understanding the tensions over achievement and status elevation within the Corinthian Christians.[36]

Malherbe also noticed that Luke's reference to the *scholē* of Tyrannus (Acts 19.9), typically understood as a lecture-hall, may in fact have been a guild hall, *scholē* being a typical designation for such buildings.[37] The references in Acts to Paul's handkerchiefs and aprons (19.11-12) and to conflict with the guild of silversmiths (19.23-41) as well as Paul's own claims to have worked with his own hands to support himself (20.34-35) are all consistent with locating Paul in the social context of handworker associations.[38] For Malherbe these convergences were clear invitations to pursue Paul's connection with professional *collegia* further.

Wayne Meeks, Malherbe's colleague at Yale, also considered the thesis of Hatch and Heinrici but came to a rather different conclusion. Meeks' search for models for the Pauline churches led him to consider the household, voluntary associations, the synagogue and philosophic or rhetorical schools.[39] As most others, he was prepared to admit

34. A.J. Malherbe (*Social Aspects of Early Christianity* [Baton Rouge: Louisiana State University Press, 1977], p. 75) bases this claim on the statement of Acts 18.3 that Paul, Aquila and Priscilla were tentmakers and on the location of the 'synagogue of the Hebrews' near the Corinthian agora, where the small shops of artisans would have been located.

35. See R. MacMullen, *Roman Social Relations, 50 BC to AD 284* (New Haven: Yale University Press, 1974), p. 77: 'What is interesting about crafts associations for our purposes is the focussing of energies on the pursuit of honor rather than of economic advantage... Associations resembled the whole social context they found themselves in and imitated it as best they could.'

36. Malherbe, *Social Aspects*, pp. 88-89.

37. Waltzing, *Etude historique*, I, pp. 221-35, 425-60.

38. Malherbe, *Social Aspects*, pp. 90-91.

39. Wayne A. Meeks, *The First Urban Christians: The Social World of the Apostle Paul* (New Haven: Yale University Press, 1983), pp. 75-84.

several similarities: both *collegia* and Pauline churches were small, face-to-face groups; both were voluntary; both included persons of a common trade; and both observed certain rituals including a common meal. And while Pauline churches were not burial societies, 'we can hardly doubt, in the face of the sort of sentiment expressed in, say, 1 Thess. 4.13-5.11 or the enigmatic reference to 'baptism for the dead' in 1 Cor. 15.29, that these groups made appropriate provision for the burial of deceased Christians'.[40]

Christian groups, like *collegia*, depended upon the largesse of wealthy patrons but, argues Meeks, unlike *collegia*, Christian churches did not reward patrons with honorific inscriptions, which may have given them reason to feel slighted.[41] He also notes that while Christians did not elect their leaders, 'democratic procedures' were at work in Pauline groups even though spirit possession and charismatic activity were complicating factors.

The differences for Meeks, however, are decisive. First, Christian groups were 'exclusivistic and totalistic in a way no club nor even any pagan cultic association was'. Baptism initiated a process of thorough resocialization in the course of which loyalty to the sect would supplant all other loyalties. Furthermore, the motivation for membership went beyond mere fellowship and conviviality to salvation 'in a comprehensive sense'.[42] Secondly, Christian groups, says Meeks, were more inclusive as regards membership. Although he acknowledges that some *collegia* drew members from various levels of society and included both men and women, there is rarely evidence of 'equality of role' among these categories, and for the most part *collegia* members were socially homogeneous.

Thirdly, Meeks acknowledges that Tertullian and Eusebius referred to Christian groups as 'factiones', 'corpora' and θιασῶται. But the paucity of any significant terminological overlap between associations and Paul's own description of his churches makes it, in Meeks' view, unlikely that churches modelled themselves on associations. Instead,

---

40. Meeks, *First Urban Christians*, p. 78.
41. Meeks refers to a paper, now published, by L.W. Countryman, 'Patrons and Officers in Club and Church', in P.J. Achtemeier (ed.), *Society of Biblical Literature 1977 Seminar Papers* (SBLASP, 11; Missoula, MT: Scholars Press, 1977), pp. 135-43, esp. p. 140.
42. Meeks, *First Urban Christians*, pp. 78, 79.

terms such as ἐκκλησία were mediated through the LXX.[43] He further
acknowledges that ἐπίσκοπος may have been taken over from the
usage of associations but states that 'it has scarcely begun to make its
appearance in Christian terminology in Paul's time'[44]—a somewhat
puzzling comment in view of the fact that along with διάκονος and
perhaps προστάτις ἐπίσκοπος, is the *only* title attested in any of the
Pauline churches.[45] Finally, he observes that Pauline churches quickly
developed extra-local links in a way that neither professional *collegia*
nor cult associations did.

3. *Methodological Issues*

The debate sparked by Hatch and Heinrici is of interest both for the
matters of substance concerned, and because it exposes important
assumptions at work in scholarship on early church polity. Some of
the arguments invoked against Heinrici and, especially, Hatch were
plainly dogmatic in nature. For some critics it was simply intolerable
that the Church should have owed its structure to paganism.[46] This
reaction should not strike us as especially surprising. For the age in

43. Meeks (*First Urban Christians*, pp. 79, 222 n. 24) states that ἐκκλησία does
not occur as the title of a club, but is used only (rarely) of business meetings. He
cites the single inscription mentioned by Poland (*Geschichte*, p. 332) but overlooks
those cited by Heinrici and Hatch (above n. 13).

44. Meeks, *First Urban Christians*, p. 80.

45. Meeks (*First Urban Christians*, pp. 80, 222 n, 29) suggests that when
διάκονος appears in the inscriptions of associations, it refers to persons who are
waiting on tables. Yet Poland (*Geschichte*, pp. 391-93), to whom he refers, states:
'διάκονος tritt *als einzelner Beamter* in Troisen, Thyrrheion and Palairos (...fünf
διάκονοι hat ein Kolleg von Meterverehrern in Kyzikos und mindestens neun ein-
schließlich eines Priesters ein κοινὸν τῶν διακόνων von Ambrakia, das ägyptische
Götter verehrte). Die Funktionen des Diakonos können wohl sehr verschiedenartig
gewesen sein, immerhin läßt die weite Verbreitung dieser Bezeichnung für den
Priestergehilfen im staatlichen und privaten Kult es nicht unmöglich erscheinen, daß
der christliche Diakonentitle aus dem heidnischen hervorgegangen ist' (pp. 391-92,
emphasis added).

46. These have been detailed in N.F. Josaitis, *Edwin Hatch and Early Church
Order* (Recherches et synthèses, Section d'Histoire 3; Gembloux: J. Duculot, 1971).
A series of Hatch's letters (reprinted by Josaitis, *Edwin Hatch and Early Church
Order*, pp. 12-14) reveals the opposition at Oxford to Hatch's nomination as the
Bampton lecturer, opposition that had to do with his (and Sanday's) perceived
'Darwinianism'.

which Hatch wrote and much of the century that followed was dominated by the notion that the message of Jesus and the original purity and simplicity of his followers' lifestyle were swiftly overlaid with hellenized, Catholic elements. Hatch, too, accepted this view, articulating it with great clarity in his Hibbert Lectures of 1888.[47] But in this later work, Hatch appears to treat the Pauline churches as part of the 'first stage of Christianity', in which the basis of association was still moral and spiritual; the transformation of Christianity—its virtual paganization—came later. But even if Hatch saw the balance tipping toward *Frühkatholismus* only in the second century, he had opened a dangerous door by daring to compare Pauline churches with Graeco-Roman religious cults. This threatened to move the fulcrum back into the first century, something, at least, that many Protestants could not tolerate.[48]

a. The Priority of 'Jewish' Models

While such theologically-motivated arguments are easily noted, there are at least two other methodological issues that the Hatch-Heinrici proposal exposed. The first concerns become plain when one asks the question, did or would Christian groups appear to be *collegia*? The answer is almost unaminous. Even opponents of Hatch and Heinrici such as Gore agreed with Hatch's statement that 'to the eye of the out-side observer they were in the same category as the associations which already existed... The basis of association, in the one case as the other, was the profession of a common religion'.[49] But Gore only conceded

47. E. Hatch, *The Influence of Greek Ideas on Christianity*, in A.M. Fairburn (ed.), *Hibbert Lectures of 1888* (repr., with a foreword by F.C. Grant; New York: Harper & Brothers, 1957 [1890]), pp. 283-309, 334-35.

48. See J.Z. Smith, 'On Comparing Words', in *Drudgery Divine: On the Comparison of Early Christianities and the Religions of Late Antiquity* (Jordan Lectures in Comparative Religion, 14; London: The School of Oriental and African Studies; Chicago: University of Chicago Press, 1990), pp. 54-84. K. Lake's treatment of Pauline baptism provides an example: 'Baptism is, for St. Paul and his readers, universally and unquestionably accepted as a "mystery" or sacrament which works *ex opere operato*...this sacramental teaching is central in the primitive Christianity to which the Roman Empire began to be converted' (*The Earlier Epistles of St. Paul: Their Motive and Origin* [London: Rivingtons, 1911], p. 385). See the reaction in H.A.A. Kennedy, *St. Paul and the Mystery-religions* (London: Hodder & Stoughton, 1913), pp. x, 2, 212, 232-36, 244, 247, 264-65 and *passim*.

49. Hatch, *Organization*, pp. 30-31.

that Christian groups would have *appeared* to be *collegia*. Decisive for
the opponents of Hatch was the distinction between appearance and
essence, or between churches incidentally resembling *collegia* and
having been *influenced* by them. For many it was more palatable to
argue that the resemblances were interesting but ultimately inconse-
quential, since NT churches had in fact been 'influenced' by the synagogue, or by Palestinian institutions, or had derived their terminology
from the LXX.

The argument, articulated variously in Sanday and Gore, and by
more recent scholars,[50] that the LXX or first century Judaism is a
'better' source for ecclesial terminology is a particularly clear example
of what Jonathan Z. Smith has described on a broader scale: the use of
'Judaism' to insulate emergent Christianity from the Hellenistic
world.[51] An instance of this line of argument is seen in the declar-
ations that the מבקר (inspector) of Qumran[52] supplied the prototype
for ἐπίσκοπος.[53] It is fair to say that the energy expended on
qualifying this proposal[54] at no time approximated that devoted to

50. See, e.g., Meeks's comments on *ekklesia* (*First Urban Christians*, p. 79).

51. Smith, *Drudgery Divine*, p. 83. Such a strategy, ironically, is frequently
coupled with assertions of the superiority of Christianity to Judaism, thus leaving
Christianity as 'unique'.

52. מבקר from בקר, 'to inspect'. See, e.g., 1QS 6.19-20: 'let his wealth and his
wages be conveyed into the hands of the inspector (מבקר) of the Great Ones who
shall enter them to his credit in the account book...'

53. E.g. J. Jeremias, *Jerusalem in the Time of Jesus: An Investigation into
Economic and Social Conditions during the New Testament Period* (London: SCM
Press; Philadelphia: Fortress Press, 1969), p. 261; J. Daniélou, *The Theology of
Jewish Christianity* (trans. J.A. Baker; London: Darton, Longman & Todd, 1964),
pp. 48-49; J. Schmitt, 'Sacerdoce judaïque et hiérarchie ecclésiale', *RSR* 39 (1955),
p. 257.

54. See, e.g., H.W. Beyer, 'ἐπισκέπτομαι, ἐπισκοπέω, ἐπισκοπή, ἐπίκοπος,
ἀλλοτριεπίσκοπος', *TDNT* 2 (1964), pp. 618-19, who asserts that 'none of the
offices denoted by ἐπίσκοπος in the Greek speaking world has so much in common
with the Christian office of bishop as to enable us to affirm the possibility of a
historical connection' (p. 618) but also points out some differences between the
Christian bishop and the Qumran מבקר. Accordingly, while he allows that synagogal
and Pharisaic (!) forms might have been in view, he concludes: 'But their [the
Christian] community, based on the great commission to preach the Gospel and to
live according to it in the most inward of all societies, was something new and
distinctive, so that for the fulfilment of its mission new offices had to be created, or
to develop out of the matter itself.' Schweizer (*Church Order*, p. 201) likewise thinks

dismissing Hatch's Greek parallels. For it evidently seemed 'more likely' that Pauline churches would have used 'Jewish' titles than Gentile ones, despite the fact that (1) there is no good evidence that Paul was aware of the technical language used at Qumran, (2) nor is there evidence that the terms ἐπίσκοπος and διάκονος at Philippi were Paul's coinage and (3) Philippi was much closer—geographically and culturally—to the Cyclades (Thera) or Rhodes than it was to an obscure Judaean backwater. Ironically, studies by Bardtke, Schneider, Dombrowski and, in particular, Moshe Weinfeld have made a compelling case that the structure of the community at Qumran is due in significant measure to the influence of Graeco-Roman associations.[55] Weinfeld observed that the hierarchy at Qumran, with priests followed by the 'official at the head of the many' (פקיד בראש הרבים,

that Qumran offers a close parallel, but observes that ἐπιμελητής is a better translation for מבקר.

55. The connection was first drawn independently by H. Bardtke, 'Der gegenwärtige Stand der Erforschung der in Palästina neu gefundenen hebräischen Handschriften, 44: Die Rechtsstellung der Qumran-Gemeinde', *TLZ* 86 (1961), pp. 93-104, and C. Schneider, 'Zur Problematik des Hellenistischen in den Qumrantexten', in H. Bardtke (ed.), *Qumran-Probleme: Vorträge des Leipziger Symposions über Qumran-Probleme vom 9. bis 14. Oktober 1961*, (Deutsche Akademie der Wissenschaften zu Berlin. Schriften der Sektion für Altertumswissenschaft 42; Berlin: Akademie-Verlag, 1963), pp. 305-309. It was developed by B.W. Dombrowski, 'היחד in 1QS and τὸ κοινὸν: An Instance of Early Greek and Jewish Synthesis', *HTR* 59 (1966), pp. 293-307; M. Delcor, 'Repas cultuels esséniens et thérapeutes, thiases et haburoth', *RQ* 6 (1968), pp. 401-25 and M. Hengel, *Judaism and Hellenism: Studies in their Encounter in Palestine during the Early Hellenistic Period* (London: SCM Press, 1974), I, pp. 243-44; II, p. 165 n. 866. Dombrowski compared the regulations of τὸ κοινὸν τῶν Σιδωνίων from a bilingual Greek-Phoenician inscription at Piraeus (H. Donner and W. Rollig [eds.], *Kanaanäische und aramäische Inschriften* [2 vols.; Wiesbaden: Otto Harrassowitz, 2nd edn, 1964–66], I, p. 13; II, pp. 73-74), the *Manual of Discipline* (1QS), and the rule of a cult of Zeus dated between 69–58 BCE (A.D. Nock, C. Roberts and T.C. Skeat, 'The Guild of Zeus Hypsistos', *HTR* 29 [1936], pp. 39-88). Dombrowski notes that the word היחד falls from use after 100 CE, and speculates that a 're-Judaizing' orthodoxy deliberately avoided τὸ κοινόν and its Hebrew equivalent as a reaction to earlier Hellenization. The most thorough study of the problem is that of M. Weinfeld, *The Organizational Pattern and the Penal Code of the Qumran Sect: A Comparison with Guilds and Religious Associations of the Hellenistic-Roman Period* (NTOA, 2; Fribourg: Editions Universitaires; Göttingen: Vandenhoeck & Ruprecht, 1986). Weinfeld draws detailed comparisons with various religious associations, including that of the Iobacchi (*SIG³* 1099).

1QS 6.14-15) and the 'inspector over the possessions of the many' (מבקר על מלאכת הרבים, 1QS 6.19-20), approximates the structure of Greek and Roman associations, with a hierarchy of ἱερεύς/*magister*, ἐπιμελητής/*curator* and ταμίας/*quaestor*.[56] Thus, the alternate to 'Hellenistic influence' is itself the product of such influence.

The attempt to use either Qumran or the LXX to isolate primitive Christianity from the Graeco-Roman world should be recognized as apologetic. Not only did Christian organizations *appear* to be *collegia*; there is a strong likelihood that they thought of themselves as such. Pliny's statement that Christians in Bithynia ceased meeting after Trajan's edict banning *hetaeriae* indicates both that the Christians involved saw themselves as constituting an association, and that this judgment was shared by Pliny.[57] The very name *Christianoi*, though perhaps initially a slur, is precisely the kind of name that associations gave themselves. Judge concludes:

> This distaste of the Christians for the name that was gratuitously bestowed upon them, however, certainly does not mean that they were unwilling to be thought of as forming an association of the usual kind. On the contrary it would hardly have occurred to them to raise the question in the first place... The term *ecclesia* (*sc.* 'meeting') itself, and the names for the various officials may have developed special connotations within the Christian community, but to non-Christians, and to Christians themselves in the early stages, they need have suggested nothing out of the ordinary.[58]

It would seem that first-century Christians were perhaps not quite so concerned to protect their biblical pedigree as were many nineteenth and twentieth century commentators.

b. *Genealogy and Analogy*
A second issue raised by Hatch's thesis has to do with the goal of comparison. Hatch's proposals were in some ways more modest, and

---

56. Weinfeld, *Organizational Pattern*, p. 20. Josephus mentions an Essene ἐπιμελητής (*BJ* 2.123, 129, 134) while Philo (*apud* Eus. *PE* 8.2.10) describes the role of the ταμίας in managing the economy of the community.

57. Pliny, *Ep.* 10.96: *quod ipsum facere desisse post edictum meum, quo secundum mandata tua hetaerias esse vetueram.*

58. See E.A. Judge, *The Social Pattern of Christian Groups in the First Century: Some Prolegomena to the Study of New Testament Ideas of Social Obligation* (London: Tyndale Press, 1960), p. 45.

his method considerably more sophisticated, than his opponents recognized. What they fixed on was the perceived claim that similarities between voluntary associations and churches implied 'influence' or borrowing. In fact, he did not use the term 'influence' and notwithstanding his comments on the episcopacy, Hatch was as concerned to identify *differences* between *collegia* and churches.[59]

> What then, if we look at the Christian communities simply on their human side as organizations in the midst of human society, was their point of peculiarity and difference?[60]

He merely assumed what was evident from ancient sources—that associations proliferated in the Imperial period and that Christian groups would *look* like just another associations.[61] What seemed to exercise most of his opponents was that he could compare Christian churches with non-Christian ones, for comparison would inevitably lead to claims of genealogy and homology. Yet Hatch was more nuanced. Comparison is not in the first instance about genealogy; it is about *understanding* the phenomema themselves:

> The importance of a comparison lies in the fact that we cannot avoid going on to the further question, how far the similar phenomena are the product of the same causes. If we find in the Roman Empire civil societies with organizations analogous to those of the Christian societies, civil officers

59. 'Influence' is used extensively in the Hibbert Lectures, but there it is in conjunction with second century transformations. See Hatch, *The Influence of Greek Ideas*, pp. 283-309.

60. Hatch, *Organization*, p. 32. In the introductory lecture, Hatch writes: '...if we assume, as I propose to assume, that—at least for purposes of study—the facts of ecclesiastical history, being recorded in the same language, and in similar documents, and under the same general conditions of authorship, belong to the same category as the facts of civil history, it is not too much to maintain the existence of a presumption that the application of historical science and the historical temper to a field of historical phenomena which they have hitherto left comparatively unexplored, may be followed by new results' (pp. 2-3).

61. Hatch, *Organization*, pp. 16-17: 'These resemblances have always been admitted, and have to some extent long been investigated. But evidence which has not been thoroughly investigated until recent years, and evidence which has only within recent years come to light—especially in the unimpeachable form of inscriptions—has shown that the resemblances are not merely general but minute. The points of comparison which have been hitherto known have to be supplemented by a large number of other points, in which the close relation between Christian and non-Christian organizations has hitherto been hardly suspected.'

230 Origins and Method

with the same names and similar functions to those of ecclesiastical officers, the question arises and must be answered, whether the causes which are sufficient to account for them in the one case are not equally sufficient to account for them in the other.[62]

If the interest in genealogy—or more precisely, in establishing the *lack* of genealogical relationship between Christianity and Hellenism—often betrays an apologetic agenda,[63] the point of analogical comparison is to identify similarity within difference in such a way that various aspects of the phenomona under consideration become intelligible.[64] What the analogy of voluntary associations might help us to understand include (a) the ways in which Pauline churches found a place (or failed to find a place) in the fabric of Imperial society, (b) the ways in which they offered benefits commensurable with—not always the *same* as—those offered by other associations, (c) the ways in which such benefits, which generations of New Testament scholars have thought of as 'religious' in character, were more than that, and (d) the ways in which the internal polity of Christian groups—with its mixture of imitation of the habitual modes of social exchange and experimentation—and the church–polis relationship mirrored (and distinguished themselves from) those of other associations.

---

62. Hatch, *Organization*, p. 17. Cf. Malherbe, *Social Aspects*, p. 89: 'Although the possibility of demonstrating genealogical relationship between the organizations of the associations and the church is unlikely, the value of the material dealing with the associations is not vitiated. If we are interested in social relations rather than organizational structure, and in analogies rather than in genealogical relationships, the material may help to clarify some aspects of both the informal relationships within the church as well as the church's relationship to the larger society.'

63. See Smith, *Drudgery Divine*, p. 83: 'In the earlier Casaubon-tradition, the effort at distinction was between Roman Catholicism and a Protestant portrait of Christian origins. The later studies have shifted focus to Jewish "backgrounds". In this latter endeavour, Judaism has served a double (or, a duplicitous) function. On the one hand it has provided apologetic scholars with an insulation for early Christianity, guarding it against "influence" from its "environment". On the other hand, it has been presented by the very same scholars as an object to be transcended by early Christianity.'

64. See the helpful discussion by Smith, *Drudgery Divine*, pp. 52-53.

4. *Churches as* Collegia?

Are there sufficient similarities to warrant the comparison of *collegia* and Pauline churches? Some of the past attempts to distinguish churches from *collegia* have done so by ascribing to *collegia* a much greater degree of uniformity than actually existed. In fact, as will become clear, there was a broad spectrum of forms of *collegia*, broad enough that most of the particularities seen in Pauline churches could fit comfortably within that spectrum.

a. *Technical Designations*
It has been observed repeatedly that Pauline and later churches did not employ the self-designation θίασος or ἔρανος but almost unanimously preferred the term ἐκκλησία . The significance of this observation is relativized, however, by the fact that associations used a plethora of terms as self-designations. Some used technical terms such as κοινόν, συνέδριον, θίασος, ἔρανος, and συναγωγή, while others used a series of names referring to membership: in addition to θιασῶται and ἐρανισταί, ὀργεῶνες, συνθύται, θυσιασταί, θεραπευταί, μύσται, τελεστῆρες, ἱερουργοί, διάκονοι, συμβιωταί, φράτορες, φίλοι, ἑταῖροι and ὁμοτάφοι. In other cases still, the names were derived from the deity worshipped ('Αγαθοδαιμονισταί, 'Αρτεμισιασταί, 'Ασκλλαπιασταί, Βακχισταί, etc.), and in yet other cases, there is no name recorded, or rather vague terms such as οἶκος appear (for example *SIG³* 985 = *LSAM*, no. 20). It is true that the term ἐκκλησία was not among the most common designations for associations, but some associations *were* called ἐκκλησία, as is clear from the inscriptions cited by Hatch (above n. 13) and by an inscription from Delos published by Foucart.[65] Whether or not Paul's use of the term ἐκκλησία was inspired by the LXX is not the point. In the environment of Greek cities, the term would almost certainly be understood (by all involved) as one of the names for a voluntary association.

As to the titles of officers, it can be observed that Paul's letters lack some of the more common terminology associated with *collegia*—

---

65. Foucart, *Des associations religieuses*, no. 43 (pp. 223-25), lines 1-2 (= *CIG* 2271): Ἐπὶ Φαιδρίου ἄρχοντες, Ἐλαφηβολιῶνος ὀγδοεῖ, ἐκκλησία ἐν τῷ ἱερῷ τοῦ Ἀπόλλωνος, Διονύσιος, Διονυσίου ἀρχιθιασίτης εἶπεν· The inscription dates from 196 BCE.

ἱερεύς (priest), ἐπιμελητῆς (superintendent), γραμματεύς (secretary), ταμίας (treasurer), and compounds with ἀρχι- or -αρχης.[66] The only titles that appear are ἐπίσκοπος, διάκονος and προστάτις, all of which also occur in the context of associations.[67] In regard to ἐπίσκοπος, the critics of Hatch were quite correct in asserting that the appearance of ἐπίσκοπος in the inscriptions from Thera and Auranitis could not support the weight of Hatch's thesis concerning the exclusively financial character of the episcopal office. In fact, the situation with those inscriptions is roughly the same as with Phil. 1.1: the lack of a context makes it impossible to determine the identity and role of the ἐπίσκοποι.[68] The same is the case with διάκονος in Phil. 1.1 and Rom. 16.1, although in the latter instance, the fact that Phoebe is also called a προστάτις suggests that she is of rather high status and thus it is unlikely that the role of the διάκονος is menial.[69]

There is no a priori reason to assume that there was uniformity among the Pauline churches, any more than one should assume a uniform organizational structure in associations.[70] On the contrary, titles were highly variable, local particularities abound, and in many instances, we have no indication of how officers were designated.[71] At

66. See a survey of such titles in Poland, *Geschichte*, pp. 337-414.

67. ἐπίσκοπος: see Poland, *Geschichte*, p. 377; διάκονος: see Poland, *Geschichte*, pp. 391-92; προστάτης/προστάτις: see, C. Wescher, 'Fragment de stèle trouvé à Athènes', *RA* NS 11 (1865), pp. 504-505; Poland, *Geschichte*, pp. 363-67.

68. Poland (*Geschichte*, p. 338) observes that there is no general rule to indicate which of several officers would take precedence over the others. In some cases, the treasurer seems to have dominated the organization, in other cases it is the priest, and in some instances, the priest also assumed the function of treasurer, secretary and superintendent.

69. See most recently, C.F. Whelan, '*Amica Pauli*: The Role of Phoebe in the Early Church', *JSNT* 49 (1993), pp. 67-85.

70. See Poland, *Geschichte*, p. 337.

71. For example, the cult association from Andania (*LSCG*, no. 65) reports ὁ γραμματεύς, ὁ ἱερεύς, οἱ ἱεροί, ὁ γυναικονόμος, οἱ ἄρχοντες, ὁ ἐπιμελητής and a ταμίας, but also a ἀργυροσκόπος (bursar?) and ῥαβδοφόροι (rod bearers). Debord (*Aspects sociaux et économiques*, p. 258) notes that it is often difficult to determine the precise type of organization of an association because the titles are so many and so diverse: 'Il est difficile de préciser le type d'organisation auquel correspond l'inscription *IG* XII, 731 qui mentionne trois épistates, un secrétaire des *hierophylakes*, un *épiskopos*, six hiéropes, un *tamias*, un sous secrétaire des *hierophylakes*'.

Thessalonica and Corinth, Paul commends persons in leadership roles without using a title, stating only that Stephanus' household has appointed itself to the service of the saints (εἰς διακονίαν τοῖς ἁγίοις ἑαυτούς, 1 Cor. 16.15), while in 1 Thess. 5.12 he uses functional descriptions of leaders (εἰδέναι τοὺς κοπιῶντας ἐν ὑμῖν καὶ προϊσταμένους ὑμῖν ἐν κυρίῳ καὶ νουθετοῦντας ὑμᾶς). Since in both instances, Paul is favourable to the leaders (and they to him), it seems likely that had they assumed special titles, Paul probably would have used them.[72] That he does not may be a function of the fact that the organizations were new enough not to have developed any official titles. The same, incidentally, appears to be the case with the Zeus cult in Philadelphia (*LSAM*, no. 20).[73]

Since so little is said of leaders in Pauline churches, a fortiori, we cannot know much about the method by which they were selected or their term of office. The implication, however, that associations elected officers and that in this respect Christian groups were distinct, is certainly false. While some associations elected (some of their) officers,[74] in other instances officers were chosen by lot (in the case of priests), appointed by superiors, or either purchased or inherited the office.[75] In the majority of cases, it is unclear how officers were chosen. Since most associations depended upon the largesse of patrons and donors, their wishes would naturally have loomed large in the choice of officers, however they were chosen. The donor may himself (or herself) have served as an officer and, presumably, continued to play this role as long as he or she wished.[76] Christian groups, too,

---

72. On the other hand, Paul refrains from calling Crispus by his title in 1 Cor. 1.14, assuming that this is the Crispus whom Acts 18.8 calls ὁ ἀρχισυνάγωγος.

73. See S. Barton and G.H.R. Horsley, 'A Hellenistic Cult Group and the New Testament Churches', *JAC* 24 (1981), p. 22.

74. E.g. the association of Iobacchi (*IG* II² 1368, 178 CE) elected a ταμίας for a two-year term (ll. 146-47: ταμίαν δὲ αἱρείσθωσαν οἱ Ἰόβακχοι ψήφῳ εἰς διετίαν), although the presiding officer, the priest, was appointed by his predecessor. The treasurer was permitted to choose his own γραμματεύς (l. 155).

75. See Poland, *Geschichte*, pp. 416-18.

76. An example of this form of leadership is probably found in the Zeus association in Philadelphia (below n. 86) and it is clearly the case with the Men cult at Sounion (*LSCG*, no. 55) where the founder, Xanthos, expressly guarded against encroachments by others in his absence and made provisions for an appointee in the case of his death. See further, W.S. Ferguson, 'The Attic Orgeones and the Cult of Heroes', *HTR* 37 (1944), pp. 84-85, 94-95.

depended upon the patronage of wealthy families. As Harry O. Maier
has recently argued, they were probably localized in wealthy households and would, accordingly, have relied upon household heads as
leaders.[77]

b. *Membership*
Meeks' point that Pauline churches were more inclusive of persons
from various social levels than associations bears some scrutiny. It is
no doubt correct that associations formed along professional lines
would have included persons of generally the same social class.[78] It is
also true that Poland's more detailed analysis of the demographics of
voluntary associations has indicated that membership was rather more
homogeneous than what Foucart had suggested. Poland noted that
while there is evidence of the participation of women in many associations, they were often—though not exclusively—involved either as
spouses of members or as benefactors.[79] Slaves were present alongside
citizens in Greek civic associations, but the social distinction was
clearly preserved insofar as slaves were subject to harsher penalties
(flogging) than citizens in the case of misconduct (see, for example, an
association in Andania, *LSCG*, no. 65). It was Roman influence, especially in Thrace and Asia Minor, that was responsible for greater and
more 'equal' participation of slaves and freedmen (and freedwomen)
in associations. This was perhaps due to the notion of the association
as a *familia*, embracing persons of diverse social ranks under the
patronage of the elite. Gager, for example, notes a Dionysiac association with some four hundred members, with members ranging from
the senatorial rank to freedmen and slaves.[80] The group, however,
included only the senator's family and clients.

77. Maier, *The Social Setting of the Ministry* (above n. 33).

78. Trades clustered in the same areas of the city and consequently, trade associations also de facto represented streets or neighborhoods. Occasionally, a person
might belong to an association not in virtue of his trade, but because of his residence.
See MacMullen, *Roman Social Relations*, pp. 70-74. Naturally, one would find only
a limited range of social ranks represented in any given locality.

79. Poland, *Geschichte*, pp. 289-98.

80. J.G. Gager, *Kingdom and Community: The Social World of Early
Christianity* (Englewood Cliffs, NJ: Prentice–Hall, 1975), p. 99.

Although Foucart exaggerated the inclusive character of associations in general, it is clear, nonetheless, that some associations were 'inclusive'. The rule of the Zeus association from Philadelphia (Lydia) mentioned above makes a point of stating that the group was open to ἀνδρά[σι καὶ γυναιξὶν] ἐλευθέροις καὶ οἰκέταις (*LSAM*, no. 20, ll. 5-6, 15-16, 53-54) and the regulations regarding sexual propriety clearly indicate that slaves as well as free were in fact involved (ll. 25-41). Similarly, the Roman burial association in Lanuvium (*CIL* XIV 2112) presupposes that citizens and non-citizens, slaves as well as freeborn and freedmen were present in the *collegia*, functioning more or less as equals.

Just as one should not generalize about the membership of associations in the Greek world, it should not be assumed uncritically that Pauline churches were all equally 'inclusive'. The evidence from the Corinthian correspondence indicates that women as well as men, slaves and free, and at least some wealthier persons were involved.[81] Phil. 4.2 indicates that women were present alongside men and Paul's references to gifts of money probably suggests that the Philippian church included more than just the urban poor. Significantly, both Corinth and Philippi were refounded as Roman cities. It would be much more difficult to prove the same case from 1 Thessalonians, where Paul's ready admission that he worked day and night (1 Thess. 2.9) and his exhortation to work with one's own hands (4.11) probably indicate that he is addressing an audience who are themselves mainly handworkers.[82] Certainly Paul does not encounter the

81. G. Theissen, *The Social Setting of Pauline Christianity: Essays on Corinth* (Philadelphia: Fortress Press, 1982), pp. 95-96.

82. Thus E. Best, *A Commentary on the First and Second Epistles to the Thessalonians* (London: A. & C. Black, 1972), p. 174; R.F. Hock, *The Social Context of Paul's Ministry: Tentmaking and Apostleship* (Philadelphia: Fortress Press, 1980), pp. 31-47; G. Agrell, *Work, Toil and Sustenance: An Examination of the View of Work in the New Testament* (Stockholm: Verbum; Lund: Håkan Ohlssons Förlag, 1976), p. 99; Meeks, *First Urban Christians*, p. 64. Paul's admission in 1 Cor. 4.12, καὶ κοπιῶμεν ἐργαζόμενος ταῖς ἰδίας χερσίν, is of quite a different character than the statements and exhortations in 1 Thessalonians. In 1 Corinthians, Paul uses this admission to underscore the *difference* in status between himself and his audience, as the preceding verses (4.7-11) indicate. Traders (*negotiatores*)—including merchants, shopkeepers and prostitutes—were subject to the *collatio lustralis*, a particularly burdensome tax which drove some to sell children into slavery. See A.H.M. Jones, 'The Economic Life of the Towns of the Roman

problems having to do with his (low) social status in Thessalonica that he faced in Corinth.[83] It is at least worth considering that the Thessalonian Christians may have been quite homogeneous, not unlike a professional association; indeed, Paul may have initially operated from within a handworker's guild in that city.[84]

c. *Other Matters*

The objection that Christian groups did not keep a common chest likewise requires further nuance. While associations commonly collected fees from their members,[85] this cannot be shown to be uniformly the case. In some instances, instead of money, members supplied sacrifical animals—the officiants were normally entitled to retain portions of the sacrifice.[86] It should be added that when funds were collected, they

Empire', in J. Firenne (ed.), *La Ville: Deuxième partie: Institutions économiques et sociales* (Recueils de la société Jean Bodin, 7; Bruxelles: Editions de la libraire éncyclopedique, 1955), p. 162.

83. On the problem of Paul's social status and the way this limited his opportunities to speak, see S.K. Stowers, 'Social Status, Public Speaking and Private Teaching', *NovT* 26 (1984), pp. 59-82.

84. Little in 1 Thessalonians, with the possible exception of 1 Thess. 4.4, gives any indication of the presence of women. But irrespective of whether one translates σκεῦος κτᾶσθαι as 'control the body' or 'get a wife' or 'guard one's member', the advice is framed from the point of view of the male. If women were present, it is entirely possible that they were so only as the spouses of members. See on this R.F. Collins, ' "This is the Will of God: Your Sanctification" (1 Thess 4:3)', *LTP* 39 (1983), pp. 27-53; O.L. Yarbrough, *Not Like the Gentiles: Marriage Rules in the Letters of Paul* (SBLDS, 80; Atlanta: Scholars Press, 1985), pp. 65-87; M. McGehee, 'A Rejoinder to Two Recent Studies Dealing with 1 Thess 4:4', *CBQ* 51 (1989), pp. 82-89.

85. The presence of a ταμίας (treasurer) in many societies is an indication of this even when there is no direct mention of dues. See, e.g., C. Wescher, 'Fragment de stèle trouvé à Athènes', *RA* NS 11 (1865), pp. 497-506 = Foucart, *Des associations religieuses,* no. 27; and Sokolowski, *LSCG*, p. 358 *s.v.* 'ταμίας'; idem, *LSCGSup*, p. 233 *s.v.* 'ταμίας'. See the general discussion of finances in Ferguson, 'The Attic Orgeones', pp. 61-140.

86. For example, an association at Sounion (Attica) devoted to Men (*LSCG*, no. 55 = E.N. Lane, *Corpus monumentorum religionis dei Menis [CMRDM]* [EPRO, 19; 4 vols.; Leiden: Brill, 1971–78], no. 13, 1.8-10; 3.7-16) stipulates no fees, but indicates that members bring meat, oil, wine, cake and fruit for banquets. The cult association of Zeus in Philadelphia (Lydia) mentions monthly and annual sacrifices but provides no indication as to how they are funded. See *LSAM*, no. 20 = *SIG*³ 985 (see on this, Barton and Horsley, 'A Hellenistic Cult Group').

were not normally redistributed to members (except in the case of certain Roman *collegia*[87]); instead, they were used for the support of the cult.[88] Hence, the question of the Corinthians, which concerned a charitable collection for some *other* group and, evidently, the mechanics of its administration and delivery, was of a quite different order from the usual collections administered by associations. The unusual character of the collection for the poor of Jerusalem would be warrant enough for an inquiry; it does not necessarily imply that the Corinthians were unfamiliar with donations to a common chest.

5. *Churches as* Collegia

If the ἐκκλησίαι of Paul can be fitted into the spectrum of formal designations, organization and membership profiles of Greek and Roman voluntary associations, we might ask whether the benefits conferred by membership were comparable. This, obviously, is not a topic that can be treated adequately in such a short space, but a few comments are in order.

It is clear that Pauline churches, like *collegia*, provided a structure of belonging[89] as well as various rituals, including a common meal. Perhaps the most striking innovation concerns the density of fictive family language. Bömer observed that in Greek associations, the use of such language (especially ἀδελφός as a designation of members) is quite rare. The Roman *fratres Arvales* were 'brothers' but membership in this elite priestly collegium naturally was not open to non-elite persons. Brotherhood appears occasionally in some inscriptions belonging to Mithraic groups and those of Juppiter Dolichenus, Dionysius Liber, and Bellona, and very occasionally, in professional and domestic clubs, but in almost all cases, Roman influence is clear.[90]

---

87. In some Roman collegia there were periodic distributions (*sportulae*) to members of a few denarii (1-6 dn., depending upon rank). See, e.g., *CIL* VI 10234: *Lex collegi Aesculapi et Hygiae*, 153 CE = Waltzing, *Etude historique,* III, pp. 268-71 (no. 1083). See Waltzing, *Etude historique,* IV, pp. 631-63, 666-72 for a discussion of *sportulae.*

88. See the study of Debord, *Aspects sociaux et économiques,* pp. 183-243; Poland, *Geschichte,* pp. 453-98.

89. See the helpful discussion of the language of belonging, separation and boundaries by Meeks, *First Urban Christians,* pp. 84-110.

90. Bömer, *Untersuchungen über die Religion der Sklaven,* I, pp. 172-78. See also above, n. 17.

In view of this, the density of ἀδελφ-language in Pauline churches—twenty times in 1 Thessalonians alone—is striking. Paul's suggestion to Philemon that a slave should be considered as an ἀδελφὸς ἀγαπητός is all the more striking in view of Bömer's observation that the extension of fraternal language to slaves is almost completely unattested, even in Roman associations.[91] It is here that one might locate the appeal of Pauline churches: the fictive dissolution of the obstinately vertical character of Graeco-Roman social life through the creation of a 'family' that transcended such boundaries.[92]

Associations did not merely supply a sense of belonging, however. As Foucart observed, associations imitated the structure of the *polis*[93] and what this meant to the nonelite who belonged was that they were able to participate in a kind of *cursus honorum* to which, outside the collegium, they would have no access. Since we know so little of the hierarchy of Pauline churches, it is impossible to determine how honours were or were not conferred. But it is clear that all could have the expectation of participation of the glorious ἀπάντησις τοῦ κυρίου (1 Thess. 4.17). It is also worth noting that especially in Philippians, Paul invokes language of citizenship (πολίτευμα 3.20) and refers to civic obligation and rewards—λειτουργία—when describing the Philippians' generosity to Paul (Phil. 2.17, 27, 30). Later he refers to them as στέφανός μου (4.1) a term particularly common in the honorific language of civic cults. Thus, even if individual members were not voted honours, the language of the Pauline churches is replete with allusions to the structures of honour and, in a markedly intensified way, to the structures of belonging.

Once the apologetic obstacles to comparison are overcome, the question asked by Hatch, whether setting associations and churches side by side might help us understand the internal dynamics and the remarkable successes of Pauline churches, may point to new and productive approaches for understanding the organization of early Christian churches.

91. Bömer, *Untersuchungen über die Religion der Sklaven,* I, p. 178: a slave is intended only in *CIL* VI 10681 and VI 37885.
92. See further, J.S. Kloppenborg, 'Φιλαδελφία, Θεοδίδακτος and the *Dioscuri*: Rhetorical Engagement in 1 Thess 4.9-12', *NTS* 39 (1993), pp. 265-89.
93. Foucart, *Des associations religieuses,* pp. 50-53.

THE AGRIPPINILLA INSCRIPTION:
RELIGIOUS ASSOCIATIONS AND EARLY CHURCH FORMATION

Bradley H. McLean

Introduction

In late Western antiquity voluntary religious associations provided a principal setting for social interaction.[1] The following inscription belongs to one such association, dedicated to Dionysos. Its organizational model, internal structures, membership and recruitment offer an instructive point of comparison with early Christian churches.

1. *Description of the Inscription*

The inscription was discovered two kilometers from Torre Nova in the Roman Campagna[2] dating to c. 150 CE. It is located on the marble base of a sculpture dedicated to Pompeia Agrippinilla, a priestess of this Dionysiac association. The statue no longer survives. Agrippinilla was the wife of M. Gavius Squilla Gallicanus, a one-time senator, consul and later proconsul of Asia Minor. This eminent senatorial family was descended from Theophanes of Mytilene, friend and historian of Pompei. The family had originally resided in Mytilene on the island of Lesbos, but subsequently moved to the Roman Campagna, bringing the Dionysiac association with it.

---

1. A.D. Nock, 'The Historical Importance of Cult-Associations', *CR* 38 (1924), pp. 105-108; M.N. Tod, 'Clubs and Societies in the Greek World', in *Sidelights in Greek History* (Oxford: Basil Blackwell, 1932), pp. 71-96; W.A. Meeks, *The First Urban Christians: The Social World of the Apostle Paul* (New Haven: Yale University Press, 1983), pp. 77-80; J.S. Kloppenborg, 'Phenomenology of Graeco-Roman Private Associations' (paper delivered to the Annual Meeting of the Canadian Society of Biblical Literature, 1990), pp. 1-17.
2. A large plain in central Italy surrounding Rome, lying between the Mediterranean Sea and the Sabine and Alban mountains.

The Agrippinilla Inscription

['Αγρ]ιππειπεινίλλαν τὴν ἱέρειαν μύσται
οἱ ὑπογεγραμμένοι[1]

I

[Μαχ]ρεῖνος[2] ἥρος[3]
[Κεθ]ηγίλλα[4] δᾳδοῦχος[5]
Ἱερεῖς[6]
[Γ]αλλικανός[7]
5 Γαλλικανός
Μαχρεῖ]νος[8]
Ὄρφιτος
Τέρτυλλος
Ὄρφιτος
10 Κέλσος

Ἱέρειαι[9]
Μαλιόλα
Μαλιόλα

Ἱεροφάντης[10]

II

Φλῶρος

Κόνων
Ἀρχιβάσσαροι[17]
Χαιρήμων
Ἴβανος

Ἀμφιθαλεῖς[18]
Λάτριος
Μένανδρος

Λικν<>αφόροι[19]
Καλλίστη
Εὐτυχίς
Νίκη

Φαλλοφόρος[20]
Καμιλλ<ι>ανή[21]

Πορφύροι[22]
Τρόφιμος
Νικηφορίων

III

ἀπὸ καταζ]ώσεως[29]
Βάκχις
Ἑλένη
Χάρις
Ὀλυμπιάς
Ἱλάρα
Σοφίας[30]
Εὐχάριστος
Χρυσόπαις
Σεούηρος
Ἰσίων
Εὔοπτος
Ἀπολλόδωρος
Κομική
Εὐήμια
Ἑλένη
Ἀφροδισία
Ἰουλία Εὐτυχία
Ζωσίμη
Ἀμάνδα
ΕΥΗΛΟΥΣ[31]
Νικοτέλεια
Θυϊάς
Μαρκία
Ζωσίμη
Ἄνθουσα
Ὀλυμπιάς
Ἑρμπτίων

IV

Φίλιππος
Εὐτυχής
Ἐπαίνετος
Ἀβάσκαντος
Ἡδονή
Ἐπαφρόδιτος
Εὔοδος
Ἀμέθυστος
Ἄθυρμα
Ἡρακλέων
Ἀπόλα(ο)υστος
Κρήσκ(ην)ης
Ἰόῦστα
Νέπος
Ἀρτεμισία
Κένταυρος
Πίττυς
Ἰσίδωρος
Ἱλαρίων
Μύρων
Συμφέρουσα

Ζωτικός
Ποτεντεῖνα
Σουκέσσα
Ἐπαφρόδιτος

V

Βάκχοι ἀπὸ
Καταζώσεως[33]
Πρειμιτεῖβος
Νίκων
Σατυρίσκος
Ἕλπιστος[34]
Ἐπάγαθος
Μηνᾶς
Σοζομενός[35]
Εὐτύχης
Νικηφόρος
Ὕλλος
Ἀβάσκαντος
Ἀκίνδυνος
Βάθυλλος
Φῆλιξ
Αὔξιμος

Βάσ<σ>χαι ἀπὸ
Καταζώσεως[36]
Ἐλπίς[37]
Σειρήν
ΛΟΙΔΗ[38]

VI

Φορτουνᾶτος
Κάρπος
Ὀνήσιμος
Γαληνός
Ὀνήσιμος
Εὐτυχής
Ἐπάνοδος
Ἀφροδίσιος
Σύμφωνος
Στεφανίων
ΠΑΜΦΙΛΑΣ[41]
Γεμέλλιον
Πάγκαρπος
Νικίας
Κόρος
Εὐκαρπᾶς
Φίλητος
Μάρκος
Φίλητος
Εὐτυχος
Ἐπαφρόδιτος
Ἑρμογένης
Ἀλέξανδρος
Ἀγαθήμερος
Ἐπάφρυλλος
Ἄγνος

The Agrippinilla Inscription (continued)

	I	II	III	IV	V	VI
	Ἀγαθόπους	Ἱερομνήμων[23]	Θρέπτη	Νάρκισσος		Ἀγαθήμερος
30	Θεοφόροι[11]	Ἄτιμητος	Χέλειδών	Ἀγγελικός		Εὐάγγελος
	Γαλλικανός	Ἀρχινεανίσκοι[24]	Ἶρις	Σύμφρουνος[32]		Εὐτύχης
	Διονύσιος	Ἐπίκτητος	Φερρά	Τροφίμη		Σκίνδιον[42]
	Ὑπουργὸς[12] καὶ		Σείμπρος	Ἑρμῆς		Ζωσιμᾶς
	Σειληνοκόσμος[13]	Ἀρχιβάσσαραι[25]	Κάρπος	Κωντιλιανός		Νίκυλος
35	Σερῆνος	Ποθούσα	Ἀσπασία	Κλήμης		Νίκων
	Κισταφόροι[14]	Συμφέρουσα	Φιλόκαλος	Βασσίλλα		Εὐχάριστος
	Φιλλῆτι	Βάκχις	Δημοσθένης	<Ε>ἰρηναῖος	Ἱεροὶ Βάκχοι[39]	Ἑρμίας
	Σαβεῖνα	Βάσσαρις	Ζηνόδοτος	Ἀντιοχίς	Ἀντίοχος	Ἑρμῆς
	Ἐφεσία		Ἑταῖρος	Παλλίων	Πίνδαρος	Κορνλιανός
40			Τρωΐλος	Εὐκαρπία	Ἀστερίων	Πρεμιτεῖβος
	Ἀρχιβούκολοι[15]	Βουκόλοι[26]	Προύδης	Πάνθεια	ΠΕΛΟΠΙΟΗΣ[40]	Ζώσιμος
	Σαβεινιανός	ΝΙΚΟΛΔΩΝ[27]	Κύκνος	Ὑγεία		Ἄνθιον
	Ἀγαθοκλῆς	Ἀβασκαντίων	Ἀφροδίσια		Νεκτάρεος	Ζώσιμος
45	Αὐξάνων	Σέμνος	Νήρεους		Θηβανός	Φίλητος
		Εὐτύχης	Ἄπερ		Διογένης	Πρόσδεχτος
	Βουκόλοι Ἱεροί[16]	Ὑπερήφανος	Εὔνους		Φιλόκαλος	Ἀγαθήμερος
50	Χρυσόγονος	ΛΟΥΞΕΝΝΟΣ[28]	Σελήνη		Διονυσόδωρος	Ἐπίκτειτος[43]
	Μελαγκόμας	Τυχικός	Βέλλα		Πίθανος	Σωτήρ
	Καῖνος	Καλλικλῆς	Στέφανος			
	Κόρινθος	Πρεισκιανός	Ῥουφεῖνα			
	Πάμμουσος	Εἰρηναῖος	Χαρτῖνος			
55	Θεόδοτος	Κάλλιστος	- - - -Α			
	Κοτονικιανός					

	VII	VIII	IX	X
	Ἔκλογος	----	[Σ]τεφανᾶς48	Κρητική
	Οὐενοῦστος	---Σ	Ἔμιτινος	Ἐπίκτησις
	Τυχικός	---Σ	Σαρδόνυξ	Σεκουνδεῖνα
	Εὐτυχίδης	---Σ		Σπένδουσα
5	Οὔικτωρ	---Ξ	Προσόδικος	Ἑλπίς51
	Νίκων	---ΟΣ	Εὔγραμμος	Τρύαλλις
	Ἴκμενος	[--]ΝΟΣ	Βάσσος	Εὐοδία
	Ἐπίκτητος	---ΟΣ	Φιλώτας	Ἀπρύλλα
	Προτογένης	---Σ	Ὀνησίφορος	Στρατηγία
10	Ἡραιατᾶς		Εὔρετος	Οὐαλερία Ἀριστεῖνα
	Ἀλβανός		Αὐξάνων	Μυγδονίς
	Σπόρος		Ἀφέλους υἱός	Νεμεσίλλα
	Μύρων		Ἔλενος	Φηλικίτας
	Ἀταέρτωρ		Ζώσιμος	Λύκα
15	Εὐτυχίδης		[Δ]ιωνᾶτος	Σέμνη
	Ῥῆνος		---	---
	Μύρσος		---	---Σ
	Οὐενιοῦστος		---	---Α
	Θάλλος		---	---Α
20	Εὐχάρης		---	[Ρ]ομουλα
	Γενέσιος		---Σ	Πρειμιγένεια
	Ἀχιλλεύς		---Σ	Αὔξησις
	Κράτερος		---Σ	Ἀπρύλλα
	Φῆλιξ		--ΝΙΑΝΟΣ	Ἀντιάνειρα
25	Τάναγρος		---ΛΑΣ	Σμύρνα
	Φορτουνᾶτος	---Ν		ΔΛΗ52
	Ἴκαρος	---Σ		Σουκέσσα
	ΒΟΥΔΙΟΝ44	---Σ		Ἐλευθέριν53
	Φιλήμων	-ΦΥΡΟΣ		Ἑρμιόνη
30	Πίθανος	[Πρ]ό[σ]φορος		ΕΤΙΙ
	Διονύσιος	[Βα]σιλείδης		Πρείμα
	Εὔκαρπος	['Ο]λυμπιάδης		

	VII	VIII	IX	X
	Δεκίβαλος	Ἀβάσκαντος		
35	Μασκελλίων	Τρόφιμος		
	Ἀράτωρ	Κοσμίων		
	Ἡλιόδωρος	Φορτουνᾶτος		
	Εὐτύχης	Ῥεστιτοῦτος		Σειγητα[54]
	Ἄτταλος	Ἔπαφρᾶς		Φίλητος
40	Σπόρος	Δημήτριος	Ἀντροφύλαχες[49]	Ἀπ[ο]λλώνιος
	Λουκανός	Πραξιδάμας	Παρθένιος	Κίννωτος
	Σάλερνος[45]	Καρπωφόρος	Πελοπίδης	Φηλικίων
	Ἰουβιλάτωρ[46]	Ὀνήσιμος		Λειβερανός
	Σεκοῦνδος	Ἔρος[47]		Γλύκερος
45	Γάμος[47]	Ἔρος		Πτέρων
	Φορτουνᾶτος	[Ν]ηΐδυμος		Κακιλία
		Εὐκτήμων		Δύναμις
		Μεγιστίων		Φιλήτη
		Ἔρμιππος		Ἐπίκτητος
50		Φορτουνᾶτος	Βάσχαι[50]	Δα<ι>δούχις
		Ἀχιλλᾶς	Τύχη	Ῥοῦφα
		Ἄριστων	Ἑρώτιον	Μουσική
			Σεουῆρα	Φοῖβος
			Λύκα	Βειθυνικός
55			Παῦλα	Νίκων
			Ναΐς	Ἱλαρίων
			Εὐτυχία	Βετταλίων
			Ἀντωνῖνα	Θάλλος
			Πρεῖμα	Πομπεϊανος
60			Εὐτυχίς	Ἀσπασία
			Εὐκαρπία	Κόσμος
			Βλάστη	
			Μοντίκλα	
			Νικαριώ	

1. 'The mystaí whose names are written below (erected this statue) of the priestess Agrippinilla.'

2. According to known genealogies, he may be Agrippinilla's brother, but more probably her nephew.

3. Nilsson suggests that the term ἥρως indicates that Macrinus had paid his contribution but died before the monument was erected (Nilsson, *Opuscula selecta*, II, pp. 524-41, esp. p. 525; Nilsson, *Dionysiac Mysteries*, pp. 51-52 n. 38). Franz Cumont, among others, disagrees and is persuaded that Macrinus is not dead but a high functionary or perhaps the head of the association ('La grande inscription', pp. 237-38). He observes that in this inscription men take precedence over women; therefore a man, not the female *dadouchos*, must be at the head of the list. The title *hero* is being used in the archaic sense of 'leader', probably a useage which had survived on Lesbos. It should be noted that Dionysus was known as the bull-god and his worshippers known as βουκόλοι, 'cowherds' (2.41; cf. 1.42, 49). In rustic speech, the chief bull of a herd was a *heros*. The *heros* in this association probably took the role of the bull-god, Dionysos. In some inscriptions the true Dionysus is distinguished from the 'Heros Dionysus' by referring to the former as 'Theos Dionysos' (cf. Quandt, pp. 153, 161; K. Kerényi, *Dionysos: Archetypal Image of Indestructible Life* [Bollingen Series, 65.2; Princeton: Princeton University Press, 1976], p. 354).

4. Daughter of Agrippinilla.

5. 'Torchbearer', second rank in the hierarchy. A torch was used to light the nocturnal feasts of Dionysus and took on the significance of purification.

6. 'Priests' appointed from the immediate family.

7. Gavius Squilla Gallicanus, consul in 150 CE and husband of Pompeia Agrippinilla.

8. Probably brother of Agrippinilla (cf. n. 2).

9. 'Priestesses' from noble family of Manlii.

10. 'Hierophant' probably proclaimed the events of the mysteries after the manner of the hierophant in Eleusis (Kerényi, *Dionysos*, p. 353).

11. 'God-bearers' would carry a statue of Dionysus on their shoulders in procession.

12. An assistant to the priests at sacrifices.

13. Probably a 'constable' who would oversee the conduct of the *mystaí*, preserve order, and perhaps punish offenders; he may have worn the ancient silenus costume.

14. Carried the mystic chest (*cista mystica*) containing sacred utensils; carried in procession (cf. *CIG* 2052 (Apollonia in Thrace)).

15. 'Chief cowherd' (cf. n. 3).

16. 'Holy cowherds', an intermediate degree between the 'chief cowherds' and 'cowherds' (cf. 1.42, 2.41; cf. n. 3).

17. The term βάσσαραι (which does not appear in the inscription) refers to 'female bacchantes', hence ἀρχιβάσσαραι (cf. 2.34) refers to the 'chief female bacchant'. In this inscription the term βάκχαι (9.49; cf. 5.24) is used instead of βάσσαραι. The unusual term ἀρχιβάσσαροι (2.5) seems to have been formed by analogy with ἀρχιβάσσαραι (2.34). Likewise, this 'chief bassaros' would oversee the two levels of βάκχοι (cf. 5.1-2, 37).

18. 'Amphiitaies': prepubescent acolytes involved in the Dionysiac mysteries, perhaps by reading a sacred text (cf. Villa Item) or carrying a thyrsus (cf. Villa Farnesina).

19. *Sic*. Λικναφόροι (cf. *CIG* 2.2052; D. 18.260; Cal. Cer. 127). The liknon is a winnowing basket in which corn was placed after threshing and thrown against the wind so as to winnow the grain from the chaff. In the archaic Dionysiac cult it had no mystic connotations (W. Burkert, *Ancient Mystery Cults* [Cambridge, MA: Harvard University Press, 1987], p. 96). In the renewed cult it became a sacred symbol of purification for both the Dionysiac and Eleusinian mysteries, driving away pollution like the chaff from the grain (see p. 264 n. 54). Likna were carried in procession by 'likna-bearers' (Servius on Virgil, *Georgica* 1.166).

20. A 'phallus-bearer' would carry a sculpted phallus—the inseparable emblem of Dionysiac worship—in procession (cf. M. Nilsson, *Geschichte der griechischen Religion* [2 vols.; Munich: Beck, 3rd edn, 1967], I, pp. 590-94, p. 35). In some processions it was of such colossal size that it was carried in a cart. Here it is small enough to be carried by a single woman (see p. 264 n. 54).

21. Vogliano, 'Grande Iscrizione', p. 229.

22. 'Fire-bearers' would bring the fire which was necessary for any sacrifice or

ritual ceremony. Though a torch could be used for this purpose, the 'fire-bearer' must not be confused with the *dadouchos*.

23. Secretary (?) or steward who had charge of the material property of the cult.

24. Those responsible for instructing the νεανίσκοι (adolescent members) and leading them in procession (cf. Latin transcription of this term in *CIL* 6.2180).

25. Cf. n. 17.

26. 'Cowherds' (cf. n. 3): probably a troop of dancers (H. Jeanmaire, *Dionysos: Histoire du culte de Bacchus* [Paris: Payot, 1951], p. 471). In Pergamum the 'cowherds' were Dyonisiac dancers led by a χορηγός (*IGR* IV, 386). These dancers were probably appropriately attired to act out the roles of various gods and wore masks for the purpose (Burkert, *Mystery Cults*, p. 189; Kerényi, *Dionysos*, p. 351; cf. Iobacchi of Athens [section 5]).

27. *Sic.* Νικολέων (Vogliano, 'Grande Iscrizione', p. 229).

28. Luscienus?

29. Undoubtedly the οἱ μύσται and αἱ μύσται (Cumont, 'La grande inscription', pp. 234). Masculine and feminine names are mixed in this category. The title signifies the idea of 'clothing oneself'. In this context, it probably refers to being clothed with the nebris (fawn skin), an act which would accompany initiation.

30. (Masc.) or Σοφιάς (fem.).

31. *Sic.* Εὔκλους.

32. *Sic.* Σύμφρονος cf. 6.11.

33. Cf. n. 3.

34. Ἔνπιστος?

35. *Sic.* Σωζομενός.

36. Cf. nn. 3, 17.

37. Fem.

38. *Sic.* Ἀλοιδῆ (Vogliano, 'Grande Iscrizione', p. 227).

39. Cf. n. 3.

40. *Sic.* Πελοπίδης (cf. 9.40).

41. Πεμφιλᾶς (Vogliano, 'Grande Iscrizione', p. 229).

42. Masc.

43. *Sic.* Ἐπίκητος (cf. 2.32; 7.8; 10.48).

44. *Sic.* Βοίδιον (Vogliano, 'Grande Iscrizione', p. 227).

45. Salerunus?

46. Ἰουβλλάτορ.

47. Masc.

48. Vogliano, 'Grande Iscrizione', p. 230.

49. 'Guardians of the sacred cave': Dionysus was said to have been born in a cave and caverns were sometimes dedicated to him. An artificial cave may have been constructed and carried in the procession.

50. Cf. nn. 17. 3. The Βάκχαι were the maenads who, in the ancient form of the mysteries, were involved in ecstatic activity.

51. Fem.

52. *Sic.* Ἅλη or Δούλη? (Vogliano, 'Grande Iscrizione', pp. 227, 228).

53. *Sic.* Ἐλευθέρις?

54. 'Those who keep silent', i.e., novices who were required to keep silent for a period of time in order to prove themselves capable of keeping the secrets. This list includes masculine and feminine names.

The inscription records the names of members (μύσται) who both belonged to this Dionysiac θίασος and contributed towards the cost of erecting the statue. Since this total number of names does not represent a complete census of the membership—but only those who made a financial contribution—the total membership must have been greater. More than half of the membership of men and women—222 names in all—is designated simply as 'holy bacchants' (ἱεροὶ βάκχοι, 5.37) and 'baccantes' (βάκχαι, 9.49) respectively. This is the category for the general male and female membership respectively, designating those who had completed the initiation process and become members in good standing, but had not been appointed to any of the more specialized ministries.

The remaining names are organized in a series of lists according to the function which each performed in the association. Many of the individual lists are followed by a blank space in order to allow for the addition of more names as new donations were made.[3] In all, the inscription lists 402 names (including lacunae). The list is not organized according to a rigid hierarchy such as the *cursus honorus* of the Roman magistrates, though it is clear that the most eminent members appear at the beginning of the list and the most lowly—the novices (σειγηταί, 10.33)—at the end. The order of functionaries is determined by their corresponding order in the sacred procession—an essential feature of Dionysiac religion. Thus, following the most honoured functionaries (*heros*, *dadouchos*, priests, priestesses and *hierophant*) are those who were charged with carrying a variety of objects in the procession: two men carry a statue of Dionysos (θεοφόροι, 1.30), followed shortly thereafter by three women carrying the mystic chest (κισταφόροι, 1.36), then further on, three more women carrying the sacred winnowing baskets (λικναφόροι, 2.14), followed by another woman carrying a sculpted phallos (φαλλοφόρος, 2.21), and later on still, two male fire-bearers (πυρφόροι, 2.25). A variety of supervisors are interspersed between these sacred bearers.

---

3. This is confirmed by the title ἀρχινεανίσκοι (2.31) which appears in the plural, but is followed by only one name and then a black space.

2. *The Text*

The inscription is now part of the collection of the Metropolitan Museum in New York. It is written in ten parallel columns arranged on three sides of a marble statue base (0.83 m high, by 0.56 m wide, by 0.44 m in thickness). Achille Vogliana has published a facsimile drawing of the inscription but he did not produce an edited text.[4] Vogliana does not number the lines of his facsimile consecutively as is customary, though the individual names are enumerated under each heading.[5] Thus, the text above is the first critical edition of the Agrippinilla inscription.[6]

3. *Organizational Model: The Familia*

That the structure of this Dionysiac association is based upon the Roman *familia* [7] can be inferred from the observation that the

4. A. Vogliana, 'La Grande Iscrizione Bacchica del Metropolitan (Mitilene) Museum', *AJA* 37 (1933), pp. 215-31, facs. pls. 27-29; also: F. Cumont, 'La grande inscription bachique du Metropolitan Museum', *AJA* 37 (1933), pp. 232-63, esp. pp. 237-38; M.P. Nilsson, 'En marge de la grande inscription bacchique de Metropolitan Museum', in *Opuscula selecta linguis Anglica, Francogallica, Germanica conscripta* (3 vols.; Svenska institutet i Athen, Skrifter, Acta, Series altera, 2; Lund: Gleerup, 1951–60), II, pp. 524-41; cf. M.P. Nilsson, *The Dionysiac Mysteries of the Hellenistic and Roman Age* (Lund: Gleerup, 1957), pp. 51-52 n. 38; cf. M.P. Nilsson, 'New Evidence for the Dionysiac Mysteries', *Eranos* 53 (1955), pp. 28-40; M.P. Nilsson, 'Dionysos Liknites', *Bulletin de la Société des Lettres* (Lund: Gleerup, 1950), No. 1; M.P. Nilsson 'The Bacchic Mysteries in the Roman Age', *HTR* 46/4 (1953), pp. 177-202; partially translated by F.C. Grant, *Ancient Roman Religion* (New York: Liberal Arts Press, 1957), pp. 56-58.

5. It is this enumeration system which he employed in his prosographical index (Vogliana, 'La Grande Iscrizione', pp. 237-331).

6. The task of numbering the lines was complicated by the fact that the size of the characters and the distance between lines varies throughout the inscription. In order to preserve the relative positioning of words between successive columns it was necessary to introduce occasional single spaces. However, the majority of the spaces in the printed text occur in the inscription itself in order to allow for the addition of further names.

7. The *familia* was made up of all persons under the authority of the head of the house (*pater familias*) including his wife, unmarried daughters and his sons (whether married or not) and his sons' families. In its widest sense it includes slaves, personal property and all real estate.

principal functionaries are all members of the senatorial family of
M(arcus) Gavius Squilla Gallicanus. Achille Vogliano has deduced the
following genealogy of this family based on inscriptional evidence.[8]

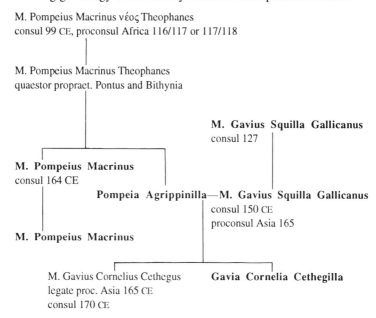

M. Pompeius Macrinus νέος Theophanes
consul 99 CE, proconsul Africa 116/117 or 117/118

M. Pompeius Macrinus Theophanes
quaestor propraet. Pontus and Bithynia

M. Gavius Squilla Gallicanus
consul 127

M. Pompeius Macrinus
consul 164 CE

Pompeia Agrippinilla—**M. Gavius Squilla Gallicanus**
consul 150 CE
proconsul Asia 165

M. Pompeius Macrinus

M. Gavius Cornelius Cethegus   **Gavia Cornelia Cethegilla**
legate proc. Asia 165 CE
consul 170 CE

The names in bold type appear in the inscription. It is immediately
apparent that the highest positions in the association were reserved for
the immediate families of M(arcus) Gavius Squilla Gallicanus and his
wife, Pompeia Agrippinilla, the priestess honoured by the statue.
Gallicanus himself and his father (?) served as priests (1.4, 5). Either
Agrippinilla's brother or nephew—both named Macrinus—was
appointed to the highest position of *heros* (1.1), while the second
Macrinus was appointed priest (1.6). Agrippinilla's daughter, Cornelia
Cethegilla (1.2), was appointed *dadouchos*, second in authority only to
the *heros*. The remaining 389 names probably consist of the balance
of the *familia*, domestic slaves and freedmen, in addition to friends,
business associates, tradesmen and newly arrived immigrants from
Asia Minor (see below).

8.   Vogliano, 'Grande Iscrizione', esp. pp. 215-26, 220-22; also: E. Groag and
A. Stein (eds.), *Prosopographia Imperii Romani Saec. I. II. III* (Berolini et Lipsiae:
de Gruyter, 1933), pp. 24-25, no. 15, p. 21, no. 98.

Private *collegia* and *thiasoi* were customarily dependent upon aristocratic individuals or families who established and financed them. Consider, for example, the founding of a *collegium* to Asclepius and Hygia, and the provision of a 50,000 sesterces endowment by a wealthy Roman woman, Marcellina, in memory of her father who had been procurator (*CIL* VI, 10234). Against this background, it seems likely that Agrippinilla, herself a wealthy aristocrat, must also have provided substantial financial aid to this Dionysiac association. The erection of a statue in her honour by the association served not only to publicly honour Agrippinilla, but equally, to encourage her patronage in the future.[9]

4. *Prosopography*

Eighty percent (323 of 402 names) of the cognomina listed in the inscription are of Greek origin.[10] Given the fact that this inscription was found in the environs of Rome, it is remarkable that only 79 of the 402 names are of Latin origin.[11] T. Frank has studied Latin and

9. M.P. Bonz, 'Differing Approaches to Religious Benefaction: The Late Third-Century Acquisition of the Sardis Synagogue' (paper delivered to the Archaeology of the NT World Group of the SBL Annual Meeting, San Francisco, 1992), pp. 1-19, esp. p. 9.

10. Iiro Kajanto persuasively argues that 'one can in most cases easily tell which cognomen are of Latin, which of non-Latin origin' ('The Significance of Non-Latin Cognomina', *Latomus* 27 [1968], pp. 517-34, esp. p. 518).

11. The Roman names as follows: Agrippinilla (dedication); Albanus (7.11); Amanda (3.20); Antonina (9.58); Aper (3.45); Aprilla (or Aprulla) (10.8); Adsertor (7.14); Bassilla (4.36); Bassus (9.7); Vitalio (10.56); Bella (3.48); Gallicanus (1.4); Gallicanus (1.5); Gallicanus (1.31); Gemellio (6.14); Decibalus (7.33); Donatus (9.15); Jubilator (7.42); Justa (4.15); Caecilia (10.45); Cethegilla (1.2); Celsus (1.10); Clemens (4.35); Coetonicus (1.56); Cornelianus (6.38); Crescens (4.13); Felicitas (10.13); Felicio (10.41); Felix (5.16); Felix (7.24); Florus (2.1); Fortunatus (6.1); Fortunatus (7.26); Fortunatus (7.45); Fortunatus (8.36); Fortunatus (8.49); Liberianus (10.42); LOUQENNOS (Luscienus?) (2.47); Lucanus (7.40); Macrinus (1.1); Macrinus (1.6); Ma(n)liola (1.24); Ma(n)liola (1.25); Marcia (3.24); Marcus (6.20); Mascellio (7.34); Monticola (9.63); Orfitus (1.7); Orfitus (1.9); Pompeianus (10.58); Potentina (4.26); Prima (9.59); Prima (10.33); Primigenia (10.22); Primitivus (5.3); Prisciannus (2.50); Prudens (3.41); Pollio (4.39); Quintilianus (4.34); Restitutus (8.37); Rufa (10.50); Rufina (3.50); Romula (10.21); Sabina (1.38); Sabiniannus (1.43); Salernus (7.41); Secundina (10.3); Secundus (7.43); Severa (9.52); Severus (3.10); Serenus (1.35); Successa (4.27); Successa (10.28);

non-Latin (that is Greek and barbaric) cognomina in order to determine the racial composition of Rome's population during the Empire.
He has concluded that the 'bearers of Greek names are in general
from the East or descendants of Eastern slaves'.[12] Scholars, building
on Frank's work, have attempted to determine the respectability of
Greek cognomina in Roman society by studying the frequency of the
transmission of parent's Greek cognomina to their children.[13] Their
findings agree that parents with Greek cognomina usually gave their
children Latin—not Greek—cognomina. For example, according to
Frank's sample, the frequency of Greek cognomina diminishes from
64 percent to 38 percent in one generation.[14] This suggests that Greek
cognomina generally had less respectability in Roman society than did
Latin ones.

   More recently, Iiro Kajanto has surveyed nine Italian towns to
determine the extent to which social and ethnic origin determined the
ratio of Latin to non-Latin cognomina. He broke down his findings
into *ingenui* (freemen), *incerti* and *liberti* (freedmen). His findings are
most instructive: 'The cognomina of the *ingenui* were everywhere
preponderantly Latin. The average is 80.8 percent'.[15] It is significant
that the percentage of Latin cognomina was lowest in Rome. However,
even in Rome, as many as 73.3 percent of the *ingenui* bore Latin
cognomina.[16] Kajanto attributes the higher incidence of non-Latin
cognomina in Rome to the higher incidence of slavery in Rome and
the higher rate of recruitment of foreign slaves, while he attributes
non-Latin cognomina among the *ingenui* to their descent from former
slaves or *peregrini* (immigrants).[17]

   Kajanto's figure of 73.3 percent Roman names among *ingenui* in

Tertullus (1.8); Valeria (10.10); Venustus (7.18); Victor (7.5).
   12. T. Frank, 'Race Mixture in the Roman Empire', *AHR* 21 (1916), p. 51;
reprinted as 'Decline and Fall of the Roman Empire', in D. Kagan (ed.), *Problems of
European Civilization* (Boston: 1965).
   13. A.M. Duff, *Freedmen in the Early Roman Empire* (Cambridge: W. Heffer &
Sons, 2nd edn, 1958), pp. 55-58; H. Thylander, *Etude sur l'épigraphie latine* (Lund:
Gleerup, 1952), pp. 159, 163; L.R. Taylor, 'Freedmen and Freeborn in the Epitaphs
of Imperial Rome', *AJP* 82 (1961), p. 127.
   14. Frank, 'Race Mixture', p. 46.
   15. Kajanto, 'Significance', p. 524.
   16. *Ingenui* (73.3 percent Latin, 26.7 percent non-Latin); *incerti* (41.6 percent
Latin, 58.4 percent non-Latin); *liberti* (28.3 percent Latin, 71.7 percent non-Latin).
   17. Kajanto, 'Significance', pp. 522-27.

Rome is significantly higher than the 19.6 percent of Latin cognomina found on the Agrippinilla inscription from the same general area. This evidence strongly suggests that many of the Greek names on the inscription are either Greek slaves or freedmen. This hypothesis is supported by other data: a comparison of 323 Greek names of the Agrippinilla inscription with an inventory of 3248 attested Greek slave names yields 141 correspondences, equalling approximately one quarter of the total inscription.[18] This should not be interpreted to

18. From fifth century BCE to third century CE, compiled by L.C. Reilly (*Slaves in Ancient Greece: Slaves from Greek Manumission Inscriptions* (Chicago: Ares, 1978). The following is organized according to title: ἱεροφάντης: Ἀγαθόπους (1.29); θεοφόροι: Διονύσιος (1.32); κισταφόροι: Φιλήτη (1.36); βουκόλοι ἱεροί: Θεόδοτος (1.55), Κόνων (2.4); ἀρχιβάσσαροι/αι: Χαιρήμων (2.6), Ποθούσα (2.35), Συμφέρουσα (2.36), Βάκχις (2.38); ἀμφιθαλεῖς: Μένανδρος (2.12); λικναφόροι: Καλλίστη (2.15[-α]), Εὐτυχίς (2.17), Νίκη (2.17); πυρφόροι: Τρόφιμος (2.26); ἀρχινεανίσκοι: Ἐπίκτητος (2.32); βουκόλοι: Σέμνος (2.44 [-η]), Εὐτύχης (2.45), Τυχικός (2.48 [-η]), Καλλικλῆς (2.49), Εἰρηναῖος (2.51); ἀπὸ καταζώσεως: Βάκχις (3.2), Ἑλένη (3.3), Χάρις (3.4), Ὀλυμπιάς (3.5), Ἱλάρα (3.6), Σοφίας/Σοφιάς (3.7; [-ία]), Ἰσίων (3.11), Ἀπολλόδωρος (3.13), Κωμική (3.14 [-ος]), Εὐφημία (3.15), Ἑλένη (3.16), Ἀφροδισία (3.17), Εὐτυχία (3.18), Ζωσίμη (3.19), Ὀλυμπιάς (3.27), Κάρπος (3.34), Ζηνόδοτος (3.38 [-η]), Ἀφροδισία (3.43), Νήρεους (3.44), Εὔνους (3.46), Στέφανος (3.49), Φίλιππος (4.2), Εὐτυχᾶς (4.3), Ἐπαίνετος (4.4), Ἡδονή (4.6), Ἐπαφρόδιτος (4.7), Εὔοδος (4.8), Ἡρακλέων (4.11), Ἰσίδωρος (4.20), Συμφέρουσα (4.23), Ἐπαφρόδιτος (4.28); Ἑρμῆς (4.33), Εἰρηναῖος (4.37), Ἀντιοχίς (4.38), Εὐκαρπία (4.40), βάκχοι ἀπὸ καταζώσεως·: Σατυρίσκος (5.5), Ἐπάγαθος (5.7), Μηνᾶς (5.8), Εὐτύχης (5.10), Νικηφόρος (5.11), Ἀβάσκαντος (5.13), Νίκων (5.14), Ἐλπίς (5.26); ἱεροὶ βάκχοι/βάκχαι: Ἀντίοχος (5.38), Διογένης (5.45), Διονυσόδωρος (5.47), Κάρπος (6.3), Ὀνήσιμος (6.4), Ὀνήσιμος (6.6), Εὐτυχᾶς (6.7), Ἀφροδίσιος (6.10), Παμφιλᾶς (6.13 [-λος]), Νικίας (6.16), Φίλητος (6.19), Φίλητος (6.21), Εὔτυχος (6.22), Ἐπαφρόδιτος (6.23), Ἀλέξανδρος (6.25), Ἀγαθήμερος (6.26), Εὐτύχης (6.30), Ζωσιμᾶς (6.32), Νίκων (6.34), Ἑρμίας (6.36), Ἑρμῆς (6.37), Ζώσιμος (6.40), Ζώσιμος (6.42), Φίλητος (6.43), Ἐπίκτησις (6.46), Σωτήρ (6.47 [-ηρία]), Εὐτυχίδης (7.4), Νίκων (7.6), Ἐπίκτητος (7.8), Εὐτυχίδης (7.15), Θάλλος (7.19), Κράτερος (7.23), Φιλήμων (7.29), Πίθανος (7.30 [-ον]), Διονύσιος (7.31), Εὔκαρπος (7.32), Εὐτύχης (7.37), Ἄτταλος (7.38), Ἀβάσκαντος (8.33), Τρόφιμος (8.34), Κοσμίων (8.35 [-ία]), Ἐπαφρᾶς (8.38), Δημήτριος (8.39), Ὀνήσιμος (8.42), Ἔρως (8.43), Ἔρως (8.44), Εὐκτήμων (8.46), Μεγιστίων (8.47), Ἕρμιππος (8.48), Ἀρίστων (8.51), Φιλώτας (9.8), Ὀνησίφορος (9.9), Εὔρετος (9.10), Ζώσιμος (9.14), Παρθένιος (9.39 [-ιον]); βάκχαι: Τύχη (9.50), Ἐρώτιον (9.51), Λύκα (9.54), Ναῒς (9.56),

mean that *all* people bearing attested Greek names were necessarily slaves, nor that people not identified in this list were not slaves. However, the fact that one quarter of the names on the inventory are attested elsewhere as names applied to slaves is an additional confirmation that many of the members of the Agrippinilla association were probably slaves or freedmen of the household of Gallicanus. The fact that parents bearing Greek names tended to give their sons Latin cognomina suggests that most of these slaves and freedmen bearing Greek names on the Agrippinilla inscription are first-generation immigrants.

With three exceptions, only the cognomina are provided (or personal name in the case of Greek names) in the inscription.[19] In other words, neither the nomen (*nomen gentilicium*) is provided for the Latin names, nor is the patronymic (or demotic) provided in the case of Greek names. Franz Cumont contrasts this state of affairs with other Dionysiac inscriptions in which names are given in the complete form of the *tria nomina*.[20] How are we to explain the omission of the praenomina and nomina in the Agrippinilla inscription? Cumont

Εὐτύχια (9.57), Εὐτυχίς (9.60), Εὐκαρπία (9.61), Ἐπίκτησις (10.2), Σπένδουσα (10.4 [-δων]), Ἐλπίς (10.5), Εὐοδία (10.7), Λύκα (10.14), Σμύρνα (10.26), Ἐλευθέρις (10.29), Ἑρμιόνη (10.30); σειγηταί: Φίλητος (10.38), Ἀπολλώνιος (10.39), Γλύκερος (10.43 [-α]), Φιλήτη (10.47), Ἐπίκτητος (10.48), Φοῖβος (10.52), Νίκων (10.54), Θάλλος (10.57), Κόσμος (10.60).

19. A Roman citizen normally had a minimum of three names, praenomen, nomen (nomen gentilicium) and cognomen. The 'nomen' named the founder of the family and was passed on to all members of the same *gens*. The nomina frequently ended in *-ius, -eius, -aius, -aeus*, or *-eus* (e.g. Gavius). The *gens* were subdivided into various *familiae*, identified by the cognomina (e.g. Gallicanus). The praenomen, usually abbreviated by a single letter (e.g. M[arcus]), was employed to distinguish one family member from another. To these names other names, agnomen (e.g. Squilla) and supernomen (cf. I. Kajanto, *Supernomina* [Commentationes humanarum litterarum; 40.1 Helsinki: Helsingfors, 1966]) might also be added. On Cognomina, see: I. Kajanto, *The Latin Cognomina* (Societas Scientarum Fennica; Commentationes Humanarum Litteratum, 36.1; Helsinki: Helsingfors, 1965); C. De Simone, *Gnomen* 38 (1966), pp. 384-88.

20. Cumont, 'La grande inscription', p. 234. A good example of this is the first-century dedication of the Dionysiac association at Pergamum which includes many of the same titles as our inscription (*I.Perg.* 485 [= *SIG*² 743 = *SIG*³ 1115 = Quandt 123]; cf. *IGR* IV, 386); also: Apollonia (*CIG* 2055 = *IGLAM* 1555), and Mesia (*CIL* III, 7437; *ILS* 4060).

suggests that in this association, the societal hierarchy with its inherent distinctions had been replaced by a spiritual hierarchy in which all were brothers and sisters:[21]

> Thus one is led to the conclusion that in the mysteries of Bacchus, or at least in particular associations of initiates, the social distinctions of the secular world were obliterated and that a religious hierarchy was substituted in place of the social stratification of public life, such that the initiates were no longer called by their surname which all possessed, nor identified as to how each was related to or belonged to a *gens*. All the bacchants were spiritual brothers.

Though Cumont's theory concerning the lack of *tria nomina* would seem to offer a clear analogy to the familial terms which Paul employs for the members of his congregations,[22] his conclusion breaks down upon closer inspection. Normally, Greeks living in the Eastern half of the Empire would have had only one name—their personal name.[23] They were not given a second name to denote the family after the manner of the Latin nomen (cf. Paus. 7.7.4), though in the Imperial period, the patronymic (usually formed from the genitive of the father's name) was sometimes applied (for example Ἀλκιβιάδης Κλεινίου).[24] In the Agrippinilla inscription, only one man is identified with his

21. Cumont, 'La Grande Inscription', p. 234; elsewhere Cumont points out that in oriental cults, the term 'brothers' is commonly employed as the equivalent for the *consacranei* or συμμύσται (cf. F. Cumont, *Religions Orientales dans le Paganisme Romain* [Paris, (4th edn, 1929)] pp. 24, 121, 269, n. 111; cf. *ILS*, 3360: *Fratribus suis*).

22. E.g. 'brothers' (*passim*), 'sisters' (e.g. 1 Cor. 7.15; 9.5; Rom. 16.1; cf. Mt. 12.50; Jas. 2.15; 2 Jn 13), and 'sons (of God)' (e.g. 1 Thess. 1.10; 1 Cor. 1.9; 2 Cor. 1.19; Gal. 1.16; 2.20; 4.4, 6; 3.27; Rom. 1.3, 9; 5.10; 8.3, 29, 32); Paul descibes himself in relation to them as a 'father' (1 Cor. 4.15); cf. also the use of the term 'household' (Eph. 2.19) to describe the relationship between Christians.

23. The naming of Greek children was the free choice of their parents. Normally, a son was given the name of his grandfather, or father, or a name derived from the father's name (e.g. Φόκος → Φόκιον) or similarly compounded (e.g. Θεόφραστος → Θεόδορος) (H.T. Peck [ed.], *Harper's Dictionary of Classical Literature and Antiquities* [New York: Harper & Brothers, 1923 (1896)], p. 1101).

24. For an example of Greek personal names with patronymics on a donative inscription, see the inscription of the Jewish community in Aphrodisias (No. 76.1) (J.M. Reynolds, R. Tannenbaum and K.T. Erim, *Jews and God-fearers at Aphrodisias: Greek Inscriptions with Commentary* [Proceedings of the Cambridge Philological Society, Supplementary vol. 12; Cambridge: The Cambridge Philological Society, 1987], pp. 5-7).

patronymic in order to distinguish him from another man with the
same name (Αὐξάνων Ἀδέλους υἱός, 9.11-12; cf. 1.45).

This raises an interesting question: are the Greek names which
appear on the inscription true Greek cognomina of full Roman names
or simply Greek personal names? Since I have established that many
of those bearing Greek names had only recently immigrated from
Lesbos as the slaves and freedmen[25] of the Gallicanus household, it is
probable that they were never given full Roman names; the Greek
names on the inscription are probably personal names—not
cognomina.[26]

In the case of freedmen (*liberti*), the situation is somewhat different. Freedmen were given their masters' praenomina and nomina and
thus became indistinguishable from the remaining members of the
family apart from their original praenomen which would become
their cognomen. Therefore, freedmen *could* be individually identified
on the Agrippinilla inscription by citing their cognomina.[27] Garnsey
notes that 'the influence of men of servile extraction reached its peak
in the West' during the Antonine era (138–92 CE), roughly the same
period as this inscription.[28] Therefore, it is probable that some of the
Greek names appearing in the inscription are of freedmen.

What can be said about the *Roman* cognomina on the Agrippinilla
inscription; why are they referred to by their cognomina alone? It
should first be said that within the context of a *familia*, both masters
and slaves were addressed by their praenomina. This was a practical
necessity since family members and slaves shared the same

25. The duties of the *libertii* continued after manumission. Many freedmen were
as useful for their masters after manumission as before (J.H. D'Arms, 'Republican
Senators Involvement in Commerce in the Late Republic: Some Ciceronian
Evidence', in J.H. D'Arms and E.C. Kapff [eds.], *The Seaborne Commerce of
Ancient Rome: Studies in Archaeology and History* [Memoirs of the American
Academy in Rome, 36; Rome: American Academy in Rome, 1980]).

26. If these Greek names are truly Greek cognomina, then it indicates that they
are either freedmen or sons of a freedman (P. Garnsey, 'Descendants of Freedmen in
Local Politics: some Criteria', in B. Levick [ed.] *The Ancient Historian and his
Materials: Essays in Honour of C.E. Stevens Farnborough* [Farnborough: Gregg
International, 1975], pp. 167-80; R. Duthoy, 'La fonction sociale', in *Epigraphica*
36 [1974], pp. 134-54).

27. The complete Roman name of a freedman would include his legal status with
the letter *l(ibertus)* (e.g. Q. Cornelius Q.l Pal. Saturninus).

28. Garnsey, 'Descendants', p. 167.

cognomen.[29] Mothers and daughters were often addressed by their cognomina, but only because few women possessed praenomina.[30] Beyond the *familia*—among friends and acquaintances—men were customarily addressed by their cognomina.[31] Thus, the fact that cognomina—not praenomina—are employed in the Agrippinilla inscription suggests that the scope of the association is wider than the members of a single *familia*. Since formal address required praenomen with either nomen or cognomen, it can also be concluded that the association is not self-consciously formal; it should rather be likened to a meeting of friends and business associates. The fact that full names are used in the inscriptions cited by Cumont (cf. n. 20) is due to the fact that they represent civic—not private—cults; the public nature of civic religious observance demanded a formal style of address.

It can also be concluded that none of the Roman cognomina are of slaves. In the Imperial period the slaves in Roman households were named by adding a slave's praenomen to the full *tria nomina* of his owner.[32] Clearly, all slaves in the Gallicanus household would have had the same cognomina (namely Gallicanus) and would be indistinguishable from other members of the family in an inscription that did not list their praenomina.[33] The only way to distinguish

29. The choice of praenomina employed by the patrician class was very limited. Generally, a given *gens* would restrict itself to a fixed number. For example, the *Aemilii* used only seven, the *Claudii* had six, the *Cornelii* used seven. In total, there were only eighteen praenomina which were employed by the patricians.

30. The praenomina of women who possessed them were not abbreviated. A woman's name usually consisted of her father's nomen in the feminine form (e.g. Pompeius → Pompeia). In the Imperial period the selection and arrangement of a woman's names was variable. A daughter's nomen could be derived from either the nomen or cognomen of her father. In our inscription, two women are identified with both nomen and cognomen, Ἰουλία Εὐτυχία (3.18) and Οὐαλερία Ἀριστεῖνα (10.10).

31. 'Names, Personal', in N.G.L. Hammond and H.H. Scullard (eds.), *The Oxford Classical Dictionary* (Oxford: Clarendon Press, 2nd edn, 1970), pp. 720-21, esp. p. 721; M. Johnson, *Roman Life* (Chicago: Scott, Foresman & Co., 1957), p. 118.

32. On inscriptions, the word *servus*, sometimes abbreviated as 'S' or 'SER', was usually appended. Thus, Martialis C. Olii Primi s means Martialis, slave of C. Olius Primus.

33. Since the only two Gallicani on the list are high ranking functionaries (priests), this possibility must be ruled out.

between individual Roman slaves of the same household would be to cite their praenomina. Since no Roman praenomina appear in the list, it can be concluded that none of the Roman names are of slaves.

What conclusions can be made regarding those who bear Roman cognomina but are beyond the immediate family of Gallicanus? One should be wary of assuming that these names belong to humble trades-men and farm hands since many plebeians did not have cognomen (for example the families of Marii, Mummii and Sertorii). Indeed, cognomina were often an indication of ancient lineage and nobility.[34] Hence, the fact that the Roman names are all cognomina suggests that few were plebeians.

The obvious range in social status presupposed by this inscription in which an ex-consul, his family and social acquaintances would partici-pate in a religious association with their slaves and freedmen suggests that hierarchical distinctions were relativized. This also explains the fact that the attested slave names are found throughout most offices and in proportion to overall number in each office: *hierophante* (1), god-bearers (θεοφόροι) (1), chest-bearers (κισταφόροι) (1), holy herdsmen (βουκόλοι ἱεροί) (2), leaders of the male and female bacchants (ἀρχιβάσσαροι/αι) (4), acolytes (ἀμφιθαλεῖς) (1), bearers of the winnowing baskets (λικναφόροι) (3), fire-bearers (πυρφόροι) (1), youth leaders (ἀρχινεανίσκοι) (1), cowherds (βουκόλοι) (5), initiates (ἀπὸ καταζώσεως) (35), male and female bacchic initiates (βάκχοι/αι ἀπὸ καταζώσεως) (8), holy bacchantes (ἱεροί βάκχοι) (69), female bacchants (βάκχαι) (22) and novices (σειγηταί) (9).[35]

This situation is reminiscent of the church in Corinth: when Paul exhorts the Corinthians saying, 'consider your call, brethren, not many of you were wise according to worldly standards, not many were powerful, not many were of noble birth' (1 Cor. 1.26), he implies that some were indeed wise, powerful and of noble birth. Despite this, the spiritual kinship of the congregation in Corinth and elsewhere was such that societal distinctions between slaves, freedmen and masters were relativized (1 Cor. 12.13; Gal. 3.26-29; Col. 3.11; Eph. 2.17-19). In the stratified world of Roman society—based as it was upon order, class, status and wealth—religious associations, whether dedi-cated to Dionysos, Christ or some other god—provided the opportunity for at least limited improvement in one's status in the world. Consider

34. Johnson, *Roman Life*, p. 121.
35. Cf. n. 18.

how Paul addresses the slave Onesimus as 'my child' (Phlm. 10) and commends him as a 'brother' (Phlm. 16). Onesimus became a member of Paul's team (Phlm. 11-13) and a trusted messenger to the churches of Colossae (Col. 4.7-9). Though it is unlikely that the slaves in the Agrippinilla association were accorded such equanimity, or were addressed in familial language, their lowly status in the hierarchical Roman society was relativized by their membership in this religious society.

As in the case of the nucleus of the Agrippinilla association, the original structure of many early Christian congregations was provided by the family.[36] It is for this reason that the Christian groups required household guidelines for governing the relation between children and parents, husbands and wives, slaves and masters.[37] Yet it is worth noting that few, if any, Roman houses could accommodate the Agrippinilla association whose membership exceeded 402 people. Clearly, the *familia* structure of this association in no way limited its growth and portability, nor the inclusion of members beyond the *familia*. It can be concluded that the growth in the membership of family-based religious associations was not limited by the size of private dwellings, nor by consanguinity with the founding *familia*. By analogy, family-based Christian congregations may also have been far larger than is commonly supposed—perhaps numbering in the hundreds. This observation should caution those who would assume that family-based churches were necessarily small, intimate gatherings.

Moreover, it is remarkable how such a large association could be successfully transplanted from Lesbos to Rome, all the while preserving its original language and probably its traditional liturgy. It is reasonable to assume that a religious association such as this may well have attracted new members from the environs of Rome. This model suggests one manner in which Christianity may have spread throughout the Mediterranean. As heads of Christian households relocated for reason of employment, whether mercantile or military, their adherent families and congregations may have prospered in new lands and attracted new, perhaps sizable, local membership.

36. E.g. 1 Cor. 1.16; cf. Acts 11.14; 16.15, 31, 34; 18.8; 20.20; cf. Meeks, *Urban Christians*, pp. 75-84.
37. E.g. Col. 3.18–4.6; Eph 5.21–6.9; Tit. 2.1-10.

5. *Internal Structures and Titles*

The archaic cult of Dionysos had virtually no structure or functionaries (see s. 6, a). However, throughout the Hellenistic and Roman periods, civil and private Dionysiac associations experimented with a variety of organizational structures and diverse titles. Sometimes this was accomplished by borrowing titles from the Eleusinian mysteries. For example, the use of the titles *dadouchos* and *hierophant* in the Agrippinilla inscription betrays the pretension to simulate the Eleusian mysteries.[38] The Agrippinilla inscription encompasses more titles than any other extant Dionysiac inscription—numbering at least twenty-two distinct titles in all (see chart below). By far the largest enrolment is under the title of '(holy) bacchants' (ἱεροί βάκχοι, 5.37 and βάκχαι, 9.49) comprising over half the membership (222/402). The second largest category, the 'initiates' (ἀπὸ καταζώσεως, 3.1), includes slightly less than a quarter of the total membership (90/402). Most of the remaining titles are extremely rare, while some occur in this inscription alone.

The only extant inscription of a Dionysiac hierarchy with a comparable number of titles is that of the Iobacchi in Athens with twelve titles.[39] The diversity of terminology is such that these two large inscriptions hold no term in common, though there are similarities.[40] It should be added that many smaller inscriptions do repeat many of the titles found in the Agrippinilla inscription.[41] Though not a mystery

38. Jeanmaire, *Dionysos*, p. 471.

39. S. Wide, *MDAI(A)* 19 (1894), p. 248; *SIG²* 1368; *SIG³* 1109; translated by M.N. Tod, *Sidelights on Greek History* (Oxford: Basil Blackwell, 1932), pp. 86-91. The cult of the Iobacchi did not include Dionysiac mysteries, but was connected with them by certain ritual observance and by its hierarchy. The inscription deals with rules for admission and rules for maintaining good conduct at banquets (Burkert, *Cults*, pp. 64-65).

40. Cf. the terms ἀρχιβάσσαροι (2.34) and βούκολοι (1.42) of the Agrippinilla inscription with ἀρχίβακχος and βούκολικός.

41. Cf. Pergamum (*I. Perg.* 485 [= *SIG³* 1115; Quandt, 123]; *MDAI(A)* 24 (1899) 179, no. 21 [= Quandt, 123; *I.Perg.* 486a]), Philadelphia (K. Buresch, *Aus Lydien* (New York: Hildesheim, 1977 [1898]), p. 11, no. 8 [= Quandt, 179-80]), Ephesus (*BMI* 602 [= Quandt, 161]; *BMI* 595 [= Quandt, 161]). Magnesia (*I.Mag.* 117 [= Quandt, 163]), Attaleia (J. Keil and A. von Premerstein, *Bericht über eine Reise in Lydien* [Vienna: Denkschriften, Akad. 1911], p. 72, no. 152, p. 76 restored [= Quandt, 183-84]), Apollonia, Thrace (*CIG* 2052), Abdera (*BCH* 62

cult, the roles assigned in the ritual of the Iobacchi are ordered on the *archibakchos* and certain officials were chosen to enact the roles of particular gods (for example Dionysos, Aphrodite, Prometheus).[42]

There is no need here to repeat the discussion of Cumont and others concerning the precise role of each of these functionaries since they are to a large extent idiosyncratic to each association and lack clear analogues in the early Christian congregations.[43] However, it is instructive to observe that various Christian groups also experimented with their own titles such as apostles, prophets, teachers, miracle workers, healers, administrators, deacons and overseers (cf. 1 Cor. 12.27-31; Eph. 2.19-21; Phil. 1.1).[44]

6. *Membership*

a. *Women*

In classical times, the Dionysiac *orgia* were held every second year; they were dominated by women (*maenads/thiades/bacchai*) because Dionysos—above all other gods—was the god of women.[45] He was known as 'mad Dionysos' (Homer, *Il.* 6.132) because of the ecstasy, terror and wildness which he incited in women, first on his mythical nurses and subsequently on all women. Wine and dance induced a state of mad intoxicated frenzy which permitted married women a temporary, socially sanctioned escape from their regulated lives as wives and mothers.[46] Walter Burkert eloquently describes

---

[1938], pp. 51ff), Perinthus (*RhM* 34 [1879], p. 211; *IGR* XII, 1.787), Rome (*ILS* 3369), Rhodes (*IG* XII, 1,155 [= Quandt, 204]).

42. Cf. the role of the *heros* (notes to inscriptions, n. 3) and 'cowherds'.

43. Cumont, 'La grande inscription', pp. 236-63; Nilsson, *Opuscula selecta*, II, pp. 524-41; Nilsson, *Dionysiac Mysteries*, pp. 45-59; Kerényi, *Dionysos*, pp. 353-54.

44. E. Schweizer, *Church Order in the New Testament* (London: SCM Press, 1961), pp. 13, 162.

45. R.S. Kraemer, 'Ecstasy and Possession: The Attraction of Women to the Cult of Dionysus', *HTR* 72 (1979), pp. 55-80; Kerényi, *Dionysos*, p. 130.

46. It would seem that only married women were permitted to be *bacchai* in the full sense (cf. Diodorus 4.3.3; Euripedes, *Phoenissae* 655-66); though Euripides' *Bacchae* seems to have virgins among the *bacchai* (controversial text), Albert Heinrich argues that the *Bacchae* cannot be used as a reliable source for the reconstrction of Maenadism since it is as much a re-enactment of myth as of ritual ('Greek maenadism from Olympias to Messalina', *HSCP* 82 [1978], pp. 121-60, esp. 122;

the significance of this temporary ecstasy:[47]

> What sets Dionysus apart, even in a predetermined framework, is the
> 'frenzy', the individual experience of ecstasy—which, of course, is not
> clearly distinguished from drunkenness... The god here desires the
> rupturing of establishment: it is his epiphany... In the private sphere,
> marriage is the principal order that is overturned... Whenever the human
> order is considered so stable, it will all the more be broken by a higher
> power and changed into its opposite. Dionysus provides the antithesis to
> the family: whereas a wife must tend the house, the maenads roam the
> wilderness; whereas a wife is modestly dressed, the Dionysiac mob raves
> in wild, lascivious, shameless nudity; whereas a wife must work,
> especially at the loom, Dionysus scares women and girls 'away from the
> looms and the spindle'; whereas a wife must love her husband and
> provide for her children, in the night of the *Agrionia* the mother kills her
> child to wound her husband. Hate and murder, instead of affectionate
> union, rule the night, which reveals what the day suppresses, the frenzied
> outburst leads to a purification.

There were few functionaries in the archaic cult; most were women
serving as high priestesses.[48] This is not the place to take up the
complex question of the role of men in the archaic cult. Undoubtedly,
it was not a homogenous phenomenon, but must be distinguished
according to geographic locale and perhaps by social class. Suffice to
say that a general trend is clear: in the archaic cult men were a
minority in both the general membership and in positions of
authority.[49] By far, the most famous of the Bacchanalia was held in

W. Burkert, *Homo Necans: The Anthropology of Ancient Greek Sacrificial Ritual
and Myth* (trans. P. Bing; Berkeley: University of California Press, 1972], pp. 184-
85, 176.

47. Burkert, *Homo Necans*, pp. 184-85; cf. Kerényi, *Dionysos*, pp. 132-33.

48. In Cos, no one except the priestess was allowed to sacrifice or perform
initiations (*SIG³* 1012). In other cities, the *orgia* seem to have been much less regulated by officials (cf. Diodorus Siculus 4.3).

49. E.g. in Mitylene (Lesbos) men were excluded except for the 'overseer of
women' ([γυναι]κονόμος [*LSCG*, no. 127]). A tomb epigram dating to the middle
Hellenistic age and ascribed to Dioscorides describes how a man led the *orgia* of the
Thyiades at Amphipolis (Nilsson, *Dionysiac Mysteries*, p. 177, n. 8) may reflect the
transition between the archaic mysteries and the new mysteries which were open to
men. Attalos II appointed a man as priest of Dionysos Kathegemon (*I.Perg.* 248;
OGIS 331). There is also evidence for female itinerant charismatics; for example, one
inscription from Miletus (276/275 BCE) tells how they would 'perform initiations for
Dionysos in the city or in the country' (*LSAM* 48, ll. 19-21; cf. *REG* 32 [1919],

Rome. However, it was brutally suppressed by the Roman senate in 186 BCE.[50] Reformed Dionysiac mysteries returned to Italy by the first century CE, probably from Asia Minor.[51]

During the Hellenistic and Roman periods, Dionysiac religion dramatically altered. Many more men were allowed into the cult of Dionysos, a boggling array of functionaries and titles were adopted and the once liberating madness of the maenads was replaced with carefully regulated hierarchical societies. In the Roman Age especially, the love of ceremony was such that hierarchies of officials and new regulations, transformed the irrational erotic dance into carefully ordered processions. The incorporation of men was most rapid in those cases in which Dionysiac societies (*thiasoi*) were incorporated into civic cults. Since men were already in positions of civil authority in the civic cults, it was a simple matter for them to dominate the civic Dionysiac cults at all levels.

Against this background of increasing male membership and the concomitant control of civic Dionysiac cults, it is instructive to observe the manner and degree to which women participated and held positions of authority in a *non-civic* voluntary association such as that of Agrippinilla. The following chart lists the number of men and women in each office. Those offices occupied solely by men, but duplicated for women, have been combined in the chart; this results in the identification of twenty-two distinct offices.

p. 256); men and women were initiated but the initiations were undertaken separately by priests and priestesses respectively.

50. Cf. Livy 39.8-19; 39.8, 3; A. Bruhl, *Liber Pater: Origine et expansion du culte dionysiaque à Rome et dans le monde romain* (Paris: E. de Boccard, 1953), pp. 82-116; R.J. Rousselle, 'The Persecution of the Bacchic Cult, 186–180 BC' (dissertation, Ann Arbor, 1982); W. Heilmann, 'Coniuratio impia. Die Unterdrückung der Bacchanalia als Beispiel für römische Religionspolitik', *Altsprachlicher Unterricht* 28/2 (1985), pp. 22-37; Nilsson, *Dionysiac Religion*, pp. 14-21; cf. n. 46.

51. E. Simon traces the Villa Item composition to Pergamum, finding links with the Telephos frieze ('Zum Fries der Mysterienvilla bei Pompeii', *Jahrbuch des Deutschen Archäologischen* 76 [1961], pp. 111-72, esp. pp. 60-69).

	Title	Men	Women	Total
1.	*heros* (ἥρως, 1.1)	1	0	1
2.	torch bearer (δαδοῦχος, 1.2)	0	1	1
3.	priests/priestesses (ἱερεῖς/ἱέρειαι, 1.3, 23, + dedication)	7	3	10
4.	*hierophant* (ἱεροφάντης, 1.28)	1	0	1
5.	god-bearers (θεόφοροι, 1.30)	2	0	2
6.	assistant and constable of Silenus (ὑπουργός καὶ σειληνοκόσμος, 1.33-34)	1	0	1
7.	mystic chest bearers (κισταφόροι, 1.36)	0	3	3
8.	chief cowherds (ἀρχιβούκολοι, 1.42)	3	0	3
9.	holy cowherds (βουκόλοι ἱεροί, 1.49)	8	0	8
10.	chief bacchants (ἀρχιβάσσαροι/αι, 2.5, 34)	2	4	6
11.	acolytes (ἀμφιθαλεῖς , 2.10)	2	0	2
12.	bearers of the *likna* (λικναφόροι, 2.14)	0	3	3
13.	phallus-bearer (φαλλοφόρος, 2.21)	0	1	1
14.	fire-bearer (πυρφόροι, 2.25)	2	0	2
15.	secretary? (ἱερομνήμων, 2.29)	1	0	1
16.	youth leaders (ἀρχινεανίσκοι, 2.31)	1	0	1
17.	herdsmen (βουκόλοι, 2.41)	11	0	11
18.	initiates (ἀπὸ καταζώσεως, 3.1)	52	38	90
19.	male/female baccant initiates (βάκχοι/αι ἀπὸ καταζώσεως , 5.1-2, 24-25)	15	3	18
20.	(holy) bacchants (ἱεροὶ βάκχοι, 5.37 / βάκχαι, 9.49)	176	46	222
21.	guardians of the sacred cave (ἀντροφύλακες, 9.38)	2	0	2
22.	novices (σειγηταί, 10.37)	15	8	23
	Total	292	110	402

In total, 27 percent (110/402) of the total names on the inscription are of women. As noted above, the statue includes only those names of people who made a financial contribution to the statue. Therefore, it is reasonable to assume that more women than men are omitted since women generally had lesser economic means. Therefore, the figure of 27 percent female names is a measure of the relative wealth of women as compared to men, as well as a measure of female membership. Despite this difficulty in interpreting the figures concerning women, it is significant that women are represented in the highest levels of the association. Of the four highest offices (*heros, dadouchos,* priest/priestess, *hierophant*), women are included in two of them, namely the second highest position (*dadouchos*) and that of priestess, though numerically, they represent only four out of thirteen names. Of course, the fact that the statue itself is dedicated to Agrippinilla, a priestess, should not be overlooked. Indeed, the force of the dedication is to honour her as the pre-eminent priestess and patron. Though Agrippinilla is known to have been the wife of Gallicanus, it is significant that she is not identified as such in this inscription. She is recognized as an individual—not as someone's wife or mother. I suggest that her position should be likened to that of a 'high priestess', but that term is not applied here because it was reserved for *civic* functionaries.

There was a growing trend throughout the first and second centuries CE to involve women—in addition to men—in the high-priestly offices of various civic cults. The first high priestess of Asia was Julia, highpriestess in Magnesia from 40–59 CE.[52] The following chart illustrates the trend towards the inclusion of women in the high-priestly office.[53]

Time	29 BCE–25 CE	26–80 CE	81–130 CE	131–179 CE	180–250 CE	Total
Men	8	11	16	26	41	102
Women	0	1	6	9	20	36

Generally speaking, women are not grouped with the men in the inscription, but ordered in their own groups, though these groups usually parallel the groups for men. Paired groups include those of priests/priestesses (1.3, 23), the chief bacchantes (2.5, 34) and the bacchant initiates (5.1-2, 24-25). Moreover, the largest category, the male 'holy bacchants' (5.37) was probably very similar, if not identical, to the female 'bacchants' (9.49) despite the fact that the latter lacks the qualifying adjective. In two cases are men and women

---

52. *I.Mag.* 158: 'The *boule* and the *demos* honoured Juliane, daughter of Eustratos (?), son of Phanostratos (?), wife of Alkiphronos, the high priestess of Asia, who was the first women to serve as high priestess of Asia, stephanephoros, gymnasiarch, priestess for life (?) of Demeter in Ephesus, because of all (her) excellence.' The next six extant high priestesses of Asia are: Antonia Caecilia (80–120 CE; Thyatira; *IGR* IV, 1238); Favia Ammion Aristio (85–130 CE; Ephesus; *IGR* IV, 1325); Stratonike (89–150 CE; Teos; *IGR* IV, 1571); Claudia Tryphaina (89–150 CE; Teos; *IGR* IV, 1571); Vedia Marcia (97–100 CE; Ephesus; *I.Eph.* IV, 1017); Skaptia Phirmille (130/131 CE; Ephesus; *I.Eph.* II, 430). I am grateful to S. Friesen for collecting this information ('Networks of Religion and Society at Ephesus: Men and Women in the Provincial Highpriesthood', [paper delivered to the Archeology of the NT World Group of the SBL Annual Meeting, San Fransisco, 1992]).

53. Friesen, 'Networks of Religion'.

combined under the same heading, namely the 'initiates' (3.1) and the 'novices' (10.37). These two classes represent the second and third largest groups after that of the '(holy) bacchants'.

There remain six offices which have exclusively male membership (18 men total) and lack a female counterpart (assistant and constable of Silenus, acolytes, secretary [?], youth leaders, holy cowherds and guardians of the sacred cave). In the case of those offices with only one for two names, it is impossible to say whether women were deliberately excluded or were simply not enrolled at the time, or failed to make a donation. However, in the case of the largest exclusively male class, the 'holy cowherds', a troop of dancers who took the roles of various gods (1.49, cf. notes to the inscription, nn. 16, 3)—with eleven male members—the more natural assumption is that women were prohibited from membership.

An examination of the roles of other women in the Agrippinilla association reveals that they had a special prominence in the Dionysiac procession: of the five classes of functionaries responsible for carrying objects in procession (a statue, a mystic chest, winnowing baskets [*likna*], a phallus[54] and fire), three are comprised exclusively of women. What is more, seven of the eleven names are of women. This fact suggests that the archaic roots of the Dionysiac mysteries as a women's cult had to some extent survived.

The stunning frescoes of the Villa of the Mysteries in Pompeii—showing another Dionysiac private *thiasos* sponsored by a wealthy family—offer a visual description of the continued role of women in a private Dionysiac association in the early first century CE.[55] Of the twenty-three figures portrayed in these frescoes, none are of mortal men, while there are fourteen images of mortal women.[56] One of these frescoes may portray a bacchic priestess and patron, perhaps

54. The 'likna-bearers' (λικναφόροι [cf. notes to inscriptions, n. 19]) and phallus-bearers (φαλλοφόρος [cf. n. 20]) were frequently the same people since the phallus was often hidden in the covered *liknon* (winnowing basket) under the grain.

55. M.I. Rostovtzeff, *Mystic Italy* (New York: Henry Holt, 1927); A. Maiuri, *La Villa dei Misteri* (Rome: n.p. 1931); Nilsson, *Dionysiac Mysteries*, pp. 66-76; Kerényi, *Dionysos*, pp. 355-63; Fierz-David,*Women's Dionysian Initiation: The Villa of Mysteries in Pompeii* [trans. G. Phelan; Dallas: Spring Publication, 1988 [1957]).

56. The remaining figures consist of a prepubescent boy, three satyrs, one winged demonic female figure, two images of the mythological Silenus, and finally the goddess Ariadne caressing the god Dionysos.

occupying a role similar to that of Agrippinilla; on a wall facing the largest scene is painted the portrait of the woman who sits with a dignified demeanor in a richly decorated chair.[57] The portrait is positioned so as to create the effect that she is watching the sacramental drama enfolding on the opposite wall. In another scene, a neophyte attends a priestess seated by a table who appears to be officiating. The priestess is crowned with myrtle and appears sumptuously dressed.[58]

When the role of women and slaves in the Agrippinilla association is compared with Pauline congregations a similar situation is observed. The distinctions in status accorded to men and women in society were to some extent relativized in Pauline churches (1 Cor. 12.13; Gal. 3.26-29; Col. 3.11; cf. Eph. 2.17-19). However, women such as Phoebe (Rom. 16.1),[59] Chloe (1 Cor. 1.11), Tabitha (Acts 9.36b-43) and Junia (Rom. 16.7)[60] did attain active and prominent roles in the churches.[61] This similarity disappears—at least in some churches—by the second century: there is evidence that the role of women was being restricted in Christian churches (for example 1 Tim. 2.11-15) at the same time as women's roles were expanding in the Graeco-Roman cults. John Gager has suggested that one of the reasons for the success of Christianity was its appeal to women, in contrast to Mithraism which excluded women.[62] The evidence of the Agrippinilla inscription would suggest that early Christian churches were no more inclusive—

57. A. Maiuri, *Roman Painting* [trans. S. Gilbert; Geneva: Albert Skira, 1953), pp. 52, 54; p. 51 for overview; Nilsson, *Dionysian Mysteries*, p. 69, fig. 10b; Kerényi, *Dionysos*, fig. 106.

58. Kerényi, *Dionysos*, fig. 110B; see plates in Fierz-David, *Dionysian Initiation*.

59. E. Schüssler Fiorenza, 'Women in Pre-Pauline and Pauline Churches', *USQR* 33 (1978), pp. 153-66.

60. B. Brooten, '"Junia... Outstanding among the Apostles" (Romans 16.11)', in Leonard and Arlene Swindler (eds.),*Women Priests: A Catholic Commentary on the Vatican Declaration* (New York: Paulist Press, 1977), pp. 141-44.

61. W. Meeks, 'The Image of the Androgyne: Some Uses of a Symbol in Earliest Christianity', *HR* 13 (1973–74), pp. 165-208; H.D. Betz, *Galatians*, (Hermeneia; Philadelphia: Fortress Press, 1979), pp. 181-201; A. Cameron, '"Neither Male Nor Female"', in *Greek and Rome* (2nd ser. 27 (1980), pp. 60-68; R. Scroggs, 'Paul and the Eschatological Women', *JAAR* 40 (1972), pp. 283-303.

62. J. Gager, *Kingdom and Community: The Social World of Early Christianity* (Englewood Cliffs, NJ: Prentice–Hall, 1975).

or perhaps less so—of women in positions of authority than were the
Dionysiac cults.

b. *Membership and Recruitment*
In the past, explanations for the recruitment and expansion of
religious associations have often been based solely on their appeal to
psychological need and ideological attachment.[63] However, more
recent studies have focused on the importance of gaining access to
certain social networks. According to Michael White, 'recruitment to
new religious groups often moves through pre-existing social
networks, especially family units'.[64] Therefore, ideological commitment to and membership in, a particular religious association may be
determined by an individual's social network. From this point of
view, 'faith constitutes conformity to the religious outlook of one's
intimates'.[65]

Religious associations created a network of fictive kinship which
served to structure relationships and nurture loyalties. A religious
association such as the Dionysiac association of Agrippinilla created
this 'kinship network' by relating individuals—especially in extended
family alliances—to a common god who acted as patron, bestowing
material and spiritual benefits. J. Davis terms this phenomenon
'godparenthood'.[66] From this perspective, such personal benefits as
were experienced were attributed to their ultimate patron Dionysos,
the giver of all benefits.

Clientellism, patronage and employment often depended upon the
'kinship' network of the religious association.[67] The social network of
the religious association was particularly efficient because of the

63. R. Stark and W.S. Bainbridge, 'Networks of Faith: Interpersonal Bonds and
Recruitment to Cults and Sects', *AJS* 85 (1980), pp. 1376-95, esp. pp. 1376-78.

64. M. White, 'Finding the Tie that Binds: Issues in Social Description', in
L.M. White (ed.), *Semeia 56: Social Networks in the Early Christian Environment:
Issues and Methods for Social History* [Atlanta, GA: Scholars Press, 1992] pp. 3-
22, esp p. 21; R. MacMullen, *Paganism in the Roman Empire* (New Haven: Yale
University Press, 1981), pp. 116-27; L.M. White, 'Adolf Harnack and the
"Expansion" of Early Christianity: A Reappraisal of Social History', *The Second
Century* 5 (1985), pp. 97-127, esp. pp. 115-20.

65. Stark and Bainbridge, 'Networks', p. 1377, cf. p. 1394.

66. J. Davis, *People of the Mediterranean: An Essay in Comparative Social
Anthropology* (London: Routledge & Kegan Paul, 1977), p. 223.

67. MacMullen, *Paganism*, p. 111; White, *God's House*, pp. 143-47.

multiplicity of social contacts that could be accessed' through it.[68] Thus, religious associations served to mediate a variety of relation-ships—whether those of master/slave, employer/employee, credi-tor/debtor, patron/recipient.[69] These social bonds which were created and reinforced in the context of religious associations could have immediate social benefits. For example, the cult of Isis in Pompeii mediated contacts for political support in city elections; in 79 CE 'all worshippers of Isis' supported Cn. Helvius Sabinus for election as *aedile* in Pompeii.[70] In another election, Cuspius Pausa was supported for election by a guild of Isiac bakers.[71]

The Agrippinilla association offers one such example of over-lapping social networks in which social relations are structured, loyalties reinforced and social mobility, clientellism, patronage and political support fostered. We can hardly overlook the fact that Squilla Gallicanus was a very prominent and powerful man. After belonging to the senate—the most prestigious status group in Roman society—he was appointed consul in 150 CE, one of the two highest magistrates of the Roman state. Then in about 165 he was appointed proconsul of Asia.[72] The governorship of Asia was one of the two highest posts in terms of prestige along with the province of Africa.[73] As proconsul of

68. White, 'Finding the Tie', p. 21; cf. Stark and Bainbridge, 'Networks', pp. 1387, 1392.

69. The bestowal of honour was not a one-way exchange. Reciprocity was also involved through the act of honouring the patron. There is evidence of women, including high priestesses, being in control of their own wealth and acting as patrons; e.g., Julia Severa (Akmonia) donated a building to two of her Jewish clients (synagogue leaders) (L.M. White, *Building God's House in the Roman World: Architectural Adaptation among Pagans, Jews, and Christians* [Baltimore: The Johns Hopkins University Press, 1990], pp. 81-82; White, 'Finding the Tie', pp. 3-22, esp. p. 19). As White observes, the fact that the clients also contributed funds for the renovation suggests that they also possessed some measure of wealth and social standing. We should not overlook the fact that they also had access to a wealthy patron (White, 'Finding the Tie', p. 19).

70. V. Tran Tam Tinh, *Essai sur le culte d'Isis à Pompéi* (Paris: Bocard, 1964), pp. 87-92; J.L. Franklin, *Pompeii: The Electoral Programmata, Campaigns and Politics, AD 71–79* (Papers and Monographs of the American Academy in Rome, 28; Rome: American Academy in Rome, 1980), pp. 87-92.

71. *CIL* 4.787; *CIL* 4.1011; cf. Franklin, *Pompeii,* pp. 22, 103-104.

72. Proconsuls were selected by lot from the senate, but only senators of appropriate seniority were eligible.

73. In the case of these prosperous urban provinces, the proconsuls were required

Asia, his staff included four junior senators, three legates (*legati*) with administrative and judicial functions and one *quaestor*. He appointed his own son, Cornelius Cethegus, as one of these legates. He would also be accompanied by a small group of attendants (*apparitores*) who acted as lectors, messengers, heralds and scribes. It was also customary for a governor to bring a body of friends and advisors. In addition, he was assigned a detachment of regular soldiers who, among other duties, provided personal protection.[74] The tenure of proconsulships was fixed by law at only one year. When Squilla Gallicanus returned to Italy at the end of his term, his administrative assistants, friends and advisors would also have returned. Romans were acutely aware of the relative degrees of importance of various magistracies (cf. *cursus honorum*) and would surely enjoin themselves to anyone who could expediate their progress through the ranks. If the Agrippinilla inscription dates after Gallicanus's proconsulship, it is possible that many of the Roman names on the inscription are of the administrative staff who returned with him to continue their careers near Rome.[75]

Clearly, there can be no doubt that Gallicanus was a man of immense power and influence; to be associated with him through a Dionysiac association was also to have access to his social network. Through such an association, newly manumitted slaves could acquire some respectability by association and, what is more, establish business contacts. It is clear that most of the Greek names of this inscription list the slaves and freedmen of the Galicanus household (see above).[76] Though some manumitted slaves would continue in the employ of their masters,[77] others would benefit from their master's

to be ex-consuls; cf. G. Burton, 'Government and the Provinces', in J. Wacher (ed.), *The Roman World* (2 vols.; London: Routledge & Kegan Paul, 1987), I, pp. 423-39, esp. p. 424.

74. G. Burton, 'Government and the Provinces', in Wacher, *The Roman World* I, p. 425.

75. If the inscription dates prior to his proconsulship, the Roman names may be people from his administration as consul (*aedile, censors, quaetors, praetors*).

76. Cf. pp. 251-52.

77. D'Arms, 'Republican Senators', pp. 115-71. Keith Hopkins has argued that the practice of manumission actually reinforced the institution of slavery by offering the inducement of advancement to slaves who performed their duties properly (*Conquerors and Slaves: Sociological Studies in Roman History* [Cambridge: Cambridge University Press, 1978], I, pp. 115-71).

good connections and become very powerful men.[78] By virtue of their membership, slaves and freedmen were accorded a degree of respect and status and some were entrusted with distinct ministries in the association.

From this perspective, studies of conversion and membership in early churches which focus on psychological need and ideological attachment, to the exclusion of the importance of social networks, are bound to be incomplete. For example, the wealthier members of the Corinthian congregation probably offered to other members, especially social isolates such as new immigrants and newly manumitted slaves, various kinds of assistance. The structured social relationships in a church such as at Corinth, with its fictive kinship, probably facilitated opportunities for patronage, clientellism, employment and social and political mobility. In this light the statements, 'I belong to Paul', 'I belong to Apollos', 'I belong to Cephas' and 'I belong to Christ' (1 Cor. 1.12) could be interpreted as patronage alliances and as godparenthood rather than as ideological affirmations.

Conclusion

The Dionysiac association portrayed in this inscription was probably established and funded by the donations of the wealthy aristocrat, Agrippinilla, while resident in Mitylene. It was then subsequently relocated to the Roman Campagna when her husband Squilla Gallicanus was transferred. The erection of the statue in her honour suggests that her patronage continued. The structure and membership of the association was based upon Agrippinilla's *familia* and other overlapping social networks.

Approximately 80 percent of the membership consisted of Greek slaves and freedmen of the Gallicanus household. Freeborn Romans made up the remaining membership, taken from the immediate and extended families, friends and business associates of Agrippinilla and Gallicanus. Membership in the association served to relativize social distinctions in an otherwise socially stratified society. The use of cognomina in the inscription suggests that the ethos of the association

78. H.P. D'Escurac discusses the complexity of the status of manumitted slaves ('Affranchis et citoyenneté: les effets juridiques de l'affranchissement sous le Haut Empire', *Ktéma* 6 [1981], pp. 181-92).

was neither that of the intimacy of a family, nor the formality of a civic cult.

Membership was not determined by ideological attachment to Dionysos (over against some other god), but rather by the pre-existing social bonds and networks. Under the patronage of Dionysos, material benefits were realized by his followers when the social network of the association mediated and nurtured other social networks such as employer/employee, patron/recipient, creditor/ debtor.

This association manifests many common features of Hellenistic and Roman Dionysiac associations such as the multiplication of titles and functionaries, the inclusion of men at all levels, and the emphasis on regulated processions of men and women in the place of the liberating ecstasy of married women in the time of the archaic cult. The inclusion of women in the highest offices is consistent with the general pattern of increasing appointments of high priestesses in civic cults.

The Agrippinilla association provides an interesting analogy to some of the churches founded by Paul. Identifiable common denominators include the family based structure, the relativizing of social hierarchy, the portability of the cult and the experimentation with different titles and functionaries. The inclusion of women, slaves and freedmen in early churches was by no means greater than their inclusion in this association. As in the Agrippinilla association, a key factor in the recruitment of membership in the early churches may have been the importance of gaining access to social networks rather than an ideological conversion or one based on psychological need. Such personal benefits as resulted would have been interpreted as the benefactions of their cult patron, Christ.

THE UNIQUENESS OF JESUS AS A METHODOLOGICAL PROBLEM

Lloyd Gaston

The uniqueness of Jesus is a given and an appropriate one in any theology which speaks of 'the only begotten Son of God'. On the other hand Christian theologians have no need to be interested in the historical Jesus and therefore no need to be concerned about the question of *his* uniqueness. To my knowledge John Hurd has never engaged in this latter enterprise, but he has consistently been attentive to questions of clear and rigourous methodology.[1] While I have also never heard him expound the Chalcedonian Definition, I am sure that if he were to speak of the two natures of Jesus Christ he would follow the injunction to do so 'without confusion.'

For most of the history of the Church Jesus was, and is, unique in the strictest sense. This is seen particularly in the two unique events which bracket his life: 'conceived by the Holy Spirit, born of the Virgin Mary' and 'suffered under Pontius Pilate...the third day he rose again from the dead'. What was in between those two events was not worth mentioning in the creed and in any case was understood in the light of them. Because of the liturgical prominence given the gospels and the pre-eminence given the Fourth Gospel in theology, the main function of Jesus during his lifetime was seen to be the proclamation of his own uniqueness. Above all, christological statements about the uniqueness of Jesus tend to be in the present tense, in Christian piety about how he relates now to the believer, or in doctrine about his eternal relation to God the Father and humanity.

Since the Enlightenment there have been many attempts to recover an historical Jesus, a Jesus about whom one speaks in the past tense, a

---

1. '"The Jesus Whom Paul Preaches" (Acts 19.13)', in P. Richardson and J.C. Hurd (eds.), *From Jesus to Paul; Studies in Honour of Francis Wright Beare* (Waterloo: Wilfred Laurier University Press, 1984), pp. 73-89, is more about Paul than Jesus but is methodologically important.

Jesus who lived between and apart from the bracketing unique events.[2] Hermann Reimarus (1778) quite properly put Jesus in the context of his own culture as a figure devoid of uniqueness, but because of his fierce anti-theological rationalism also presented a Jesus guilty of a serious mistake and disciples guilty of fraud. D.F. Strauss distinguished myth from history, with uniqueness belonging only to the former, but the myth was no longer christological but expressed the relationship between God and humanity as such. Liberal lives of Jesus reacted by continuing critical study of the Gospels and the distinction between history and myth, now called 'the Jesus of history' and 'the Christ of faith', but reintroducing the uniqueness of Jesus. This uniqueness now referred not to traditional Christology but to the historical Jesus, hidden in such terms as 'religious genius' or unparalleled 'God-consciousness'.[3] Jesus' uniqueness was no longer a given but had to be argued for, almost always by contrasting him with his historical context.

Rudolf Bultmann professed to be uninterested in the historical Jesus, apart from the mere fact of his death.[4] In principle there is nothing kerygmatic about the historical Jesus and uniqueness ought not to be

2. 'The historical and substantive presupposition for modern research into the life of Jesus is emancipation from traditional christological dogma on the basis of the principle of reason' (H. Conzelmann, *Jesus* [Philadelphia: Fortress Press, 1973], p. 5). I have found to be very helpful R. Morgan, 'The Historical Jesus and the Theology of the New Testament,' in L.D. Hurst and N.T. Wright (eds.), *The Glory of Christ in the New Testament: Studies in Christology in Memory of George Bradford Caird* (Oxford: Clarendon Press, 1987), pp. 187-206.

3. 'When Christology appears in the form of a "Life of Jesus," there are not many who will perceive the stage manager behind the scenes, manipulating, according to his own dogmatic script, the fascinating spectacle of a colorful biography' (M. Kähler, *The So-called Historical Jesus and the Historic Biblical Christ* [Philadelphia: Fortress Press, 1964], p. 56).

4. That it is really only the 'thatness' and not the 'how' can be seen in such statements as: 'What is certain is merely that he was crucified by the Romans, and thus suffered the death of a political criminal. This death can scarcely be understood as an inherent and necessary consequence of his activity; rather it took place because his activity was misconstrued as a political activity. In that case it would have been—historically speaking—a meaningless fate. We cannot tell whether or how Jesus found meaning in it. We may not veil from ourselves the possibility that he suffered a collapse' (R. Bultmann, 'The Primitive Christian Kerygma and the Historical Jesus', in C.E. Braaten and R.A. Harrisville [eds.], *The Historical Jesus and the Kerygmatic Christ* [New York: Abingdon Press, 1964], pp. 15-42, 24).

attributed to him. Nevertheless, in his famous chapter on the message of Jesus as only a presupposition for New Testament theology can be found statements like: 'Jesus' message is a great protest against Jewish legalism'.[5] All that is left of the uniqueness idea is the conviction that Jesus' relationship to Judaism is always to be seen in terms of a sharp contrast. Bultmann does not often argue for the authenticity of sayings of Jesus, but one place where he does so in passing is an expression of this desire for contrast and an anticipation of the future:

> Where in opposition to Jewish morality and piety the distinctive eschato-logical tone which characterizes the preaching of Jesus is expressed, and where on the other hand there are no specifically Christian features, one may more probably conclude that one has a genuine parable of Jesus.[6]

The new quest for the historical Jesus arose out of the desire to find at least an analogy between the Christ of faith and the Jesus of history. In order to avoid the charge of arbitrariness which could be levelled against the selectivity of the old questers, it became necessary to develop explicitly certain objective criteria of authenticity. The most important of these has undoubtedly been the so-called criterion of dissimilarity or discontinuity. It was given its classic formulation in the address given by Ernst Käsemann which launched the new quest:

> 'In only one case do we have more or less safe ground under our feet: when there are no grounds either for deriving a tradition from Judaism or for ascribing it to primitive Christianity, and especially when Jewish Christianity has mitigated or modified the received tradition, as having found it too bold for its taste.[7]

His first application is to the three words 'But I say' from the antitheses of the Sermon on the Mount, from which he concludes, 'The Jew who does what is done here [setting himself above Moses] has cut himself off from the community of Judaism'.

---

5. R. Bultmann, *Theology of the New Testament* (New York: Charles Scribner's Sons, 1955), I, p. 11. 'It is the Christian fear of Judaism that has led to the placing of such an inordinate premium on originality and uniqueness' (L.E. Keck, introduction to D.F. Strauss, *The Christ of Faith and the Jesus of History* [Philadelphia: Fortress Press, 1977], p. cv).

6. R. Bultmann, *Die Geschichte der synoptischen Tradition* (Göttingen: Vandenhoeck & Ruprecht, 4th edn, 1958), p. 222.

7. E. Käsemann, 'The Problem of the Historical Jesus', *Essays on New Testament Themes* (London: SCM Press, 1964), pp. 15-47, esp. p. 37.

Norman Perrin was probably the most influential advocate of this criterion, as 'the fundamental criterion for authenticity'. His formulation is as follows:

> the earliest form of a saying we can reach may be regarded as authentic if it can be shown to be dissimilar to characteristic emphases both of ancient Judaism and of the early Church, and this will be particularly the case where Christian tradition oriented toward Judaism can be shown to have modified the saying away from its original emphasis.[8]

His first application, following Jeremias, is to the two words 'Abba' and prepositive 'Amen,' where he sees 'a phrase unique in Judaism'[9] and a 'radical difference from Judaism'.[10]

All three of the formulations cited so far contain what could be called a further criterion, 'the criterion of modification by Jewish Christianity'.[11] It can be seen in its crudest and rather unpleasant form ('If Jesus is sometimes made to sound Jewish, it is the fault of his later Jewish followers') in E. Stauffer, *Die Botschaft Jesu; Damals und heute*.[12] It strangely reappears in E.P. Sanders, *Jesus and Judaism*,[13] where one would least expect it.

The dissimilarity test has come in for a considerable amount of criticism, particularly in Great Britain.[14] It is not hard to see why.

---

8. N. Perrin, *Rediscovering the Teaching of Jesus* (London: SCM Press, 1967), pp. 39.

9. Perrin, *Rediscovering*, p. 38. But see J. Barr, '"Abba" Isn't "Daddy"', *JTS* 39 (1988), pp. 28-47.

10. Perrin, *Rediscovering* p. 41. But see J. Strugnell, '"Amen, I Say Unto You" in the Sayings of Jesus and in Early Christian Literature', *HTR* 67 (1974), pp. 177-82.

11. R.H. Stein, 'The "Criteria" for Authenticity', in R.T. France and D. Wenham (eds.), *Gospel Perspectives* (Sheffield: JSOT Press, 1980), I, pp. 225-63, 245-46.

12. E. Stauffer, *Die Botschaft Jesu; Damals und heute* (Bern & Munich: Franke, 1959).

13. 'There is a layer of material, primarily in Matthew, which presents us with a Jesus who...calls his followers to be more righteous than the Pharisees by the same standard' (E.P. Sanders, *Jesus and Judaism* [Philadelphia: Fortress Press, 1985], pp. 260-61).

14. See especially F.G. Downing, *The Church and Jesus; A Study in History, Philosophy and Theology* (London: SCM Press, 1868); M. Hooker, 'Christology and Methodology', *NTS* 17 (1970-71), pp. 480-87; 'On Using the Wrong Tool', *Theology* 75 (1972), pp. 570-81; D.G.A. Calvert, 'An Examination of the Criteria

Given our limited knowledge of both early Judaism and early
Christian movements, the argument must be basically an argument
from silence (or ignorance). It contradicts the criterion of environment by distancing Jesus from his Jewish Galilean context. It helps to
create a Jesus distinct from and superior to Judaism, which at least for
some has been a hidden theological agenda. It does not discover what
was characteristic of Jesus but what was peculiar to him, which is not
at all the same thing.[15] Finally, it discovers or creates a Jesus who was
unique. One might suspect that this is the driving force behind the
persistent use of this criterion.[16] It is hard otherwise to explain its
continued prominence in the two most recent discussions of the
criteria[17] and in the procedures of the Jesus seminar.[18] Incidentally,
since the use of the traditional christological titles does not pass the
dissimilarity test, it has become popular to call Jesus a 'charismatic' as
a code name for uniqueness. However, insofar as the term has any
content at all, Jesus was the exact opposite as a sociological type, as
Malina has shown.[19]

Not quite the same as the criteria for authenticity are more general
a priori considerations of how Jesus' words and deeds are to be understood. W. Walker puts it this way:

> Any adequate picture of the historical Jesus, therefore, must satisfy three
> basic criteria:... [A] it must set Jesus convincingly within the context of

for Distinguishing the Authentic Words of Jesus', *NTS* 18 (1971–72), pp. 209-18;
R.S. Barbour, *Traditio-Historical Criticism of the Gospels; Some Comments on
Current Methods* (London: SPCK, 1972). R.H. Fuller seeks to defend the criterion
against these critics in 'The Criterion of Dissimilarity: The Wrong Tool?', in
R.F. Berkey and S.A. Edwards (eds.), *Christological Perspectives: Essays in
Honor of Harvey K. McArthur* (New York: Pilgrim, 1982), pp. 42-48.

15. Hooker, 'Christology', pp. 481.

16. 'This tool attempts to isolate those sayings and deeds attributed to Jesus
which would help to account for the transition from Judaism to Christianity'
(D.L. Mealand, 'The Dissimilarity Test', *SJT* 31 [1978], pp. 41-50, esp. p. 45). Is
this really where the transition is to be sought?

17. D. Polkow, 'Method and Criteria for Historical Jesus Research', *SBL 1987
Seminar Papers* (Atlanta: Scholars Press, 1987), pp. 336-56; M.E. Boring, 'The
Historical-Critical Method's "Criteria of Authenticity": The Beatitudes in Q and
Thomas as a Test Case', *Semeia* 44 (1988), pp. 9-44.

18. R.W. Funk, *The Gospel of Mark: Red Letter Edition* (Sonoma: Polebridge,
1991), pp. 29-52.

19. B.J. Malina, 'Jesus as Charismatic Leader?', *BTB* 14 (1984), pp. 55-62.

first century Palestinian Judaism... [B] it must show why his life ended in
execution at the hands of the Roman authorities... [C] it must account for,
or at least illumine, the birth of the Christian community.[20]

If A seems to point away from dissimilarity, B is a very strong
restatement of it. If A would allow for ordinariness, C comes close to
asserting uniqueness. I suggest that all three of these statements are not
really criteria for doing history at all but are highly charged
theological postulates disguised as historical method.

To take first the statement that we must understand Jesus' life in
such a way as to adequately account for his death, on the face of it it is
absurd. History knows too many examples of meaningless deaths, of
the execution of the innocent, of judicial mistakes, for this not to be an
equally plausible explanation.[21] And yet those who insist on seeing a
connection do so not really as historians but with an a priori theological 'must'.[22] That Jesus must have been a Jew is also a theological
statement and is, I believe, an essential one.[23] Whether or not the
beginning of the later Christian church is relevant depends on how
one answers the prior theological question: whether Christology has
its origins in an act of God confessed in the kerygma or in something
extraordinary in the character of its 'founder'. The theological Jesus is

20. W.O. Walker, 'The Quest for the Historical Jesus: A Discussion of
Methodology', *ATR* 51 (1969), pp. 38-56, esp. p. 55.

21. See R.J. Miller, 'The (A)Historicity of Jesus' Temple Demonstration: A Test
Case in Methodology', *SBL 1991 Seminar Papers* (Atlanta: Scholars Press, 1991),
pp. 235-52.

22. Jesus' 'death on the cross cannot be understood without the conflict between
his life on the one hand and the law and its representatives on the other. If this is
true, then through his death the prevailing law calls him into question, as one who by
his freedom in life and preaching had called into question this understanding of the
law... His execution *must* be seen as a necessary consequence of his conflict with the
law.' (J. Moltmann, *The Crucified God* [London: SCM Press, 1974], pp. 131-32);
'Jesus' trial and execution has a hermeneutical bearing on precisely what it was that
he taught and did. His message and conduct *must* have been of such a nature that
they were bound to cause deep offence to (at least) the (conventional) Jewish belief
and praxis of the time.' (E. Schillebeeckx, *Jesus: An Experiment in Christology*
[London: Collins, 1979], p. 97). Contrast Bultmann above, n. 4.

23. See especially P. van Buren, *A Theology of the Jewish-Christian Reality;
Part 3, Christ in Context* (San Francisco: Harper and Row, 1988). See also
B. Hebblethwaite, 'The Jewishness of Jesus from the Perspective of Christian
Doctrine', *SJT* 42 (1989), pp. 27-44.

by definition unique, but to use theological postulates to establish historical criteria is to mix categories inexcusably.

One of the best recent books on Jesus is in my opinion E.P. Sanders's *Jesus and Judaism*. He is a master at unmasking faith statements parading as historical ones, especially those having to do with uniqueness.[24] He rightly claims to 'have been engaged for some years in the effort to free history and exegesis from the control of theology; that is, from being obligated to come to certain conclusions which are predetermined by theological commitment',[25] but I wonder if he has been completely successful. His book is a major contribution to seeing Jesus within the context of Judaism, the first of Walker's three basic criteria, but he also insists on using Jesus' death and the rise of Christianity to understand his life.[26] His reason for doing so is, to be sure, not theological but because it is more 'satisfying historically'.[27] Is that an adequate reason? Following Martin Hengel,[28] he insists that Jesus' saying 'Leave the dead to bury their own dead' (Q 9.60) has 'no true parallels', is to be understood not metaphorically but literally, is authentic and in effect unique.[29] He concludes that 'the novelty and offense of Jesus' message was that the wicked who heeded him would be included in the kingdom even though they did not repent'.[30] If that is stretching the point (and I think it is), why does he do it? It may be that we also need to be rigourous and self-conscious in our theological methodologies.

At one point Sanders says that he is no longer 'interested in the debate about the significance of the historical Jesus for theology'.[31] Such a statement can only be applauded, for I believe that to posit such

24. See his *Jesus and Judaism* (Philadelphia: Fortress Press, 1985), pp.137-38, 238-40, 320, etc.; E.P. Sanders *The Question of Uniqueness in the Teaching of Jesus* (London: University of London, 1990).

25. Sanders, *Jesus*, pp. 333-34.

26. He is under no illusion that this is easy. 'It is difficult to make his teaching offensive enough to lead to execution or sectarian enough to lead to the formation of a group which eventually separated from the main body of Judaism' (Sanders, *Jesus*, p. 4).

27. Sanders, *Jesus*, p. 22.

28. M. Hengel, *The Charismatic Leader and His Followers* (Edinburgh: T. & T. Clark, 1981).

29. Sanders, *Jesus*, pp. 252-55.

30. Sanders, *Jesus*, p. 207.

31. Sanders, *Jesus*, p. 12.

significance can only lead to theological and historical distortions. But what about the significance of theology for the historical Jesus? Unless we are exceedingly careful conscious or unconscious theological presuppositions will enter into our approach to the historical Jesus, especially in the use of such 'objective' criteria as that of dissimilarity or in the hidden or open desire to find uniqueness. While it is possible to make the historical judgment, 'It is implausible that a controversial new religion owed its origins to someone utterly indistinguishable',[32] it is also possible to deny it. On the other hand, a theological statement like, 'If we deny that there is anything remarkable about Jesus, if Jesus really was an ordinary, fallible human being and no more, then our Christology has no basis in fact',[33] would require of historical research what it cannot provide and is also, I believe, bad theology.

The concept of uniqueness is a very slippery one. Its meaning ranges from the older 'of which there is only one' to a more modern 'uncommon, unusual, remarkable'. It is important not to slide from the latter meaning into the former. Or again, there is a sense in which every human being is unique in comparison with all other humans while at the same time being a very typical and ordinary human. It is conceivable that Jesus had individual characteristics which made him interesting and significantly different from his contemporaries, but one cannot assert that this must have been so and then try to exalt the differences into absolutes. Since it is not really possible to progress from the historical Jesus directly to the Christ of faith, anyone attempting to do 'Christology from below' must sneak their theological presuppositions into the 'historical' portrait of Jesus, much like the unknown God sneaking divine sparks into the creatures of the Demiurge in some forms of Gnosticism. No one has put the problem better than J.Z. Smith:

> The uniqueness of the 'Christ-event', which usually encodes the death and resurrection of Jesus, is a double claim...ontological...[and] historical... For many scholars of early Christianity, the latter claim is

32. Mealand, 'Test', p. 47.
33. S.W. Sykes, 'The Theology of the Humanity of Christ' in S.W. Sykes and J.P. Clayton (eds.), *Christ, Faith and History* (Cambridge: Cambridge University Press, 1972), pp. 53-72, esp. p. 65. Is not Kierkegaard's Divine Incognito at least a possible way of doing Christology? In fairness it must be said that Sykes is aware of the problems involved.

often combined with the former, so as to transfer the (proper, though problematic) theological affirmation of absolute uniqueness to an historical statement that, standing alone, could never assert more than relative uniqueness... This illicit transfer from the ontological to the historical [is what causes the problem].[34]

The pervasiveness and depth of the situation Smith describes is so great that stringent measures are required to combat it. I suggest that the hall in which the historical Jesus is studied should be entered, either with commitment or with a detached sympathy, only through the anteroom of theology. There the Christian might consider that theology takes precedence over Christology[35] and that what God has done in Christ makes him a figure whose uniqueness does not need to be demonstrated. The Christian will continue to make statements about the significance of Jesus Christ for the church today[36] and might not bother to go into the study hall at all, since nothing would be gained by it that is not gained by any other historical study. Similarly, the non-Christian, if interested, may inquire about the historical Jesus without the necessity of explaining the rise of a Christian church[37] and with the possibility of finding a figure essentially undistinguished from his contemporaries. All talk about Jesus should begin by asking what

34. J.Z. Smith, *Drudgery Divine; On the Comparison of Early Christianities and the Religions of Late Antiquity* (Chicago: University of Chicago Press, 1990), p. 39. Note earlier: 'Uniqueness...in the case of Jesus appears to be a modern inference from theological presuppositions or perhaps a human substitute for divine attributes' (H.J. Cadbury, *The Peril of Modernizing Jesus* [London: SPCK, 1962], p. 68); 'Perrin is using a Christian apologetic motif ("Jesus is unique") as a standard of judgment' (Downing, *Church and Jesus*, p. 116); 'the hidden presupposition [that] the historical Jesus' person and work must be shown to be unique... partly historical, partly christological or apologetic... a consequence of certain apologetic assumptions' (Barbour, *Criticism*, pp. 16-17); the dissimilarity criterion is 'biased toward uniqueness' (Sanders, *Jesus*, p. 16); D. Nineham, 'Epilogue', *The Myth of God Incarnate* (London: SCM Press, 1977), pp. 186-204.

35. See the work of John Hick.

36. To say that Jesus is a feminist might be to make an important theological statement for today; to say that Jesus was a feminist is to make an historical statement which is probably false and in any case tendentious.

37. 'We are sometimes told that the unique attractiveness of the central figure of Christianity as presented in the synoptic gospels was a primary factor in the success of Christianity. I believe this idea to be a product of nineteenth-century idealism and humanitarianism' (A.D. Nock, *Conversion* [Oxford: Clarendon Press, 1937], p. 210).

is typical of a first century Galilean Jew, which is indeed one source of knowledge about Jesus, before going on to ask about individual peculiarities.[38] The criterion of dissimilarity must be reversed so as to say that anything that makes Jesus sound like a first century Jew is to be preferred to anything that makes him sound like a Christian or an object of Christian devotion. In addition to good qualities one would also expect to find defects in Jesus' moral character.[39] Only so can the methodological error of using the criterion of dissimilarity to prove uniqueness be broken.

I close with two theological considerations which might help in keeping inappropriate apologetic out of the quest for the historical Jesus, one serious and one playful. Maurice Wiles, in his important Bampton Lectures, argues that it is inappropriate to speak of God's action in the world, whether in terms of history or of the lives of individuals. What has been called 'providence' is really 'best understood as a form of retrospective interpretation of experience'.[40] Wiles consistently applies this also to Christology, to 'God's action in Christ'. At no point did God deprive Jesus of his human freedom and responsibility by intervening in his life to effect an event or a decision. We could then speak of a retrospective incarnation. God did not cause the birth of Jesus (or of anyone else) but it might seem appropriate to give theological significance to a human being conceived in a brutal rape.[41] God did not cause the death of Jesus (or of anyone else) but it might seem appropriate to give theological significance to one who died by crucifixion.[42] The point is that Jesus' life was completely contingent, if one may put it that way, and not necessary, and we are free to investigate it without having anything to prove.

38. While this was often neglected in the past, see Sanders, *Jesus*; R.A. Horsley, *Jesus and the Spiral of Violence* (San Francisco: Harper and Row, 1987); and J.D. Crossan, *The Historical Jesus: The Life of a Mediterranean Jewish Peasant* (San Francisco: Harper & Row, 1991).

39. See, for example, J. Bowden, *Jesus: The Unanswered Questions* (London: SCM Press, 1988).

40. M. Wiles, *God's Action in the World* (London: SCM Press, 1986), p. 83.

41. See J. Schaberg, *The Illegitimacy of Jesus: A Feminist Theological Interpretation of the Infancy Narratives* (San Francisco: Harper & Row, 1987).

42. See B.L. Mack, *A Myth of Innocence: Mark and Christian Origins* (Philadelphia: Fortress Press, 1988) and Crossan, *The Historical Jesus*.

The playful consideration has to do with the legend of the Lamedvovniks, the thirty-six righteous.[43] It is perhaps a peculiarly Protestant obsession to insist that no human being is completely righteous and that to be so would be to be unique, but it has not always been so.[44] The legend says that there are in every generation thirty-six righteous people, undistinguished people, unknown to themselves or others, for the sake of whom the world is maintained. Let us suppose this indeed to be the case and that sometime in the first century God needed such a relatively righteous Jew, someone who would be 'adequate',[45] as the catalyst for founding a Gentile church. Any of them would do, but as it happened God chose Jesus (as Christians believe). He could have chosen Hanina ben Dosa, say, or any of the others, but in fact he chose Jesus. Hanina ben Dosa and Jesus have much in common,[46] but there are of course also individual differences. We are free to investigate those similarities and differences, if we want to, because neither person is unique, being only one of thirty-six. All this is meant to be only tentative and unprofound but to suggest that anyone interested in the historical Jesus first be conscious about theological presuppositions and thus avoid the methodological trap of assuming that Jesus must be unique and that the criterion of dissimilarity is the objective way to establish this.

43. See G. Scholem, *The Messianic Idea in Judaism and Other Essays on Jewish Spirituality* (London: George Allen and Unwin, 1971), pp. 251-56.

44. See, for example, Zechariah and Elizabeth, who 'were both righteous before God, walking in all the commandments and ordinances of the Lord blameless' (Lk. 1.6) or Paul, who 'as to righteousness under the law [was] blameless' (Phil. 3.6).

45. J.A.T. Robinson, 'Need Jesus Have Been Perfect?' in *Christ, Faith and History*, pp. 39-52, 44.

46. See G. Vermes, *Jesus the Jew; A Historian's Reading of the Gospels* (London: Collins, 1973).

THE SON OF MAN PROBLEM AS AN ILLUSTRATION OF THE *TECHNE* OF NEW TESTAMENT STUDIES

Walter E. Aufrecht

My friend and esteemed colleague, John Hurd, has contributed not only to the study of the New Testament, but to the study of Aramaic language and literature. So I am happy to offer in his honour these few remarks on *techne* in NT studies as seen through the prism of 'son of man'.

There are several reasons why son of man is a good topic to illustrate the art of New Testament studies. First, it is one of the most explored in NT studies and, as such, gives sufficient opportunity to examine a variety of views.[1] Secondly, it is a theologically 'neutral' topic. That is, there are no dogmas based on or derived from it, such as with 'Son of God', 'Messiah', 'Lord', etc.[2] Thirdly, the debate over this phrase exposes virtually every issue and methodology current in NT studies, and every presupposition that scholars bring to the NT.[3] My aim, therefore, is not to solve the son of man 'problem', even if that were possible, but to use it as an example of method in the study of the New Testament.

---

1. For recent surveys, see W.O. Walker, 'The Son of Man: Some Recent Developments', *CBQ* 45 (1983), pp. 584-607; J.R. Donahue, SJ, 'Recent Studies on the Origin of the "Son of Man" in the Gospels', *CBQ* 48 (1986), pp. 484-98; C.C. Caragounis, *The Son of Man, Vision and Interpretation* (Tübingen: Mohr, 1986).

2. For discussion of this aspect of the problem, see Walker, 'Recent Developments', pp. 604-606.

3. As many scholars have pointed out, the son of man debate touches on issues such as the documentary hypothesis, the identity of the religio/cultural matrix from which Christianity emerged (Judaism, Hellenism, etc.), semitic linguistics, the quest for the historical Jesus, the development of the synoptic tradition, methodological concerns (form criticism, redaction criticism, etc.), and the theology of the New Testament and of the later church.

The phrase 'son of man' has led to extensive discussion because, with four exceptions in the NT,[4] it is found only on the lips of Jesus.[5] It appears that this phrase is a self-descriptive designation. Furthermore, the phrase appears in the whole range of gospel traditions: the Sayings Source Q, Mark, Special Matthew, Special Luke and John. These multiple attestations, in the view of many scholars, lend credence to the authenticity of the phrase and further intensify investigation. What seems curious, however, is that Jesus never applies it to himself in so many words. Rather, he speaks without exception of the son of man in the third person. This has been interpreted to mean that the phrase is a title, a somewhat peculiar situation which has led to several questions. First, whether the evangelists have preserved correctly Jesus' use of this phrase. Secondly, what the relationship is of the proclaimer of the title to the title itself. Thirdly, what is the christological content of the phrase.[6]

The modern discussion began with Bultmann's *Theology of the New Testament*,[7] in which he recognized that three groups of son of man sayings can be differentiated from one another.[8] And although some

4. Acts 7.56, Rev. 1.13, 14.14, and possibly Heb. 2.6 quoting Ps. 8.4.

5. An apparent exception is Jn 12.34. Some would also add Mk 2.10. On this, see Donahue, 'Recent Studies', p. 498, n. 68.

6. It is not as well recognized as it should be that christological titles are not a description of Jesus' nature, but are an attempt to capture the *meaning* of his life, works and teachings. I call this the 'Lone Ranger Syndrome' of the New Testament. That is, in the *Lone Ranger* television series, after the events of the story have unfolded, the one who has been saved asks, 'Who was that masked man?' The answer invariably is 'Why, that's the Lone Ranger', as if the content of that title is self-evident. So too with Jesus: he performs saving acts, and then a title is given to make these acts *meaningful*. Soteriology precedes Christology, both logically and historically. As W. Marxsen has pointed out, 'Repetition of the *proclamation* of Jesus is...not the exhaustive expression of what Jesus means for faith', *The Beginnings of Christology: A Study in Its Problems* (Philadelphia: Fortress Press, 1969), p. 45.

7. R. Bultmann, *Theology of the New Testament* (New York: Charles Scribner's Sons, 1965), I, pp. 29-30.

8. W.O. Walker has pointed out ('Recent Developments', pp. 590-91 n. 32), that the threefold division had already been suggested by F.J. Foakes Jackson and K. Lake, *The Beginnings of Christianity* (London: Macmillan, 1920), I, pp. 368-84, and worked out in J. Héring, *Le royaume de Dieu et sa venue: Etude sur l'espérance de Jésus et le l'apôtre Paul* (Paris: Alcan, 1937), pp. 88-110.

scholars have suggested other groupings,[9] Bultmann's treatment has become normative. In the first group, Jesus speaks of the son of man at work in the present. This group of sayings, while not statistically extensive, appears in all strata of the tradition.[10] In the second group, Jesus speaks of the son of man who suffers and is raised from the dead. This group is absent in the Sayings Source Q, John and Revelation.[11] In the third group, Jesus speaks of a coming son of man. This occurs for the most part in an apocalyptic sense.[12]

Once the three groups have been identified and isolated, certain interesting patterns begin to emerge. First, it is discovered that the first group is virtually empty of all theological meaning. It is the widespread, though by no means unanimous, opinion of scholars that the phrase 'son of man' in this group represents a translation from the Aramaic, where it stood for 'man' or 'I'.[13] Secondly, in no instances

9. J. Knox, *The Death of Christ: The Cross in New Testament History and Faith* (London: 1959); G. Vermes, *Jesus the Jew: A Historian's Reading of the Gospels* (London: Collins, 1973); B. Lindars, 'Re-enter the Apocalyptic Son of Man', *NTS* 22 (1975), pp. 52-72; M.P. Casey, *Son of Man: The Interpretation and Influence of Daniel 7* (London: SPCK, 1979); A.Y. Collins, 'The Origin of the Designation of Jesus as "Son of Man"', *HTR* 80 (1987), pp. 391-407; Caragounis, *Vision and Interpretation*, p. 146.

10. Mk 2.10 (= Mt. 9.6, Lk. 5.24); Mk 2.28 (= Mt. 12.8, Lk. 6.51); Mk 10.45 (= Mt. 20.28, Lk. 22.27 has 'I'); Mt. 16.13 (Mk 8.27 and Lk. 9.18 have 'me'); Mt. 8.20 (= Lk. 9.58); Mt. 11.19 (= Lk. 7.34); Mt. 12.32 (= Lk. 12.10); Lk. 6.22 (= Mt. 5.11 has 'my'); Mt. 13.37; Lk. 19.10 (9.56 in some MSS).

11. Mk 8.31 (= Lk. 9.22, Mt. 16.21 has 'he'); Mk 9.21 (= Mt. 17.12); Mk 9.31 (= Mt. 17.22, Lk. 9.44); Mk 10.33 (= Mt. 20.18, Lk. 18.31); Mk 14.21 *bis* (= Mt. 26.24 *bis*, Lk. 22.22 changes once to 'he'); Mk 14.41 (= Mt. 26.45); Mt. 26.2; Lk. 22.48, 24.7.

12. Mk 8.38 (= Mt. 16.27, Lk. 9.26); Mk 9.9 (= Mt. 17.9); Mk 13.26 (= Mt. 24.30b, Lk. 21.27); Mk 14.62 (= Mt. 26.64, Lk. 22.69); Mt. 12.40 (= Lk. 11.30); Mt. 24.27 (= Lk. 17.24); Mt. 24.37 (= Lk. 17.26); Mt. 24.44 (= Lk. 12.40); Lk. 12.8 (Mt. 10.32 has 'I'); Mt. 10.23, 13.41, 16.28, 19.28, 24.30a, 24.39, 25.31; Lk. 17.22, 17.30, 18.8, 21.26.

13. Among those who disagree with this so-called circumlocutional use are F.H. Borsch, *The Son of Man in Myth and History* (Philadelphia: Westminster Press, 1967); C. Colpe, 'ὁ υἱὸς τοῦ ἀνθρώπου', *TDNT*, VIII, pp. 400-77; J. Jeremias, 'Die älteste Schicht der Menschensohn-Logien', *ZNW* 58 (1967), pp. 159-72; H. Boers, 'Where Christology is Real: A Survey of Recent Research on New Testament Christology', *Int* 26 (1972), pp. 300-27; J.A. Fitzmyer, SJ, review of M. Black, *An Aramaic Approach to the Gospels and Acts* (Oxford: Oxford

do two of the groups appear together in the text. That is, they seem to have entirely distinct meanings. Thirdly, the third group, sayings about the coming son of man, are incompatible with the second group, sayings about the suffering and rising son of man. The reason for this is that it is hard to see how Jesus could speak both of the son of man who is to come and the son of man who has come. We have no evidence that he spoke of two sons of man.[14]

Attempts have been made to harmonize the three groups. Some scholars, for example, have suggested that the second group preceded the third and logically leads to it. Thus, there is a progression in salvation history: suffering, dying and rising (second group), leading to parousia (third group). But as Marxsen has pointed out,[15] (1) the motifs of dying/rising on the one hand, and parousia on the other, are never found together in the text; (2) it is likely that the second group, the suffering sayings, are more recent from a literary point of view: they are absent in the Sayings Source Q and do not make their appearance until Mark; and (3) the second group cannot be explained in terms of early Judaism and thus cannot be prior to the third group in terms of the history of the development of thought. In short, the groups appear to have nothing in common with each other except the phrase 'son of man'.

These data have led to a variety of interpretations, of which there are three basic types. First, there are those who argue that all sayings are the product of the early church: none of the son of man sayings is an authentic saying of Jesus. This view is associated with the following scholars: Vielhauer, Conzelmann, Teeple, Perrin, Walker and Donahue.[16] For the moment, only one argument of these scholars

University Press, 1967), in *CBQ* 30 (1968), pp. 417-28; P.M. Casey, 'The Son of Man Problem', *ZNW* 67 (1976), pp. 147-54; *idem, Son of Man; idem*, 'Aramaic Idiom and Son of Man Sayings', *ExpTim* 96 (1984–1985), pp. 233-36; *idem*, 'The Jackals and the Son of Man (Mt. 8.20 // Lk. 9.58)', *JSNT* 23 (1985), pp. 3-22; *idem*, 'General, Generic and Indefinite: The Use of the Term "Son of Man" in Aramaic Sources and in the Teaching of Jesus', *JSNT* 29 (1987), pp. 21-56; B. Lindars, *Jesus Son of Man: A Fresh Examination of the Son of Man Sayings in the Gospels* (Grand Rapids: Eerdmans, 1983); Caragounis, *Vision and Interpretation*, pp. 23-29; Walker, 'Recent Developments', pp. 586-87, 593-95.

14. W. Bousset, *Kyrios Christos, Geschichte des Christunglausbens von den Anfäng des Christentums bis Irenaeus* (Göttingen: Vandenhock & Ruprecht, 1921).

15. W. Marxsen, *The Beginnings of Christology*, pp. 24-25.

16. P. Vielhauer, 'Gottesreich und Menschensohn in der Verkündigung Jesu', in

needs to be mentioned. The second group of sayings cannot be authentic because they are prophetic and prophecy must take place after the event. What is implicit in this argument, or its variations, is an attack on prophecy perceived as predictive, as a kind of crystal-ball phenomenon.[17]

The second group of scholars hold the view that all, or nearly all, of the son of man sayings are authentic. Names associated with the view in one or more of its forms are Stauffer, Bammel, Moule, Hooker, Marshall, Longenecker, Kim and Caragounis.[18]

Aufsätze zum Neuen Testament (Munich: Kaiser, 1965), pp. 55-91; *idem*, 'Jesus und der Menschensohn, Zur Diskussion mit Heinz Eduard Tödt und Eduard Schweizer', in *Aufsätze*, pp. 92-140; H. Conzelmann, *An Outline of the Theology of the New Testament* (New York: Harper & Row, 1969), pp. 135-36; H.M. Teeple, 'The Origin of the Son of Man Christology', *JBL* 84 (1955), pp. 213-50; N. Perrin, *A Modern Pilgrimage in New Testament Christology* (Philadelphia: Fortress Press, 1974); *idem, Rediscovering the Teaching of Jesus* (New York: Harper & Row, 1967); W.O. Walker, 'The Origin of the Son of Man Concept as Applied to Jesus', *JBL* 91 (1972), pp. 482-90; *idem*, 'The Son of Man Question and the Synoptic Problem', *NTS* 28 (1981–82), pp. 374-88; *idem*, 'Recent Developments', pp. 589-95; Donahue, 'Recent Studies', p. 496.

17. Those who would argue the opposite, viz., that the second group of sayings are authentic, must then explain why God would act so consistently in all other respects in dealing with the world and humankind, and so inconsistently in this one instance, i.e., Jesus could predict the future with such precision. Such a view undermines the Christian doctrine of salvation, at least as classically stated: Jesus was human in all respects and that because of this, salvation is available for other humans.

18. E. Stauffer, 'Messiah oder Menschensohn?', *NovT* 1 (1956), pp. 81-102; E. Bammel, 'Erwägung zur Eschatologie Jesue', *Studia Evangelica* 3 (1964), pp. 3-32; C.D.F. Moule, 'Neglected Features in the Problem of "Son of Man"', in J. Gnilka (ed.), *Neues Testament und Kirche, für Rudolf Schnackenburg* (Frieburg: Herder, 1974), pp. 413-28; M.D. Hooker, 'Is the Son of Man Problem Really Insoluble?', in E. Best and R. McL. Wilson (eds.), *Text and Interpretation: Studies in the New Testament Presented to Matthew Black* (Cambridge: Cambridge University Press, 1979), pp. 155-68; *idem, The Son of Man in Mark: A Study of the Background of the Term 'Son of Man' and its Use in St. Mark's Gospel* (London: SPCK, 1967); I.H. Marshall, 'The Synoptic Son of Man Sayings in Recent Discussion', *NTS* 12 (1965–66), pp. 327-51; *idem*, 'The Son of Man in Contemporary Debate', *EvQ* 42 (1970), pp. 67-87; R.N. Longenecker '"Son of Man" Imagery: Some Implications for Theology and Discipleship', *JETS* 18 (1975), pp. 3-16; *idem*, '"Son of Man" as a Self-Designation of Jesus', *JETS* 12 (1969), pp. 151-58; S. Kim, *The 'Son of Man' as the Son of God* (Grand Rapids:

Scholars of the third group are the most numerous, for they try to deal with two issues. First, like the others, they are interested in the question of whether or not a given saying or set of sayings is authentic. When this question is raised, the answer is likely to be that one of the groups of sayings is more authentic than the others, and once that is determined, then other sayings can be related to it. Secondly, these scholars are concerned with locating the whole range of sayings in the history of the development of the church and its Christology. The principle is if one wishes to deny a *Sitz im Leben* in the life of Jesus for a Gospel pericope, one must produce a convincing substitute in the life of the early church. In this way, one deals with the *evidence as presented to us* without making up data which we do not have (a concern of the first group of scholars); and on the other hand, takes seriously the possibility that Jesus did speak about the son of man (a concern of the second group of scholars).

There are basically two points of view: (1) those who give priority to sayings in the third group: Bultmann, Hahn, Tödt, Fuller, Taylor, Higgins, Marxsen, Jüngel, Bornkamm, Knox, Collins and Boring;[19]

Eerdmans, 1985); Caragounis, *Vision and Interpretation*.

19. R. Bultmann, *The Theology of the New Testament*; *idem*, *History of the Synoptic Tradition* (New York: Harper & Row, rev. edn. 1969); *idem*, 'Reich Gottes und Menschensohn', *TRu* 9 (1937), pp. 1-35; F. Hahn, *The Titles of Jesus in Christology: Their History in Early Christianity* (London: Lutterworth, 1969); H.E. Tödt, *The Son of Man in the Synoptic Tradition* (Philadelphia: Westminster Press, 1965); R.H. Fuller, *The Foundations of New Testament Christology* (New York: Charles Scribner's Sons, 1965); V. Taylor, *The Names of Jesus* (New York: St Martin's, 1953); *idem*, 'The "Son of Man" Sayings Relating to the Parousia', *ExpTim* 58 (1946–47), pp. 12-15; A.J.B. Higgins, 'Son of man-*Forschung* since *The Teaching of Jesus*,' in A.J.B. Higgins (ed.), *New Testament Essays: Studies in Memory of Thomas Walter Manson* (Manchester: 1959), pp. 119-35; *idem*, 'The Sign of the Son of Man (Matt. xxiv:30)', *NTS* 9 (1962–63), pp. 380-82; *idem*, *Jesus and the Son of Man* (London: Lutterworth, 1964); *idem*, 'Is the Son of Man Problem Insoluble?', in E.E. Ellis and M. Wilcox (eds.), *Neotestamentica et Semitica: Studies in Honour of Matthew Black* (Edinburgh: T. & T. Clark, 1969), pp. 70-87; Marxsen, *The Beginnings of Christology*; E. Jüngel, *Paulus und Jesus: Eine Untersuchung zur Präzisierung der Frage nach dem Ursprung der Christologie* (Tübingen: Mohr, 4th edn, 1972); G. Bornkamm, *Jesus of Nazareth* (New York: Harper & Row, 1960); Knox, *The Death of Christ*; Collins, 'The Origin of the Designation'; M.E. Boring, *Sayings of the Risen Jesus, Christian Prophecy in the Synoptic Tradition* (Cambridge: Cambridge University Press, 1982), pp. 239-50, 290-94.

and (2) those who give priority to sayings in the first group: Schweizer, Vermes, Bowker, Casey, Lindars, Black, Leivestead, O'Neil, Tuckett, Mearns and Hare.[20] (The second group of sayings are considered by all to be secondary because of their passion predictions).

Those who give priority to the third group of sayings point out that all of these sayings have something in common: Jesus and the son of man are explicitly distinguished from one another. It is argued that these sayings are authentic by the criterion of dissimilarity. They are dissimilar from Jewish apocalyptic and from later church Christology. It hardly appears imaginable, so the argument goes, that such a saying could have arisen in the church after the title 'son of man' had already

20. E. Schweizer, 'Der Menschensohn (Zur eschatologischen Erwartung Jesu)', *ZNW* 50 (1959), pp. 185-209; *idem*, *Lordship and Discipleship* (London: SCM Press, 1960); *idem*, 'The Son of Man', *JBL* 79 (1960), pp. 119-29; *idem*, *Erniedrigung und Erhöhung bei Jesus und seinen Nachfolgern* (Zurich: Zwingli, 2nd edn., 1962); *idem*, 'The Son of Man Again', *NTS* 9 (1962–63), pp. 256-61; G. Vermes, 'The Use of *br ns'/br ns* in Jewish Aramaic'; M. Black, *An Aramaic Approach to the Gospels and Acts* (Oxford: Oxford University Press, 1967), pp. 310-30; *idem*, 'The Present State of the "Son of Man" Debate', *JJS* 29 (1978), pp. 123-34; *idem*, 'The "Son of Man" Debate', *JSNT* 1 (1978), pp. 19-32; J. Bowker, 'The Son of Man', *JTS* 28 (1977), pp. 19-48; Casey, *Son of Man*; *idem*, 'The Son of Man Problem'; *idem*, 'Aramaic Idiom'; *idem*, 'The Jackals'; *idem*, 'General, Generic, and Indefinite'; Lindars, 'Re-Enter'; *idem*, *Jesus Son of Man*; *idem*, 'Response to Richard Bauckham: The Idiomatic Use of Bar Enasha', *JSNT* 23 (1985), pp. 35-41; M. Black, 'Unsolved NT Problems: The "Son of Man" in the Old Biblical Literature', *ExpTim* 60 (1948–49), pp. 11-15; *idem*, 'Unsolved NT Problems: The "Son of Man" in the Teaching of Jesus', *ExpTim* 60 (1948–49), pp. 32-36; *idem*, 'Servant of the Lord and Son of Man', *SJT* 6 (1953), pp. 1-11; *idem*, 'The Son of Man Problem in Recent Research and Debate', *BJRL* 45 (1962–63), pp. 305-18; *idem*, *An Aramaic Approach to the Gospels and Acts* (Oxford: Oxford University Press, 1967); *idem*, 'The Throne-Theophany Prophetic Commission and the "Son of Man": A Study in Tradition History', in R. Hamerton-Kelly and R. Scroggs (eds.), *Jews, Greeks and Christians: Religious Cultures in Late Antiquity, Essays in Honour of William David Davies* (Leiden: Brill, 1976), pp. 57-73; *idem*, 'Jesus and the Son of Man', *JSNT* 1 (1978), pp. 4-18; *idem*, 'Aramaic Barnasha and the Son of Man', *ExpTim* 95 (1984), pp. 200-206; R. Leivestad, 'Exit the Apocalyptic Son of Man', *NTS* 18 (1971–1972), pp. 243-67; J.C. O'Neil, 'The Silence of Jesus', *NTS* 15 (1968–1969), pp. 153-67; C. Tuckett, 'The Present Son of Man', *JSNT* 14 (1982), pp. 58-81; C. Mearns, 'The Son of Man Trajectory and Eschatological Development', *ExpTim* 97 (1985), pp. 8-12; D.R.A. Hare, *The Son of Man Tradition* (Minneapolis: Fortress Press, 1990).

been transferred to Jesus; and Jewish apocalyptic would not have included the element of the present in them; rather, they would have been completely future oriented.[21]

If some or all of these sayings are accepted as authentic, then we must treat differently the other groups of sayings because they are incompatible. It is suggested that the early church, after the resurrection, identified the risen Jesus with the coming son of man and proceeded to read back the title into the early ministry of Jesus.[22] In effect, when we look at sayings from groups one and two, the son of man is no longer one who is to come, but one who has *already* come.[23] The title which indicated the future has been filled (given meaning) with material drawn from the past, with the deeds, suffering, dying and rising of Jesus.[24] And so the proclaimer becomes proclaimed.

There is a hidden presupposition here that undergirds the argument: Jesus had in mind a son of man figure about whom his listeners knew when he spoke of it. Such a presupposition has been challenged by the scholars who claim that the first group of sayings are primary. '...[i]s it credible that Jesus, who certainly avoided apocalyptic speculations about the time of the coming events, and descriptions of the catastrophe or the future glory, etc., used, in such a central position and without further introduction, a term unknown to the Judaism of the Pharisees and the Qumran group, known at best in small apocalyptic circles?'[25] In short, there was no 'son of man' *title* in Judaism. Rather, what Judaism had was an expression for 'man', which Jesus took up because it was not yet a definite title. It was only an attempt by the later church to take the teaching of Jesus and make it more apocalyptic that the phrase 'son of man' becomes a title for a figure in the future. On the lips of Jesus the phrase had no theological content, it simply referred to him as a human being.

There are, therefore, two opposing views: the first group of sayings has priority or the third group has priority. This situation has led to the question: 'Is the son of man problem insoluble?'[26] If the debate is

21. Marxsen, *The Beginnings of Christology*, pp. 28-31.
22. Marshall, 'The Synoptic Son of Man Sayings', p. 332.
23. Marxsen, *The Beginnings of Christology*, p. 38.
24. Marxsen, *The Beginnings of Christology*, p. 38.
25. Schweizer, 'The Son of Man Again', p. 257.
26. Higgins, 'Insoluble'.

maintained in these terms, the answer clearly is, 'yes'.[27]

It is obvious that the debate on son of man has taken shape because of the influence of Bultmann's analysis of the phrase in his *Theology of the New Testament*. Indeed, there seems hardly an area of New Testament study that does not begin with Bultmann's stating of the matter. His influence is so great (and perhaps at this point even unconscious in the minds of many New Testament scholars), that the three classifications now may be referred to as 'trajectories'![28] In one way or another, scholars seem to be forced into arguing on Bultmann's terms: if not accepting the classification, then attacking it.[29] Unfortunately with regard to son of man (and, one wonders, with regard to other aspects of New Testament *techne*), Bultmann's stating of the matter has led New Testament scholarship to a dead end. In such a circumstance, it is useful to re-examine the premises upon which the debate rests.

Almost no one has recognized that the three-fold division of son of man sayings is not a form-critical distinction.[30] It is a distinction based on content. It is, therefore, methodologically impossible to find a *Sitz im Leben* for these sayings on form-critical grounds. A *Sitz im Leben* in form criticism is the setting in life of a *form* and a serious confusion has arisen in applying to *content* the rules of form criticism. One legitimately may be concerned with locating a saying or a group of sayings in the history of the development of the church and its Christology. But the major tool for doing this, form criticism, does

27. There are two other interrelated dimensions of the New Testament son of man discussion that are used to bolster this or that point of view already arrived at on other grounds. Because the literature on both of these is enormous, limitations of space permit only their mention here. First, there is the problem of where this phrase came from and how it was used prior to the Christian formulation of it. See summary and discussion by Caragounis, *Vision and Interpretation*, pp. 35-144, 168-243. Secondly, there is the issue of philology, i.e., the language of the phrase and its precise meaning in Hebrew, Aramaic and Greek. See Caragounis, *Vision and Interpretation*, pp. 9-33.

28. See Mearns, 'The Son of Man Trajectory'.

29. A recent discussion of son of man ends with Bultmann's formulation: 'Bultmann set forth this... analysis in classical form'. R.M. Grant, *Jesus After the Gospels: The Christ of the Second Century* (Louisville: Westminster/John Knox, 1990), p. 24.

30. See now Hare, *Son of Man Tradition*, pp. 5-8.

not apply to the threefold discussion of the son of man sayings as established by Bultmann.

Norman Perrin, in a series of articles now collected in his *A Modern Pilgrimage in New Testament Christology*[31] has demonstrated this without saying it directly. He argued that in their *present form*, all the son of man sayings are the work of the evangelists, but that *behind them* stands a long development. This development is seen first in the son of man traditions outside of the Gospels: *pesher*-like traditions based on Daniel 7 and other Old Testament texts. This independent son of man tradition, which owes its development to early Christian scribes, was merged by the evangelists with other independent traditions.

If one looks at the so-called third group of sayings, they reflect definite *forms*: apocalyptic promises, eschatological judgment pronouncements, eschatological correlatives, exhortations to watchfulness—to which the son of man has been added. *There is no third group of sayings*. Likewise, an investigation of the so-called first group of sayings will betray a variety of origins, some of which *may* go back to Jesus, but which, of course, are void of theological meaning. The second group, according to Perrin, are the work of Mark based on his development of an earlier *paradidonai* tradition, another form-critical analysis.

In short, 'there is no "Son of Man" concept but rather a variety of uses of Son of Man imagery'.[32] Few, if any, of the New Testament son of man sayings in their present form are original. If the phrase 'son of man' has been added to a previously existing tradition in order to deal with a problem in the life and work of the church, then the issue cannot be which category of son of man sayings is prior. The issue is one of how and why they were developed in the church. This, of course, leads to redaction-critical questions and answers, something impossible with regard to the Bultmanian stating of the case. Here, it seems, we have a genuine advance in the discussion on the son of man, one that can be built on by others.[33]

31. N. Perrin, *A Modern Pilgrimage in New Testament Christology* (Philadelphia: Fortress Press, 1974).

32. Perrin, *A Modern Pilgrimage*, p. 26.

33. For example, M. Eugene Boring has explored the place of the phrase 'son of man' in early Christian prophecy in his *Sayings of the Risen Jesus*. Though still tied to the Bultmanian classification, Boring has advanced the discussion by recognizing

Another important development is the recent exploration of the notion of 'authenticity' by scholars such as R.H. Stein[34] and C.C. Caragounis.[35] Caragounis, especially, is concerned with the son of man problem. He states that what New Testament studies offers at present 'is the conspicuous absence of objective, valid and universally accepted criteria'[36] for determining authenticity. He shows how the issue of authenticity is often bound up with assumptions and presuppositions having nothing to do with the biblical text. But this discussion begs a prior question: what *is* 'authenticity'? What is meant by it, and why is it important? Clearly, more discussion of this term is necessary, as well as discussion of the hidden theological presuppositions with which it is associated.[37]

As a means of clarifying the son of man problem, and, indeed, virtually all other aspects of New Testament study, more work needs to be done on exactly how the New Testament traditions developed. There appear to be at least two alternatives, ably spelled out by

that the sayings are the work of early Christians, not Jesus. Work of this kind increasingly will require not only redaction criticism, but the use of techniques developed in the social sciences, a burgeoning aspect of New Testament scholarship. See the remarks by Donahue ('Recent Studies', pp. 495-96), which call attention to the work of G. Theissen, especially his *The Sociology of Early Palestinian Christianity* (Philadelphia: Fortress Press, 1978), pp. 24-30.

34. R.H. Stein, 'The "Criteria" for Authenticity', in *Gospel Perspectives, Studies of History and Tradition in the Four Gospels* (Sheffield: JSOT Press, 1980), pp. 225-63.

35. Caragounis, *Vision and Interpretation*.

36. Caragounis, *Vision and Interpretation*, p. 149.

37. The problem of theological presuppositions is discussed brilliantly by David Tracy in his book *The Analogical Imagination* (New York: Crossroad, 1981), pp. 3-46. Tracy argues that there are three audiences for the theologian (and, one might add, the New Testament scholar): society, academy and church. A great deal of the son of man debate may be seen as a manifestation of the three vocabularies used by various scholars in addressing these three audiences. The argument between those who accept all the sayings and those who reject all the them, can be seen roughly in terms of a debate between those who are speaking to the church and those who are not. Those who argue for the third group as having priority are primarily concerned with speaking to the academy. The support of one group of sayings over another invariably reflects the audience to which an appeal is being made. Each group emphasizes one aspect of the theological enterprise over the other and none of the groups seems capable of speaking in terms that are acceptable to the needs of another group.

Gerhardsson.[38] One might argue, for example, that the message of
Jesus was 'in the air' so to speak and transmitted more or less by
happenstance.[39] Or one might argue that there was a Christian scribal
tradition modelled more or less after the Jewish tradition. The
problem here is knowing just what Jewish scribal traditions to point to
in drawing an analogy. Perrin chose Qumranic traditions as a model,
as have Stendahl and others.[40] Robinson and Koester suggested a
mixture of Graeco-Roman and Jewish scribal traditions.[41] Still others
suggest that the traditions behind the Targums or another type of
Jewish literature may serve as model.[42] All of this will have important
consequences for the son of man debate and certainly will throw
clearer, if indirect, light on our understanding of the phrase.

Finally, on the subject of the Aramaic sub-stratum of the New
Testament, a great deal of work needs to be done, not the least of
which is to decide whether or not there is such a substratum.[43] On
this, the best work is done by Fitzmyer.[44] His words need to be
repeated:

38. B. Gerhardsson, *Memory and Manuscript, Oral Tradition and Written
Transmission in Rabbinic Judaism and Early Christianity* (Uppsala: Gleerup, 1961);
idem, Tradition and Transmission in Early Christianity (Lund: Gleerup, 1964).

39. This view follows from the dogma of the Bultmann school that the New
Testament is a falling away from the pristine *kerygma* of earliest Christianity.

40. K. Stendahl, *The School of St Matthew and its Use of the Old Testament*
(Uppsala: Gleerup, 2nd edn, 1967 [1954]); Walker, 'Recent Developments',
pp. 595-98.

41. J.M. Robinson and H. Koester, *Trajectories through Early Christianity*
(Philadelphia: Fortress Press, 1971).

42. B. Chilton, 'Targumic Transmission and Dominical Tradition', in *Gospel
Perspectives, Studies of History and Tradition in the Four Gospels* (Sheffield: JSOT
Press, 1980), I, pp. 21-45.

43. For the arguments regarding a possible literary formulation in Aramaic behind
the Sayings Source Q, see J. Kloppenborg, The *Formation of Q, Trajectories in
Ancient Wisdom Collections* (Philadelphia: Fortress Press, 1987), pp. 59; and the
response by M. Black, 'The Aramaic Dimension in Q with Notes on Luke 17.22
Matthew 24.26 (Luke 17.23)', *JSNT* 40 (1990), pp. 33-41.

44. J.A. Fitzmyer, SJ, 'The Study of the Aramaic Background of the New
Testament', *A Wandering Aramean, Collected Aramaic Essays* (Missoula: Scholars
Press, 1979), pp. 1-27; *idem,* 'The Contribution of Qumran Aramaic to the Study of
the New Testament', pp. 85-113; *idem,* 'The New Testament Title "Son of Man"
Philologically Considered', pp. 143-60.

In treating the Aramaic background of the New Testament, and especially of the sayings of Jesus within it, one has to reckon with (*a*) the well known refractory process of underlying oral tradition; (*b*) the coloring of the tradition by a later faith-experience of the early Christians; (*c*) likely additions to the traditional collections of sayings, made perhaps in a spirit of genuine extensions of his words or an adaptive reinterpretation of them to new situations; (*d*) words actually put on his lips by early Christians... and (*e*) the language of the given evangelist.[45]

To this may be added an investigation of the NT manuscripts and their treatment of son of man. It may be that the Greek phrase in later manuscripts reflects a late-Aramaic expression (*pace* Vermes).[46] One way of helping to determine this would be to compare the various manuscripts and their traditions, an enormous task in New Testament textual study.

These few remarks have tried to illustrate methodology in New Testament scholarship by reference to the study of the phrase 'son of man'. Despite the difficulties involved, the phrase will continue to be analyzed by New Testament scholars, because, at the very least, it presents a compelling challenge to strive for methodological clarity. This is proof enough that the *techne* of NT studies is alive, well, and successful in the pursuit of knowledge.[47]

45. Fitzmyer, 'The Study of the Aramaic Background', p. 10.

46. On other grounds, some scholars have argued that son of man Christology developed among Greek-speaking, not Aramaic-speaking, Christians. See H. Lietzmann, *Der Menschensohn* (Freiburg: Mohr, 1896); Teeple, 'Origin'; Walker, 'Recent Developments', pp. 602-604.

47. I am indebted to Professors John S. Kloppenborg, Bradley H. McLean, Wayne O. McCready, and Benedict T. Viviano, OP for their helpful suggestions which have improved this paper in numerous ways.

ANCIENT AND MODERN QUESTIONS ABOUT AUTHENTICITY

Robert M. Grant

The church historian Eusebius of Caesarea raised several questions about the authenticity of New Testament books that later Christians found disturbing, or at least interesting. Since he was primarily concerned with external testimonies to the books, he rarely dealt with ideas, style or vocabulary, though non-Christian analysts were accustomed to treat such matters. He quoted the treatise *On Promises* by Dionysius of Alexandria but neglected the critical methods used in it. For this reason his treatment of both the Epistle to the Hebrews and the Apocalypse of John is inconclusive and incomplete.

1. *Questions about Tradition*

Questions about Hebrews and Revelation had been raised by the very learned Roman presbyter Gaius, who was opposing Montanist arguments in the time of Zephyrinus. Eusebius quotes some fragments, citing Gaius' opponent on the tombs of Philip and his daughters at Hierapolis (3.31.4)[1] and Gaius himself on the tombs of Peter and Paul at Rome (2.25.6-7). The Montanists and Gaius probably raised literary questions about the Epistle to the Hebrews (6.20.3) and the Apocalypse of John (3.28.2); Gaius rejected both books. Eusebius does not wish to know that he also raised questions about the Gospel of John.

Eusebius promises to discuss Hebrews (3.3.5). He can believe that Hebrews is by Paul and also Philonic–Therapeutic in tone (2.17.12) since he relies on 'historical' analysis to suggest that the Therapeutae were early Jewish Christians who used allegory (2.16-17). He thinks that Clement of Rome, fellow-worker of Paul, wrote a letter to the

---

1.　All references without author or work are to Eusebius's *Ecclesiastical History* (*EH*).

Corinthians (3.5-16; Phil. 4.3) in which he used Hebrews (character of style, ideas, 3.38.1-3), though some say Hebrews is rejected at Rome (3.3.5 = Gaius and later, 6.20.3). Eusebius also quotes Clement of Alexandria along with the 'historical' tradition he followed. Paul wrote Hebrews for Hebrews in Hebrew, and Luke translated and published it. This historical fantasy explains why the same χρώς[2] (color) of style is found in Hebrews and Acts. Again, when writing to the Hebrews Paul refrained from calling himself an apostle (6.14.2-4, with a similar statement by 'the blessed presbyter').

Eusebius himself makes promises about John but fails to keep them. He provides a general promise on canonical/uncanonical writings (3.3.3; 5.8.1) and proposes to list authors who used the writings of 'the apostle and evangelist John, condemned to Patmos' (3.18), next reporting on what Irenaeus and Clement of Alexandria said about John (3.23). The point that some recognize Revelation and some do not is to be illustrated by quotations (3.24.18). But Eusebius avoids discussing disagreements between John and the synoptics (treated by Gaius at length) by simply insisting that John intended to supplement them by adding 'what was done by Christ at first, at the beginning of the proclamation' before the imprisonment of John the Baptist and by emphasizing Christ's divine origin rather than his genealogy (3.24.8-12). John taught Papias of Hierapolis and was buried in one of the two 'tombs of John' at Ephesus (3.39.6-7). Papias's reading of the millennium was perverse and literal, for he did not understand that the apostles wrote 'mystically' and therefore he had a bad influence, notably on Irenaeus—though in 3.39.12-13 Eusebius does not repeat the extraordinary quotation from John via Papias that Irenaeus provides.[3] Justin ascribed the Apocalypse to the apostle John (4.18.8), and Theophilus quoted the Apocalypse in writing *Against the Heresy of Hermogenes* (4.24).[4] Irenaeus used the Apocalypse and dated it under

2.   Equivalent to χρῶμα, colour or complexion of style as in Dionysius of Halicarnassus to Ammianus (*Amm.* 2.2), χρώματα, 'special features that colour his style.' Perhaps Eusebius owes the relatively unusual word χρώς to Dionysius of Alexandria as cited in 7.25.21.

3.   Papias in Iren., *Her.* 5.33.3-4.

4.   Tertullian's *Ad Herm.* which I showed relies on Theophilus (Vigiliae Christianae 3 [1949], 228-29 = *Christian Beginnings: Apocalypse to History* [London: Variorum, 1983], Essay XV), cites the Apocalypse, especially in *Ad Herm.* 24, though without naming its author.

Domitian (3.18.3; 5.8.5-6).[5] The anti-Montanist Apollonius quoted
from the Apocalypse and said that John raised a dead man at Ephesus
(5.18.14).[6] In the fifth book of his *Commentary on John*, written at
Alexandria, Origen says that John wrote both Gospel and Apocalypse
(6.25.9-10).

Eusebius' rather mechanical method for dealing with the history of
the canon is poorly executed. He neglected the influence of the
Apocalypse on Montanism, partly because he had read no Tertullian
except the *Apology* in Greek. Of course, since Montanists were
heretics their testimony was invalid. He did not know that Tertullian
defended a millennial kingdom on earth by appealing not only to a
Montanist oracle but also to Ezekiel and the apostle John (Rev. 21.2).[7]

He omits the rejection of the Apocalypse by Gaius of Rome because
he fails to understand that Gaius was writing not about 'Cerinthus' but
about Revelation (3.28.2) and was the source of Dionysius (7.25.1-3;
cf. 3.28.4). Indeed, the idea that Cerinthus was a Gnostic millenarist
owes its existence to Eusebius' uncritical use of Gaius. Gaius was
simply trying to denigrate the Apocalypse by assigning it (and the
Gospel of John as well) to him (3.28.1). Eusebius explains away the
contradictory Gnostic teachings of Cerinthus as summarized in
Irenaeus *Heresies* 1.16.1 by not quoting them but calling them
Cerinthus's 'more esoteric doctrines' (3.28.6), since they do not
include a millennium. More reliably (?) he insists (twice) that the
apostle John refused to enter a bath with Cerinthus inside (3.28.6,
4.14.6).[8] He does not discuss any of Gaius' arguments against either
the Gospel or the Apocalypse.[9] In addition, he does not know that
Origen came to doubt the apostolic origin of Revelation.[10]

5.   Iren., *Her.* 5.30.1.
6.   For such resurrections cf. *Acts of John* 24 and 46.
7.   Tert., *Ad Marc.* 3.24.4.
8.   From Iren., *Her.* 3.3.4.
9.   These are known from Epiphanius (*Her.* 51) and the translation of the
commentary of Dionysius bar Salibi on the Apocalypse by I. Sedlacek (*Corpus
Scriptorum Christianorum Orientalium* [Scriptores Syri, 110; Rome: de Luigi,
1910]).
10.   O. Guéraud and P. Nautin, *Origène sur la pâque* (Paris: Beauchesne, 1979),
p. 119 n. 23; p. 172, lines 16-17.

2. *Literary Arguments*

Strictly literary arguments came to the fore only in the third century. When Origen discussed Hebrews he was concerned more with literary matters than with tradition and noted that the character of the λέξις was better than Paul's. For Origen, λέξις involved φράσις, σύνθεσις (composition) of the λέξις, and νοήματα (ideas). He concluded that the marvelous ideas are the apostle's, but the style and composition are due to someone who took notes, maybe Clement or Luke (6.25.11-14). Eusebius himself counted fourteen Pauline epistles, obviously including Hebrews (3.3.4).

Though Eusebius does not say so, Dionysius of Alexandria proved that the Apocalypse was not written by the apostle by making full use of the critical method and technical terms (7.24-25).[11] He began by summarizing the arguments of Gaius (without naming him) and summarizing his conclusion, that the Apocalypse was unintelligible and ἀσυλλόγιστος (irrational) and had a false title (1); it was a πλάσμα (fiction) (2). He then 'closely examined the whole book...and showed that it cannot be understood literally' (6). In other words, Dionysius apparently used Gaius' arguments against the book simply to overthrow the literal sense.

Dionysius bases his own judgment on the ἦθος (character of the authors), the εἶδος τῶν λόγων (different kinds of discourse[12]), and the διεξαγωγή (arrangement). Thus the Evangelist/Epistoler did not name himself, whereas the Apocalyptist John did so. This shows that the authors are different (8–16). The effort to divide the two (three) books continues into theological terminology (νοήματα, conceptions; ῥήματα, terms; and σύνταξις, arrangement, 17). On the one hand, the Epistle uses the same language as the Gospel, 'slightly altered.' The books have the same anti-docetic purpose and the same 'headings and terms,' twenty-one of which Dionysius lists, sometimes paraphrasing them in the interest of his theological argument. He claims that the language of the Apocalypse is quite different, though some of his statements are wrong. 'Turning from darkness' occurs in

11. Text and commentary in C.L. Feltoe, *The Letters and Other Remains of Dionysius of Alexandria* (Cambridge: Cambridge University Press, 1904), pp. 106-26.

12. As in Isoc., *Or.* 13.17.

neither Gospel/ Epistle nor Apocalypse. 'Grace' occurs four times in the prologue to the Gospel and not in 1 John, but twice in the Apocalypse. 'Remission of sins' is found explicitly in no Johannine book, though the verb is present. 'Faith' too is not a noun but a verb in John. 'Adoption' appears in Paul, not in any of these documents. Dionysius obviously believed that he was setting forth what John meant, whether or not it was expressed in just these words. The 'colour' of Gospel and Epistle is the same (17-23),

Finally, the φράσις (style) reveals the difference between Gospel/Epistle and Apocalypse. The Greek of the former books is faultless, and their diction (λέξεις), reasonings (συλλογισμοί) and constructions (συντάξεις) express literary skill, while the language of the Apocalypse contains barbarism, solecism[13] and vulgarity. All these points indicate the ἀνομοιότης (dissimilarity) of the writings (24-27). Eusebius seems to have found the arguments rather convincing but refused to revise his own confused ideas about Revelation.

3. *Historical Problems*

Eusebius' interpretation is also wrong because he fails to understand the apocalyptic eschatology of early Christianity and is concerned primarily with justifying the semi-Alexandrian theology of his own time.[14] He thinks that Philo described the early Christians when he wrote about the Therapeutae of Egypt (2.16-17) and believes that heretics employ a character of style far different from the apostolic ethos. Their judgment and their Tendenz is far from 'true orthodoxy' and their writings are ἀναπλάσματα (forgeries) (3.25.7), often verbose and lengthy (3.38.4). Thus the apocalyptic eschatologist Papias could not have been a 'hearer and eyewitness of the apostles' (even though Irenaeus says he heard John, 3.39.1), for he related 'strange parables and teachings of the Savior' and other 'rather mythical accounts.' His ideas about the millennium were perverse because he did not understand that the apostles' accounts were figurative and mystical. Unfortunately, though he was stupid he was also 'ancient' and his ideas therefore infected traditionalist authors like

13. 'A barbarism is a mistake in one expression, while a solecism is a mistake in putting together ungrammatical expressions', A.D., *Synt.*, p. 198, 7 (Bekker).

14. Cf. B.E. Daley, *The Hope of the Early Church: A Handbook of Patristic Eschatology* (Cambridge: Cambridge University Press, 1991).

Irenaeus (3.39.11-13). Eusebius neglects the Jewish apocrypha and pseudepigrapha used by most early Christians. Thus he is unaware that Papias's description of eschatological productivity comes from the Jewish apocalypse 2 Baruch, though cited by Irenaeus, and he does not note that the Roman Hippolytus accepts this tradition.[15]

As for authors later in the second century, Eusebius passes over what Justin wrote: 'I and every other completely right-minded Christians know that there will be a resurrection of the flesh and a thousand years in a rebuilt, ornamented, and enlarged Jerusalem, as the prophets Ezekiel and Isaiah, and others, acknowledge'.[16] Eusebius refers to *Dialogue* 81 and 82, but not to this passage (4.18.8). He does not mention that according to Theophilus's treatise *To Autolycus*, after resurrection and judgment humanity will return from its exile to paradise, 'of earth and planted on the earth',[17] but is content to call the treatise 'elementary' (4.24). His improbable paraphrase of Hegesippus makes the grandsons of Jude tell Domitian that the kingdom of Christ is 'not worldly or earthly but heavenly and angelic' (3.20.4).

As for the Alexandrians, Eusebius does not report that Origen's 'school for souls', though located 'in the heavenly regions', began its course of post-mortem instruction in Paradise, 'in some place located on earth'.[18] Nor does he admit that Dionysius's arguments about the Apocalypse were not universally convincing. Indeed, when the millenarian Coracion acknowledged defeat by the bishop's words, 'some (οἱ μέν) of the other brethren present rejoiced over the conference and the mutual deference and unanimity displayed toward all'. The sentence requires οἱ δέ to continue (others, however); but we do not learn anything about their attitude (7.24.9). Presumably they did not agree.

In other words, the early Christian hope was more complex and more contradictory than Eusebius suggests, and he misunderstands it because his view of orthodoxy is unhistorical and incomplete. He had no room in his history or other works for Origen's statement contrasting what the apostles handed down with what was reserved for

15. Hippol., *Comm. Dan.* 4.60.
16. Just., *Dial.* 80.5. Admittedly in *Apol.* 1.11 he insists that the kingdom will not be 'human'.
17. Theophil., *Auto.* 2.26 and 24.
18. Or., *Prin.* 2.11.6-7.

later investigation.[19] (Origen does not refer to apocalyptic eschatology but raises similar important questions.) This failure kept Eusebius from accurately assessing the nature and origin of biblical books.

4. *Ancient and Modern*

Every attentive student of the Bible must have noticed the way in which trends take over the scene rather regularly. Our examination of Eusebius' comments on Hebrews and the Johannine literature shows that the ancient situation was not very different from the modern. Basically Eusebius' analysis is faulty because it is both prejudiced and incomplete. Many of his problems are technical in origin. His studies are incomplete and inconclusive because he would not (or could not) make them complete and conclusive. He is unsystematic because there was no real way for him to be systematic. The reader will realize that this paper has now reached its main point: to pay tribute to John Hurd for his zeal in taking biblical studies beyond the Eusebian point by using the word-processor. The word-processor makes possible, though it does not ensure, the accuracy and completeness that lie at the foundation of literary research. To be sure, a measure of common sense, broad reading, and even intelligence is needed beyond that. But without what Eusebius could not, or at any rate did not, provide it is impossible to move toward understanding. The New Testament books need to be set in a properly understood historical context of early Christian life and theology. The 'traditions' about them need to be analyzed, though not necessarily rejected. For their style and vocabulary we need to follow, and go beyond, the Alexandrians, not Eusebius—though we should be grateful to him as to any pioneer. As the editor of these studies suggests, greater attentiveness to method can reshape our understanding of early Christianity and Judaism.

19. Or., *Prin.* preface 3-10.

DISCONTINUITY, METAMORPHOSIS AND COHERENCE:
METHODOLOGIES FOR COMPUTER-ASSISTED TEXTUAL ANALYSIS,
WITH REFERENCE TO THE *METAMORPHOSES* OF OVID

Willard McCarty

In order to dominate a changing situation, full of contrasts, [the intellect]
must become even more supple, even more shifting, more polymorphic
than the flow of time: it must adapt itself constantly to events as they
succeed each other and be pliable enough to accommodate the unexpected
so as to implement the plan in mind more successfully... Victory over a
shifting reality whose continuous metamorphoses make it almost
impossible to grasp, can only be won through an even greater degree of
mobility, an even greater power of transformation.

Marcel Detienne and Jean-Pierre Vernant[1]

1. *The Biblical Hintergrund*

The last century of biblical criticism, particularly in the work of
Julius Wellhausen and his followers, has made us aware of the fact
that the central text of our culture is historically many texts by many
hands from many sources.[2] Although happily no longer the ruling

1.   *Cunning Intelligence in Greek Culture and Society* (trans. J. Lloyd; Chicago:
University of Chicago Press, 1991), p. 20.
2.   This school of criticism, best known for its division of the narrative into
separate authorial strands (usually called J, E, P and D), succeeded in reducing the
text to an increasingly complicated network of sources combined in an equally
complicated series of redactions. See the penetrating analysis of the failures of the
Wellhausen school in E. Voegelin, *Order and History*. I. *Israel and Revelation*
(Baton Rouge: Louisiana State University Press, 1956), pp. 149-62; and for a
constructive reaction, G. von Rad, *Genesis: A Commentary* (trans. J.H. Marks;
The Old Testament Library; Philadelphia: Westminster Press, rev. edn, 1972), p. 42;
and esp. B. Childs, *Introduction to the Old Testament as Scripture* (Philadelphia:
Fortress Press, 1979). See also N. Frye, *The Great Code: The Bible and Literature*
(Toronto: Academic Press Canada, 1982), and *Words with Power, Being a Second*

critical approach, the reduction of the canonical edifice to its component gravel renewed the impetus to understand its architecture. The fundamental discontinuities of the biblical text, its numerous compositional gaps, repetitions and inconsistencies, might make the notion of an 'architecture' seem inappropriate for the rough and sprawling pile that we find. Yet if for no other reason than the effects its perceived or presumed unity has had, the importance of following the traces of design in the text and of attempting to understand the overall principle of composition, is impossible to ignore.

For the Christian Bible the first great design issue is, of course, the division of the Testaments, whose unity has been argued from the beginning by the principle of typology: *quanquam et in Vetere Novum lateat, et in Novo Vetus pateat,* Augustine wrote, 'in the Old the New is concealed, in the New the Old is revealed' (*Quaest. in Hept.* 2.73). However polemical its use became, typology has deeper roots: it seems not only to have been the working principle by which the NT authors themselves read Hebrew Scripture,[3] and to have antecedents in Jewish liturgy,[4] but also to be based on a habit of mind found in the Hebrew Bible itself, as studies by Jean Daniélou and others have shown.[5] To a

Study of 'The Bible and Literature' (Toronto: Penguin, 1992).

3. Frye, *The Great Code*, pp. 79-80; cf. L. Goppelt, *Typos: The Typological Interpretation of the Old Testament in the New* (trans. D.H. Madvig; Grand Rapids: Eerdmans, 1982), pp. 4-5; J. Daniélou, *The Lord of History: Reflections on the Inner Meaning of History* (trans. N. Abercrombie; London: Longmans, 1958), pp. 227-32; B. Childs, 'Prophecy and Fulfillment: A Study of Contemporary Hermeneutics', *Interpretation* 12 (1958), pp. 263-64.

4. R.P.C. Hanson, *Allegory and Event: A Study of the Sources and Significance of Origen's Interpretation of Scripture* (London: SCM Press, 1959), p. 72.

5. J. Daniélou, *From Shadows to Reality: Studies in the Biblical Typology of the Fathers* (trans. D.W. Hibberd; London: Burns & Oates, 1960); H.D. Hummel, 'The Old Testament Basis of Typological Interpretation', *Biblical Research* 9 (1964), pp. 38-50; B.W. Anderson, 'Exodus Typology in Second Isaiah', in B.W. Anderson and W. Harrelson (eds.), *Israel's Prophetic Heritage: Essays in Honor of James Muilenburg*; New York: Harper & Brothers, 1962), pp. 177-95; G. von Rad, 'Typological Interpretation of the Old Testament' (trans. J. Bright, in C. Westermann and J.L. Mays [eds.], *Essays on Old Testament Hermeneutics*; Richmond, VA: John Knox, 1963), pp. 20, 32-3; Goppelt, *Typos*, pp. 38-41 n. 99. In the above work, Daniélou specifically points to the three great antitypes in the Hebrew prophets as proof of Old Testament typology: the messianic kingdom and its king, which the prophets envision as a new Paradise and a new Adam (pp. 12-16);

literary scholar, the typological habit of mind is interesting because it operates like metaphor, asserting the identity of two very different things or events while not eliminating their differences. This is essentially Eric Auerbach's argument for the idea of 'figural interpretation,' which reveals in the strictly typological view of a work structured by correspondence between old and new stories, type and antitype, a more generalizable, and more specifically textual theory of how the Bible achieves unity from its radically discontinuous narrative.[6]

A figural reading of the Bible is predicated on an equal if paradoxical recognition of putative coherence and of the textual facts that appear to disrupt it. Accordingly, we are not to bridge linked stories by rationalizing prose; rather, we are to assume unity, then attempt to imagine from the facts at hand the greater story this unity adumbrates. Apparent irrelevancies and contradictions are neither explained nor discarded but held, as it were, in tentative suspension, awaiting a more complete understanding. This understanding may come from rereading, spontaneous insight, or phenomena outside the text altogether; more interestingly from a literary point of view, it may also come from the addition of other stories drawn in by association. Thus, for example, by their rough juxtaposition, the two stories of creation still discernible in Genesis—first of dry land out of watery chaos (Gen. 1.1-2.3), then of the watered garden from a primeval desert (2.5-25)—attract and bring together the apocalyptic parting of the Red Sea (Exod. 15.1-19) and the vision of the desert that 'shall rejoice, and blossom as the rose' (Isa. 35.1). With changes in understanding brought about by such metaphorical accretion, some of what was formerly deemed irrelevant becomes relevant, and

the second cataclysm, of which Noah's flood is the type (pp. 73-74); and finally, the new Exodus, which will have all the features of the old one, though transformed (pp. 155-56). As well, the second cataclysm and the new Exodus combine in Isaiah, 'who describes the crossing of the Red Sea as a new victory of Yahweh over Rahab, type of both Egypt and the great Abyss (Isa. 51.9-11)', and in Hosea the messianic age is an antitype of the first Wilderness period, 'a return of the time in the desert when the Nuptials of Jahweh with his people were celebrated' (p. 154).

6.   '"Figura"', (trans. R. Mannheim, in *Scenes from the Drama of European Literature* [Theory and History of Literature, 9; Manchester: Manchester University Press, 1984]), esp. pp. 58-60. See also *Mimesis: The Representation of Reality in Western Literature* (trans. W.R. Trask; Princeton: Princeton University Press, 1953), p. 17.

therefore a new, more inclusive meta-story (as it might be called) is imaginatively provoked. Strictly speaking this meta-story is beyond telling. Like the events of history on which the Bible is predicated,[7] the text provides a glimpse of a truth beyond itself, but unlike an allegorical reading, this truth is accessible in no other way; it cannot be rendered into an independent statement but remains, as Paul said of fallen perception, ἄρτι δι' ἐσόπτρου ἐν αἰνίγματι (1 Cor. 13.12).[8]

Auerbach eloquently argues that the Bible is consequently open-ended, forever able to expand within and beyond itself, but also forever provoking the hermeneutical quest ('"Figura"', pp. 58-60). The text remains indispensable, its most troublesome feature—the radical discontinuities we have observed—essential signposts to a hidden coherence. Thus, it might be argued, we are preconditioned by the Bible in relation to all written texts.

2. *Literary Application*

To the literary critic Auerbach's theory is intriguing because it points to a principle by which other discontinuous collections may be read— and thus provides me with a bridge wherewith to cross over from biblical studies onto very different ground. In the remainder of this essay, that is, I wish to discuss the methodological aspects of computer-assisted research based on just such a collection of stories as Auerbach's principle helps to illuminate: the *Metamorphoses* of the Roman poet Publius Ovidius Naso (43 BCE–18 CE).[9] Interestingly, the

---

7.   On the biblical conception of history, in addition to Auerbach's '"Figura"', see Voegelin, *Israel and Revelation*, esp. his notion of 'paradigmatic history' developed in ch. 4; B.S. Childs, *Myth and Reality in the Old Testament* (Studies in Biblical Theology, 27; London: SCM Press, 2nd edn, 1962), pp. 100-106; G.B. Caird, *The Language and Imagery of the Bible* (Duckworth Studies in Theology; London: Duckworth, 1980), esp. ch. 12.

8.   For the contrast of typology and allegory, see Hanson, *Allegory and Event*, chs. 3–4; Auerbach, '"Figura"'; R.A. Markus, 'Presuppositions of the Typological Approach to Scripture', *Church Quarterly Review* 158 (1957), pp. 442-45; Daniélou, *The Lord of History*, pp. 143-45, and 'The Problem of Symbolism', *Thought* 25 (1950), p. 438; and Anderson, 'Exodus Typology in Second Isaiah', pp. 178-80.

9.   My discussion of Ovid is based on research currently in progress; for a preliminary description of my project, see W. McCarty, 'Finding Implicit Patterns in Ovid's *Metamorphoses* with *TACT*', in T.R. Wooldridge (ed.) *A TACT Exemplar*,

Bible and the *Metamorphoses*, however culturally remote, are not entirely dissimilar from a structural point of view. Both are radically discontinuous works comprised of numerous traditional stories; both depict a human progression in time and space, from creation out of chaos and initial blessedness, through a sudden fall into an inferior existential state and a world-engulfing deluge, in and out of a bewildering variety of disastrous events, to an apotheosis of man and a holy city.

I am not attempting to slide over the profound gulf between the two works, nor am I claiming anything whatever about an historical relation between them. Nor, as it may seem, do I intend to slip deviously into a literary analysis of the *Metamorphoses*, which would hardly be appropriate to the volume in which this essay appears. Rather, with the similarities of these works in mind, I intend to discuss how the methodology of computer-assisted textual analysis, as it is evolving in my electronic 'edition' of Ovid's poem, affects its study, and so by extension to suggest what might be done for biblical research, despite the many linguistic and structural differences between the two works. Because the genre that I am about to describe has so few examples, and these so primitive, the attempt to make an electronic edition of the Bible in my sense would likely also contribute substantially to the emerging field of humanities computing, which owes so much to the mental habits of biblical exegesis as well as to the direct contributions of its practitioners, such as Professor Hurd.

3. *The Electronic Edition and TACT*

I will define an 'electronic edition' broadly as a machine-readable version of an established text together with software designed to assist its study. Implicit in this definition is the subservience of both software and raw text to the entity they constitute. Although it is undoubtedly true that both will, indeed must remain separable,[10] nevertheless

CCH Working Papers 1; Toronto: Centre for Computing in the Humanities, 1991), pp. 37-75; 'Peering Through the Skylight: Towards an Electronic Edition of Ovid's *Metamorphoses*', in *Research in Humanities Computing '92* (Oxford: Clarendon Press, forthcoming).

10. To date no standards for encoding of texts have been implemented in analytical software; despite broad similarities (such as the COCOA conventions used by both TACT and Oxford Concordance Program), each software package has invented

from the scholarly user's perspective, the composite entity is what matters.

Emphasis on the importance of a composite entity has been rare; so also the potential for such an entity itself to communicate the editor's understanding of a text. Most computer-assisted projects seem to have focused on results and given scant attention to process,[11] perhaps because of the prevalent tendency to view the computer as 'just a tool'—a criterion no tool, properly understood, could satisfy—hence to ignore its inherent characteristics and their far-reaching implications. (I will return to these implications later.) Thus studies have tended to overlook the idea of the repeatable, modifiable experiment as the norm for the computer-assisted aspects of scholarship,[12] and the notion that this experiment might itself constitute a new form of

its own encoding scheme, so that a text prepared for a specific package is in effect not usable elsewhere. With the standards currently under development by the Text Encoding Initiative, however, it will be possible to encode texts independently of software, hence allow different programs to be applied to the same text without re-encoding. See C.M. Sperberg-McQueen, 'Text in the Electronic Age: Textual Study and Text Encoding, with Examples from Medieval Texts', *Literary and Linguistic Computing* 6 (1991), pp. 34-46; L. Burnard, 'Tools and Techniques for Computer-assisted Text Processing', in C.S. Butler (ed.), *Computers and Written Texts* (Applied Language Studies; Oxford: Basil Blackwell, 1992), pp. 3-8.

11. Note, e.g., L.T. Milic's criterion that computer-assisted scholarship should turn out results which diverge sharply from what has been done before, in 'Winged Words: Varieties of Computer Application to Literature', *CHum* 2 (1967), pp. 24-31, cited by R. Potter, 'Statistical Analysis of Literature: A Retrospective on *Computers and the Humanities*, 1966–1990', *CHum* 25 (1991), p. 403. See, however, n. 12.

12. Note C. Delcourt's perceptive comment, quoted by Potter in 'Statistical Analysis of Literature', p. 413, that 'many studies…are more satisfied with the easy identification of monsters, i.e., literary phenomena unexplained by wrong models, than with the laborious research of models fitting the textual data well'. See the emphasis on recursive modelling in W. van Peer, 'Quantitative Studies of Literature. A Critique and an Outlook', *CHum* 23 (1989) p. 306, discussed by Potter, 'Statistical Analysis of Literature', p. 407; and cf. the scientific notion of 'hypothesis testing' in R.W. Bailey, 'The Future of Computational Stylistics', in R. Potter (ed.), *Literary Computing and Literary Criticism: Theoretical and Practical Essays on Theme and Rhetoric* (Philadelphia: University of Pennsylvania Press, 1989 [1979]), pp. 5-11; Potter's own essay, 'From Literary Output to Literary Criticism: Discovering Shaw's Rhetoric', *CHum* 23 (1989), pp. 333-40. I have in mind a looser notion than Potter's, of a recursive, exploratory experiment, which does not necessarily begin with a specific hypothesis (see p. 314, below).

publication. As we will see, the electronic edition is such a form.

Several existing text-retrieval packages may appear to qualify as the basis for editions, but when we consider traditional scholarly practice, it becomes obvious that most of them are far too unsophisticated for the task.[13] Even by the limits of current technology, which are formidable, much more can be done to change and deepen our understanding of texts than they permit. TACT, the analytical system on which my edition is based, is an exception, as I will illustrate in detail.[14]

In simplest terms TACT is an evolutionary development of the concordance system, that is, a device for generating lists of words in context. Unlike older, 'batch-oriented' systems, which were designed to produce printed lists, its central component is interactive and provides a number of dynamically manipulable displays. It is thus by nature a tool for exploration and experiment rather than production of a finished product. To the basic functions of concording it adds two significant kinds of enhancements: tools for the automatic detection of textual patterns, and others that allow the user to declare and record patterns. These two kinds suggest a corresponding distinction in the approaches that may be taken to computer-assisted analysis of text. As I will argue, in principle these approaches converge; in practice they are sometimes found together. Each, however, tends to be suitable for a distinct range of phenomena, involve divergent assumptions about

13. For a survey see B. Brainerd, S.R. Reimer and I. Lancashire, 'Text Analysis', in *The Humanities Computing Yearbook 1989–90* (Oxford: Clarendon Press, 1991), pp. 477-503.

14. TACT has been developed by John Bradley and Lidio Presutti at the University of Toronto with the support and encouragement of the Centre for Computing in the Humanities; for several years John Hurd served as chair of the committee that oversaw the development of TACT, and so a project with TACT at its core has him in part to thank. See J. Bradley, *TACT: User's Guide, Version 1.2* (Toronto: Centre for Computing in the Humanities, 1989); for examples of applications see T.R. Wooldridge (ed.) *A TACT Exemplar*. Both publications are available only in hardcopy from TACT Distribution, Centre for Computing in the Humanities, University of Toronto, Robarts Library, 130 St George Street, Toronto, Ontario M5S 1A5, Canada; telephone: (416) 978-4238; fax: (416) 978-6519; Internet: cch@epas.utoronto.ca. The software is available from the CCH or by anonymous-ftp from epas.utoronto.ca, /pub/cch/tact/. TACT version 2.1 is scheduled to be published by the Modern Language Association of America.

the nature of text, and reveal to the practitioner different aspects of the material under study.[15]

4. *Algorithm versus Meta-text*

Let us call the two approaches to textual computing the 'algorithmic' and the 'meta-textual'.[16] My work with the *Metamorphoses* has so far emphasized the latter, although several of the algorithms in Tact have provided important clues for an understanding of the poem.[17]

As the term suggests, the algorithmic emphasizes application of sophisticated automatic procedures, for example to discover exactly repeating phrases, or compute the density with which selected words cluster. Algorithmic analysis may begin with the abstract formulation of a theory about text, which is then implemented in some programming language; with a procedure borrowed from another field, such as statistics; or, in the case of statistical analysis, simply apply one or

15. Applications of computing to texts are surveyed and otherwise classified by E. Irizarry, 'Literary Analysis and the Microcomputer', *Hispania* 71 (1988), pp. 984-95 (by area of application and by technique); C. Butler, *Computers in Linguistics* (Oxford: Basil Blackwell, 1985), ch. 2 (by linguistic unit and by area of application); Bailey, 'The Future of Computational Stylistics' (by techniques).

16. As far as I know, the distinction I make is new. Literary and linguistic computing has, it seems, emphasized computation in the modern rather than etymological sense, i.e. numerical analysis instead of generic organization, as in the French term *l'ordinateur*. Note, for example, that Potter's 'Statistical Analysis of Literature,' the review article on literary computing in the anniversary issue of the major North American journal in the field, *Computers and the Humanities*, deals only with the application of numerical techniques. Similarly, J.F. Burrows's insightful review in 'Computers and the Study of Literature', although contrasting the more inclusive idea of *ordonnance* with computation, discusses only numerical means of analyzing the order(s) of text, in Butler (ed.), *Computers and Written Texts*, pp. 167-204. In that same collection of essays, Lou Burnard discusses both textual markup and database management systems, but not the combination of the techniques. Many studies have employed markup without giving much attention to the analytical possibilities of dense encoding, e.g., Irizarry, 'Literary Analysis and the Microcomputer', p. 988; T. Snelgrove, 'A Method for the Analysis of the Structure of Narrative Texts', *Literary and Linguistic Computing* 5 (1990), pp. 221-25; N.M. Ide, 'Meaning and Method: Computer-Assisted Analysis of Blake', in Potter (ed.), *Literary Computing and Literary Criticism*, p.128; Butler, *Computers in Linguistics*, p. 16.

17. See my article, 'Finding Implicit Patterns in Ovid's *Metamorphoses* with *TACT*', pp. 64-74.

more functions of an existing package, such as SPSS or SAS.[18] Because implementation requires specialised skills, once they are developed algorithms tend to be accepted as set-pieces, their assumptions and procedures inherited (rather than necessarily examined) by users.[19] Ideally an algorithm reveals phenomena that cannot normally be detected as such; or it affords its users a clarifying distance from their own preoccupations, so that they may better see the surface phenomena of the text.

In contrast, the meta-textual approach emphasizes editorial codes or 'markup', which the individual scholar puts into the text to identify selected objects for later processing, for example, names of people and places or hypothetical structures.[20] Meta-textual analysis begins with an encoding 'language', which defines how phenomena of interest may be identified. In using this language the encoder applies one or more theories about the text to its actual phenomena—or, more interestingly, discovers and develops a theory through interaction with them. Meta-textual analysis, then, involves its practitioners intimately with their own preoccupations as again and again these are challenged by the translation into markup and by textual detail. Since it is easily modified, a given encoding is exemplary rather than final, inviting critical dialogue rather than simple acceptance. The burden of consistency and cogency lies with the individual encoder, however.

Both approaches, as I have suggested, bring with them assumptions about the nature of text and involve interpretations of the work under study. The computer, especially in algorithmic analysis, has in the past often seemed appealing because of the objectivity, hence scientific rigour it was presumed to bring to the notoriously unsystematic study

18. Note mathematician Stephen Smale's warning (quoted by Bailey, 'The Future of Computational Stylistics', pp. 8-9) that good models begin with 'a penetrating study and understanding' of the phenomena to which they are applied, thus that borrowed procedures can be seriously misleading.

19. In 'Statistical Analysis of Literature,' Potter looks forward, amid several complaints about the impenetrability of statistical arguments, to the time when statistically unsophisticated users will be able to use mathematical models without understanding the basis on which they are constructed (p. 413). More cautiously, Burrows recognises the problem but has no clear answer ('Computers and the Study of Literature', p. 188).

20. Note esp. Sperberg-McQueen's fine article on the intellectual implications and potential of textual encoding, 'Text in the Electronic Age', which deserves close study.

of literature. Without careful qualification, however, this putative objectivity can be seriously misleading. Even if we assume that the user has no chance to affect results significantly (as by adjusting the parameters of an algorithm, or by choosing one algorithm over another), and that these results require no interpretation (seldom if ever the case), even so an automatic procedure, or an accepted encoding, necessarily imposes the assumptions of the maker. These assumptions may be innocuous, but they can also be dangerous if the user is ignorant, credulous, or cannot check the text, for example, because it is too large. In any case, the notion of pure objectivity is a dangerous illusion.[21]

Equally misleading is the related assertion that meta-textual analysis in particular is *necessarily* infected by a crippling subjectivity, since the text reflected back to the scholar is primarily shaped by the markup he or she has imposed on it.[22] Let us for the sake of argument put aside the irrational distrust of the imagination, hence the hungering after an external (and often non-literary) criterion by which literary criticism may be measured.[23] Two assumptions remain: that our perceptions cannot be trusted, whereas a machine we have programmed can, or that our whole understanding of a text is merely the sum of component observations, hence that it does not involve

21. Note Sperberg-McQueen's argument that computers do not process data but representations of data, and that 'Representations are inevitably partial, never disinterested; inevitably they reveal their authors' conscious and unconscious judgments and biases' ('Text in the Electronic Age', p. 314); Burrows' comment that 'the analysis of patterns always entails a degree of intervention and distortion... the eye of the beholder is never a transparent medium' ('Computers and the Study of Literature', p. 168).

22. The charge is old and persistent: see, e.g., R.R. Dyer, 'The New Philology: An Old Discipline or a New Science?', *CHum* 4 (1969), pp. 53-64; and cf. Frye's comment that 'unthinking people often accuse scholars in every field of finding only what they have previously wanted to find, as though all genuine discoveries resulted from ignorance or pure chance' (*Words with Power*, p. 7).

23. The dependence on non-literary criteria is observable, e.g., in content analysis, where the appeal is often to some kind of external consensus; see n. 35. Frye's central thesis seems to me crucial (and echoes Stephen Smale's warning, n. 18), that 'To subordinate criticism to an externally derived critical attitude is to exaggerate the values in literature that can be related to the external source, whatever it is... If criticism exists, it must be an examination of literature in terms of a conceptual framework derivable from an inductive study of the literary field'; see *Anatomy of Criticism: Four Essays* (Princeton: Princeton University Press, 1957), p. 7.

forgetting, weighting or altering details in the act of assimilating them to larger patterns. Both assumptions are utterly unproductive, implying the obsolesce of reading and thinking, or the kind of text no one would care to read or think about.

In any case, the meta-textual approach makes one of its principal contributions by giving the scholar a means of recording detailed observations and the factual basis for hypotheses, then bringing all back relentlessly, despite whatever results may be hoped for. The quality of those observations is of course the scholar's look-out, as I have noted. The meta-textual approach provides, then, in part a kind of memory; it allows us to study the point at which individual readings become ideas, and so gives us greater insight into critical processes. Thus human intervention (inevitable in any case) need not only bedevil us with human inconsistencies;[24] it can be the source of enlightenment.

Obviously we need to take scholarly care and apply discipline to the task. This discipline has, however, special implications in the case of encoding, since it means taking on the mental framework of the encoding language, that is, thinking in its terms. (Thus the meta-textual approach is more than a kind of memory, since an encoding language is not so much a means of recording facts otherwise arrived at, as it is a cognitive tool, a means of thinking about text.) Part of what an encoder does in this frame of mind is to extend what the computer can do; as it were, paradoxically to play the computer, which he or she can sometimes do better than the computer can, if not always as fast. Thus, one might argue, the analytical approaches I have distinguished here are in principle the same, and in practice will tend to converge, differing only in that the meta-textual approach employs covert 'algorithms' which are beyond our current abilities or patience to formulate. Note the assumption in this argument, however.

The reasons why we cannot write out these algorithms (if that is what they are) and efforts in the field of artificial intelligence to overcome the problems, lie outside the scope of this essay. We can observe, however, that algorithmic analysis, like the methods of modern science, has indeed proved itself valuable for revealing textual phenomena beyond the normal range of vision or extent of time. (Such phenomena may escape human detection because they are

---

24. Potter, 'Statistical Analysis of Literature', p. 418.

scattered over a very large text or themselves are unusually complex, numerous, or otherwise difficult for the unaided scholar to record.[25]) Contrastingly, meta-textual analysis tends to be suitable to sets of phenomena within this range of vision and time, that is, for the close study of a work sufficiently long and complex to make unassisted study difficult. It is unsuitable for individual short works, since what may be discovered will already be obvious, and tends to be unsupportable for very long texts, where the labour of encoding can be formidable. The norm for a meta-textual project is, then, the electronic edition of a substantial work such as the Bible, Ovid's *Metamorphoses*, Dante's *Divina Commedia*, Milton's *Paradise Lost*, or collections of smaller works such as sonnet sequences.

I have urged the point that neither approach can avoid assumptions and interpretations. In fact both not merely begin with but essentially tend towards the hypothetical, so that we may formulate better questions. Both follow the recursive cycle that moves from the text, through hypothesis and experiment, back to the text, then on to alteration of the hypothesis, further experimentation, and so forth— the essentially and gloriously endless activity of interpretation (see n. 12).

Both approaches also confront us with the signifying dissonance between the computational model and the common phenomena of imaginative language.[26] The recursive cycle I just described is perfective up to the point at which no existing algorithm can detect or declarative markup render what seems to be in the text. Scorning the limitations of the computer is easy at this point but not enlightening (except in the deeper darkness cast by mindless enthusiasts). More fruitful is to notice the interesting and significant questions indicated by the failure to get answers to the questions with which one began. Thus, for example, we might begin by asking which words and phrases constitute Ovid's erotic vocabulary, and so attempt to construct a list sufficient to recall all relevant passages, and only these. We find, however, no such list is possible: many passages escape the

25. See, e.g., Burrows, 'Computers and the Study of Literature', and esp. N.M. Ide, 'A Statistical Measure of Theme and Structure', *CHum* 23 (1989), pp. 277-83 (cf. Potter, 'Statistical Analysis of Literature', p. 424); I. Lancashire, 'Phrasal Repetends in Literary Stylistics: Hamlet III.i', in *Research in Humanities Computing '92* (Oxford: Clarendon Press, forthcoming). See also n. 17.

26. Cf. van Peer, 'Quantitative Studies of Literature', pp. 302-306.

net, and too many irrelevant ones are caught. Clearly the assumptions behind the initial question are wrong. The question then becomes how *eros* is communicated: by collocates? by conventional associations? by broader contextual effects—and, if so, what effects? What in fact is *eros* in literature? Thus, computer-assisted analysis may provoke a metamorphosis of questions that rapidly takes us beyond the limits of our knowledge. It is probably unsafe to assert, in the manner of eighteenth and nineteenth-century histories, that this boundary is a fixed barrier forever separating human and non-human analysis. It does, however, throw light into the obscurity of how we know what we know, towards *was eigentlich geschiet*.[27]

5. *Tagging in TACT*

Let us now turn from the basics to the specifics of meta-textual analysis with the program TACT. Although current work in text-encoding standards already goes well beyond the markup language of TACT (see n. 10), as yet no analytical software implements these standards. Meanwhile, then, we can learn much from experiments with what has fallen most advantageously to hand.

In the encoding language of TACT tags have two possible functions. First, they may designate locations and thus be used to mark structure.[28] Such tags assign a name to each type of division, such as 'book', 'speaker' or 'story' and to each occurrence of each type, a number or name as appropriate, for example, the number of the book, the name of the speaker or the title of the story. Structural markup is then used either to define how the distribution of objects, such as a group of semantically related words, is presented or to determine which of them are selected. For example, we may have all words related to hunting displayed according to speaker or select all such words that occur only within a given story. TACT allows many competing structures to be defined then used as needed.

---

27. L. von Ranke's famous phrase rendered in the present tense, describing the primary duty of the historian; see G.B. Caird, *The Language and Imagery of the Bible* (London: Gerald Duckworth, 1980), p. 201.

28. In the terminology of TACT locations may be marked by 'Text References,' which use COCOA-like tags (e.g. <speaker Romeo>), or 'Labels', whose type is specified by the kind of bracket used (e.g. {Romeo}, where {...} indicates a speaker).

The objective of structural tagging is to demarcate as many useful schemes as possible. To qualify, a structural scheme need not only be conventionally accepted or just cogent in itself, but each of its divisions also must designate enough text so that recalling words within it will be rewarding (an experimentally determined amount). For the *Metamorphoses* it is more important to realise that narrative divisions are possible almost down to the level of the phrase than it is actually to attempt marking all of them.

The second function of tags in TACT is to constitute 'meta-words' which are editorial comments pertaining to content rather than structure. In brief, they identify and classify verbal phenomena that are difficult or impossible to detect algorithmically, such as the antecedent of a pronoun, a place-name or a lengthy personal epithet. Good scholarly practice dictates that meta-words are always distinguishable as such, but to the software they are simply character-strings in the text and so appear in word-lists and may be searched for just like authorial words. In my edition of the *Metamorphoses*, all meta-words begin with a unique character, so that they are not only unambiguously selectable but are also grouped together in generated lists and concordances.

The objective of meta-words is twofold: to capture as much relevant information in each instance as possible and to classify it so that all like items are easily identified and will occur together in alphabetical listings. As a result of consistent tagging it becomes possible to list, for example, all the ways the Roman goddess Juno is named in the *Metamorphoses* (for example, *Iuno, Saturnia, coniunx Iovis, regina deorum, illa*), to study her attributes and to retrieve contexts for each of these so that the relationship between manner of naming, character and action may be discovered. In a complex work like the *Metamorphoses* an alphabetical list of tags is most useful as it abstracts significant textual objects from the contextual swarm, groups like with like and so presents a simplified view of the work, for example, as the set of all named individuals.

In my edition I have defined a syntax for meta-words that allows most if not all information about the tagged objects to be gathered. Thus meta-words may have several parts. The first part is a standard name, which may or may not correspond to usage in the text but which is always attached to the same *persona*; the second part, if any, specifies how that character is actually referred to and may contain the name or names of other characters indirectly referenced; and the third, also optional, lists the attribute (possession, state of mind, offspring, etc.). As example, take the gift of destruction bestowed on Hercules by Juno, his step-mother, to whom he cries, *decet haec dare dona novercam*, 'this is a fitting gift for a step-mother to give' (Ov. *Met.* 9.181); in my scheme, the resulting tag is

$$= Juno = noverca/Hercules/-dona$$

which may be read, 'a reference to Juno, occurring as *noverca*, with reference to Hercules, concerning her *dona*'. The initial equals-sign designates a name-tag, as I mentioned.

I remarked that tagging simplifies by eliminating context selectively. It is also inherently reductive in a more serious and interesting way because its primitive pseudo-language renders explicit what in imaginative writing is often ambiguous and suggestive. The above example is hardly either, but a thoroughgoing attempt to encode all references to persons in the *Metamorphoses*, for example, clearly shows how the limitations of the computational model illuminate what it fails to capture. Apart from the implications of this failure, at the very least such an attempt raises, perhaps unexpectedly, the fruitful questions of what constitutes a personal reference, and especially in a mythological text, what may be considered a 'person'.

Here I wish to consider not only the significant limitations of tagging but also, briefly, their philosophical and interpretative context: specifically the tendency for the ontological categories of narrative (being, action and setting) to break down. In a Graeco-Roman mythological text such a breakdown or metamorphosis is not merely an authorial characteristic or attribute of the genre; rather, it is central to a culture that made no rigid distinction between divine and human, or sentient and mindless phenomena.[29] Therefore, the

29. The fluidity or ambiguity of ontological distinctions in Graeco-Roman culture comes out, for example, in the tendency to deify or hypostasise abstract ideas; in the 'spiritual landscape' of pastoral; and, more generally, in the 'catoptric' nature of the gods (from Greek κάτοπτρον, 'mirror'). See, respectively, H.L. Axtell, *The Deification of Abstract Ideas in Roman Literature and Inscriptions* (Chicago: University of Chicago Press, 1907); B. Snell, *The Discovery of the Mind: The Greek Origins of European Thought* (trans. T.G. Rosenmeyer; New York: Harper & Row, 1960 [1953]), ch. 13, 'Arcadia: The Discovery of a Spiritual Landscape'; and W. McCarty, 'The Shape of the Mirror: Metaphorical Catoptrics in Classical Literature', *Arethusa* 22 (1989), pp. 161-95. Depictions of the gods thus provoked

encoder of the *Metamorphoses* is bound to encounter problems making such distinctions. These problems are not to be avoided or ignored but treasured, as they reflect fundamental properties of the text. Furthermore, the nature of mythological fiction, perhaps all fiction, shows clearly that names of beings (however tentatively a being may be defined) are not 'rigid designators'[30] that is,

comment as early as Xenophanes (born c. 570 BC), who wrote that if beasts could paint each kind would depict gods in its own form (fr. 15, in Clem. A., *Strom.* 5.109.3); cf. E.R. Dodds, *The Greeks and the Irrational* (Berkeley: University of California Press, 1951), pp. 181-82. Similar remarks are to be found in Cicero (*Tusc. disp.* 1.26.65; cf. *de nat. deor.* 1.27.77); Pliny (*HN* 2.5.15-18, 21); Sextus Empiricus (*adv. math.* 1.29; cf. 1.23); Lucretius (6.63-64; 4.591-92); and of course in Christian writers such as Augustine (*de civ. Dei* 4.26, 9.8, 18.13), Arnobius (*adv. nat.* 3.16,19), and Tertullian (*ad nat.* 2.2, 7, 11). The modern interpretation of ancient spirituality as the product of a psychological 'projection' (e.g. by Dodds *passim*) is anachronistic, since there are no words for such an act in either Greek or Latin; classical criticism of the gods is concerned with the opposite, i.e. discovering that the gods stem from psychic affections (e.g. Sextus Empiricus, *adv. math.* 1.186-88). Ovid's remark in the *Ars*—*expedit esse deos*, 'it is expedient that there are gods', *et, ut expedit, esse putemus*, 'and since it is expedient, let us suppose that they exist' (1.637)—points us in the right direction: to their assimilation into that metaphorical language by which otherwise unreachable phenomena of the mind could be detected and represented.

30. Analytical philosophers have argued that proper names are 'rigid designators': see, e.g., D.M. Braun, 'Proper Names, Cognitive Contents, and Beliefs', *Philosophical Studies* 62 (1991), pp. 289-305; M. Pendelbury, 'Why Proper Names are Rigid Designators', *Philosophy and Phenomenological Research* 1 (1990), pp. 519-36. Arguments for the connotative function of names have been made from linguistic evidence and broader cultural contexts, e.g. by A.S. Marmaridou, 'Proper Names in Communication', *Journal of Linguistics* 25 (1989), pp. 355-72; F. Niyi Akinnaso, 'Names and Naming Principles in Cross-Cultural Perspective', *Names: Journal of the American Names Society* 29 (1981), pp. 37-63; R.B. Barnes, 'Personal Names and Social Classification', in D. Parkin (ed.), *Semantic Anthropology* (ASA Monograph, 22; London: Academic Press, 1982), pp. 211-26. For comparative literary treatments, see, e.g., D. Lamping, *Der Name in der Erzählung: Zur Poetik des Personennamens* (Wuppertaler Schriftenreihe Literatur, 21; Bonn: Bouvier Verlag Herbert Grundmann, 1983); the several essays in the 'Special Issue on Theory about Names', *Names: Journal of the American Names Society* 33 (1985); two essays in *Names and Their Varieties: A Collection of Essays in Onomastics* (comp. K.B. Harder; New York: University Press of America, 1986): K. Malone, 'Meaningful Fictive Names in English Literature', pp. 53-65, and W.F.H. Nicolaisen, 'Names as Verbal Icons', pp. 246-52. For classical literature, see J. Peradotto, *Man in the Middle Voice: Name and Narration in the* Odyssey

homosemous, but *loci* of association where ontological boundaries are often confused.

As I have already suggested proper names on the one hand and stories on the other bracket a continuum of fictional devices in the *Metamorphoses*. These include familial aliases such as patronymics, eponyms, abstractions, substantive phrases and epithets, which in length may be only arbitrarily distinguishable from brief tales.[31] Thus, as actions coalesce into names through attribution of this and that deed, so names themselves tell tales of deeds and events, sometimes implicitly, sometimes explicitly in forms tending to the narrative. Every 'he' is a 'he who...' every 'she' a 'she who...' even if through accident or poetic intention we now are unable to complete the clause.

Being and action may not be exactly interchangeable but they mirror each other and so imply the potentially disturbing, semiotically rich ambiguity resulting from the dissolution and metamorphoses of identity. Separable identity, in works like the *Metamorphoses*, is also compromised structurally by the collocative association of stories that, as Auerbach argues for figural interpretation, adumbrates a unity beyond itself. The reader of a discontinuous anthology such as the Bible or the *Metamorphoses* perhaps most often enters the work at some point other than the beginning, to refer to a particular story rather than to read the work from first to last. (The educated reader may be presumed to have read the entire work at least once, others to have absorbed significant portions of it indirectly.) A corollary to the collocative principle is that the focal story in such a reading becomes

(Martin Classical Lectures, NS, 1; Princeton: Princeton University Press, 1990); S. Goldhill, *The Poet's Voice: Essays on Poetics and Greek Literature* (Cambridge: Cambridge University Press, 1991), ch. 1; E. Fraenkel, 'Namenwesen', in PW; and the brief comments on neoteric practice in Roman poetry by D.O. Ross in *Backgrounds to Augustan Poetry: Gallus Elegy and Rome* (Cambridge: Cambridge University Press, 1975), pp. 62-63; and in '*Uriosque Apertos*: A Catullan Gloss', *Mnemosyne* 26 (1973), pp. 60-62.

31. Thus *Agenorides*, 'son of Agenor', for Cadmus; *Athena*, goddess and city; *Invidia*, personified 'envy'; *rex superum*, 'king of those above', for Jupiter; and for Liriope, mother of Narcissus, *caerula Liriope, quam quondam flumine curvo / implicuit clausaeque suis Cephisos in undis / vim tulit...* (*Met.* 3.342-4). She is named twice here, once as 'sea-blue Liriope', the other as 'she whom once Cephisos embraced with his curved stream and took by force in his enclosing waters'—name and story simultaneously.

the measure as well as destination of the rest, the lens, as it were, through which the work itself is viewed. As a result, the focal story is universalized. Thus with Narcissus in mind we discover that Actaeon, Pentheus, Cadmus, Callisto, Proserpina and others manifest narcissean tendencies in themselves, and that they in turn transform Narcissus from the callow youth who falls fatally in love with his own image into a 'narcissean presence' of forbidden, destructive self-regarding.

In the *Metamorphoses*, then, ontological ambiguity is one aspect of the profoundly metamorphic nature of the whole poem, in which all things change, opposites mingle, and souls migrate from form to form.[32] Indeed, as the distinction between being and action is compromised, so also between being and non-being, or sentience and mindlessness. In the poem, for example, it is impossible to determine with the consistency demanded by markup when *sol*, 'sun,' indicates merely the mindless ball of fiery light in the sky (for example *Met.* 1.63?), when the sentient god Phoebus (2.31-32), who is sometimes identified with Apollo (1.473; 11.306). Markup brings such questions to light and forces some kind of decision, which by its arbitrariness can be a source of insight.[33] The entity *luna* ('moon') is more elusive, trying the extreme limits of being: at times perhaps only the moon (2.117)—if, again, 'only' makes sense in a Roman context—at other times the shadowy natural counterpart of the lunar goddesses Diana and Hecate (2.453; 7.179), in a sisterly relationship with *sol* (2.453), and distantly associated with Medea and Circe through witchcraft (7.179; 14.367). How is she (or it) to be tagged?

Unfortunate mortals, demi-gods and nymphs become ontologically ambiguous through punitive or accidental metamorphosis; such radical changes of being raise the difficult question of when occurrences of their names or nominal indicators are to be tagged as personal references, when otherwise, or omitted altogether. Daphne, for example,

---

32. Note particularly the argument for metempsychosis, or transmigration of souls, that Pythagoras makes at the end of the poem, concluding with the argument that all flesh is human, all eating of flesh a 'Thyestean banquet' (*Met.* 15.459-78). The argument is significant, since it gives context to the many figures of predation and devouring throughout the poem, e.g. Tereus.

33. Apollo, Phoebus, and *sol* can of course be kept completely separate in the markup, but then one loses the benefit of a collation under one heading. My compromise relies on the syntax of the name-tag, which always preserves the actual name used in the text, e.g., = Apollo = Phoebus = sua-oracula.

changes into a laurel tree to avoid her would-be lover, Phoebus (1.452-567); as she changes, he addresses her—simultaneously sentient being and, in the distant future, both guardian tree of Augustus' portals and the source of branches signifying victory (1.557-65). At what point does she cease being Daphne and become the mindless laurel, if ever?—if, again, anything in the Ovidian world can be termed purely mindless. Perhaps we need a better question. Narcissus manifests a similar ambiguity in his relationship to his own reflected image, which he at first mistakes for another being, then continues to love despite the realisation that it is his reflected self (3.341-510). How an editor tags references to this catoptric selfhood depends very much on his or her reading of the poem. If an editor decides to tag names consistently and thoroughly, then in several instances no neutral tagging is possible.

Literary critics may be excused for reacting to the impossibility of a purely 'objective' markup by not wanting any of it. Thus, even if we grant that a marked-up text is useful to the encoder, we need to wonder what value it might have for anyone else. The argument I have made and suggested is that this markup is in essence exemplary rather than final, provoking reevaluation and further work. Meta-words may seem particularly dubious if not dangerous in this regard, since their total effect is the cumulative result of many small acts of interpretation, daunting to check or change. Is, however, the ground of such electronic scholarship necessarily any less solid than, for example, any other formed by painstaking interpretation of the evidence? The necessity for review of scholarly work of course remains, but (I would argue further) the evidence is at least all there so that the minute basis of comprehensive statements may be examined.

6. *Lexicon and Thesaurus*

With markup, I have argued, the tentativeness of textual phenomena is not the issue, rather the consistency with which they can be defined. Experience with the *Metamorphoses* suggests that things like proper names and textual structures are formally consistent enough to qualify. Other phenomena, such as themes and images, are less securely attached to individual words, hence are better handled by another, more changeable device. In TACT this device is the 'rule' or retrieval statement, which is external to the textual database. Such rules are normally composed with a wordprocessor and are stored in rule-files. In my application rule-files constitute a lexicon, from which is derived a thematic thesaurus.

In terms of the basic approaches to textual analysis I sketched earlier, rules belong to the meta-textual variety. Although not placed in the text, a thematically organized rule constitutes a kind of encoding in that it assigns the occurrences of the listed word-forms to a named class. Rules are simply easier to manipulate and review than tags, and their extra-textual status is a useful reminder of their intentional mutability.

If you think of markup proper as establishing the topography and landmarks of a text, then rules constitute the twists and turns of an actual journey through it. Thus they are suitable to queries that must shift with the twists and turns of complex, hermeneutical investigation.

Each rule specifies one or more character-strings to be matched against those in the text. Rules may be used, for example, to define parts of speech with distinctive endings, words with specific prefixes, or any fixed pattern of letters. The chief use in my edition, however, is to construct entries that gather the inflected forms of interesting words under their dictionary headwords or 'lemmas'.[34] Thus an entry for *ignarus* ('ignorant'):

= *ignarus*
   ignara,ignaram,ignare,ignari,ignaro,ignaroque,ignaros,ignarum,ignarus

(The equals-sign here marks the lemma as such; in TACT selecting the rule '= ignarus' from a rule-file would then retrieve all occurrences of the inflected forms listed) Such entries could be applied directly as rules, but for purposes of literary study, one often needs to group words by their perceived semantic relation (for example hunting or love) rather than by position in the alphabet. Ordering the lexicon by such relations is not a good idea, however, as it eliminates the stable lexicographical reference point. Polysemous words will tend to belong to more than one of these groups, and interpretations will vary in time and from person to person. Without the reference point, such

34. For my edition of the *Metamorphoses*, the *Oxford Latin Dictionary* (*OLD*) is the authority for definitions as well as for lemmas, e.g. to determine whether a given participle is to be considered a separate word or listed under its verb.

interpretative structuring would rapidly either slip below the level of conscious thought, into prejudice, or render the lexicon obtuse, especially to a subsequent user.

To avoid such difficulties I construct a *thesaurus proprius* or 'conceptual glossary' of words occurring in the poem by copying entries from the lexicon, then arranging them under the appropriate semantic headings.[35] Whereas the base lexicon is as interpretively neutral as possible (finally authoritative, stable in its arrangement, and equally useful to all), the thesaurus expresses the interpretations of its maker throughout. It is, then, presumed always to be changeable if not changing, useful to others primarily as an exemplar or means of checking conclusions based on it, should these be of any interest.

My thesaurus is loosely hierarchical. Large semantic groupings such as the vocabularies of hunting, warfare or love constitute files in

35. For the notion of a *thesaurus proprius* see Irizarry, 'Literary Analysis and the Microcomputer', p. 988. On the grouping of words by image, theme or vocabulary, see also Butler, *Computers in Linguistics*, p. 17; the three essays that constitute 'Part II: Theme and Semantic Analysis', in Potter (ed.), *Literary Criticism and Literary Computing*: P.A. Fortier, 'Analysis of Twentieth-Century French Prose Fiction: Theoretical Contexts, Results, Perspective', pp. 77-95; J.D. Goldfield, 'Computational Thematics, a Selective Database, and Literary Criticism: Gobineau, Tic Words, and Riffaterre Revisited', pp. 97-122 (the most methodologically explicit); Ide, 'Meaning and Method', pp. 123-41; and C.W. Anderson and G.E. McMaster, 'Computer-Assisted Modeling of Affective Tone in Written Documents', *CHum* 16 (1982), pp. 1-9. Fortier, Goldfield, Ide, and Anderson and McMaster all use external authorities for their groupings: synonym dictionaries of the period (Fortier and Goldfield), a dictionary of semantic profiles (Anderson and McMaster), the consensus of critics (Goldfield), or a symbol dictionary with supposed universality (Ide); Goldfield begins, however, with an 'inductive and subjective' listing of interesting words, although he apparently does not differentiate between an alphabetical lexicon and a thematic thesaurus. He refers to the seminal work of K.M. Schmidt in 'content analysis', which is based on the construction of a general content-analysis dictionary or thesaurus by which a text may supposedly be reduced to its component concepts; see 'Concept versus Meaning. The Contribution of Computer-Assisted Content analysis and Conceptual Text Analysis to this Disputed Area', in *Méthodes quantitatives et informatiques dans l'étude des textes / Computers in Literary and Linguistic Research* (Colloque International CNRS, Université de Nice, 5–8 June 1985; Geneva: Slatkine-Champion, 1986), pp. 780-95. According to Schmidt, content analysis emerged from attempts to build 'a powerful tool for reducing the amount of reading'; the basic, anti-literary tendency to move away from the text to an abstract conceptual scheme remains central. Schmidt's basic appeal is to consensus achieved by a high level of abstraction.

themselves, each with internal subdivisions: for example in the case of hunting, for equipment (nets, chains, snares, spears, etc.), techniques, predators, prey, associated numina (Diana, Bacchus, Apollo) and so forth. Not surprisingly many of these large groupings overlap and so share terms; this sharing is expressed easily enough in the thesaurus by duplicate entries, which again are copied from their single authoritative source, the base lexicon.

The electronic lexicon could have an additional function, namely to allow reference from English senses to Latin headwords, and thus to locations in the *Metamorphoses*.[36] Because of the extraordinary polysemy of the language, it is especially true that the full thematic and imagistic potential even of a small Latin lexicon is difficult to determine, especially for subsequent users, who cannot depend on the derived thesaurus to reveal it. A solution would be to add all the definitions for each word from a standard source (in my case, the *OLD*), then to compile the electronic lexicon into a lexical database, so that an alphabetical list of all sense-words with reference to their respective headwords may be derived. Preliminary experiments with the *OLD*, and experience with the *Oxford English Dictionary on CD-ROM*, have shown me that a Latin lexical database would indeed be a potent tool, but the labour involved for a lexicon the size of the *OLD* (approx. 40,000 entries) is forbidding.

7. *Words and Ideas*

We have seen that with markup we run into fundamental problems because the complex effects of imaginative language do not survive well the translation into the crude terms of the encoding pseudo-language. Similarly, the building of a semantically organized thesaurus, no matter how complete the collection of words, will almost inevitably fail to capture passages that a human reader will have no trouble recognizing, as I noted earlier. It seems reasonable to suppose that the more suggestive the text, the more the expressive

36. This corresponds to Schmidt's 'semasiological' function of the content-analysis dictionary, supplementing the 'onomasiological' or reference from words to ideas ('Concept versus Meaning', p. 788). Unlike his notion of the content-analysis dictionary, however, my electronic lexicon does not restrict or reduce interpretation, only show additional possibilities. Lexicographers and philologists, however good in their fields, cannot be presumed experts in literary interpretation.

potential of language speaks through it, the higher the failure-rate will tend to be. As with markup, the near inevitability of failure does not mean that the exercise is not worth doing, rather that the electronic edition answers queries by raising methodological questions.

If we make a concerted and intelligent effort to set down the words of a particular vocabulary, we will of course get a serviceable list with which to begin a study of the corresponding ideas, either in one work or, comparatively, amongst several. Using such a list TACT can then produce a distribution graph that will show the areas where the vocabulary is concentrated and where it is scarce.[37] Several iterations of word-gathering and graphing may be necessary before the vocabulary is as complete as can be; when it is, the next step is to compare the graphic evidence with what we as readers know. The differences may of course show that a careless reader is wrong, or that a prejudiced one is blind to evidence, but an intelligent reader is more likely to uncover interesting, non-trivial questions, especially why the explicit vocabulary concentrates here or there but not in other places where the idea represented by that vocabulary is obvious. Let me illustrate with the vocabulary of ignorance in the *Metamorphoses*.

The story of Arachne and Minerva (*Met.* 6.1-145) provides a good example: clearly about ignorance, the story nevertheless contains very few of the relevant words.[38] The discrepancy in fact points to the poet's ironic indirection: he treats ignorance by focusing on its opposite, knowledge, which in the *Metamorphoses* is a forbidden knowledge that spells an end to all knowing, and so a final, irreversible ignorance. Thus, in a contest of skill, mortal Arachne and divine Minerva, both gifted weavers, depict the nature of the gods in their tapestries. Arachne's skill proves the greater, her report of divine

---

· 37. Considerably more sophisticated kinds of distribution than TACT provides are possible by applying mathematical functions to the data. See, for example, J.B. Smith, 'Computer Criticism', in Potter (ed.), *Literary Computing and Literary Criticism*, pp. 25-31; N. Ide, 'A Statistical Measure of Theme and Structure', *CHum* 23 (1989), pp. 277-83; cf. Goldfield p. 102. Note, however, that TACT output can itself become input to a numerical analysis package; I use a spreadsheet program.

38. Apart from Minerva's quoted speech (obviously suspect), in only one place is ignorance of any variety attributed to Arachne: the poet notes that *perstat in incepto stolidaeque cupidine palmae / in sua fata ruit*, 'she persists in her challenge and rushes on her fate, stupified by desire for glory' (*Met.* 6.50-51). Such is a typical effect of desire in the *Metamorphoses*.

nature the more accurate. She shows in her weaving exactly what the poet has shown in his verse: the unbridled, destructive libido of the gods. Minerva, however, weaves the divine establishment's party-line. Enraged at Arachne's success, she—the 'goddess of knowing'—destroys the evidence of divine misdeeds and silences the weaver by changing her into a spider, thus manifesting her opponent's truth. But the opposition is not quite that simple. However wise to divine failings, Arachne acts ignorantly (the outcome of any such challenge is a foregone conclusion) or is rendered effectively ignorant by pride in her own skill and by desire for glory. Knowledge, then, leads to the extinction of knowledge in mortals and gods alike. The scholar who studies ignorance must also study its categorical opposite.

Not all discrepancies between words and ideas are so rewarding, however. Clearly, as has been noted for some time, a methodological question is raised by the failure of single words to capture the sense of a text. Logically the next step is to offer tools for dealing with multi-verbal constructs. TACT offers a wider range of these than any other program of which I am aware.

Fixed phrases—more accurately, fixed sequences of words—are the simplest. Collecting these for later study is simply a mechanical process with obvious applicability to highly formulaic texts (such as Anglo-Saxon poetry or modern government documents), where fixed phrases function much like single words. Allow me to note in passing, however, that phrasal repetition is more common than we suppose, and that in particular fixed phrases are surprisingly plentiful and useful in the *Metamorphoses*, clearly a non-formulaic text. In fact, inflection and Ovidian *variatio sermonis*, both of which would seem to minimize the occurrence of exactly repeated phrases, almost guarantee that they will be significant when they do occur—not so much as reliable bearers of meaning themselves, of course, but as links between stories. The paradigm for all such in the poem is Echo's partial echoing of Narcissus: her repetitions, John Hollander has noted, deconstruct the youth's intended meanings 'into their hidden but operative *ultimae*',[39] revealing an erotic selfhood that will grip him fatally when he sees his own alluring image in the water. For the *Metamorphoses*, then, phrasal repetition is yet another device to help us see unsuspected coherence beneath the disparate appearance of events.

39. *The Figure of Echo: A Mode of Allusion in Milton and After* (Berkeley: University of California Press, 1981), p. 12; see also pp. 26-31.

A more general form of the 'phrase', because it is not bound by contiguity, is the collocate or occurrence of two or more words nearby each other. The assumption is that collocates which tend to fall within an experimentally determined span will betray a semantic relationship and so indicate an associated idea. In TACT the user may choose amongst three kinds of collocational analysis: of specified words or word-groups; of all collocates of a given word or word-group; and of all collocates of every word. The latter two kinds also compute for each collocation its Z-score, a statistical value designed to measure the degree to which the collocation is unusual for the text under study.[40]

Intuitively one can understand how related words will tend to be found close together and how, through that relation, the polysemy of these words might be focused into meaning. The computational model, as it were, allows us to draw a boundary around a segment of text, then to single out the significant collocates within it conveniently. The primary limiting assumption of the model is of the text as a linear string of equivalent objects. Readers also experience the text more or less linearly on first reading, but as it is internalized in memory, the text becomes something like a simultaneous presence. Furthermore, to the reader words are never merely equivalent objects; and once the text becomes simultaneous, its component words differentiate according to their significance in the work, and find their semantic neighbours sometimes irrespective of linear distance. The technology of collocation is of little help here.

Again, the model obviously has something right, but its failure in certain key respects points to a root problem: that the combination of character-strings and word-separators—that is what words, fixed phrases and collocates are to the computer—do not constitute language. If the machine cannot at present go beyond the bare linguistic signs to signification, then at least it may show us everything that can be done with them. If the machine is to bring, as is often claimed, a new interpretative rigour to the study of texts, then it will be because we increasingly know where the bare evidence leaves off and the imaginative world begins. Illuminating the boundary between the two is, I have suggested, where the technology is apt to make its most significant contribution.

40. Bradley, *TACT: User's Guide*, p. 13.

Conclusion

In 'Literary Studies as Flight From Literature?' Leonard Forster
describes in the history of that discipline a recurrent impulse to turn
away 'from hollow abstractions in search of the concrete, the specific,
the characteristic, the natural'.[41] In time yearning for direct
confrontation with the text, which demands so much of the reader, is
itself replaced by yet another flight into the safety of abstraction and
ideology (p. xxvii). The revolutionary fervour of textual computing
marks, perhaps, one such recurrence of this impulse to seek the
concrete, with its combined sense of return from arid theory to what
is actually on the page, and of new perspectives leading to fresh
discoveries. The history of revolutions suggests, however, that the
decline of creative impulse, through revolutionary chic, into reactionary senescence is inevitable. If so, then the real question is what
lasting contribution might be taking shape. Here I would like to
develop the suggestion I made briefly in the previous section and in
conclusion say what I think its effects might be.

The genre of research and publication I have described in this essay,
the electronic edition, returns not just to the text itself (no more than a
concatenation of character-strings?) but, because it is a participatory,
interactive medium, also to the ancient scholarly passion for commentary and exegesis: the struggle to interpret from τὸ γὰρ γράμμα
ἀποκτέννει, the 'letter that killeth', τὸ δὲ πνεῦμα ζῳοποιεῖ, the
'spirit that giveth life' (2 Cor. 3.6), and to spread the quickened word.
It also manifests once again our need for and fascination by the
methodologies and mechanisms of study that we have been devising at
least since the invention of the alphabet,[42] which brought with it an
elegant and powerful means of listing and organizing textual elements,
and so the concordance, and so TACT. Fascination with the latest such
device is, perhaps, sometimes more obvious than the utility of applying it, but the cultural significance of this fascination is undeniable
and, I would argue, important for our understanding of the role of the
computer in textual study. On the one hand we are warned of the

41. *Modern Language Review* 73 (1978), p. xxii.
42. See T. McArthur, *Worlds of Reference: Lexicography, Learning and Language from the Clay Tablet to the Computer* (Cambridge: Cambridge University
Press, 1986).

'pernicious tendency in the human mind to externalize its own inventions, pervert them into symbols of objective mastery over us by alien forces':[43] for example, the troubling myth of Daedalus, *ingenio fabrae celeberrimus artis* (*Met.* 8.158) and builder of the Labyrinth, who is characteristically trapped by his own ingenuity; and the Psalmist's characterization of idol-worship as a snare of destructive self-referentiality (Ps. 115.8; cf. 106.36; Isa. 44.9-20), on which Paul elaborates in Romans 1.21-32. On the other hand, the venerable notion of a *homo ludens* suggests positively the extent to which discoveries in the arts and sciences arise out of the serendipitous interplay of mind and material, to which belongs playful delight in the mechanisms of knowledge and the craftsmanship of knowing.[44]

At the same time as we gain perspective from and are both warned and encouraged by the heritage of computer-assisted methods, we also need to sharpen our minds to the realisation that the electronic medium and its devices are very, very new. Such things are by nature slow to assimilate. Scholarly applications of the computer still largely imitate old methods; far too little attention has been paid to the inherent qualities of the medium, hence to what methods may be particularly appropriate to the new device.[45] This is understandable, since these qualities are difficult to distinguish from the accidents of current implementation, which is often obscure and unstable. Nevertheless, we should now at least realise that imitation is severely limiting and be prepared to speculate on the gross outlines of what lies beyond it. Perhaps even more importantly, we should know what it is that we want—what scholarly fruits we would harvest from 'the fields of desire' (Isa. 32.12, על שדים ספדים).

My example has been the *Metamorphoses*, in which mutability is the subject, so it is perhaps not surprising that I should emphasize the

43. N. Frye, 'Literary and Mechanical Models', in I. Lancashire (ed.), *Research in Humanities Computing 1* (Oxford: Clarendon Press, 1991), p. 10.

44. Note the discussion of 'serious play' in my article, '*HUMANIST*: Lessons from a Global Electronic Seminar', *CHum* 26 (1992), p. 212, esp. n. 27. Potter expresses impatience with play and, more seriously, with undirected exploration and its consequent threat of 'data inundation'; see 'Statistical Analysis of Literature', p. 427, and 'From Literary Output to Literary Criticism', p. 333.

45. Sperberg-McQueen comments that 'tools always shape the hand that wields them; technology always shapes the minds that use it' ('Text in the Electronic Age', p. 34); cf. my discussion of tools as perceptual agents in '*HUMANIST*', p. 38.

same quality in the device made for studying it. Changeableness, however, is as basic to thinking as to living, so to all texts as artifacts of living and material of thought. Thus I would argue that however problematic it may be in some respects, the mutability of the electronic medium is perhaps its most valuable characteristic.[46] To echo the agonistic language of Detienne and Vernant with which I began, this changeableness speaks to the contest in which we pit our interpretative cunning against the text as it is quickened into life by reading, attempting to gain 'victory over a shifting reality whose continuous metamorphoses make it almost impossible to grasp'. I would argue further that because of this changeableness the electronic edition promises to improve upon its predecessor to a significant degree for the purposes of trial and experimentation with its text, and for presenting the processes and methods of understanding it. As a stable repository of editorial wisdom, crucial to further interpretative work, and as a means of reading the text, the electronic edition seems to me much less well suited than the codex, which does the job so admirably well.

Mutability, properly recognized and put to work, bears directly upon the area I suggested as the most promising for computer-assisted textual study: exploring the differences between literary and mechanical models. Quite clearly the genius of the electronic edition moves us quickly away from the imitative and perverse emphasis on 'productivity' (that is, the efficient processing of received knowledge) towards the swiftly moving, nimble, experimental spirit of inquiry, which in some respects is less well served by printed editions. Just as clearly, however, imitation of human mental operations is of the essence, and so the recursive process of perfective imitation that characterizes the application of particular techniques and programs, and the development of the technology as a whole. Like Daedalus we first build an image of our own cleverness, then must become more clever to escape its limitations.

46. The problems caused by the mutability of electronic texts are legal and technological; the latter are easily solved by software that verifies the integrity of files; the former, less easily, over time by the usual mechanisms of the law. Here I am using the notion of 'mutability' in the broadest possible sense, including for example the ease with which electronic texts are replicated and transmitted. Note Irizarry's brief discussion of the 'mobility' of electronic text ('Literary Analysis and the Microcomputer', p. 993).

Northrop Frye mischievously suggests in 'Literary and Mechanical Models' that literary critical schools are 'better thought of as programming models,' and that 'the importance of the computer is in bringing them down to manageable scope, so that their assumptions can be worked through in a reasonable time...' (p. 7). Although little has been done explicitly in this direction, John B. Smith described some years ago the convergence of certain modern schools with the kind of methodology most easily accommodated on the computer.[47] Smith proposed that 'Computer Criticism' might itself form a separate school, based on 'its expanded concept of abstract structure and the resulting shift in the critic's conceptualization of the text and its meanings' (p. 25). As the basis for a school of criticism rather than a critical instrument, however, the computer would seem to represent an ultimate 'flight from literature' into programmatic abstraction, and thus an end to its value for literary studies. The fact that such a school has not yet formed (although others have come and gone) may be only historical accident, but there may be a deeper and more interesting reason. At the same time as the computing machine focuses attention on what seems the stable 'materiality' of text,[48] it subverts that stability by rendering the fixed word of print into immaterial patterns

47. 'Computer Criticism', pp. 21-25, citing Russian Formalism, New Criticism, French Structuralism, and the London Formalist school; cf. Burrows, 'Computers and the Study of Literature', pp. 183-88; Fortier, 'Analysis of Twentieth-Century French Prose Fiction', pp. 78-83; Bailey, 'The Future of Computational Stylistics', pp. 6-8. The debt to New Criticism is most often noted, e.g. as a failing by Susan Wittig in 'The Computer and the Concept of Text', *CHum* 11 (1978), pp. 211-15. Citing Wittig's study, Rosanne Potter observes in 'Statistical Analysis of Literature' that although the New Critics may be out-moded, 'that textual surfaces (style) no longer merit analysis is a political, rather than a scientific, statement' (pp. 405-406); Burrows similarly comments that 'as Johnson said of the Metaphysical poets, to write on their plan it was at least necessary to read and think' (p. 186). Note also M.D. Harris's computational application of a theory about discourse, 'Analysis of the Discourse Structure of Lyric Poetry', *CHum* 23 (1989), pp. 423-28; Snelgrove's implementation of reader-response criticism, in 'A Method for the Analysis of the Structure of Narrative Texts', pp. 221-25. In 'Statistical Analysis of Literature', Potter claims that 'the empiricism of quantitative approaches to literature puts computational analysis at odds with our times' (p. 426); the same might be said of the metatextual approach. As I suggested at the beginning of this section, however, contrary empiricism may be precisely what makes machine-assisted *ordonnance* so attractive.

48. Cf. Smith, 'Computer Criticism', pp. 21ff.

of energy that must be dynamically maintained even to be perceived.[49] It furthermore subverts the fixity of theoretical dogma, when we can figure out how to program it, by inviting and facilitating change, thus probing and testing of theory. Again, mutability is the ruling principle of the medium, hence interactivity, hence the recursive cycle of hypothesis and experimentation that pushes us not into the false and limiting security of another critical school, rather to the limits of articulate theories.

To return to another theme of this paper, Frye notes the potential of the computer in the discovery of the recurrent entities of literary text (p. 6): not merely the characteristics of an idiolect or explicit markers of narrative relationship, but what he calls the 'archetypes' or basic cultural elements out of which a literature is written. These of course are more than mere character-strings, although expressed through them, and likely harder to detect even than what we often mean by 'theme' or 'meaning', which tend to be local and contextually determined. Yet they are by definition the kind of thing that should emerge out of great masses of text, through which the computer is tireless at sifting. Indeed, a sifter that is synchronic by nature (or, more accurately, that imitates synchronic access most easily), and so pays no attention to contextual meaning, may be just what is required. The question is of course what mesh will catch these archetypes, and to discover that implies considerably more work in computer-assisted textual analysis of all kinds, including the sort I have described for Ovid and proposed for the Bible. Since the discovery of molecular programming in DNA, is it not possible to suppose a modern realisation of a dream at least as old as Homer: the creation of a machine like ourselves? ὄφρα οἱ αὐτόματοι θεῖον δυσαίατ' ἀγῶνα / ἠδ' αὖτις πρὸς δῶμα νεοίατο, θαῦμα ἰδέσθαι, 'that the self-moving machines might enter the gathering of the gods at [the craftsman's] wish and again return to his house, a wonder to behold' (Homer, *Il.* 18.376-7).

49. Thus prior to a theory of literature we need a theory about text that is more sophisticated than one which asserts its 'materiality,' as Smith does. For a good beginning, see Sperberg-McQueen, 'Text in the Electronic Age;' S.J. DeRose, D.G. Durand, E. Mylonas, and A. Renear, 'What is Text, Really?', *Journal of Computing in Higher Education* 1 (1990), pp. 3-26.

Again, we come back to the cognitive problem of how we know what we know, or as one scientist put it, 'how we may think'.[50] I have argued that the computational model is valuable as much or more for its limits in the exploration of imaginative language as its powers—hence its power to push the limits of understanding. Perhaps it is, then, a model of ourselves in a broader sense than is usually discussed. Within its confines, the mechanical model provides a simulacrum of thinking that shapes further thought about thinking, and so a view of things 'by means of a mirror in an enigma'. Yet, to follow the physical metaphor, it is a model also in the sense that having built it we can view a particular mental form from the outside, in perspective, as a feature in the landscape of the imagination. The pragmatic value cannot be doubted, but close, philosophical attention to the implications of actual practice, it may be argued, is the beginning of a renewed scholarly wisdom.

.

50. The title of a seminal article by Vannevar Bush (proposing a mechanical model of scholarly work he called the 'memex'), in the July 1945 issue of *Atlantic Monthly*; see also 'Memex Revisited', in *Science is not Enough* (New York: William Morrow and Co., 1965), pp. 75-101.

PART III
NEW UNDERSTANDINGS OF THE RELATIONSHIP
BETWEEN JUDAISM AND CHRISTIANITY

PHILO AND EUSEBIUS ON MONASTERIES AND MONASTICISM: THE THERAPEUTAE AND KELLIA

G. Peter Richardson

This paper attempts two experiments: first, and most important, to see how well one can use ancient literature to develop an architectural reconstruction of the buildings used by a Jewish group in the early Christian period; secondly, and more speculatively, to enquire into the influence of that group and its structures in a later period of Christian history; before I conclude I will endeavour also to connect these matters with John Hurd's interest in Corinth.

The Jewish group is the Therapeutae/Therapeutrides. There are many remarkable aspects of this group, which must have flowered in the first century BCE and the first century CE; one is that it has complementary names for female and male participants, complementary activities and equivalent kinds of leadership positions. In brief, it is a rare group in antiquity providing an important outlet for religious Jewish women in Egypt within a celibate but mixed community.[1] But the point of interest here is the group's buildings, as described by Philo, for they form one of the few complexes known to us from that period of antiquity housing a monastic community. The other well known community is, of course, also from the Jewish world, the one at Qumran.[2] This latter is a truly communal enterprise,

---

1. See P. Richardson and V. Heuchan, 'Jewish Voluntary Associations in Egypt and the Roles of Women' (paper delivered at the Canadian Society of Biblical Studies meeting in Charlottetown, P.E.I., June 1992), for a study of both Therapeutae and the temple community at Leontopolis.

2. See G. Vermes, 'Essenes and Therapeutae', in *Post Biblical Jewish Studies* (Leiden: Brill, 1975), pp. 30-31; E. Schürer, G. Vermes, F. Millar and M. Black, *A History of the Jewish People in the Age of Jesus Christ* (Edinburgh: T. & T. Clark, 1979), vol. 2, Appendix A, pp. 591-97: 'the hypothesis that the Therapeutae were members of an Egyptian Branch of the Palestinian Essene movement deserves serious consideration' (p. 597). This section seems to me to make several serious

whereas the Therapeutae/Therapeutrides form a quasi-communal group of persons—both male and female—in which the focus is on a life of solitary contemplation.[3] To put it in later Christian terms, Qumran is a cenobitic community and the Therapeutae form a quasi-eremitic group.

My main point of comparison will be an early monastic group of buildings recently excavated at Kellia in Lower Egypt that reflect the activities of a quasi-eremitic group. I will point out that there are unusual similarities between Kellia and the description of the Therapeutae in Philo. The middle term between these two points of comparison is Eusebius's description of early Egyptian monasticism, a description that he borrows very largely from Philo.

The Therapeutae may seem an odd place to begin this investigation of Judaism and Christianity. When the Therapeutae flourished Christianity had hardly begun; knowledge of the group is very limited—we have really only one source, Philo—and it seems to have soon passed from the scene leaving hardly a mark on Judaism. What can this strange, little-known, ascetic group teach us, apart from how complex Judaism was in the first century CE?

1. *Eusebius on the Therapeutae*

Eusebius (born about 260 CE) enters the picture because he had second-hand knowledge of this group; he believed it had so many features similar to the Christianity of his day that he claimed that the Therapeutae were Christians.[4]

Book 2 of Eusebius's *Ecclesiastical History (EH)*[5] deals with the apostles in the period from Tiberius to Nero; after discussing Simon

---

errors interpreting Philo: the 'communal sanctuary' is not referred to as a κοινὸν μοναστήριον, the assembly and refectory are not the same building, and the resemblances between the buildings at Qumran and for the Therapeutae are not very close.

3.   For the claim that both Qumran and the Therapeutae practise contemplation, see P. Geoltrain, 'La contemplation à Qumran et chez les Thérapeutes', *Semitica* 9 (1959), pp. 49-57.

4.   See T.D. Barnes, *Constantine and Eusebius* (Cambridge, MA: Harvard University Press, 1980), pp. 195-96.

5.   Eusebius, *History of the Church* (Harmondsworth: Penguin, 1965); K. Lake and J.E.L. Oulton, *Eusebius Ecclesiastical History* (2 vols., LCL; Cambridge, MA: Harvard University Press, 1932 [1926]). Quotations are from the Penguin edition.

the arch-heretic, Eusebius introduces Peter into the account as the exposer of Simon (2.13-14). He then deftly connects this incident with Mark, Peter's follower and the author of the Gospel (2.15), who was also the first Christian to go to Egypt to preach and establish churches there, especially in Alexandria (2.16-17):

> So large was the body of believers, men and women alike, built up there at the first attempt, with an extremely severe rule of life, that Philo decided that he must record in writing their activities, gatherings, meals, and everything else about their way of living. (17) It is also recorded that under Claudius, Philo came to Rome to have conversations with Peter, then preaching to the people there. This would not be improbable, as the short work to which I am referring, and which he [Philo] produced at a considerably later date, clearly contains the rules of the Church still observed in our own day. And again, when he describes the life of our ascetics with the greatest precision, it is plain enough that he not only knew but welcomed with whole-hearted approval the apostolic men of his day, who it seems were of Hebrew stock and therefore, in the Jewish manner, still retained most of their ancient customs.

This contains a remarkable blend of fact and fiction, knowledge and speculation.[6] Eusebius knows that Philo visited Rome during Claudius's reign (fact, see earlier in 2.4-5)[7] but he asserts that he came to talk to Peter (fiction). He knows of his writing *de Vita Contemplativa* (fact) but he believes that this work speaks of ascetic Christians (fiction). He understands that the earliest Christian apostles were Hebrew in manner of life and race (fact) and thinks that Philo was intimate with them, almost one of them (fiction). He claims that there was a large body of Christians in Alexandria (fact?) and thinks they behaved like ascetic Jews (fiction?). He argues that Peter preached in Rome (fact?) but that it was as early as the reign of Claudius (fiction). And so on.

6.   A kinder estimate than that of F.C. Conybeare, *Philo: About the Contemplative Life* (Oxford: Clarendon Press, 1895; repr. New York: Garland, 1987): 'hallucinations' (p. 318); 'impenetrable... darkness' (p. 319); 'rubbish' (p. 326).

7.   'Philo became widely known as one of the greatest scholars, not only among our own people but also among those brought up as pagans. By descent a Hebrew, he could not hold his own with any of the eminent occupants of official positions in Alexandria.' When speaking of Philo's embassy he refers to a work of five books, and he compares this with Josephus's account. Eusebius then explicitly attributes the 'calamities' in Alexandria in the late thirties–early forties to the 'consequence of their crimes against Christ', linking this in turn with Sejanus and Pilate.

The features of the Therapeutae that especially attract Eusebius include their renunciation of property, their life of contemplation ('the prophetic way of life'), their location 'over' (or 'beyond') Lake Meriotis,[8] their seclusion in houses with individual 'sanctuaries' (or 'monasteries'), their 'spiritual discipline' (ἄσκησις) including their study of Scripture,[9] their self-control in matters of food, the conduct of their meetings. He quotes liberally from *de Vita Contemplativa* and is careful to attribute it to Philo. He points out that he has selected these various items for comment because they are 'those in which the characteristics of Church life are displayed' (δι᾽ ὧν τὰ χαρακτηριστικὰ τῆς ἐκκλησιαστικῆς ἀγωγῆς ὑποτίθηται).

But beginning at this very point in his description his comments on the Therapeutae start to have a strong defensive ring to them; his view that they are Christians appears to have been controversial:

If anyone does not agree that what has been described is peculiar to the gospel way of life but thinks it applicable to other people too, he will surely be convinced...

These statements...seem to me to refer plainly and unquestionably to members of our Church (περὶ τὸν καθ᾽ ἡμᾶς).

...if...someone insists on denying it, he will surely...be convinced by still clearer evidence which cannot be found anywhere but in the religious practices of Christians...

...the regular spiritual discipline still practised among us...

...in precise accordance with the practice observed by us and us alone to this day...

...anyone can see that he [Philo] had in mind the first preachers of the gospel teaching and the customs handed down by the apostles from the beginning.[10] (*EH* 2.17)

8.   Eusebius and Philo before him use ὑπέρ. The natural meaning of the preposition when used of relative geographical position is not 'above' but 'beyond' or 'farther inland'; cf. ἐξ Αἰθιοπίας τῆς ὑπὲρ Αἰγύπτου cited in Liddell-Scott-Jones. See further below.

9.   Eusebius conjectures that Philo has actually listened to the exposition of the Therapeutae and thinks that the writings they were studying were 'the gospels, the apostolic writings and in all probability passages interpreting the old prophets, such as are contained in the Epistle to the Hebrews and several others of Paul's epistles'. This is another aspect of Eusebius's effort to make Philo almost a Christian (*EH* 2.17).

10.   Note especially the double emphasis: not to other people, to us alone. The

Two obvious and significant observations flow directly from even a cursory glance at this curious situation: first, Eusebius does the best he can with the information available to him to make sound historical reconstructions, though inevitably he fails and sometimes leads wildly astray;[11] secondly, in the fourth century he values the ascetic life of a first-century group he claims was Christian, and he wishes the Church to emulate that group. Two other points bearing on monasticism are also significant. Thirdly, Eusebius is an important witness to the fact that in his own day Christian monasticism has developed to the point he can describe its characteristics, even if it be in terms borrowed from Philo. He knows that Egyptian monasticism manifests some of the very same features that he finds in Philo's description. Fourthly, its history must be sufficiently long that he can claim, presumably with some degree of plausibility, that these monastic characteristics actually go back two hundred and fifty or more years to the time of Mark's supposed founding of Egyptian Christianity. Whether Eusebius himself believed this does not matter much; what matters more is that he can make this type of claim, and that this claim becomes evidence for Egyptian practice in his lifetime.[12]

In short, Eusebius provides us with important evidence for Egyptian monasticism in the first few years of the fourth and the late third century.[13] Can one substantiate these inferences about this early

character of this series of statements is not unlike earlier *adversus Iudaios* literature; what Christians now have no longer applies to anyone else, whatever claims the others might once have had.

11. On Eusebius's sources, see Barnes, *Constantine and Eusebius*; R. Grant, *Eusebius as Church Historian* (Oxford: Clarendon Press, 1980), pp. 52, 73-75; M. Gödecke, *Geschichte als Mythos: Eusebs 'Kirchegeschichte'* (Frankfurt: Peter Lang, 1987).

12. Barnes, *Constantine and Eusebius*, p.130; R.L. Wilken, *The Myth of Christian Beginnings* (Notre Dame, IN: University of Notre Dame Press, 1980), p. 73: 'In Eusebius's history, nothing really happens or, more accurately, nothing *new* happens. The history of the Church is a history of an eternal conflict between the truth of God and its opponents.'

13. This evidence from Eusebius pushes back the origins of the movement, or at least advances the pace of development a little. It is strange that D.J. Chitty, *The Desert a City: An Introduction to the Study of Egyptian and Palestinian Monasticism under the Christian Empire* (Oxford: Basil Blackwell, 1966), and A. Guillaumont, *Aux origines du monachisme chrétien* (Spiritualité orientale, 30; Bégrolles-en-Mauges: Abbaye de Bellefontaine, 1979), make so little use of Eusebius in their otherwise careful studies.

Christian monasticism from archaeological evidence? The short answer is no. There is, quite simply, no verifiable archaeological evidence in Egypt—or indeed anywhere else—for Christian monasteries in this very early period. There is, however, one very suggestive site.

2. *The Kellia*

About fifty five kilometers south of Alexandria is the site of one of the most massive collections of monastic establishments in antiquity, the Kellia.[14] It lies just south of Nitria, another monastic centre, and north of Wadi Natroun—or the Scetis—which still has four monastic establishments today.[15] All three areas lie within sixty kilometers of each other, and the first two were related. All three are on the edge of the great Western or Libyan Desert; together they form one of the greatest flowerings of the urge to flee society and go into the wilderness to live a life of prayer, self-denial and worship of God (fig. 1). Here is a very early centre of one of the two great streams of the monastic movement.[16]

Kellia derives from a Greek transliteration (κέλλα) of the Latin *cella* ('room', 'chamber' or simply 'cell')—a name indicating something of the character of the buildings that have been recovered there. It is this site from among the three just mentioned that is relevant to this paper, because Kellia gives evidence of some of the earliest structures to have been thrown up by the fledgling monastic movement. More important, these have been the object of intensive archaeological rescue work sporadically since 1964, for agriculture

14. A basic bibliography on Kellia includes: R. Kasser, *Kellia 1965: Topographie générale, mensurations at fouilles aux Qouçoûr* (Geneva: Georg, 1967); F. Daumas and A. Guillaumont, *Kellia I, Kom 219: Fouilles exécuté au 1964 et 1965* (2 vols.; Cairo: L'Institut français d'archéologie orientale, 1969); R. Kasser, *Kellia: Topographie* (Geneva: Georg, 1972); R. Kasser, *Survey archéologique des Kellia (Basse-Égypte) Rapport de la campagne 1981* (2 vols.; Leuven: Peeters, 1983); *Les Kellia, ermitages coptes en Basse-Egypte* (Geneva: Editions de Tricorne, 1989).
15. Some numbers: Nitria is said to have had 5000 monks, Kellia 600, Oxyrhynchus 10,000 monks and 20,000 virgins; a nineteenth-century estimate was 70,000 monastics altogether. Details in Daumas et Guillaumont, *Kellia I*, pp. viii, xiv. Though these are exaggerated figures, the numbers in this area were large.
16. Further details in Guillaumont, *Origins*, and Chitty, *The Desert a City*.

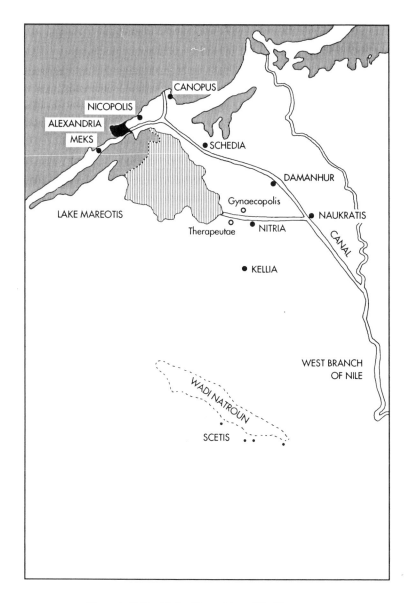

Figure 1. *Kellia, Nitria, Alexandria and the Therapeutae*

has already taken over much of the site and threatens to take over the whole area. The excavated structures clearly put a primary emphasis on the individual 'cell'; they express in their built form the ideal of the life of solitary devotion. According to the literary evidence, nearby Nitria was actually used as a kind of novitiate for a couple of years before monks adopted the more withdrawn form of life at Kellia. Regrettably excavation there has not been done and it is now not possible.

The excavations at Kellia give extremely strong fifth-, sixth- and seventh-century evidence of quasi-eremitic monasticism—emphasizing withdrawal—but blending this with communal elements; this was distinct from either total seclusion with no communal elements or an emphasis on community, so-called cenobitic monasticism.[17] Though most of the large number of buildings at Kellia witness to the practices of the sixth and seventh centuries, a fair number reflect fifth-century practices,[18] and the excavators have concluded that there are also earlier stages that go back to fourth-century structures. Literary evidence confirms the development of the site in the late 300s. The excavators have done an exemplary job in putting together the resources to carry out these emergency excavations and they have drawn in other scholars associated with them in studying the implications of these important remains.[19] The following summary is confined to the earliest substantial evidence—for the period of the fifth century—but much of it also applies to the evidence that pertains to the fourth century.[20]

a. In the fifth century there is a clear pattern of clusters of 'houses' of mud brick with vaulted rooms (this clustering probably applies in the fourth century as well), following more or less the pattern shown in fig. 2; all houses are oriented in the same direction.

17. P. Bridel, 'La dialectique de l'isolement et de l'ouverture dans les monastères kelliotes: Espaces reservés—espaces d'accueil', in *Le site monastique*, pp. 145-61.

18. Kasser, *Survey*, especially the drawing on p. 56 identifying specific sites pre-500 CE.

19. See the colloquium on Kellia, *Le site monastique*, especially the contributions by Weidmann, Grossman, Krause, Thierry, Al-Tawab.

20. D. Weidmann, 'La construction des plans des monastères', in *Le site monastique*, pp. 257-60; R.-G. Coquin, 'Evolution de l'habitat et évolution de la vue érémitique au Kellia', pp. 261-72.

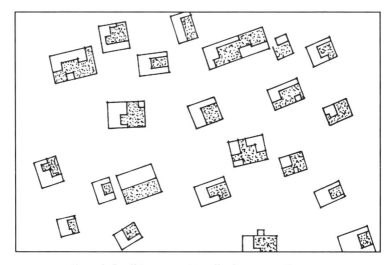

Figure 2. *Small Portion of the Kellia Site* (Les Kellia, p. 18)

b. A low wall encloses a courtyard of each house, on two sides of which are erected quarters for a monk in a rather primitive suite of rooms, the most important of which is the room for prayer and meditation. This is typically entered through a small vestibule and off it, in turn, is a small cell for sleeping, along with storage rooms. In all the earliest buildings the prayer room is typically in the north-west corner of the structure (fig. 3).[21]

c. The prayer rooms typically have a niche on the east wall (a customary direction for prayer) in which may be a fresco to aid devotion—a picture of Christ or something similar (fig. 3).[22]

d. As time went on the houses became more complex, first of all admitting two persons, a senior monk and a junior 'disciple', then accommodating a number of monks in one larger and more complex structure, often now around a central courtyard.[23]

21. *Les Kellia*, figs. 12-15; R.-G. Coquin, 'Evolution de l'habitat', especially figs. 1 and 2, p. 252.

22. Guillaumont, *Origines*, chs. 8, 9, 11; *Les Kellia*, figs. 19-29; P. Corboud, 'L'oratoire et les niches-oratoires: Les dieux de la prière', in *Le site monastique*, pp. 85-92.

23. Details in the various archeological reports, especially Daumas et Guillaumont, *Kellia I*; D. Weidmann, 'Dispersion et concentration'.

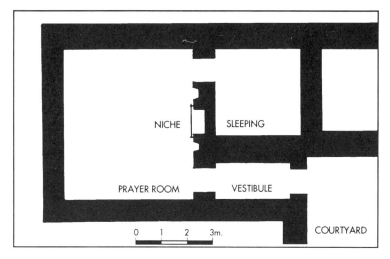

NICHE   SLEEPING

PRAYER ROOM   VESTIBULE

0   1   2   3m.   COURTYARD

Figure 3. *Primitive Apartment for One Monk*

e. For the most part there are few major communal buildings, although some primitive ones seem to have existed even in the fifth century and others certainly developed later.[24] But it appears that for some purposes the communal function was carried out (perhaps only in the very earliest period) at Nitria, some distance away but still functioning as a kind of mother house.[25]

3. *Egyptian Monasticism*

Eusebius writes just at the time that Egyptian monasticism emerges from the activities of three persons:[26] Antony (251–356 CE) the first anchorite, whose activity was originally just south of Alexandria;[27]

24. Daumas et Guillaumont, *Kellia I*, chs. 3, 7; G. Descoeudres, 'L'architecture des ermitages et des sanctuaires', in *Les Kellia*, pp. 47-55.

25. Guillaumont, *Origines*, ch. 10.

26. On monasticism in Egypt, see especially Chitty, *The Desert a City*, and Guillaumont, *Origines*.

27. Antony is usually considered the first monk, but he may have been a disciple of Paul of Thebes (d. 340) who fled to the desert (according to Jerome in *Vita Pauli*) around 249–51 CE. If Jerome's account of Paul is correct (and it is doubtful) he was a true hermit. The name anchorite derives from the Greek ἀναχορεῖν 'to withdraw',

Pachomius (290–346 CE) the first cenobite;[28] and Athanasius (296–373 CE) the Bishop of Alexandria who encouraged these earliest 'monks.'[29] It is in Athanasius's *Life of Antony* (*Vita Antonii*, c. 357 CE) that one finds introduced into Christian literature the terms 'monk' and 'monastery', both associated with Antony. Antony's long career included two periods as a hermit, the earlier in the last quarter of the third century, with a short interval between, during which he seems to have organized a community (probably between 306 and 313 CE). The references in *Life of Antony* purport to describe the period around 306 CE.

Antony's first period of activity prior to 306 CE is usually located in the desert to the south of Alexandria and west of the Nile Delta[30], near the remains at Kellia, Nitria and the Wadi Natroun (in the Scetis depression).[31] Literary evidence puts these monastic foundations in the early fourth century (between 330 and 340 CE); as just noted the archaeological evidence is very strong for the fifth to the seventh centuries, and confirms their origins in the fourth century.[32] In other words, the literary and archaeological evidence converge in an important and satisfying way.

At almost precisely this same period Eusebius was writing his

'retire' or 'flee to the country'; it is used of monks who adopt a life of solitary seclusion; see further P. Miquel, *Lexique du désert: Etude de quelques mot-clés du vocabulaire monastique grec ancien* (Spiritualité orientale, 44; Bégrolles-en-Mauges: Abbaye de Bellefontaine, 1986), pp. 67-72.

28. Pachomius is associated with the Thebaid, as is Paul of Thebes, specifically the area immediately adjacent to Nag Hammadi where the library of Coptic Gnostic books was found. The word cenobite derives from the Greek κοινός or 'common', and refers to monks who live in a communal setting in a monastery.

29. The roots of both the solitary form of asceticism and of the communal form are undoubtedly complex, though in part at least both go back to Origen.

30. At almost the same time a similar development occurs in Palestine, also associated with three persons: Chariton (founded the first monastery c. 330 CE), Euthymius (376–473 CE) and Sabas (439–532 CE). The earliest was Euthymius's establishment on the ruins of Herod's fortress of Hyrcania (Khirbet Mird). These too were quasi-eremetic, though others used individual caves along a wadi linked with a mother house or *laura* (e.g., St. George Koziba in Wadi Qelt).

31. His later activity is located farther south near the Red Sea where a monastery bears his name; J. Doresse, 'Les monastères de Saint-Paul et de Saint-Antoine au désert de la Mer Rouge', in *La site monastique*, pp. 163-72.

32. See Guillaumont, *Origines*, chs. 6, 10; F. Daumas, 'Essai d'interpretation du couvent', in *Kellia I*, pp. 135-45.

church history with its account of the Therapeutae; it is still generally held that most of the first seven books were written before 303 CE, the final version c. 324 CE. In his description of the community of the Therapeutae, whom he believes to be Christian, Eusebius carefully quotes Philo's reference to the *monasterion* (see below), the only time prior to Athanasius's use of the word in connection with Antony that the word has been found in Greek literature. Thus, Athanasius (c. 357 CE) uses *monasterion* of Antony's activities, referring to the first few years of the century. Eusebius (c. 306 CE) derives *monasterion* from Philo's description of the Therapeutae. In the preceding few years the earliest instance of individual withdrawal can be found in Antony. Antony withdraws from society immediately south of Lake Meriotis. Fourth century remains of quasi-eremitic establishments have been found in this same region. The Therapeutae, another quasi-eremitic group, is also found on the margins of Lake Meriotis. Is this a remarkable set of coincidences or is there something historically significant in these associations?

4. *Philo on the Therapeutae and Therapeutrides*

Having highlighted in *EH* 2.16 that this was a large group.[33] Eusebius goes on to particularize, 'both men and women alike' and then he refers to Philo's *de Vita Contemplativa* and to the group's name (in *EH* 2.17): 'Therapeutae and their womenfolk Therapeutrides'. He thinks the name (here following Philo) comes from either the root 'to heal' or 'to worship' and that this name (now making up an explanation himself) was used 'because the title Christian was not yet in general use'. Eusebius seems intrigued by the emphasis on women; he claims that the clearest evidence of the Christian character of the group is to be found in the presence and the roles of women there, 'most of them elderly spinsters who have remained single' (citing Philo): for Eusebius this group's inclusion of celibate women is evidence that they are Christian.[34]

---

33. It is doubtful if there is any basis in fact for this claim; it is much more likely that Eusebius requires a large number in order to explain why Philo is attracted to them. Philo does, in *Contemp.* 18-22, imply that there are a lot, but he seems to mean contemplatives in general.

34. Egyptian monasticism made provision for women ascetics (see Chitty, *The Desert a City*), though the evidence, apart from Eusebius, is not strong.

What about Philo's account itself?[35] It includes of course much more material than can be found in Eusebius's precis of it; it is now agreed—after nineteenth-century doubts—that it is genuine and that it describes a Jewish group in Egypt. It may even be first-hand[36] for the group has its principal and perhaps its only community on the lake near Alexandria.[37] The members have fled from society to Lake Mareotis[38] where there is a community of farm buildings (*Contemp.* 22–23) or 'houses collected together' (*Contemp.* 24). Certain distinct activities set the group apart: the use of laws and oracles, dream activity, prayer, meditation and contemplation, reading and interpretation of Scripture, singing of hymns and psalms, seventh-day assemblies, hierarchical seating and so on (*Contemp.* 25–31).

Each day the members of the Therapeutae, in isolation, pray twice a day, at dawn and at evening (*Contemp.* 27–28). Between these times

35. F.H. Colson, *Philo* (LCL, 9; Cambridge MA: Harvard University Press, 1941), pp. 103-69.

36. P. Geoltrain, 'La Traité de la vie contemplative de Philon d'Alexandrie', *Semitica* 10 (1960), pp. 1-61, esp. pp. 25-26; F. Daumas and P. Miquel, *De Vita Comtemplativa* (Les Oeuvres de Philon d'Alexandrie, 29; Paris: Cerf, 1963), pp. 32-34.

37. Daumas locates the Therapeutae's community in a western suburb of Alexandria two kilometers west of Dikhela, between Mex and Agame: Daumas and Miquel, *Contemp.*, pp. 39-46 (with map); F. Daumas, 'La "solitude" des Thérapeutes et les antécédents égyptiens du monachisme chrétien', in the colloquium *Philon d'Alexandrie* (Lyon, 11–15 September 1966; Paris: CNRS, 1967), pp. 347-59. Conybeare, *Contemplative Life*, pp. 294-97, argues for a location north-east of Alexandria, a little beyond Nicopolis. As noted earlier, Philo, and Eusebius quoting him, both used ὑπέρ whose natural meaning in the context is 'farther inland', i.e., on the other side of the lake altogether, very close to Nitria, one of the first centres of Christian monasticism (this interpretation is made very difficult by the reference to the sea in *Contemp.* 23). See fig. 1.

38. See Strabo, *Geography* 17.1.7, 10, 14, 22 for descriptions of the lake and its importance, using two different names for the lake: *Mareia* and *Mareotis*. The size of the lake was larger in antiquity, extending farther south and east (see fig. 1), so that it came almost as far as Nitria: a canal joined the lake to the Nile at Naukratis, which was between Schedia and Memphis on the western arm of the Nile. Strabo refers in passing (17.1.22) to a village by the name of *Gynaecopolis*, somewhere south of Schedia (for his route see 17.1.16). His description, though imprecise, says 'on the right [are] a very large number of villages extending as far as Lake Mareia'. Is the name a jesting reference to Therapeutae—the town of women, i.e., the place where women have surprisingly large roles?

they contemplate scripture as allegory and study the writings of their founders. They also compose hymns and psalms 'in all sorts of metres and melodies', hymns suitable for processions or in libations at the altars or for the choruses. This daily activity occupies them for six days during which they eat and drink only at night, some eating only every third day and others abstaining for seven days.

On the seventh day there is a general assembly (*Contemp.* 30). The senior person (πρεσβύτατος) gives a discourse, they eat common bread flavoured with salt and hyssop and drink water. On the fiftieth day they are called by a member of the Rota (ἐφημερευταί, *Contemp.* 65–66) to line up in an orderly manner and pray. The seniors (πρεσβύτεροι, *Contemp.* 67) recline in rows according to rank. The President (πρόεδρος, *Contemp.* 75) discusses a question arising from Scripture or one propounded by a member, treating the Scripture allegorically (*Contemp.* 77–78).[39] Then the young male attendants bring in food on tables, following which is a sacred all-night vigil (*Contemp.* 77, 81, 83). After this they all depart to their houses or cells to pursue philosophy and repeat the fifty-day cycle again.[40] As compared with Qumran[41] the two most outstanding differences are the roles of women[42] and the nature of the monastic organization.

39. Despite the equivalence of women among the Therapeutae/Therapeutrides, in the three latter cases Philo seems to assume men are in control.

40. These and other elements leave little doubt that most Greeks or Romans observing such a group would think of it as a voluntary association—a *collegia* or a *thiasos*. See further, Richardson and Heuchan, 'Jewish Voluntary Associations'; Conybeare, *Contemplative Life*, pp. 297-99.

41. Philo specifically draws attention to the connection with Essenes in the first paragraph; whether he intends readers to imagine that the Therapeutae are an Egyptian variant on a group in the Holy Land is not clear. But he does distinguish them as 'active' and 'contemplative'.

42. See D. Sly, *Philo's Perception of Women* (Atlanta: Scholars Press, 1990); R.S. Kraemer, 'Women in the Religions of the Greco-Roman World', *RSR* 9 (1983), pp. 127-39; *idem*, 'Jewish Women in the Diaspora World of Late Antiquity', in J.R. Baskin (ed.), *Jewish Women in Historical Perspective* (Detroit: Wayne State University Press, 1991), pp. 43-67; *idem*, 'Monastic Jewish Women in Greco-Roman Egypt: Philo Judaeus on the Therapeutrides', *Signs* 14 (1989) pp. 342-70; A.J. Levine (ed.), *'Women Like This': New Perspectives on Jewish Women in the Greco-Roman World* (Atlanta: Scholars Press, 1991); C.A. Brown, *No Longer Be Silent: First Century Jewish Portraits of Biblical Women* (Louisville: Westminster/ John Knox, 1992); L.A. Archer, *Her Price is Beyond Rubies: The Jewish Women in Graeco-Roman Palestine* (Sheffield: JSOT Press, 1990); E. Schuller, 'Women in the

5. *Buildings of the Therapeutae*

Philo also provides an important description of the group's buildings,
though we lack archaeological evidence of the structures, regrettably,
to verify his description and to aid in trying to recreate the character
of the structures.[43] He begins by describing imprecisely their 'houses'
(οἰκία, *Contemp.* 24; οἴκημα, 25), perhaps with the emphasis on cells
or cubicles, clustered along Lake Mareotis but 'neither near together
as in towns... nor yet at a great distance' (*Contemp.* 24), with a
dispersed rather than a unitary character as at Qumran[44] (fig. 4),
though not so dispersed as to destroy the sense of κοινωνία (*Contemp.*
24). Each individual house has its own ἱερόν or 'shrine', also called a
σεμνεῖον or 'sanctuary' and μοναστήριον 'cubicle'[45] in which
persons are 'initiated' into the 'mysteries' of the sanctified life (ἐν ᾧ
μονούμενοι τὰ τοῦ σεμνοῦ βίου μυστήρια τελοῦνται,
Contemp. 25). Philo's use of these words is confusing; it is difficult to
know how to translate them and challenging to imagine how he visual-
ized the 'houses' or 'cells'. For example, towards the end he refers to
each member going back to a σεμνεῖον after the vigil (*Contemp.* 89),
meaning the private contemplative space; in *Contemp.* 30 he uses
μοναστήριον for the same function; in *Contemp.* 25 both words are
used to explain ἱερόν which is merely part of an οἴκημα, though
οἴκημα, (like οἰκία in *Contemp.* 24) is used of the space that each
person has, not of a group house.[46] The most obvious solution is that

Dead Sea Scrolls' (publication forthcoming, Canadian Society of Biblical Studies,
Charlottetown P.E.I., 1992), in which some very important suggestions are made
and questions raised about the usual views of the place of women in Qumran.

43. On the following *realia* see Daumas and Miquel, *Contemp.*, pp. 35-39.

44. The buildings at Qumran have a more communal character than seems the
case with the Therapeutae; it is possible, however, that the caves at Qumran had
something of the same role as Philo's 'houses' among the Therapeutae, i.e., as cells.
The recent attempt to claim the main group of buildings at Qumran as a Roman villa,
not a community building, is far-fetched and unimpressive.

45. Philo's use of μοναστήριον (e.g., *Contemp.* 30; see also Colson, *Philo*
9.519-20) is said to be the only instance until the late fourth century of the use of the
word, though Colson and others overlook Eusebius's citation of Philo. Later, Philo
uses the words 'unembellished and makeshift... for utility only' (*Contemp.* 38).
When Eusebius alludes to the buildings he claims that Philo is speaking about
churches in the area (περὶ τῶν κατὰ χώραν ἐκκλησιῶν).

46. There is a somewhat similar ambiguity in *Contemp.* 20 and 23 with respect to

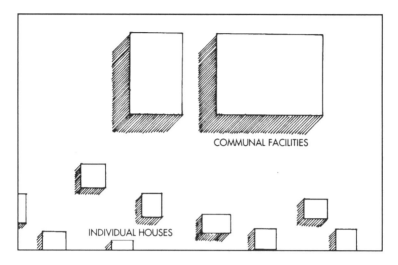

Figure 4. *Therapeutae: Schematic Community*

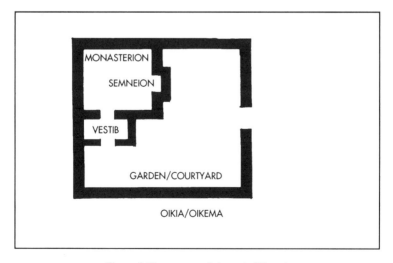

Figure 5. *Therapeutae: Schematic 'House'*

he visualizes a 'shrine' (not more accurately described), within a special room for contemplation and devotion, within a somewhat larger house—all set within a garden or field that contributes to its solitary character (see fig. 5).

They have two larger buildings also. The first is a 'common sanctuary' (κοινὸν σεμνεῖον *Contemp*. 32) for seventh-day worship. When introducing the description of this building Philo refers to the degree of isolation of the individual cells (*Contemp*. 30): the members do not pass beyond the courtyard (αὔλειος)[47] of their individual houses, 'not even looking out from their isolation' (ἀλλ' οὐδὲ ἐξ ἀπόπτου θεωροῦντες). The individual chambers for contemplation are separate from the assembly building, far enough away or else arranged in such a fashion that the members cannot see it. Within the common sanctuary is a double enclosure (διπλοῦς περίβολος) providing space on one side for men, on the other for women—'for women too', says Philo, 'regularly make part of the audience with the same ardour (ζῆλον) and the same sense of their calling' (*Contemp*. 32).

At this point Philo describes, for the first and I think the only time in antiquity, a 'dividing wall' in a Jewish building for ritual purposes:

> The wall between the two chambers rises up from the ground to three or four cubits built in the form of a breastwork, while the space above up to the roof is left open. This arrangement serves two purposes: the modesty becoming to the female sex is preserved, while the women sitting within ear-shot can easily follow what is said since there is nothing to obstruct the voice of the speaker (*Contemp*. 33).

It is now commonplace to argue that synagogues in this period did not have a dividing wall between men and women.[48] I share that view; there is no evidence either literary or archaeological for a division— whether horizontal or vertical—at this stage of synagogue development. Here, however, is a description of just such a wall in an

---

the overall character: in 23 he speaks of ἐπαύλεις ('farm buildings' or 'country house') and he suggests that they form κῶμαι ('villages') but in 20 he stresses that they live ἐν κήποις ἢ μοναγρίαις ('in gardens or solitary fields', the latter word being very rare).

47. Translated by Colson 'outside door'; this can be implied, but it is preferable to translate 'courtyard' as the root suggests.

48. See among others B. Brooten, *Women Leaders in the Ancient Synagogues* (Chico, CA: Scholars Press 1982).

assembly building, though in a structure different from a synagogue.[49] The wall could recall the barrier between the outer court and the so-called court of the women in the Jerusalem Temple,[50] though I consider that to be a remote analogy in the context. Philo's language—here περίβολος—implies an outdoor space, though he also refers to a roofed room attached to the exterior space. περίβολος commonly applies to the space before or around a temple, and I take it that way here, though this is neither explicit nor strong. These hints suggest a double stoa enclosing a defined double space, off which is an assembly room divided down the middle by a breast-high wall (see fig. 6).[51]

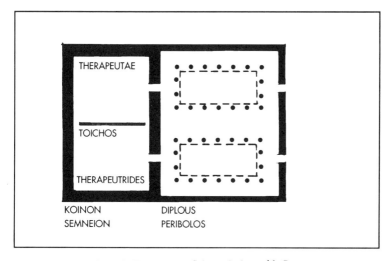

Figure 6. *Therapeutae: Schematic Assembly Room*

49. Conybeare, *Contemplative Life*, p. 130, argues strongly for a synagogue or possibly a school—a *bet ha-midrash*.

50. Recently E.P. Sanders has commented on the development of this court in the Temple in *Judaism: Practice and Belief 63 BCE to 66 CE* (London: SCM Press, 1992), pp. 57, 61-62; *idem, Jewish Law from Jesus to the Mishnah* (London: SCM Press, 1990), pp.104 -105.

51. The description in Ephesians 2.14-15 of a μεσότοιχον τοῦ φραγμοῦ (cf. Philo's τοῖχος) is not in my opinion a reference either to the Temple in Jerusalem or to another Jewish building but to the Temple of Apollo at Didyma. P. Richardson, 'Ephesians 2.11-22 and the Temple of Apollo at Didyma' (unpublished paper, SNTS, Dublin, July 1989).

The second common building is a refectory (συμπόσιον), apparently not divided in the same way as the first (see 83; 'they rise up all together and standing in the middle of the refectory...'). Initially men recline on one side and women on the other (*Contemp.* 69), but as the meal proceeds into the vigil they all come together into a single choir. The benches are not soft, says Philo, but 'plank beds of the common kinds of wood, covered with quite cheap strewings of native papyrus, raised slightly at the arms to give something to lean on' (*Contemp.* 69). The guests at banquets are arranged in rows in order of precedence according to years in the community (*Contemp.* 75, 80). Portable tables are brought in filled with food only after scripture exposition and hymns (*Contemp.* 81). When the meal is over, the members remain in the dining room and hold the sacred vigil (see fig. 7).[52]

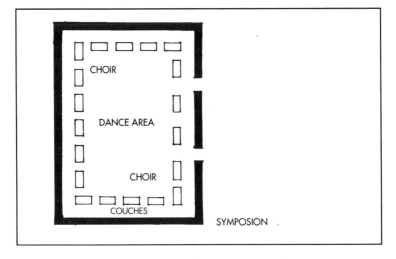

Figure 7. *Therapeutae: Schematic Banquet Room*

52. My reconstruction is analogous to other large dining rooms in the Graeco-Roman world. For another literary description of a Jewish monastic *symposium*, apparently in a messianic context, see 'The New Jerusalem' (5Q15), col. 2, with space for 22 couches in a room 19 by 12 cubits.

While the συμπόσιον is not unusual, I know of no building exactly similar to the assembly room in antiquity, and I conclude that Philo is here describing a unique solution to this group's unique equivalence between men and women (incidentally strengthening the view that Philo may have seen the buildings for himself), though it has an obvious resemblance to later synagogues. The combination of the two large structures with a number of smaller houses or 'cells' integrated into a single complex is also very unusual in the first century, though it has obvious resemblances to later Christian monasteries.

One final observation on the Therapeutae. We have no information whatsoever about the end of the group; scholars tacitly presume it did not survive beyond the first century CE. This assumption is precarious. As compared with the temple community at Leontopolis which filled a fairly obvious Egyptian military function and which may have been a place of last resort for Judean revolutionaries in the early seventies, there is no evidence at all of any military importance attached to the Therapeutae, and presumably therefore no reason for Roman military action against it in mopping up exercises.[53] Perhaps it could have been involved in some way in the Jewish revolt in Egypt in 115/116 CE, but we have no explicit or inferential evidence of this. I see no possibility one way or the other to infer from any literary or historical datum when the community disappeared. It may have lasted for some time.

6. *The Therapeutae and Kellia*

It will already be clear that there are strong resemblances between the actual character of the buildings excavated at Kellia and the inferrred character of the buildings of the Therapeutae as described in Philo. Those resemblances can be briefly summarized as follows:

a.   the Therapeutae (and it is a not bad description of Kellia also) had 'houses' resembling farm houses clustered together allowing complete privacy for each individual; the emphasis in both communities was on withdrawal, seclusion, the life of individual contemplation (figs. 3, 5);

53. Leontopolis, a few miles to the south-east in the delta region, was destroyed by the Romans in 73 or 74 CE. (Jos., *BJ* 7.421, 433-35). Josephus's silence on the fate of the Therapeutae raises doubts about its end.

b.   in both cases the structures and the pattern of life were designed in such a way that a life of seclusion was balanced with communal activities (figs. 2, 4);

c.   the individual living quarters of members of both Kellia and the Therapeutae contained a 'shrine' on which devotion focused (figs. 3, 5);

d.   in both cases the main assembly buildings were remote (in Kellia this seems to be so in the early period, though it later changed—figs. 1, 4);

e.   those living the life of seclusion in both communities met with others in seventh-day assemblies, in both cases including community meals and community worship in common facilities;

f.   both communities were located in the same area around Lake Mareotis, and it is possible that both were on the far side of the lake (fig. 1);

g.   these two communities are the only ones during the whole period to have the word μοναστήριον applied to the community;

h.   in both cases there is literary evidence that women participated in the celibate life of withdrawal on more or less equivalent terms.

The resemblances apply both to the built forms of the two monastic settlements and to the organization of the life within those structures. There are differences, perhaps the main one being the difference in the relationship between the cells at Kellia and the 'mother house' at Nitria, of which distance (15 km) there is no hint in Philo's description of the Therapeutae. There may also be differences in the exact nature of the individual shrines (we cannot be sure of this) and of the size of the community itself (this is certainly the case in the more developed stage at Kellia). In general, however, if one wants some idea of what the buildings of the Therapeutae were like one cannot do better than to look at the structures at Kellia.

7. *Once again, Eusebius and Philo*

Writing early in the fourth century CE Eusebius claims that the first-century Therapeutae are Christians. The distinct echoes of Philo's description of the Therapeutae in the developing monastic practices of

Eusebius's own day at sites such as Kellia prompt Eusebius, I suggest, to identify the Therapeutae as Christians. The fact—for it is a fact— that within early Christianity groups similar to the Therapeutae did develop quasi-eremitic monastic establishments, and that this occurred in Egypt, does not of course mean that there was any influence of one on the other. It may be that the resemblances are indirect, fortuitous, or unexceptional—there are only so many ways to build and organize a monastery.[54] Because monasteries existed before Eusebius's time, he can imagine when he comes to write his history that Philo's description of the Therapeutae is simply a description of an early version of the Egyptian Christian monasteries he knows from first-hand observation. It is not difficult to understand why Eusebius might apply this earlier description to something he knows, if it squares closely with his observations. There may, then, be no great mystery in Eusebius's application of Philo to Christians of Eusebius's period. It is an honest mistake.

Is Eusebius, however, not just making a mistake, as I at first thought, when he applies Philo's description to Christian monks? Or does he know what he is doing when he takes a Jewish group of the first century and calls it Christian, as I now wonder? The evidence is slight, but tips in favour of the latter view. First, the statements referred to earlier indicating controversy over his claim tumble over each other in the last portion of *Ecclesiastical History* 2.17; this requires vigorous oposition to Eusebius's view that the Therapeutae are Christians. Though he does not expand on these contrary views, it is not amiss to think Eusebius's opponents know that the group is *not* Christian but Jewish, and believe that one should not use Jewish customs to establish Christian practices. (His opponents may even argue that the life of withdrawal and contemplation is itself wrong, that Judaism had practised monasticism but that apostolic Christianity had not.) Secondly, Eusebius certainly knows that Philo is not a Christian, so why would he write about a Christian group? Thus, Eusebius goes out of his way to make up a reason for Philo's interest in Christianity—because of the size of the group (*EH* 2.16). Thirdly, Eusebius's personal contacts with Egypt might have informed him of

54. Daumas ('La "solitude" des Thérapeutes') hints at the connection but does not pursue the matter. Guillaumont (*Origines*, ch. 2) in the end thinks the evidence of Philo on monasticism was real but limited and more Jewish Christian than Philonic. This conclusion needs reassessment.

the true character of the Therapeutae, for he spent some time in Egypt.

Whether Eusebius knows what he is doing or not, the gap between the apostolic period and his day makes it relatively easy for him to absorb the group into his history of Christianity as one of the original forms of behaviour and organization, even though others argue against this model for Christian activitiy. Eusebius takes the Therapeutae over as an explanation, perhaps even a defence, of the fledgling monastic movement of his day. His justification is his conviction that if it exists in his day it must have existed in the apostolic period also.

This much may be a reasonable inference regarding Eusebius's motivation. Even if true, however, it does not go very far towards accounting historically for the development in a Christian group of the very same monastic practices and monastic structures as the earlier group had developed. To put the issue differently, is there an earlier influence before Eusebius's use of the ancient description of Philo? Before Eusebius's day was monasticism actually being influenced by direct or indirect knowledge of the practices of the Therapeutae? This is a more difficult, and ultimately unanswerable, question. Since we do not know how long the Therapeutae survived as a group we cannot guess how much knowledge there was of the group's organization and buildings nor what impact they might have had. Is it plausible that Christians in an earlier period (second century? or early third century?) knew of the group, and that they found themselves attracted to it? In such a scenario the attractions would be the quality of the life, its emphasis on celibacy and virginity, its attention to the contemplative spiritual life, and the devotion of the group to scripture and worship.

We cannot know the answer to this question; it is only just plausible speculation. At the end of the day it does not even matter very much. What stands out as remarkable is the very close similarity of the life of two groups and the very closely similar buildings that they developed to meet the needs of the two communities.[55] Some architects might wish to say, of course, that the same set of needs—

---

55. Though the literary evidence of the flowering of the two movements is something like 250 years apart, and later is directly dependent on the earlier evidence, I have suggested (above) that the actual gap is not likely that great, though I do not believe they ever co-existed as communities.

even many years apart—might generate identical solutions. This particular case is set apart by two factors: the earliest commentator, Eusebius, actually draws a direct connection between the one and the other, admittedly making a different point from the one I am raising here, and both communities arise in the same region in lower Egypt.

Regrettably, we cannot know whether to let this suggestive connection first promoted by Eusebius's use of Philo affect our views of the earliest developments in Christian monasteries and monasticism. The most we can say confidently is that there is an unusually close similarity between a first-century form of Jewish monasticism and a fourth-century form of Christian monasticism. It is not expected, nor commonly said, but the points of similarity are surprisingly exact.

8. *The Therapeutae, Some Concluding Comments*

My main interest in this paper has been the first-century Therapeutae; it is thus worth asking whether the group had any other lasting influences on either Christianity or Judaism? Within Judaism the only close contemporary parallel for this type of closed community with a distinctive set of buildings is Qumran.[56] In important respects Qumran is not truly similar, but it is the best that can be found. Yet Qumran helps to underscore one significant aspect of the Therapeutae; in broad terms both are communities dedicated to scriptural exposition, common life, withdrawal from society, full-time religious activity. For a period of time (we do not know how brief or long), Judaism had a monastic tradition, pehaps more influential than we can now recover with confidence. When it disappeared is not known. To underline a point made earlier, there is a correspondence between two accessible forms of Jewish monasticism—Qumran being cenobitic and the Therapeutae being quasi-eremitic—and two forms of Christian monasticism—Lower Egypt being mainly quasi-eremitic and Upper Egypt being mainly cenobitic. It is a desideratum to investigate as

56. Two non-Jewish analogies come to mind. There were at Alexandria and also at Memphis (Cairo) major Sarapeia that may have formed loose 'communities'. In some cases there were living quarters for the priests within the complex, and in the Asklepieia for participants as well. Both were sometimes found in a somewhat withdrawn location. But in neither was the community closed, nor was the primary function contemplation. The Therapeutae are at one edge of a growing and important tendency among the religious variations of the Graeco-Roman and Jewish worlds.

carefully and thoroughly as possible this monastic stream in post-
biblical Judaism. Perhaps as we understand better Christian monasticism we can begin to understand better Jewish monasticism and its
impact.

Despite the fact that the Therapeutae seem to have left no direct
footprints in Judaism in the subsequent period, there is one slight but
suggestive later connection with this almost forgotten Egyptian group:
the division between males and females in the assembly room
(*Contemp.* 32). Ironically, the group that experimented most successfully with equivalence between males and females may have
bequeathed to Judaism a wall that has symbolized the division between
the sexes ever since. I cannot prove that later synagogues that used
such a wall derived it from the Therapeutae; yet there are no other
documented first century walls (except for the Temple in Jerusalem
which is hardly similar),[57] there were later ones, and the description
of such a wall in Philo sounds exactly similar to these later walls. The
Therapeutae's buildings offer a fascinating piece of evidence not much
considered; they may be a curious middle term on the way towards
later synagogues as well as towards later Christian monasteries.

Did the Therapeutae influence first-century Christianity in any way?
Since there is only slight first-century Christian flirtation[58] with
monasticism such a thought may seem unlikely. But it is worth
recalling that there was a somewhat similar attitude to women, marriage, the celibate life and virginity in some quarters, most obviously in
the church in Corinth.[59] Pierre Benoit, a scholar not known for his

57. The wall in the temple, it need hardly be said, was between Jews and non-
Jews, not males and females; though there was a court of women distinct from the
court of Israel, this did not force a sharp separation.

58. *Barn.* 4.10 hints at an early form of Christian seclusion, though not
'monasticism'. If I am correct to see Barnabas as early (late 90s), this evidence is
especially important; see P. Richardson and M.B. Shukster, 'Barnabas, Nerva and
Yavnean Rabbis', *JTS* 34 (1983), pp. 31-55; M.B. Shukster and P. Richardson, 'A
Temple and *Bet Ha-Midrash* in the Epistle of Barnabas', in S.G. Wilson (ed.), *Anti-
Judaism in Early Christianity* (Waterloo, ON: Wilfrid Laurier University Press,
1986), II, pp. 17-31.

59. Guillaumont (*Origines*, chs. 1, 2, 4, 13) emphasizes the importance of the
first-century church on the roots of monasticism, especially 1 Cor. 7.32-40. He also
stresses the importance of the notion of the 'holy,' especially as it pertains to Moses
and to the priesthood, in this development, and argues that a temporary need became
a permanent custom. These latter observations could be applied to the Therapeutae

radical views, hinted some time ago at the possibility of influence; he suggested that the Therapeutae are a middle term between Judaism and the gnosticism of Asia Minor, and that Apollos is a vehicle for that influence.[60] Issues with a resonance in Corinth are the abandonment of marriage (1 Cor. 7.1-7), celibacy and virginity (1 Cor. 7.32-40), women's roles and their 'liberation' (1 Cor. 11.2-16; 14.33b-35). Some persons in the church in Corinth, influenced by leaders other than Paul, held exaggerated views—as Paul sees things—of women's right to act independently of but alongside men; the same persons may have held stringent views of flesh, the body and self-denial. In several respects these views are similar to the independent virginal and celibate lifestyles of the Therapeutae, though without the secluded life of contemplation. Is it possible that Benoit is right, and that members of the church in Corinth learned these views from Apollos, who learned them in turn from the Jewish monastic group in Egypt?[61] Were this so the Therapeutae would have left two footprints on later Christian monasticism, one through the shaping of ascetic ideas in the influential church in Corinth, and the other through the shaping of the ideal of the withdrawn life and the outlines of its practice. It is not possible to prove these outrageous suggestions, but they might be left hanging for Professor Hurd—whose contributions to our understanding of Corinth have been so great—to shoot down.

(see further, Richardson and Heuchan, 'Jewish Voluntary Associations').

60. Summary in J. Murphy-O'Connor, *The Ecole Biblique and the New Testament* (Freiburg: Universitätsverlag, 1991), pp. 55-56, citing P. Benoit, 'Colossiens (Epitre aux)', *Dictionnaire de la Bible* (Paris: Letouzey & Ané, 1961), supp. 7, pp. 157-70, esp. pp. 159-63; Grant (*Eusebius*, p. 75) also hints at such a connection. It is not necessary to posit a *general* influence as Benoit seems to do to hold the possibility of an influence on one or a few small Christian communities.

61. On similar questions see P. Richardson, 'The Thunderbolt in Q and the Wise man in Corinth', in P. Richardson and J. Hurd (eds.), *From Jesus to Paul* (Waterloo, ON: Wilfrid Laurier University Press, 1984), pp. 91-111; *idem*, 'On the Absence of Anti-Judaism in 1 Corinthians', in P. Richardson (ed.), *Anti-Judaism in Early Christianity* (Waterloo, ON: Wilfrid Laurier University Press, 1986), I, pp. 59-74.

SECTARIAN SEPARATION AND EXCLUSION—THE TEMPLE SCROLL: A CASE FOR WHOLISTIC RELIGIOUS CLAIMS

Wayne O. McCready

1. *The Drive Toward Wholistic Religious Claims*

Jacob Neusner, in *From Testament to Torah*, has advanced an important thesis for researchers of Second Temple Judaism and the beginnings of Christianity.[1] Neusner's proposal is that formative Judaism, of approximately 500 BCE to 700 CE, began with Hebrew scriptures representing a *testament*. Eventually, there emerged a more wholistic religious expression represented in the single word *torah* that encompassed a complete religious system. The term *torah* represents a generative or procreative symbol, the total expression of the religion. *Testament* is a designation for a religious system or a text that was limited and lacked formative potential. It did not achieve the long-term and procreative consequence of *torah*.[2]

Part of Neusner's methodological approach is to consider that religion, in this case Judaism, in a formative stage typically deals with urgent questions raised in society. If society is faced with topics of extreme urgency, the response can be creative for long-term religious definition that sponsors both belief and practice. The task for the modern researcher is to identify significant 'questions' that generated answers evident in written sources of specific religious systems. By

---

1.   In a forthcoming article 'Testament, Torah and the Temple Scroll', in Z.J. Kapera (ed.), *Festschrift for Jósef T. Milik* (Kraków: Enigma Press and the Polish Academy of Sciences, forthcoming) I deal with wholistic claims in columns 29.3-30.2 and 56.12-59.12 of 11QTemple. This presentation broadens the assessment of wholistic claims to political and social contexts, as well as in the Temple Scroll generally, in order to estimate formative aspects of sectarian self-definition. See J. Neusner, *From Testament to Torah* (Englewood Cliffs, NJ: Prentice–Hall, 1988), pp. 164-70 for a comparison between *testament* and *torah*.

2.   Neusner, *Testament to Torah*, pp. 135-38, 149-52.

investigating the thrust and focus of 'answers' in written sources—and their historical, social, political, as well as larger religious contexts—researchers can learn a great deal about formative stages of religion.

Specific to Neusner's study of Judaism from 500 BCE to 700 CE, he estimates that destruction of the first and second temples at Jerusalem, as well as Christianization of the Roman empire were topics of such urgency that they forced a response on the part of all religious systems in Judaism. Gedalyahu Alon in volume one of *The Jews in their Land in the Talmudic Age* made a similar case for the primacy of the destruction of the second Jerusalem temple and Christianity becoming the official religion of the Roman empire. Alon advanced a point of some substance that a third formative factor for emerging Judaism was Christianization of ancient Palestine as sacred territory.[3] Out of diverse religious systems that made up Judaism in the formative era there eventually was a single, definitive and normative Judaism that supplanted the multiplicity of religious claims that had been prior and it sought to speak for all Jews. Talmudic Judaism was the religious system to survive while others did not because it joined together stress on sanctification of Israel with a message of salvation. The combination of sanctification of life style and expectation of salvation successfully characterizes Judaism from the post-Constantine period to the modern.[4]

The Judaism that emerged as normative did so because it best answered penetrating questions related to loss and recovery that started with the destruction of the first Jerusalem temple. The combination of destruction of a major cultic centre with all of homeland Judaism under foreign domination made loss of land, as well as negation of political independence, urgent topic matters. Previously a Jewish homeland and political independence had been justified through claims of election verified through some semblance of national autonomy. The degree of foreign domination in the exilic

3.   G. Alon, *The Jews in their Land in the Talmudic Age* (trans. and ed. G. Levi; Jerusalem: Magnes Press, 1980), pp. 18-38. Alon noted that anti-Jewish legislation under Emperor Theodosius II dismissing the patriarchate and prohibiting new synagogues was representative of a turning point for formative Judaism. The status of Judaism in ancient Palestine was not only reduced but the profile of Palestine as a Christian territory was raised to justify suppression of pagan religions and deviant Christian sects for the sake of catholic orthodoxy.

4.   Neusner, *Testament to Torah*, pp. 119-20.

circumstances that eliminated all national worship centres was a severe challenge to religious affirmation. In the post-exilic era Judaism regained some homeland territory. The intensity of land as something lost and then regained raised a particular consciousness of peoplehood, land and nationalism that progressively became more fundamental to Jewish self-definition. Part of the response to these topics included an emphasis on specific ways of being religious in daily life patterns to ensure a particular peoplehood and nationalism—that is, sanctification. Others attempted to provide a renewed or new vision for Judaism through claims of salvation. Such enterprises produced a series of *testaments* that stressed either sanctification or salvation but they did not necessarily combine these principles into a procreative whole for all of Judaism.

A case can be made that the drive toward a single Judaism was evident well before the turn of the common era, and the combined principles of sanctification and salvation can be found in Jewish sectarian writings. Specific to this presentation is that a wholistic system can be detected in the Temple Scroll. The principles of sanctification and salvation were fundamental to the content and details of this text. Neusner's estimation that formative Judaism was involved in a transition from *testament* to *torah* can be maintained and it is an important assessment for researchers of western religions.[5] The emphasis of this study is that formative Judaism, as well as the beginnings of Christianity, inherited the ambitions of Jewish religious parties and sectarians, or proto-sectarians, to present a whole and complete religious system.[6] The Temple Scroll represents such an attempt and its endeavour was an essential part of the religious fabric that contributed to emerging normative Judaism. Furthermore, Temple Scroll (11QTemple) formulations of a wholistic system were a response to societal factors that can be identified with the Hasmonean dynasty in the time frame of approximately 140 to 65 BCE and these societal factors were fundamental to claims of sanctification and salvation in

---

5.   Neusner, *Testament to Torah*, pp. 68-72.
6.   By party, I refer to those who held specific views of things Jewish and accommodated their opponents. Sectarians also had particular views but they were unwilling to accommodate their opponents. They excluded them as rightful heirs of Israel. *Secta* was not a negative designation in antiquity. It did not have the meaning of deviant. See S.J.D. Cohen, *From Maccabees to Mishnah* (Philadelphia: Westminster Press, 1987), p. 125.

various segments of Jewish society. There was a drive toward establishing a single, definitive and normative account of things that was significantly influenced by the Hasmonean dynasty, as well as by parties and sectarians responding to that dynasty. In a curious development, sanctification and salvation principles advanced in 11QTemple included aspirations of separation and exclusion that were essential and necessary to the wholistic claims of the Temple Scroll. A point to be noted is that even in peculiar religious formulations such as those found in 11QTemple—the principles of sanctification and salvation that served normative Judaism well, and contributed to its long-term success—can be found in sectarian Judaism.

2. *The Hasmonean Dynasty: Testament and Potential Torah*

A consequence of the Maccabean revolt against Syrian policies in ancient Palestine was the establishment of the Hasmonean dynasty that sponsored national programmes intended to provide identity for homeland Judaism, as well as to confirm the legitimacy of the monarchy. The initial conflict between Syrian policies and early Maccabean warriors had less to do with the right of a Syrian king to impose laws on subjects and more to do with the imposition of laws that were determined to push the definition of being Jewish outside the widest possible boundaries acceptable to Mattathias and his supporters.[7] If one was to use Neusner's terms it involved a conflict of *testament* against *testament*. One 'limited system' against another 'limited system'. The Maccabean warriors and their Hasidaean allies represented a 'family' of Judaism concerned with religious self-definition,[8] and they were involved in responding to a crisis in society. The irony of Mattathias' response to policies of Antiochus IV Epiphanes was that Mattathias's decision to defend the ways of the

---

7. See E. Bickerman, *From Ezra to the Last of the Maccabees* (New York: Schocken, 1962), p. 97. Bickerman notes that the initial conflict did not have to do with individual conscience and freedom of religion but a clash between a secular power and those who held a particular religious position that was understood as God's revelation.

8. See J. Neusner, W.S. Green and E.S. Frierichs (eds.), *Judaisms and their Messiahs at the Turn of the Common Era* (Cambridge: Cambridge University Press, 1987), pp. ix-xiv for summary comments on the pluralistic dimension of Judaism at the turn of the common era.

ancestors, vested in Jewish law, involved not only interpreting the law (such as whether fighting constituted a definition of 'work') but imposition of law on the population of ancient Palestine. The point to be noted in this study is that such an imposition of law was by Jews upon fellow Jews. The Maccabees and their associate Hasidaeans were committed to replacing what they interpreted as unacceptable compromises with Hellenism by active resistance that effected Jews more than Gentiles. The Maccabean military force moved from village to village not only destroying what they interpreted as idolatrous altars, but imposing their views of law with threat of punishment and execution of fellow Jews (cf. 1 Macc. 5, 7; Jos., *Ant.* 12.327-53). In later developments Simon took Gaza. He expelled his opponents from their homes and city—and he replaced them with people who met his expectations of purity and 'who observed the law' (1 Macc. 13.48). Simon's Jerusalemite opponents were starved into submission (1 Macc. 13.49-50). In the combined office of secular power and high priest, both priests and lay people were forbidden to nullify Simon's decisions or oppose what he said (1 Macc. 14.44-45).

Earlier, Judas Maccabeus had deliberately opposed a member of the high priestly family, Jakim, who had taken the hellenized name Alcimus. Substantial investigation of Alcimus' pedigree resulted in agreement on the appropriateness of his appointment as high priest. Indeed, the Hasidaeans supported Alcimus (1 Macc. 7; 2 Macc. 14.3-10). Although the Maccabean's historians vilify Alcimus, it is apparent that the topic being dealt with in the historical details had less to do with conflict between traditional Jewish living versus Gentile overlords, and more to do with legitimacy of religious leadership. Alcimus' version of the conflict in Palestine to Demetrius I was that the Maccabees were 'keeping up war and stirring up sedition' (2 Macc. 14.6). The emerging primacy of the Maccabees as secular and religious leaders was fortuitously confirmed through a treaty with Rome (1 Macc. 8). Alcimus was prevented from assuming full authority as high priest for supposedly participating in pagan festivals and sacrifices during the persecutions of Antiochus IV Epiphanes (2 Macc. 14.3). Jonathan, Judas Maccabeus's brother and successor, managed to have himself appointed as high priest even though he did not belong to the traditional high priestly family of Zadokites. The irony of Jonathan's appointment was that it came by authority of Alexander Balas, a Gentile and pretender of the Syrian monarchy

(1 Macc. 10.18-21), as well as Demetrius I the reigning Syrian king (1 Macc. 10.22-44).

The initial figures in the Maccabean family had been motivated by a perceived threat that hellenization would compromise their view of traditional Judaism. Judas Maccabeus both in fact and folklore represents a middle ground between Neusner's *testament* and *torah*. On the one hand this hero of the Maccabean wars provided a paradigm for dealing with questions concerning the challenges of Hellenism that potentially could consume Judaism. The political and theological theory of Jeremiah that viewed Gentiles as God's instrument of punishment for disobedience was rejected.[9] On the other hand Judas was time specific and did not realize a generative symbolism for Jewish self-definition in the second century BCE. Elias Bickerman observed that Judaism quickly forgot Judas. In later Jewish tradition, Mattathias and his grandson John Hyrcanus were the principal figures of Hanakkuh commemoration. Indeed, it was Christianity that honoured Judas as a model of knighthood and preserved his place as a hero from antiquity.[10] Judas had potential to be a generative symbol for Judaism. By virtue of the Maccabean commitment to a life style and society based on ancestral traditions, a way (*torah*) was made available to reject full immersion into common Hellenistic culture. To be Jewish included some sort of commitment to the laws of Moses and some form of separation from Gentiles.[11] Judas represented a first principle for determining a working relationship with Hellenism. Potentially, he offered a 'world creating' system in both symbolic and factual terms. His efforts to establish a Jewish territory raised expectations to be able to practice religion without undue interference from non-Jewish traditions to a significant level. Palestine could organize itself according to the 'laws of Moses'. How strictly it would adhere to such laws and the interpretative traditions that would

9. See Cohen, *Maccabees to Mishnah*, pp. 27-30 on how Jeremiah provided a political theology for dealing with Gentile rule of homeland Judaism.

10. Bickerman, *Ezra to Maccabees*, pp. 134-35.

11. See E.P. Sanders, *Judaism Practice and Belief 63 BCE–66 CE* (Philadelphia: Trinity Press International, 1992), p. 20. Sanders observes that response to 'extreme hellenization' included not sacrificing to foreign gods, dietary observances and circumcision. These factors were recognized as representative of being Jewish. Further, Jews expected to be able to continue their beliefs and practices. Other than during Hadrian's regime, such rights were granted to Jews in antiquity.

become societal policy was open to debate. As was noted above with reference to 1 Macc. 13.48, Simon attempted to bring independent Hellenistic cities in Palestine (such as Gaza) under Mosaic law and when opponents refused he expelled them from their cities.[12]

Part of the reason that Judas Maccabeus—and the emerging Hasmonean dynasty—failed to provide full generative potential was that his brothers and their heirs did not take advantage of the substance of initial victories of the Maccabean revolt. Although they combined both offices of king and high priest, and they extended Jewish control over a significant portion of Palestine, they managed to eventually turn Palestine into a Hellenistic principality.[13] This was largely the consequence and the necessity of becoming involved in the international politics of the eastern region of the Mediterranean world.[14] For the sake of international alliances, Jonathan executed fellow Jews (1 Macc. 10.59-89). In the cut and thrust of regional politics it was difficult to divorce foreign interests from the ambition to solidify Hasmonean control of Palestine. 1 Macc. 11.20-37 indicates that when Jonathan took control of the citadel at Jerusalem he appeased Syrian suspicions by taking silver, gold, clothing and other gifts to King Demetrius. As a consequence of that action (and 300 talents), Jonathan managed to free Judaea, and three districts in Samaria from tribute as well as confirm his authority in Jerusalem. International politics, Jewish nationalism and Jewish religion became blurred in their orientations. While religion and politics for ancient Judaism always had been profoundly interrelated, the Hasmonean policies involved homeland Judaism as a proactive player in the international scene. It is impossible to separate the success of the Hasmoneans from their diplomatic skills in dealing with Egyptian, Syrian and Roman policies. Although these foreign governments were minimally interested in Palestine during the second and first centuries BCE, an inappropriate alliance or unwise treaty could have changed the fate of Jewish autonomy in short order. Both Jonathan and Simon gambled on being able to orchestrate the internal conflicts of Egyptians, and especially Syrians, to their best advantage. In order to

---

12. See Sanders, *Judaism*, p. 20.

13. Bickerman, *Ezra to Maccabees*, p. 139.

14. For specific details of involvement with both Egyptian and Syrian politics, see M. Stern, 'Judaea and her Neighbors in the Days of Alexander Jannaeus', *Jerusalem Cathedra* (Detroit: Wayne State University Press, 1981), I, pp. 23-45.

do that successfully, they had to be on intimate terms with the right players at the opportune time.

The momentum of being involved in international Mediterranean politics became a driving force for Hasmonean kings, even when the Syrian empire fell into extreme confusion during John Hyrcanus' reign. It included being fluent in Greek, adopting Greek names, raising an army of substance that necessitated foreign mercenaries paid by opening the tomb of David and taking treasures supposedly deposited there (Jos. *Ant.* 13.249), annexing more territory (such as Samaria and Idumea) and requiring circumcision and commitment to the law of Moses as signs of loyalty for forced converts to Judaism (*Ant.* 13.257-258; 13.275-279). Such acts were understood to be signs of being Jewish. Although the early Maccabean warriors had resisted Gentile impositions on Jews, in the later Hasmonean dynasty there was active imposition of things Jewish on Gentiles which recreated a Hasmonean form of Hellenism.[15]

The 'world-creating' feature of *torah* as a generative principle required the setting of boundaries that assisted the formulation of a particular world view, and a specific way of living.[16] The Hasmonean regime represented by Jonathan and Simon, and certainly by John Hyrcanus and Alexander Jannaeus, failed to provide leadership for a distinctive and clear Jewish world view and way of living as it imposed Judaism on Gentiles. A crisis of self-definition emerged because Hasmonean policies, internal to Palestine as well as its foreign affairs, progressively challenged Jewish identity and societal structures. Also, the salvific vision that Maccabean warriors had for homeland Judaism based on commitment to ancestral traditions did not match its initial ambitions. It is against the failed potential of the Hasmonean dynasty as *torah* inspiring that the Temple Scroll can be compared.

15. Bickerman has a chapter entitled 'Genesis and Character of Maccabean Hellenism', in *Ezra to Maccabees*, pp 153-65. He makes a telling point (pp. 158-60) about legal title of land. Greek tradition accepted legal claim of territory based on original ownership. Thus, opponents of the Hasmoneans resisted annexation of Gentile territory with claims of original land claims. Rather than countering with claims of divine promise, the Hasmoneans accepted the Greek principles and sought to find an historical basis for determining Jewish territory. This included combining biblical traditions with original land claims.

16. Neusner, *Testament to Torah*, pp. 165-67.

3. *The Temple Scroll and its Historical Context*

A consensus of Temple Scroll scholarship is that this text reflects an early phase in the history of those responsible for the Dead Sea Scrolls.[17] Precise dating of the Temple Scroll is frustrated by the nature of the manuscript as it is a compilation of various sources including revisions of material from Deuteronomy, festival calendar details and an extensive description of a temple complex that seems to be a modification of Ezekiel's vision for a new Jerusalem.[18] Also, the text may not have been written by Qumranites but it was part of the Qumranite library because it represented a viewpoint attractive to some of the sectarians.[19] Some researchers estimate that 11QTemple was a response to circumstances in the early post-exilic period when Persia controlled Jerusalem.[20] The majority of scholars judge that the

17. The relationship of the scrolls to the ruins at Qumran has recently come under review. For an estimation of intimacy between the scrolls and the ruins, see F. García Martínez and A.S. Van der Woude, 'A "Groningen" Hypothesis of Qumran Origins and Early History', *RevQ* 56 (1990), pp. 521-41; also see F. García Martínez, 'Qumran Origins and Early History: A Groningen Hypothesis', *FO* 25 (1988), pp. 113-36. For a view that there is reason for suspecting a relationship between the scrolls and the ruins, see N. Golb, 'The Problem of Origin and Identification of the Dead Sea Scrolls', *PAPS* 124 (1980), pp. 1-24; *idem*, 'Les manuscrits de la mer Morte: Une nouvelle approche du problème de leur origine', *Annales ESC* 5 (1985), pp. 1133-149; *idem*, 'Réponse à la "Note" de E.-M. Laperrousaz', *Annales ESC* 6 (1987), pp. 1313-320; *idem*, 'Who Hid the Dead Sea Scrolls', *BA* 28 (1987), pp. 68-82; *idem*, 'The Dead Sea Scrolls', *AS* 58 (1989), pp. 177-207.

18. Source analysis of 11QTemple suggests that material based on Hebrew scripture was brought together by a redactor. See Y. Yadin, *The Temple Scroll* (Jerusalem: Israel Exploration Society, 1983), I, pp. 71-88. For sophisticated and convincing source analysis see A.M. Wilson and L. Wills, 'Literary Sources of the Temple Scroll', *HTR* 75 (1982), pp. 275-88 and M.O. Wise, *A Critical Study of the Temple Scroll from Qumran Cave 11* (Chicago: The Oriental Institute of the University of Chicago, 1990); also H. Stegemann, 'The Literary Composition of the Temple Scroll and its Status at Qumran', in G.J. Brooke (ed.), *Temple Scroll Studies* (Sheffield: JSOT Press, 1989), pp. 123-48.

19. See Stegemann, 'Literary Composition', pp. 125-26, 128; P. Davies, 'The Temple Scroll and the Damascus Document', in Brooke (ed.), *Temple Scroll Studies*, p. 208, suggests that content of 11QTemple may not have been influential among Qumranites because it was dated in light of perception of a new dispensation.

20. See J. Maier, 'The Architectural History of the Temple in Jerusalem in the

Temple Scroll reflects the Hasmonean dynasty, although the sources that make up the final text may date from an earlier period.[21] The latter position will be taken in this presentation although the specific identification with one of the Hasmonean kings is not my concern. I estimate that it is the momentum of Hasmonean policies that produced a crisis that the Temple Scroll responded to, and thus the reigns of John Hyrcanus or Alexander Jannaeus make the same point.[22]

Light of the Temple Scroll', in Brooke (ed.), *Temple Scroll Studies*, pp. 23-62; also, P. Callaway, 'The Temple Scroll and the Canonization of Jewish Law', *RevQ* 13 (1988), pp. 239-50 and H. Stegemann, '"Das Land" in der Tempelrolle und in anderen Texten aus den Qumranfunden' in G. Strecker (ed.), *Das Land Israel in biblischer Zeit* (Göttingen: Vandenhoeck & Ruprecht, 1983), pp. 156-57; also Stegemann, 'The Literary Composition', pp. 239-55, as well as Stegemann, 'The Origins of the Temple Scroll', in *Congress Volume, Jerusalem 1986* (VTSup, 40; Leiden: Brill, 1988), pp. 235-56. Professor Stegemann holds that 11QTemple was a supplement to the Pentateuch and a sixth book of the Torah section of Hebrew scriptures that was minimized by the reforms of Ezra.

21. Some researchers make a precise identification of 11QTemple with the reign of John Hyrcanus. See Yadin, *Temple Scroll*, p. 390. Also see M. Broshi, 'Le Rouleau du Temple', *MB* 4 (1978), pp. 70-72; A. Caquot, 'Le Rouleau du Temple de Qoumrân', *ETR* 53 (1978), p. 446; M. Delcor, 'Explication du Rouleau du Temple de Qoumrân', *AEPHE* 92 (1983-84), pp. 246-47; A.S. van der Woude, 'De tempelrol van Qumrân (I)', *NedTTs* 34 (1980), p. 180. Other scholars prefer to date 11QTemple contemporary with the reign of Alexander Jannaeus, Hyrancus's successor. See M. Hengel, J.H. Charlesworth and D. Mendels, 'The Polemical Character of "On Kingship" in the Temple Scroll: An Attempt at Dating 11QTemple', *JSJ* 37 (1986), pp. 28-38. Cf. J. Milgrom, 'The Qumran Cult: Its Exegetical Principles', in Brooke (ed.), *Temple Scroll Studies*, pp. 165-80; M. Delcor, 'Le statut du roi d'après le Rouleau du Temple', *Henoch* 3 (1981), pp. 47-68; Delcor, 'Is the Temple Scroll a Source of the Herodian Temple?', in Brooke (ed.), *Temple Scroll Studies*, pp. 84-85; E.-M. Laperrousaz, *Qoumrân: L'établissement essénien des bords de la Mer Morte. Histoire et archéologie du site* (Paris: Picard, 1976); Laperrousaz, 'Note à propos de la datation du Rouleau du Temple et plus généralement des manuscrits de la mer Morte', *RevQ* 10 (1981), pp. 447-52; Laperrousaz, 'Does the Temple Scroll Date from the First or Second Century BCE?', in Brooke (ed.), *Temple Scroll Studies*, pp. 91-97; L.H. Schiffman, 'The Temple Scroll and the Systems of Jewish Law of the Second Temple Period', in Brooke (ed.), *Temple Scroll Studies*, pp. 123-48. For comparative research on 11QTemple and other important texts of Qumran that may contextualize 11QTemple, see Davies, 'The Temple Scroll', pp. 201-10. Also, J.C. VanderKam, 'The Temple Scroll and the Book of Jubilees', in Brooke (ed.), *Temple Scroll Studies*, pp. 211-36 and Wise, *Temple Scroll*, pp. 136-54.

22. See Wise, *Temple Scroll*, pp. 189-94 for dating 11QTemple contemporary

4. *The Temple Scroll and a Wholistic Vision of Sanctification*

The Temple Scroll represents itself as a new or renewed *torah* of Moses.[23] Although the redactor of the Temple Scroll was clearly in possession of disparate materials dealing with multiple topic matters, the compilation and end product was something other than a collection of scattered texts. It is a well-planned document profiling the sanctity of temple, land and people, as well as ideal principles for government and society in general. Michael Wise has correctly observed that the Temple Scroll redactor followed the ambition of Mosaic law to provide a comprehensive 'law for the land'. Indeed, the redactor understood that he was a new Moses.[24] Sources were ordered to profile sanctification of three vital areas—temple, land and people— that affected all of Israel and had the consequence of perfecting cult, society and government.

The Temple Scroll's 'law of the land' focused on temple with details of the sanctuary, its courts and access to holy areas (11QTemple 3.1-13.8; 29.8b-46.3a), as well as a calendar of sacrificial ritual (13.9-29.8a). The architecture of the proposed temple included a huge third courtyard that was so large that all of ancient Jerusalem would have

with Jonathan (c. 150 BCE) based on a comparison between 1 Macc. 10 and 11QTemple 43 and 52. For those who date 11QTemple in the Herodian period see B.E. Thiering, *Redating the Teacher of Righteousness* (Sydney: Theological Explorations, 1979), p. 207, and 'The Date of Composition of the Temple Scroll', in Brooke (ed.), *Temple Scroll Studies*, pp. 99-120; also see R. Eisenman, *James the Just* (Leiden: Brill, 1986), pp. 87-94.

23. See my article, 'A Second Torah at Qumran?', *SR* 14/1 (1985), pp. 5-15. Cf. Yadin, *The Temple Scroll*, I, pp. 60-73; Stegemann, 'Literary Composition', p. 131. Also see S.A. Kaufman, 'The Temple Scroll and Higher Criticism', *HUCA* 53 (1982), pp. 29-43, and G. Brin, 'The Bible as Reflected in the Temple Scroll', *Shnaton* 4 (1980), pp. 182-225. Also, B.Z. Wacholder, *The Dawn of Qumran: The Sectarian Torah and the Teacher of Righteousness* (Cincinnati: Hebrew Union College Press, 1983), p. 15.

24. Wise, *Temple Scroll*, p. 200. Also, see Stegemann, 'Das Land', pp. 154-71. Part of Wise's thesis is that the redactor was a member of the sectarian community who sponsored the Damascus Document. Festival calendar laws that originally were particular and germane to entry and maintenance in a sect were extended to address all of Israel by applying them to topics relating to either temple or temple-city. See Wise, *Temple Scroll*, p. 154.

been enclosed within sacred parameters.[25] Source material that parallels Deuteronomy 12–26 and had general application for society was reworked to emphasize temple.[26] Specific laws that promoted the unique religious importance of Jerusalem had the consequence of sanctifying not only the sacred city but all of the land. When Jerusalem was appropriately protected from impurities an established order was in place for all of society (47.3b-18).[27] Jacob Milgrom has suggested that 11QTemple represents a 'maximalist' view of purity that sought to impose maximum conditions of holiness demands upon minimalist space—the temple-city of Jerusalem.[28] Milgrom estimates that the exegetical principle was that all Israel attained holiness at Sinai. Since 11QTemple understands that the temple-city was of equivalent holiness, the Sinaitic regulations must prevail in the city. The people were sanctified by purity laws of general application (48.3–51.10), as well as government organizational laws (51.11–56.11; 60.1–66.17).

The redactor of the Temple Scroll crafted his sources to establish a particular hierarchical order sponsoring a concentric notion of holiness that increased by degree as one moved from the periphery toward the centre.[29] This exegetical use of source material had the ambition to create a legal system that redefined the entire Jewish society and religion according to sectarian standards. The distinctly sectarian nature of the details and content of Temple Scroll *halakhah* is abundantly clear.[30] The thrust of the legal system was to recreate

25. See M. Broshi, 'The Gigantic Dimensions of the Visionary Temple in the Temple Scroll', *BARev* 13 (1987), pp. 36-37.

26. Wise, *Temple Scroll*, p. 200.

27. For identification of a historical context of laws protecting the sanctity of Jerusalem see a comparison between 11QTemple 47 and Jos. *Ant.* 12.146 in my article, 'The Sectarian Status of Qumran: The Temple Scroll', *RevQ* 42 (1983), pp. 183-91. Wise, *Temple Scroll*, pp. 179-82, estimates that column 47 is almost certainly a free composition of the redactor.

28. Milgrom, 'The Qumran Cult: Its Exegetical Principles', pp. 165-80.

29. See M. Delcor, 'Temple Scroll a Source of the Herodian Temple?', p. 70; cf. C. Daniel, 'Nouveaux arguments en faveur de l'identification des hérodiens et des esséniens', *RevQ* 7 (1969-71), pp. 396-402.

30. Cf. Schiffman, 'The Temple Scroll and the Systems of Jewish Law', pp. 240-41. Also, see L. Schiffman, *The Halakhah at Qumran* (Leiden: Brill, 1975); Yadin, *Temple Scroll*, I, pp. 397-404, and 'Is the Temple Scroll a Sectarian Document?', in G.M. Tucker and D.A. Knight (eds.), *Humanizing America's Iconic*

conditions of holiness in the land that would be equivalent to the
sacred camp of Israel in the wilderness with purity laws for the camp
and tabernacle applied to Jerusalem.[31] A motivating principle of the
halakhah was to separate and exclude 'pure' from 'impure'. For
example, a ditch one hundred cubits wide was to be dug around the
temple in order to separate the sanctuary from the rest of Jerusalem
(46.9-12). The ditch was to ensure that no one entered the temple
without being ritually pure according to the halakhah of 11QTemple.
In addition, three days of purification was required before admission
to Jerusalem (45.7b-10a) and only 'pure' food and drink was allowed
into the temple-city carried in skins of pure animals that had been
slaughtered in the Jerusalem temple (47.7-18). Thus, all impurity was
excluded from the temple-city. Concerted effort was made to address
any topic that might compromise the sanctity of Jerusalem. Sexual
intercourse was not permitted in Jerusalem (45.11-12) and privies
were to be located 3000 cubits from the temple-city (46.13-16a).
Women apparently were not to live in Jerusalem for fear of
compromising the sanctity of the city during a menstrual period or
from child birth (48.16-17). Special burial cities were to be
established (48.11-14) and the festival calendar of 11QTemple was
based on a solar year of 364 days.

However, the sectarian nature of 11QTemple is not the point I wish
to emphasize. Given the sectarianism of its legal system, one might
expect that there would be indifference or even hostility toward larger
society.[32] But the opposite is true. I propose that the Temple Scroll
was aware of the importance of peoplehood, land and nationalism as
the basis of religious self-definition and—even in a particular halakhic
context—there was an attempt to establish a programme for all of
society that was procreative and wholistic in scope and in detail.
Laws—regulating the sanctuary and its courts, details outlining access

Book (Chico, CA: Scholars Press, 1982), pp. 153-69; Wacholder, *Dawn of
Qumran*, pp. 33-98; M. Lehman, 'The Temple Scroll as a Source of Sectarian
Halakhah', *RevQ* 9 (1978), pp. 579-87.

31. Wacholder, *Dawn of Qumran*, p. 16; cf. Stegemann, 'Literary Composition',
p. 142, and J. Maier, 'Die Hofanlagen im Tempelentwurf des Ezechiel im Licht der
Tempelrolle', in J.A. Emerton (ed.), *Prophecy: Essays presented to Georg Fohrer on
his 65th Birthday* (Berlin: de Gruyter, 1980), pp. 55-67.

32. See B.R. Wilson, 'An Analysis of Sect Development', in B.R. Wilson
(ed.), *Patterns of Sectarianism* (London: Heinemann, 1967), pp. 23-24.

to holy areas, as well as specifics relating to cultic calendar, holy city and behaviour—established proper degrees of sanctity for all aspects of society. The Temple Scroll envisioned a 'world-creating system' by systematically ordering a way of life and providing a structural model for society that made the temple exclusive—and fundamental—for any definition of Israel. The primacy of the temple made its holiness a first principle in dealing with the crucial question of maintaining land and nationhood that was fundamental to Second Temple Judaism and had become progressively more problematic for some segments of society in light of the complexities of internal and external politics, as well as the Jewish Hellenism that was sponsored by Hasmoneans such as John Hyrcanus and Alexander Jannaeus.

5. *Covenant and the Temple Scroll*

Details found in columns 29.3–30.2 are frequently judged to be fundamental to the Temple Scroll.[33] This section of 11QTemple is a transitional passage. The thrust of this material is that sacrifices made in the festival cycles already outlined (13.2–29.2), and offered in the temple detail in the columns that follow this section ensure the presence of God among the people. Following Yigael Yadin's translation the important lines are as follows.[34]

> And I will accept them (?), and they shall be (?) my people, and I will be theirs for ever, [and] I will dwell with them for ever and ever. And I will consecrate my [t]emple by my glory, (the temple) on which I will settle my glory, until the day of blessing on which I will create my temple and establish it for myself for all times, according to the covenant which I have made with Jacob at Bethel (29.7.10).

Without dealing with the eschatological nature of the temple in 11QTemple,[35] it is clear that the basis of a covenantal relationship with God is outlined. Sacrificial offerings in columns 13 to 29 were a condition of God's covenant, and consequences of obeying God's stipulations included the establishment of a nation, as well as the

33. See M.O. Wise, 'The Covenant of Temple Scroll XXIX, 3-10', *RevQ* 53 (1989), pp. 49-60. Also, Wilson and Wills, 'Literary Sources', p. 276, and P. Callaway, 'Exegelische Erwägungen zur Tempelrolle XXIX, 7-10', *RevQ* 12 (1985–87), p. 95.

34. Yadin, *The Temple Scroll*, II, pp. 128-29. Also see I, pp. 182-87.

35. See Wise, 'Covenant of Temple', pp. 52-54.

continuing presence of God. The combination of the terms *torah* and *mishpat* in 11QTemple 29.4 makes for a difficult translation. The line details prescriptions about burnt offerings being made on the proper day according to the 'law of this ordinance' as Yadin translated it.[36] Professor Wacholder judges that the combination of the two terms *torah* and *mishpat* was fundamental to 11QTemple because it established the primacy of material found in this scroll that made it something greater than an alternative to other torahs. The conjunction of the two terms had the ambition to make the scroll—*the* torah.[37] The damaged text at the top of column 30 does not allow for full assessment of the idea of Jacob's covenant in the Temple Scroll, but the basic point of the formative nature of God's presence among his people is clear from the existent text. Stipulations of the covenant, concerning the festive sacrifices (columns 13-29), and the material that will follow, constitute the legal-religious bond between people and their God. Although the religious stance of the Temple Scroll is particular, 11QTemple 29.3-10 has a wholistic vision that includes all of Israel. It concerns not only a covenant to build a temple: it is a reaffirmation and reapplication of the covenant made with the patriarchs (Jacob, Isaac and Abraham) that promises God's presence, and possession of the land.[38]

If it is correct to associate the Temple Scroll with the Hasmonean period, the scroll reflects challenges in society that forced homeland Judaism into a continuing preoccupation with defining itself.[39] Exile and return, foreign occupation by Persians and Greeks—as well as the independent state under the Hasmonean dynasty—suggested that independence and statehood could not be taken for granted. Indeed, foreign occupation and national independence proved to be problematic for different reasons but they added up to the same basic question—the definition of being Jewish within the context of a larger

36. Yadin, *The Temple Scroll*, II, pp. 127. Cf. Wacholder, *Dawn of Qumran*, p. 18, and p. 238 (n. 106) who suggests that generally in Qumran literature *mishpat* and its cognates refer to written traditions.

37. Wacholder, *Dawn of Qumran*, pp. 18, 22-23.

38. Stegemann, 'Literary Composition', p. 131. Wise, 'Covenant of Temple', p. 57. Wise suggests that there are significant parallels with the Damascus Document on covenant, pp. 58-59.

39. Neusner suggests that ancient Israel distinguished itself among nations with a preoccupation of self-definition (cf. *Testament to Torah*, p. 12).

>5

non-Jewish world. By developing a priestly vision of human existence based on the temple, and its orderly and meticulous service to God,[40] the Temple Scroll presented a particular response to questions of Jewish self-definition. The definition of Judaism as a special group in the context of the larger world was to be based primarily on the first principle of the temple's holiness that defined peoplehood and nation. A particular Judaism is presented by 11QTemple advancing the idea that sanctification of Israel was sustained by a fundamental commitment to holiness of time and place, but it also had a central component that envisioned all of Israel.

6. *The Temple Scroll and Claims of Salvation*

In later rabbinic Judaism, as well as in developing Christianity, claims of salvation included messianic expectations.[41] However, Judaism in the period prior to the turn of the common era does not exhibit a uniform or definitive concern for messianism.[42] The Dead Sea Scrolls, in general, placed greater emphasis on expectation of a 'better day' than on messianism. It is less than clear that the term 'messiah', as it is commonly understood, is compatible with the expectation of the 'anointed ones' cited in limited sources in the Dead Sea Scrolls.[43] Indeed, the dominant factor in the scrolls was an expectation of a new epoch of history immediately in the future and the role Qumranites were destined to play—through 'community' activities—in the coming-to-be of that better day. A case could be made that emphasis of sanctification evident in 11QTemple meant that a better day came through sanctification of temple, land and people. However, a more specific claim of salvation does play an essential role in the schema of

40. Cf. J.N. Lightstone, *Society, The Sacred, and Scripture in Ancient Judaism* (Waterloo: Wilfrid Laurier University Press, 1988), pp. 21-43.

41. See Neusner, *Testament to Torah*, pp. 73-77 for comments on stress of sanctification to the near exclusion of salvation and messianism.

42. See W.S. Green, 'Introduction: Messiah in Judaism: Rethinking the Question', in J. Neusner, W.S. Green and E.S. Frierichs (eds.), *Judaisms and their Messiahs at the Turn of the Common Era* (Cambridge: Cambridge University Press, 1987), pp. 1-13.

43. Cf. S. Talmon, 'Waiting for the Messiah: The Spiritual Universe of the Qumran Covenanters', in Neusner, Green and Frierichs (eds.), *Judaisms and their Messiahs*, p. 115.

the Temple Scroll especially highlighted in the section called 'statutes of the king' in columns 56.12–59.21.

The material in the 'statutes of the king' appears to be a work of the redactor in contrast to the more explicit reworking of other source material found elsewhere in the Temple Scroll.[44] Kingship is the primary topic matter and 56.20 indicates that the content of this section of 11QTemple is torah for the king, as it states 'and when he sits on the throne of his kingdom, they shall write for him this torah from a scroll before the priests'.[45] The king was not to write the laws of kingship as this responsibility rested with the priests. Shemaryahu Talmon has noted that Qumranite expectations of a new age had a 'real-historical character'. Although Qumranites believed that they were on the threshold of a new phase of history, it was not 'other-worldly' or historically alien from preceding stages of Jewish history.[46] This characteristic is evident in 11QTemple as the laws for kingship are this-worldly, rather politically specific and seem to counter an already existing kingship (56.18-21). The polemic against foreign mercenaries guarding the king (57.8b-11),[47] the requirement of the queen to be Jewish, and for the king and queen to have a monogamous relationship (57.15b-19a),[48] the concern for defensive strategies against potential enemies (58.3-15a),[49] and the polemic

44. 'Statutes of the King' appears to be based on Deut. 17.14-20. See Y. Yadin, *The Temple Scroll: The Hidden Law of the Dead Sea Sect* (New York: Random House, 1985), pp. 192-94. See Stegemann, 'Literary Composition', pp. 141-42, for a view that this section deals with matters relating to kings of Judah or Israel from a Deuteronomic tradition; cf. Wilson and Wills, 'Literary Sources', pp. 287-88. Also, see Z.W. Falk, 'The Temple Scroll and the Codification of Jewish Law', *JLA* 2 (1979), pp. 33-44.

45. Cf. Hengel *et al.*, 'On Kingship', pp. 31-32. The king is to obey the law written for him by priests (56.20b-21), not by the king himself as in Deut. 17.18; cf. 1 Sam. 10.25, 2 Kgs 11.12.

46. Talmon, 'Waiting for the Messiah', p. 126.

47. See Jos., *Ant.* 13.249, 374-75. Cf. Yadin, *The Temple Scroll*, I, pp. 348-49.

48. Although there were biblical tales about Solomon and others (2 Sam. 3.2-11; 12.8; 5.13; 16.20-22; 2 Chron. 11.21; 13.21), Alexander Jannaeus was notorious for his concubines; cf. Jos., *Ant.* 13.380. Cf. Yadin, *The Temple Scroll*, I, pp. 353-57.

49. Lack of defensive strategy during the period of Alexander Jannaeus against the threat of outside invasion was a primary concern for ancient Judaea. Cf. M. Stern, 'Judaea and her Neighbors', pp. 22-46. Cf. Jos., *Ant.* 13.324, 337,

against a king living on booty (58.11c-15a)[50]—all point to circumstances that can be identified with the Hasmonean era.

The laws for king negated religious or priestly duties, and qualified his judicial responsibilities. He was to function as a military figure only. The king's status as judge was one among thirty-six elders, priests, and levites. The stipulation of Deut. 17.20 not to raise the king above his brothers was used to create a royal council that bound the king to the council's decisions.[51] The king would be subject to the council even on military matters, and the judicial section of 11QTemple is intended to guard against errors of judgement in handling political and military matters.[52]

On one level the section on 'statutes of the king' appears to reflect the context of the Hasmonean dynasty. Although 11QTemple is reactionary to the momentum of Hasmonean policies, the tone and content of the material is positive and constructive. The primacy of priestly concerns shaped not only the reaction to kingship, but it offered a constructive directive for societal benefit and order. On another level the 'statutes of the king' respond to societal questions relating to political standing and possession of land by offering a salvific vision of the future based on a kingship and priesthood operating in. harmony. Success in military and political matters would be guaranteed if the king did not act on his own accord, but on the instructions of the high priest (58.20b-21). Column 59 details the curses that would fall upon the king and people if the king did not observe the statutes, and the blessings if he did.[53] Past kings are condemned for violating God's covenant and despising divine laws. However, there is an alternative for future expectations. Following

345-47, 390-91. Also see Hengel *et al.*, 'On Kingship', pp. 34-36.

50. See Yadin, *The Temple Scroll*, I, pp. 359-62; Hengel *et al.* 'On Kingship', 36; J. Milgrom, 'Studies in the Temple Scroll', *JBL* 97 (1978), pp. 520-21.

51. See J. Maier, *The Temple Scroll* (Sheffield: JSOT Press, 1985), p. 126. The responsibilities of the council include dealing with issues relating to *mishpat* and *torah* —the two terms used in combination that was noted in column 29.4 above.

52. Hengel *et al.*, 'On Kingship', p. 33. See Yadin, *The Temple Scroll*, I, pp. 349-53, for a comparison between the judicial council of 11QTemple and those of 1QS and CD.

53. The blessings and curses are based on Deut. 28, Lev. 26, 2 Chron. 20; cf. Yadin, *The Temple Scroll*, II, p. 265.

Yadin's translation of column 59.11-13, the text promises the following.[54]

> I will save them from the hands of their enemies, and deliver them from
> the hand of those who hate them, and bring them to the land of their
> fathers and deliver them, and I will multiply them and take delight over
> them, and I will be their God, and they shall be my people.

The thrust of this column seeks to profile a religio-political programme of a kingship guided by priests who in the forthcoming better day would be an essential component for constituting the people of Israel. The early Maccabean warriors had inspired a vision of kingship that became progressively more important to expectations of a better day. The realities of the Hasmonean failure to realize better days, from a sectarian perspective, did not negate or minimize the role of kingship in systems of salvation in Second Temple Judaism. The 'statutes of the king' represents a fundamental principle for the salvific vision of 11QTemple. Redemption will come when the king observes the *torah* of the king, and it is a necessary condition that compliments the endeavours to sanctify and make perfect cult, land and people.

Conclusion

If we return to Neusner's thesis that Judaic writings in the fourth century CE successfully joined together stress on sanctification of Israel with a message of salvation and these principles defined Judaism in the medieval and modern periods—both of these principles are evident in the Temple Scroll. The text seeks to be generative and procreative with claims of sanctification and salvation. Further, the Temple Scroll functioned as a wholistic system in response to societal factors contemporary with the Hasmonean dynasty. There is a correlation between the wholistic ambitions of the Temple Scroll as *torah* and the 'potential' but failed generative symbolism in the kingship of the Hasmoneans in that both sought to deal with peoplehood, land and nation. The distinctive feature of the Temple Scroll as *torah* is that the salvific factor that gave rise to the Hasmonean monarchy as defenders of traditional Judaism is balanced with precise details for organizing a society based on 11QTemple.

54. Yadin, *The Temple Scroll*, II, p. 268.

Hope for the future as well as specifics for living are complimenting principles for the Temple Scroll. Although ancient Jewish sectarianism was particular in its vision of who constituted the people of God and what were the essential principles for such a group that resulted in exclusivism, and exclusion of non-sectarians, the Temple Scroll suggests that there was an attempt to provide a single, definitive and wholistic alternative for those attracted to claims of sectarians. Formative Judaism and Christianity inherit such an endeavour. This study suggests that even an ultra-conservative form of sectarianism, represented by the Temple Scroll, wished to incorporate all of society in its view of things by balancing the principles of sanctification and salvation.

THE BIBLE AND TRANSLATION: THE TARGUMS

Ernest G. Clarke

I am pleased to contribute and dedicate this article to my friend and colleague Professor John Hurd. My association with John goes back some fifteen years when we began to discuss the possibility of producing a K(ey) W(ord) I(n) C(ontext) concordance to the Aramaic *Targum Pseudo-Jonathan* of the Pentateuch.[1] Out of his large experience with computers he provided me, first of all, with his programme for producing a KWIC concordance and then continued to advise and assist. There was the added challenge for John in that he was required to deal with a Semitic alphabet, structured differently from his familiar Greek. This whole exercise began at a time when computer work was less sophisticated. For instance, because of the costs associated with on-line use of the main-frame computer much of the initial preparation was done by key-punching the targum text. The number of homographs in a semitic language was quite extensive. So he devised a method of checking for them. Finally the question of printing the final text in Aramaic required John to write a computer programme to estimate the width of the Aramaic letters to prevent text spilling over the end of the lines in the wrong place (namely at the left margin rather than at the right margin as it must be for a semitic language).

In modern Hebrew the word 'targum' simply means translation. So a modern translation from one language to another such as from English to French would be called a 'targum'. In the context of Biblical Studies, however, 'targum' has a specialized meaning; namely, the translation of the Hebrew Bible into the Aramaic language. It is in this sense that the term is used in this paper. Also, for the purposes of

---

1. E.G. Clarke with the collaboration of W.E. Aufrecht, J.C. Hurd and F. Spitzer, *Targum-Jonathan of the Pentateuch: Text and Concordance* (New York: Ktav, 1984).

this paper I use the word 'Bible' in its narrower sense to refer to the Hebrew Scriptures, called by Christians, the Old Testament.

We are familiar with translations from one language into another. And we recognize the fact that no modern translation is ever totally neutral/objective. Within the target language there are conventions which dictate that a certain word in the original language can be translated in the target language with a specific word dictated by context. On the other hand, often there is no way that a phrase or expression in one language can be translated literally in order to express the same idea in the target language. Thus, the modern translator has to supply, explicitly, what is implied in the source language, found in the connotative network of a given text. So it is that translation is always inflationary. George Steiner[2] speaks of three principal approaches to translation: (1) strict literalism, with its attendant distortions and incoherence, (2) faithful but autonomous restatement and (3) that of imitation, re-creation, variation, interpretive parallel. This latter sheds the usual modern translation scruples and deems it legitimate for the translator to allow his personal emotions, convictions and motives to enter his target language version. As this study will show the meaning of targum as translation is closer to Steiner's third category.[3] What E. Levine[4] refers to as 'a conversation' with the common text, that is, the Bible and S.P. Brock suggests that 'the translation co-exists in a symbiotic relationship with the Hebrew original'.[5]

Already in ancient times one can see the tendency not to translate literally. From the eighth century BCE comes the Tell Fakhariyah

---

2. G. Steiner, *After Babel: Aspects of Language and Translation* (London: Oxford University Press, 1975), p. 253.

3. P.S. Alexander, 'Jewish Aramaic Translations of Hebrew Scriptures', in M. Mulder and H. Sysling (eds.), *Mikra* (Philadelphia: Fortress Press, 1988), pp. 217-53: corresponds to that of the Latin *interpretatio*, i.e., it covers both 'translation' from one language into another and 'explanation' of a text...'; cf. also S.P. Brock, 'Aspects of Translation Technique in Antiquity', *GRBS* 20 (1979), pp. 69-87 and P.S. Alexander, 'The Targumim and the Rabbinic Rules for the Delivery of the Targum', in J.A. Emerton (ed.), *Congress Volume, Salamanca 1983* (VTSup, 36; Leiden: Brill, 1985), pp. 14-28.

4. E. Levine, *The Aramaic Version of the Bible* (BZAW, 174; Berlin: Töpelmann, 1988).

5. S.P. Brock, 'Translating the Old Testament', in D.A. Carson and H.G.M. Williamson (eds.), *It is Written: Scripture Citing Scripture: Essays in Honour of Barnabas Lindars* (Cambridge: Cambridge University Press, 1988), p. 87.

inscription which is a bilingual text. As S.A. Kaufman writes, 'In the ancient world, two versions of a bilingual inscription are rarely, if ever, mere word-for-word equivalents. Each version is informed by the cultural context of its respective language and is phrased somewhat differently according to the linguistic and stylistic norms of that language.'[6] There are, to be sure, instances of slavish imitations of the Akkadian style and language, in this inscription, but there are deviations. As I hope to demonstrate, the targums go further; nevertheless Tell Fakhariyah demonstrates the fact that literal translation is an unacceptable principle on which to affect translation, even in the ancient world.

To return to the argument that translations provided the hearer with a text understandable in the language of the day: at an earlier stage of targumic studies it was also argued that the Targums arose because the people did not understand the Hebrew of the Bible. The validity of this argument is closely related to the time of the emergence of the Aramaic language as the spoken language for the people of Palestine; especially, when Hebrew died out as a spoken language. Discoveries at Qumran (before 70 CE), Murrabba'at (first/second century CE) and the extensive inscriptional material (to the sixth century CE) found in Palestine written in Hebrew would suggest that the date for the transition from Hebrew to Aramaic was later than had earlier been thought. M.H. Segal[7] argued for the continued use of Hebrew as a spoken, everyday language at least until the fifth/sixth centuries CE. Segal writes:

> M(Middle) H(Hebrew) had an independent existence as a natural living speech, growing, developing, and changing in accordance with its own genius and in conformity with the laws which govern the life of all languages in general...so long as the Jewish people retained some sort of material existence in Palestine MH continued to be the language of at least a section of the Jewish people living in Palestine.

1. Translating the Hebrew Bible into Aramaic has a much more complex set of reasons than just to provide a text for people who no longer understood the original. In the first place, the translation has to do with the fact that for Judaism (and the Christians who wrote the New Testament) the Bible (Old Testament) was a living document.

6.   S.A. Kaufman, 'Reflections on the Assyrian-Aramaic Bilingual form Tell Fakhariyah', *Maarav* 3.2 (1982), p. 153.

7.   M.H. Segal, *A Grammar of Mishnaic Hebrew* (Oxford: Clarendon Press, 1927), p. 13.

Early Judaism sought, therefore, to up-date the Scriptures, to actualize them in terms of current needs, to make the Bible meaningful and relevant to its contemporary audience, whenever that period was.[8] D.J. Harrington[9] calls the process 're-writing the Bible'.[10]

The discovery of a large variety of texts at Qumran, as well as Jewish writings known before Qumran, has shown that Judaism had a number of different ways to re-write the Bible, to up-date its meaning for a contemporary audience. The variety can be broken down into two major categories. First, the re-working of Scriptures took a literal form called *peshat* (literal explanation) and *derash* (interpretative explanation). *Peshat* is expressed by 'targum' and *derash* by 'midrash'. These terms 'targum' and 'midrash' are both methods of up-dating as well as genres of literature. As a literary genre 'targum' is always a verse by verse and chapter by chapter explanation of the biblical text. By contrast, 'midrash' as a literary genre, although it is an explanation of the biblical text, does not necessarily arrange its explanations in a verse by verse order. We shall return to discuss the inherent nature of the targumic way of dealing with Scripture. P.S. Alexander[11] observes differences between the terms 'targum' and 'midrash' by observing that Targumim never quote 'rabbinic authorites by name'. Midrashim 'often quote verses of Scripture intoduced by citation formulae' whereas Targumim never quote Scripture overtly. Midrashim are argumentative in style whereas Targumim 'give conclusions and are careful to conceal the bones of exegetical logic'. Midrashim often 'introduce variant and conflicting interpretations' whereas Targumim 'are careful to smooth away any conflicts'.

8. D.M. Golomb, 'The Targumic Renderings of the Verb *lehistahawot*: A Targum Translation Convention', in *Working with no Data: Semitic and Egyptian Studies presented to Thomas O. Lambdin* (Winona Lake, IN: Eisenbrauns, 1987), pp. 105-18 esp. p. 107.

9. D.J. Harrington, 'Palestinian Adaptations of Biblical Narratives and Prophecies', in R.A. Kraft and W.E. Nickelsburg (eds.), *Early Judaism and its Modern Interpreters* (Philadelphia: Fortress Press, 1986), pp. 239-40.

10. Alexander, 'Jewish Aramaic Translating', pp. 238-39. For this reason I find it difficult to accept A. Shinan's argument ('The "Palestinian" Targums—Repetitions, Internal Unity, Contradictions', *JJS* 36 [1985], p. 87) that *Targum Pseudo-Jonathan* 'seems unworthy of the designation "Targum"; it is better described... by Vermes as "the re-written Bible"'. If Targum is not a re-written Bible then I do not know what it is.

11. Alexander, 'The Targum', in Emerton (ed.), *Congress Volume*, p. 16

The second category employed in updating Scripture is called *Pesharim* or interpretation, understood as the unravelling of mysteries.[12] The *Pesharim* developed under the influence of the book of Daniel where the interpretation of the mysteries appeared to be so important. So within Judaism, attempts to actualize Scripture could be expressed in the *pesher* form.[13] This literary genre is written in Hebrew and consists of a lemma of the biblical text, plus the word *pšr* plus an extended explanation in Hebrew of what the biblical text meant in the contemporary situation.

Only the Targums appear in Aramaic. The Midrashim and Pesharim are written in Hebrew. These last two literary genre, given their form, could in no way suggest that they are God's original Word. By contrast, the Targums which are a translation of the biblical text, following exactly the same verse and chapter order, might be mistaken for God's Word if they had been written in Hebrew. Levine[14] noted that even mediaeval Christian Monks believed that God spoke only Hebrew and so they quickly learned Hebrew in old age in order to be able to converse with God in the next life. Although God's Word was written in Hebrew, nevertheless, unless there is some ongoing interpretation of that Word of God it would soon become meaningless and irrelevant. Hence Judaism sought continuously to contemporize the Scriptures by these various processes. The Bible was translated into Aramaic not because the people did not understand the original but rather so that the biblical text could be actualized and made relevant for the contemporary audience. As D.M. Golomb writes, 'The targumim are rabbinic documents, not popular ones, and the rabbis would have paled at an attempt to rewrite the Bible from one Hebrew to another—Aramaic was the language of comment, of meaning, of explication'.[15]

The desire to actualize the Bible in contemporary terms was not in itself unique to the Targums. In the biblical text itself this process was already operative.[16] Within the tradition of the biblical text there has

12. M.P. Horgan, 'The Bible Explained (Prophecies)', in Kraft and Nickelsburg (eds.), *Early Judaism and its Modern Interpreters*, pp. 248-49.

13. D. Dimant, 'Qumran Sectarian Lecture', in M.E. Stone (ed.), *Jewish Writings in the Second Temple Period* (Philadelphia: Fortress Press, 1984), pp. 503-504.

14. Levine, *Aramaic Version*, p. 14 n.3.

15. Golomb, 'The Targumic Renderings', p. 107.

16. I.L. Seeligman, 'Indications of Editorial Alterations and Adaptations in the

been an ongoing process of editing and re-editing to reflect the meaning of the 'Word of God' at any given moment. For instance in a prophetic book there is no indication within the text itself that a given passage stems from one hand or several; or even from one specific time. The object of the biblical text is not to credit a specific author with certain words but to present God's Word to his people. Within the Targums themselves, following good biblical practice, there was no barrier to re-working in a later age, the original targumic text.

And so a very clear reason for an Aramaic translation of the Bible is related to the need to up-date the Bible for the contemporary audience at whatever point in time the translation is being presented. There are inconsistencies in the biblical text which need to be resolved. There is a view that the biblical text represents a coherent whole so separate incidents need to be reconciled. A contemporary identification needs to be made for now obscure biblical terminology, such as geography. And, current theological positions need to be elaborated. As well, different rabbinic interpretations of the biblical text need to be presented.[17]

M.L. Klein wrote an article a number of years ago in which he examined passages where the Targum inserted a negative into the translation of a biblical passage or dropped a negative. Klein argues that 'the wide gamut of surviving targumim, ranging indeed from the very literal to the most expansive midrashic paraphrases indicate that, in fact no standard of interpretation prevailed. Moreover, even individual targumim are rarely consistent in their translational method'.[18]

One can see this fact of the Targums, observed by Klein, in several ways. For the Pentateuch there is an Official Targum, called *Targum Onqelos*, which appears, on the surface, to be a literal word for word translation of the Hebrew text. But on looking more closely at the targumic text one notices that the Aramaic words chosen to translate the Hebrew are loaded with all sorts of interpretation. The deviations from the biblical text in *Targum Onqelos* are often very subtle, reflected by a change of a single word of vocabulary or a brief added

Massoretic Text and the Septuagint', *VT* 11 (1961) pp. 201-21; D.W. Gooding, 'Problems of Text and Midrash in the Third Book of Reigns', *Textus* 7 (1969), pp. 1-29.

17. Alexander, 'Jewish Aramaic Translating', pp. 226-73.

18. M.L. Klein, 'Converse Translation: A Targumic Technique', *Biblica* 57.4 (1976), pp. 515-73.

item.[19] On another level the fact that there are two other complete Targums of the Pentateuch (*Pseudo-Jonathan* and *Neofiti*) plus an incomplete (or Fragmentary) Pentateuchal Targum, as well as Geniza Targums with different targumic texts, points to the fact that there was extant a variety of interpretations of the biblical text. All these witnesses follow the biblical order, verse by verse but in addition contain a large amount of extra material explaining the meaning of the biblical text. The existence of *Targum Onqelos* in contrast to the other Targums of the Pentateuch has much to say about the fixing of the text of the Hebrew Bible as a consonantal and official text. When that happened there was much need for a pseudo-canonical translation in the Aramaic language and as close as possible to the original which had become canonical or official.[20] And so, much of the extra explicative material was not included in the official Targum (*Onqelos*) of the Pentateuch. When this process of standardization took place, it is impossible to date exactly; but it is clear from many studies that the targumic text familiar to the writers of the New Testament is preserved now mainly in the other 'unofficial' Targums. Furthermore, these other Targums of the Pentateuch must have not been completely rejected otherwise they would not be extant today.

The fact that a number of different complete and incomplete Targums still exist shows that there was no uniform, standard, accepted interpretation at any one point in time. The difference between Targums recognized as official (*Onqelos* for the Pentateuch and *Jonathan ben Uzziel* for the Prophets) and the other Targums is a result of the acceptance of one text of the Hebrew Bible being recognized as normative and authoritative.

2. A second factor contributing to the nature of *Targumim* is the fact that the present text of the Targums, especially in the Targums of the Pentateuch and the Prophets, was worked and re-worked often; so there are layers of interpretation. We have observed that there are three complete and one incomplete Targum of the Pentateuch. And many studies have tried to come to terms with the differences found by which the different Targums translate the same passage.[21]

19. G. Vermes, 'Haggadah in the Targum of Onqelos', *JSS* 8 (1963), pp. 159-69; J. Bowker, 'Haggadah in the Targum of Onqelos', *JSS* 12 (1967), pp. 51-65; Berliner (1814) also gave a limited number of examples.

20. Alexander, 'Jewish Aramaic Translating', p. 242.

21. Cf. J.T. Forestell, *Targumic Tradition and the New Testament* (Chico, CA:

S.D. Fraade in a review of Churgin's *Targum Jonathan to the Prophets* which has been re-issued with an extended essay by Smolar and Aberbach[22] called it '"progressive composition" having no single author but comprising both early and late translation tradition'.[23] In actual fact it is possible that the process of up-dating could continue to the point when a text is actually preserved in a specific mediaeval manuscript. That may be the final possible date of fixation of a Targum but, of course, in general, the major work of the Targum/translation took place closer to the beginning of the process than to the end.

The Targum is always determined by how a specific text is to be understood by the believing community at the point at which the translation was made or modified. The difference stems from the fact that to an initial translation are added later interpretations sustained by the belief that the Targum is an expression of God's living Word to the believing community. There is a continuum of principal tradents—generations of translators—working and re-working the same text. Golomb[24] wrote 'the Targum is the authorized community standard of what the word of Torah means. In discussing a difficult verse in Zechariah (12.11) in *b. Meg.* 3a, R. Joseph comments "if it were not for the Targum of that verse, we would not know what it means"'.[25] And, I believe that is an extension of the process already noted for the biblical text itself.

Within any given Targum there are divergent readings which illustrate the point that Targums were an on-going exercise in which additions and modifications were being made. Part of the explanation for this is found in the process of producing a Targum and partly in the purpose. B.D. Chilton discusses this duality in the same text with

Scholars Press, 1979); R. Le Déaut, *The Message of the New Testament and the Aramaic Bible (Targum)* (Rome: Biblical Institute Press, 1982) and many other articles by Le Déaut; E.G. Clarke, 'Jacob's Dream at Bethel as interpreted in the Targums and the New Testament', *SR* 4.4 (1974), pp. 367-77; B.D. Chilton, *Targumic Approaches to the Gospels* (Lanham, MD: University Press of America, 1986); M.G. Steinhauser, 'Noah in his Generation: An Allusion in Luke 16.8b', *ZNT* 79.1.2 (1988), pp. 152-57.

22. L. Smolar and M. Aberbach, *Studies in the Targum Jonathan to the Prophets and Targum Jonathan to the Prophets by Pinchas Churgin* (New York: Ktav, 1983)

23. S.D. Fraade, *JQR* 79.4 (1985), pp. 392-415.

24. Golomb, 'The Targumic Renderings', p. 8.

25. The Babylonian Talmud uses this phrase quite often; in addition to *b. Meg.* 3a cf. *b. M. Qat.* 28b, *b. Sanh.* 84b, *b. Ber.* 28b, etc.

reference to the Targum of Isaiah by saying 'if we were dealing with a composition which was a literary document, *de novo*, one might be inclined to infer that a pre-temple destruction source has been con-flated with a post-temple destruction source. He further observes that the fact that 'the Targum was oral in practice...such a process which must have influenced the literary production of the Targum as a document, would have tended to blur the lines between one layer and another'.[26]

Therefore these differences in the same document may represent biblical interpretation at different periods in time (diachronically). However, it is possible that differences represent the thinking of different scholars synchronically. For instance the Wilderness of Shur in the Hebrew Text is translated by 'Hagra' and 'Halusa' in the pentateuchal Targums. In *Targum Pseudo-Jonathan* both words are used in different passages whereas both words appear in the same verse in other Targums. Noah is called both 'a righteous person' and a 'pure/innocent person' in the same passage in different Targums. The examples from *Targum Pseudo-Jonathan* and the other pentateuchal Targums could be chronological but could also represent two different contemporary ways of translating the same word/idea in the Hebrew text (On the matter of Noah's character the Midrashim tell us that in the third century there existed two different opinions which were debated by the Rabbis in their schools). In either explanation the inconsistency now exists in the same document and represents stages or layers rather than different documents which have been conflated.

When an analysis of the Aramaic language, into which the Targums are translated, is made one observes, as well, an inconsistency in vocabulary, morphology and syntax within the same text. For the Pentateuchal Targums these inconsistencies represent the long period over which the Targums were worked and re-worked to reach their present form—a period in which language also changed. The differ-ences in language just noted are further compounded by scribal activity in copying manuscripts. Many of the mediaeval scribes knew only the Babylonian Aramaic of the liturgy and so they often changed a word or phrase into the Babylonian Aramaic, with which

26. B.D. Chilton, *The Glory of Israel* (JSOTSup, 23; Sheffield: JSOT Press 1983), p. 21.

they were familiar, for the unfamiliar Palestinian word(s).[27] Golomb[28] calls this a copyist's error.

3. A third factor contributing to the nature of Targumim with its various levels of interpretation in the source text is that it was used for liturgical purposes and was required to be presented orally. That having been said, the Targum at the oral stage was never a haphazard, random, extemporaneous translation but rather it was a fixed, traditional, authorized version which was memorized and recited. Oral did not mean spontaneous. It may well be that the main reason for presenting the Targum orally was to avoid confusion with the Word of God, found in the Bible which was read from a written text.[29] Nevertheless, the fact that the Targum was presented orally allowed for the introduction of new, up-dated interpretations according to the rabbinic norms of the day. And I believe these latest up-datings were eventually incorporated into the existing written text. As noted in rabbinic literature anyone could recite the Targum for the day but there is no evidence that the translator was free in what he recited. The Babylonian Talmud says that 'He who translates a verse verbatim is a liar. And he who alters it is a villain and a heretic'.[30] So even in early times a literal, verbatim translation was unacceptable. And yet, the translator must not be so free as to deviate from acceptable norms. In fact, there were probably written Targums on which the meturgeman's oral presentation was based. Certainly the arguments against written Targums show that written Targums did exist. The fact that a Targum of Job was found at Qumran shows that written Targums existed from at least the first century BCE.

I have spent time discussing the nature of the Pentateuchal Targums. To a large degree the same can be argued for the official Targum of the Prophets by Jonathan Ben Uzziel. The fact that Goshen-Gottstein has collected a large number of Fragmentary Targums of the Prophetic

27. E.Y. Kutscher, *Studies in Galilaean Aramaic* (trans. M. Sokoloff; Ramat Gan, Israel: Bar-Ilan University Press, 1976), p. 2.

28. Golomb, 'The Targumic Renderings', p. 15.

29. Alexander, 'The Targumim', p. 25 'Every effort had been made to avoid confusing the targum with the written text of Scripture... two different people. The Scripture reader had to be clearly seen to be "reading" from the scroll; the translator had to recite targum from memory...'; cf also Alexander, 'Jewish Aramaic Translating', pp. 238-39.

30. *b. Qid.* 49a.

books suggests that other interpretations existed but were not preserved intact when an official Targum of the Prophets was established.[31]

The books of the third section of the Bible (*Ketubim*) also have Targums. Here, however, I believe the process is different. The long extended period when the text was worked and re-worked did not operate. With respect to the Targum of Qoheleth (Ecclesiastes), which I now want to discuss in more detail, it was most likely put together (translated) over a much shorter period of time so there are not the layers of interpretation. There is much more of a coherent whole to the Targum of Qoheleth. In only the area of the language of the Targum of Qoheleth is there obvious inconsistency. The text of the Targum is said to be in Palestinian Aramaic. Nevertheless, there is a large degree of Babylonian Aramaic found in most of the manuscripts ranging from a heavily babylonized text in MS Vaticanus to a purer text form in MS Paris 110. One explanation for these differences, which are not contained in all manuscripts, is that the mediaeval scribes copying the text substituted Babylonian Aramaic words for the less familiar Palestinian Aramaic words.

The consistency of theme which appears in the Targum of Qoheleth can be seen in a number of ways. Probably the most basic attempt to make the biblical text intelligible to a contemporary audience is to be found concerning the identification of Qoheleth with King Solomon. Although one's understanding may have associated Qoheleth with Solomon, the Bible does not actually say so. All the Bible says is 'the word of Qoheleth (the 'Preacher' in most English translations) the son of David, king in Jerusalem'. The Targum reads 'the words of prophecy which Qoheleth, that is, Solomon the son of David the king who was in Jerusalem prophesied'. Consistently the three passages where the Bible reads Qoheleth, the Targum adds Solomon.[32] Likewise the passages where the first person pronoun is used, referring to Qoheleth, the Targum substitutes Solomon. A second shift found in the Targum of this verse identifies Solomon with prophecy because only prophets are understood to convey God's message to the people. In the text Qoheleth/Solomon is certainly expressing God's message. Also God does not speak directly to people, and so it is effected through prophecy. Already as reflected in the Targum of 1 Kings

31. M.H. Goshen-Gottstein, *Fragments of Lost Targumim* (Ramat Gan, Israel: Bar-Ilan University Press, 1983) (Hebrew), part 1; part 2 (1989).

32. Qoh. 1.12; 7.27; 12.9, 10.

(5.13) there was a tradition which identified Solomon as a prophet which reflects the Targumist's understanding of the wholeness of the biblical text.

There is a move to greater specification in the Targums generally. And so in the Targum of Qoheleth there are examples of that emphasis. The general phrase 'all who were before me' are identified as sages. In Qoh. 2.4 where the biblical texts lists some of Qoheleth's activities, 'great works' become 'good works'; and 'I built houses' becomes 'I built for myself houses, the temple to atone for Israel and the royal summer palace, the chamber, the porch and the courthouse of hewn stones where the sages and judges sit in judgement. I built a throne of ivory for a royal seat...'; 'I planted vineyards' becomes 'I planted vineyards in Jabneh opposite the grape vineyards so that I and the Rabbis of the Sanhedrin might drink wine from them and also make from them libations of wine old and new on the altar'. Because the Targumist has identified Qoheleth as Solomon the whole tenor of the Targum is set in the specific historical period when Solomon lived. And because Solomon, according to the Bible, was the builder of the Temple, specific passages are associated with the temple, cultus, and things related to the temple, even though in the Hebrew text the references are less specific, and more general.

This move to specificity is also found in the Targumist's tendency to give precise historical identification. The words 'that youth', in Qoh. 4.15-16, is interpreted, in the Targum, as referring to Rehoboam, Solomon's son who lost the kingdom to Jeroboam because he sought the advice of young counsellors rather than that of the elders.

There are many other instances where the Targum sought to with specific statements what seems to be abbreviated in the biblical text. The famous passage in ch. 3 dealing with time: 'A time to be born, and a time to die, a time to plant and a time to pluck up what is planted', etc. becomes in the Targum as a 'Time chosen to bear sons and a time chosen to kill rebellious and blasphemous sons, to kill them by the order of the judges; a time to plant a tree and a time chosen to uproot a planted tree', etc. What is happening here is that the Targum seeks to make specific what can be considered non-specific in the biblical text. By examining each expansion one can gain an understanding of how the Targumist viewed the verse being translated. While a large number of expansions can be treated as mere expansions they are all intended to elucidate the biblical text.

There is certainly a theological thrust to the Targum of Qoheleth. The emphasis on wisdom and the study of Torah which is emphasized in the biblical book, is more fully developed in the Targum. Since Solomon is considered to epitomize wisdom in the Bible and since Solomon is considered the author of the book of Qoheleth, wisdom determines much of the interpretation of the book as far as the Targum is concerned. In 12.12 it is said that 'of making many books there is no end, and much study is a weariness of the flesh'. To the Targumist the many books created are all books of wisdom and study of them is the study of Torah and study does not weary the flesh but one examines the weariness of the flesh. Furthermore, the general word 'wisdom' of the biblical text is regularly modified in the Targum to be 'the wisdom of the righteous' (9.16), 'wisdom of the wise' (9.18; 8.1), 'wisdom of the sages' (10.1), 'wisdom of Torah' (7.11,12; 8.16). Solomon explored the books of Wisdom (12.9) and tried in his wisdom to judge the people (12.10) and 'to teach wisdom to those empty of knowledge' (12.11).

Another aspect of this Targum is the eschatological dimension. Many of Qoheleth's observation concerned what happened 'under the sun, in this world'. The Targumist considers the phrase 'under the sun' to refer to this world.[33] By contrast the Targumist considers the phrase 'in this world', to actually refer to the world to come.[34]

Finally, the idea of the study of Torah as the main emphasis of Qoheleth's toil is found frequently developed in the Targum. Even such an obscure phrase as 'it is good that you should take hold of this' (7.18) is identified as the book of Torah.[35]

We could multiply the illustrations from the Targum of Qoheleth but suffice it to say that there is a thematic coherence to this Targum which is less clear in the Targums of the Pentateuch. Even the Targum of Qoheleth, however, is intended to translate the biblical text in terms of how it was understood at the time the translation was

---

33. Cf 1.3, 9, 14, 17, 18, 19, 20, 22; 3.16; 4.1, 2, 7, 15; 5.12, 17; 6.1, 12; 8.9, 15(2×), 17; 9.3, 6, 9, 11, 13; 10.5.

34. 2.16; 9.6 cf. 1.3; 2.10, 11, 26; 3.15, 22; 4.8, 9; 5.10, 18; 6.4, 5; 7.12, 14, 15; 8.12, 13, 14; 9.4, 5; 10.19; 11.1, 'world *to come*'.

35. 'it is good that you grasp the affairs of the world to do good to yourself in the way of the merchant and also from this book of Torah do not abandon your position...'

made. Translation, therefore, is interpretation and thereby the people of the Book remain true to the Word of God while being a creative, living, and evolving community of believers.

John Coolidge Hurd, Jr: *Cursus Vitae*

1928	Born 26 March, Boston, Massachusetts
1948	Married Helen Porter, 20 December
1949	BS (Chemistry), Harvard University
1952	BD, Episcopal Theological School, Cambridge, Massachusetts
1952	Ordained Deacon, Diocese of Massachusetts, 7 June
1952–53	Curate, St Thomas Church, New Haven, Connecticut
1953	Ordained Priest, Diocese of Massachusetts, 27 June
1953–54	*Locum tenens*, Trinity Church, Branford, Connecticut
1954–58	Priest-in-Charge, Christ Church, Bethany, Connecticut
1958–60	Instructor, Department of Religion, Princeton University
1960–67	Professor of New Testament, Episcopal Theological Seminary of the Southwest, Austin, Texas
1961	PhD, Yale University
1964	Christian Research Foundation Award for *The Origin of 1 Corinthians*
1964–65	Faculty Fellowship, American Association of Theological Schools
1965	Elected to membership in the Studiorium Novi Testamenti Societas
1966–69	Editor-in-chief, *Anglican Theological Review*
1967–	Professor of New Testament, Trinity College, Toronto
1967–69	Member, Committee on Cooperation in Theological Education in Toronto (COCTET, the founding committee for the Toronto School of Theology)
1967–70	Honorary Assistant, Grace Church on the Hill, Toronto
1967–91	Director of Advanced Degree Studies, Trinity College
1970–	Honorary Assistant, The Parish of St Clement, Eglinton

1972–73   President, Canadian Society of Biblical Studies

1976   Cross-appointed as a founding member of the Centre for the Study of Religion, University of Toronto

1974   Award for curriculum innovation, Council of Ontario Universities, for computer-assisted instruction in Greek

1976   Martin Memorial Lecturer, College of Emmanuel and St Chad, Saskatoon

1977–78   Award by the Association of Theological Schools for development of computer-assisted instructional materials for Greek

1978–84   Chairman, Working Group on Computer-assisted Research, Society of Biblical Literature (CARG)

1980–85   Chairman, Humanities Computer Interest Group, University of Toronto

1980–85   Chairman, Computer Users' Committee, University of Toronto

1981–84   Chairman, Biblical Department, Toronto School of Theology

1984–85,
1986–88   Chairman, Advanced Degree Council, Toronto School of Theology

1986–91   Chairman, Software Development Committee, Centre for Computing in the Humanities, University of Toronto

1992   Visiting Scholar, Faculty of Divinity, University of Edinburgh

1992–93   Dean (*pro tem*), Trinity College

BIBLIOGRAPHY OF JOHN C. HURD

1. *Publications*

The Origin of 1 Corinthians (London: SPCK; New York: Seabury Press, 1965; reprinted with a retrospective preface, Macon, GA: Mercer University Press, 1984).

A Bibliography of New Testament Bibliographies (New York: Seabury Press, 1966).

'Pauline Chronology and Pauline Theology', in *Christian History and Interpretation: Studies Presented to John Knox* (Cambridge: The University Press, 1967).

'Bibliography of the Work of John Knox', in *Christian History and Interpretation*.

'The Sequence of Paul's Letters', *CJT* 14/3 (July, 1968), pp. 189-200.

'Isaiah's Curse According to Mark' (Presidential Address), *BCSBS* 33 (1973).

A Synoptic Concordance of Aramaic Inscriptions (production and computer programming; text prepared by W.E. Aufrecht from edition of H. Donner and W. Roellig; International Concordance Library, 1; Missoula, MT: Scholars Press, 1975).

'Romans', '1 Corinthians', '2 Corinthians', 'Galatians', in *The Oxford Study Bible: New English Edition* (New York: Oxford University Press, 1976).

'Paul, Apostle', 'Pauline Chronology', '1 Thessalonians', '2 Thessalonians', 'Offering for the Saints', in *The Interpreter's Dictionary of the Bible: Supplementary Volume* (Nashville, TN: Abingdon Press, 1976).

'Observations about Good Proposals', *Theological Education* 16 (Autumn, 1979).

From Jesus to Paul: Studies in Honour of Francis Wright Beare, ed. with P. Richardson (Waterloo, ON: Wilfrid Laurier University Press, 1984).

' "The Jesus Whom Paul Preaches" (Acts 19.13)', in *From Jesus to Paul*.

'Bibliography of Francis Wright Beare', in *From Jesus to Paul*.

'Seminar on Pauline Chronology', ed. and 'Introduction': Part 4 of B. Corley, *et al.* (eds.), *Colloquy on New Testament Studies: A Time for Reappraisal and Fresh Approaches* (Macon, GA: Mercer University Press, 1983).

Targum Pseudo-Jonathan of the Pentateuch: Text and Concordance, programming and production; text prepared by E.G. Clarke and W.E. Aufrecht for the International Targum Project (New York: Ktav, 1984).

'Paul Ahead of his Time: 1 Thess. 2.13-16', in P. Richardson with D. Granskou (eds.), *Anti-Judaism in Early Christianity*. I. *Paul and the Gospels* (Waterloo, ON: Wilfrid Laurier University Press, 1986), pp. 21-36.

Index to Volumes 61–100 (1942–1981) of the JBL, for the SBL (Atlanta, GA: Scholars Press, 1987).

Revisions and supplementary bibliography for F.W. Beare, *The Epistle to the Philippians* (Black's New Testament Commentaries; repr.; London: A. & C. Black, 3rd edn, 1988).

'1 Corinthians' and 'Francis Wright Beare', in *Dictionary of Biblical Interpretation* (Nashville, TN: Abingdon Press, forthcoming).

2. *Papers Delivered to Learned Societies*

'The Structure of 1 Thessalonians', for the Paul Seminar of the SBL, annual meeting, Los Angeles, 4 September 1972.

'The Gospel of Mark', Martin Memorial Lectures, College of Emmanuel and St Chad, Saskatoon, Sask., 3–7 May 1976.

'Certain Uncertainties in New Testament Studies', for the Thessalonians Seminar of the SBL, annual meeting, New York, 15 November 1979.

'Psychological Considerations in Computer-assisted Instruction and the *Greek Tutor*, a Language Instruction Package', for the Symposium on Biblical Studies and the Computer, University of Michigan, 21 February 1980.

'Computers and the Humanities', for the 11th Ontario Universities Computing Conference, Queen's University, 6 June 1980.

'Concerning the Authenticity of 2 Thessalonians', for the Thessalonians Seminar of the SBL, annual meeting, Dallas, Texas, 19–22 December, 1983.

'The Authenticity of 1 Thessalonians 2.13-16', for the Paul Section of the SBL, annual meeting, Atlanta, GA, 22 November, 1986.

'Concerning Character Fonts for Humanists and Simple, Multilingual Word Processing for Humanists', for the Canadian Society of Biblical Studies, annual meeting, June 1985.

'The Integrity of 1 Corinthians 1–6', a response to Gerhard Sellin, '1 Kor 5–6 und der "Vorbrief" nach Korinth', for the 1 Corinthians Seminar of the Studiorium Novi Testamenti Societas, annual meeting, Dublin, 24–28 July 1989.

'The Human Side of Computer Assisted Instruction', for the Computer Assisted Research Group of the Society of Biblical Literature, annual meeting, New Orleans, 17 November 1990.

'Uncertain Certainties in Pauline Theology', for the New Testament Seminar of the University of Edinburgh, 20 April 1992.

INDEXES

INDEX OF BIBLICAL REFERENCES

HEBREW BIBLE

Genesis		*1 Kings*		2.4	391
1.1–2.3	304	5.13	390, 391	4.15-16	391
2.5-25	304			7.11	392
		Isaiah		7.12	392
Exodus		32.12	328	7.18	392
12.18-19	178	35.1	304	7.27	390
15.1-19	304	44.9-20	328	8.1	392
20.10-11	178	51.9-11	304	8.16	392
23.22	125	60.17	87	9.16	392
		66.6	125	9.18	392
Leviticus				10.1	392
17.7-9	178	*Ezekiel*		12.9	390, 392
17.10-12	178	1.26	164	12.10	390, 392
18.6-26	178	1.28	167	12.11	392
26	377			12.12	392
		Psalms			
Deuteronomy		8.4	283	*Daniel*	
12–26	371	9.17	176	7	291
17.18	376	106.36	328	7.13	164
17.20	377	109.8	88	10.18–11.1	137
25.4	87	115.8	328	12	163, 164
28	377			12.1-3	163
		Qoheleth			
		1.12	390		

NEW TESTAMENT

Matthew		12.8	284	16.21	284
5.11	284	12.32	284	16.27	284
8.20	284	12.40	284	16.28	284
9.6	284	12.50	253	17.9	284
10.23	34, 284	13.37	284	17.12	284
10.32	284	13.41	284	17.22	284
11.19	284	16.13	284	19.28	284

20.18	284	17.22	284	17	169
20.28	284	17.24	284	18.3	222
24.27	284	17.30	284	18.5	132
24.30	284	18.8	284	18.8	257
24.37	284	18.31	284	19.9	222
24.39	284	19.10	284	19.11-12	222
24.44	284	21.26	284	19.22	132
25.31	284	21.27	284	19.23-41	222
26.2	284	22.22	284	20.4	132
26.24	284	22.27	284	20.20	257
26.45	284	22.69	284	20.28	86
26.64	284	24.7	284	20.34-35	222
28.16-20	85			21.24-25	182
		John		21.25	59, 181
Mark		12.34	283	22.17	169
2.10	283, 284	13	253	23.1	115
2.28	284	21	34	26	170
8.27	284			26.24-29	171
8.31	284	*Acts*			
8.38	284	1.9-11	169	*Romans*	
9.9	284	1.20	88	1.3	253
9.21	284	1.21-26	169	1.9	253
9.31	284	1.21-22	88	1.16	167
10.33	284	2.17	169	1.21-32	328
10.45	284	7.56	283	2.20–3.25	204
13	34	9.10	169	2.28-29	147
13.26	284	9.36-43	265	5.3	168
14.21	284	10.3	169	5.10	253
14.41	284	11.5	169	6.18	93
14.62	284	11.14	257	6.22–7.19	204
		15	30, 45,	7.24	167
Luke			89, 173	8	166, 167
4.42	137	15.1	173, 175	8.3	253
5.24	284	15.5	175	8.10	167
6.22	284	15.19-21	181	8.13	167
6.51	284	15.20	59, 181	8.15	147
7.34	284	15.29	59, 181	8.17-18	168
9.18	284	15.32	132	8.17	167
9.22	284	16	86	8.18	167
9.26	284	16.14-15	83	8.21	147
9.44	284	16.15	83, 86,	8.29	166, 167,
9.56	284		257		253
9.58	284	16.19	83	8.32	253
11.30	284	16.25	83	9–11	167
12.10	284	16.31	257	12.2	165-67
12.8	284	16.34-35	86	12.6-8	83
12.40	284	16.34	83, 86	12.8	89
13.17	125	16.40	83, 86	13.4	102

15.8	102		157, 167	10.1	149
15.25	31	5.9-12	45	10.25	57
15.31	59	5.11	67	11.2-16	359
16.1	102, 232,	6.14	39	11.2	33, 143,
	253, 265	6.18	69		149
16.2	87	6.19–7.22	206	11.30	32, 37
16.7	265	7–16	156	11.33–	
16.15	86	7–14	188	12.23	204
16.20	151	7	46, 55,	12	154
16.25-27	151		60, 61,	12.1	149
			62, 64,	12.4-13	170
1 Corinthians			156	12.13	256, 265
1	46	7.1	60, 61,	12.27-31	239
1.9	253		63, 67	12.28	90
1.10–4.21	203	7.1-7	64, 359	12.28-30	83
1.10-11	149	7.2	62	13	52, 154
1.11	67, 265	7.5	62	13.12	305
1.12	47, 53,	7.7	61	14	154
	68, 269	7.8	61	14.6	149
1.12-13	56, 51,	7.9	62	14.8	109
	52, 54	7.12	62	14.20	149
1.13	52	7.15	253	14.26	149
1.16	257	7.24	149	14.33-35	359
1.17-18	97	7.26-27	61	14.39	149
1.18-19	94	7.29	149	15	37-40, 46,
1.26	149, 256	7.32-40	358, 359		48, 64-69,
2.1	149	7.34	61		156
3.1	149	7.36	62	15.1	68, 149
3.1–4.21	161	7.37-38	61, 62	15.2	68
3.1-2	150	7.38	60, 61	15.3-4	68
3.4	53	8	46, 55,	15.5-7	68
3.5	32, 102		57, 60,	15.5	53
3.19	167		62-64,	15.12-28	135
3.21-23	52		154	15.12	64, 65,
3.22	53	8.1	54-57		67, 69
4.1-4	150	8.4	55, 57	15.13-14	65
4.6	53, 149	8.6	56	15.15-16	37
4.7-11	235	8.7	57	15.15	38
4.7–6.19	204	8.9	57, 58, 62	15.29	64, 126,
4.12	235	8.10-13	55, 62		223
4.14-15	147	8.10	59	15.44	66
4.15	253	8.13	69	15.45	169
4.17	132	9	154	15.48	38
4.18-21	148	9.1	169	15.49	167
5	55, 200	9.5	53, 253	15.50	39, 149
5.1–16.18	202, 203	9.9	87	15.51-52	37, 38, 66
5.1	67	9.13–10.11	206	15.52	38
5.9	32, 58,	10.1-11	154	15.54-57	39

15.56–16.24   204
15.58   149
16   31
16.1-4   219
16.2   31
16.3   109
16.5   233
16.10-11   132
16.12   32
16.13-18   156
16.15   86, 149
16.19   86, 203
16.20   151
16.21   151
16.22   151

2 Corinthians
1.2-3   147
1.3   150
1.8–2.13   205
1.8-9   41
1.12–2.8   206
1.16   168
1.19   253
3.1   50
3.6   102, 327
3.16–4.6   167
3.18   167
4.4   167
4.6   165
4.14   40
4.15-17   167
5   40, 41,
               48, 65-
               67
5.1   40, 66
5.1-4   40
5.3   66
5.14-27   147
5.20   126
6.14–7.1   45, 58,
               62
6.14   62
6.16-17   58
7.1   62
7.5-6   205
8–9   31
8.2   168

8.19   84, 90
10.5   49
10.7   47, 53
10.10   49
10.12-14   50
11.5-6   49
11.6   49
11.23   102
11.30   49
12   170, 172
12.5   49
12.9-10   49
12.10   126
12.14–13.13   206
13.4   49
13.5-11   156
13.11-13   205
13.12   151

Galatians
1   169
1.1-5   157
1.1   147
1.3-4   147
1.4   167
1.6–5.16   205
1.6–5.12   205
1.6-10   157
1.6   150
1.10-12   153
1.10-11   153
1.12–2.14   158
1.13–2.21   153
1.13-14   197
1.14   143, 197
1.16   166, 253
2.7-9   59
2.15-21   159
2.20   253
3.1–6.18   159
3.1–6.1   154
3.1–4.31   159
3.3-21   203
3.7   147
3.10–4.9   206
3.16   147
3.26-29   256, 265
3.27   253

4.4   253
4.6   147, 253
4.19   150, 166
5.1-12   203
5.2-12   203
5.2-3   175
5.10–6.17   206
5.13–6.10   205
5.16–6.10   156
6.6   90
6.11-18   205
6.11-17   151
6.11-15   157
6.11   151
6.12-14   94, 97
6.15   147
6.16-18   157
6.17   205

Ephesians
1.1-2   205
1.3–3.5   206
1.3–2.10   205
2.11–3.21   205
2.11-22   351
2.14-15   351
2.17-19   256, 265
2.19-21   259
2.19   253
3.5–5.3   206
4.1–6.20   205
5.3–6.24   206
5.21–6.9   257
6.21-25   205

Philippians
1.1   83, 86,
               90, 102,
               232, 259
1.3-26   204
1.3-11   203
1.7-8   150
1.12–2.30   97, 203
1.12   167
1.13   110
1.27–4.2   114
1.27–2.4   98
1.27-38   124

1.27-30	112-14, 116, 126	4.2-6	156	2.18	133
1.27	102, 115-17, 119, 120, 124, 127	4.3	123, 296	2.19-20	154, 155
		4.15	32, 87	3.1-8	155, 156
		4.20	151	3.1	130, 155
1.28	124			3.2	102, 135
1.29-30	168	*Colossians*		3.3-4	168
1.29	126	1.1-2	205	3.5	133
1.30	123, 126	1.3-29	205	3.6	130
2.3-5	98	2.1–3.4	205	3.7	130, 135
2.5-10	97	2.8–3.8	206	3.8	155
2.9-11	116	3.4	167	3.9-13	155
2.11	147	3.5–4.6	205	3.9	155
2.12-16	98	3.11	256, 265	3.10-12	130
2.12	114	3.17–4.17	206	3.16	130
2.17	238	3.18–4.6	257	4	37-39
2.19	83	4.7-9	257	4.1–5.22	156
2.22-24	132	4.7-18	205	4.1–5.11	156
2.25	83, 109, 119	4.15	86	4.1-12	203
2.27–3.30	204			4.1-8	156
2.27	238	*1 Thessalonians*		4.1	139, 142, 143
2.28	119	1.1	134	4.3-8	154, 156
2.29	119	1.1-2	147	4.3	143
2.30	238	1.2–5.22	156	4.4	143, 236
3.2	92	1.2–2.16	154-56	4.7	143
3.2-12	102	1.2-10	155	4.9–5.11	203
3.2-11	92, 93, 97	1.3	156	4.9-12	156
3.3-11	94, 95, 97	1.4	130, 147, 150	4.9	203
3.3	147	1.6	150, 168	4.10	139
3.4-11	98	1.7-8	155	4.11	139, 235
3.6	173	1.9-10	34, 35	4.12-13	142
3.7-8	97	1.9	142	4.13–5.11	130, 131, 156
3.10	165, 166	1.10	155, 253	4.13-18	34-37, 156, 203, 204
3.12-16	98	2.1–3.13	203		
3.12	166	2.1-12	155, 156		
3.17–4.1	113	2.7-8	150	4.14	35, 142
3.17-21	92-95	2.9	235	4.15-18	35, 156
3.17-18	98	2.12	139, 140, 155	4.15-17	154
3.18	92-96, 98, 101	2.13	130, 142	4.15	37
3.19	92-94, 98	2.13–5.4	204	4.16	37
3.20-21	165	2.13-16	154, 155	4.17	66, 238
3.20	116	2.14-15	155	4.18	139, 156
4.1	98, 238	2.14	130, 168	4.19-22	142
4.2	83, 235	2.16	130, 155	5.1-22	203, 204
4.2-3	87	2.17–3.13	155, 156	5.1-11	156
		2.17-20	155	5.1	203
		2.17	155	5.2-8	154, 156

5.5-7	139	2.7	138	*2 Timothy*	
5.8	109	2.8	138	1.1-2	208
5.10	204	2.11	138	1.3-7	208
5.11	139, 156	2.12	130, 135	2.3	109
5.12-22	156	2.13	130, 138,	6.9-22	208
5.12	233		143		
5.14	139, 140,	2.15	129, 133,	*Philemon*	
	204		135, 136,	1	109, 150
5.19-22	139		142	2	86
5.21	139	2.17	139	10	257
5.23	143	3.1-15	129	11-13	257
5.26-27	151	3.4	139	16	257
5.26	151	3.6-15	129, 140,		
5.27	148		141, 205	*Hebrews*	
		3.6-12	141	2.6	283
2 Thessalonians		3.6	139, 140,	2.16-17	295
1.1-2	205		142	13.1-19	207
1.3–3.16	206	3.7	140	13.20-25	207
1.3-12	205	3.10	139		
1.4	132, 135	3.11	130, 140	*2 Peter*	
1.5-13	136	3.12	139	3.16	190
1.5-12	132	3.16-18	205		
1.5	131, 135	3.17	130, 133,	*Revelation*	
1.6	131		134	1.13	283
1.7-8	130	4.1-2	130	2.14	186
1.7	131	4.1	130	2.20	186
1.8	131, 135	4.10-12	130	2.24	186
1.9	131, 136	5.23	130	6.10	131
2	137			7.14	131
2.1–3.5	205	*1 Timothy*		11.18	131
2.1-12	131, 140	1.1-2	208	12.7-9	137
2.1-2	129	1.9-10	201	13.6	131
2.2	129, 130,	1.12-17	172	14.14	283
	133, 136	1.16	173	19.12	131
2.3-15	129	2.11-15	265	19.14	131
2.3-12	130, 132,	3.1	88	20.10	131
	136	5.18	87	21.2	297
2.6-7	136	6.21	208		
2.6	138, 141				

Aberbach, M. 387
Agnew, F.H. 84
Akinnaso, F.N. 317
Alexander, P.S. 381, 383, 385, 386, 389
Alon, G. 361
Anderson, B.W. 303, 305
Anderson, C.W. 322
Arnold, E.V. 109
Auerbach, E. 304, 305
Axtell, H.L. 316

Bailey, J. 130
Bailey, R.W. 307, 309, 310, 330
Bammel, E. 286
Barbour, R.S. 275, 279
Bardtke, H. 227
Barnes, R.B. 317, 335, 338
Barr, J.M. 87, 274
Bassler, J.M. 192, 193
Bauer, W. 139
Baur, F.C. 191
Beare, F.W. 97, 100, 103, 111
Beker, J.C. 192, 193
Benoit, P. 358, 359
Berger, K. 84
Berger, P.L. 193
Betz, H.D. 84, 158-60
Beyer, H.W. 87, 88, 226
Bickerman, E. 363, 365-67
Black, M. 284, 288, 294, 334
Boers, H. 284
Boman, T. 86
Bömer, F. 217, 237, 238
Boring, M.E. 275, 287, 291

Bornkamm, G. 27-30, 32, 33, 287
Borsch, F.H. 284
Böttger, P.C. 101
Bousset, W. 56, 60, 65, 71-76, 78, 79, 285
Bowker, J. 288
Bowden, J. 280
Bradley, J. 308, 326
Brainerd, B. 201, 308
Branick, V. 86
Braun, D.M. 317
Braun, H. 88
Brewer, R.R. 115, 116
Brin, J. 370
Brock, S.P. 381
Broshi, M. 369, 371
Brown, R.E. 85
Bultmann, R. 48-51, 66, 67, 272, 273, 276, 283, 284, 287, 289, 290, 293
Burkert, W. 259, 260
Burnard, L. 307, 309
Burrows, J.F. 309-11, 313
Bush, V. 332
Butler, C. 309

Cadbury, H.J. 279
Caird, G.B. 314
Callaway, P. 369, 373
Calvert, D.G.A. 274
Campenhausen, H. von 90, 91
Caquot, A. 369
Caragounis, C.C. 282, 285-87, 289, 292
Casey, M.P. 284, 285, 288
Cerfaux, L. 191

Charlesworth, J.H. 369
Childs, B. 302, 303, 305
Chilton, B.D. 293, 387, 388
Clemente, G. 100
Cohen, S.J.D. 362, 365
Collins, A.Y. 284, 287
Collins, J.N. 89, 90
Collins, R.F. 236
Colpe, C. 284
Cotter, W. 100
Conzelmann, H. 91, 134, 207, 272, 285
Crossan, J.D. 280
Cumont, F. 247, 252, 253, 255, 259

Dahl, N. 145, 146, 159, 160, 178
Daniel, C. 371
Daniélou, J. 226, 303, 305
Dassmann, E. 90
Davies, P. 368, 369
Davies, W.D. 190
de Robertis, F.M. 100
Delcor, M. 369, 371
Delcourt, C. 227, 307
Deissman, A. 191
DeRose, S. 331
Desjardins, M.R. 56
Dettienne, M. 302, 328
Dibelius, M. 88, 89, 91, 126, 207
Dimant, D. 384
Dobschütz, E. von 90
Dodd, C.H. 191
Dodds, E.R. 317
Dombrowski, B.W. 227
Donahue, J.R. 282, 283, 286, 292
Donfried, K.P. 128, 133-35
Doty, W.G. 202, 203, 205, 207
Downing, F.G. 113, 274, 279
Durand, D. 331
Dyer, R.R. 311

Earl, D. 105, 106
Eisenman, R. 370

Falk, Z.W. 376
Farmer, W.R. 30
Filson, F.Y. 86
Fischer, K.M. 135

Fitzmyer, J.A. 88, 284, 293, 294
Forestell, J.T. 386
Forster, L. 327
Fortier, P.A. 322, 330
Foucart, P. 213, 214, 231, 235, 236, 238
Fraade, S.D. 387
Fraenkel, E. 318
Frank, T. 249, 250
Friedrich, C.J. 91
Frierichs, E.S. 363
Frye, N. 302, 303, 311, 328, 330, 331
Fuller, R.H. 275, 287
Funk, R.J. 148, 152, 275

Gagé, J. 221
Gager, J.G. 234, 265
Garnsey, P. 254
Gaston, L. 174, 175
Georgi, D. 88, 89, 94
Gerhardsson, B. 293
Giblin, C.H. 136-38
Gnilka, J. 94
Golb, N. 368
Goldfield, J. 322, 324
Goldhill, S. 318
Golomb, D.M. 383, 384, 387, 389
Goppelt, L. 303
Gore, C. 218, 219, 225, 226
Granskou, D. 145
Grant, R.M. 289, 338
Green, W.S. 363, 375
Guillaumont, A. 338, 339, 342-44, 355, 358

Hahn, F. 287
Hainz, J. 88, 89
Hall, R. 159
Hanson, R.P.C. 303, 305
Hare, D.R.A. 288, 289
Harnack, A. 109, 217, 218
Harrington, D.J. 383
Harris, M.D. 330
Hatch, E. 82, 212-15, 217, 218, 220, 224, 225-32, 238
Hawthorne, G. 113, 126
Hays, R.B. 193
Hebblethwaite, B. 276

Heinrici, G. 215-21, 224, 225
Hengel, M. 227, 277, 369, 376, 377
Héring, J. 283
Hick, J. 279
Higgins, A.J.B. 287, 289
Holl, K. 50
Holland, G.S. 136, 137, 138
Hollander, J. 325
Hollmann, G. 130
Holmberg, B. 90, 141
Holsten, C. 218
Hooker, M.D. 274, 275, 286
Horgan, M.P. 385
Horsely, R.A. 280
Hübner, H. 191
Hughes, F.W. 129, 133
Hummel, H.D. 303
Hurd, J.C. 26, 30, 31, 44-46, 51-55,
    58-64, 67-71, 76-78, 80-83, 95,
    105, 128, 145, 154-57, 162, 178,
    186, 188, 190, 199, 202, 204,
    212, 271, 282, 306, 308, 334,
    359, 380

Ide, N.M. 309, 313, 322
Irizarry, E. 309, 322, 328
Isenberg, W.W. 68

Jeremias, J. 153, 154, 226, 284
Jervis, A. 148
Jewett, R. 92, 130, 135
Johnson, L.T. 194
Jones, A.H.M. 110, 235
Josiatis, N.F. 224
Judge, E.A. 228
Jüngel, E. 287

Kähler, M. 272
Käsemann, E. 49-51, 53, 273
Kaufmann, S.A. 370, 382
Kajanto, I. 249, 250
Keck, L.E. 88, 273
Kennedy, H.A.A. 225
Kennedy, G.A. 159
Kenny, A. 201, 202
Kierkegaard, S. 278
Kim, S. 165, 286
King, K.L. 56

Kirk, J.A. 84
Kirk, K.E. 82
Klauck, H.J. 86, 221
Klein, M.L. 385
Klijn, F.J. 102

Kloppenborg, J.S. 81, 103, 238, 239,
    293
Knox, J. 28, 31, 284, 287
Koeberlein, E. 138
Koester, H. 92-94, 97, 172, 293
Korschorke, K. 69
Kuhn, T. 194-98
Kümmel, W. 201, 202
Kutscher, E.Y. 389

Lake, K. 45, 183, 225, 283, 335
Laperrousaz, E.-M. 369
Lamping, D. 317
Lancashire, I. 308, 313
Larsen, J. 103
Lazenby, J. 119-22
Le Déaut, R. 387
Lehman, M. 372
Leivestad, R. 288
Levine, E. 381, 385
Lewis, N. 100
Liebenam, W. 216
Lietzmann, H. 88, 219, 294
Lightfoot, J.B. 217
Lightstone, J.N. 375
Lindars, B. 284, 285, 288
Loening, E. 219
Lohse, E. 89
Longenecker, R.N. 286
Louw, J.P. 141
Lund, N. 154

McArthur, T. 327
McCarty, W. 305, 316
McCready, P.
McCready, W.O. 147, 148
Macdonald, M.Y. 91
Mack, B.L. 280
McLean Harper, G. 102
McMaster, G.E. 322
MacMullen, R. 99, 100, 101, 110, 222,
    266

Maier, H.O. 221, 234
Maier, J. 87, 368, 372, 377
Malherbe, A. 107, 110, 171, 221, 222, 230
Malina, B.J. 275
Malone, K. 317
Markus, R.A. 305
Marmaridou, A.S. 317
Marshall, I.H. 286, 289
Martinez, F. Garcia 368
Marxsen, W. 283, 285, 287, 289
Mealand, D.L. 275, 278
Mearns, C. 288, 290
Meeks, W. 86, 110, 111, 146, 147, 222-24, 226, 234, 235, 237, 239, 257, 265
Miller, R.J. 276
Milligan, G. 141
Milgrom, J. 369, 371, 377
Moltmann, J. 276
Morgan, R. 272
Moule, C.F.D. 286
Milic, L.C. 307
Mylonas, E. 105, 331

Neusner, J. 360-63, 367, 374, 375, 378
Neyrey, J.H. 193
Nicolaisen, W.F.H. 317
Nida, E.A. 141
Nilsson, M.P. 247, 259, 261, 264, 265
Nineham, D. 279
Nock, A.D. 239, 279
Novak, D. 178-80

O'Brien, P. 112, 123
O'Neil, J.C. 288

Patte, D. 161, 192, 193, 196
Peel, M.L. 68
Peer, W. van 307, 313
Pendelbury, M. 317
Peradotto, J. 317
Perrin, N. 274, 285, 286, 291, 293
Poland, F. 100, 102, 103, 216, 220, 232-34, 237
Polanyi, M. 195
Polkow, D. 275
Potter, R. 307, 309, 310, 312, 313, 322, 328, 330
Presutti, L. 308

Rad, G. von 302, 303
Räisänen, H. 191
Ranke, L. von 314
Reimarus, H. 272
Reinhold, M. 100
Reitzenstein, R. 49
Rénan, E. 215, 216
Renear, A. 331
Rengstorf, K.H. 84
Richardson, A. 84-86
Richardson, P. 145, 178, 334, 347, 351, 358
Robinson, J.A.T. 281
Robinson, J.M. 68, 79, 80, 293
Rohde, J. 89

Sanday, W. 217, 218, 226
Sanders, E.P. 192, 274, 277, 279, 280, 351, 365, 366
Schaberg, J. 280
Schenke, H.M. 83, 135
Schiffman, L.H. 369, 371
Schillebeeckx, E. 82, 276
Schmidt, K.M. 322, 323
Schmithals, W. 47-54
Schmitt, J. 226
Schmittals, W. 92-94
Schneider, C. 227
Schöllgen, G. 90
Scholem, G. 281
Schubert, P. 151
Schüssler Fiorenza, E. 87, 91, 265
Schulz, S. 94
Schweitzer, A. 190, 191
Schweitzer, E. 220, 226, 288, 289
Schweizer, E. 82, 87, 259
Seeligman, I.L. 384
Segal, A.F. 186, 189, 194
Segal, M.H. 382
Selwyn, E.G. 135
Sherwin-White, A.N. 104
Shinan, A. 383
Smale, S. 310, 311
Smith, J.B. 324, 330, 331
Smith, J.Z. 225, 226, 230, 278, 279

Smolar, L. 387
Snelgrove, T. 309, 330
Snell, B. 316
Sperberg-McQueen, C.M. 307, 310,
    311, 328, 331
Stauffer, E. 274
Stegeman, H. 368-70, 374, 376
Stein, R.H. 274, 292
Steiner, G. 381
Steinhauser, M.G. 387
Stendahl, K. 293
Stern, M. 366, 376
Stewart, J.S. 191
Stowers, S. 147, 158, 160, 236
Strauss, D.F. 272, 273
Strugnell, J. 274
Stuhlmacher, P. 118
Sykes, S.W. 278

Talmon, S. 375, 376
Taylor, V. 287
Teeple, H.M. 285, 286
Theissen, G. 235, 292
Thiering, B.E. 370
Tödt, H.E. 287
Tracy, D. 292
Trilling, W. 130, 131, 135, 142
Tuckett, C. 288

Vaage, L.E. 81
Van Buren, P. 276
Vander Stichele, C. 142, 143
VanderKam, J.C. 369
Vermes, G. 281, 284, 288, 334, 386
Vernant, J.P. 302, 328
Vielhauer, P. 385

Vitringa, C. 215
Voegelin, E. 302
Vogliana, A. 247, 248

Wacholder, B.Z. 370, 372, 374
Waddington, W.H. 213
Walker, W.O. 275-77, 282, 283, 285,
    286
Waltzing, J.P. 99, 100, 103, 222, 237
Wanamaker, C.A. 131
Watson, D.F. 112, 113, 121
Weinfeld, M. 227, 228
Weingarten, H. 215
Weiss, J. 219, 220
Wellhausen, J. 302
Whelan, C.F. 232
White, J.L. 97, 152, 202, 203
Whiteley, D.E.H. 27
Wiles, M. 280
Wilken, R. 20, 338
Wills, L. 368, 373, 376
Wilson, A.M. 368
Wilson, B.R. 372, 373, 376
Wilson, S.G. 172, 178, 182-84
Winter, J.G. 150
Wise, M.O. 368-71, 373, 374
Witt, R. 138
Wittig, S. 330
Woolridge, T.R. 308
Woude, A.S. van der 368, 369
Wrede, W. 130, 131
Wuellner, W. 160, 161

Yadin, Y. 368-71, 373, 374, 376-78

Zachner, R.C. 166

JOURNAL FOR THE STUDY OF THE NEW TESTAMENT

Supplement Series

11 THE LETTERS TO THE SEVEN CHURCHES OF ASIA IN THEIR LOCAL
SETTING
Colin J. Hemer

12 PROCLAMATION FROM PROPHECY AND PATTERN:
LUCAN OLD TESTAMENT CHRISTOLOGY
Darrell L. Bock

13 JESUS AND THE LAWS OF PURITY:
TRADITION HISTORY AND LEGAL HISTORY IN MARK 7
Roger P. Booth

14 THE PASSION ACCORDING TO LUKE:
THE SPECIAL MATERIAL OF LUKE 22
Marion L. Soards

15 HOSTILITY TO WEALTH IN THE SYNOPTIC GOSPELS
Thomas E. Schmidt

16 MATTHEW'S COMMUNITY:
THE EVIDENCE OF HIS SPECIAL SAYINGS MATERIAL
Stephenson H. Brooks

17 THE PARADOX OF THE CROSS IN THE THOUGHT OF ST PAUL
Anthony Tyrrell Hanson

18 HIDDEN WISDOM AND THE EASY YOKE:
WISDOM, TORAH AND DISCIPLESHIP IN MATTHEW 11.25-30
Celia Deutsch

19 JESUS AND GOD IN PAUL'S ESCHATOLOGY
L. Joseph Kreitzer

20 LUKE
A NEW PARADIGM (2 Volumes)
Michael D. Goulder

21 THE DEPARTURE OF JESUS IN LUKE–ACTS:
THE ASCENSION NARRATIVES IN CONTEXT
Mikeal C. Parsons

22 THE DEFEAT OF DEATH:
APOCALYPTIC ESCHATOLOGY IN 1 CORINTHIANS 15 AND ROMANS 5
Martinus C. de Boer

23 PAUL THE LETTER-WRITER
AND THE SECOND LETTER TO TIMOTHY
Michael Prior

24 APOCALYPTIC AND THE NEW TESTAMENT:
ESSAYS IN HONOR OF J. LOUIS MARTYN
Edited by Joel Marcus & Marion L. Soards

25 THE UNDERSTANDING SCRIBE:
   MATTHEW AND THE APOCALYPTIC IDEAL
   David E. Orton
26 WATCHWORDS:
   MARK 13 IN MARKAN ESCHATOLOGY
   Timothy J. Geddert
27 THE DISCIPLES ACCORDING TO MARK:
   MARKAN REDACTION IN CURRENT DEBATE
   C. Clifton Black
28 THE NOBLE DEATH:
   GRAECO-ROMAN MARTYROLOGY
   AND PAUL'S CONCEPT OF SALVATION
   David Seeley
29 ABRAHAM IN GALATIANS:
   EPISTOLARY AND RHETORICAL CONTEXTS
   G. Walter Hansen
30 EARLY CHRISTIAN RHETORIC AND 2 THESSALONIANS
   Frank Witt Hughes
31 THE STRUCTURE OF MATTHEW'S GOSPEL:
   A STUDY IN LITERARY DESIGN
   David R. Bauer
32 PETER AND THE BELOVED DISCIPLE:
   FIGURES FOR A COMMUNITY IN CRISIS
   Kevin Quast
33 MARK'S AUDIENCE:
   THE LITERARY AND SOCIAL SETTING OF MARK 4.11-12
   Mary Ann Beavis
34 THE GOAL OF OUR INSTRUCTION:
   THE STRUCTURE OF THEOLOGY AND ETHICS
   IN THE PASTORAL EPISTLES
   Philip H. Towner
35 THE PROVERBS OF JESUS:
   ISSUES OF HISTORY AND RHETORIC
   Alan P. Winton
36 THE STORY OF CHRIST IN THE ETHICS OF PAUL:
   AN ANALYSIS OF THE FUNCTION OF THE HYMNIC MATERIAL
   IN THE PAULINE CORPUS
   Stephen E. Fowl
37 PAUL AND JESUS:
   COLLECTED ESSAYS
   Edited by A.J.M. Wedderburn
38 MATTHEW'S MISSIONARY DISCOURSE:
   A LITERARY CRITICAL ANALYSIS
   Dorothy Jean Weaver

39   FAITH AND OBEDIENCE IN ROMANS:
A STUDY IN ROMANS 1–4
Glenn N. Davies

40   IDENTIFYING PAUL'S OPPONENTS:
THE QUESTION OF METHOD IN 2 CORINTHIANS
Jerry L. Sumney

41   HUMAN AGENTS OF COSMIC POWER:
IN HELLENISTIC JUDAISM AND THE SYNOPTIC TRADITION
Mary E. Mills

42   MATTHEW'S INCLUSIVE STORY:
A STUDY IN THE NARRATIVE RHETORIC OF THE FIRST GOSPEL
David B. Howell

43   JESUS, PAUL AND TORAH:
COLLECTED ESSAYS
Heikki Räisänen

44   THE NEW COVENANT IN HEBREWS
Susanne Lehne

45   THE RHETORIC OF ROMANS:
ARGUMENTATIVE CONSTRAINT AND STRATEGY AND PAUL'S
DIALOGUE WITH JUDAISM
Neil Elliott

46   THE LAST SHALL BE FIRST:
THE RHETORIC OF REVERSAL IN LUKE
John O. York

47   JAMES AND THE Q SAYINGS OF JESUS
Patrick J. Hartin

48   TEMPLUM AMICITIAE:
ESSAYS ON THE SECOND TEMPLE PRESENTED TO ERNST BAMMEL
Edited by William Horbury

49   PROLEPTIC PRIESTS
PRIESTHOOD IN THE EPISTLE TO THE HEBREWS
John M. Scholer

50   PERSUASIVE ARTISTRY:
STUDIES IN NEW TESTAMENT RHETORIC
IN HONOR OF GEORGE A. KENNEDY
Edited by Duane F. Watson

51   THE AGENCY OF THE APOSTLE: A DRAMATISTIC ANALYSIS OF PAUL'S
RESPONSES TO CONFLICT IN 2 CORINTHIANS
Jeffrey A. Crafton

52   REFLECTIONS OF GLORY:
PAUL'S POLEMICAL USE OF THE MOSES–DOXA TRADITION IN
2 CORINTHIANS 3.12-18
Linda L. Belleville

53 REVELATION AND REDEMPTION AT COLOSSAE
   Thomas J. Sappington

54 THE DEVELOPMENT OF EARLY CHRISTIAN PNEUMATOLOGY
   WITH SPECIAL REFERENCE TO LUKE–ACTS
   Robert P. Menzies

55 THE PURPOSE OF ROMANS:
   A COMPARATIVE LETTER STRUCTURE INVESTIGATION
   L. Ann Jervis

56 THE SON OF THE MAN IN THE GOSPEL OF JOHN
   Delbert Burkett

57 ESCHATOLOGY AND THE COVENANT:
   A COMPARISON OF 4 EZRA AND ROMANS 1–11
   Bruce W. Longenecker

58 NONE BUT THE SINNERS:
   RELIGIOUS CATEGORIES IN THE GOSPEL OF LUKE
   David A. Neale

59 CLOTHED WITH CHRIST:
   THE EXAMPLE AND TEACHING OF JESUS IN ROMANS 12.1–15.13
   Michael Thompson

60 THE LANGUAGE OF THE NEW TESTAMENT:
   CLASSIC ESSAYS
   Edited by Stanley E. Porter

61 FOOTWASHING IN JOHN 13 AND THE JOHANNINE COMMUNITY
   John Christopher Thomas

62 JOHN THE BAPTIZER AND PROPHET:
   A SOCIO-HISTORICAL STUDY
   Robert L. Webb

63 POWER AND POLITICS IN PALESTINE:
   THE JEWS AND THE GOVERNING OF THEIR LAND 100 BC–AD 70
   James S. McLaren

64 JESUS AND THE ORAL GOSPEL TRADITION
   Edited by Henry Wansbrough

65 THE RHETORIC OF RIGHTEOUSNESS IN ROMANS 3.21-26
   Douglas A. Campbell

66 PAUL, ANTIOCH AND JERUSALEM:
   A STUDY IN RELATIONSHIPS AND AUTHORITY IN EARLIEST CHRISTIANITY
   Nicholas Taylor

67 THE PORTRAIT OF PHILIP IN ACTS:
   A STUDY OF ROLES AND RELATIONS
   F. Scott Spencer

68 JEREMIAH IN MATTHEW'S GOSPEL:
   THE REJECTED-PROPHET MOTIF IN MATTHAEAN REDACTION
   Michael P. Knowles

69   RHETORIC AND REFERENCE IN THE FOURTH GOSPEL
      Margaret Davies
70   AFTER THE THOUSAND YEARS:
      RESURRECTION AND JUDGMENT IN REVELATION 20
      J. Webb Mealy
71   SOPHIA AND THE JOHANNINE JESUS
      Martin Scott
72   NARRATIVE ASIDES IN LUKE–ACTS
      Steven M. Sheeley
73   SACRED SPACE
      AN APPROACH TO THE THEOLOGY OF THE EPISTLE TO THE HEBREWS
      Marie E. Isaacs
74   TEACHING WITH AUTHORITY:
      MIRACLES AND CHRISTOLOGY IN THE GOSPEL OF MARK
      Edwin K. Broadhead
75   PATRONAGE AND POWER:
      A STUDY OF SOCIAL NETWORKS IN CORINTH
      John Kin-Man Chow
76   THE NEW TESTAMENT AS CANON:
      A READER IN CANONICAL CRITICISM
      Robert Wall and Eugene Lemcio
77   REDEMPTIVE ALMSGIVING IN EARLY CHRISTIANITY
      Roman Garrison
78   THE FUNCTION OF SUFFERING IN PHILIPPIANS
      L. Gregory Bloomquist
79   THE THEME OF RECOMPENSE IN MATTHEW'S GOSPEL
      Blaine Charette
80   BIBLICAL GREEK LANGUAGE AND LINGUISTICS: OPEN QUESTIONS IN
      CURRENT RESEARCH
      Stanley E. Porter and D.A. Carson
81   THE LAW IN GALATIANS
      In-Gyu Hong
82   ORAL TRADITION AND THE GOSPELS: THE PROBLEM OF MARK 4
      Barry W. Henaut
83   PAUL AND THE SCRIPTURES OF ISRAEL
      Craig A. Evans and James A. Sanders
84   FROM JESUS TO JOHN: ESSAYS ON JESUS AND NEW TESTAMENT
      CHRISTOLOGY IN HONOUR OF MARINUS DE JONGE
      Edited by Martinus C. De Boer
85   RETURNING HOME: NEW COVENANT AND SECOND EXODUS AS THE
      CONTEXT FOR 2 CORINTHIANS 6.14–7.1
      William J. Webb

86   ORIGINS AND METHOD: TOWARDS A NEW UNDERSTANDING OF JUDAISM
      AND CHRISTIANITY—ESSAYS IN HONOUR OF JOHN C. HURD
      Bradley H. McLean
87   WORSHIP, THEOLOGY AND MINISTRY IN THE EARLY CHURCH: ESSAYS IN
      HONOUR OF RALPH P. MARTIN
      Edited by Michael Wilkins and Terence Paige